THE
LETTERS OF
Sean O'Casey
1955-58

SEAN O'CASEY, 1958

THE
LETTERS OF
Sean O' Casey
1955-58

VOLUME III

Edited by
DAVID KRAUSE

The Catholic University of America Press
WASHINGTON, D.C.

Library of Congress Cataloging-in-Publication Data
(Revised for vol. 3)

O'Casey, Sean, 1880–1964.
The letters of Sean O'Casey.

Vol. 3– has imprint: Washington, D.C. :
Catholic University of America Press.
Includes bibliographical references and indexes.
Contents: v. 1. 1910–41. —v. 2. 1942–54.—
v. 3. 1955–58.
1. O'Casey, Sean, 1880–1964—Correspondence.
2. Dramatists, Irish—20th century—Correspondence.
1. Krause, David, 1917–   ed. II. Title.
PR6029.C33Z53   1975   822'.9'12   74–11442
ISBN 0–02–566660–6 (v. 1)
ISBN 0–02–566670–3 (v. 2)
ISBN 0–8132–0651–0 (v. 3)

CONTENTS

INTRODUCTION

A<small>T</small> the age of seventy-five, at the beginning of this final decade of his life, the near-blind O'Casey was still an active if seldom produced controversial playwright; still a devoted husband and father of three children; still a self-exile from his native Dublin, living in a rented flat in Devon; and still a prodigious letter writer. The friends and strangers to whom he wrote regularly remained his most loyal and necessary audience. In this third volume of his letters, he continues to reveal his unguarded and unpretentious self-portrait, probably one of the most memorable and enduring characters he ever created. He emerges informally with all his strengths and weaknesses in full view, all his paradoxical excesses of Irish eloquence and insecurity, kindness and vindictiveness, compassion and pride, anger and idealism, skepticism and faith. Although he had suffered all his life from deprivation, illness, and the threat of blindness, he never succumbed to despair. In his characteristically positive manner he wrote to a university student in South Carolina in February 1955: "God has given, or man has developed, a mind to conquer the things that plague us. I am with the army of conquerors."

O'Casey always believed that the inevitable conflicts that arose between individuals and nations had to be confronted and conquered with words rather than with violence. A self-taught laborer from working-class Dublin who did not become a writer until he was in his mid-forties, he learned from the dynamic Irish labor leader Jim Larkin, under whom he had worked as an unpaid union assistant during the 1913 General Strike, that words are the best weapons of the dispossessed. By nature a man of shy as well as strong feelings, he tolerated only verbal violence. Almost everything he wrote during the last forty years of his life raised some form of controversy, over his unconventional treatment of tragicomic themes and non-realistic theatrical techniques, his comic profanation of Irish and British sacred cows, his unorthodox political and religious views, and his absolute refusal to accept compromise or moderation for the sake of expedience or popularity. He remained stubborn in his defense of his artistic vision. As a result, his letters, as well as his plays, essays, and autobiography, consistently indicate that he stood among the most eloquent and persistent word-fighters of the twentieth century.

Although O'Casey won many of his verbal battles on paper, he often lost the financial wars in the theatre. Therefore his victories were primarily of the spirit, except for his early triumphs in the Abbey Theatre. After the Abbey rejected _The Silver Tassie_ in 1928, he became an itinerant playwright without a regular theatre. In terms of popular success and material rewards, then, he has to be considered something of an heroic failure throughout his long writing career, particularly during the last decade of his life. Nevertheless, he was one of those stoical and incorruptible artists who seem to grow stronger and more resolute under the burden of defeat and neglect. His letters provide an intimate record of his hardship and heroism.

O'Casey wrote five new plays between 1955 and 1961: two visionary comedies, _The Bishop's Bonfire_ (1955) and _The Drums of Father Ned_ (1960), and three short satiric comedies, _Behind the Green Curtains_ (1961), _Figuro in the Night_ (1961), and _The Moon Shines on Kylenamoe_ (1961). He also wrote over forty articles and two books of new and collected essays, _The Green Crow_ (1956) and _Under a Colored Cap_ (1963).

First performed in his native Dublin in 1955, _The Bishop's Bonfire_ produced something of a critical bonfire when the nervous local reviewers rejected it as anti-Irish and anti-Catholic, in spite of its colorful Irish clowns and an idealistic young priest. _The Drums of Father Ned_ was symbolically burned, or banned, in Ireland before it could be performed. In 1958 the play was scheduled to be presented at the annual Dublin drama festival, but what amounted to an unofficial prohibition arose when the Catholic Archbishop, who had not read the play or the dramatization of Joyce's _Ulysses,_ which was also to be produced, announced that he would not open the festival with the traditional Votive Mass if works by O'Casey and Joyce were included on the program. Confronted by the Archbishop's indirect ban, and a frightened theatre company looking for a face-saving way to drop the play by demanding permission to rewrite some unspecified "structural" flaws, O'Casey decided he had no choice but to withdraw his play. In a gesture of sympathetic protest, Samuel Beckett withdrew his mime plays, which were also on the program. Ironically, it turned out, O'Casey and Joyce and Beckett were not welcome in Ireland in 1958.

As a result of this unofficial censorship, O'Casey decided to counterattack by prohibiting all professional productions of his plays in Ireland, a ban he maintained for the next six years, even though he and his family could well have used the valuable royalties. Furthermore, his frustration had been compounded by the fact that for the past year, from February

1957 to March 1958, the Irish Customs Office had mysteriously imposed an unofficial ban on his new book of essays, *The Green Crow*. For a year, without any explanation, the book was not allowed to be distributed or sold in Ireland, a fact that meant another loss of royalities. Whether by accident or tacit design, the Archbishop and the Customs Office had unofficially prevented O'Casey from reaching his Irish audiences and readers. Perhaps he had anticipated this situation when waggishly he had once told the director of the Irish Association of Civil Liberties, "In Ireland they wear the fig leaf on the mouth." Not unexpectedly, then, he enjoyed a sharp and merry laugh of revenge in his last three short comedies, which deal with the relevant themes of repressive fear, unofficial censorship, and hypocritical piety.

It was the sanctimonious piety of the clergy that often prompted O'Casey to insist that he was anti-clerical, not anti-Christian. He was very sensitive on this point and tried to balance his censure of what he thought were blatant Irish Catholic sins of commission with equally strong protests against what he called the cowardly Irish Protestant sins of omission. He scolded the clergy of both churches for preaching that the outrageous economic and social servitude of the Irish lower classes at the turn of the century was due to the will of God rather than to the will of man. This cruel and unchristian fallacy was one reason why in his early twenties O'Casey gave up the Protestant faith into which he had been born and raised and eventually turned to the militant socialist labor movement of Jim Larkin. When the unamused Irish reviewers rejected *The Bishop's Bonfire* in 1955 because, among many other supposed transgressions, they charged that the play was "idolatrous," he wrote to a Dublin Catholic friend in March to stress a greater sin against God and man: "But there are other idolatries in Ireland, and elsewhere, that I am against, for instance that poverty and disease are the will of God."

It is not surprising, therefore, that O'Casey singles out as one of his personal heroes the dissident Irish Catholic priest, Dr. Walter McDonald, Professor of Theology at Maynooth College, who early in the century had been suppressed for writing controversial books exposing what he believed to be the reactionary and unchristian practices of the church hierarchy. Dr. McDonald's name shines forth as a symbol of religious enlightenment in O'Casey's autobiography and all volumes of the letters.

Having grown up among the poor Catholics on the severely depressed northside of Dublin, where his closest friends were Catholic, O'Casey naturally had sympathies with these people with whom he shared common hardships rather than with the well-to-do and distant Protestants. He once wrote a very moving response to the ritual of the Catholic faith, the poetic symbolism and beauty of which he said he accepted, even if he was not a believer. His friend Desmond MacCarthy, in a good review of *Inishfallen, Fare Thee Well,* stated that O'Casey "loathed the Church of Rome"; O'Casey replied in a 7 February 1949 letter, Vol. II, that he could not possibly loathe the Catholic liturgy: "I loathe those . . . the cardinals and bishops . . . who are turning her liturgy into vulgar nonsense and her temples into dens of thieves. Dante said this about the famous monastery of Monte Cassino—that the monks had turned the place of St. Benedict into a den of thieves." Then he made this revealing comment on the divine liturgy: "The idea of the Incarnation, the ascent, the coming of the paraclete, and all the moral philosophy, the poetic tales connected with these, are beautiful; and, though not accepted either in substance or fact, remain beautiful, and I am not one to loathe the lovely."

The unpredictable O'Casey created a secular liturgy of his own whenever he invoked the names of the great literary figures in an attempt to glorify the brotherhood of man through his unorthodox vision of evangelical Communism. He wrote a letter to Brooks Atkinson, drama critic of the *New York Times* and his long-time friend, on 11 April 1949, Vol. II, in which he proclaimed his unique faith: "Of course I am a Shelleyan Communist, and a Dickensian one, & a Byronic one, and a Miltonic one, and a Whitmanian one, & one like all those who thought big & beautifully, & who cared for others, as I am a Marxian one, too." Earlier in this letter, O'Casey, the poetic Communist, in one of his typical recourses to religious symbolism, expressed his constant need to improve his art in this manner: "God forgive me, I never shall be satisfied with what I do; I am always demanding the grace from the Holy Ghost to do better."

Now, in the third volume, when Atkinson teasingly reminds him of the aesthetic Communism he had professed in that 1949 letter, O'Casey replies in an August 1956 letter that he is still the same kind of symbolic Communist, an independent and intuitive believer. Then he makes a special point of adding that he had never joined the Communist Party because he always placed his art before his politics, before everything: "No, for, like Shaw, I wished first to be a good playwright before anything else. That is a thing many Communists seemed unable to learn—that a man must be first excellent at what his hand findeth to do before he could be a Communist at all." It is also in this letter that he makes a strange and unconvincing attempt to excuse the brutalities of Stalin by saying "He wasn't infallible." Nor was O'Casey on this crucial point. One of his personal reasons for stubbornly defending what seems to be indefensible in an instance like this was his refusal to provide capitalist apologists with an opportunity to use his words as a weapon against Russia and against his idealistic Communism.

Although he held strong political views, O'Casey invariably took an aesthetic stand by insisting that the artist in any country must be free from the pressure of politics. It is the craft of the artist, he claims, not his ideology, that controls and expresses his art. "There is no 'class consciousness' in art," he says in an April 1956 letter to a friend in Washington, "there is but bad painting and fine painting. It is the mind of the artist that creates the art." He himself prefers the classical and French Impressionist painters, but he defends the modern abstract art of Picasso and Braque, and adds that an artist need never feel guilty if his paintings carry no political or social significance: "A body isn't a 'traitor to the struggle around him' if he paints a lovely bunch of roses, a kid aswing on a gate, a cow in a meadow, or a house on a hill."

Here and elsewhere O'Casey mocks the Soviet dogma of Socialist Realism with its automatic charge of decadent "formalism" in Western art. In a July 1955 letter to a young British miner he says: "The worst formalism that I know is the formalism of the chattering phrases uttered and muttered by the Communists themselves." And, although he never waivered in his long commitment to socialism, he warns the young socialist miner: "Remember that Life comes first, even before socialism; and that socialism must be adapted to life, not life to socialism."

For an uncommon socialist like O'Casey, the life of the artist was always a primary concern. Probably the best statement he ever made on the subject of the inviolable independence of the artist, and his freedom from all outside pressures, appears in Vol. I in the letter he wrote to Lady Gregory on 28 March 1928: "And one thing is certain—that so long as God or Nature gives us one atom of strength, we must continue to use that atom of strength to fight on for that which is above & before all governments & parties—Art & Literature which are the mantle & mirror of the Holy Ghost, and the Sword of the Spirit."

Nevertheless, he could also celebrate the holiness of ordinary events, and he liked to write to his friends about his experiences with birds and flowers and trees, all of which expanded his rituals of daily curiosity and pleasure. Except for a rare occasion when he had to travel to London to visit an eye specialist, O'Casey spent all of his time in or around his flat in St. Marychurch, a suburb of Torquay near the sea. When he was not writing or reading in his room, he was busy with his wife and three children; he took his daily walk around the village; he listened to music or talks on BBC radio; he prowled about in his garden among the flowers and watched the birds. In the summer of 1957 he befriended "a blackbird, a robin, and a cock and hen bullfinch, all of whom I feed with scraps of fat and biscuit-crumb as well as supplying them with water."

O'Casey was deeply concerned about family life and often inquired about the happiness and health of the children of his friends. In 1956 his own health broke down when he had to undergo two major operations—prostate and kidney stone—in the early months, followed by a siege of bronchial pneumonia and a long post-operation infection. At the end of the year he and his wife suffered their greatest tragedy when their 21-year-old son Niall died suddenly of leukemia.

O'Casey was devastated by the cruel loss. Many of his letters in 1957 reflect the lingering pain of Niall's death, and in February he wrote to a woman in New York who had also experienced a tragic loss and extended his sympathy to her. He had lost a dear friend as well as a son, and his heart is still bruised as he tries to comfort the woman and himself: "Well, you see, lass, there's no one who hasnt had a sorrow, and sorrow is the one sacrament that binds us together, all men and women the world over; you with yours, me with mine, and ours with others—an endless chain of a bond of sisterhood and brotherhood." In many letters he had to exorcize his sorrow by writing about it.

Ironically, two days before his son died at the end of 1956, a revival of his 1940 play *Purple Dust* opened successfully in New York in an off-Broadway production. It proceeded to run for just over a year, the longest run ever for an O'Casey play. It turned out to be his only sustained success in the theatre since *The Plough and the Stars* was acclaimed in the midst of riots at the Abbey Theatre exactly thirty years earlier. *The Plough,* together with *Juno* and *The Gunman,* continue to be revived from time to time all over the world, but the remaining eight full-length plays and eight short plays, some of which are occasionally produced by university and art theatre companies, still await proper professional productions. Over twenty years after his death, O'Casey is still on the whole a playwright without a theatre. In his final years he took a philosophical view of the neglect. When ambitious productions of *The Gunman,* a musical version of *Juno,* and *Cock-a-Doodle Dandy* all failed in New York in 1958, he told Brooks Atkinson in an end-of-the-year letter about his disappointment, particularly over the *Cock,* his favorite play, but he refused to concede ultimate defeat: "Somehow, some day, somewhere, the characters will leap & laugh a way into life. Meanwhile, they are safe in limbo."

When consoling himself or his friends or even strangers over various misfortunes, O'Casey was always a man of faith who could never take a defeatist attitude toward art or life. He seemed to have a special gift for understanding and consoling the lonely or despairing women who were strangely attracted to him. He wrote as a wise confidant who shared their anxieties, and he urged them to endure their sorrows with courage, as he had done. He offered profuse sympathy and practical advice. And even when he disagreed with them, he never lost their trust. Among his many memorable letters to women, several that stand out are his 31 May 1956 letter to a woman who says she is "lonely among the lonely," whom he tells to fight against despair by relying upon whatever natural talent she has to "satisfy God and pacify man"; his 3 June 1956 letter to a grieving woman who says she has given up all hope, to whom he replies with the lyrical stoicism of his "We cannot always suffer ecstasy" letter—these and any of his letters to Georgie Cooper, Mrs. R___ or Mrs. Nora ___. For young people, high-school and college students who sought him out, he had a similar feeling of rapport, and he became for them a compassionate voice of hope. Whenever he wrote to parents, he urged them to encourage their children to liberate themselves from the fears and constraints of the adult world.

In spite of chronic illness, near-blindness, and prolonged grief over the death of his son, O'Casey somehow manages to maintain his friendly vigor, with something of what he once called a "wild prance" in spirit if not always in body. He is totally candid and open-hearted with strangers as well as with friends, people in the theatre or ordinary people all over the world whom he accepts as equals. He is ready to discuss any subject and quick to identify his likes and dislikes. He reserves his greatest praise for writers, for Shakespeare and Milton; all the Romantic poets, except Wordsworth; all the classics; Hawthorne and Melville, Emerson and Whitman, Twain and Fenimore Cooper, Joyce and Yeats, Ibsen and Shaw, Strindberg and O'Neill. Writing to his doctrinaire Communist friends in Russia, he does not hesitate to defend great poets who are out of favor there, such as the ostracized Pasternak or the reactionary T. S. Eliot. Unlike the American and Russian government officials who are so antagonistic toward each other, he has no difficulty in admiring both countries and expressing his warm feelings toward his capitalist and Communist friends.

He encourages amateur companies to produce his new plays because he no longer believes in a commercial theatre committed to profit, not art. He damns the new Abbey Theatre directors for betraying the artistic principles of Yeats and Lady Gregory, even though the latter two rejected his *Silver Tassie*. In public letters to the Dublin newspapers he boldly criticizes many instances of what he considers repressive or stagnant practices and attitudes in Ireland, but it is also apparent that his love for his homeland remains undiminished. He cries out in an October 1956 letter, "Oh, God, this grip that Ireland gives!" He is in constant rebellion against all forms of injustice, but he tells an Irish friend in July 1957 that he is against the continuing violence of the gunmen: "I don't agree with the methods of the present IRA. I never believed in Irishmen killing Irishmen, for enough of that has been done already."

O'Casey prefers to fight and play with words. Although he had not spoken regularly in Gaelic for over forty years, his letters in his native tongue are articulate, if not always grammatical. Lively and argumentative, they translate into a colorful and often comic idiom. He manages to capture some of that vigorous spirit of the oral Celtic tradition in his English writing. The language of his letters is often colloquial and nonliterary; nevertheless, he can also assume a high style when the occasion demands, when he becomes outraged or visionary and reaches for his version of biblical or Elizabethan rhetoric. His conversational prose style may sometimes betray his lack of formal education, not in his mature vocabulary and wide range of allusions and quotations, but perhaps in the easy way he allows some of his paragraphs and sentences to accumulate and run to inordinate length. In his self-taught manner he likes to expand the scope of a sentence by resorting to many commas and, particularly, his favorite semicolons to develop a series of parallel and emphatic clauses. Ideas and impressions proliferate. The extended construction of these fulsome sentences suggests the natural pattern of speech rather than the deliberate order of formal discourse. If grammatical unity is sometimes strained in these flowing and variously qualified sentences—in the way that spontaneous speech can take grammatical liberties—the rhythmic stress and meaning are seldom lost.

O'Casey's uninhibited words take on the distinctive quality of an intimate and authentic voice. It is always apparent that he enjoys the sound of words as they leap and stretch his imagination. The common man is revealed in the uncommon style. He is therefore a powerful and persuasive writer of letters, sounding like a man talking, not writing, to his friends and strangers.

TEXT AND
ACKNOWLEDGMENTS

ALL the letters in this edition are printed in their entirety, exactly as O'Casey wrote them, except for several instances where some pages have been lost or misplaced by the owners of the original copies. Since he often made carbon copies of his typed letters, I have been able to preserve letters that some editors of newspapers and magazines refused to publish, letters that some private owners have refused to let me see or copy, letters that their owners have destroyed or lost, and letters to people I have been unable to locate.

Although O'Casey's handwriting and typing became erratic in his final years, when he was practically blind and wrote largely by instinct and sheer determination, I have, with a few exceptions, been able to transcribe his writing with what I trust is complete fidelity. His spelling was remarkably accurate, though in some instances I have corrected a misspelled word or name that he wrote in haste and previously had spelled correctly. When in his near-blindness he hit the wrong key—"I dont always strike the right quay"—I have made the logical correction. All letters to newspapers and magazines would normally be addressed, for example, "To the Editor of *Irish Times,*" but here this introduction has been shortened to, "To *Irish Times.*" For the translation of Gaelic phrases and letters written in Gaelic, I have relied upon the valuable aid of Mr. Alfrid MacLochlainn and Dr. Bruce Boling, as well as upon Dinneen's *Irish-English Dictionary.*

A collection of letters that gives only one side of a natural dialogue can be frustrating to the reader. In the hope of alleviating some if not all of this problem, I have tried to supply the other side of the dialogue in a variety of ways: by including several letters written to O'Casey, several letters and news stories in newspapers and magazines about him, and several controversial reviews to which he responded. I have also tried to tell the story behind the letters in a general introduction, in separate introductions to each year, and in the footnotes, where the necessary background and context are provided. Because O'Casey was always vitally curious about playwrights and plays, I have tried to identify and date the plays he mentions; and because he was deeply concerned about the actors who appeared in his plays, I have included the casts of his premieres, as well as the leading players in notable revivals.

My personal friendship with O'Casey during the last decade of his life, 1954 to 1964, when I was able to visit him at his home in St. Marychurch almost every summer, proved to be an invaluable help in clearing up many vague and puzzling references in the letters. Particularly during the final two and a half years of his life, I was able to ask him direct questions about complex situations and controversies. His replies were usually straight and unequivocal. If he sometimes did not recall exactly when certain events took place—he could be vague about dates—he had a phenomenal memory about what had happened and why. This edition of his letters could not have been completed in its present form without his great good help, as well as the very kind and generous assistance of his wife Eileen.

Over a period of twenty-five years I have collected some 2,500 letters, 2,436 of which will finally appear in the four volumes of this edition. I suspect that several hundred letters are missing: some destroyed, some lost, some withheld. I know a number of people who are withholding their letters for various private reasons, and it is likely that more letters will turn up in the years ahead.

The letters are collected in four separate volumes: Volume I, 1910–1941 (published in 1975); Volume II, 1942–1954 (published in 1980); Volume III, 1955–1958; Volume IV, 1959–1964, with an Appendix for letters that turned up after the publication of the early volumes.

Volume I contains 653 letters by O'Casey; 124 letters to or about O'Casey; 21 news reports and reviews of O'Casey's work—a total of 798 entries.

Volume II contains 807 letters by O'Casey; 15 letters to or about O'Casey; 5 reviews of O'Casey's work; 1 article by O'Casey; 1 statement to the press by O'Casey—a total of 829 entries.

Volume III contains 506 letters by O'Casey; 3 letters to or about O'Casey; 1 news report about O'Casey—a total of 510 entries.

Volume IV tentatively contains 469 letters by O'Casey; 6 news reports about O'Casey—a total of 475 entries.

All the letters in Volume III were written in O'Casey's home at Flat 3, 40 Trumlands Road, St. Marychurch, Torquay, Devon.

*   *   *

I have used the following code to identify the form of the original letter:

MS. Manuscript copy
TS. Typescript copy
TC. Typed carbon copy
PC. Printed copy

The location of each letter can be found in the following list of
sources.

A. Institutions
Berg Collection, New York Public Library
California State University Library, Fullerton
Cornell University Library, Ithaca
League of Dramatists, London
Uppsala University Library, Sweden

B. Periodicals
Inniu, Dublin
International Literature, Moscow
Irish Press, Dublin
Irish Times, Dublin
Manchester Guardian, London
New Statesman and Nation, London
New York Times, New York
Plays and Players, London
Sean O'Casey Review, New York
Sunday Times, London
Times Pictorial, London

C. Private Owners
Abraham Lincoln Brigade, New York
John Allen, London
T. W. Allen, Brooklyn
Brooks Atkinson, New York
Oriana Atkinson, New York
Ronald Ayling, Edmonton, Canada
Mrs. R. S. Beattie (Joan McAlevey), Brooklyn
John Beary, New York
John Bell, Newry, N. Ireland
Guy Boas, London
Mary Bromage, Ann Arbor, Michigan
J.P.R. Budlong, New York
Marguerite Buller, Oxford, England
Philip Burton, New York
Moses Cammer, Larchmont, New York
Kay Carney, New York
Ken Coates, Nottingham, England

Barbara A. Cohen, New York
Voja Čolanović, Belgrade, Yugoslavia
Edward B. Connolly, Philadelphia
Mrs. John T. Cooper, Fort Dodge, Iowa
Elizabeth Coxhead, Gerrards Cross, Bucks.
Hume Cronyn, New York
Thomas Quinn Curtiss, Paris
Cyril Cusack, Dublin
Maureen Cusack, Dublin
Vincent C. De Baun, Aurora, New York
Jay Deiss, New York
Alan Dent, London
George Devine, London
R. L. De Wilton, New York
Joseph W. Donohue, Jr., Amherst
Dr. Hugh Doran, Torquay
Mrs. Hugh Doran, Torquay
Barrows Dunham, Philadelphia
R. F. Ewer, Grahamstown, South Africa
Elizabeth Gurley Flynn, New York
Rev. Michael E. Gallagher, S.J., Tokyo
Patrick Galvin, Dublin
John Gassner, New York
Robert Emmett Ginna, New York
Eric Gorman, Dublin
Robert D. Graff, New York
Christopher Murray Grieve (Hugh MacDiarmid), Lanarkshire, Scotland
Tyrone Guthrie, London
G. W. Head, Detroit
Mrs. Stanley J. Hochdorf, Washington, D.C.
Robert Hogan, Newark, Delaware
William Honan, Charlottesville, Virginia
Clare and Stan Howard, New York
Rosamond Jacob, Dublin
Augustus John, London
Harold D. Jones, Brooklyn
Seamus Kavanagh, Dublin
May Keating, Dublin
Elizabeth Kelly, Dublin
Helen Kiok, Queens Village, New York
Alice Kornbluth, New York
David Krause, Providence, R.I.
Major A. E. Leach, Maidenhead, England
Doris Leach, Maidenhead, England
A. J. Leventhal, Dublin

Joan McAlevey (Beattie), Brooklyn
Proinnsias Mac an Bheatha, Dublin
Frank McCarthy, London
Rex MacGall, Dun Laoghaire
Patrick McLaughlin, Liverpool
Francis MacManus, Dublin
Peter MacManus (Peadar MacMaghnais), Dublin
Macmillan & Co. Ltd., London
Richard Magat, Elmhurst, New York
Ria Mooney, Dublin
Dr. Frank Morrell, New York
Franklin D. Murphy, Los Angeles
Isabella Murphy, Dublin
Peter Newmark, Guildford, Surrey
Conor O'Brien, Dun Laoghaire
John O'Donovan, Dublin
Tarlach Ó hUid, Dublin
J. J. O'Leary, Dublin
Coiril Ó Mathuna, Galway
Kay O'Riordan, Dublin
Michael O'Riordan, Dublin
Sean O'Rourke, Dublin
Arvid Paulson, New York
Mrs. R＿＿ and Miss A＿＿, England
Horace Reynolds, Belmont, Massachusetts
Stanley Richards, New York
Agnes Agatha Robinson, New York
Marianne Roney, New York
Dr. Gilbert Ross, New York
Paul and Nan Ross, New York
Clara Rotter, New York
Jane Rubin, New York
Rose Russell, New York
Seumas Scully, Dublin
Louis Sheaffer, New York
Miss Sheila ＿＿, London
Mrs. Muriel Shlosberg, Far Rockaway, New York
Paul Shyre, New York
Jeffrey Simmons, London
Brendan Smith, Dublin
Walter Starkie, Los Angeles
Joseph Stein, New York
J. J. Sullivan, Manchester, England
W. Suschitzky, London
Jessica Tandy, New York

Abigail Wanamaker, London
Jessica Wanamaker, London
Zöe Wanamaker, London
Richard Watts, Jr., New York
Eugene Weintraub, New York

For kind permission to publish copyrighted material in letters and a news report, I am grateful to the following: W. A. Newman for his letter of 14 March 1955 to O'Casey; Gabriel Fallon for his "Open Letter to O'Casey," *Irish Press,* 30 March 1955; Plays and Players for Bourke William's "Reply to Sean O'Casey," June 1955; *New York Times* for the news report, "SHOUTERS AT PLAY CHIDE O'CASEY," 7 October 1958.

While it is impossible to list everyone who has helped me in my work, I must express a very deep debt of thanks to those who have over the years given me valuable aid, counsel, and information—singling out these heroic helpers: Mr. Alfrid MacLochlainn; Mr. Brian McKenna; Mr. Robert Lowery; Mr. John O'Riordan; Mr. Timothy O'Keeffe; Mr. R. L. De Wilton; Mr. Jim Scully—and also the following: Mrs. Eileen O'Casey; Mrs. Mina Carney; Mr. and Mrs. Cyril Cusack; Mr. and Mrs. Eric Gorman; Mr. Francis MacManus; Mr. Michael Hewson; Mr. Seumas Scully; Mrs. R. Kloegman; Mrs. Valerie Plunkett; Mr. Michael Martin; Mr. Francis Mins; Dr. Bruce Boling; Professor Elmer Blistein; Mr. Ray A. Roberts.

Finally, this third volume could not have been completed without the very valuable help of a fellowship from the National Endowment for the Humanities.

Last and not least important, I have been fortified and blessed through many years of work by the love and help of my wife Anne, and the patient understanding of our four children, who gradually realized why so much of my time was devoted to Sean O'Casey.

O'CASEY
CHRONOLOGY

(30 March 1880, is born in Dublin; 18 September 1964, dies in Devon)

1955	February 22	*The Bishop's Bonfire* opens in Dublin at the Gaiety Theatre, presented by Cyril Cusack, directed by Tyrone Guthrie
	May 15 to June 5	Radio Eireann's "O'Casey Festival" is presented on four successive Sunday night broadcasts with performances of *The Shadow of a Gunman, Juno and the Paycock, The Plough and the Stars,* and *Red Roses for Me,* with recorded introductions by O'Casey
	June	*Juno and the Paycock* is recorded in Ireland by Cyril Cusack Productions for Angel Records, supervised by Alan Dent
	September	Publication of *The Bishop's Bonfire* by Macmillan
	November 1	*Cock-a-Doodle Dandy* opens in New Haven, performed by the Yale School of Drama, directed by Frank McMullan
	December 28	*Red Roses for Me* opens in New York at the Booth Theatre, presented by Gordon W. Pollock, directed by John O'Shaughnessy
1956	February	Undergoes prostate operation at Torbay Hospital

	March	Undergoes kidney stone operation at Torbay Hospital
	March	Publication of *The Green Crow*, a collection of essays in New York by George Braziller
	March 18	*I Knock at the Door*, adapted by Paul Shyre, directed by Stuart Vaughan, is performed as "A Concert Reading" in New York at the Kaufmann Auditorium, Y.M.-Y.W.H.A.
	May 27	*Pictures in the Hallway*, adapted by Paul Shyre, directed by Stuart Vaughan, is performed as "A Concert Reading" in New York at the Kaufmann Auditorium, Y.M.-Y.W.H.A.
	September 16	*Pictures in the Hallway*, adapted by Paul Shyre, directed by Stuart Vaughan, opens on Broadway at the Playhouse Theatre
	October	Publication of *Mirror in My House*, the two-volume edition of the autobiography, by Macmillan, New York
	December 27	*Purple Dust* opens in New York at the Off-Broadway Cherry Lane Theatre, presented by Paul Shyre, Howard Gottfried, Noel Behn, and Lewis Manilow, directed by Philip Burton
	December 29	Son Niall dies of leukemia at the age of twenty-one
1957	January 3	Niall O'Casey's ashes are dispersed in the Garden of Remembrance, Golders Green Crematorium, London
	February	Publication of *The Green Crow* in London by W. H. Allen; and copies sent to Ireland are seized without explanation by the Irish Customs Office, resulting in an unofficial ban of the book
	May	Receives from Moscow the publication of Russian translations of *The Shadow of a Gunman* and *Juno and the Paycock; I Knock at the Door* and *Pictures in the Hallway*
	August	Finishes writing *The Drums of Father Ned*
	September 29	*I Knock at the Door*, adapted by Paul Shyre, directed by Stuart Vaughan, opens on Broadway at the Balasco Theatre

October 10	The Dublin Toastal Council accepts *The Drums of Father Ned* for a premiere production at the Tostal Theatre Festival of 1958
1958 January	Publication of Russian translation of *The Bishop's Bonfire* in *Zvezda* (Star), Leningrad, organ of the Union of Soviet Writers
January 5	*Purple Dust* closes at the Cherry Lane Theatre, after a run of over a year, since 27 December 1956, the longest ever for an O'Casey play
January	The Archbishop of Dublin disapproves of the plan to present *The Drums of Father Ned* and a dramatization of Joyce's *Ulysses* at the Tostal Festival
February	As a result of the Archbishop's disapproval, the Dublin Tostal Council rejects *The Drums of Father Ned* and the dramatization of Joyce's *Ulysses,* and as a gesture of protest Samuel Beckett withdraws his two mime plays from the Tostal Festival
March	The unofficial banning of *The Green Crow* by the Irish Customs Office is lifted without explanation, and after a year's prohibition the book is released for sale in Ireland
April 8	George Jean Nathan dies at the age of seventy-six
July	Publication of *Five One-Act Plays* by Macmillan, London
July	As an aftermath of the banning of *The Drums of Father Ned* from the Irish Tostal, O'Casey decides to ban all professional productions of his plays in Ireland, a prohibition he maintains until 1964
October 13	Lennox Robinson dies at the age of seventy-two
November 12	*Cock-a-Doodle Dandy* opens in New York at the Off-Broadway Carnegie Hall Playhouse, presented by Lucille Lortel, Paul Shyre, and Howard Gottfried, directed by Philip Burton
November 20	*The Shadow of a Gunman* opens in New York at the Bijou Theatre, presented by Actors' Studio, directed by Jack Garfein

ILLUSTRATIONS

THE
LETTERS OF
Sean O'Casey
1955-58

I

GOD AND MAN
AND GODOT
1955

OF course there is fear in the United States just as there is fear here, & in many other places—Ireland, for instance—because of the tremendous change that has come, and is continuing to come, over life everywhere. Most of us are afraid of change; afraid of the future, afraid of the unknown. That is why we rush back to our old gods and cling around their mouldering altars; and shout at and threaten those who go by bravely to face what is to come. Man is still fighting fear, and many have to suffer for it as Socrates did when he drank down the hemlock. But things that have lost their value will have to go. God's stout fingers are tearing outworn things to pieces."

"Beckett? I have nothing to do with Beckett. He isnt in me nor am I in him. I amnt waiting for Godot to bring me life; I am out after life myself, even at the age I've reached. What have any of you to do with Godot? There is more life than Godot can give in the life of the least of us. That Beckett is a clever writer, and that he has written a rotting and remarkable play, there is no

doubt; but his philosophy isnt my philosophy, for within him
there is no hazard of hope; no desire for it; nothing in it but a
lust for despair, and a crying of woe, not in a wilderness, but a
garden."

At the beginning of 1955 O'Casey was getting ready for the Dublin
premiere of his new play, *The Bishop's Bonfire,* and toward the end of the
year he was awaiting the New York premiere of *Red Roses for Me,* an
older work written in 1942 that had not been performed in America.
Since these two visionary plays are tragicomedies dealing with his favorite
subjects, religion and politics, with an irreverent mixture of serious and
comic twists, it is understandable that his letters during this period often
show him trying to justify the ways of God to man, man to God, and man
to man. Although Christianity and Communism may appear to be anti-
thetical to orthodox Christians and Communists, the unorthodox O'Casey
was deeply drawn to both concepts in paradoxical ways that suggest he
sought the spiritualistic faith of one and the materialistic hope of the
other. He was a self-professed if somewhat evangelical Communist, and
by practice he was no longer a Christian, yet he often wrote in his letters
as if he were still trying to link the Red Star to the Star of Bethlehem, as
he had done in an earlier play, *The Star Turns Red* (1940). In his own
eccentric way he seems to be talking about the universal goodness of
mankind when he says in a May letter, "All who do good are Communists."

In a January letter to Cyril Cusack, who, while rehearsing for *The
Bishop's Bonfire,* apparently objected to the use of songs in serious situations, O'Casey defends his theatrical method by characteristically invoking
Christian, Hebrew, and Celtic symbols, and presenting the Blessed Virgin
as a socialist singer: "There is nothing wrong in a gay moment. 'Let us
come before His Presence with a song.' The Blessed Virgin broke into a
socialist song when she heard the Message from the Angel of the Annunciation. Moses broke into song when his band had crossed the Red Sea,
and Miriam banged the tambourine. Cuchullain as he died, laughed loud
at the comic raven slipping in the blood flowing away from the Hero's
life."

O'Casey censures the Christians whenever they fail to practice what
they preach, and he censures the Communists whenever they practice their
preaching in abstract clichés and party platitudes. A day before he told
Cusack how the Christians should sing out their joyous faith, he wrote to
an American doctor, warning how Communists should not parrot their
political theories: "Life comes before theory; and we have to fit theory to
life, not life to theory. . . . I have heard many Communists chattering
this way, till the head aches & the heart is sick. You'll never reach the

mind of anyone talking this way. It is just jargon. Soviet articles, plays, & stories have been full of it, till the minds & hearts of listeners & viewers have been bored & tired, so that now it is plain that many are revolting against this wearying sing-song nonsense. . . . Go away from it, and quietly read Keats or Shakespeare for a month or two."

It is curious that instead of pointing to Marx, O'Casey refers to the Bible and Shakespeare and Keats when scolding Communists for their "sing-song" theory-parroting; and in an April letter he enlightens an innocent critic with this comment: "All that is stated in the writings of Engels and Marx, books and books, is enshrined in fourteen lines of a poem of Keats"—in "Isabella; or The Pot of Basil." He always prefers poetry to dogma and is most likely to talk about Langland and Chaucer, Shakespeare and Dryden, Shaw and Emerson—Emerson with whom he heartily agreed that "Every day is a holy day."

Even in hard times, when the Dublin critics savagely attacked him and his new play, O'Casey refuses to abandon hope and writes in March to a friend: "No, I'm not a damned bit pessimistic, a mhic! On the contrary, never so convinced that life is going forward." He recognizes and often cries out against the pain and unjust suffering in the world, but he feels that fear and ignorance are the enemies of promise; he is convinced that the human condition will improve; and in an almost mystical way he declares that "things that have lost their value will have to go. God's stout fingers are tearing outworn things to pieces."

In his own unique way O'Casey sounds like a man of deep faith who believes in the potential enlightenment and salvation of humanity. He writes long letters to a Yale Divinity School student about the intolerant ways the various churches attack each other as they pursue their narrow creeds; he is suspicious of "the blather" of self-proclaimed prophets like Billy Graham; and he continues to invoke the theological wisdom of Dr. Walter McDonald, quoting passages from the dissident Maynooth priest's book questioning all claims of theocratic fiat and infallibility. In late January he urges this student to trust the miracles of art more than the sermons of would-be prophets: "To me, there is more in a picture by Greco, Titian, [Augustus] John, in a Symphony by Beethoven, a Concerto by Mozart, a play by Shakespeare; more glory to God, more Epiphanic insight, than a life's roaring from B. Graham."

A week later in early February, replying to an Irish Catholic in Manchester, he rejects the "bombastic" Catholicism of G. K. Chesterton, who was "as much a catholic as a toby jug." He goes on to defend his criticism of the Catholic Church for not practicing what it preaches: "I have never yet said anything against what is the Catholic Faith, though I've said a lot about what is called Catholic practice. There is a big difference, you know. . . . I want Irish Catholicism to be the most courageous, the most enlightened Catholicism in the world. Is that a bad wish?"

More courage and more enlightenment were always O'Casey's goals, for his own life and work, and for people everywhere who had to fight against fear and ignorance. This is the advice he offers to all the strangers who write to tell him about their problems and aspirations—students and teachers, miners and bus drivers, doctors and laborers, housewives and lonely women—people who somehow sense that, even if O'Casey happens to doubt them or disagree with them, he will reply with understanding and friendship. To the heartbroken widow in New York who told him of her sorrows, her late unlamented parents brutalized by drink and the recent loss of her husband and her only comfort, he replies with a compassionate parable: "You remember the woman who came to Buddha appealing to Him to restore a dead child to life; following him everywhere appealing, till he promised to raise the child to life again, if she but brought a pinch of salt from a household that did not know the sorrow of death. And she searched here, there, everywhere, for days, for weeks, for months; but at last had to come to tell Him that nowhere was there a household void of the sorrow that comes from the death of a loved one; nowhere."

In matters of controversy O'Casey feels forced to adopt an aggressive manner when he writes to the Dublin papers to scold and mock the reviewers who in the spirit of Irish malice mercilessly attacked him personally as well as his *Bonfire*. In March he tells Cusack he is convinced that "if an Angel did the Production of an O'Casey play, and another had leaned over me shoulder when writing it, it would still be a wretched work to the Irish Professional critics." In this wounded state he gets his only comfort from his loyal friends in New York, the drama critics George Jean Nathan and Brooks Atkinson. His hopes are revived by September, when he begins to rewrite some scenes of *Red Roses for Me* for the New York premiere; and he urges the director to avoid Stage-Irish cliches: "One warning: don't let any exclamation of 'be japers' creep into the text. No Irishman ever uses the phrase, now; and I greatly doubt if any Irishman ever did."

Although O'Casey has been away from Ireland for twenty-nine years, he remains very proud of his heritage; but in June, when writing warmly to an Irish-speaker, he insists bluntly that he does not want to be mistaken for a nationalistic hero: "I am no patriot; I am simply an Irishman." Earlier in March, however, in his more mystical mood, he had written to a young Dubliner who was thinking of leaving the country, warning him that it was no simple thing to become an exiled Irishman: "But you won't escape from Ireland. Your children might, but you cant. Ireland has a touch from God in her—go to the ends of the earth, and you'll find her beside you." By the terms of his Celtic birthright, then, the idealistic O'Casey was an Irishman before he was anything else, one who could never escape that "touch from God" which his special Irish spirit had bestowed upon him.

It may have been that independent Irish spirit which prevented O'Casey from accepting the Soviet dogma of propagandistic art for his own work and for all art. He releases his Celtic wrath against the Communist theory of "socialist realism" in his July letters to a young British miner: "Remember that life comes first, even before socialism; and that socialism must be adapted to life, not life to socialism. . . . Zhdanov didn't know what he was talking about." Comically ready to concede that "a lot of Communists are as dogmatic as any cleric," he mocks Zhdanov's ruthless campaign against the "formalism" of Western art by turning the rigid theory against itself: "The worst formalism that I know is the formalism of the chattering phrases uttered and muttered by the communists themselves."

It was in the same spirit of enlightened protest that O'Casey defended T. S. Eliot in February, saying he had written to the USSR Commission on Foreign Writers to claim that "the venomous criticisms of Eliot were shameful and false." A month earlier he had defended Eugene O'Neill in a letter to a German translator who felt that O'Neill lacked political optimism: "Who there, or here, as a playwright is greater than he? If you say this one, or that one is greater as a propagandist for a particular opinion, you may be right; but the pressing home of an opinion alone not only doesnt make one a fine playwright, but may make one a damned bad one." This did not mean that O'Casey rejected some didacticism in art, for he had reminded an Irish friend in March that "The Sermon on the Mount was poetry as well as teaching."

O'Casey was convinced that it was an indirect function of literature to improve and celebrate life. Writing to his American publisher in November, he sent his "lay Bishop's blessings" to the socially conscious Arthur Miller. If at the end of the year he withheld his blessings from *Waiting for Godot*—"I amnt waiting for Godot"—he was rejecting the defeatist attitude in "a rotting and remarkable play," not Sam Beckett the artist, whom he placed on a level with the great Ibsen. For the yea-saying O'Casey, mankind was "not in a wilderness, but a garden," and he was determined to do everything he could to help it flourish.

To Carmen Capalbo[1]

TC. O'CASEY

4 JANUARY 1955

Dear Carmen Capalbo,
    I dont know how far you have gotten with the play [*Purple Dust*], though I'm hoping, of course, that you have succeeded in getting on a

---

[1] Carmen Capalbo (1925–   ), American theatre director and producer who had taken an option to present *Purple Dust* but later gave it up. See O'Casey's first letter to him, 15 November 1954, Vol. II.

good way towards a production. G. J. Nathan has told me that you have had some difficulty—or are having some difficulty—in getting a Cast—the difficulty that every, or almost every play of any worth has to meet. I do hope you may surmount the difficulty. I mentioned in a previous letter that our Breon was doing a design for the scene of the play. I am sending this to you under another cover, and hope you may like it. Breon has written a few notes on the edge to guide to its meaning. The two side-pieces, representing a kind of tapestry on the walls symbolises the spirit of the play: to the right, the animals of the country, to the [left], trees, and a blue meandering strip of blue, the River.

The back top is open, and through this, and the back window, the countryside is visible, the designs changing with each act, though the main structure remains the same.

The two figures in armour could be done in plywood, silvered over; a figure standing at either side of the tapestry.

The three chief episodes of comic-Action are the Scene with the "Bull"; the one with the Garden-roller; and that with the Bureau, a sketch of which goes with the scene-design.

There could be a window-hatch in the door-way on left, back, which could suddenly fall, at an appropriate moment, through which the "Bull" could thrust his head to bellow—this head should be a comical stylised one, with twisted horns, like the "cow with the crumpled horn" of the nursery song; the face should show a look of bewildered wonder. The door should swing open a little (at the beginning Barney should rush to shut it, before he flees away, right); it should open again and he should rush back to shut it; then fussily and clumsily put the mattress, etc, against it, Poges shouting at him to be quick, and generally, action of this sort to accentuate the fight they are all in.

The scene with the Bureau, the "quattro-quentro," could be done through the door on left at back, or by the Window at back, which, I imagine, should open, or two-thirds of it, two panels of panes, which would provide another entry and exit, and a picturesque one, too. It is important that the work round the bringing in of the Bureau should be clearly seen, for it can be a very funny episode; and the action, though noisy, shouldnt be rapid, and should allow the words to be heard.

The third scene—the one with the roller: See that the doorway through which Poges obstinately persists in shoving it is wide enough to allow it to pass easily; or that the roller be made to suit the doorway: the roller neednt be too big. It might be good to bring it IN by the window, though you will of course easily manage some other way.

The open back-scene has many advantages. It shows the aspect of the outer world, the river, the sky, the fields. One more very important thing, it allows the Song at the end of the play to be heard clearly, which is essential, for it is on the note of the song that the play should end—"Far from all moulderin' ashes we row," etc. In a boxed-in scene, this is hardly heard at all, and the end is blurred, if not spoiled. I suggest, too, that the boat might pass by the window rowing through the flood. If this be done, I should have a gayly-coloured boat to do it, giving an emphasis to the hope and bright resolution of the song.

I shall send on the design in a day or so by ordinary post, for Air Mail is a bit costly. It should reach you within a fortnight.

Thanks for the Christmas Card—the song of the CHERRY TREE LEGEND; a song not usually liked by Christians, for it is too human for them, and puts Holy Joseph in a curious position of distrust, and by-passes the story of the Angel explaining everything in a dream to him. Dreams are handier things than Freud thought them to be!

Irish Catholics shun the Cherry Tree song. There was a fine row about it once, with Yeats mixed up in the wordy melee.[2] It is rarely, if ever sung among the other carols.

We are having many a flood here; and for the past week, we are in the midst of gales. As I write this, the winds are shaking the house, for we live near the sea, only a few steps away, and the winds blow the gulls over the roof of the house. Our flat is on the higher floor, so the winds get us more easily than they do those who live below.

All good wishes to you, and may you succeed in all your endeavours.

Yours sincerely,
Sean O'Casey

[2] When W. B. Yeats defended the "Cherry Tree Carol" as a traditional masterpiece, after a Christian Brother had burned it as "devilish literature," Professor Alfred O'Rahilly, a Catholic apologist, scornfully responded: "Mr. Yeats regards himself as a much better judge of blasphemy than a mere Christian Brother." For a full account of this controversy, see O'Casey's letter to Gabriel Fallon, ? May 1926, note 3, Vol. I. See also O'Casey's letter to the *Irish Times*, 12 April 1961, note 3, which was refused publication because he called O'Rahilly "that curious little ecclesiastical cuckoo-clock."

To Mrs. Muriel Schlosberg[1]

MS. SCHLOSBERG

4 JANUARY 1955

Dear Mrs. Schlosberg,

Thank you very much for your kind letter and for your kinder words. I am very glad that you liked my books, and that you appreciated the love

[1] Mrs. Muriel Schlosberg, 1121 Beach 24th Street, Far Rockaway, N.Y.

of life, and the call for a safer and happier life that echoes through them. Glad, too, I am, that your Mother has rallied out of her illness. I hope she may live longer to enjoy life & all that goes with it to the stout in heart and the generous in thought. Yes, your Country must be a lovely one, & must have many wonderful and beautiful places. I know New York, Boston, and Philadelphia a little; but no more. So you have three children too, as we have—two boys and a girl. Our girl's name—Shivaun—is the Irish equivalent for "Susan." In Irish, it actually means "a fair fairy," *shidhe bhán;* in Hebrew, it means "a lily," so there's not much difference. My mother's name was Susan. Our eldest, Breon, is now 23; our second, Niall, now a gunner in the Royal Artillery, is 20; & our girl is 15. So give my love to Susan & to each of your boys. Though near the sea—only a few steps away—, we are now surrounded with snow, & it is very cold. I'm not sure whether you live in Far Rockaway or Los Angeles, but you gave the former address on the envelope; so I'm sending this note there. From the Devon Sea, I send my love via the Hudson and the Susquehanna (both of which I know) to your husband & to you.

Yours very sincerely,
Sean O'Casey

To David Krause

MS. KRAUSE

5 JANUARY 1955

My dear Dave:

I hope you are well and thriving; doing well in your work which is so important for the years to come. The Teacher. They number some fine names, Dave—Jesus, Aristotle, Socrates, Buddha, Confucius, Darwin—hardly one who drew breath, worth more than an Irish damn, but had some of the teacher in him; Shaw, Larkin, Emerson. Only poets like Eliot do not teach, though they trot before to lead, scornful of the instructive word. Is this a lecture I'm giving, or what?

I wrote to the Macmillan Company about your proposed book. They liked the idea, & said they would get into touch with you. But all the time, Dave, remember not to let this book if you still happen to be doing it, not to let it do harm to your teaching. This must come first all the time. This is what you have set yourself to do, & you must try to do it well.

"Sunset & Evening" has met with a barrage of abuse & scorn in Ireland. I enclose one by Austin C.[1] Curious outlook over O'Casey. A deep depression with breezes trying to look like a stormy wind. He even uses a quotation I took from the very paper he writes for, written by one "Thersites"[2], alias Hogan, alias Thomson, and attributes it to me, tho' the words are marked as quoted in the book. The Irish writers, on the whole are afraid to write opinions over their names, & then become more fearful than ever when they see their opinions in print. One of them, referred to in my book, P. Galvin, sent me a stupid, impudent (to me) "Open Letter," followed by a letter of abuse because I had written him to say I couldn't bother to comment on his Open Letter.[3] I put a few phrases into the book, & now the laddo is in a phrensy, calling for an apology (which he won't get), & threatening an action for breach of copyright. A Solicitor of mine, Harold Richenstein, tells me there is a technical infringement, but it is so trivial that he thinks no solicitor would take the case. It is odd how many love abuse, & yet dread to see it in front of them afterwards. The Irish writer is always in dread of something. They'd love to shout, but are afraid of the neighbours hearing. By the way, A. Clarke wasn't a gassoon in 1926;[4] he was 30, & should have known better; envying Yeats, he wanted a sly slap at him thro' me.

"The Bishop's Bonfire" is to be seen in Dublin. Cyril Cusack— one-time Abbey actor—is taking it under his wing. There'll be a chance for all the critics. Oddly enough, Cyril is a very good fellow, with a lovely sense of humor, with an intelligent wife who has a sense of humor, too. In the recent competition, the Abbey Theatre got 47 plays, and (they say) not one good enough to warrant even part of the £250 prize. Wish they'd give me the Prize for "The B.'s Bonfire." But the Abbey, too, goes about now on tiptoes, singing its song in a whisper.

Well, Dave, the Calendar says we're in another year, and we must try to make the best of it. Here, we are surrounded by snow, and fierce winds shake the windows; but, soon, the daffodils will be sprouting.

---

[1] Austin Clarke, "Cock-a-Doodle Dandy," *Irish Times,* 6 November 1954, a review of *Sunset and Evening Star* (1954).

[2] For the background of the O'Casey-Galvin controversy, see O'Casey's letters to Francis MacManus, 1 June 1954, note 8; David Marcus, 28 July 1954, note 1; G. W. Head, 31 December 1954, note 2, Vol. II.

[3] Thomas Woods (1923–61), Irish literary figure and diplomat. Woods wrote a regular column on the book page of the *Irish Times* under the pseudonym of "Thersites"; he wrote articles and reviews under the pseudonym of "Thomas Hogan"; and for many years he was an official in the Department of External Affairs, serving as Ireland's Permanent Representative to the Council of Europe at the time of his death.

[4] In a letter to the editor of the *Irish Statesman,* 20 February 1926, Austin Clarke had written: "Several writers of the new Irish school believe that Mr. O'Casey's work is a crude exploitation of our poorer people in an Anglo-Irish tradition that is now moribund." In a letter in the same issue, Liam O'Flaherty wrote a bitter attack against Yeats and O'Casey.

I send a little sketch done for the spine of "I Knock at the Door" oh, long, long ago.

My love to you and yours.
As ever,
Sean

Spine for book — 'Knock at the Door'

To Cyril Cusack[1]

MS. CUSACK

6 JANUARY 1955

Dear Cyril,
     With this go 3 Photos—which I hope may give you one suitable for the Souvenir. You are going it, aren't you? Since you like Tyrone Guthrie,

---

[1] Cyril Cusack (1910–   ), Irish actor and producer, began his acting career with the Abbey Theatre in the 1930s, distinguishing himself in the plays of Synge and O'Casey, and thereafter played in many notable productions in Dublin, London, and New York, as well as in many films. See letters to him in Vol. II.

I can have no objection. He is Irish, and should know a lot about the strange idiom of Irish character & conduct; he is a true man of the Theatre, & all it hopes to do.

The only thing troubling me is the cost. Have you counted it? You have a big responsibility on you, and I'm one who knows what responsibility is: so be careful, unless you can get some one to back you.

I'm sending by Registered Post the final text of the play. You'll see the "hiding of the bottle" scene changed completely; and, also, the scene between Foorawn & The Codger in the 2nd Act, "The way to the tomb," changed too, and a great deal for the better, I think.

The photo—any of them—mustn't be published outside of the Souvenir without Gjon Mili's consent—6 East 23rd Street, New York City, New York. I've risked the Souvenir, for Gjon is a friend of mine, and, I know, would readily give me permission to use one of his in this way.

As another Souvenir, maybe you'd like to keep one of them for the mantelpiece. If you do, you're welcome to any one or the other.

I've written 100 to 150 words for you. I've made no effort to explain the play—there'll be enough of these when the play has been produced.

I've just given a few notes on a muted cornet as an introduction to the play. I hope you may find it satisfactory.

I don't know what feature to give the play—tragedy, comedy, historical, pastoral, pastoral-comical, or what: there's something of all in it. But as you say, "tragi-comedy" is as good as any, so let's decide on that much explanation. Sorry, you didn't care for the "Interior." I thought myself that the "doors" were awkwardly placed for movement, especially for the scene of carrying in the "palms," etc. You can emend it, leaving in anything you like.

I am so glad to hear that the little ones are well again. So much anxiety shoved into the past. Maureen is trying to do too much, apparently. Good for her that she shone so fine in the play; but tell her to take care of herself, & not to let all her energy loose.

Eileen who is in London, has just rung up to say she saw "The Matchmaker," & she thought the Production very fine indeed—another affirmation for T.G.[2]

Please acknowledge Gjon Mili under picture of Photo in Souvenir. "Photo by Gjon Mili."

My love to Maureen, the children, & to you.
Sean

Enclosures:
3 Photos
Slip of my phrases for Souvenir

[2] Tyrone Guthrie directed Thornton Wilder's *The Matchmaker,* which opened in London on 4 November 1954.

THE BISHOP'S BONFIRE[3]

Here's what's called a play by what is called a playwright. O'Casey's the name, and here he is trying once more to dance a polka on the stage. See him dance the polka. He hopes you'll like it, and he hopes you'll laugh. We writers are inclined to be a cocky crowd, thinking so often that what we say should be, not written down on paper, but graven deep down in marble so that newcomers to life won't miss the great news; when, in reality, most of what is written by us are but plumes of smoke getting into the eyes to make them water, and into the nose to make us sneeze. Apart from the great geniuses like Shakespeare, Tolstoy, or Shaw we writers are, in our artistry, of no more importance than the artistry in the energy of the farmer, the miner, the builder, and the housewife in keeping the home and bringing a family safely through the earlier years of life.

Well, here's another plume of smoke which I hope may have a little flame in it to light up life for a moment or two; to make us think again of some of the problems Ireland has to face in the midst of the sound from the singer's song and the politician's shout.

So with the gallant orchestral help from the Producer and the Actors, here's O'Casey trying out another polka-play on an Irish stage. He hopes you'll like it and he hopes you'll laugh.

Sean O'Casey

[3] These comments were printed in the theatre program, with a photograph of O'Casey taken by Gjon Mili.

To Paul Ross[1]

MS. ROSS

7 JANUARY 1955

My dear Paul,

Thanks, dear man, for the gift & the card from you all. It is well that Gil is away now from the Ceremonial, and has set his feet on the road to the doing of things; leaving behind the fossils buried in the ice of their status quo. It is funny how these think that because they stand still, the world does, too. But, as you tell me, there among the petrified ones, a young boy & a young girl meet; and life takes a new step. I share your hope that Joyce and Gil may be very happy; not free from struggle, of

[1] Paul L. Ross (1902–78), Brooklyn, New York, lawyer and social activist, made an unsuccessful race for mayor of New York City in 1950. In his law practice he frequently defended left-wing figures in civil rights cases. See letters to him in Vol. II.

course—for that would be as fossils are—but happily united in meeting all difficulty & anxiety with patience, courage, and resolution.

The picture by Breon in the "Bonfire" isn't bad.[2] He has suggested sending you an earlier one which I don't like, because I don't think it a good one. I have, of course, told him so; and haven't given him your address. So say no more. If he does a better one (I have told him, I am willing to sit again. Indeed, so far, I've sat 4 times for him. He has done a full-size one; but it is far too big to send away; &, anyway, he wants to keep it for a possible show). I shall tell you about it. I do hope Nan will take care of herself. You all look fine in the photo, & I only wish Joyce had been with you. Thanks, too, for your kind cable. It seems to have been a fine production; & I hope it may have been something of a fine play. Anyway, I've no doubt it's better than Mr. [Walter] Kerr makes it out to be. I would be surprised if any play of mine failed to split opinion; I hope there will always be in a play of mine the heat & explosion of a bursting drama-atom.

My love to Nan—tell her I hope she will mind herself—, to Gil, my young friend, to his Joyce, and to you, my older one.

As ever,
Sean

[2] A portrait of O'Casey painted by his son Breon appears as the frontispiece of the published edition of *The Bishop's Bonfire* (1955).

To Cyril Cusack

MS. CUSACK

8 JANUARY 1955

Dear Cyril,

I forgot to mention this in my letter to you:—If you use Breon's Design for exterior, could you mention his name in the Programme?[1] I know he would like to see his name there—he's young, not like an old stager as I am who for many years hasn't cared whether his name is in darkness or in light.

Sean

[1] Breon O'Casey's design for *The Bishop's Bonfire* was not used. The sets were designed by Michael O'Herlihy.

To George Jean Nathan[1]

MS. CORNELL

8 JANUARY 1955

My very dear George,

1955 Greetings to Julie and to you, sweet Prince. I do hope you are well, & that the spring, now in front of us, will bring us all a few fine roses. I'm glad you liked the last Autobiography [*Sunset and Evening Star*] by and large. It was the best I could do. There is still hope of the "Purple Dust" coming into view. Our elder boy is trying out a set for it, & I have made a few alterations in the Script. I'm mortally busy at present. There has been an odd development with "The Bishop's Bonfire." A young Catholic (Irish) producer read the play, got enthusiastic, & is working to put it on in the Gaiety, Dublin, & thinks of carrying it over to England. Tyrone Guthrie is to be the Producer (Director); they're getting out a "Souvenir Program," if you please, with a decorated cover, a photo of O'Casey, a comment by a Benedictine Monk (Irish) whose two loves are "God and James Joyce"; and another comment by a Jesuit.[2] God, I'd love to see it! Breon, again, is trying out an outside & inside set. It keeps his hand in, & gives him something definite to do with colors. "The Book Find Club" has taken on "Sunset & Evening Star," & wants me to collect articles I've written, combine them with the "Flying Wasp," & make a book of it.[3] Radio Eireann is to put on an "O'Casey Festival of Plays,"[4] & wants me to do 3 or 4 quarter-of-an-hour Broadcasts; and all the while, I'm being bombarded with shocking Irish Reviews of "Sunset & Evening Star." It's a goddamned curious country.

Another young Irish poet [Patrick Galvin], who sent a vicious "Open Letter" to the Press, & another, supplementing what he said in it, phrases

---

[1] George Jean Nathan (1882–1958), drama critic, author, editor; wrote over thirty books on drama and theatre; began writing reviews for the *New York Herald* in 1905; co-editor with H. L. Mencken of *Smart Set,* 1914–24; regular drama critic of the *New York Journal American,* 1943–56; early champion in America of the works of Ibsen, Strindberg, Shaw, O'Neill, O'Casey, and Saroyan. In 1955, at the age of seventy-three, he ended his bachelorhood and married the actress Julie Haydon. He was converted to Roman Catholicism shortly before he died. For O'Casey's reaction to his conversion and death, see his letter to Brooks Atkinson, 16 April 1958. See O'Casey's letters to him in Vols. I and II. See also *My Very Dear Sean, George Jean Nathan to Sean O'Casey, Letters and Articles* (1985), edited by Robert G. Lowery and Patricia Angelin.

[2] The statements in support of O'Casey by the Benedictine monk and the Jesuit priest did not appear in the souvenir program of *The Bishop's Bonfire.* Instead, there was a quotation from Francois Mauriac, "God and Mammon"; and three statements in praise of O'Casey, one by Cyril Cusack, one by Gerard Fay, and one in Irish by Micheal MacLiammoir. And, finally, there was O'Casey's comment on the play; see his letter to Cusack, 6 January 1955.

[3] It became *The Green Crow* (1956), published by George Braziller, who also ran the Book Find Club.

[4] See O'Casey's letter to Philip Rooney, 29 April 1955, note 1.

of which I put into my last book, threatens a law action for "breach of copyright." Macmillan's here apologised to him; but he'll wait for one from me. Some time ago, the same lad wrote asking implicitly for £50, and explicitly for £5, to keep a magazine going of which he was the Editor. Well, I haven't, & never yet had, £50 or £5's to give away; so I didn't agree; & I imagine—tho' I may be wrong—that this denial of mine had something to do with the "Open Letter." However, the "infringement" is so trivial, according to a solicitor of mine, that he may find it hard to get a solicitor to take up the case. It isn't an infringement coming within the concern of the Authors' Society. It is all my own stupidity in taking any notice of his "Open Letter," but he pestered me into commenting on it; or, rather, into refusing to comment on it, which brought him to write an abusive letter, a phrase or two of which I quoted in "S. & E. Star."

Well, George, the Abbey Theatre's Play Competition (prize £250) brought them 47 plays, not one of which was even half-way good enough for them even to give a consolation prize. And yet, they'll do none of mine. They knew about "The B.'s Bonfire," but simply ignored it. It is very curious. For this reason alone, I hope Cusack may succeed in bringing the play to the Dublin stage. It is more plausible in Dublin than the more gay and imaginative Cockadoodle Dandy: there was no hope for that one.

Well, let me know how you are. You are near an old-married man now, & should be getting used to it. I don't know how you stuck staying on your own for so long. I couldn't have done it. The house (or flat) feels empty when Eileen's away, even for a few days in London.

I hear P. V. Carroll is to have a new play—"The Wayward Saint" on in New York soon.[5] Maybe, that may blaze a trail for other Irish plays—mine, of course, first of all. So I hope it may do well.

Give Julie a kiss for me. I wish I could spend an evening with you both. Ah, well, never mind.

My love to her, &, dear George, to you.

As ever,
Sean

[5] Paul Vincent Carroll's *The Wayward Saint* opened in New York on 17 February 1955, and closed after 21 performances.

To Miss Elizabeth Barber[1]

TS. LEAGUE OF DRAMATISTS

11 JANUARY 1955

My dear Miss Barber,

No, dear; I'm too old now to let my name go on to any Council, bar that of the Communion of Saints, and there's little chance of me getting asked to join that one.

A little while ago, I refused to let my name go down as one of the Vice-Presidents of a new Dramatic Group recently formed, with a lot of big names attached to it. I have long tried to keep my name from appearing in this way, except with those activities concerned with Peace among Nations; concerned with Peace; and I am anxious to go on with this practice.

Please give your Executive my sincere thanks for the kind thought of wanting me to add my name to the Council of the League, to which be all good and useful achievements during this present year.

Yours very sincerely,
Sean O'Casey

1 Elizabeth Barber, League of Dramatists, London.

To Otto Brandstädter[1]

TC. O'CASEY

12 JANUARY 1955

Dear young friend,

Thank you for your letter of the 27 Nov. 1954. I have been very busy, and still am, so I couldnt take time to reply to you before this time. Thanks for the bibliography,[2] which may be very useful to me from time to time in replying to the various American students who ask me to help them in locating references to my work; though I'd far rather they would

1 Otto Brandstädter, German bibliographer and translator of O'Casey's works. He wrote the introductory essay for Georg Goyert's translation of *I Knock at the Door,* under the title *Ich Kloppe An* (Leipzig: Paul List Verlag, 1957). Subsequently he wrote essays for translations of the five remaining volumes of the autobiography. In 1966 Irmhild and Otto Brandstädter published a German translation of eleven O'Casey plays. *Rote Rosen Fur Mich. Ausgewahlte Dramen.* See letters to Brandstädter in Vol. II.

2 Otto Brandstädter, "Ein O'Casey-Bibliographie," *Zeitschrift für Anglistik und Amerikanistik* (Berlin, 1954).

say what they think themselves rather than to delve opinions out of the opinions of others. I daresay, though, we all learn from each other—if not from what others do well, then from what others do badly. I should be glad of a copy of the Magazine of English and American studies. I dont know much German myself, but our elder lad knows a good deal, and would be interested in it too.

There is a good deal to be said for the claim that O'Neill was the top of American drama, and still remains so. Who there, or here, as a playwright is greater than he? If you say this one, or that one is greater as a propagandist for a particular opinion, you may be right; but the pressing home of an opinion alone not only doesnt make one a fine playwright, but may make one a damned bad one. Would you call Strindberg a fine playwright? Yet he was in a number of ways as "pessimistic" as O'Neill. Shakespeare himself, you know, could be damned pessimistic; terribly so at times, both in his plays and his sonnets. There is a lot of evil in life, and while we fight for and encourage the good, we must not be afraid of facing the evil. And people and persons are driven at times by "mysterious forces," by emotions neither they themselves nor anyone else can as yet explain. My dear friend, we do not know everything about life yet. Perhaps, as you say, O'Neill is portraying a "decaying society." But decay is but another word for change; and society is always in a process of change to make room for a new form. Even though it may appear that it would last forever (as it did in China) always underneath the seeming sleep, great forces are moving and stirring, till, some time or another, the change smites the eyes of some, and gladdens the eyes of others. The best of authors can but write from what their senses take in, illumined by whatever imagination God or nature may have given them; that is draw on what they meet, see, hear, touch, which presents bewildering variety of theme in every place on earth; and mixed with all this is the writer's own psychology, his own misfortunes, his own disappointments, his own sorrow, as well as his own laughter and sense of joy. That is why the Democratic writing or so much of it falls far below what life is, or what imagination can make it. The stories are all the same, colored a little differently by change of location. But this is all literary controversy, and would need a year and a big book to describe.

I am busy at the moment during a few changes to a new play, THE BISHOP'S BONFIRE, which is marked for a production in Dublin some time next month; and with the proofs of the same play for publication. Indeed, Dr Franke[3] seems to be a man of great energy, full of action and planning. May the work go well with him.

Macmillan's have written to say that they have no objection to Dr. Franke taking over the Biography from the Henschel Publishing Firm; and I am very glad.

It will be a "hard task" to translate me into German, or any other

---

[3] Dr. Franke of Paul-List-Verlag, Leipzig.

language, for my work is quite different from other Irish work; not quite so hard as Joyce would be; but hard enough.

If you take a part in the translation to help, I hope you can get a fee for your work. You are young, and must think out your own life. If you arent married, you probably will be, which may mean a family, and many responsibilities; so think of Otto before you think of Sean. If you do take on to help, and get a fee, and are doubtful about anything, let me know the difficulty, and I shall be glad to try to explain the problem.

All good and cordial wishes to you.
Yours sincerely,
Sean O'Casey.

To Brooks Atkinson[1]

MS. ATKINSON

15 JANUARY 1955

My dear Brooks and Oriana,
A good New Year to you both, & a bouquet of thanks for the kind package of pleasant goods you sent to us all. We are all pegging along firmly, if not merrily. Breon is now at an Art School in London; Shivaun still at Dartington; Niall a Lance Bombardier in the Royal Artillery in Germany; & Eileen & I keep guard here till they come back (as I write, Shivaun, home for the Sunday, is at my side & we are discussing Hazlitt's review of Shakespeare's Richard the II, which she has to discourse upon for a school essay). You know I wrote a play called "The Bishop's Bonfire"? Now, I want you and Oriana to pray for my intentions. Cyril Cusack, one-time Abbey man, has taken the play on for a production in the Dublin Gaiety Theater; & Dublin is agog, waiting—waiting for Lefty. Tyrone Guthrie is to Direct, & a "Souvenir Program" is in hands, with comments by clerics & lay, a few words from me around a photo; and Dublin once again is to be the place of an O'Casey First Night. This play isn't as fine as "Cockadoodle Dandy," but is fine enough to merit a good production; & Cusack is doing his best to secure one; so pray for his intentions too. London is sending over writers to have a look at it, & take down all that happens. It will be interesting to see how it goes—in London too. Cyril C. is a very ardent Catholic, & had just come back from a pilgrimage to St. Patrick's Purgatory when he read the play. He is calling it a Tragi-comedy.

---

[1] Brooks Atkinson (1894–1983), American drama critic and author; drama critic of the *New York Times*, 1926–60; conducted a special column, "Critic at Large," *New York Times*, 1960–66. See letters to him in Vols. I and II.

The Abbey Theater's Play Competition last year was a failure; tho' a prize of £250 was offered for the best play. 47 were sent in, but none, it was declared, was good enough for a thought—production; & so no prize was given. Wish they'd have given me the £250 for B.'s Bonfire. Never mind: the world wags that way, & we must rise above the wag of the world.

I hope you had a good and a restful time in the Summer. Do you & Oriana ever sit down? George Jean tells me you agree that Cockadoodle Dandy was the better play for Carmen Capalbo to do. I agree. I often wished it had been that play; but didn't like to say so for fear of annoying a friend who had made his choice.

God be good to you Brooks and to dear Oriana.

As ever,
Sean

To Mrs. Doris Leach[1]

MS. LEACH

17 JANUARY 1955

Dear Doris,

These floods! This snow! And all because we don't prepare for them; because we don't remember what our own land does. Too busy peering into the affairs of others. [Edward] Crankshaw knows more about Moscow than he does about London. He counts the Slavic flakes of snow as they fall, & gives the statistics in the Sunday Papers.

Well, dear, I hope you, your husband, & your mother, have escaped the clutch of the river. We know what a flood is: we had one last winter in Tingrith; but whereas yours came up from below, ours came down from above. A huge tank under the roof, burst; no-one knew where the main was to cut the supply off; so, before one who knew came, the water cascaded down for two hours, flooding everything we had; we running round in macks & bare feet, doing everything but asking God to turn off the waters. It is infuriating to find what Eileen calls "our little bits & pieces" soaked and soiled because of the carelessness in the first fixing of things. We have had fierce weather here, and "glorious Devon" is in the grip of ice, snow, sleet, blocked roads, shattered pipes, & when the grip loosens, the thaw comes, then the deluge! Uranium, plutonium—it's amazing what we can do; amazing what we don't do. In Ireland, the same—as if no-one

[1] Mrs. Doris Leach, 2 Chantry Road, Maidenhead, Berkshire. See letters to her in Vol. II.

ever asked a Saint to help them. Year in, year out, the people have to flee from the Shannon, the Barrow, & the Nore. I do hope you have managed to keep the Thames out of the house.

I have had to waste a bit of time over a P[atrick]. Galvin whom I quoted & commented upon in "S. and E. Star." He demanded an apology for quoting him without permission (I should never have got it), & threatened a law-action if the apology didn't come. He alleged "breach of copyright." Macmillans readily gave one, but, then, the "Open Letter" of Galvin didn't apply to them. I understand, the "breach" was technical, and so insignificant that no solicitor would like to take the case. He (Galvin) is still (appealing now) asking for his apology. "Please!" he calls out in his last letter. I am always ready to take a risk to make these fellows stand up to the challenge of their own words!

I'm busy now with "The Bishop's Bonfire" for it is very probable that Dublin will see the first production done by Tyrone Guthrie, with special Programme, including design, comments, & photo. The first performance is down for 28 Feb. If it does come thro' (there's no knowing what may happen in Ireland), it will be interesting to see how it is taken or attacked.

The accident you mention was, indeed, a sad one; but, possibly, one of so many due to our clinging so aimlessly to worn-out ways. Anyhow, logically & actually, it couldn't make a flood in your home any less distressing or destructive. Both things are bad; & will continue till we all get sense to act collectively to make life safer & time less wasteful.

My love to your husband and to you.

As ever,
Sean

To Dr. Frank Morrell[1]

MS. MORRELL

17 JANUARY 1955

Dear Frank,

No one can separate himself from "Social issues"; but, if he is to be a qualified man in his particular science, he can't allow his mind to be always making a thesis of them. Gilbert [Ross]—like us all—will have to

---

[1] Dr. Frank Morrell (1926–   ), neurophysiologist, Montefiore Hospital, New York; Professor and Chairman of the Neurology Department, Stanford University, 1961–69; since 1969, Professor of Neurology, New York Medical College. In the summer of 1952, when Dr. Morrell was an intern in a London hospital, he stayed with the O'Caseys in Totnes for a week. See letters to Dr. Morrell in Vol. II.

fight & force his way thro' the raw things within & without our humanity; and, as an intelligent lad, he will learn from them more than from any book of theoretical value. Life comes before Theory; & we have to fit theory to life, not life to theory; & that can be done by learning from experience; trial & error. You can't stuff Communism into a soul no more than you can stuff Christianity into it. A stuffed Communist isn't a Communist at all, no more than a stuffed shirt is a man. Young people are often cynical. Nan & Paul [Ross] shouldn't worry; or you either. If you aren't careful, you'll make his cynicism permanent. Don't take too much notice of it; & don't argue too much with him. You'll just succeed in making cynicism exciting to him. Let him think out things for himself; & don't think you have all the truth; even all the facts. Listen to yourself again: "In a more positive sense I believe we have a public responsibility or obligation, taking men as they are and society as it is, to actively promote those trends, both scientific and economic, which insure the utilization of scientific knowledge for the benefit of the largest number of people." And all your paragraphs are similar to this one—full of cliches and platitudes that have nothing in them but questions hidden away among the words, too timid, or too submerged, to ask them. I simply hear a politician speaking over the radio for his Party: pouring out phrase after phrase that tell the listener nothing. Indeed, I've heard many Communists chattering this way, till the head aches & the heart is sick. You'll never reach the mind of anyone talking this way. It is just jargon. Soviet articles, plays & stories have been full of it, till the minds & hearts of listeners & viewers have been bored & tired, so that now it is plain that many are revolting against this wearying sing-song of nonsense.[2]

No wonder you yourself say you are tired. How could you escape wearyness of soul packing your poor head with all these stereotyped arguments?

Go away from it, and quietly read Keats or Shakespeare for a month or two, till you forget for a while your anxiety for Gil's young soul.

My love to you.

Sean

[2] For Dr. Morrell's reaction to this advice to avoid political jargon and fanaticism, see O'Casey's letter to him, 22 May 1955, note 1.

To Cyril Cusack

TS. CUSACK

18 JANUARY 1955

Dear Cyril,

Thanks for your letter from Chelsea. It's not good to be in bed these days with a cold within adding fuel to the cold without. A cold in winter is hard to bear, and more lasting too. Take care of yourself when you feel better, tho' by the time you get this, the warning (like most warnings) will be too late to be of any use. Anyhow, I hope you are allright now. I imagine that you are, maybe, trying to do too much. It's usually the way with acting, producing, writing, too much to do, or idleness without any apparent hope.

The "goose-stepping to the tomb" is really an allusion to the play, "On the Way to the Tomb." It has no religious implication. We are all on our way there, starting the second we are born, but there is no reason, that I can see, why we should sing a dirge all the way there; and one doesnt go any more readily with a dirge in our heart than we do when we chant a gaysome song. That's the Codger's way, anyhow, and he infects Foorawn with his own idea for the moment in the play. There's nothing wrong in a gay moment. "Let us come before His Presence with a song." The Blessed Virgin broke into a socialist song when she had heard the Message from the Angel of the Annunciation. Moses broke into song when his band had crossed the Red Sea, and Miriam banged the tambourine. Cuchullain, as he died, laughed loud at the comic raven slipping in the blood flowing away with the Hero's life. The Codger is one who queueing up for the Judgement might forget the solemnity of it, and break into song, and, maybe, none of God's Spirits would shout out Silence!

As for the razor-edge of the bottle-scene—no recorded saint is concerned; and, actually, the whole incident is one indicative of the frailty of man's good resolutions; his pompous manner of declaring a change for the better; of turning over a new leaf; accompanying the declaration with a bugle blast; Here goes! Codger, wiser man, sceptical of the loud alarums, seeing the breaking of it almost as soon as it has been made; warning silently that a resolution to be effective must be done in quietness, silently, in one's own heart; watched and remembered till the change becomes a habit. I dont think there is much more in the incident, bar its coloring in a heightened Irish way. Anyway, while we live, it is said that the soul is united with the body, and, even—as Dr. [Walter] McDonald thought—formed a substantial part of the body according to the decree of the Council of Vienne. So we cant leave our souls behind us; we go; they go with us; and the soul is part of whatever song we sing. So we neednt be afraid of an old man dancing when he thinks of death; or shrink when a poor soul puts a good resolution under the skirt of a saint. In this ritual of timed thought, we "make the worship more important than the god." By the way, I have remembered a point you raised in one of your early letters, that of fearing the "hob-nailed" boots of Ran [Rankin]; and The Prod [The Prodigal]; would sound curious when they jumped from the platform. Well, "tradesmen" dont wear hob-nailed boots. Sturdy boots, but not studded with nails. This is one way of distinguishing them from the "laborers."

I've seen most of the references, here and in America. A Column-writer in the Manchester Edition of THE NEWS OF THE WORLD wrote to me too about it. I usually get a lot of publicity; but success depends on the play, the production, and the acting. It is hard now to pick and choose a cast—there are so many competing interests. I see Liam Redmond is in the USA to go into a production of P. V. Carroll's play, THE WAYWARD SAINT; and that Siobhan [MacKenna] is to open on the 1st of Feb. in the West End in St. Joan. I knew a lass Ingrid Burke, young, pretty, who did well here, but got married, and I've never seen any word of her since. She lived, I think, in 1 Cheyne Gardens, Chelsea. Did you ever hear of her? Did you ever think of Eddie Byrne as one of Cast? Actors arent so plentiful as one would think after reading of the crowds of names that act everywhere there is a shack standing in any street or field in Ireland.

If I remember right, Juno was first put on in Lent. Anyway, Lent merely means Spring, from the word Length, on account of the days lengthening out in that season; so, maybe, the play's theme of a desire for spring (springtime is ringtime), is appropriate enough.

I do hope you may be able to get a good Cast, tho' no more strongly than you do yourself.

We are glad that your children have risen out of illness; from my experience, it is always a sad sight to see children ill.

All the best to Maureen and to you.

Sean

Some day you might slip down for an hour with Tyrone Guthrie? But don't, if you are tired, or have more useful things to do.

To Clayton Garrison[1]

TC. O'CASEY

24 JANUARY 1955

Dear Clayton Garrison,

You present the problem of a thesis. No one seems to know what is a tragedy in drama. I dont. It has travelled a long way from the Goatsong. When I started to write a play, I knew as little as him who knew most. Early on, I had read many, many plays, mostly melodramas, sold for one penny a copy, with Goldsmith's, Sheridan's, and Shakespeare's thrown in to make weight. Most of them are forgotten now—just as most, if not all, those written during my lifetime have been forgotten too. I remember Dion Boucicault's only, and some called FISH OUT OF WATER, THE WIDOW SMITH, GREEN BUSHES, PEEP O' DAY BOYS, and maybe a few others if I tried to think. These I daresay gave me some tinge of the melodrama, and, at least, I remain very fond of a "good curtain" as well as a good title. I'm inclined to think that many tie themselves to old rules and old "unities." We still cling to Aristotle's cloak, though all have forgotten its color and its shape. The golden rule, said Shaw, is that there is No rule. So say I, too. It is said that a tragedy is a play that ends in sorrow or disaster, brought about by fate, by weakness of will, by psychological maladjustment, or by social pressure. But arent all these within what is called "fate"? No one really knows what "fate" is any more than one knows what is "original" or "mortal" sin. No playwright, if he wants to write a play, can be stopping to ask himself "Is this or is that not fate"? Rather than torment myself with such a question, I'd shove the character into singing a song. At this period of time, I couldnt even guess why I called "Juno" a tragedy. To me now, I like to leave it to others to say. This play to some will be a comedy, to others a tragedy, to a few a tragi-comedy; to me—a play. My latest play which is to be done in Dublin is to be called a tragi-comedy, because the Producer thought it had to be called something. In the published version I am calling it "A Sad Play with the Tune of a Polka." I understand that the "Will" plot is of the melodrama, oldfashioned theme; and so it is; but I didnt realise this when the play was being written. I knew all the characters; the "Will" is depicted exactly as it happened. "Mrs. Boyle" came to me (we all lived in the same tenement) and read me a copy of the "Will." It was I who told her that she wouldnt get a penny from it; that it would all be swallowed up in law costs; but she couldnt or wouldnt believe this, till she was forced to do it, and face the future; which she didnt face quite so bravely as is shown in the play; for the character is a blend of "Mrs. Boyle" with another woman of great courage and quiet resolution, of which one finds many in the Dublin slums. It is all tragedy, even the

---

[1] Clayton Garrison, a student at Palos Verdes College, Rolling Hills, California.

comedy. It is the tragedy of vanity and of subservience to vanity. There is a touch of Boyle in all of us. We strut along thinking that our shadows shine. There's a touch of Joxer in a lot of us; saying yes when we ought to say no. And I hope there is some of Mrs. Boyle in us all. To be brave even at the eleventh hour. So shall we save our souls, even though the "no" be wrong, for none is infallible.

Mary's attachment to Bentham isnt vanity. She is of those who want to be brighter in life. She sees in Bentham, in a very dim-souled way, a beginning out of the morass of the tenement, which Jerry doesnt offer in manner, though he does in his cry that he'll soon have a bigger wage. Bentham to Mary is a higher civilization, though she isnt educated enough technically or by experience of life to see that he is a veneer. But these are no more than spontaneous opinions, for I amnt good at analysing my own plays (or any others for that matter); and, as I said before, JUNO is such a long, long way off that I could never bring my mind back to the mood of that time.

Well, that's about as much as I can think of about JUNO; for my mind is now engaged with work that is being done, or with work I hope to do in the days ahead.

[*Sean O'Casey*]

To Marguerite Buller[1]

MS. BULLER

25 JANUARY 1955

My Dear Marguerite,
Greetings! I do hope you have long ago recovered fully from the effects of your illnesses, & that you are yourself again. You must be more careful to try to keep away from infection.

I'm glad you read my book, and thank you for your kind words about it. I hope it may give some a sense of what war is like, though we seem to keep close to the edge of its danger. Generals today, it seems to me, talk too much. If I remember, it wasn't so in my younger days. The Generals then had a curious dignity they don't seem to possess now. When I was a young man, I was in the midst of Lord Roberts, General Sir Redvers Buller, Colonel Burnaby, General Gordon, Gen. Butler, and Field Marshal Wolseley.—We had a calendar once with colored portraits of them all. A change came, I think, first with Kitchener. But we must take things as they are, & do our best with them.

[1] Marguerite Buller, 104 Banbury Road, Oxford. See letters to her in Vol. II.

I thank you for your two very charming presents—Eileen uses the little decorated box, and I have the shrine for the twine beside me as I write. It is very attractive and bright, and very useful to me, too. Thank you very much.

I am very busy at the moment with a production of my last play—"The Bishop's Bonfire"—to be given in Dublin next month; and I am curious about what re-action it may provoke there. I'm busy, too with proofs of the play which is to be published next May.

We are settling down here. It is a pleasant place, though the winds blow in a little too often from the sea; and we have had our share of ice and snow. England has had a bad time of it this winter; but maybe the worst is over now. I long for the Spring.

Now take greater care of yourself; keep warm till the sun gets friendlier.

I send you my love.

Yours very sincerely,
Sean.

To Moses Cammer[1]

TS. CAMMER

27 JANUARY 1955

Dear Mr. Cammer:

I have but time to thank you for your very kind letter, and to say I am glad that you have liked my books. Of course there is fear in the United States just as there is fear here, & in many other places—Ireland, for instance—because of the tremendous change that has come, and is continuing to come, over life everywhere. Most of us are afraid of change; afraid of the future, afraid of the unknown. That is why we rush back to our old gods and cling around their mouldering altars; and shout at and threaten those who go by bravely to face what is to come. Man is still fighting fear, and many have to suffer for it as Socrates did when he drank down the hemlock. But things that have lost their value will have to go. God's stout fingers are tearing outworn things to pieces.

I know Orwell's work is clad in purple and fine linen; but open a button or two, and underneath we see a poor skeleton of crumbling bones. The God of Isaac and of Jacob, & Abraham, or the God of the Christians doesn't humble Himself in Hollywood: He is not there: He is with the people who are demanding the greatness of a full life.

---

[1] Moses Cammer, 91 West Garden Road, Larchmont, N.Y.

I prefer Whitman's view of animals before that of Orwell.

Well, thanks again, and all good wishes to you.

Sean O'Casey

To Cyril Cusack

TS. CUSACK

27 JANUARY 1955

Dear Cyril,

I hope things are going well with you, and that you have fully recovered from your recent cold. I presume you are in Ireland, and so send this there. Breon has written to me saying that you arent going to use his designs for the scenes of the play because Tyrone doesnt think them quite suitable. That cant be helped of course, and we must be satisfied. However, there is one point on which I'd like to put in a word about whatever design may be selected. It is this: the design shouldnt be drab in any way; it should be colorful, and that part of the house seen should be brightly painted—though NOT with the colours of Green, White, and Yellow. Red, green, bright yellow, black, and white; any of these, though if black and white, bright ones should be added; primary colours, not pastels. The Tri-color should be gay, too. I'd like the play to be done within, as it were, an array of glassy jewels. Touching on your and my discussion as to what we should call the play, comedy, tragedy, tragi-comedy—you remember?—I dont like these terms—though, of course, you can use the term "Tragi-comedy" as we decided—and I have, in the published version changed the description to "A Sad Play Within the Tune of a Polka" which I'm telling you of as a reason for, and a guide to, the format of the designs, and why I'd like them to be bright, if not gay. Get me? Since you are not using Breon's, would it be too much trouble for you or for Mr. [William P.] Ryan to let him have them back, addressing them here?

I have had a request from New York asking for the play. The Agent had refused, and so I was written to; dont know where they got the script, for I have now only the galley-proofs; and an inquiry from Berlin. I was amused at your reference to the pieces appearing in the Press here, "all for free." I usually get a lot of publicity, and, I daresay, you saw the piece in EVERYBODY'S?[1] The writer rang me up, asking permission to quote; he, too, had read the play, saying he read galley-proofs given by Macmil-

---

[1] "O'Casey at Sunset," *Everybody's Weekly,* London, 29 January 1955, a preview of *The Bishop's Bonfire,* in the "Compère Spotlight" column.

lan's; but I dont [think] Macmillan would do that without asking me first. However, no harm done.

I'd like to know how the Cast is going, and if you have overcome all, or most, of your difficulties there. I hope you got my last letter wherein I suggested, if possible, and if you were in London, or thereabouts, you and Tyrone might slip down here for a night and a day. But don't kill yourself running about: I'll understand. One more: aren't you taking a part in it—that is, one of the Cast? Apropos of what you said about the "razor-edge" aspect of the bottle scene and the "goosestepping scene," I enclose pictures comical (and satiric) of scenes in a Benedictine Mon. done by a Benedictine (Is he your Ben. from the I. of Wight?), taken from the New Y. Times, and published by the Catholic Firm of Sheed & Ward.[2] Aren't these "razor-edged" criticisms? I believe Brother (now Father, I think) Gerard of the Franciscans, Capuchin, was stopped from drawing his gracious cartoons of the Brethren in The Capuchin Annual, but I amn't sure. Father Senan[3] might be interested in seeing these. If you send them, give him my best wishes, & the same to Brother (Father?) Gerard. I know them both.

All the best to Maureen, the children & to you.

I see the "Irish" Pantomime collapsed silently after the tenth day.[4] Who writes the "lyrics"?

As ever,
Sean

2 Brother Choleric, *Cracks in the Cloister* (1954), a collection of cartoons. Brother Choleric is the pseudonym of Hubert Van Zeller.
3 Father Senan, O.P., editor of the *Capuchin Annual,* Dublin. Brother Gerard was his assistant.
4 *Sonia agus an Bodach* (Sonia and the Peasant), the Abbey Theatre Christmas Pantomime, closed on 8 January 1955.

To Anthony E. Harvey[1]

TC. O'CASEY

29 JANUARY 1955

Dear Anthony,

Greetings to you and your pal. You ask me many more questions than I am able to answer. Your half-sister seems to be taking a lot for granted. Granted that that may suit her, but it doesnt suit others. She asks no questions, therefore she can never know the truth, never even part

1 Anthony E. Harvey, Yale University Divinity School, New Haven, Connecticut.

of the truth which is only what each of us can grasp. Probably, the whole truth would destroy us; we shouldnt be able to bear it. I mean here the contemplation of the Universe, not of course, the poor blather of Billy Graham. I have heard many Billy Grahams in my time; and I found them wise only in the business of making a good thing out of what they conceived to be a revelation straight from God. If a God there be, then Billy Graham isnt the only manifestation of Him. And what does any of us know about these things outside of our experience? You have but to look around to see (and be bewildered) by the multitude of groups that think in violently different ways about these things—the Buddhist, Islam, and, among Christians, the savage way they have contested their different beliefs about the self-same things: Anglicans, Roman Catholics, the Orthodox Church, the Maronites, the Coptics, not to mention the lesser groups, Methodists, Salvationists, Presbyterians, and so on. It is a medley. Even the rigid R. Catholics have been divided about dogmas: The Dominicans opposed for years the Dogma of The Immaculate Conception; so did St. Theresa; and for long a bitter dispute raged over the Dogma of Infallibility; and no one yet seems to be able to define this Dogma, or is able to simply say what Bull or exclamation from the Pope is fallible or infallible. There's a whole world of books setting out the beliefs of the warring sections of the Christian Church alone; war among themselves. And where here does the bould Billy come in? We must think things out for ourselves, and not depend on the noises that proceed out of the big mouth of Billy Graham. He is far too familiar with God. Look up what happened when Moses made the request to see God. The sight would have destroyed him and so, as God passed by, He placed His hand over the eyes of Moses, so that He shadowed Himself from the view of Israel's Leader. Paul says somewhat the same thing when he remarks, "Here we see things as in a glass darkly"; but B.G. seems to have a front seat in heaven seeing all plainly with the naked eye. Life in great part is a vital activity of questions.

Listen to these: "Congregations and commissions would have us depend almost altogether on traditions, and shut our eyes to difficulties that strike us in the face. Was St. Paul right in his outlook on the pagan world of Greece and Rome? Were these poor idolaters as inexcusable as he represented them to be? Are we bound to the arguments for the existence of God set forth in the Book of Wisdom, or by St. Paul (Acts 14–16)? Was Cain—who, in St. Luke's Gospel, appears among the progenitors of our Lord—a real personage? Or did the authors of the Septuagint, from which St. Luke quotes, insert him by mistake? Did the human writers of Genesis mean to teach that the world was made in six days of twenty-four hours, that the deluge was absolutely universal and destructive of the life of land animals everywhere, that any species surviving did so by being brought into the ark, that all men of the time were present at the building of Babel, and that it was there and then that diversity of tongues arose? So too in the history of Papacy and Episcopacy: when there were no monarchial Bishops anywhere, can we believe there was one in Rome? Did St. Augustine, with his belief in the necessity of divine charity, recognise the sufficiency of attrition to remit mortal sin? Or if charity was necessary, did he think mortal sin first remitted by the Sacraments? Were, in fact, sacraments of the dead instituted and administered for the remission of guilt, or only for that of punishment, and for the giving of graces to live a purer life in future? And, then, grace and virtues: supernatural qualities? But what is a quality, and how does it contribute to action? How does grace operate, and when is it given? Before or after justification? Can human souls be supernaturalised in part—in the intellect, while the will remains in its natural state? Where does the supernatural begin in the roots of faith? Can faith be lost without formal mortal sin? What is the testimony of modern life in this respect? What is mortal sin indeed? How does it stand with regard to charity—in its commission and its remission? In what sense is the soul a substantial part of the body?"[2]

These are but a few of the questions posed by Dr. McDonald, for forty years Professor of Maynooth R. Catholic College—a great and a very brave man. Where would he be with Billy Graham, who, according to himself, has all the answers? He goes on, "On these and many such questions, I have found peace at last, on lines no little divergent from the tradition." You see, he had to make his own faith out; and so must we all. Dr. McDonald couldnt answer these questions; neither, of course, can I. All I know is that the Bible isnt a sure and infallible guide. Why, there are two sets of Commandments (see Frazer's "Folklore of the Old Testament") and two descriptions of the creation, the one differing from the other in the same book of Genesis. No; dear young friend, you must solve these things yourself. Be sure, for one thing, B.G. lacks humility, and St. Augustine said "The first step to heaven is humility, the second step is humility, and the third step to heaven is humility."

Lift up your heart, lad—God wont send you sliding down the drain because you dont understand everything about Him. Keep under His blue sky as much as you can for your health's sake. To me, there is more in a picture by Greco, Titian, [Augustus] John, in a Symphony by Beethoven, a Concerto by Mozart, a play by Shakespeare; more glory to God, more Epiphanic insight, than a life's roaring from B. Graham. Graham Greene's a good Catholic; though the Bishops dont like his plays; he has been banned in Dublin. No; the R.C. Church dont allow suicide for any reason whatsoever. The girl in G.G.'s play would Not be considered a martyr.[3] In my play, the B's Bonfire, I give a picture of a differently-minded priest, tho' the question isnt one of a girl seeking union with a married man.

---

[2] These are selected passages from Walter McDonald, D.D., *Reminiscences of a Maynooth Professor* (1925), pp. 399–401.
[3] Rose Pemberton in Graham Greene's *The Living Room* (1953).

Many believe that, like Mauriac, there is a deep tinge of Jansenism in G. Greene. My play, the B's B. gets its first production in Dublin's commercial theater, The Gaiety, next month. I am very busy with it. It will be published in May—or is to be.

Give my love to Dr. Grellet Smith; he sent me the Bulletin—or was it you—of Randolph-Macon; a fine Journal, with a fine poet peeping out of its pages. Whatever influence R-M may have had on you, it seems to have helped a lot in making you a most intelligent lad. Tell that to the Girl. Dont know Miss [Nora] Nicholson, yet. Now, my love to you and to George; and to all your family, and to Dr. Grellet Smith.

As ever,
[Sean O'Casey]

To Paul and Nan Ross

MS. ROSS

29 JANUARY 1955

My dear Paul and Nan,

We are grieved to hear of Nan's illness. The first thing is to get her well again. You must see, Paul, that she takes full care of herself. Women are braver than men; take more risks; and are apt to be careless of their own condition. Don't let her go to "Juno" till she is quite well; till the doctor gives her a definite visa to go; don't let her stir from her bed, her home, till she is really fit. And give her my love and Eileen's; but, even then, she must be careful for pneumonia leaves the lungs delicate for a time.

Thanks for your kind words about "Sunset and Evening Star." The article in Life[1] did a lot of good, I think, in easing the hard idea that a Red had but one idea in his head; and hated all different ones in other heads. I'm afraid the "Reds" in the USA & here have themselves to blame for a lot that has happened: so many of them seem to lack grace and knowledge. To Americans, Emerson, Whitman, Jefferson, et al, are more important than Lenin or Engels. We must learn first from our own dear kin.

If I took to myself all the kind things said of my work by Americans, I'd be, indeed, a foolish Cockadoodle Dandy; but, thank God, I am never satisfied with what I do; & start an article and play with a tension & fear that would suggest I was but a beginner—as indeed, I am; as we all are; always but beginning. I had a long letter from Frank Morell, full of theory & aflow with words. He seems to turn everything into a theory; & has no

[1] "The World of Sean O'Casey," *Life,* 26 July 1954.

time for the song of a lark in the clear air. Such an excellent lad, I wish he would go more softly for his own sake; & more sensibly, too.

About Breon doing a picture of me for you, we'll talk of it when we hear from you that Nan has completely recovered. "The Bishop's Bonfire" is to be produced in Dublin next month—of all places! We are waiting for an interesting time. Then it may come to London.

It is fine to hear Gil is to graduate in June. Oh, I hope he may be a good Doctor, as he is a good lad; & that in the years to come, he may serve man with his knowledge & his spirit. Well, Paul, you appeared in good company with Einstein, Chaplin, [Lillian] Hellman, [Arthur] Miller, an' all! But be wise as a serpent; & don't strain your energy in causes that can have no effectiveness on present-day life.

My love, our love to Nan, to Gil, & to you.

Warmly,
Sean

To Douglas M. Jacobs[1]

TC. O'CASEY

30 JANUARY 1955

Dear Mr. Jacobs,

Thank you for your letter. I have been very busy with a new play which is for production in Dublin next month; and with the proofs of the play, for it is to be published in May; so I had to leave your letter aside for the time being. I quite agree with your Airman friend: I'm afraid the Dublin Players[2] are pretty poor. However, they were doing the play before I knew anything about it. One has to put up with these disappointing things. All actors cant be of the best—no more than all playwrights. As for the First Editions—I have never put much of a pass on them. The only first editions I have, or rather that are in the flat, are the copies I gave to Mrs. O'Casey and our three children—inscribed to each of them. For myself, I havent one. That doesn't bother me in any way however. It would be hard, I think, to get first editions, for the first edition was never a large one. It is only now that they have become larger; only now that I have become a little better known. But why 1st Editions? Wouldnt any edition be as welcome to a library—that is, of course, if the library

---

1 Douglas M. Jacobs, bookseller, P.O. Box 187, Ridgefield, Connecticut.
2 Ronald Ibbs's Dublin Players performed *Juno and the Paycock* as part of their repertoire during their 1954–55 tour of America.

thought well of the writer? I agree with you that collecting for collecting sake is rather foolish. Or so it seems to me. I suppose there is something in it. My MS—what I have of it—is a curious sight! I dont think I've a single MS word of my first three plays; though here and there, on widely differing notes on differing subjects, there may be a paragraph that came into my head suddenly, and was jotted down for future use. My first writings of plays and biographies are scattered about on various slips, in various books, among many many things, and even the rough typescript of the first draft is a scattered thing, very different from the last thing decided. Many have asked me about this, and one script is in either Harvard or Yale. A number of Universities—why, God only knows—have asked me for MS, but up to now, I have had no time to look about me to see what I have. Worse still, we have recently moved from our house to a Flat, and things are scattered worse than they were; so that it would be an unbearable chore to look through things at the moment. If I ever do it, I must wait till I have plenty of spare time, and after a good rest. As for your kind offer to send me any book I was in need of, if I was a bad man, and ready to use you, I'd demand thousands. So keep off these kind of offers. I shall write to Murray soon as I get a chance; but I have many, many letters to answer. I dont know of any bibliographies of my work; dont think there are any, bar those appearing in theses written by students in various colleges.

You seem to have a fair collection yourself. Cant make out how you came by the page proofs. I think I have never done any in the USA. All these have been done by the publishers here. If you be in London, you'll have to ring me up, for I couldnt say whether I'd be free or no. . . .[3]

[3] Page missing.

To Barbara A. Cohen[1]

TS. COHEN

31 JANUARY 1955

Dear Barbara,

Thanks for your letter and for the fine present, though you mustnt do anything like sending anything again. It was very kind of you and Marianne [Roney] to think of us. We're keeping it till Easter till we are all together—our lad who is in London trying to become a painter, our

[1] Barbara A. Cohen, Caedmon Publishers, New York. See letters to her in Vol. II.

other lad who's a Lance Bombardier in the Royal Artillery stationed in Germany, and our lass who is still at school; so that we may have a family feast.

I expect to be doing three or four quarter-of-an-hour tape-recordings for Radio Eireann—the Irish Broadcasting system. I hope to have it done by a Donald Aldous who does tape-recording here for a variety of recording, music, plays, etc.; for those mostly who want to hear themselves time and again after the excitement of a public show has passed away. I wish I had known about Aldous when you first asked me to record—it might have saved you a lot of expense. I hope the "overwhelming" you mention was due to a mighty rush for your various records. I have had a request to do several recordings from a Miss Pearl Hayes Hackett of 898 West End Av., New York 25, who suggests that she might be able to get them on to Radio and television. She suggests I should speak on Freedom of Thought in Eirinn, or on Conscience, or something like these. I dont intend to do anything for her; but am interested to know if you have ever heard of her. She acts as hostess to Irish poetry readings, and coaches in reading, and, I suppose, in elocution. If you havent heard already of her, dont, for God's sake waste time trying to find out anything; for I have no intention of even answering her letter. She is just trying to horn in on the additional knowledge of me that has come to many Americans during the last year or so. She sends me a card announcing a lecture from a professional R. Catholic Lecturer [Maurice Leahy], who, years ago, wrote, when I had sent him a subscription, praising my work to the skies. Later he went to Dublin, and, on account of the feeling there, could hardly find words bad and venomous enough about the work he had praised in his letter, which he had evidently forgotten. I published his letter in the Irish papers, and embarrassed him deeply.[2]

I'm afraid Gordon [Rogoff] has chosen the wrong way of life. The curse of many young people is that they pine, not to do great things, but to be thought of as great, suddenly, and without the patient toil and sacrifice that goes with those who are gifted, and seek no outward applause. I havent done the recording for R. Eireann yet; waiting for Aldous to come here. He lives but five minutes from here, but his tape isnt the same speed as that of R.E.; so he is getting his amplified or speeded up, and is sending a sample to R.E. to see if they will pass it. I hope they do. A. was the man who did recording for [Gjon] Mili, and I like him and am easy with him. If he doesnt do it, I may only do one recording, for, believe me, I amnt anxious to send my voice farther than my own fireside. I hope Marianne had a fine time in Cuba. I am busy with a production of the new play, THE BISHOP'S BONFIRE which is to be given in Dublin's big commercial theater next month—an utterly unexpected event. We are waiting to see what happens.

[2] For the Maurice Leahy controversy, see O'Casey's letters to the *Irish Times,* 29 August and 6 September 1938; and to the *Irish Press,* 17 October 1938, Vol. I.

Love to Marianne, to Peter [Bartok], to Gordon—if you see him, &
to you.

as ever,
Sean

To Raymond Broad[1]

TC. O'CASEY

1 FEBRUARY 1955

Dear Raymond Broad,

Thanks, many, for your letter and for the whispering article on G.B.S.
I am very glad to have it indeed, as a memento of the gayer time when
the Sage appeared to be physically immortal.

Looking over it, I dont feel like a jump into the air; still, if I go on
with the proposed book, I shall send it in as it is, with but two brief sentences added, and one amended that seemed to be confused.

I should be glad if you would let me have the brochure on the work
of the Arts Council, for reference, if I decide to write the proposed article.
I am very busy at the moment preparing a broadcast for Radio Eireann,
and with a play to be done in Dublin next month; so it may be some
time before I can throw my mind into anything else. Besides, an article
always presents difficulties to me, though most people do not believe this.
It is, all the same, quite true. I have never developed a facility in writing.
Each time I begin a new play, I begin as a beginner; or so I feel till the
most of it has been quarried out from a mass of ideas and notes.

I should like to do the article, or try to do it, and, as soon as I can,
I'll think about it; and, if I cant, I'll let you know.

Thanks again, and all good wishes to you.

Yours sincerely
Sean O'Casey.

[1] Raymond Broad, *Municipal Review,* Victoria Station House, London. SW1.

To Mrs. R——

MS. PRIVATE

5 FEBRUARY 1955

Dear R.,

Thanks a lot for your kind letter, & generous offer of a Sub. to give me "Soviet Union." Thanks a lot, again, but I already get it monthly, with Soviet Literature, Soviet News, etc. I have been in touch with the USSR for years—while I was still in Dublin, in 1924; and have here a snapshot of the first diesel locomotive that came to the USSR, at that time; with a crowd of thin & poorly-clad children, people, & soldiers, wearing their odd cloth helmets, looking at it with wonderment, & surrounding it as a very precious thing—which it was. It was a fertile loco. I wonder how many have they now! And the West thinks the East are sending out creeping spies to snatch little secrets from their nuclear energy plants; when the fact is that the Soviet Scientists know as much—if not more— than we do about the linking of the force of nature to the skill of man: See Sir Francis Simon's article, "The Atomic Rivals" in the "Atomic Scientists" Journal for January, 1955 Vol. 4. No. 3. It would open—or it should open—the eyes of those who think the Russians can learn nothing but by looking over other shoulders to see how things are done!

I have been an associate member of the Atomic Scientists' Association for years & if only more of us were, in the USA & here, we shouldn't be so damned ignorant of what the Russians can do without us.

I do hope your daughter will do well as an actress—a hard job & a precarious one. Our own daughter, now over 15, still at school, has fixed her mind on being one, tho; & I am very anxious about it. Our elder lad is trying to be a painter—and this bewildering problem. The younger lad is a Lance Bombardier in the Royal Artillery station in Germany: Lord knows what he may want to be. I & Eileen have always left it to themselves to choose. It is their life, & not ours.

A fool mind it is who wishes Gandhi dead. He can't die. He is immortal, like Shaw.

Thanks for your kind words about the Biography.

My love to your daughter & to you.

All good wishes,
Sean O'Casey

To Peter Newmark[1]

MS. NEWMARK

7 FEBRUARY 1955

My dear Peter,

Glad to hear from you. You tell me a little about yourself this time, but not a damn word about Monica. How is she sticking you? I hope you are both very happy together.

No, not a "1 acter"; a new "3 acter," named "The Bishop's Bonfire," to be published in May. The event seems to be causing a stir in Ireland. A very intelligent actor, Cyril Cusack, of Cyril Cusack Productions, has taken the play—he wrote asking me to let him read it, after he had come back exhausted from a Pilgrimage to St. Patrick's Purgatory; liked the play greatly (he said), & requested I'd give him a Licence to produce it in Dublin, with an option for London and New York. I gave him what he asked for readily as a tribute to his courage in presenting it to Dublin. It's an outspoken play, with a good deal of humour, & some sad moments. I have called it, for publication, "A Sad Play Within the Tune of a Polka." They're getting out a Souvenir Program, & Tyrone Guthrie is to produce it: & that's as much as I know about it. Odd, the Abbey never asked to see it: It is as if I had died to them after the "Plough & the Stars." They had a Competition last year—£250 prize; got near 50 plays, but not one of them worth as much (they said) as a minor consolation prize.

After a correspondence, in which [Patrick] Galvin demanded an apology (he got it from Macmillans), and my laughing refusal, it has apparently died away; & I haven't heard from him for a long time. I'm used to this. You may remember, W. B. Yeats threatened me in the same way when I revealed what he thought of "The Silver Tassie."[2] Didn't read "William's" book;[3] but, if I am right, he's quoted by Irish critics when they refer to my work, particularly one, Gabriel Fallon. But I haven't time to stop to consider: I'm far too busy.

Very glad you got an article taken by Boris Ford (don't know him: seems a half Irish, half Russian name); but I do hope you have been, or will be paid for it.

Don't worry if you are thrown out of the Labour Party. So long as you aren't thrown out of life, you needn't care much. Indeed, we need a few Independents everywhere, in Parliament & out of it.

---

[1] Peter Newmark, a teacher in London, was an undergraduate at Cambridge University in 1936 and attended O'Casey's talk there on "The Holy Ghost Leaves England"; see the draft to Alfred A. K. Arnold, 18 January 1936, Vol. I. See also letters to Newmark in Vols. I and II.

[2] See "The Abbey Directors and Mr. Sean O'Casey," *Irish Statesman,* 9 June 1928, Vol. I.

[3] Raymond Williams, *Drama From Ibsen to Eliot* (1952), which contains some unfavorable comments about O'Casey, in a "Note" at the end of a chapter on Synge.

Had an intelligent worker from Unity here yesterday. Told him a few things I felt about mannerisms of Communists. Convinced him that a bad actor was no good on the stage however grand he might be as a Communist; or that a surgeon who couldn't heal a wound, or a physician who couldn't deal with an illness, was no good, however rigid his devotion to the Party might be.

Well, all good wishes, my old friend & old critic, to Monica & to you.

Yours as ever.
Sean

To J. J. Sullivan[1]

TS. SULLIVAN

7 FEBRUARY 1955

Dear Mr. Sullivan,

Thanks for your letter. Shaw was merciful, and held back his punches. He was intensely sensitive about hurting the feelings of others. He often, as he told Mrs O'C, after refusing to do a foolish thing, crucified himself for not having done it, and so escaped wounding the feelings of those who had asked him to do it. A lot of us Irish are like that: we do foolish things for fear of hurting ourselves in displeasing others. I, myself, have often held myself in when discussing things with others, afraid to hurt them when they are face to face with me; say things I shouldnt say; refrain from saying what should be said. You are wrong when you say that I "couldnt forgive him (Chesterton) for becoming a Catholic." I don't care a damn what he thought within himself, but I do care about what he tries to force on others. He never became a Catholic. He used the outward and visible signs, and that was all. He was as much a catholic as a toby jug; the stick he carried, and which he so often threw down before his opponents, never turned to a serpent, never even blossomed, though he shouted out Look! at what he saw himself, but none other could see; except romantic Catholics who knew about as much as he did himself. Most intelligent Catholics are a little ashamed of him now, and pass his name from their mouth with a good deal of pity, and a little contempt. He has been referred to as "the poor, foolish knight." Listen to his detective-poet [Father Brown] plays now being broadcast by the B.B.C., with their tinsel-stuff propaganda of what he thought to be the C. Faith. Compare him with Dr. Walter McDonald of St. Patrick's College, Maynooth, Professor of Theology. The one so sacreligiously bombastic, the other so

---

[1] J. J. Sullivan, 6 Penryn Avenue, Brooklands, Sale, Manchester.

reverently anxious to know, to prove, to exalt the Faith; so eager to make Irish Catholicism a leader of thought in Christian speculation and Catholic truth.

You mention my "many dislikes," but only one of my "likes," though I had many, and record them. Chesterton's book on SHAW[2] is a moist, sodden sample of his awful sentimentality, and wouldn't be accepted anywhere as a literary work of art. I point out a woeful error of his in his explanation of the character of Miss Reilly (Nora);[3] Understand Shaw? He didn't understand Nora! I knew G.B.S. well: we talked of many literary figures, but he never mentioned Chesterton, his biographer; the "only man who understood him"; never once mentioned him; never crossed either of our minds; too unimportant. You jibe at me saying he went to live in a middle-class flat in Battersea; and point out, that I did the same.[4] So I did. You say he moved thence to Beaconsfield, and that I went down to Devon. So I did; but you miss the point completely. I stated—not implied, mind you—that he went to Battersea to live among the workers. There is no harm in living in a middle-class flat, but it is another thing when the flight there is used to give a false halo to the one who goes there; again, he went to Beaconsfield, and again it was stated he went to live in the country. Beaconsfield is no more the country than is the Green Park adjacent to Piccadilly. Now, as you bring up this point of me going to Devon to a middle-class residence, even that escapade was very different from his removal. I didnt buy the house I lived in in Devon as he bought Tree Tops. Indeed, after living there for 17 years, the landlord said he wanted the house to live in, and gave us notice to quit. He didnt want it to live in, and well we knew it, and others, too; but we had to go, and we were hardly round the corner when the notice of FOR SALE topped the wall. But there's no blame to be put on anyone for buying a home—if he can—; but there is if a public man uses it to declare to others what a wonderful fella he is; and to use the removal for quasi-religious propaganda reasons; or when it is used by others to boost his name. Generosity has nothing to do with criticism of a public man's actions or with his literary work. One is either a critic or he isnt. You mistake me about the Catholic Church. I have never yet said anything against what is the Catholic Faith, though I've said a lot about what is called Catholic practice. There is a big difference, you know. The Catholic Faith as defined isnt anything like what most Catholics believe to be the Faith. For instance, Celibacy for the Clergy isnt a dogma, tho' many Catholics believe it to be one. But take the chief ones, the Incarnation, the devotion to the Blessed Virgin, for instance; the Mother and Child. This is a long tussle between Zeus and the Triple Goddess—the Maid, the Nymph, and the Mother. Aphrodite, Astarte, now

[2] G. K. Chesterton, *George Bernard Shaw* (1909).

[3] Nora Reilly, the heroine of Shaw's *John Bull's Other Island* (1907).

[4] See O'Casey's comments on Chesterton in "A Drive of Snobs" and "Shaw's Corner," *Sunset and Evening Star* (1954), *Autobiographies II*, pp. 460–66, 602–606.

appear in the cult of the Mariannae. Mary's blue mantle is the old mantle of the Triple Goddess; it is a beautiful and poetic conception; high above the trivial and tawdry accounts given of the various "apparitions" given by various kids from time to time. You have an Irish name. Very well: you'll allow that Ireland is, mainly, a Catholic country, and is likely to remain one. No miracle would convert the Catholics to protestantism. Well, then since that is so, I want Irish Catholicism to be the most courageous, the most enlightened Catholicism in the world. Is that a bad wish? So did Shaw—see Larry Doyle in JOHN BULL'S OTHER ISLAND where he declares his wish that the Irish Catholic Church should lead the world of religion; so did Dr. W. McDonald, Professor of Theology in Maynooth for 40 years. You have but to read the popular C. Press to see pandaring to sensationalism and tawdry pietistic nonsense. And C.T. [Catholic Truth] booklets arent much better. Take again the Pope's laughable fiat against "modern art," allowing only that which is in the "true traditions," etc—as stupid as the declaration made by Zdanov before he vanished into death. Dont think, now, that "stupid" is a hard, O'Casey word: I heard an eminent Catholic—R[obert]. Speaight—refer over the wireless to what he called "a stupid Pope." And, God Almighty, how many stupid bishops are there! My friend, there are still many questions to be asked. McDonald has asked many; tremendous ones, too. I will quote but one from a crowd: "Can faith be lost without formal mortal sin? What is the testimony of modern life in this respect? What is mortal sin, indeed? How does it stand with regard to charity—in its commission and its remission?" You see how One question opens up a dozen—like to search into the atom—the solving of one question postulates a dozen more. Can you answer these questions put by Dr. McDonald? No, life isnt solved with an ora pro nobis.

The new (or old) dogma of the Assumption doesnt appear to him who thinks over it as clear and plain from the Irish priest's declaration from the pulpit that "God hoisted Her up to heaven holus bolus, body and bones."!

You see now why Dr. McDonald, and others like him, interest me far more than Chesterton; and maybe why the poor foolish man's off-hand and self-satisfied declarations make me mad.

I dont want to disturb you, but most of what I have said in my books are facts; and, outside of these, the comments are just opinions, said sincerely and honestly, but they have in no way, whatsoever, any claim to infallibility.

Now, all good wishes to you.

Yours sincerely,
Sean O'Casey.

To Tyrone Guthrie[1]

MS. GUTHRIE

11 FEBRUARY 1955

Dear Tyrone,

Just got your letter. Thanks. About the change—I'll probably change it (2nd act) to "tacking down the carpet." I'll send you the few necessary remarks soon as possible. It is a very trivial change. Boheroe shouldn't *act* "as if he had God Almighty in his pocket": with all his foreseeing courage, there should be the inner assurance of humility. He mustn't be bumptious—or so I meant, &, God forgive me, if I didn't make this apparent. You are probably right about the ending of the act—though I like the sigh God gives. He has to do it often in Ireland—and everywhere. But I see your point of a colliding sigh and laugh; so do it the way you see it to be better than that way I chose.

You are, of course, positively right about "Danny." He must (or is meant to be) be the boisterous, ready lad, forcing forward, especially in his scene with Boheroe & Keelin; & the change should be a shock to F. Boheroe & to Keelin. It needed but a few words for F. Boheroe to get him to hoist all sail, &, then, a few more words from Reiligan to furl them all quiet again & stow them away. This character is important, & Cyril should certainly take your advice. It is foolish to be soft-hearted in getting a Caste together. The lad will have to take a bump—we all have to take them at times, hard ones, too. Lots believe that all of us Irish are grand natural actors: we aren't; for the theatre remains a hard, hard job for all who have anything to do with it.

Don't worry about Breon. He has a lot to learn. Over his shoulder, I suggested the practical side of scene-designing, as he was doing it; &, I'm sure, tho' unattentive, like all the young, some of it sunk in; and it was all good training for him. The venture has given him a little experience. He takes it all very quietly.

Before I forget it, Don Burke, charge of England's LIFE Branch, phoned me today to say he would probably go to Dublin to see rehearsals, & try to make a "story" for New York. Ask Cyril to be kind to him, if he goes to Dublin. He's a fine lad, & will be a friend in any way he can.

I can see Tony[2] as too "acty" and womanish; tho' the original was womanish without being like a woman at all; he should be positive in his assertions—"It's my brick" assertive & resentful, as many of these are when they don't get their own way; & savage, too, when their inner impulses are almost revealed, & they get frightened, subconsciously, into a scream—as with Keelin in the 1st act. Try to get him to put a little spon-

---

[1] Sir Tyrone Guthrie (1900–71), theatrical director and author; director of *The Bishop's Bonfire,* which opened in Dublin on 28 February 1955; knighted in 1961.

[2] Tony Quinn played the role of Richard Rankin.

taneous spirit into his acting; but, I fear, between ourselves, Tony has become dry & a little rusty.

Thanks, very much, for taking on the hard, hard job you're doing, &, in some cases, of making bricks with the straw of natural acting to bind the material together.

What about the "Porter"? This is a good part, & has an important part to play around the "lad with the Buckineeno."

All good wishes to you, a mhic o.[3]

> *Yours very sincerely,*
> Sean

[3] My son.

To Times Pictorial

11 FEBRUARY 1955[1]

Mr. The Editor
Pictorial Times, Dublin.

Dear Sir,

Aside answers to your questions sent by telegram:[2]

1. I don't know. Will depend on how I feel and the mood of the Irish Sea.
2. Don't know either. A bit afraid of the anger of Ireland's Triple God—Woods, Hogan, and Thersites.[3]

Your telegram went to Tingrith, Totnes, and had to be telegraphed to St. Marychurch, for which the P.M.G. charged eleven shillings; so I am keeping the reply-paid form, for I cant just fling away eleven shillings with a laugh.

> *All good wishes.*
> *Yours sincerely,*
> *Sean O'Casey*

[1] This letter was printed on the front page of the *Times Pictorial*, 26 February 1955.

[2] Text of the telegram sent to O'Casey by the *Times Pictorial*, which appeared with his reply in the issue of 26 February: "Times Pictorial, Dublin, would appreciate answers to the following stop are you coming to Dublin for production your new play stop if not could you state reasons for continued absence from Ireland stop regards."

[3] See O'Casey's letter to David Krause, 5 January 1955, note 3.

To Tyrone Guthrie

TS. GUTHRIE

12 FEBRUARY 1955

Dear Tyrone,

I have been reading again the end of the 2nd Act, keeping in mind your suggestion about cutting the episode of the "darkening scene." If I am right, you suggested it should end with the Monsignor's ". . . to have a friendly chat with our Bishop."

I agree about the "darkening," but I have a lingering love for Keelin's sombre exclamation, and suggest it should end with her lines ". . . I love him, an' he's lost to me now!"

But, if you think otherwise, well and good.

I am a little worried about "Rankin." I think he should be as whisperingly fierce when he denies looking at Keelin, head down low as he whispers fiercely; head up—away from her—and consciously trying to get his mind away from "unholy thoughts"; seeking from his look at the sky to get a glimpse of the "swalla," as if it might be a guardian angel to him. I knew the Original well; worked many a time with him. He was a Mason, and his name was Johnnie Rankin. He liked me because once, when sitting down to our lunch, a number of Prods and a Cath. started an argument on the "Faith," and I defended the Catholic viewpoint from the bible and the Prod. Prayerbook. But the poor man was obsessed with a sense of guilt. Once, when I argued with him that it wasnt so hard to go through life decently, giving little offence to God (in an endeavour to win him from his obsession), how I remember the way he wheeled to face me, bring his face close to mine, as he spittily hissed out, "There's always concupiscence!" Rankin is at war with the world, the flesh, and the devil, and these are embodied in all those around him; there is always fierceness in him, even in his silences. T.Q. [Tony Quinn] should remember this.

I enclose a suggestion for the alteration in the opening of the 2nd Act, which, I hope, may be satisfactory. What was it Yeats said? I think, "My curse on plays that have to be devised in fifty ways!"

Yes, I'm sure there's a stir with you about the play—how much of it friendly, one cant tell; but all curious, which is a good thing in itself.

Pity you couldnt have got Liam Redmond. He is a fine actor, but a note I read some time ago, gave the news that he was in the U.S.A. to play an important part in P. V. Carroll's new play to be done there—"The Wayward Saint." I hope this may be a success, and so open a way for other Irish plays.

Joseph [Tomelty] is good, too, but I daresay Cyril could not get him. But, on the whole, you seem to have a good Caste, and with T. Guthrie leading them, they should do well.

By the way, Mrs. O'C., and Breon, saw your "The Ladder,"[1] a little time after she had been with G.B.S., and both of them liked it immensely.

All good wishes to you.
Sean

enclosure

Suggestions for Scene Two

What about the following for Ending of Scene Two, to give a hint of the courage you mentioned?

_____

After

Keelin (brokenly)—What am I to do, Father; oh, what am I to do! Dan hadnt the courage, etc. . . . I love him, and he's lost to me now!

F. Boh (gently)—My poor child, my poor child. (A little more hardihood in his voice) Courage girl. (With a tinge of impatience) Courage, woman! The fight isnt over. There will be another time, another place, and a better, but another man.

Keelin—I want my Danny!

_____

The older version will have to stay in the book of the play; and, anyway, it is truer to what is in Ireland, I think. By the way, the persistent rebel is really the Codger. One of the characters the Fenians created; or, later on, the Parnellites.

Nahum means "Comfort," and, like Irish, the vowels get longer stresses than is usual in the English. He was certainly no comfort to Nineveh. What great invectives!

Elijah in Hebrew means Jehovah is God, and, I fear, the sounds have been emasculated by translation into English. Hebrew is akin to Arabic.

Thanks heartily for all your trouble. I am very glad indeed that you have been the Director of the play.

Yours very sincerely,
Sean

[1] *Top of the Ladder*, written and directed by Tyrone Guthrie, opened in London on 11 October 1950.

To Cyril Cusack

TS. CUSACK

14 FEBRUARY 1955

Dear Cyril,

Thanks for your letter. I'm glad to hear, naturally, that the 1st night is gone before booking.[1] Of course, we want more than that, a lot more, and I, too, hope we'll get it. I think the play deserves it, and I'm sure the acting will deserve it, too. Here's hoping!

About Breon's designs: He wants them back, and prefers not to have them hung in the foyer. He needs them for show in some students' exhibition in St. Martin's Art School. He is in no way hurt because they weren't used. He has seen me sticking stout-hearted through so many disappointments that he has become aware that in art as well as in life, there's many a slip twixt cup and lip. So dont worry about the matter at all. I've already told this to Tyrone, who very kindly wrote about it in his letter to me. I should like though, if you sent Breon a couple of guineas—two or three—; no more, for I have already given him a few for his work for me in designing the sets. But I know, he'd like to feel he had got something for work done from one unconnected with him. It would give him a proud feeling—being a "new commencer."

Tyrone did send me some suggestions which I have agreed to, as he may have told you by now. I have sent him an alternative opening for the 2nd act, using a V ladder in place of a fireplace; and giving you a verse of the "Bless'd be th'day." It is a song I did recently for a Radio Broadcast in May; and I have agreed to the suggested altering of the end of the same act. By the way, in one of my letters, I pointed out that "tradesmen" in Ireland never wore "hob-nailed boots." Sturdy ones only, but no nails. This note was in reference to yours querying the noise they'd make in their business of jumping from the platform on to a floor.

About Foorawn crossing herself before the statue, I'd very much rather she didn't. Let us look upon the statues as unblessed, for they are but fantasies, and as such, need no gesture. The whole idea (from my point) is a cry against the habit of using the Saints by believers to do work for them they can damn well do for themselves.

I'll look up "falsify," think over it, and let you know later. It takes me awhile to think over a word.

Tyrone was mentioning "Danny" as being bad. That's serious, Cyril, and no heart, however soft, should let itself be cajoled into tolerating incompetence. You, as much as I, have a big burden to carry, and one who can't help should be mercilessly jettisoned.

About going over—Eileen, Shivaun, and a friend, a Dublin girl, will

---

[1] *The Bishop's Bonfire* was to open at the Gaiety Theatre on 28 February 1955.

certainly be going, and I want you to get three tickets somewhere in the House for the 1st night. Sydney Bernstein of Television and Cinema with some friends will be going over, too.

I hope you may successfully manage Equity. They are a force that one has to meet and satisfy; though I wish they'd take more trouble about making their members capable. A Union carpenter, plumber, or electrician must be a first-class worker; his Union guarantees him; but Equity here and in New York don't seem to have any set standard for acting; they are, or seem to be, content when Union fees are paid. In New York they give an additional week for a more "difficult" play. This concession was given to WITHIN THE GATES.

I'm glad you liked "Brother Choleric."[2] Evidently, a very clever artist, and one who has a grand sense of humour—very different from [Ronald] Searle's, whose work, I don't like at all.

And I'm glad Father Tom[3] "couldn't lay down 'Sunset and Evening Star.' " Give him my good wishes—if he'll have them.

I think that's all for the moment, except to wish well to Maureen, the children, and you, with my love as a bow to the wish.

Yours sincerely,
Sean

P.S. The "falsify" is right, Cyril, for it refers to Keelin's sense of "being a lady." He suggests that her love for him should falsify that feeling; make it false, show her that it wasn't a true feeling, or a natural one. But your point is a fair one, and falsify might be given the idea you mention. It is obscure. I suggest therefore the following—

Let your love fortify your truer feeling, an, etc.

It might be better this way.

Or, "falsify your falser feeling," but I think the first to be the better one.

2 See O'Casey's letter to Cusack, 27 January 1955, note 2.
3 Father Tom, a Benedictine monk, friend of Cusack's.

To Joan D'Alton[1]

TC. O'CASEY

14 FEBRUARY 1955

Dear Miss D'Alton,

Thanks for your letter regarding my proposed broadcasts.[2] I dont think you have got it quite right. Last November, Mr. M[icheál] O'hAodha (who, I hope, is getting better) wrote to me suggesting these broadcasts. I replied giving reasons for a keen hesitation in consenting to do it: encroaching on the time and space that might be given to younger writers; anxious to avoid resentment from some of the writers who might be annoyed at my getting the privilege (and pay) of speaking over Radio Eireann, et al.

I also made it clear to Mr. O'hAodha that I wouldnt talk about my plays, but would rather speak—if I spoke at all—in an informal way about things that moved about in my mind at the moment of writing the script. I never talk about my work, except during the time of a play-production when I damn well have to.

My 2nd theme was a commentary on a statement made by a writer in a Dublin Evening paper; and the third one I thought of doing would be some comments about war, with a few extracts from old songs dealing with it. I am far away from the mood and the moments of the plays you mention; my thoughts are on newer things, as I hope you may see (if I have written well) in the newer play—"The Bishop's Bonfire."

I am still hesitant, and, if you are in any way doubtful, I am quite prepared to withdraw from the idea; but I think the one I have submitted should be done solely on account of the fact that I am committed to the engagement of Mr. [Donald] Aldous, and feel he should suffer no loss if the idea of talks be abandoned.

I may remark, also, that Mr. O'hAodha said the talks were to be 2000 words, lasting fifteen minutes each, and so I tried to keep close to this request from Mr. O'hAodha.

Frankly, I should like to talk over Radio Eireann—I have never done so—but not about my plays. I write or chat only about what interests me, and to talk about my plays would not interest me at all—only bring embarrassment.

Please let Mr. O'hAodha know that I sincerely hope he may soon be allright again.

With all good wishes to Radio Eireann and to you.

Yours sincerely,
Sean O'Casey.

[1] Miss Joan D'Alton, Assistant Productions Director, Radio Eireann, Dublin.
[2] See O'Casey's letter to Philip Rooney, 29 April 1955, note 1.

To David Krause

MS. KRAUSE

14 FEBRUARY 1955

My dear Dave:

Thanks, rosy ones, for your kind letter of good words; but God would have to help me if Conceit had been my besetting sin. Not all would agree with you, & the Irish writers, if they read it, would give a loud, sardonic hoot. You should have read what the "Statesman & Nation" said about the Cambridge chapter; adding that he (the critic) had been a graduate in Cambridge when O'Casey came, & so knew better.[1] One who had been there, looked up the Register, and found that the critic had graduated years before I came down there.[2] So, you see, how one has to fight, not honesty, but sly deceit. The young man (middle-aged now) who had been there, wrote in to say the other had not; but, of course, his letter didn't get printed. Not that it matters a damn—except to the moral of the critic. Of course, you're right about Creda;[3] no one knows, or knew, what happened; but she was bent on forcing her view on me. She's a well-known lass & writer, &, I've seen references to her & one bearing the same name (a man), & I'm sure it's the husband back again. She has written since a number of things about the USSR, but no longer mentions the husband. I'm doubtful about those who yell, or yodel, out their opinions (without good reasons backing them), Conservatives or Communists. We must reason together: "Come, let us reason together, saith the Lord of Hosts." Ay, let us reason together since we have to live, to work, &, in the end, die together.

Of course, [T. S.] Eliot is a fine writer, and a most sincere man. I wrote to the Chairman of the USSR Commission of Foreign Writers, telling him so; and that the venomous criticisms of Eliot were shameful and false. So was Yeats; but not Orwell, in my opinion. He was no Joyce, and, again, he should have known more about English Literature, if he wanted to go for me. He was like a wolf mad with the mange, as Hitler was a wolf mad with a jaundice against the Jew.

What I wanted to say, really, was to warn you against thinking too much about my work in your book. You like me (as I you), and so you've

---

[1] See O'Casey's letter, "Sean and Mr. Worsley," *New Statesman and Nation,* 6 November 1954, note 1, Vol. II.

[2] See O'Casey's letter to Peter Newmark, 10 November 1954, note 1, Vol. II.

[3] See the "Creda Stern" incident in "The Dree Dames," *Sunset and Evening Star* (1954).

got to be careful. I enclose two cuttings that may give you pause, & give you, maybe, a jolt to a "double-think." A Orwellian-Joycean effort!

[Patrick] Galvin has, I imagine, given up the idea of a law action—I haven't heard from him for a long time. I'm worried about these young Irish writers. They're afraid of losing any job they have; afraid of the clerics; afraid of their genuine opinions; & they're afraid now of "Thersites"—the triple Woods—Thersites—Hogan; Ireland Triple Coddess.[4] They try to show part of bravery lost by attacking any braver than themselves.

Now, less of them and me, & more of yourself. Do take care of that cough. A lingering, whoreson cough is usual after a bout of the damned grippe. Keep warm, and rest as much as possible; & avoid a chill. You may have gone to work too soon. Wrap yourself up well till the cough goes. I hope you may have a good and happy time with the course of modern drama; and, most important, that it will mean more money for you. Professors and Teachers don't get paid as well even as Film Starlets—that's our holy civilization. "Lillibulero" is a Protestant song, certainly composed when James II came to the throne; reputed to have been written by Lord Wharton. A favorite in Belfast for years: now superseded by "The Protestant Bugs"—James was the "dog" and Tyrconnell the "ass." Yeats mixed him & Ormond in a poem. Yeats had an idea he was descended from the Butlers-Ormond. He put Ormond on James's side in the "Battle of the Boyne"; but Ormond, cuter than Tyrconnell, fought for King William.

We have had a lot of violent weather here, but I'm bearing up brave. Busy with The Bonfire. Dublin gives its first performance this month. Tyrone Guthrie is producing it—directing it. Dublin excited. 1st night booked out before bookings start. Oh, boys, what can the mather be?

My love, dear Dave to you.

As ever,
Sean

---

[4] One of the cuttings enclosed in this letter was an attack on O'Casey by "Thersites" (Thomas Woods—see O'Casey's letter to Krause, 5 January 1955, note 3) in his column "Private Views," *Irish Times,* 5 February 1955, where he says: "But we are expected to take the rejection of a play [*The Silver Tassie*] that he himself must know to be third-rate as the excuse for Mr. O'Casey's prolonged tantrums in exile, and for his six-volume venting of venom on people like George Orwell, who was worth twenty of him any day of the week. We ought to have coddled Mr. O'Casey; we ought to have tucked him in comfortably every night and fed him with pre-digested Marx and Engels for breakfast, dinner and tea, and humbly accepted without question every word the Master deigned to write."

To Oxford University English Club

TC. O'CASEY

THE PRESIDENT OF THE OXFORD UNIVERSITY ENGLISH CLUB.
CORPUS CHRISTI COLLEGE, OXFORD.

14 FEBRUARY 1955

Dear friend,

I couldnt make your name out, so I take the liberty of addressing you as friend, for it is time that friendship should be honored in the observance than in its breach.

I thank you for your very kind invitation to go to Oxford to have a chat with the Members of your Club; but, unfortunately, it isnt possible to go. I'm too old now to run round thoughtlessly or thoughtfully—75 next month—, and I have work before me that will keep me going till I'm gone.

Of course, I'd be delighted to go, and, of course, I'd enjoy the visit, but I shall have to be content with the rambling visit I paid to Oxford away back in 1926.

A new play of mine, "The Bishop's Bonfire" is to get a first production in Dublin this month, and many appeals have come to me to be present when it shows itself for the first time; but I have had to refuse, and be pleased to wait till it comes to London, as all who are busy with it hope it may.

I used to run round and speak on platform and in street, but now, like His Holiness the Pope, I must be content to speak from my window to any passer-by who is interested enough to pause, look up, and listen.

My good wishes to all your Members, and to you.

Yours sincerely,
Sean O'Casey.

To Cyril Cusack

MS. CUSACK

17 FEBRUARY 1955

Dear Cyril,

This to tell you that Don Burke of "Life" is flying over tomorrow to see something of the rehearsals; so do what you can to please him. I imagine, I told Tyrone already, but amn't sure. Please tell him, again, if I haven't done so in my letter. A member of the staff is to come down here on Wednesday next to have a preliminary chat before going over to Dublin to "cover the First Production." They may take photos. Anyway, Don says they are going to "cover" the event in "Life." Don and Mrs. Burke have read the play—proofs given to Don by Macmillans—, & he tells me they "both thought it wonderful." I wonder are they anyway near the mark? Well, that will all depend on Woods-Thersites-Hogan, Eire's triple Coddess. I wonder what we could do to placate her? Hope things go well with you.

Yours sincerely
Sean

To Frank McCarthy

MS. McCarthy

17 February 1955

My dear Frank,

There's a lad—not altogether a lad, for he must be near or there to forty—I know who is looking for a job, & I imagine you might advise him. He worked for Shell Mex, in Dublin, for God knows how many years, and some months ago—say a year—got his docket thro' "redundancy." He looked & looked for a job in Ireland; he was Secretary of the Irish Students' Debating Society for years; he's a very good Catholic; he knows everyone in Dublin from Erskine Childers down; & yet couldn't get a job anywhere. In desperation, he came to England—foolishly, I think; & is searching busily, but unsuccessfully for the present-day pearl of great price—a job. I thought you might give him the bend on the better way to go about it; or at least, suggest lodgings where he wouldn't have to pay so much as he's doing. The trouble is, I think he was a clerk, & it's devilishly hard for a collar-and-tie man to find an opening, once he's been shooed away from the desk he worked at. Perhaps, you could give him a few words of advice. He's a good fellow, tho' inclined to be something of an interminable talker. His address is:—

Seumas Scully
West London Hotel,
Kensington Gardens Square,
London, W.2.

But don't bother, don't do anything to worry yourself, if you aren't feeling fit. A duodenal ulcer is enough for anyone to mind; and needs constant caution in diet. Beware of intoxicants, & try to live quietly, & be austere in drinking and eating.

I'd have written sooner, only I've been very busy with a Dublin production of "The Bishop's Bonfire." Cyril Cusack Productions has taken it on, & Tyrone Guthrie is producing it. It is causing a great stir in Dublin, & is to be first performed at the end of this month.

I do hope you are feeling fit, & that you are taking care of yourself.

As ever,
Sean.

To Seumas Scully[1]

MS. SCULLY

18 FEBRUARY 1955

Dear Seumas,
I am very sorry you had to come to London—wish you had come 20 years ago. You see it is particularly hard to get clerical work here, or anywhere else. It is not only incredible that you could get nothing in Ireland; it seems to me to be bitterly disgraceful. I have written to a friend of mine asking him to have a chat with you. He is not one who can plant you in a job—just an ordinary worker of very high intelligence. He is a Frank McCarthy, born Drumcondra, brought up a Protestant, & none the better for that, thank God. He was a sergeant in the British Army in last war, was torpedoed by the Japs in the Pacific Ocean, while in bed, tossed about in the sea 48 hours, naked, save for an oilskin-bag round his neck carry[ing] a photo of G. B. Shaw. He knows the common ropes of London (& Dublin) well, & his knowledge may be of great use to you. He has worked in lots of places—a restless chap—, pubs, hotels, Eton College—, & today—if he is there still—in Passfield Hall, Endsleigh Place, London W.C.1 in Bloomsbury, not far from British Museum. It is attached—a hostel, I think—to the London School of Economics. I've written him asking if he would see you, & gave him the address you've given to me. If he will see you, go, for he is an experienced lad, & can advise you on many common things; & might even suggest what chance of a job you had in London. London is a tougher place than Dublin. Frank might be able to put you in the way of cheaper digs. There are a number of places in Bloomsbury cheaper than where you are—Michael Scott stayed once—

---

[1] Seumas Scully (1910–   ), born in Moore Street, Dublin, worked as a clerk; theatre enthusiast, and Secretary of the Dublin Technical Students Literary and Debating Society. See letters to him in Vol. II.

a Mrs. Sullivan—many, many years ago. Bloomsbury Hotel might be cheaper than where you are. We—Eileen & I stayed there once; but I don't know what the charges are now. There was an Irish lass at the desk, & an Irish porter. Lots of Irish in Bloomsbury—district of W.C.1, or part of it. Guildford St. Bloomsbury St. Theobalds Rd. etc. Ask Frank, anyhow. Take a chance, if you have an idle hour, to go to his place of employment. Say I sent you, of course.

Let me know what happens.

Keep the pecker up—you're not dead yet. You can't expect to jump from Dublin (that you know) to London (that you don't know) & be flung into a job in no time. After all, you spent some time in Ireland looking for one.

Ask Frank—if you see him—to tell you what *he* thinks: whether it is worth waiting on, or better to go back to what you know; but first see those to whom you have letters.

Yours as ever,
Sean.

To Cyril Cusack

MS. Cusack

19 February 1955

Dear Cyril,

I have read your letter to Eileen. Seems fine. I'm glad you forced yourself into getting a new "Danny."[1] You surely have done him good by shunting him off the stage, tho' you may not have done well to Waldron by bringing him on to it: it is always so hard to be sure: he might make a far better actor than he would a doctor; and, anyhow, either Profession is as precarious as the other.

I amn't worrying about the result of Tyrone's work and yours: I have full and quiet confidence in you both as far as the Production goes. A run in London is what I hope for so that the work done may receive a fit reward.

It isn't the strain of or tension in, a first production that halts me here. I have long, long ago, reached a philosophy that is quiet about all these things. It is really the physical of 75 that keeps me put. I have to last as long as I can, and so must recognise my limitations. However, I will go, of course, to London to see you all; hoping Tyrone may be there, too; tho' papers say he's off to Canada soon.

---

[1] Aiden Kerrigan eventually played the role of Daniel Clooncoohy.

By the way, Cyril, you haven't mentioned anyone for the part of the "Porter" or the "Lieutenant."[2] The "Porter" is a good part; the L. not so good. I hope you may have a good man for the "Porter."

I hope the new opening for the Second act is satisfactory.

All the Best to Maureen, the children, & to you, and

Bail ó Dhia ar an obair.[3]

As before
Sean

By the way, for the book of the play, I have put in as a quotation the first two Gaelic lines of the song, Caoine for Kilcash.[4]

[2] Harry Hutchinson played the Porter, Godfrey Quigley the Lieutenant.

[3] The Blessing of God on the work.

[4] The following lines from "The Keen of Kilcash" appear on the title page of *The Bishop's Bonfire* (1955):

> *Cad dheanfamaoid feasta gan adhmad,*   x20.6
> *Ata deire na g-coillte ar lar.*
> (What shall we henceforth do without timber.
> The last of the forest trees is down.)

See O'Casey's letter to Kay Carney, 15 February 1958, where he gives the above translation.

To George Jean Nathan

MS. CORNELL

19 FEBRUARY 1955

My very dear George:

I hope you are keeping well, and watching yourself. But then, you've Julie to do that for you, thank God. I am possessed of a few aches, for the weather here is bitterly cold, with snow and blustering, blistering winds. But the yellow crocuses are out, and that is a sign of fairer & fuller flowers to come.

I am very busy. "The Bishop's Bonfire" is in full rehearsal; first performance on the 28 Feb; with Tyrone Guthrie directing. It is causing a big stir in Dublin, with the theater (the Gaiety—not the Abbey) booked out & over before the bookings opened. It will be the first production of a play of mine in Dublin for 30 years;[1] a thing that rather surprised me when I looked it up. Lots from London are going over, & so are Eileen, with

[1] The last premiere performance of a full length O'Casey play in Dublin was the Abbey Theatre's production of *The Plough and the Stars* on 8 February 1926. His one-act play, *The End of the Beginning*, was first performed at the Abbey Theatre on 8 February 1937.

Shivaun, and a very charming friend we have made here—a Jewess,[2] as Dublin as they make them, with her husband—two doctors working in Torquay. The long journey & the Irish Sea are too much for me this.

I've been asked to record two or three broadcasts for Radio Eireann, who are putting on four plays of mine (O'Casey Festival!), & they wanted me to speak about the plays—a subject too old to interest me. I said no to this, & suggested my own choice, and sent them a rough script for one of the talks. They have agreed—I think reluctantly—to this one; but have again asked me to speak about my plays; I've said no; and wait their final decision. I'm prepared to withdraw, for I've a suspicion I may be wasting my time.

John O'Shaughnessey has signed a contract with me, thro' Miss Rubin, for the play "Red Roses For Me," which he hopes to do in the Fall. Looks like the USA & Eire for me. For the last three months I have got some hundreds from the U.S.A. and 3 guineas from England. Is it any wonder I prefer the Stars & Stripes to the three crosses of the Union Jack: And the Book Find Club has taken "Sunset & Evening Star." Hail Columbia!

Seriously, my very dear George, I do hope you are keeping well. My love to Julie for her own sake & for yours, and my love, dear lad, to you.

As ever,
Sean

2 Dr. Madeleine Epstein.

To Suzanne Rhem[1]

TC. O'CASEY

20 FEBRUARY 1955

Dear Miss Rhem,

Oh, my dear, what a choice. Could you not have chosen to write a Thesis about someone who had some more of a knowledge of religion besides me? What do I know, so what can I tell, about religion, or in fact, about anything else? And what religion, and which church? There are hundreds of them, and all claiming to be the one and only way of getting to God. A great orchestra playing together, but each instrument playing a differing tune; and you want me to make an ordered symphony from the sounds? The real important thing is, my dear, to form your own opinion of what O'Casey thinks about Church and Religion from what he has

1 Miss Suzanne Rhem, 1513 Pendleton Street, Columbia, South Carolina.

written: you'll probably be as near to what he believes as he is himself. What is religion, anyhow. And what is a Church? I will try to say a word or two concerning your terrible questions. I have read a lot about comparative religions, and of course, have Experienced those believed in by R. Catholic and the various Protestant denominations. I have read Coulton's FIVE CENTURIES OF RELIGION, and know that the Medieval Church wasnt what Anglican and R. Catholic set her out to have been; I have read Frazer's THE GOLDEN BOUGH, leading me to the anthropological facts that show the origin of many beliefs held today by multitudes; I have read a lot about Evolution, and have rejected because of its revelations the story of man's creation, of the creation of the living and inanimate world around us. To lay out all the thoughts surrounding these discoveries in science, and those made through experience, would make a book and a half. I have read Frazer's FOLKLORE OF THE OLD TESTAMENT and his STORIES OF THE ORIGIN OF FIRE, and no longer believe that man's moral development was quite so simple as told in the older books of the Bible. I am more curious than sceptical. I am always asking why, whither, whence, what? All things are amazing to me; I love to look long at the wing of a butterfly, just as I am interested in nuclear energy; so much so that I am an Associate Member of the British Atomic Scientists' Association. Everything around us is living, and full of potential energy; and we are but beginning to realise it. These are the big, big things. You arent quite right in assuming that I am annoyed with whatever God there be because I have been in circumstances where, apparently, "people were forsaken by God." There is no evidence that God forsook anyone; but there is a lot to prove that man can be very foolish, and that many unhappy and miserable conditions are due, not to God, but to man himself. God has given, or man has developed a mind to conquer the things that plague us. I am with the army of conquerors. How, when, and where, did man conceive the idea of a God? You know that early man had to give some answer for the phenomena of the mysterious universe around him: the sun, stars, wind, fire, water, and their angers, darkness and light, as well as man himself. We have gone a long way from primitive speculations, though the idea of the priest-god still lives. It has evolved now into the speculative christian idea that the material world was created by a pre-existent mind, and is sustained by non-material beings and forces—which is no explanation at all. To enter into the definite christian world, one has to embrace a lot more than this opinion: Incarnation, Resurrection, etc; which many modern clerics have rejected, regarding these beliefs but as symbols: Bishop Barnes, Father Tyrell, et al. I believe in revelation, not by direct communication by God to man; but by man's experience alone. Life is battling, but battling towards truth, not error. You seem to think I am one of the first of sceptics, but they existed from the dawn of thought. The minute opinions came into existence, opinions began to differ. See the Elizabethans, and earlier records of man's ideas.

See Shelley, Byron, Shakespeare, Wordsworth. Nothing more blasphemous or terrible can be thought of than Shakespeare's "Like flies to wanton boys are we to the gods; they kill us for their sport." So, you see, I am not the only one who has sceptical thoughts. As for positive belief, I can think of nothing better than Shaw's declaration—through the character of Father Keegan in his play, JOHN BULL'S OTHER ISLAND: his glorious human church of three in one and one in three. It is the last speech of Keegan towards the very end of the play. Read it, my dear; it is very beautiful. Religions are like shells on a seashore—you pick one up to throw it down; pick up another that finds your fancy, and you bring it home to place it on the mantelpiece over the fire.

I seem to see the Church as a great monetary and political power—the bigger banks in Italy are owned by it; the church in Spain owns vast properties, as in all places where they have the majority power; so I am anti-church as Christ was when he drove the money-changers out of the Temple. Card. Spellman can give Dublin £10,000 for charity: Dublin's R.C. Bishop can fling out a £1000 without winking; Card. Griffin here can fling out £5000 without a wrinkle of care: St. Peter said once, Silver and gold, have I None. . . .

"Anti-clericalism" is a common thing now—everywhere, strongest in R.C. countries; an old fight—the church versus the state. It exists in your own country. Remember Card. Spellman's attack on Mrs Roosevelt? It is not peculiar to me. Of course I hate hypocrisy, cant, and humbug—not only among clerics, but among all sections of the community. Read Mencken's "Americana."

Yes; the clergy have great power in Ireland but there have been a few fine souls left who still raise a voice against its abuse; and, fortunately, we Irish are warm-hearted, and so, when we are engaged in social life, sectarianism is forgotten, and the Irish are immersed in music and song and good feeling.

Of course, I have affectionate feelings for those I know whose religion, or lack of it, differs from my thoughts; I am indifferent to what one believes in, politics, religion, or anything else so long as she or he isnt a bore; is intelligent; likes art, the theatre, and literature, music or science; in short, one who is alive, regardless of race or creed. My feelings as a young man were towards life with all its shapes, color, and vivacity; my feeling now (74) are towards life with all its shapes, color, and vivacity. No more time, my lass; very busy with play to be produced next Monday in Dublin. Au revoir. My love and good wishes to you, and may you soon be waving your Master's Degree.

[Sean O'Casey]

To Tyrone Guthrie

TS. GUTHRIE

21 FEBRUARY 1955

Dear Tyrone,

Thanks a lot for your letter of the 16th. Glad the alternative bit for the [ending] 2nd Act suited. I have been thinking of what you say about encouragement instead of mere consolation; and there is a lot in it. But it doesnt run that way in Ireland up to now. You may remember Father Flanagan,[1] who fought and spoke, and finally sank into silence; Father Sheedy,[2] friend of Dr. McDonald, who defended a P.P. before a bishop, and wasnt long till he found himself faraway in the silences of Altoona, Pennsylvania; Dr. McDonald himself, who had to see that his "Reminiscences" were published after his death;[3] whose picture appears in "History of Maynooth College," but whose name in the Index is the only one that hasnt a page-number set against it. Father O'Hickey[4] who fought the Bishops over Irish in the University, even went to Rome, came home a broken man, and who wasnt given even the meanest job on "The Mission"—Holy Ireland, you know, is still in Partibus infidelium, and the R.C. Ministry is still a Mission; the Irish or Ireland, rather, is a heathen land. The priest on whom I drew the part of F[ather]. Boheroe, I met in a Rest Home for Nuns in Wicklow. He was sent there because he was "naughty." Questioned things. Eileen had gone there to see a relative who was a nun. I went off to have lunch with the taxi-driver who brought us down. When I came back, I was told Father _____ —I cant remember the name—wanted to see me. Reluctantly, I went in to chat with the young and ardent Levite, who was a grand lad, who had no one to talk to, for none of the nuns had a second idea in a head; so we talked of many things, and I came away with a handclasp that I can feel still. Where's he now? I dont know. He said good-bye, and the rest is silence. Again, a priest's (Anglican or R. Catholic) tendency is almost invariably, in cases of personal sorrow or disappointment, towards resignation, not rebellion or resistance. It is almost a reflex action, automatic. I am wondering, all the same, if your suggestion would be better.

No; I think My Bonnie[5] is allright. It is a charming old folk-song, and even chorussing Trinity Students couldnt spoil it. In my opinion, it relates closely to the circumstances between Foorawn and Manus. I looked

---

[1] For comments on Father Michael O'Flanagan see O'Casey's letter to Francis MacManus, 14 January 1946, note 8, Vol. II.

[2] For comments on Dr. Morgan Sheedy see O'Casey's letter to Brooks Atkinson, 5 March 1949, notes 4 and 5, Vol. II.

[3] Dr. Walter McDonald's *Reminiscences of a Maynooth Professor* was published in 1925, five years after his death on 2 May 1920.

[4] See O'Casey's chapter on Dr. Michael O'Hickey, "Lost Leader," *Drums Under the Windows* (1945).

[5] "My Bonny's Gone Over the Ocean," a song in *The Bishop's Bonfire*.

over many songs when I was writing the play, and found none to compare
with it. Of course it is satirical, but, to me, pathetically so; whereas the
other—when Irish Eyes are smiling—is comically satiric. I'd rather let it
stay. "Green Bonnets" is another matter: The real "Border" never entered
my head. It hadnt lasted long when I left, so I never could see any border
in Ireland. I see your and their point. I think you and they are right. But
not Let Erin Remember. I've heard that sung with Tom Moore playing
accompaniment, and Robert Emmet listening, after The Marseillaise had
been played, and it was terrible—in AN IMAGINARY CONVERSA-
TION.[6] I enclose two suggestions for this scene between Danny, F.
Boheroe, and Keelin.

You are right about the "vernacular." It was lovely when it was a
novelty; but, no—It wont do by itself. But a lot think it as dewy and as
fresh as ever. It isnt. It didnt last as long as Cleopatra. Imagine you being
in Israel. I had a friend out there who directed plays in the Kibbutz—is
that the right term?

You are right about the London critics: they never allow any sympathy to go out of them to an experimental play. I believe they always
seek a night's amusement; except when they go to a Shakespeare show;
then they put on their top-hats. It is very depressing when after a long
time of work, a play that has in it the heart of the playwright, goes down,
and the critics pooh pooh a brave effort. And so little comes out of it; a
few pence in the purse, and a black disappointment in the heart. I know
it all. Certainly Breon and Mrs O'C. talked a lot about THE TOP OF
THE LADDER.

I'm sure Harry [Hutchinson] and Tony [Quinn] will do well. They
have to work hard for a living, and they arent young any longer. Too many
of us have to keep working too long. I have to keep hard at it, though
I'm 75, with no investments, not even a Savings Certificate. It's just as
well to have to face active life to the end. But I'd like a more frequent
reward, and, I daresay, so would you. But then, recently in Dublin, it was
settled that artists thrive on suffering. Good, sound christian doctrine!

God send that all of us will snatch a few brands from the burning of
the bishop's bonfire.

> *With all good wishes,*
> *Yours very sincerely,*
> *Sean O'Casey*

2 sheets enclosure[7]

[6] Conal O'Riordan's *An Imaginary Conversation,* a one-act play about Robert
Emmet and Tom Moore, opened at the Abbey Theatre on 13 May 1909, under
O'Riordan's pseudonym of "Norreys Connell."

[7] The 2 sheets are missing.

To Mrs. R——— and Miss A———

TS. PRIVATE

22 FEBRUARY 1955

My dear two friends,

Thank you, thank you very much, but I could never think of accepting your gift of £150; and so I return the check with this letter. I dont need it, and, so far, have managed allright. If you were another of Shaw's Millionairesses, it might be another matter. It was very good of you to think of me, but you must also think of yourself and of A. If you have this amount to spare, I suggest that you put it aside for her.

I listen to quite a lot of music—we have a wireless; though the Third Programme is impossible here; and I enjoy it all very much. And with three children—the oldest 25, the lad trying to be a painter—I am always in the know of what the young think and what the young do; and that—through Time—means everlasting life.

Indeed, at the moment, I have no time to think of anything except work in hand—which is good, though I have to refuse a lot of it, lacking the energy to keep going forever.

Unfortunately, the Dramatists League gave Unity [Theatre] last June a tentative permission to do a play of mine, subject to a possible professional offer, without telling me. If they had, I should never have given it for the play, for I know they would have given it a shocking production. In the meantime, I signed a contract for the same play with an American Producer, who some years ago, did it in Houston, Texas, and caused a furore.[1] It was then I learned that permission had been given to Unity. Oh, I wish these Communists would realise the greatness of England's heritage; and not have their eyes forever on the faraway; would tell their people through the English mind what the Great English did, and what the great English said.

For instance, as Shaw said, there are a few lines of Keats that embrace all the hopes, all the propaganda, that Marx and Lenin took years and volumes to say.[2]

Well, I must stop so as to get on with some changes in a play to be done in Dublin next Monday, and with the proofs of the book of the play, which have just come. Thanks again, and my love to both of you.

Yours very sincerely,
Sean O'Casey

P.S. Dear lass, do be careful how you hand out money. A generous hand will always find soiled paws stretched out to get some.

[1] For an account of the protest against a production of *Red Roses For Me* in Houston, Texas, in 1951, see O'Casey's letter to George Jean Nathan, 26 May 1951, note 2, Vol. II.

[2] For the two relevant stanzas from Keats's "Isabella," see O'Casey's letter to David Krause, 12 April 1955, note 2.

To Robert Emmett Ginna[1]

MS. GINNA

4 MARCH 1955

My dear Bob,

Today, I was doing two 15 minute broadcasts (tape recording) for Radio Eireann,[2] & I got the Recorder to bring a machine which could do the Record you sent us; and so Breon & I heard your voice again mingling with my own.[3] Eileen & Shivaun are in Dublin; Niall in Germany—artillery—, so they couldn't hear it. I & Breon were delighted with it. It was really grand, and, by God, you did me proud. I do hope I & the home may be something like the picture you give of it. Eileen, certainly, deserves all you say about her. Our recording friend will bring the Machine here again—I've to do another recording—, & then Eileen & Shivaun will hear it, & I shall hear it again. It was very kind of you to make the record, & kinder to send it on to us. We shall treasure it indeed. It was odd to hear your voice from the record, differing from the sound I was familiar with while you were with us. But my own voice from a record, disk or tape, startles me.

Thanks & thanks, dear Bob.

As you may have heard, my "Bishop's Bonfire" is on in Dublin. Street where the theater is—the Gaiety—packed out; cheering & boos; in the theater, the same, boos & cheering. However, they expect the play to run for 4 or 5 weeks; & then, maybe, come to London. Irish Critics damned every scene, every action, every word of it; but the English critics gave it a fine press, which is odd; so good a press that there is good hope of it getting the chance of a London run. I have been denounced by the "Standard," & getting a lot of letters warning me of the Judgement Day.

Thanks, too, for the Magazine[4] which I am reading with great interest—Science is one of my loves; &, for years, I've been an Associate of the Atomic Scientists Association.

When I've read them, I'll send them on to Niall.

[1] Robert Emmett Ginna (1925–   ), New York, an editor of *Scientific American* and *Life* magazines. See letters to him in Vol. II.

[2] He gave three talks for the Radio Eireann "O'Casey Festival," radio dramatizations of four of his plays broadcast from 15 May to 5 June 1955. For details see the letter to Philip Rooney, 29 April 1955, note 2.

[3] Ginna had sent him a record of the sound-track for the television program, "A Conversation with Sean O'Casey and Robert Emmett Ginna," presented on 22 January 1956 on NBC-TV. For details see the letter to George Braziller, 9 November 1955, note 1.

[4] *Scientific American.*

I do hope, dear friend, that you are happy in your new post; & that it gives you good satisfaction; for you are a clever lad as well as being a lovable one.

Breon sends his love to you, & so do I.

As ever,
Sean

Thanks again, Bob, for the very charming record—wish it had been longer; but it was grand.

Just reading article on "Bridges"—lovely Photography. What power there is in the bridges shown! A beautifully turned-out magazine, Bob. The Cover is really majestic of the George Washington Bridge. I've seen no Soviet Photo—& they're pretty good—to compare with it in selection of form & imagination. A grand photograph!

By God, you Americans are some Engineers—& Editors—and Photographers. A grand magazine.

Sean

To Cyril Cusack

Ms. Cusack

5 March 1955

Dear Cyril and Maureen, and the children,

Thanks for a lot—for the Production, for the acting, & the taking of the play, in which you all had a share.[1]

Take as much rest as you can, & don't bother too much about G.F.[2] Try to pass by on the other side of his comments. As for me, & his comments about this play and the other play, he and the others are wild about the interest taken in it all. Eileen has just come back, & tells me she was at the play on Friday, & that it went splendidly; and that the comedy went over grand, as I hoped it might. She tells me the "Jeep" scene is very

[1] Cyril Cusack Productions presented the premiere of *The Bishop's Bonfire* on 28 February 1955 in Dublin at the Gaiety Theatre, directed by Tyrone Guthrie, settings by Michael O'Herlihy, with the following cast: Seamus Kavanagh as Dick Carranaun (the Prodigal); Tony Quinn as Richard Rankin; Eddie Byrne as Councillor Reiligan; Paul Farrell as Canon Burren; Denis Brennan as Manus Moanroe; Aiden Kerrigan as Daniel Clooncoohy; Maureen Cusack as Keelin; Cyril Cusack as Codger Sleehaun; Patrick Leyde as Father Boheroe; Sheila Brennan as Foorawn; Godfrey Quigley as Lt. Michael Reiligan; Harry Hutchinson as the Porter.

[2] Gabriel Fallon, "The 'Bonfire' Never Did Really Blaze Up At All," *Evening Press,* Dublin, 1 March 1955.

comic. I see G.F. couldn't even keep quiet over my little tweet in the programme. He takes it word by word, and bites at it. He can't swally it! Does
the chap imagine that I shall henceforth think of what G.F. will think of
what my thinking might say? It is an odd conceit, and, possibly, has some
Freudian explanation.

I shall write again. I hope it may go to London for all our sakes.

I'm delighted that Maureen was so good. English Press much kinder
this time; bar "Statesman"—but then that was a Gael-critic—Donough
Donat.[3] He was particularly hurt by the phrase of "Where's me Da?"

My love to Maureen, to you, & to the children.

Sean

Eastward Ho!

[3] Donat O'Donnell (Conor Cruise O'Brien), "No Bishop, No Bonfire," *New
Statesman and Nation,* 5 March 1955.

To Ria Mooney[1]

MS. MOONEY

7 MARCH 1955

My dear Ria,

Many thanks for the tie of pure Irish wool, dyed a very charming
crimson—a religious and a secular symbol: The Precious Blood and the
Red Flag.

Thanks, too, a thousand, for your kindness to Eileen and Shivaun.
Shivaun seems to have become more Irish than the Irish themselves; more
Irish than I, even. Oh, Ria, the young!

Now a few questions, &, be sure, I'll not mix you up in anything I
may say, if I ever say anything; for I know the writer-fellas in Dublin.

1. Who is "S"?[2] Ess? Less! Is this the Caidhp cúl árd, or Caidhp
   bhás,[3] of Seamas Kelly, the "drama critic"?

[1] Ria Mooney (1900–73), Abbey Theatre actress and director, who had played
the role of Rosie Redmond in the first production of *The Plough* in 1926. She directed
the London premiere of *Red Roses For Me* in 1946; for details of the production see
O'Casey's letter to Mrs. Una Gwynn Albery, 6 March 1946, note 1, Vol. II. See letters
to Miss Mooney in Vol. II.
[2] Seamus Kelly, drama critic of the *Irish Times,* wrote reviews under the initials
"S" and "K," and wrote a regular column under the name of "Quidnunc."
[3] *Caidph cúl árd,* "High Caul Cap," the name of an Irish dance; *Caidph bháis*
(pronounced Ky-bosh), Cap of Death, possibly derived from the pitch-cap torture
of the insurgent Croppy Boys by the British during the 1798 rebellion.

2. Who is Donat O'Donnell?[4] Isn't he one who occasionally writes, or wrote, for "The Bell," or for "Irish Writing"?

3. Is "The Bell" still ringing?[5] Some time ago I sent a year's sub, but haven't heard a word since. Twice I sent my new address, but so far, the "Bell" has always trickled here to me from "Tingrith" Totnes.

Well, allana [dear], you all seem to have had an exciting time, & Dublin seems to have warmed her hands, & aroused her mind, at the B.'s Bonfire.

By the way, Ria, have you read the pastorals?[6] From what they denounce—from immodest dress, dances, drink, gambling, etc,—one would imagine poor oul' Ireland was a "den of infantry." Looks like "The Poor Old Woman" was always now on the razzle dazzle. And hardly a sentence in them with even an echo of a thought, or the shadow of a sparkle.

I wonder does any one ever read them? I sometimes think they are read only by the lone, lorn atheist—communist here in Devon.

All the best to you, and thanks again.

As ever,
Sean

---

[4] Conor Cruise O'Brien (1917–   ), Irish writer, diplomat, teacher, and politician who wrote under the pseudonym of Donat O'Donnell.

[5] *The Bell* magazine ceased publication in December 1954.

[6] The pastoral letters issued by the Roman Catholic Bishops each year at the beginning of Lent.

To Cyril Cusack

TS. CUSACK

10 MARCH 1955

Dear Cyril,

It is impossible for me to go to Dublin. First, an X-ray examination some few years ago showed that healed scars on the lungs had puckered them in such a way as to pull the heart out of its proper place behind them; rendering it dangerous to undergo any strain; so, if I went, it couldnt be by plane (prohibited), but by the long journey of sea and rail. This would mean that I might well be not an aid, but a burden and a bloody nuisance to you. I amnt well just now, and a journey, even under favorable conditions of weather, is out of the question. I rarely mention these things for they are purely a personal concern, cant be helped by anyone; but must be recognised and fought against by myself alone. I mention them now, between ourselves, in confidence, simply because I have to in order to explain the full circumstances.

Of course, it is difficult to be perfectly accurate about receipts for the first few nights; you know that what happened, crowds, etc, was probably unprecedented in theatrical Dublin experience. I certainly didnt imagine there would be such scenes. I thought there would be a good deal of interest in the play, a steady denunciation of it beforehand and after, by the STANDARD,[1] and a solid unanimous denial of anything even sketchily worthwhile in the work by the Dublin drama critics. These things, I knew would happen; but not the wild happenings, or the presence of so many outside or inside the theatre. Of course, I thought, too, that you realised that you wouldnt escape the STANDARD, or that the Dublin drama critics could deal with the play as a play, rather than as a work by O'Casey. I shouldnt worry over these things; they were inevitable. Take these things easy; they dont matter in any way. These things—for they arent minds or men—have no influence (save perhaps a good one) outside of the coasts. They tried their best to injure me when Mili and Ginna were in Dublin for the article in LIFE, but they showed their malice too clearly—as I knew they would, and so advised Mili and Ginna to seek them out—to do any harm. Ginna has since spoken about me and the family over the American Television and Wireless,[2] and Gjon Mili has shown a little film he made of us to friends everywhere in the C. of New York. The records I made for Caedmon are in many Colleges and schools, and even in private families, which is good for me and you, if the play ever goes across the Atlantic. After all, the denunciations of the D.D. critics deal mostly with me, and if I'm chirrupy and indifferent, why should you worry? Hurt business? I dont think so. If people want to go, they go, for there must be a lot of talk about the play, and talk like this, even curiosity, should entice them to go and have a look for themselves. Of course, you scarcely always have a capacity house; but the play, I think, should run safely for five weeks. The important thing to me is LONDON; to you, too, maybe. Well, a few plays done in Dublin could have had a better send off, in publicity and attention, than THE B'S BONFIRE. The Critics here have been really very fair, and, on the whole, have given the play a good chance.[3] Some of them have even almost demanded that the play be seen in London; all were intensely interested—bar one in THE STATESMAN AND NATION, who hadnt a good word for any part of it; but he was another of the solid phalanx of

---

[1] *The Standard,* 18 and 25 February 1955, in sensational front-page articles attacked O'Casey two weeks before the play opened, and then reviewed it in predictably negative terms, 4 March 1955. The critics of the other Dublin papers agreed with *The Standard,* though in a less abusive manner, that the play was a libel against Ireland and an artistic failure. See O'Casey's reply to his Dublin critics, "Bonfire Under a Black Sun," *The Green Crow* (1956).

[2] See O'Casey's letter to George Braziller, 9 November 1955, note 1.

[3] The London drama critics generally praised the play, especially the comic scenes. The play ran for five weeks but did not go on to London.

Dub. critics—Donat O'Donnell, who doesnt count, for, I am sure one cannot escape from the assurance that these critics arent interested in what I do, but only in doing me as much harm as they can. There is great interest in London at the moment; Sunday, Darlington of THE DAILY TELEGRAPH, on the Television, spoke about the play; a good talk, I'm told, and recommended that it be produced in London. Last SUNDAY TIMES had a picture of me taken five years ago! THE OBSERVER wanted to send down a photographer to take one, but I was too tired of having this done, so I suggested a reproduction of [Augustus] John's picture. I dont know whether they'll do it or no. Last week I listened to ANY QUESTIONS concerning theatre and drama, and several in the course of the debate, said "it was a disgrace the way O'Casey was neglected." If the play comes to London, I think we shall get a good Press. Personally, I'm not anxious or eager; if it werent for the economic side of it, I shouldnt care a damn. But, I venture to say, Cyril, that few plays done in Dublin would have had such a Press, or would have received such attention; so, from your point of view, it couldnt have been much better.

(THE OBSERVER has just sent a telegram to ask again to come down to take a picture. They say it will take but ten minutes, so I am agreeing. I hear that J. C. Trewin, the drama critic, has an article about the play in some paper—the SPHERE or TATLER, giving it a good notice.[4] This is all more important to us than what the professional Dub. critics spout out of them.) Dont forget that I am working here for the play as you are in Dublin. I know the picture will take more than ten minutes—they all say that; but the OBSERVER is a very important Journal. I really detest having my picture taken, and this represents real work on my part. "If it werent for the wife and kids," I'd just content myself with writing, or trying to write, a few more songs; and a few more opinions about the life I see and hear around me. Now for the technical parts of your letter to me: First, I cant see how THE STANDARD can stop you. If that be so, then Ireland's no more; but I dont think it has that power among Catholics, bar the ones who can barely read or write; like the fanatical "Prods" of Manchester, Liverpool, Toronto, and Belfast, who can barely read or write either. Now if, as you say, the audiences are showing an interest in it, That is the main thing. I'm glad they enjoy the comedy, which is a good sign. I've heard that a well-known critic, who very often writes as if he were the Angel of the Annunciation sent to tell the world

---

[4] J. C. Trewin, "Wonderful Reception," *The Sketch*, 9 March 1955, an article on booing and first night receptions, which begins with the following reference to the Dublin reception of *The Bishop's Bonfire:* "The gallery is in the news again. Not the London gallery this time, but one in Dublin. It has been booing a new play by a grand man of the theatre, Sean O'Casey. I was not over there, but I know the reputation of these Irish playgoers when their blood is up. This time there was no Yeats (as there used to be at the Abbey) to stride on indignantly, with waving mane, to denounce the booers. Otherwise, I gather, it was the usual pattern."

things, kept laughing joyously at the "funny parts." A friend of mine there was watching him.[5] Enjoying it, too, without paying for his seat. Makes one mad to think of it! I daresay the play ends on "a weak hand," and I know that is, naturally, an actor's bane; but I shouldnt worry too much. MAJOR BARBARA, J. BULL'S OTHER I., end on weak hands, too. It isnt a happy ending; and, possibly, may be a mistaken one. I'm not sure; but it cant be altered in Dublin. If you like, I'll think of a possible alternative for London; though a change wouldnt appeal to me; but I might think of something which would give a longer space between the death and fall of the curtain. That is, if you think it might be wise, and if M[aureen]. agrees with you. As for neglect of "line," "character," "language" for "atmosphere," Tyrone seems, by most accounts to have given a good production. Character, line, and language must, mainly, depend on the actors. Some will be best, some better, some good; and, if accounts be accurate, there is no bad one in the play.

I dont see how you could have gotten a better Caste. As for the Canon, he isnt a comic character, unconsciously so, of course, in his efforts to bring unity to the household for the Bishop's visit; I'd say he is meant to have a coarse dignity; perhaps, ruthless to do all he can for the temporal welfare of the church, especially in Ballyoona, where he only can do it—a kind of "Distant Point" in the Church Catholic. But then you have the actor; no actor can give what he hasnt got. Like all walks of life, some have one, some two, some five talents, and each has to make the most of what he has got. No one else can do it for him. Whether a change might be beneficial for London, I'm not sure, for who else is there? Liam Redmond, but he isnt available. I mentioned one, Ingrid Burke, but you didnt seem to notice it; for, anyway, it was wise to get someone whom you yourself knew. Of course, we must remember that there was an additional strain on the actors in this play; the natural one of a first night in an (to an audience) unknown play; and that of the venomous opposition of the STANDARD and its henchmen; so that they couldnt have been at their best: even you were distressed in this way— an attack on two fronts. In London that strain wont be there. As for the Production, it wouldnt be fair to deal drastically with Tyrone's conception. For good or ill, it is his work, and he wouldnt be pleased (and rightly so) if we manhandled it. Dont mind what THE TIMES says too much: other critics admired the Production. If you see any portion too stiff—especially in comedy parts—then soften it; and, above all, let the characters speak so that they can be heard. Look for perfection, but dont be too unhappy if you dont find it. Take me, do you think that I am satisfied with the play as I've written it? By God, I'm not! But it was the best I could do in the mood of the moment, and to that extent I am satisfied—and it is a great extent. I'm very glad Leyde[6] is improving; but dont forget that he is a lad

---

[5] He later identified this critic as Gabriel Fallon.
[6] Patrick Leyde played the role of Father Boheroe.

of little experience, and dont think he can be expected to be as you are. As he is sensitive and intelligent and young, he will improve. Of course Harry H.[7] has a world of experience behind him; he's an old trooper, and always can be trusted to give a competent performance. The OBSERVER photographer is coming down this evening to take the picture tomorrow, and another American is to be here on Monday next, so you see I have to be busy, too. Of course, when you come to London, I'll go up—if I'm able to crawl—, and we can go over it quietly, maybe touching a little change in here and there, but leaving the Production unharmed. Remember that Tyrone is an "alien" to production in Dublin, and there will be jealousy against him; but if an Angel did the Production of an O'Casey play, and another had leaned over me shoulder when writing it, it would still be a wretched work to the Irish Professional critics. Now, you, relax; dont read the STANDARD; dont read anything to irritate you. Take all the rest you can. Dont be blathering about not being as good as you'd like in your part: Eileen tells me you are grand, and Eileen is a damn good judge.

I will let you know the amount of the Cheque when it comes; but havent you an accountant to do an audit for you? My love to Maureen, to the children, and to you.

Sean

[7] Harry Hutchinson played the role of the Porter.

To Frank McCarthy

MS. McCARTHY

10 MARCH 1955

My dear Frank,

Thanks for your letter. Dr. Soper's article is a fine and a timely one.[1] I, too, have been fighting this magic business among Catholics—their rosaries, their medals, etc., making a Punch & Judy show of their Faith. Of course, I don't mind your putting me in "The Messenger."[2] As I should have been proud to be alongside Dr. W. McDonald, 40 years Professor of Theology in Maynooth College, so I am delighted to be shoved up beside such a man as Dr. Soper. We're all "leathering away with the wattle o'."

[1] A reference to Dr. Donald O. Soper's article on magic and superstition in religion in the March 1955 issue of the *Kingsway Messenger,* the Methodist magazine of Dr. Soper's West London Mission at Kingsway Hall.
[2] An editor of the *Kingsway Messenger,* McCarthy reprinted part of O'Casey's letter to him of 28 June 1954 in the issue of April–May 1955.

Yes, the play has caused a stir in Ireland, and seems to have caused something of a stir here. The Irish Papers are sputtering away with indignation—against the play, but really against the O'Casey. Not one Irish professional critic had a single good word to say about the play or about me—even stretching along to "The Statesman." All to the good, for their unanimous roar of condemnation shows their solid solidarity against O'Casey. I must be a long knife in their bowels. They went too far, trying to imbue the bewildered English critics with their own venom. They did their best, too, with the two LIFE representatives some time ago; but TIME was there for the play, taking notes & taking photos. I've just done 4 15-minute broadcasts for R. Eireinn to be given in May, I think. I hope they may not shelve them. They are simple, easy-going talks, quietly persuasive, or calmly sarcastic, with a snatch of a song in each of them.

Pity Seumas [Scully] didn't seek the Assist. Warden's job. But he is probably afraid of doing anything that might infringe the Faith. He does talk, but he is a decent chap, & it's disgraceful that the Knights of Columbanus didn't give him some kind of a job.

"Hall of Healing," I fear, is out of the question. One-act plays are tabu in the Professional Theatre; only Amateurs & Reps do them now.

Don't worry too much about Seumas: you have yourself to look after. Keep to your diet; never eat hastily; don't drink much spirits or beer: the body is very important: the soul can do little without it.

My love to Dr. Soper & to you.

As ever,
Sean.

To Cyril Cusack

MS. CUSACK

11 MARCH 1955

Dear Cyril,
Enclosed is a picture of a young lass who looks fine, and who might be a promising catch in the future for you: worth putting down on your list. Hope things still go well. Curious that the Leader-writer in TIMES PICTORIAL caught a good glimpse of what the play meant, tho' he isn't a "Professional" drama critic; even the shot at the end of the play.[1]

[1] George H. Burrows in his column "Talking It Over," *Times Pictorial,* 12 March 1955 (this Dublin weekly appeared on 8 March for the week ending 12 March), praised *The Bishop's Bonfire* but confessed that he was not a drama critic, and he concluded with this comment: "Commerce is in control in Ireland and maybe

Curious critics forget that a shot ends "Hedda Gabler," & a shot ends "The Wild Duck"; curious these fellas who call themselves critics don't know that Shakespeare doesn't always despise melodrama or slap-stick; or Moliere, or even Aristophanes. God, what an ignorant lot of theatrical chaperones they are! And THE STANDARD flapping bony wings & crowing that she is Almighty God's guardian-eagle angel. As for the character of "The Canon," don't they remember Pope Pius XI said, "insisted" a Catholic paper says, that "the priest today must be healthily modern," & the present Pope has said "the priest must accommodate his faculties to present complex conditions"; "Give them big ideas" advised an Archbishop, as he sent a young priest to be professor of a Seminary; or that a recent book, written by a Catholic—priest for all I know—says "celibacy, if it is purely negative, can lead to a selfish hardening of the heart, & to the emergence of an order of 'Clerical Pashas.' " I've just read these things, so no one can say I build my play on out-of-date ideas. The critics themselves are just rusty runabouts, dead to the world around them. Indeed, the play is pertinent, so much so that they yell in agony when their splenetic ignorance is poked back into their eyes and echoed back into their poor dull ears.

No cheque has come so far—Friday, midday. By the way, you mention in your letter something about giving a blank cheque. That doesn't seem business. I've got a lot of letters (English) all of which seem to think the play is a great success—taking their views from English critics, of course; they could hardly take it from our Irish friends—and that it will come to London. I hope so.

The Observer has just ended taking a picture.

All good wishes
As ever
Sean

O'Casey was wise even beyond his own knowing when at the end of the bonfire he made a character use a gun to destroy the thing he loved and lost awhile." For several more quotations from Burrows, see O'Casey's letter to the *Sunday Times,* 20 March 1955.

To Mrs. Maureen Cusack

MS. CUSACK

11 MARCH 1955

Dear Maureen,

I've just written a long letter to Cyril. He should have it now. The story you tell of the C[ivil] Service Spinster saying over coffee (not beer, not spirits) that "she couldn't stop laughing," is a good sign. The addition of "I didn't clap at the end," is to be expected. You can't expect an audience to let themselves go at such a new kind of play. But if audiences enjoy themselves, they are bound to tell others—as the C. S. Spinster did—, and so bring more into the house. My presence would bring you but one more hand-clap—me own; and what use would that be? Probably, not even one more, for I could hardly clap my own play; &, if I clapped the acting, they'd all say O'Casey was clapping himself.

I am to be photographed tomorrow for the "Observer," & an American is coming on Monday. There will probably be others I shall have to see, & other things to do, in the hope London may be interested. On the whole, we are very fortunate—what if the comedy hadn't come over!

Tell Cyril—he asked me to keep check—the cheque hasn't yet come; but it may arrive with the midday post.

It is very cold here still, & the winds blow fierce.

My love to you.

Sean

To Rev. Francis Cawley[1]

TC. O'CASEY

12 MARCH 1955

Dear Father Cawley,

Your letter wasnt explicit enough for me to venture an answer to what you said. "According to accounts the play [*The Bishop's Bonfire*] wasnt successful," is vague. Do you mean what you have heard, or what the archaeological specimens, that are called Irish drama critics, have written about it? Critics are rarely agreed, and the solid agreement of the Irish critics tell a tale, not of criticism, but of antagonism: they doth protest too much. And "successful" is a word having different meanings to different minds. You may remember Christ and His critics. He wasnt very successful then, and, according to the Bishops' Pastorals, He doesnt seem to be successful now. As for the "Vow of chastity and the spoiled priest elements being out of date," I dont quite get what you mean. Does not the Vow of Chastity still exist? And is it that there is no young man nowadays, entering a Seminary to become a priest, who ever fails to go on to the end of the road? Only the other day, talking to an Irish Catholic of obvious intelligence, we commented on the work of a well-known Irish

---

[1] Rev. Francis Cawley, St. Nathy's College, Ballaghadereen, Co. Roscommon, Ireland.

writer, and the comment of this most intelligent Catholic was "In his work, I always get the smell of a spoiled priest." The Clergy are no more "tricky" to draw in a novel or in a play, than any other human being: we are all tricky, in one way or another. Even the human characteristics of a St. Peter didnt change when he became an Apostle. He still could curse and swear like a fisherman. At least, it is so recorded. Supposing I put St. Peter on the stage, and in the midst of his fervour and his fear, I made him curse and swear, what would the holy men and women of your STANDARD think? Indeed, what would you think? I dont quite know what you mean by "normal." Few of the Saints were "normal" as contrasted with human normality. Surely, you remember that on the Day of Pentecost, when the Apostles, all who were gathered together, were "filled with the Holy Ghost," those who saw and heard them said that they were drunk? Of course I know priests who lived and worked, live and work, ay, and who were born there too, in Ireland. As for the "liberal" curate you so scornfully allude to, they are becoming more numerous, as was foretold by Dr. McDonald, 40 years Professor of Theology in May-nooth College. But all this is rather beside the point: the work I did must be judged, or should be, before bothering about this element or that one. It is a Play. Its intrinsic value is drama, and it stands or falls by the accuracy and delight of that medium. And, of course, above and before all, I do not hold that I am an infallible mortal.

   With sincere good wishes to you,

Yours very sincerely,
Sean O'Casey.

To Patrick Galvin[1]

TS. GALVIN

12 MARCH 1955

Dear Mr. Galvin,

   Thank you very much for thinking of sending me one of your Records,[2] but, very unfortunately, the disk came broken in two.

   No one, save an expert packer, should attempt to pack these fragile things.

   I do hope you are making something out of your singing. The loaf of bread is still just as important as the book of verse.

[1] Patrick Galvin (1927–   ), Irish poet, playwright, journalist, and balladeer. See references to him in Vol. II.
[2] Galvin's recording of Irish political songs for Stinsons of New York.

Please do not try to send another Record. It would probably be wasted, for we havnt yet learned to handle fragile things gracefully.

With all good wishes,
Yours sincerely,
Sean O'Casey

To George Jean Nathan

MS. CORNELL

12 MARCH 1955

My very dear George:

I hope you are well a vic o, & that the Winter hasn't been too hard on you. It has been a keen one here, it still is bitterly cold, with a ferocious wind blowing. Just a day ago, the snow departed, but the frosts stay. My "Bishop's Bonfire" is still burning in Dublin—3rd week. It caused a stir that I didn't quite anticipate. Crowds gathered round the theatre struggling to get in; those who couldn't lit bonfires in the street, & sang songs. Among those who couldn't get seats for 1st night were Mrs. Pandit Nehru and the American Ambassador. Confused business: if I'd been there, they would; but the bookings were so unexpectedly heavy that the Management seemed to be thrown into confusion. A tremendous battle of talk and argument is going on everywhere; and such excitement hasn't been known in Dublin since the time of the first production of the "Plough & the Stars"—with this big difference that the "noes" haven't yet ventured to be violent. I guessed this myself, for Dublin can't be aroused so much on a Sectarian question as they can on a National one. So far, as far as I know, no cleric has said a word against the play. The Irish critics have declared against it to a man: a solid phalanx of opposition, surging out of the country when they get a chance in an English paper. But so far, it hasn't kept the people from going, & the play plays so far to packed houses in the Gaiety Theater, 3 times bigger than the Abbey. About 30 English critics went over, & their opinions differ greatly from the Irish critics, & the Irish ones are mad about it. All of them say the play should be brought to London, making the Irish ones madder still. The Black Market in theater tickets appeared in Dublin for the first time. I wish it had happened twenty years ago when I was young enough to go over and mix myself in the tumult. I have just done four Sixteen-minute broadcasts (recorded) for Radio Eireann, to be broadcast during an "O'Casey Festival" in May—during Tostal Week, maybe. They wanted me to speak on each play before it was broadcast; but this I wouldn't, couldn't do; so I talked of various things, and sang some old songs, and two new ones of my own making.

But I haven't heard from you for some time, and I am wondering about you—as to how you are; for you are nearer to me than any broadcast. Indeed, I don't think I'd do them at all, if it were not for the bit of money they will bring to the kitty.

Now, how are you, very very dear George? God send you are well, and putting the winter away bravely.

My love, sincere & deep, to Julie and to you.

> As ever,
> Sean

Clippings enclosed.

To Don Burke[1]

TC. O'CASEY

14 MARCH 1955

My dear Don,

I delayed answering your letter with the televising suggestions till I felt sure you had completely recovered from your bad cold, and your temperature was again normal; for you Americans are inclined to be impulsively-generous even without one.

Now, listen, lad: first of all dont forget that you have yourself, Helene, and the coming baby to think of first of all. And, my lad, they are Big things. Then you have your job which must be a busy one, and which you must do well, so you cant let yourself disperse your thoughts too much into other and outside activities. Remember, too, Don, agra, that you have done a lot for me already.

I, too, believe that a good many of my plays would make good television; though they might be difficult to do, seeing that Television is a different art from the drama. I have no commitments with any television company, here or in the U.S.A. I, of course, would be agreeable to any U.S.A. Company taking an interest in the plays; and your methods, as set out in your letter, are admirable.

All, except one. I couldnt allow you to "arrange the necessary backing"; I wouldnt have anything like that. If any Television Company is interested, and is ready to back its idea, well and good; but I wont allow

[1] Don Burke, *Time,* London.

my friends to commit themselves to any such thing when they have other important things to do, and other lives to guard and cherish.

Now, Don, lad, this is final. You have done a lot for me, as I have said, and I appreciate it greatly; but I am determined to keep that American generosity within reasonable bounds as far as I myself am concerned.

The play in Dublin is playing to full houses still, which is fine— for me.

So, my love to your Helene, and my blessing on the coming Child, and my love to you.

> *As ever,*
> [*Sean*]

To Joan D'Alton

TC. O'CASEY

14 MARCH 1955

Dear Miss Joan,

The praties are dug an' th' frost is all over! I have finished croaking into the microphone; have done to the best of me ability, the four broadcasts that were arranged for some time ago; and Mr. [Donald] Aldous has carried them off under his arm.

I tried to think of talking about my plays, as suggested, but, dear lass, it was more than I could do. It was altogether too embarrassing. Believe it, I hate to talk about my work; and whenever an Interviewer comes here, it is usually I who interview him. I am intensely interested in what other people do and think. Today, gulls are flying about past my window, and I am hard set to stop watching their flight and their gliding in order to write this letter to you.

Well, I have talked (or cawed, as I call it) about various things in the Broadcasts; have some snatches from some old songs, and have sung two new ones, which I hope you'll like—me own make.

Just got a number of cards from New York, with little, handsome cottages on them, all roofed with Shamrocks. I hope you may have a happy St. Patrick's Day.

> *Yours very sincerely,*
> *Sean O'Casey.*

From W. A. Newman, Editor, Irish Times

TS. O'CASEY

31 WESTMORELAND ST.
DUBLIN
14 MARCH 1955

Dear Mr. O'Casey,

It goes to my heart to return a letter from you, but this one breaks one of our most rigid principles, which is that we do not print adverse comments on other papers. I gather that the man you are after is the critic of the *Standard.*

Need I say that, if it should interest you to comment on either our own notice or on the notices of the Dublin critics in general, I should be only two happy to print such a letter—as, indeed, I always do publish anything over your name.

Yours very sincerely,
W. A. Newman
Editor.

To Irish Press[1]

15 MARCH 1955

"The Bishop's Bonfire"

Dear Sir,—I am very interested in Archeology; in the Sumerian, the Minoan Civilizations, the astonishing graves found in the Egyptian sands, the prehistoric pictures brightening the dark walls of French caverns, the ruins of the Temple of Mithras, recently dug into view in London, the unveiling of the River-dwellings from under the waters of the Irish lakes.

Now, Ireland is a fascinating study of this subject, for there are many examples of living archeological remains there as well as a few dead ones. Among the Archeological specimens of what are jovially called "dramacritics," there is one that is most astonishing and ancient—the one establishing his stone head on the columns of the paper calling itself the royal Standard of God Almighty.[2] Who is, what is this fascinating figure? Where

[1] This letter was refused publication by the *Irish Times.* See the letter of explanation by the editor, W. A. Newman, 14 March 1955.

[2] A reference to Seamus Byrne, who reviewed *The Bishop's Bonfire,* "The Shadow of an O'Casey," *The Standard,* 4 March 1955. Byrne wrote a play called *Design For a Headstone* (1950), hence the tone of O'Casey's letter and the reference to "stone head." All the following quotations are from Byrne's review.

was he found? Is he of the earlier or the later stone-age? On the columns where the figure stands are odd and eerie ogham scratchings which would be a delight to interpret; such as "Whose earlier work resuscitated," "The healthier proclivity," "former fiancé," "the general factotum," "adequate motification and without function," "no homogeneous structure," "looked for a moment as if his entry heralded plot development," "exacted the maximum value, but still no plot development" "author injected harshness into the concept," "difficult job in the part in that it lacked matter."

What do these phrases mean? Are they slogans, clichés, coronacha, catchcries? Is there ne'er a scholare in the Colleges of Dublin, Galway, Cork, or Belfast with wit enough to decipher them? What's coming over Ireland? The saints are there right enough—but where are the scholars? Is the ogham writing so exoteric that it is beyond the power of the greatest scholar to explain? Or are they but the careless scratching in an idle moment of some poor wandering Irish R.I.P. Van Winkle? Couldn't the neighbour who sent me the paper persuade the School for Advanced Studies to probe the problem?

Yours sincerely,
Sean O'Casey.

To Dr. Walter Starkie[1]

TC. O'CASEY

15 MARCH 1955

My Dear Dr. Starkie,

Well, well, it's fine to get a letter from you, and out of "Old Madrid," too. I hope you have more sun there than we have here, though there is a glimmer out today.

I am sending your letter to the League of Dramatists, 84 Drayton Gardens, London, S.W.10, who do the business end of the matter. But you can go ahead, for I am in agreement with your request and with the terms sent to me; and my blessing on the venture.

Eileen (Mrs. O'C.) has met you, but I never have—just caught a glimpse of you once or twice flitting through Dublin. I know you through your Romany writings however, and enjoyed the sparkle of your wander-

---

[1] Dr. Walter Starkie (1894–1976), Irish-born writer and teacher specializing in Spanish literature; a director of the Abbey Theatre in 1928, he alone wanted to accept O'Casey's *The Silver Tassie*—see "The Abbey Directors and Mr. Sean O'Casey," *Irish Statesman*, 9 June 1928, Vol. I; wrote books about his adventures among the Spanish gypsies, notably *Spanish Raggle Taggle* (1934); lecturer at the University of Madrid, 1948–56.

ings—like another Oisin—through the curious and picturesque world of the Gypsey.

The "Bishop's Bonfire" did cause a great stir in Dublin, and people had to fight their way to get into the theatre on the 1st night—Madame Pandit and the American Ambassador couldnt get in, which was bad and impolite management. The talk is still active, dispute, argument, hisses and handclaps, and the play is playing to full houses—though I havent had any royalty yet out of it, and am beginning to wonder. Still I'm used to that by now.

Ah, the old days! I'm afraid the Abbey isnt what it was then. No initiative, no vision, just a calm plod along the open road.

Eileen sends her best wishes to you, and so do I.

> Yours very sincerely,
> Sean O'Casey.

To J. J. O'Leary[1]

MS. O'LEARY

17 MARCH 1955
ST. PATRICK'S DAY

Dear Mr. O'Leary; or, J.J.—if you'll allow,

Thanks a thousand for your great kindness to Eileen and Shivaun during their stay in Dublin of the Golden Goblets. It was a tremendous experience for Shivaun, who, now, seems to have anchored her soul there forever. She talks of Dublin now as if she had never been without its walls. Of course, she heard only the song of Dublin, and wasn't within reach of her wail. I'm very glad she heard the song first, as all young life should. She chats about running around with J.J.; and came back tired, but it was a tiredness that glory gives. I am very glad she came back happy with all that Dublin gave her. The city was Dublin of the Golden Goblets to her. Yes, and Eileen had a fine time, too, thanks a lot to you.

I am glad to hear that, so far, no more audible commotions of rage have rippled over the audiences. Seems like the Standard's gun-peal and slogan-cry were woeful, but weak: saltpeter bangs and gull-squeals. I see Thersites has stripped me of the last rag of honour: Lady G., he says, stamped out the ideas, and the Abbey actors carried them into creation.[2]

---

[1] J. J. O'Leary, director of Cahill's Printing Works, Dublin; and a close friend of the actor Barry Fitzgerald.

[2] "Thersites" (Thomas Woods), "Personal Views," *Irish Times,* 12 March 1955, devoted his column to a retrospective view of O'Casey's career and wrote:

They no longer belong to me, il poverino! But I question one of his theories. In a previous article he says "O'Casey expected to be fed on Engels & Marx"[3]—or words with a meaning of this effect. In a later article he mentions me as "a member of the Communist Party"; & later, in this same article, he says, "O'Casey is, obviously, a man with a mind of his own."[4] Now, within the limits and circumstance of this writer's thoughts, how could a one, crying to be fed with Engels & Marx, a Communist, too, possibly, have obviously a mind of his own? Will he answer me *that*?

A lot of the critics seem to be troubled into agony that Foorawn is able, after being shot, to write a few words; yet in *The Plough,* Bessie, after being shot, is able to curse & to sing a verse of a hymn without a protest. They forget; or, they don't want to remember. I wish I had time to talk to a few of them.

Possibly, if finances allow, and if the summer be good, I may go over to see me homeland again; not for interviews or any commotion of reception: just a quiet sojourn under Ireland's magenta skies.

Evermore thanks again for your goodness to Eileen and Shivaun.

Yours very sincerely,
Sean O'Casey.

"There is no doubt a good deal to be said for the theory that the Great Trilogy was as much a product of the Abbey—meaning by that the actors and the management, and in particular, Lady Gregory—as it was of Mr. O'Casey himself. Certainly the 'character,' with which most people associate Mr. O'Casey—Seamus Shields, Joxer Daly, and Fluther Good—were far more actors' creations, the creations of F. J. McCormick and Barry Fitzgerald, than they were the creations of the dramatist."

[3] See O'Casey's letter to David Krause, 14 February 1955, note 4.

[4] In his column of 12 March 1955 "Thersites" compared O'Casey with the American novelist Theodore Dreiser: "The parallel between Dreiser and O'Casey could be pursued very far—they both ended up, for instance, as uncritical admirers of the Communist Party. But the analogy would be too dangerous, though it will suffice in so far as it refers to two writers who have had the greatest difficulty in endeavouring to communicate what they have got—or what they think they have got—to say. It was Mr. O'Casey's tragedy that his first efforts at self-expression were caught up in a machine called Lady Gregory. I do not know whether there is any truth in Dr. Gogarty's theory that it was Lady Gregory who wrote most of Yeats's plays—and probably Synge's as well. Certainly her mark must lie heavily on Mr. O'Casey's first three plays. But Mr. O'Casey obviously has a mind of his own and he was able to get himself free of these attractive tentacles. He went on to follow his own furrow. Whether he was wise to do so is another matter."

To Cyril Cusack

TS. CUSACK

19 MARCH 1955

Dear Cyril,

Thanks for your letter. Whenever you are in London, you should have a dekko at Bernadette. Yes, I have received the cheque for royalties for the first week, and have sent a receipt to Bill for the amount. It was accompanied with Statement, including list of Houses for the week. It seems that the interest in the play continues, which is rather remarkable, after the cap of death, woven so whole-heartedly by a unanimous crowd of Irish critics, in English and Irish papers, had been flung over the play to commit it to the outer and inner darkness of complete rejection. Apparently, Vox Dei isn't Vox Criteria. And in Lent, too. I'm glad that you think the play will go for the full five weeks—it might go even longer.

About London: The Duchess Theatre wouldn't be much good, for it is small, and would hardly bring in enough to be satisfactory; the Embassy is a bigger Theatre. But, if you are at all doubtful about Funds—increase of wages, etc—I shouldn't recommend you to come. With the withdrawal of so many in the Caste, too, it would be made more difficult. I can't understand Harry Hutchinson's demurral, and can't see how his connection with the B.B.C. would interfere. He went on tour with the company doing PURPLE DUST, and was ready, far as I know, to go on, if the play had been put on in London. I thought Eddie B[yrne] would have been very interested in London; but, if he isn't, it can't be helped. It presented, I thought, a fine chance for them all. The Prodigal of course is another matter, attached as he is to Radio Eireann.[1] But it is a deep pity that he can't show his fine acting over here; show Ireland isn't dead yet, far as the acting profession is concerned; and you, too, and Maureen. And the Lieutenant. But it can't be helped. If they can't, they can't; if they won't come, they won't.[2] If the play doesn't come to London, it won't in any way, be an amazing disappointment to me. So don't let that trouble you. The main thing, Cyril, is that you mustn't take any undue risks with what you have. I should be unhappy and worried if you did. After all, you have done a tremendous achievement in Dublin; and, however things may go, you have really lighted a big theatrical bonfire in Dublin that will be long remembered; and that is far more than something. Even in spite of the Critics, who, like the old prophets of Baal, poured water over it to prevent its burning.

To be fair to the critics, they weren't perfectly unanimous, according

---

[1] Seamus Kavanagh, who played the role of Dick Carranaun, the Prodigal, had a full-time job as program director of Children's Programs at Radio Eireann. See O'Casey's letter to Kavanagh, 27 September 1955.

[2] From these remarks it is apparent that the play did not go to London after its five-week run in Dublin because the actors were unable or unwilling to go.

to reviews in T.C.D. and THE LEADER, with a leading article in TIMES PICTORIAL[3]: so we have a few friends. A young Irish journalist wrote to me to say that all he spoke to were astonished the play was far from what the critics said it was; and enjoyed it mightily. Of course, word of mouth is always more effectual—bad or good play—than the critics' verdict. The way the critics wrote, one would think that I had written to the press, bellowed over the radio that it was a great, great play; and that they were determined to show me up. I don't remember ever saying any play of mine was great—how the hell could I know? A letter from some O'Sullivan appeared in THE SUNDAY TIMES last week. I have written a few words in reply, and have [asked] the O'Sullivan Bear a few questions. I hope the letter may appear.[4] Leather away with the wattle O!

A representative of an American Publisher was here with us last Sunday. He had travelled down with a Mill Hill Father, who repeated what the I. critics had said about the Bonfire. He himself had been a Jesuit for nine years, and gave me a full story of the difficulties he had met with when he realised he had no vocation. Instead of talking about business, we spent almost all the time talking of theology. He is as much a Catholic, is married to an Irish Catholic wife, has a child, with another coming—a strange history.

I have another friend who was six years one of the Salesian Order. He is now a labourer out in the Woomera Range, a laborer, where the Bomb Tests are made—another odd history. It is surprising how many odd histories come my way. I have a friend, a doctor in Harrow, who was six years in Maynooth, and was a student there when Dr. McDonald was a Professor. The doctor is very vehement about all that happened when he was there, and is very bitter about it all; even after these years. He left Maynooth as a young lad in 1913 to collect for the locked-out men. He is eloquent about his Clan, the MacSorleys, all they suffered at the hands of Sean the Proud, how they fled to Tyrone, and some of them to Breadalbane—Scotland's Breast, where a group of them still live. He refers to his P.P. when he was a lad, as "drunken, cruel, and malicious." God, he is bitter! I tell you, Cyril, I come into contact with things and men that the I. critics wot not of; and, anyhow, so full are they of themselves, that wouldn't interest them. I have another friend, who was very beautiful in her youth—she isn't old yet—who took up to be a nun, couldn't stick it, left, keeping the vow of chastity; but is a bundle of nerves. Without in any way suggesting to her any change in her thoughts, I think I have done

---

[3] These three exceptions were weekly periodicals of relatively minor influence. A very favorable unsigned review appeared in *T.C.D.*, "A College Miscellany," 4 March 1955. The favorable review in *The Leader*, 12 March 1955, was written by "X" (Valentin Iremonger), who wrote again on the play, "Sean O'Casey: A Postscript," *The Leader*, 9 April 1955. For the favorable comments in the *Times Pictorial*, see O'Casey's letter to Cusack, 11 March 1955, note 1.

[4] See "Sean O'Casey and Dublin," *Sunday Times*, 20 March 1955, which is a reply to a D. MacNamara, not an O'Sullivan.

something to steady the poor lass; for her letters were at times very hysterical, and my heart pitied her. The last one I got says, "I will take your advice go down to Wiltshire to our cottage, and go steady with my nerves. They do get bad. God bless you." Poor lass.

The second cheque has just come from Mr. [William P.] Ryan. The week's receipts are very good—£1451.19.0. We have been very fortunate, I think. It couldn't be anything better, so far, and could easily have been a lot worse. I hope, and believe, now, that the audiences will be good through the five weeks. Most important of all is that they enjoy the play on the whole. It really is much better than the critics tried to allow; not so good as COCKADOODLEDANDY, but good enoughsky. The critics found it so feeble, so poor, so childish that there seems to be no reason whatever that each of them shouldn't easily write a better one, and make a stir for themselves and for Dublin. I'd like to see any of them doing it. Well, my love to Maureen, the children, and to you.

Yours very sincerely,
Sean

Eileen, too sends her love.

To Peter Newmark

MS. NEWMARK

20 MARCH 1955

Dear Peter.

The "Statesman" doesn't click with you—or me. Well, it can't be helped. Anyway, the Statesman's critic was an Irishman, Donat O'Donough, whose real name is Conor Cruise O'Brien, a high-up official in Eire's Department of External Affairs,[1] a Depart. that has to do, for one thing, with the presentation of Ireland's achievements in Lit. & Art, & all Culture; and anyway, he was no worse than Worsley.[2] I suppose you type your letters, for no Editor will now even glance at a long-hand script. However, if the Statesman is set, then there's no use of you or of me bothering. The Irish critics, to a man, almost, wrote as Donat did; they certainly did their best to blast the play; but the odd thing is that the audiences were pleas-

[1] Dr. Conor Cruise O'Brien (Donat O'Donnell) was Counsellor in charge of Information and Cultural Sections in the Department of External Affairs; and in July 1955 he was appointed Counsellor in the Paris Embassy. See O'Casey's letters to Cyril Cusack, 5 March 1955, note 3; to Ria Mooney, 7 March 1955, note 3.

[2] See O'Casey's letter, "Sean and Mr. Worsley," *New Statesman and Nation*, 6 November 1954; and his letter to Peter Newmark, 10 November 1954, note 1, Vol. II.

antly surprised to find the play anyway like the critics said it was, and are still filling the big Gaiety Theatre, so that a scheduled run of three weeks will probably be extended to five. The play all over Dublin now is referred to as "The Bonfire," a sign of how it has been, and is still, talked about. The critics seem to have gone too far, & to have injured their own hope by combined and concentrated resolve to banish all but a week's struggling performance. No, I'm not a damned bit pessimistic, a mhic! On the contrary, never so convinced that life is going forward. All the stir is a sign of life—even that over [Aneurin] Bevan; & the reception of "The Bonfire" shows me even Ireland is beginning to cry out again. Just imagine Cyril Cusack & Maureen, his wife, good, genuine, & determined Catholics, blessed with quick intelligence & a sense of humour, taking and doing the "Bishop's Bonfire," and risking the little collection of coins they have in its production—great courage & resolution, shaming the Abbey with its £5000 a year grant from the Government.

I am so glad to hear of your promotion—which, I take it, means more pay—you are getting on. Well, all you needed was more confidence in yourself: you have many gifts, but just didn't know how to go about using them. I'm sure Monica has helped you to get to know yourself. I am very glad indeed.

[John Foster] Dulles can't pull everything down with him; a greater one, Hitler tried, but couldn't do it. No man can. The bigger urge of life is to build, not to destroy. That is why women are such a power for peace: they are so near to life.

All the best, with my love to Monica & to you.

As ever
Sean

Enclosure may interest you. Odd, that from the U.S.A. I should get most 90% of my living. By the way, I've just done 4 quarter-of-an-hour broadcasts for Radio Eireann to be broadcast in May. Talked of various things, & sang snatches from old songs, & two ones of my own making.

To Sunday Times

20 MARCH 1955

LETTERS TO THE EDITOR
Sean O'Casey and Dublin

Sir,—Referring to "The Bishop's Bonfire," Mr. MacNamara tells us that the verdict of the Irish critics was one of dismissal, and not of condemnation; that "Dublin accepted the greater iconoclasms of Kavanagh and Behan because they felt them to be true, whereas with O'Casey the ire was wasted against an unreal formula."[1]

Mr. MacNamara evidently dwells in London. Here is a comment by one who dwells in Ireland, which appeared in the (Dublin) "Times Pictorial";[2]

> One thing is clear—O'Casey is not misinformed on contemporary Ireland. I should say there are more contradictions in Irish life today than there were in the days of Joxer and Fluther Good.

And he adds

> O'Casey in his bonfire has put into words the thoughts of a great many people in Ireland today.

Dismissal of an O'Casey play by Irish critics is no new thing. All of them were dismissed, even from the first.

The one instance MacNamara gives of O'Casey's "unreal formula" is the use of the term "gin" as a symbol of drink. MacNamara says "gin is as widely drunk in Ireland as porter in Belgravia." Gin was rarely drunk in Ireland fifty years ago, but oftener now; and is a favourite drink with girls—gin and it—in dance-halls and restaurants in country and town. But the word was chosen just because it was a finer-sounding symbol than porter or whiskey. Hogarth, for one, made it famous. I've never heard the term "a porter-palace" but often that of "gin-palace." It is a sharp word, and so I selected it as a symbol.

MacNamara mentions no other. But is he aware, for instance, that a well-known figure going about today had a sister (both of them Irish) who took the vow of chastity to help him towards the priesthood? That fifty years ago the Bishops met in solemn conclave to condemn "immodest dress"; and that they do the same today? He can hardly deny emigration. Has he read the Bishops' Pastorals? Is he aware that a Catholic firm has issued a book, recommended to priests, one of the paragraphs saying "The unmarried state, if it is purely negative, can lead to a selfish hardening of the heart, and to the emergence of an order of 'clerical Pashas' "? Published long after I had made the character of the clerical pasha, the Canon, in my play.

Does MacNamara mean to say that one, dedicated to the Irish priesthood and sent to a seminary, helped by the scraping sacrifices of parents, with an addition, maybe, from the Bishop, after some years of preparation, finding himself unfit for the priesthood, suffers from no sense of agonised frustration, and, in a lot of cases, is hesitant to return to his country town or village where everyone knows him?

As for Agriculture, I ask MacNamara one question: Do Irish farm-

---

[1] D. MacNamara, a letter to the editor, *Sunday Times,* 13 March 1955.
[2] See O'Casey's letter to Cyril Cusack, 11 March 1955, note 1.

ers, as a rule, regard grass as just a thing that grows, a gift from God; or do they value it as a crop, the same way in which they regard barley, wheat, oats, or sugar beet?

It is the MacNamaras and the rest who, for years being blind and deaf, now go about bothered. I would tell this critic that no dramatist worth a damn sets down things from their "immediate experience." They have to think about what they have seen, heard, and felt before a play can come into the mind.

But the biggest error of all is the fact that MacNamara and the rest have sat down to consider the work purely as a document, and not as a play. Is MacNamara aware of the description given recently in an Irish magazine of a dance-hall where the parish priest sat at one end of the hall, and his curate assistant sat at the other to see that the couples never came too close together? Oh, no one so blind as he who will not see.

Sean O'Casey

Totnes

To W. A. Newman

TC. O'CASEY

21 MARCH 1955

Dear Mr. Newman,

Thank you very much for your kind letter. I'm sorry you couldnt publish my letter, but understand fully the sense of the rule that made refusal necessary.

Well, as for your kind suggestion of commenting on yours and the other Dublin critics, where in the name of God would I begin, and when would I end?

There are so many, so bewildering, so foolish in their cleverness, that it would take me a long time and much space to do them injustice. They are like those glass beads we see on road signs which remain so dull and dead till a sudden light from another object makes them shine and sparkle with a brightness that isnt their own.

I am enclosing a short piece that is critical of at least one aspect of the Dublin critics' criticism of my plays. If you can find space to print it, I shall be pleased.[1]

All good wishes to you.
Yours sincerely,
Sean O'Casey.

[1] See "The Bishop's Bonfire," *Irish Times,* 23 March 1955.

To Guy Boas[1]

TS. BOAS

22 MARCH 1955

My dear Guy,

Many thanks for your "Shakespeare and the Young Actor." [1955] It is a fine book, a very fine book, and should be read by every young actor, every old actor, and by all who have seen a candle lighted, a torch blaze, a sword drawn; or heard a trumpet blown, a drum beat, or a voice say or shout a word upon an English stage. Odd, you should think boys are preferable to girls in Shakespeare's plays. Gordon Craig in one of his "The Mask" numbers wished girls off the stage altogether: he thought they were bound to interfere with the true, careless, and curious rhythm of a drama. You have done a fine work in the making of the book, as you have done wonderful work on that narrow, testy stage in Sloane School. How I went the first time, bravely, to be bored, and how the hall became a lovely magic casement opening out into all the beauty and the boisterousness of Shakespeare![2] What lads they were! Lads after my own heart. I was just one of them; and now they live again with me in this book of yours. They were probably nervous, and some knees may have shaken a spell under a toga; but I don't know how, or where, or from whom—from God and Guy Boas, I guess—they got their ease; but there they were doing these great plays as if to the manner born.

You have done more, Guy, than you will ever be able to conceive. These plays must have had a never-ending influence on the lads. It brought them close to great literature in a serious rollicking way that must have gone down to the core of the soul.

And the lads are so handsome; and were so serious, so boyish. Well, Guy, they and you gave me an experience that I shall never forget, and never want to forget, which is a blessed thing.

It is a very fine book.

Le Theatre Sloane—hurrah!

The pictures are delightful, and grand, really grand, you looking yourself—a homely, Shakespearean touch—buckling on the armour of the Romans.

[1] Guy Boas (1896–1966), teacher and writer; headmaster of Sloane School, Chelsea, 1929–61. See letters to him in Vols. I and II.

[2] See "Shakespeare Lives in London Lads," *The Flying Wasp* (1937), reprinted in *The Green Crow* (1956), O'Casey's review of *A Midsummer Night's Dream*, performed by the pupils of the Sloane School, directed by Boas.

My love to Cicely and Robin and to you; and to all the lads of Sloane School, past and present.

Yours very sincerely,
Sean

To Peter Lennon[1]

TC. O'CASEY

22 MARCH 1955

Dear Peter,

Thanks a lot for your letter. It was kind of you to write to tell me that the audiences think the play, THE BONFIRE, far better than the Dublin critics made it out to be. I havent the slightest misgiving about the determination of these critics to kill the play, not because they thought it bad, but simply because it came from O'Casey. They just protested too much; they overdid it. The Bonfire blazed a little too warmly for them: they singed more than their little hands trying to put it out. I'm afraid, the English critics had a laugh at them, and, when I send their reviews over to the USA, the American critics will have another. I'm afraid I take a little delight in showing how venomous and foolish most of them are. I've just sent letters to THE IRISH TIMES and to THE IRISH PRESS giving an example of what one famous American critic thinks of them.

Yes, I daresay, things are said in a pub that wouldnt be said in the open air; shout many a thing to the devil, but never a whisper for God. I've read Honor Tracy's *Mind you, I didnt say anything.*[2]

I hope you may succeed in learning French, and that you may have a good time, some day, in Paris. But you wont escape from Ireland. Your children might, but you cant. Ireland has a touch from God in her—go to the ends of the earth, and you'll find her there beside you. Even Bernard Shaw was never out of her sight.

No presumption whatever in writing to me. The one snag is that I find it hard to find time to write to all who write to me; and, too, my eyes get tired quick, and I have to rest them.

I hope Jim McGuinness is doing well as Editor of THE IRISH PRESS. He rang me up once, long ago, when he was in the London Office.

[1] Peter Lennon, 61 Adelaide Road, Dublin.
[2] Honor Tracy, *Mind You, I've Said Nothing!* (1953), Forays in the Irish Republic.

Since then, I read how he was chosen to be Editor. I hope he is well and easy in his chair—an Editor's job isnt quite so soft a job as many think.
Hope THE BONFIRE is still burning.
All good wishes,
Yours sincerely,
Sean O'Casey

To R. L. De Wilton[1]

TS. DE WILTON

23 MARCH 1955

Dear Mr. De Wilton:
Thank you for the $230 Check, fee for inclusion of COCKADOO-DLE DANDY in the Anchor Books Anthology.[2]

I wonder could you send a copy each of SUNSET AND EVENING STAR and ROSE AND CROWN to the undermentioned?

Philip Houtz,
Executive Director,
National Jewish Hospital
3800 East Colfax Avenue, Denver Colorado, and

charge them to my account. They have written to ask me for one to interest the patients, though I'm afraid neither book will soothe any of them.

The First night of THE BONFIRE was astonishing. The management was overwhelmed with appeals for tickets, and for the first time in Dublin, Theatre tickets were sold on a black market. Thousands couldn't get in, and those who couldn't lit bonfires on the street, staying there till the play was over, singing songs and cheering. Neither the American Ambassador nor Madame Pandit Nehru could get a seat—which was bad management, for if Mrs. O'C. had known she and our daughter would readily have given their seats to them. There was a raging controversy over the play, and it's raging yet. The Gaiety Theater is a big theater, four times that of the Abbey, and Cyril Cusack was afraid they wouldn't be able to fill the place, for the three weeks; but it will do so for five, and would for longer only the theater had definitely arranged for SHOW BOAT months before. The Dublin critics, almost to a man, dismissed it as abject, foolish, feeble, with a world of other epithets, but the audiences found the play, "far, far better

---

[1] R. L. De Wilton, O'Casey's editor at the Macmillan Company, New York. See letters to him in Vol. II.
[2] *Modern Theatre*, Vol. 5 (1957), edited by Eric Bentley.

and far more enjoyable than the critics made it out to be." They went too far. "The still-born blind Irish critics," Nathan calls them; but I believe the wholesale and unanimous condemnation to be woven well into hatred and venom, purely personal envy of one who persists in trying to do things instead of looking over a pub-counter and complaining of life.

All good wishes to you with my cordial regards.
Yours sincerely,
Sean O'Casey

To Irish Times[1]

23 MARCH 1955

"THE BISHOP'S BONFIRE"

Sir,—Strange news comes to me from Ireland. It comes from one who comes from God knows where. It says that those who go to see "The Bishop's Bonfire" are surprised to find the play far better than the Irish critics made it out to be. As I hoped myself, the audience liked it and the audience laughed. But why should they be surprised? Do they think the Irish critics know a good play when they see one—or, if they do, that the critics will say so? Especially when it is O'Casey who writes the play? Do they think that the Dublin critics are the one and only wise ones God gave the world? That all the rest are fools? Well, maybe they know their own know now.

Their reviews are a bewildering mass of dismissals, denials, denunciations, declensions, and deviations from their party line. I have neither time nor space to analyse them now, but, Time sparing me a few more years, I intend to write a book wherein I shall try to have a laugh at some of the things they think and more of the things they say; laugh at these fluttering drama-angels of the denunciations.[2] I am so used to them now that anything nice from them would get me down. Though I venture to say that I amn't in the least put out by their cries of music-hall humour, farce, or even a snatch of slapstick. Shakespeare had all of these scattered among his plays, and didn't shy at a touch of melodrama; and Aristophanes didn't hesitate to love a little slapstick.

Fifteen years or more ago, the same kind of complaint about my work was made by no less an authority than St. John Ervine—that O'Casey was

---

[1] A copy of this letter, with slight modifications in punctuation, appeared in the *Irish Press,* 24 March 1955.
[2] See "Bonfire Under a Black Sun," *The Green Crow* (1956).

mostly superb music-hall, with here and there the hint of a poet. Here are George Jean Nathan's remarks on that Ervinian opinion:—

"The derogation of O'Casey by certain critics as mere superb music-hall seems to me not only obvious critical snobbery, for superb music-hall remains nonetheless still superb, but equally obvious critical superficiality, inasmuch as it overlooks the plays' rare comedy scenes' deep roots in dramatic character. They are Moliere full of Irish whiskey, now and again, Shaw off dietetic spinach, and full of red meat. Flanagan and Allen (if such critics insist) in the classical garb of Falstaff and Dogberry. Furthermore, to derogate O'Casey as a mere hint of a poet, which these same critics do (Dublin critics, nota bene), is an even larger betrayal of critical sense. Where in the drama of living Irishmen is there greater and more genuine dramatic poetry than you will find in the mighty sweep of 'The Plough and the Stars,' or in the boozy low measures of parts of 'Juno,' or in the riff-raff of 'Within the Gates,' and their periodic utterance, or in the speech of the workmen in 'Purple Dust,' or even in passages of the otherwise dubious 'Star Turns Red'? The answer is: nowhere."[3]

The quotation is from the Preface to "'Five Great Modern Irish Plays" [1941], published by Random House, New York City. The same critic thinks "Cockadoodle Dandy" to be one of O'Casey's greatest plays, and says fine things about "The Bishop's Bonfire." Well, I have said little in the blathering medley of criticisms that broke against my play: I have left those who go to see it to judge for themselves; but, now that things have settled down a little, I have produced a witness for the defence. What the witness says to the critical buckineeno[4] boys of Dublin is evidence; and it may provoke them to stick their necks again out of their thick, enveloping hoods, and give them something more to think of and talk about.—Yours, etc.,

Sean O'Casey.

Devon, March 21st, 1955

P.S.—Just got a letter this morning from G. J. Nathan, which says: "It is very gratifying to hear about the excitement stirred up in Dublin by 'The Bishop's Bonfire,' but sad to read of the stillborn blindness of the Irish dramatic critics." Blindness? Maybe, he's right.

---

[3] See also Nathan's "The Best of the Irish," *Newsweek,* 29 January 1940; reprinted in Vol. I; a direct reply to a letter from Ervine to Nathan attacking O'Casey.
[4] See the letter to John O'Donovan, 30 March 1955, note 6.

To Charles Rosenberg and Martin Kesselman[1]

TC. O'CASEY

23 MARCH 1955

Dear Mr. Rosenberg and Mr. Kesselman,

Thank you for your letter which Macmillans have forwarded on to me. I cannot understand it. Are you sure about this? Did you see it yourselves, or were you just told about it? Where was the Film shown and when and in what Cinema?

The one version of JUNO AND THE PAYCOCK in film form was done twenty-five years ago, the producer was Hitchcock. I never saw it, but Mrs. O'Casey did. There was no conception in it such as you describe. Kelly wasnt the name of the character, but Nugent. What you call "anti-Semitism" had no connection with the play. I presume you mean bias against the Jew. This "anti-semitism" is a parlour word, and I dont like it. I prefer the more honest term of ignorant and stupid hatred or fear of the Jew. It is just ridiculous; though at times truly terrible, as was shown so horribly during the god-damned Hitler rule. Well, he met the same fate he so brutally and murderously shoved on to so many unhappy Jews. But, never forget, it is lawful and quite natural to laugh sometimes at a Jew, just as one may laugh at an Irishman, or a Briton. Indeed the Jew often does it himself, as in Sholem Aleichem. The Jew takes his place equally with all other races; and secures equal praise, equal laughter; a man full of the nature of all men.

Now, about this Film. The Film rights of JUNO are mine alone; the rights of the one [they] did died fifteen years ago, and the rights came back to me. No one has any right whatsoever to do this Film—if it be the one done by Hitchcock—without my permission; or of my Agent, Miss Rubin, Richard Madden Play Co., 522 Fifth Avenue, New York, 18. NY. I should be glad if you could let me have the full details. Are you sure that it was JUNO AND THE PAYCOCK?

Was it maybe a Film that copied some of the material from the original one; and done under another name, changing it a lot, including the name Kelly, the tailor for that of Nugent?

It must be a different one, for the original Film was shown everywhere, and no word or whisper came about any stated or implied bias against the Jew. Anyhow, such a thing was just impossible, for it could

---

[1] Charles Rosenberg and Martin Kesselman, 2133 Chadbourne Avenue, Madison, Wisconsin. Having seen a re-run of Alfred Hitchcock's 1930 film version of *Juno and the Paycock,* in which the character of Needle Nugent, the tailor, was changed to Mr. Kelly and played by an actor with a Stage-Jewish accent, without O'Casey's permission or knowledge, Rosenberg and Kesselman wrote a protest to O'Casey stating: "We felt that the figure of Kelly, the tailor, was a whimsically vicious anti-semitic caricature." Fred Schwarz played the role of Mr. Kelly. For the cast of the film, see O'Casey's letter to Gabriel Fallon, 28 February 1929, note 4, Vol. I.

never occur to me to think of the Jew in any other way than as a man like myself, or like others; having his own peculiar national characteristics, like every other Race.

Well, let me know, if you have made a mistake, and that what you saw was some bugger using some of my dialogue, etc. to try to make his work better than he could ever make it himself.

Yours sincerely,
Sean O'Casey.

To Major A. E. Leach[1]

MS. LEACH

25 MARCH 1955

Dear Major Leach,
Thank you very much for your kind and able reply to Tribune's Findlater,[2] who, for one reason or another, thinks brotherhood should welcome humbug and hypocrisy as coming out of the arms of God. It is odd how mad Findlater was at any idea of a criticism of Orwell's desire for a pat on the back from O'Casey when it suited his purpose; or a criticism of Orwell's die-hard nationalisms in condemning what he called a special regard for anything written by an Irishman. So wrong, too; for Yeats had as much opposition as had Hardy; & Joyce more. Pity, they didn't publish your letter; but a friend of mine—who was a Student in Cambridge, when I talked there—wrote a reply to the "Statesman," pointing out that the Register in Cambridge shows Worsley had graduated years before I went down (he had claimed to be a graduate there during my visit);[3] & another letter criticising the Review of "The Bishop's Bonfire"; but neither letter was published. Seemingly, they can't bear my deviation from the Party Line. It is funny how many Party lines there are here & in Ireland; more rigid than the one so bitterly assailed in the USSR.

Poor Dr. [Donald O.] Soper, too, has deviated from the party line of his church; and Bevan from the Labour Party line; and God only knows how many more there are knocking about.

There was a tremendous todo over "The Bishop's Bonfire" in Dublin: the theatrical like of which hadn't been seen there for thirty years—the

---

[1] Major A. E. Leach, husband of Doris Leach, 2 Chauntry Road, Maidenhead, Berks.

[2] Richard Findlater, "This Little Man," *Tribune*, 28 January 1955, a review of *Sunset and Evening Star* (1954).

[3] See O'Casey's letter to Peter Newmark, 10 November 1954, note 1, Vol. II.

Thirty Years Peace! Now, I've broken it; & the Controversy still rages. However, in spite of the critics, the play is going on to full houses; scheduled for 3 weeks, it is running 5, & would go 6, but for commitment by the theatre to do "Show Boat"! The audiences like it well, & it has made a great impact.

I hope all is well with you. Anyhow, the Spring seems to be in sight at last. My love to Doris and to you.

> *Yours very cordially,*
> *Sean O'Casey*

To Jack Lindsay[1]

PC. *S. O'Casey Rev*[2]

27 MARCH 1955

Dear Jack,

Many thanks for your letter. Never mind looking for the List[3]—I'm always putting things in a safe place, and never finding them again. M. Apletin is an old friend; we have almost heard the bells chime at midnight. Glad to know that he is still active. I havent had time to write as frequently as I should have liked, for I am in many battles at home, here, in England, and out of home, there, in Ireland.

I'm glad, too, that they are thinking of doing some of my work, though it wont be an easy job. I've never suggested it to them. I've left them to do it, or not do it, as they might wish. Indeed, D. N. Pritt, when he was there some years ago, pressed them to do THE STAR TURNS RED—Unity was destroying it then in a 2nd production; in contrast with the fine 1st one.[4] His secretary wrote to know if she could get the script (book out of print) from Unity, and sent it on; but I wouldnt have this:

---

[1] Jack Lindsay (1900–   ), poet and historian, active in the British Communist Party. See letters to him in Vol. II.

[2] A copy of this letter appeared in the *Sean O'Casey Review*, Fall 1975.

[3] Lindsay had just returned from Russia with a list of the O'Casey plays and volumes of autobiography that Mikhail Apletin, head of the English Department of the Foreign Commission of the USSR Writers Union, had drawn up for a planned Collected Works of O'Casey to be published in Russia. The first two volumes of the autobiography appeared in translation: *Ya Stuchus' V Dver'. Na Poroge* (Moskva: Izd. inostr. lit., 1957). A volume of seven plays appeared in translation: *P'Esy* (Moskva: Iskusstvo, 1961): *Juno and the Paycock, The Plough and the Stars, The Star Turns Red, Purple Dust, Red Roses For Me, The Bishop's Bonfire, The Drums of Father Ned*.

[4] *The Star Turns Red* opened at Unity Theatre on 12 March 1940, directed by John Allen; it was revived at Unity on 31 July 1946, directed by Ted Willis.

if the USSR didnt do anything of mine out of their own desire, I didnt want, and wouldnt allow, anyone to shove me under any Russian nose. However, I am very glad they are interested in the work for the work's sake, and not for the friendship I have always had for them, or for the belief I have always had in their great achievements. I dont mind a cut here and there; but I do sympathise with the one who ventures on a translation.

I have been through a battle royal with a play of mine getting its first production in Dublin—the first first-production of a play of mine for thirty years. The Irish critics formed a solid phalanx of condemnation, almost to a man, overflowing even into the English Journals, but in spite of this, the audiences like it—though in some fear of it—and laugh and make merry during its performance. Cyril Cusack, who is a very good, self-respecting Catholic, showed extraordinary courage in deciding to do it; and has had to fight his way forward, too. I wish, Jack, Communists here would show more savvy. In the midst of the fight, they sent over a reporter demanding a ticket for the first night, which wouldnt be given to them; so they sent me a telegram near commanding me to intervene. They couldnt leave us free to fight, but they must try to interfere and complicate our movements in the fray; an interference that might have ruined Cusack's determination to overcome venomous and, in many instances, unscrupulous opposition. The fight is on still. I sent them a sharp reply telling them to get out of the way. They seem to have no sense of sensible tactics. And they wont listen. They dont understand a drama, and invariably praise for the wrong reasons.

I'm hopeful of a change coming in the USSR through the New Phase—not in fundamentals of course; but in Art and Literature. Their present architecture, for instance, is just old-fashioned, costly and ostentatious. They seem to have forgotten that Corbussier ever lived, and that he is living still, and busy planning roads in India. The USSR is always behind the USA in this important matter—bar the generous and grand wideness of their streets, a lot of their workers' houses and the tremendous engineering skill of their construction work. But the spirals and turrets are things of a far-gone past, and no longer satisfy the seeing powers of the present-day eye. Another thing; they should prefer the young rather than the old to come to them. The editor of "Ogonyek"—a grand lad—was here with me last Summer, asking me to come; and I told him it is the young, the young are the ones to go to the USSR, for it is they who will have to build, and not we. Remember Ibsen in "The Master Builder"? "The young are knocking at the door." Don't tell me you live in a castle![5] But then, there are castles in Spain and castles in Ireland, and neither are suitable to live in.

My love to you, and I hope your books go well.

Yours very sincerely,
Sean O'Casey

[5] The "Castle" in Lindsay's address referred to the village where he lived, Castle Hedingham, not his house.

To Cyril Cusack

TS. Cusack

28 March 1955

Dear Cyril,

Of course, the failure to come to London straight is disappointing to us all; but we can't expect the play to get there on a hare's back. We just have to submit to circumstances. We cant help it. It may be that it will get there before the last rose of summer dies. Anyhow, we must be philosophical, and take things as they go and come. About the Script for B[ronson]. Albery, I shouldn't like to send a Typescript—I want to keep them for myself; or rather one for myself, and one for you, if you should wish to keep it as a kinda souvenir. I suggest that you ask Macmillans, St. Martin's Street, London, W.C.2., to send a copy of the page proofs which would be far easier to read, anyhow. If they can't, I could send the copy I have. If he can't get one from Macmillan's, let me know, and I'll send on the one I have.

Regarding the request of the B.B.C. Third Programme, it seems allright, if you think it won't damage the play's chance for London; and, if—this most important—that the Caste YOU have does the part given over the wireless; preferably the "jeep" scene. If your Caste doesn't do it, I shouldn't be in favour of it at all. The "jeep" scene, or any other, done by others could be very bad, and spoil all. So, I am willing only if it be done as set down above—by YOU.

I see that G.F. is becoming an authority on what is and what isn't art; an authority on Shaw, Shakespeare, and Tolstoy:[1] knows all that was in their minds as well as what is in their plays. Says no Art tries to teach; no Art has even a whiff of teaching in it; Art may, apparently, be destructive, but never constructive. "Didactic," he calls it. What a word! Shakespeare was never didactic, he says. I wonder how he explains Shelley's "Poets are the trumpets that call to battle; they are the unacknowledged legislators of the world." Or would he say that the Parables were Art? Or merely didactic? Was Jesus only a Preacher, and nothing of a Poet? That is, of course as touching His Manhood: as Man, was He a Poet as well as

[1] Gabriel Fallon, "Why Sean O'Casey Has Failed This Time," *Evening Press,* 5 March 1955, attributed the failure of *The Bishop's Bonfire* to didacticism: "Shakespeare was never didactic . . . Tolstoy was didactic only in a limited sense. Shaw's middle name was didacticism. His survival *as a dramatist* is problematical." Fallon also condemned the play in his regular review, "The 'Bonfire' Never Did Really Blaze Up At All," *Evening Press,* 1 March 1955; and in his Saturday column, "Theatre Notes," *Evening Press,* 12 March 1955, he attacked the English critics for liking the play.

a Preacher? A Teacher? And He commented on the life around Him; in no uncertain voice too!

G.F. seems to have his knife in you too. He didn't like the little engaging word, "engagé."[2]

Just got a letter from a Catholic Irishwoman, living in England, but who often goes to Ireland. She tells me that when she was there last, she went to a dance, and there, she heard a young lad she knew, who was in a seminary (home for a holiday) pleading with his people and friends that "he had no Vocation," and begging to be released. But no—the shame would be too terrible, and the lad had to go on.

Now that I think of it, connecting with what's above again—what of St. Paul's song about Charity? Direct teaching, if anything is, and yet, in its own way, it has a lyrical quality like unto "The quality of mercy is not strained. . . ."

By the way, if B. Albery takes the play up, it must be with you, and your Cast and T. Guthrie's production; and not with a scratch Cast, and a different, and, probably, scanty production. I had an experience before. Don't understand why T.G. wants to shift the Porter seeing as how even the E. critics liked his work. You are a harassed man. The theatre is like the sea—the devil; an old devil now.

I got a number of letters warning me of the Judgement; that I am on the margin of the grave; others calling attention to "immodest dress," another saying I should be in "Grangegorman";[3] and quite a lot of ones that thunder, but few have an identity.

Well, that's all for the present, with a strong hope that the play comes to London.

Eileen sends her love—she is to write to you—to Maureen, the children, & to you; and so does *Sean*.

---

[2] In the souvenir program of *The Bishop's Bonfire,* Cusack had described O'Casey in the following manner: "O'Casey—now become, since 'Juno and the Paycock' and 'The Plough and the Stars,' fiercely *engagé,* increasingly provocative and controversial; the same O'Casey who, long ago swaddled in the sulky swirl of Anna Livia Plurabelle, long ago mother-propelled madly out of doors, now angrily clowns round the closed-in arena of the world, at the end of a crooked wand spinning his globe into a green map of Ireland."

To which Fallon replied in the *Evening Press,* 5 March 1955: "I'm afraid this *ici-on-parle francais* attitude, even when frilled over with Joycean jolly-pops, is not conducive to right thinking in the theatre."

[3] A well-known mental hospital in Dublin.

To Cyril Cusack

MS. Cusack

29 March 1955

Dear Cyril—Your letter came just now. Don't worry about the London Show—I amn't, & won't. You should be fairly sure of financial covering from loss, before you . . . plunge. The overheads seem a lot. Tony Q[uinn]. is about right concerning the Embassy. If my memory serves me, that is about what Sinclair took in when he was there; but that was long ago. Of course, £900 a week is good for the Embassy.

Transferring to the Olympia is a good idea, if it can be done, for it keeps you where you are, uses you without much additional expense, and gives a chance of three or four more weeks.

Yes, I daresay, the Lenten Retreats have affected the House; but £1355 odd is good going—I got the check for 3rd week yesterday morning. Yes, we got a lot of papers, including G.F.'s article in the E. Press. And a mhic [my friend], be careful what you write down about them. Allright to me; but G.F. wouldn't hesitate to make things unpleasant for you & for me if we said indiscreet things; or worse, wrote them. If you say anything, confine it to comments on what he says himself. I wonder did he listen—in to Tolstoy's play last night?[1] "Tolstoy," he says, "was didactic, only here and there." He says that, now, does he? Oh, boys!

And, for goodness sake, don't abandon Harry H[utchinson]. He has evidently made a hit, & who are we to go against vox populii vox Dei? Don't worry about Embassy—a financial loss to you would do me no good. You won't, of course, do anything in the Olympia, or anywhere else, in Holy Week. Whenever it is possible, I shall be delighted to see you.

All the best again to Maureen, to the little ones, & to you.

Tell Maureen beware of sucking doves.

Sean

I enclose a few more opinions from Amer. critics.

[1] A radio dramatization of Tolstoy's short novel, *Family Happiness,* was broadcast on the B.B.C. Home Service on 28 March 1955.

By Gabriel Fallon

30 MARCH 1955

Irish Press, Gabriel Fallon Writes An Open Letter to Sean O'Casey[1]

What in the name of good fortune is the matter with you?

George Jean Nathan tells you that you are not only the greatest living Irish dramatist but a fine poet to boot. J. C. Trewin has described you
as a lord of the English language. Most of the English drama critics have
highly praised *The Bishop's Bonfire.* The *Daily Mail* speaks of "the sheer
poetry of it." The *Daily Express* cries out that it is written in "language of
piercing beauty." And I could, and you could, and we all could quote
dozens of others who have paid tribute to what A. E. Wilson calls your
"stick of dramatic dynamite."

And yet you stamp and fume and choke with rage simply because an
insignificant handful of Dublin drama critics find that they cannot see eye
to eye with the world's view of you, and more particularly with your
world view of yourself. The gentle old man who came upon a Dublin
stage to dance ("see him dance the polka" you said), on the strength of a
few remarks from a few Dubliners, has turned into a foaming, whirling
Dervish.

What's wrong with you, man? Why can't you count your blessings
and keep your mouth shut? Consider how fortunate you are. The British
stage, for all its current guff, saw fit to neglect you for years. Broadway,
in spite of Nathan's panegyrics, turned its back on you.

Then out of the blue, or rather out of the green, white and gold,
comes an offer from one of Ireland's greatest actors to present your new
play and to present it in the capital of a country which wilfully you have
not seen for years, a country which you have spent much of your time
and talent in reviling. This actor engages the most distinguished producer
in the British theatre to produce your new play for you. Irish audiences,
as Irish audiences will, flock to see it, making the royalties mount for you.
British and American critics fly in. There is great excitement, and a few
hisses, but your sponsor fights them off in order to describe you as "a
great religious dramatist." The Editor of an Irish weekly claps you on the
back for the fine fellow you are: and a neophyte Abbey dramatist publicly
bows to Devon while verbosely castigating the Dublin critics for their
ignorance of your genius and the theatre.

What more do you want than that, and why should the unfavorable
opinions of a few Dublin critics upset you? Well, I'll tell you, Sean
O'Casey. In the first place it is because your overweening vanity is severely
hurt. You don't like criticism, Sean O'Casey; you only like praise.

You are making a great fuss now out of the fact that the critics are
Irish critics. But you made even greater fuss when the critics were English

[1] See O'Casey's reply, "The Bonfire," *Irish Press,* 12 April 1955.

critics. You remember Jimmy Agate, don't you? You know what you did to him? You haven't forgotten George Orwell, have you? You took him out of the grave to pulverise him. And there were other, many other, English critics. But you, the great *Flying Wasp,* buzzed and stung them all.

When you launched your first massed attack on the Irish critics (in *Irish Writing*—don't you remember?) you told them a thing or two. One of the things you told them was that there hadn't been a critic in the country since William Butler Yeats. And did you think they had forgotten what the critic Yeats had said about *The Silver Tassie,* or what you had said about Yeats's qualifications as a critic? Pull yourself together, man; try to order your memory with some of the efficiency you devote to that black book in which you record the misdeeds of modern Ireland.

But, vanity apart, there is another reason why the unfavorable opinions of these Irish critics have so upset you. Like them, you are Irish. For all your long, wilful exile, you are a slice cut from the loaf. Deep down in you nags the possibility that the Irish critics may be right. Time was when you acknowledged one of them as your "first friend in literature and the drama," when you claimed that "his friendship and talent was, and is, a wonderful gift to his friend and buttie, Sean O'Casey." Isn't there an awful possibility that such a fellow may not have lost his wits completely and that with a spark of that talent left he may, like his colleagues, be visionary enough to see what pride and wilfulness can do to a greatly gifted writer?

Have a titther o' sense, man! The critical buckineeno boys of Dublin wish you well. They hope time will spare you to return to your former dramatic greatness. They hate to see you eating your heart out because praise has been denied you by those you are pleased to describe as knaves and fools.

Never mind the book about them; more than one can play at that game; and the long view of posterity may turn out to be a poor one. Forget *The Bonfire* and get on with the next play; and this time, who knows, it may be the buckineenos' turn to cheer.

Gabriel Fallon.

To Rex MacGall[1]

TS. MACGALL

30 MARCH 1955

A Rex, a mhic,

First, thanks for your kind letter. Yes, I can read it easily,[2] for in my time, I've read [Pádraig] Pearse—a little stilted, like [Geoffrey] Keating—Canon O'Leary,[3] Torna,[4] and a lot of others, including M. na Copaleen's AN BEUL BOCHT.[5] But I havent spoken Irish now for thirty years, and the tongue, I fear, is a bit rusty. Indeed, a lot of present-day Irish seems to me to be a bit stilted; little flow in it, less music. Dr. [Douglas] Hyde set a bad example, with his Sinn Fein Amhain Irish.[6] However, he wasnt a bad old chap, and deserved his post as President; for he fought when the going was bad. I'm glad you liked the play, and am sorry you arent what you call a "clear-critic," or judge. An ugly word, this 'leirmheastoir.'[7] 'toir' sounds harsh. Why not simply 'Measaire'?[8] Measaire ceoil or measaire drama?[9] Who decides on the shape of words to come? I'm afraid I havent much concern with, or esteem for, the Irish drama critics; they still live mentally in a white-washed cottage. I'm glad, and a little surprised, that you should be among the chosen few who think "gur Crioch Ceart fior a bhi ann."[10]

No, the clergymen in the play werent meant to belong to any protestant section of the Christian Church. They are, rightly or wrongly, meant to be Catholic priests. Dont you think there are such men as "Father Boheroe" in the Mission? I built my idea of the man on a young priest I met and had a long talk with some years ago in a place called Kilternan. He had been "naughty" to his Bishop, and had been exiled to serve a convalescent community of nuns. He and I had a long, long talk. He was, after, exiled to a lonely African post, where he died a little while ago. What about the worker-priests in France? Did you ever read Dr. W. Mc-

---

[1] Rex MacGall, pseudonym of Deasún Breatnach, journalist and author of books in Irish; Pairc Leaca na Sceice, Dun Laoghaire.

[2] MacGall's letter was written in Irish.

[3] Canon Peter O'Leary (1839–1920) translated the Bible and *Aesop's Fables* into Irish, and wrote historical novels in Irish, notably *Seadhna* (1904) and *Niamh* (1907).

[4] Torna, pseudonym of Todg O'Donoghue (1874–1949), Irish-speaking poet and Professor of Irish at University College Cork, 1916–44.

[5] Myles na gCopaleen, *An Béal Bocht* (1941), "The Poor Mouth," a satiric novel that mocks the Irish-language enthusiasts; written by Brian O'Nolan (1912–66), novelist, playwright, columnist, who wrote under the pseudonyms of Flann O'Brien and Myles na gCopaleen, the latter from a character in Dion Boucicault's *The Colleen Bawn* (1860).

[6] Ourselves Exclusively Irish.

[7] estimater or critic.

[8] Estimater.

[9] Music critic or drama critic?

[10] that it was a Right and True Ending.

Donald's book? And many before them—Lammenais, for instance, or Laconnaire? I'm not sure I have the spelling right. And earlier on, and earlier still. As for the "Canon," there are many of them flourishing in Ireland still. I'm afraid I dont quite get your meaning that the clergy dont make their work clear to the people, before the eyes of the many, and that they do what they do secretly. They do a lot very quietly indeed, but they do a lot openly, too. A Liverpool Catholic has just written me an angry letter telling me of the expenditure of 5 millions on a new Cathedral; modified from the original plans; for, if they had been carried out, the church would have cost 27 millions —the Archbishop's own words, for the friend sent me the Diocesan Record. He also told me A. Bishop Downey[11] died worth 55 thousand, and didnt leave "a penny to the Catholic schools." There, the stones of the church are worth a valley of roses. I'm glad, too, the play was liked by your wife.

The Basque People are not Spaniards. They are a distinct race. Lloyd George claimed them as Kelts; but he wasn't right, I'm afraid. Their language, I believe, is akin to Sanscrit. I have two Basque friends, who help to teach our daughter—Marina & Marita—refugees from the Spanish Civil War. They are very proud of their people. Their father was shot dead in the boat that was rowing them to safety. I don't know that your last remark is correct, making out the play to be "true, religious drama." If it be so, then what harm, anyway?

Blessing & Victory to you, too, a mhic, and to your kind wife.

Yours very sincerely,
Sean O'Casey

Liverpool friend told me the 55,000 wasn't mentioned in the Catholic Press. "A cuid oibre fé rúin," ineadh?[12]

[11] The Most Rev. Richard Downey (1881–1953), Archbishop of Liverpool.
[12] "His secret work," perhaps?

To John O'Donovan[1]

TS. O'DONOVAN

30 MARCH 1955

Dear John O'Donovan,

Just this moment read your letter in the STANDARD.[2] It was a surprise. I thought I was seeing visions or having a dream: your old men

[1] John O'Donovan (1921–   ), Irish playwright, journalist, music critic, radio and TV broadcaster; 10 Upper Mount Pleasant Avenue, Dublin.
[2] "Mr. O'Donovan and The Bishop's Bonfire," *The Standard,* 25 March 1955,

shall dream dreams. I was awake allright. It is a most unkind cut at the
critics, sir; and G.F. seems very hurt about it. He shouldnt be; he should
be in some agreement. Here he is whispering in 1938: "Art—how are you!
Lookit, if an anti-O'Casey government promised to increase the subsidy
and give them all tidy salaries into the bargain, provided they refused to
produce O'Casey's plays,—O'Casey's plays, my dear fellow, would be
neither art nor drama—simply dung!" In the first essay, he rebukes what
he calls the didacticism in the play; in this little note of reply to you, he
seems to be angry that the didacticism wasnt clear enough. He proclaims
that Shakespeare was never didactic. What, never? Not only didactic, but
full of prejudices. See how he taught the English how to think of La
Pucelle; his opinion of international war in the discussion between a king
and two soldiers; what he thought of civil war in his Enter a father who
has killed a son; enter a son who has killed a father. Kings, princes, queens,
soldiers, peasants, and workers are full of opinions on all kinds of things.
And his theology! "As flies to wanton boys are we to the gods; they kill
us for their sport." If that isnt blasphemy, what is? As for vulgarity, who
could be more so? "It is a platitudinous fact," says a critic, "that some of
the grantedly greatest art that the world has known has been as vulgar as
pigs' feet. What would fastidious critics say today of an artist whose characters talked of whores and intimate biological functions, discoursed of
human sex indulgence in terms of animals; named certain women characters after social diseases, and descended to the lowest form of gutter
speech; whose characters after the act of copulation, drank themselves into
a state of stomach sickness, indulged in a prodigious belching, never
failed to speak of disgusting odours, and swore like bohunks?" "That is,
conceiving a second coming of an artist like Shakespeare?"

Do these fellows really know anything about the Bard? Do they really
bother to read his plays or his sonnets? Or his poems? I can hardly believe
it. As for a lesson wrapped in poetry, I wonder would G.F. deny that Jesus
was a poet? Would he deny that the parables—he *taught* them in parables—were, in themselves, poetry? Would he deny that the Sermon on the
Mount was poetry as well as a teaching? Would he deny the loveliness in
the phrase "Consider the lilies of the field; they toil not, neither do they
spin; and yet I say unto ye that even Solomon in all his glory was not
arrayed like one of these," because it enveloped a lesson? Would this genie
say that there is no art in St. Paul's rhapsody on Charity, which, in its own
way, has a lyrical manner akin to Shakespeare's "The quality of mercy is
not strained." Or what would he think of Shelley's "Poets are the trumpets

---

an exchange of angry letters between O'Donovan, then chief sub-editor of the Dublin
Evening Press, and Gabriel Fallon, drama critic of the *Evening Press* and one-time
drama critic of *The Standard.* O'Donovan's first letter rebuking Fallon for his review
of O'Casey's play, and his attacks on O'Casey, *Evening Press,* 1 and 5 March 1955,
had originally appeared in the *Evening Press,* 11 March 1955; and Fallon's reply had
appeared in the *Evening Press,* 12 March 1955.

that call to battle; they are the. . . ." Or of Polonius's whisper of precepts into the ear of Laertes; or even of the poet of pure poetry, Keats's fourteen or fifteen lines carrying all the implications within the writings of Engels and Marx.[3] Well, there's a few to go on with for the critics.

I see that an O'Flaherty has a picture in his mind of me staggering back horrified at the vision of all the Irish Catholics prostrating themselves before stocks and stones; and that I have an "ambition to stamp out the idolatrous practices to be found in Ireland."[4] Poor me! A smasher of holy pictures and holy images! Well, I'll have to make a start in my own home, so I will; get rid of the picture of the Madonna and Child from my wife's room, first of all; but it is a Raphael print, and far too lovely to be taken down. But what about the golden-brown and green print of the Angel of the Annunciation done in the Botticellian manner, hanging now right in front of me? Why not tear that one down? Ah, but that is far too lovely a thing to part with, or to hurt, or to treat in any other way than the way of admiration and of love. It's rather a lousy thing to try to associate me with such a stupid desire. I believe it was started by G.F. himself.[5] But there are other idolatries in Ireland, and elsewhere, that I am against, for instance that poverty and disease are the will of God; that the Saints are ready to respond to help any who may be too lazy to scratch themselves; that I agree with St. Teresa in the precept that a believer should pray as if everything depended upon God, and work as if everything depended on himself; and I'm against the preference for foreign saints over our own; that an Irishman's thought—if he thinks of a Saint at all—should be first for the fine Saints flourishing Irish names, Irish manners, and Irish honesty. The Saintly Kelt is different from the Saintly Saxon; he has a holy tang like the tang of the salty sea.

So many seem to think of Canon Burren as an impossibility that it is odd a book, recommended to priests, and published by a Catholic Firm, should say, among other things, "When a celibate state becomes negative, it is apt to degenerate into selfishness, and so some parish priests develop into parochial pashas." Pashas! If I said that! There's a lot said about "the laity's reverence for their priests"; but what of the priests' reverence for their laity? That's one of the many things that troubled Dr. W. McDonald. The way some of the *Standard* buckineeno[6] boys yell, one would think the

---

[3] See O'Casey's letter to David Krause, 12 April 1955, note 2.

[4] Desmond O'Flaherty's letter to the editor, "A 'Playgoer' and 'The Bonfire,' " *The Standard,* 25 March 1955.

[5] See Fallon's open-letter, "CALLING MR. O'CASEY," *The Standard,* 9 August 1946, reprinted in Vol. II; and O'Casey's reply, "AND SEAN O'CASEY WROTE," *The Standard,* 9 August 1946, note 1, Vol. II. This was the occasion of the break of their 23-year friendship, when Fallon accused O'Casey of "coldly calculated bigotry" in *Red Roses For Me.* Fallon repeated his charge of bigotry in his Saturday theatre column in the *Evening Press,* 29 January 1955, when, preparing his readers for the opening of *The Bishop's Bonfire,* he referred to *Red Roses For Me* and "the bigoted hocus-pocus of its Our Lady of Eblana sequences."

[6] In *The Bishop's Bonfire* there is a statue of St. Tremolo, the Bishop's patron

Church consisted only of Bishops, Priests, and Deacons. And Casabianca and Tremolo are "decidedly dangerous." It was near time the play was written. Indeed, the whole curious, hysterical display in the *Standard,* proves that O'Casey was surer than even he ventured to think himself to be.

But let us end, for the time being. What really concerns me most is your courage in writing the way you did. You have made enemies, ignorant enemies, and enemies intelligent, but malicious ones, and dangerous too. The writing in the *Standard,* or a lot of it, seems to remind me of what I once knew as "felon-setting."[7] I hope you have thought to count the possible cost of what you have done. I pray God you may not suffer for it. But the fact is, suffer or no, there are many, who if they could, would make you suffer for your temerity.

> *With all good wishes,*
> *Yours very sincerely,*
> *Sean O'Casey.*

saint who was a martyred Roman Legionary famous for the miraculous powers of his horn or *buccina,* and the comic characters in the play call him "the buckineeno boyo."

[7] Felon-setting: in politics, a deliberate attempt to create an atmosphere of suspicion about a person that would lead to his disgrace and/or arrest; in the journalistic reference to the *Standard,* it means a newspaper smear-campaign aimed at destroying a person's character.

To Barrows Dunham[1]

MS. DUNHAM

31 MARCH 1955

My dear Barrows:

I wonder how you are, your dear wife and son? It's some time since I heard from you. Last, it was away, away on the West Coast, and you wondering round like Raftery the poet.

[1] Barrows Dunham (1905–   ), writer and teacher, until 1953 Professor and Chairman of the Philosophy Department at Temple University, Philadelphia, Pennsylvania. On 27 February 1953 Dunham was declared guilty of contempt of Congress by the House Un-American Activities Committee, which was investigating alleged Communist influences in American colleges, when he invoked the Fifth Amendment privilege against self-incrimination and refused to answer questions about his educational background and occupation. He was dismissed from his position at Temple after his appearance before the committee. For the account of his exoneration in the Federal Court two years later, see O'Casey's letter to Dunham, 11 November 1955. See also letters to him in Vol. II.

Things seem to be easing up a little, though that may but seem so only because we are far from the struggle.

Yet, [Senator Joseph] McCarthy, at least, seems to have had a briele chun chroidhe—"a thump to the heart"—that has deprived him of his breath for the moment; and seems to have conjured himself into a corner. Heaven grant it may prove a tight one. There's one grand thing come to pass, anyway—there's an end forever to the winning of a war. Laurels of victory have turned to ashes. The bomb that destroys an enemy now destroys the friend; and at the same time too. We're all within the hot-blast now. The fieldglass & the marshal's baton are no damn use now. The only thing left to do is to sit down with an enemy, and share your bread with him.

A play of mine, "The Bishop's Bonfire," got a first production in Dublin five weeks ago (first "first" production I've had there for 30 years), and raised a storm that's raging yet. The Irish critics, almost to a man, condemned the play from first to last; but the audiences rallied to it, and it has run to full houses in Dublin's big commercial Theater.

I do hope you, Alice, & Clarke are all well, & doing, at least, fairly; that you have been a very brave man, & have fought the good fight, keeping the faith that man may never be reduced to a frightened shadow.

Eileen sends her love to all, and so do I.

As ever,
Sean

To George Bidwell[1]

TC. O'CASEY

3 APRIL 1955

Dear Mr. Bidwell,

Thank you very much for sending me the copy of your article that appeared in the *Polish Daily News*. It was, naturally, very interesting, and, to some extent, flattering; saying more good things about me than I'd like to hear with an open ear; for one has to be careful of the good things said of one as well as the bad things said; more careful, in fear that they might give one an opinion of oneself that might weaken common-sense and banish a sensible foresight.

My first four autobiographical books are, I fear, out of print; but I

[1] George Bidwell, Marszalkowska 7 m. 11, Warszawa, Poland.

am writing to my Publishers, Macmillan & Co., St. Martin's Street, London, W.C.2, to ask them if copies that might be sent to you are available.

My lastest play, *The Bishop's Bonfire* is to be published in May, and I shall ask my Publisher to send you a copy. It has caused something of a storm in Dublin, the Irish critics, almost to a man, condemning it, with the addition of a number of clerics advising the people to keep away from the theatre where it is showing. All the same, the audiences liked it, and it has played to packed houses, amid cheers and hisses. It was the first production in Dublin of a play of mine for over thirty years. The production then caused a storm too, and this one repeated it so strongly that, five weeks after the first night, the controversy is still raging. All to the good.

I should, of course, love to visit Poland, but I am too old now to be travelling about, more's the pity; but, anyway, the new life there and eastwards far as China, is for the Young; and, as I have often said to Russian friends, no one over thirty—except very special persons—should be invited to go to see the new energy and new resolution alive and working among you all. If collected funds ever allow, and if an O'Casey goes East, then it will be Breon, my son, 25, Niall, 20, or Shivaun, a daughter, 15, who will go, and not the old, near-sighted Sean.

Please note that I no longer live in Totnes. The Landlord of the house we had there, suddenly said he wanted the place for his mother and her daughter, gave us notice to quit, and so we had to leave after 18 years residence.

All good and cordial wishes to your clever wife and to you.

> *Yours sincerely,*
> *Sean O'Casey.*

To Mrs. Maureen Cusack

MS. CUSACK

3 APRIL 1955

My dear Maureen,

Joe Kerrigan was right, of course; but remember the important point is "if you look after it." It's wonderful what a heart can stick and do; but it just can't stick too much of a bad thing. It is evident that you have been trying to do too much, & that's just not good enough. You have a husband, children, and a house, and God knows these are enough to try even an amazon. I know, for I've been home always, & have experienced what a woman has to think of, has to do, & has to foresee.

Now, you must begin to take things more sensibly, and learn to realise your limits: what you can do; & what you shouldn't do. You know, as well as good with husband, children, and house, you are always, as well, a wise little head over Cyril's shoulders; and that, alone, is always a tremendous help, and a deep comfort.

First of all, you rest fully and determinedly all through Holy Week; and fix in your mind the things you will have to give up doing. No hard physical strain, and as little mental strain as possible. Don't rush around. Take your meals quietly, &, if you can at all, rest awhile after them. Stop doing anything, the moment you feel tired; that is, begin to feel tired. Thank heaven the play ended so that you can forget it, & sleep and read, or lie motionless & relaxed—if, & for so long, you can escape from the children. There are lots you can do, so long as you don't insist on going on when you feel tired.

Do listen to what I've said to you; for I'm something of a doctor as well as a playwright; and a fairly wise old owl into the bargain.

Eileen has written, and has, I daresay, told you that the butter came safely, & that we all enjoyed it all.

And, now, my dear, do take care of yourself. With reason on your side, you'll find Joe K. was right; and that reasonable care can bring anyone into his or her hundredth birthday.

My love to Cyril, to the children, and to you.

Yours very sincerely
Sean

To Miss Joan McAlevey[1]

MS. MCALEVEY

4 APRIL 1955

Dear Joan,

Thank you for the Shamrock Card. No, I wasn't at the first night of "The Bishop's Bonfire"—too old to travel thro' the frost & the snow, of which, I believe, you have had a heavy share recently. My wife and daughter were there, and had a lively & giddy time of it. The play caused a storm, and the controversy is raging yet; but the audiences liked it, & we have had full houses.

But never mind the "Bonfire," and concentrate on the Thesis. Try, if you have time, to read Shaw's Prefaces, too. I like Dryden, but he isn't quite so luminous or humorous as Shakespeare; but an elegant fellow.

[1] Miss Joan McAlevey, 241a Windsor Place, Brooklyn 15, N.Y.

Chaucer's "Canterbury Tales" are fine, but, to some, hard to read in a lively way; he is full of broad & dry humour; cider & dry sherry. A great man; but far more cautious than Langland. Of course, one can't help Spring coming with its budding and its golden daffodils; but, look, if we read Chaucer & Shakespeare as they should be read, we find Spring there; ay, and Summer, too,—all the seasons, in fact.

I hope you may do well in your teaching job. Remember, Joan, none of us can escape routine. We all have to put up with it. To be always enjoying ourselves, always gay, would kill us before our time. Routine is often a rough name for rest. Yes, let me know how your Thesis goes by all means.

My love to you and yours,
Yours very sincerely
Sean O'Casey

To Irish Press

5 APRIL 1955

"THE BISHOP'S BONFIRE"

Dear Sir,—Among the scintillating assembly in the Irish sky of the fairy lights, catherine wheels and sparklers let off by the Irish drama critics, I'd like to add a little more noisy hilarity to the tumult of talk aroused by "The Bonfire."

It has often surprised me that so many turbulent defenders of the faith of their fathers seem to know so little about it. One of these defenders, a drama critic, gave voice to a grave error in his review of my play. Carving his views out on what is a plaque of what poses to be Catholic thought, one would imagine that Seamus Byrne should know more and know better.

In his review, he says: "We met Foorawn's former fiancé" (this word isnt pronounced Fie nancy, as some poor scholars might think, but as fee nong see, to show how good we are at French): well, his whole sentence is: "We met Foorawn's former fiancé, Manus Moanroe, who, at some earlier stage has thought of entering the Church."[1]

I waited to see if any of the other theologically-minded critics noticed this extraordinary and fundamental error; but divil a one did: they were all too busy burying O'Casey without pomp or ceremony. Not a drum was heard, not a funeral note. Well, let me correct the error: Manus

---

[1] Seamus Byrne, "The Shadow of an O'Casey," *The Standard,* 4 March 1955.

Moanroe never had a thought of entering the Church; he was too young to have one.

Like all children born to Catholic parents (and to most Protestants, too) he entered the Church before he had time to think. A soul enters the Church not through the priesthood, but through the Sacrament of Baptism. I wonder that the drama critic who goes about, figuratively, in a glossy topper, among the lesser soft-hatted ones, didn't correct this error; but he took no notice.

Even the gentle Carmel Nolan[2] didn't either; too much taken up with what she calls "the preservation above all of the reverence for the holy priesthood for which Ireland has always been outstanding." Not a word about the reverence due from the holy priesthood to the holy people. One would think that the Church consisted of Bishops, Priests and Deacons only.

That was one of the things that troubled the mind of Dr. Walter McDonald, forty years Professor of Theology in St. Patrick's College, Maynooth: the separation of the clergy by the clergy of the people from the people.

In all charity, I advise Mr. Byrne to think a little before he chooses a fancy word—like "resuscitated," for instance—to study drama a little more before he writes about it; and to have another dekko at the Penny Catechism.

Sean O'Casey.

Devon.

[2] Carmel M. Nolan, "Protest," *The Standard,* 25 March 1955, a letter to the editor.

To Michael and Kay O'Riordan[1]

TS. O'RIORDAN

5 APRIL 1955

Dear Michael and Kay,

I have been very busy for a long time and will be for a long time to come, with many things to do, and dozens of letters to answer. Besides, I

[1] Michael O'Riordan (1917–), a Dublin bus conductor who fought for the Loyalists in the Spanish Civil War in 1938; thereafter active in the Irish Workers' Party and became its General Secretary in 1964; continued to hold this position when the IWP became the Communist Party of Ireland in 1970. For references to O'Riordan, see O'Casey's letters to Sean Nolan, 21 May 1951, note 2, Vol. II; and to Mrs. Kay O'Riordan, 19 February 1954, Vol. II.

have a lot to do in the home, and have to take an interest in the lives of our three children, so I'm a pretty busy bolshevist bugger. Well, I got your letter of Feb. and Kay's of the 3 of Mar—to Mrs O'C.—but both of us—she busier than I—had no time to answer. This one must be brief.

I am too old, and the weather was too bad, for me to go over to Dublin. Well, it has been a bit of a rouser! It certainly caused a bigger stir than I thought it would. I hope the critics are tired rushing round in mind and body by now, and can take a rest in this Holy Week. Don't worry about the intellectuals; they aren't the worst. We have to worry about our workers more, for few of them yet do much to learn things so as to stand up intelligently on equal terms with those who have had a better chance. I should very much like to see the workers (all who earn their bread, of course, are workers; intellectuals as well as dockers) but here I mean particularly the class that I belong to, the dockers, laborers, railwaymen, etc, who must, if they are to take a proper place in life, become acquainted with those holy things that have been hidden from them so long—science, art, literature.

The laborer's little lad and the laborer's little lass should know the shape of a violin, a piano, and a guitar; should be in a position to handle them, and make them speak—one or the other of them; should know something about color, line, and form in a good picture; and should be able to read, recite, and enjoy Shakespeare, and all the richness of literature which is their heritage as well as the heritage of all the others. All the things that Jim Larkin brought into the fight for bread; the great Jim Larkin; Jim Larkin with a loaf under his oxster and a rose in his hand.

Tell Kay I didn't hear A' Raibh Tu ar an gcarraig,[2] for Radio Eireann comes through to us here only in short spurts, which is very annoying; but can't be helped. Even the Third Programme cant be but faintly heard; the payment for the Hydrogen Bomb keeps us from learning, knowledge, music, and fine talk. We cant afford to live now that we are preparing to die.

I enclose a cheque for Four Guineas—two towards the expenses of your recent election fight, and two towards IRISH WORKERS' LEAGUE. By the way, the time's too soon to stand for election of a Socialist ticket; we must be patient awhile.

All the best to Kay, to you, and to those you love.

Sean

PS. However, I know A'raibh tu ar an gcarraig well. Have it here; just been reading it from "Fuínn na Smól."[3]

---

[2] "Were You at Carrick," a song.
[3] Padruig Breathnach, *Fuínn na Smól* (1913), "The Airs of the Thrushes," a book of songs.

To Mrs. May Keating[1]

MS. KEATING

6 APRIL 1955

Dear May,

Yes, I remember about the Peace Meeting. I am still working in the Peace Movement—just sent a letter & sub. to the British Peace Committee. It is comic & tragic to see people putting their trust in God and the Red Tabs of the Generals.

Thank you very much for your encouraging letter, & for the letter that replies so skillfully to Donat O'Donnell.[2] Several wrote to the Statesman about it, but the letters were refused publication. It doesn't frighten me Statesman or the Galloglass Donat. If Donat had read Dr. McDonald's book he'd find out how curates become Canons or even P.P.'s. He warned them, if they wanted to "get on," not to have any opinions of their own: and Donat can hardly say this man knew nothing. Indeed, my Boheroe was built on a young priest I met some years ago in Kilternan. He had been "naughty" to his Bishop, & had been banished as chaplain to a lonely little convalescent home for Nuns. Mrs O'C. had a cousin a nun there; & we went to visit her. Eileen talked to the nun, & I talked to the young cleric— for a long time. I remember still, & feel it still, too, the clasp of his hand, & the lonely look of him, as we left. Afterwards, I heard he had been sent to some lonelier place in Africa, where he died some few years later. And Father O'Flanagan, Father Sullivan, Father Sheedy, & God knows how many more.

Well, the Kellys, the Donats, the Byrnes, or the Fallons won't stop me talking.

All good wishes to you & yours.

Sean

P.S. It must have been a bitter sight to the critics to see the people going to the play.

---

[1] Mrs. May Keating, a Dublin woman active in the Irish labor movement.

[2] Mrs. Keating wrote a reply to the review of *The Bishop's Bonfire* by Donat O'Donnell (Conor Cruise O'Brien), "No Bishop, No Bonfire," *New Statesman and Nation,* 5 March 1955, but it was refused publication.

To Jack Lindsay

PC. S. *O'Casey Rev*[1]

6 APRIL 1955

Dear Jack,

I am glad that the young people in Moscow, who know English, like me. I am usually happier with the young, unless the old be as young as G.B.S. was at 95. A big exception is [Mikhail] Apletin, who is, probably, as young as I am myself. Late last summer, the Editor of "Ogonik" was here with us—a grand chap.

I'm delighted the Congress was such a success.[2] I wrote some sharp things to Apletin the time Zdanov was bullying writers into his narrow shell of literature.[3] At the time there were savage attacks on T. S. Eliot in the Soviet Press; and I wrote pointing out that while T.S.E. wasn't a friend, he was, at least, an open foe, and honestly antagonistic; at the same time warning them against larding Priestly with too much praise. Apletin didn't like it, I think, but a few months later, he found Priestly wasn't the godsend he had promised to be. What a curious fatty-complacent opinion of himself he has! Nothing for now. I'm glad you don't live in a castle. They're cold places. Yeats tried it for a day or two. He and Spenser are the only two poets I know who lived in a castle. Anyhow castle or cottage, the times now are hard for writers. I hope you manage fairly well.

I enclose a note for your Tatar friend which tells, as far as I can remember, my date of signing an agreement of friendship with the USSR. It may save you the bother of writing it out yourself—always a bother to an author.

All good wishes and love,
Sean O'Casey

[1] A copy of this letter appeared in the *Sean O'Casey Review,* Fall 1975.
[2] Lindsay had attended the Second Writers Congress in Moscow in 1954.
[3] See O'Casey's letter to Mikhail Apletin, 10 February 1950, Vol. II.

To Mrs. R——

MS. PRIVATE

8 APRIL 1955

My dear R——,

I take it that I have set down your name correctly. First, I thought it might be "R.," but it is R., isnt it? Or, as I have so often done before, am I making a big mistake?

I daresay, the D. Glass picture is good; but nothing like as good as one taken by Jane Cown of "The Observer."[1] The one by D.G. was taken 6 years ago. He had phoned & written from Plymouth—where he had a studio—asking me to sit for him; but I said no. One Sunday in Summer, he drove into "Tingrith"—where we lived before we came here—with a car packed high with parapharnalia; & before I recovered from the uninvited visit, he had the place wired & great lights going. He begged me to let him do a picture, for he said he had only got into the "Sunday Times," & wanted to plant himself fairly there—said he was to get £50 a week. I let him do it. He had lunch with the family; then we drove to the sea where we had rented a hut for two months; here we walked & talked, till it was time to return. A week later, a letter from him told me the picture was with the printers, & would appear next week. It did appear—six years later. I've never had a word from him since the letter telling me the printers had the picture. I don't like such fellows—they serve their masters too well. Thanks, R., and thank A. for the birthday present of good wine and spirits. Tho' practically a non-drinker, I take a little this or that evening before a meal; but have seen the effects too often to give it affection. And thanks for the "tribute." Tony Gallagher of the Irish News Agency, was eloquent over the telephone, telling me of the Broadcast from Moscow. From Moscow, mind you, he kept saying, as if bewildered and in a spiritual haze. I've just finished a tape-recording of 4 quarter-of-an-hour broadcasts for Ireland, the first time ever my voice will be heard on Radio Eireann. And a big crowd will listen to them. They are simple, though I think my voice—raucous as a crow, an American critic said—will come over clearly, giving a little advice, & few comments, and singing a few songs—two of them my own.

Thanks again go to you & to A. for your & her kindness, & my love to you both with the thanks.

Yours very sincerely,
Sean

[1] The photograph of O'Casey by Douglas Glass appeared in the *Sunday Times*, 6 March 1955; and the one by Jane Cown appeared in *The Observer*, 6 March 1955.

To George Braziller[1]

TC. O'CASEY

9 APRIL 1955

Dear George,

Your Representative, as you know, has come and gone, and I hope he did well for you among the wary English publishers. Far as I can see, there's little being put forth from the Presses that is worth even a paper cover. Even the better ones mightnt appeal to an American public. What about a vol of the best of F. O'Connor's short stories? A reprint of Hardy's TRUMPET MAJOR, FAR FROM THE MADDING CROWD, or THE MAYOR OF CASTERBRIDGE? I'm afraid we have to go back to the earlier ones who wrote like ones with fire in the blood. What about Dickens or some of Thackeray's? It is very hard to suggest anything to you, for the risk is too big. You take on a big new job when you take on that of a publisher on your very own. Dave Krause's book is, in my opinion, a likely proposition—not because of his interest in me, but because I believe him to be a very clever lad, and that within him are the qualities of a writer.

I havent yet done anything to get the articles, etc, together, to make a new book. I have been very busy with a lot of things. I did four quarter-of-an-hour broadcasts, on a tape-machine, for Radio Eireann (Ireland), and, later, the engineer who took them found that two of them had been recorded on the wrong tape; so these had to be done again: I did them yesterday, after a lot of silent cursing. They are to be broadcast soon after Easter.

The new play, given its first production in Dublin, caused a hell of a stir, roused great excitement, and ran for two weeks longer than the time arranged, to full houses; and would easily have gone far further if the theater hadnt been committed to another show. I hope it may come to London.

I must soon begin the search for any articles that I may have here. Maybe, the collection might be better than I think. George B[rantl]. when he was here, told me you'd let me have any books I'd like to have; and, I think, you said the same in a letter to me; so I choose a few, named underneath, but with the proviso, that, if you let me have them, you will deduct the cost from whatever royalty may be in future due to me. This is an indispensable condition, and a fair one.

The Future of Architecture. F. Lloyd Wright
Masterpieces of the Japanese Color Woodcut. Willy Boller

---

[1] George Braziller, publisher, New York. He was preparing to publish *The Green Crow* in 1956, a collection of eleven essays from *The Flying Wasp* (1937), four short stories from *Windfalls* (1934), and twelve new essays, most of which had previously appeared in magazines and newspapers. See O'Casey's letter to Braziller, 19 July 1955, notes 2–7.

African Folktales and Sculpture. Paul Radin and J. J. Sweeney
N591. Book of Costume. Millia Davenport.

> *Remember the proviso.*
> *My love to Marsha and to you.*
> *As ever,*
> *[Sean]*

To Patrick Galvin

MS. GALVIN

11 APRIL 1955

Dear Patrick Galvin,

Thanks a lot for the Record, which came safely this time. It is simply and charmingly sung—the songs. "Monahan's Motor Car" is, I think, the better of the two: has much more humour & wit in it. P. Cearnaigh[1] didn't quite reach the plane of a singer. He faltered always somewhere in every song he composed. He was a curious blend of audacity and timidity; the latter always succeeding the former, and letting it down. But the songs are attractive, & sung very well; & it is a very interesting record.

I can't let you send me this, & t'other one, without covering the cost; & so I enclose a guinea. You can't afford, I guess, to be giving out largesse this way.

Please accept this so that you will not, at least, be out of pocket; or, if not, I should have to return the record.

I do hope you are making something out of what you do in this way. People, I find, are always ready to listen to a song; but not always ready to drop a coin in the cap. Remember Raftery's curse.[2]

> *All good wishes to you.*
> *Yours very sincerely,*
> *Sean O'Casey*

[1] Peadar Ó Cearnaigh, known as Kearney (1833–1942), writer of patriotic songs and poems, among them "The Soldiers' Song," set to music by Patrick Heeney, which is now the national anthem of the Irish Republic. O'Casey knew Ó Cearnaigh when they were studying Irish in the Gaelic League in 1907. Ó Cearnaigh was an uncle of Brendan Behan.

[2] See O'Casey's letter to Roger Hayes, 24 November 1945, note 5, Vol. II:

> "I am Raftery with my arse to the wall
> Playing music for sweet damn all."

To Irish Press

12 APRIL 1955

THE BONFIRE[1]

Dear Sir—I see that a Certain Party has given vent to a terrible blast from his Buckineeno.[2] Oh! Me years, me years!

But the blast ends with a pathetic twittering aria. When the Certain Party tremulously says: "Isn't there an awful possibility that such a fellow may not have lost his wits completely"; the Certain Party seems to forget that there still remains the more awful possibility that such a fellow has.

O'Casey.

Devon.
April 5, 1955

[1] A reply to Gabriel Fallon's "An Open Letter to Sean O'Casey," *Irish Press,* 30 March 1955. See also O'Casey's letter to Rex MacGall, 28 April 1955. For his comment on the break with Fallon, see O'Casey's letter to *The Standard,* 9 August 1946, note 1, Vol. II.

[2] See O'Casey's letter to John O'Donovan, 30 March 1955, note 6.

To David Krause

TS. KRAUSE

12 APRIL 1955

My dear Dave:

Thanks for your dear letter, and for the good wishes surrounding the seventy-fifth year of the day I was born. Oh, Lord, a short time! Yes, indeed, the BONFIRE caused a commotion in Dublin never experienced since the production of the PLOUGH AND THE STARS thirty years ago. The professional critics were in a fine temper, and raged like the heathen furiously together. I have never had such a vehement and such a unanimous denunciation of a play before. It was everything ridiculous, bad, and feeble, disgracing the annals of dramatic art in Ireland, and, indeed, of the world. And yet, I had a few champions that bewildered and dumfounded the critics; allies that I never expected to have, in strange places, right in the midst of the enemy's camp. One is the chief sub-editor of the Daily in which the principal mouth of criticism speaks—Gabriel Fallon. The sub-editor, John O'Donovan, lashed out at Gabriel, and the two of them are circling round each other still. I sent in a few simple letters myself, short and snappy, which so enraged Gabriel that he bawled at me to "keep my mouth shut." And the principal writer in a weekly, called THE LEADER, gave another blocking blow to the critics saying that "O'Casey remains one of the few living dramatists—and the only Irish one—who bears with him always the unbearable vision we call poetry, great poetry."[1] Oh, boys! He added, too, that "We must remember that O'Casey is one of the small body of persons who may hand on a torch to the younger generation." Oh, boys!

However, all this may, or may not, be, it is encouraging to find that a lonely one has even in Ireland a few who will risk a blow for what they believe to be good and worthy of some regard. Cyril Cusack was a very brave man—he is a very conscientious Catholic, and so is his wife, Maureen; they have three children, so aren't without deep and dear responsibilities—but, I am very happy to say that his courage has been splendidly vindicated, and, not only has he lost nothing, but gained a lot through the adventure. The play, skeduled for three weeks, ran to crowded houses for five, in a big theater, and would have gone on longer but that the theater had been committed to the production of SHOW BOAT. I never thought that the play would go so well; no one did; and the critics hoped for, and were sure of, a dismal and humiliating flop. The best laid plans of mice and men. . . .

Each of us, Dave, is a pulpit; we preach by everything we say and do. It isn't necessary to be a cleric, a politician or a journalist; we do it every moment of our lives, we all try to teach each other; and this is the only way to go forward. Some have a finer gift than others for teaching, but each of us has at least one talent, though others have five. As for poets and artists, they are always at it—in spite of Eliot and those liberals who say no art can display or conceal a message. All that is stated in the writings of Engels and Marx, books and books, is enshrined in fourteen lines of a poem by Keats.[2] I have put a few questions to the Irish critics, of

---

[1] "Sean O'Casey: A Postscript," *The Leader,* 9 April 1955, by "X" (Valentin Iremonger).

[2] Keats's "Isabella; or The Pot of Basil" (1818), stanzas 14–15:

> With her two brothers this fair lady dwelt,
>   Enriched from ancestral merchandize,
> And for them many a weary hand did swelt
>   In torched mines and noisy factories
> And many once proud-quiver'd loins did melt
>   In blood from stinging whip;—with hollow eyes
> Many all day in dazzling river stood,
> To take the rich-ored driftings of the flood.

> For them the Ceylon diver held his breath,
>   And went all naked to the hungry shark;
> For them his ears gush'd blood; for them in death
>   The seal on the cold ice with piteous bark
> Lay full of darts; for them alone did seethe
>   A thousand men in troubles wide and dark:
> Half-ignorant, they turn'd an easy wheel,
> That set sharp racks at work, to pinch and peel.

which one is "would they affirm or deny that St. Paul's rhapsody in Charity was, or was not, lyrical literature?"

The Jews wrote literature whenever they prayed or sang a psalm.

I hope you have seen George Braziller. He has entered into the publishing business, and has already sent out some very fine books beautifully framed in format and style. It would be finer if he took on your book for publication. Don't make it too big; and, remember, I have quite a lot of literary faults. Don't hesitate to point them out.

I have done four quarter-of-an-hour broadcasts for the Irish b. system—Radio Eireann. It will be interesting and, I hope, amusing to read what is said about them. They are simple here and there caustic, and each of them has a song, two of the songs, my very own.

I hope by now that you have banished the effects of the Influenza. I daresay, you have, for you didn't mention a cough in your last letter.

I am sending this to your home address, for I guess the University has gone into the rest of Easter; and that you can lie a little later in the mornings. Don't forget to take prudent exercise during the recess, and keep out in the air as much as you can.

Eileen has just left for London. Niall comes on leave after six weeks of manoevering in Germany, to have an interview with the Secretary of London University so as to get his name fixed for studentship when his army time ends; though we don't know yet where the money for fees and livelihood is to come from—from The U.S.A., I trust, where the most of it has come from already. I think I'll hang the Stars and Stripes over the flat.

All good wishes, Dave, a mhic, to you and yours.

Yours very sincerely,
Sean

To Harold D. Jones

MS. JONES

14 APRIL 1955

Dear Mr. Jones,

Thank you very much for sending me the Program of "Juno," done in the Greenwich Mews Theater.

It was very interesting to read of the Union of Races in the play; and that Jew and Gentile co-operated in showing forth my play to whomsoever came to see it.[1]

I hope the activities of the Mews Theater may continue to prosper.

Yours sincerely,
Sean O'Casey

[1] The Greenwich Mews Theatre, which produced *Juno and the Paycock* in February 1955, is a community project sponsored by the Village Presbyterian Church and the Brotherhood Synagogue.

To Irving Sandler[1]

TC. O'CASEY

14 APRIL 1955

Dear Mr. Sandler,

Remember that I understand few things, though I think a lot about most of them. You are a Jew and a Historian—two damn important things. I am Irish and not an historian. Dont write history as I try to write my biography, for it would be something of an imitation, and so bad. Besides, it isnt History; bar being the his story of one item of life. But all histories should have a pulse and a punch, too; for none can be written without the participation of the one who writes, and he must have an opinion about what he records, and willy nilly, that opinion creeps or jumps into the work he does. The fact that one man is a Jew, another an Irishman does matter; we dont know how, and I, for one, dont care a damn how; it just is, and there it is, and remains so for ever. There's nothing to be proud of in it, but there's nothing to be ashamed of in it either. Most Irish are Catholics; I amnt; not even a Christian; but I'm Irish allright; so though religion has something to do with it, religion isnt everything. There is the tie of generations; of country, religion, language, of tradition, of curious weave and warp of the mind. Besides, this is good, bringing a fine variety to life, and giving each race a chance of doing things other races cant do; of thinking in ways different from others. You are an American citizen as I am a British one; but you are a Jew and I am an Irishman; though, of course, all are within the one glorious family of the whole human race.

The central problem is the work itself that you have in your mind to do. As well as having the gift of being chosen, you must weigh the surrounding circumstances: if you are married, about your wife; if you have

[1] Irving Sandler, 134 East 17th Street, New York City.

children, about them; if you havent a safe job, how you may live while the work is in progress; and, if you go on, who may publish the book or books when the work is finished.

These are all very pertinent problems which you would do well to consider before you begin: in other words, to sit down, and count the cost.

I dont half like the doubts you mention. If the urge was irresistible, you would have none. I think a history of the Jews done in a new way—I have read that of Josephus—would be a fine thing to do; but it would be a gigantic task, for the Jews have made history everywhere—Disraeli in England, for instance—but even a partial history would be important, for like all peoples, the Jews are changing, though forever remaining the same, the Jew.

Your story has one flaw—there is no next time.[2] We often do things though we know not why we do them.

I fear my advice is of little use to you. The problem is entirely your own. May the God of Abraham, of Isaac, and of Jacob enlighten you.

Yours very sincerely,
Sean O'Casey.

[2] Sandler had written that he felt like the Jew in the following story: "A Jew endured the horror of a Nazi concentration camp, only to be plopped into a displaced persons camp. Finally escaping this he reached Eretz Israel, just in time for the war against the Arabs. And then after the war, he was just about to settle into the glory of austerity when he died. Naturally this Jew went to Heaven. But there he created a row. He demanded to see God face to face, mortal eye to the heart of the sun. The Angels tried to dissuade him, and the Seraphim and Cherubim too. But he would not be halted. He stormed through all the seven heavens, demanding to see God. And finally he made it. He stood at the throne of the great Yahweh himself. Looking the Creator in the eye, the Jew demanded: 'God, next time don't choose me.' "

To Mrs. R——

MS. PRIVATE

[? APRIL 1955]

Dear R——,

Thanks for the beautiful book showing the beautiful picture done by Fra Angelico—one of my first-born favorites. Curious, the Church, far as I know, [never] gave him a post-mortem honor, even that of "the Blessed." Think, I suppose, beautiful painting doesn't interest God. Bores him? Or any Composer of lovely sounds after St. Cecelia. Or even the man who made St. Peter's Funny. Let us decamp from heaven's gate and go among the sinners: I've never been to Donegal, but know something about it "The Rosses," "Irishowen," & "Gweedore." A poor county, very beauti-

ful. Beyond the coast fishing & Donegal tweeds, there's only the small un-
economic farms. If I were you, I shouldn't be too eager to find employment
for the poor bewildered people. The letter of the girl, I think, shows she
hasn't had even an elemental education. What would she do here? Couldn't
be a nurse or even a factory worker; only a domestic servant. Leave this
problem to themselves. You really can't help. Most of the men are on the
roads making the way wide for the motor-car; or as navvies. Two of them
were killed by a cave-in of a trench the other day. The second man trying
to rescue his pal. Seems the trench wasn't safely shored. I've dug myself
in these trenches, & there was always the risk of a cave-in, if you hadn't a
brave & careful foreman.

I shouldn't invest in property in Donegal, either. I didn't know you
were in a furnished flat, & it is good to get a place of your own, but take
care of the choice. A house may have a lot of snags, & it is always wise to
pay a surveyor to have a look at anything you think you like.

Delighted to hear A. & J. are happy. May they long continue so. Have
been very busy, & glad the birthday business is over. Refused all requests
for interviews, but had to answer phone-calls, when I was alone, from Canada, USA., London, & Ireland. But I survived.

I've had to reduce my reading & writing, for age & early trouble have
dimmed my eyes, & it is something of a struggle now to read or write; but
I write & I read.

All good wishes to A., J., & to you, my friend.

Fine to hear S. is allright.

As ever,
Sean

To Mrs. Nora ____[1]

TC. O'CASEY

22 APRIL 1955

Dear Mrs. Nora ____

Yours is a rather sad letter, for, indeed, you must have had a sad time
when you were a child; a sad time to have a sadness; for a child is no phi-

[1] This woman in New York wrote the following letter to O'Casey on Easter
Sunday, 10 April 1955: "Mr. O'Casey a cara, A salute to your indomitable courage,
perpetual youth—And to your patience and fortitude. 'Sunset and Evening Star' leaves
me—what shall I say?—breathless! Panting with wonder—admiration and hope. 'I
Knock at the Door' lays on my modest 'desk' for many a year.

"My childhood ('God bless the mark') was spent—better misspent—in Ireland.
The kindest words uttered by my unlucky father, who was blown into eternity by an

losopher, and cant face things with thought. I have known many a one
like you while I lived away in Ireland; a man most often the culprit, but
frequently a woman; and, at times, both, with the poor children ground to
hopelessness between the foolish, frantic pair.

Drink is still a potent curse in Ireland, for in many districts there is
little else to do during the leisure hours snatched from the earning of
bread. Gambling is added to the drink now, with betting offices, licensed
by the Government, sprouting out finely from sheltered corners; and the
people, the young, still flee the land in thousands. But of course, the Will
of God remains, and Christ the King is Ireland's unofficial President.

But there are a few brave souls left there trying to bring about a
change; to make two blades of grass grow where but one was grown before; and, occasionally, when a chance comes, I send in a word or two by
a play, a book, or a simple recorded broadcast. But the clerics dont like
me, and do a lot to preach me as an enemy of the people. A few weeks
ago, a play of mine, THE BISHOP'S BONFIRE, done in Dublin, caused
a stir and a commotion that hadnt been felt for over thirty years.

I am sorry to read that you are alone, having lost a husband. Well,
that is another sad sorrow that you will have to face. It isnt an easy thing

---

alcoholic (atomic) fart of his own making, nine years after my unwanted arrival
into this world, ran something like this: 'God stiffen and damn you I wish I never
saw you nor the sky over you'—'After I am gone ye'll all be under the table eating
skins.'

"Now a few words about our unhappy Mother: Poor woman, her majestic
dreams of love and romance were shattered by Jameson, Hennessy, and Guinness,
Inc. (manuvering close—a small whimpering voice whispered: 'I feel sick.' 'Sick!—
Sick!! you big heap of dung. If you get sick I'll break your bloody back. Where, you
selfish bitch, do you think I'll get the money to bury you—.' Hers was a gentle soul.)

"A few years passed bringing to an end the short-lived tragic lives of these oddly
matched parents who carelessly trampled across their children's lives. On that sad
late day there was no table left to hide under to say nothing about the skins.

"They come: the great ships come. Oh! softly, softly the tides are moving out
of the harbor.

"For God stiffen and damn you brats, the fears of their childhood—which have
never subsided—and the rags of their arses flogging them to death on their way!

"This being Easter week an old 'Irish Republican' bringing Easter Greetings to
my modest 'studio' gazed a few moments upon a tiny reproduction, Picasso's: 'The
Race'—'Yerrah!' 'Praise be to his holy name—' he softly muttered—'if I put a wet paint
brush in me backside and turned a summer-sault I'de do better.'

"The years flow by like water and it's spring again. The new green is everywhere. The sun dances in the sky. Once more hope fills the awakening world. Soon,
too soon, Autumn, with all its glory, will come followed by Winter: evenings of acute
loneliness, the wailing cry along the river's edge. Nights of grey frost and utter silence—of words unspoken (my candles are burning down). The marvellous moon will
move up into the magic heavens blazing down upon the uneasy world.

"So, I lift my glass—a toast to life and death. To my late lamented husband
whose arms were my only home.

"And, too, a tender thought for the late God-stiffen-you-and-damn-you and his
bride.

"For (and with) you, Sean O'Casey—a rousing—ringing—'Hurrah!'
"Very sincerely yours, Nora _____."

to do without a companion who has been an intimate, and who is a supporter and a shield. But all of us have to face such a deserted world sooner or later. Death comes to all of us, and it very often leaves a dreadful void behind.

You remember the woman who came to Buddha appealing to him to restore a dead child to life; following him everywhere appealing, till he promised to raise the child to life again, if she but brought a pinch of salt from a household that did not know the sorrow of death. And she searched here, there, everywhere, for days, for weeks, for months; but at last had to come to tell Him that nowhere was there a household void of the sorrow that comes from the death of a loved one; nowhere.

It is the one thing we share together, irrespective of class, creed, or race; so there is no reason why we shouldnt be brave, and face forward till our own time comes to go. We can do no more; we should do no less.

And, anyway, it was the drink that shouted your father's wild words, and not your father's soul; so you can remember him with some pity—though, frankly, I have myself, little regard for these irresponsible souls, dead or alive—; and your mother with sympathy, who suffered so much through a misbegotten dream.

Try not to be too lonely.

[*Sean O'Casey*]

To Irish Times

27 APRIL 1955

PERILOUS SEAS

Sir,—In an English stage journal, a review of "The Bishop's Bonfire" tells all who read the magazine that "the Ireland of the young O'Casey is dead . . . the priest is no longer a power in the land and the O'Casey tirades against him no longer rouse the 'heretics' to rebellion or the angels to anger. As Joseph Tomelty is currently pointing out in the Abbey, the people are no longer priest-ridden—it is the priest who is people-ridden!"[1]

Now, what do yous think of that? The review was written by a Mr. Bourke MacWilliam, a drama-critic (another of the B. Boys) who evidently knows something no one else knows. In a reply to this announce-

[1] Bourke MacWilliam, *Plays and Players*, April 1955. See O'Casey's letter, "Sean O'Casey Complains," *Plays and Players*, May 1955; and MacWilliam's "Reply to Sean O'Casey," *Plays and Players*, June 1955, reprinted below. Joseph Tomelty's *Is the Priest at Home?* (1949) was revived at the Abbey Theatre for a two-week run on 11 April 1955.

ment, I ventured to point out the incidents that whirled round the Students' Debating Society, the ecclesiastical hand that stretched out from Maynooth and tore the Mother and Child Bill straight in two, and the latest toreador-declaration by the Bishop of Cork[2]—all happening, I'm told, within living memory of all who live in Ireland. To these has to be added the yarn that a representative of the Irish people, questioning the claims of the said bishop, is afraid to sign his name to his objection for fear of "finishing his political career before he had well begun it."

Is the Ireland of the young O'Casey dead? Is Joe Tomelty's people-ridden priest but a lipso facto? Dead it may be; but it won't lie down. Mr. Bourke MacWilliam must have been having a die-dream.

I'm telling you, when a Bill Mullarkey[3] fits a mitre on his head and grips a crozier in his fist, he can make the Kellys, the Burkes and the Sheas hop, and hesitate, and hide. Meanwhile the Orangemen, even the workers, hold on to the tail of King Billy's white horse, and who can blame them? Mullarkey stands guard on the border.—Yours, etc.,

Sean O'Casey.

Devon, April 25th, 1955

[2] On 13 April 1955 the *Irish Times* reported that a speech had been given on the previous day by the Most Rev. Dr. Lucey, Bishop of Cork, at the tenth congress of Christus Rex in Killarney, in which the Bishop stated that when the Roman Catholic hierarchy intervened four years earlier against Dr. Noel Browne's Mother and Child Health Plan, they did so because "they were the final arbiters of right and wrong even in political matters." An editorial titled "Perilous Seas," *Irish Times*, 14 April 1955, protested against the Bishop's views: "Dr. Lucey's use of the phrase, 'even in political matters,' we can only regard as unfortunate, and more than likely to revivify the charge—which His Lordship decries—that 'we are being ruled from Maynooth rather than Leinster House.'" The "Perilous Seas" controversy continued in the letters column of the *Irish Times* for a month.

[3] Bishop Bill Mullarkey is the title character in *The Bishop's Bonfire*, and though his power and presence are felt throughout the play, he never appears.

To Rex MacGall

TC. O'CASEY

28 APRIL 1955

Dear Rex,

Thanks for your letter. Yes, I have seen and I have read the "Leitir ar Leatheadh" [An Open Letter] written by a Certain Party, and windowed in the IRISH PRESS.[1] How anxious and loving the laddo is. All for my

[1] See Gabriel Fallon's "An Open Letter to Sean O'Casey," *Irish Press*, 30 March 1955, reprinted below.

good. He'll even venture to tell a fib to prove it—his reference to Orwell. I gave the punch to Orwell years before he died. It was sent to the OB-SERVER in 1945, the Literary Editor sent it on to Orwell—I have the Editor's letter saying so; but, like the humbug he was, Orwell sang dumb.[2] The Attack of mine was a defence, not only of myself, but of every Irish writer who published a book in England. Orwell's review was an attack on Ireland as well as on me, and I defended myself and Ireland from him—see the "song" in S. and Evening Star. But the Certain Party seems to fret and fume because I refuse to mould myself on his dictation. It has made me a lot of enemies; I knew it would, but Orwell had to be told a thing or two, and I was the man to do it. It is an odd conceit that orders one as to what he must do and what he must write, and how he must go. He wears a miragical mitre allright. And the Certain Party threatens to write a book—"more than one can play at that game." Now that IS interesting. What a delightful thing if the Certain Party did![3] Better still, if each of the drama critics wrote a book about the drama; best of all, if the whole of them, in combination, wrote a masterpiece. Food for the cods.

Thanks for *Inniu*.[4] The Gaelic to me seems rough. It doesnt glide as the Gaelic can, like a wild river, or like Tennyson's Brook. Not much music in it; and not enough of honest to God criticism, as there used to be in *Iris*.[5] For instance, "Bhi Seachtain na gCrann ar fud na tire."[6] How could that be? The week of the trees was throughout the land—doesnt ring right to me. It needs something like celebrated, or honored, or brought to the fore, and, anyway trees cant have a week to themselves. The week of honor to the trees, of care for the trees, or week of the planting of trees, would, in my opinion, be better. But, then, I really am talking of what I know nothing about.

> *All good wishes to you, a mhic.*
> *Yours very sincerely,*
> *Sean O'Casey.*

[2] See George Orwell, "Green Flag," *The Observer*, 28 October 1945, reprinted in Vol. II; and O'Casey's unpublished reply, 29 October 1945, Vol. II.

[3] Gabriel Fallon's book did not come out until a year after O'Casey's death: *Sean O'Casey: The Man I Knew* (1965).

[4] *Inniu* (Today), a current Irish language weekly newspaper.

[5] *An Iris* (The Journal), a defunct Irish language monthly magazine. See O'Casey's letter to Francis MacManus, 14 January 1946, note 1, Vol. II.

[6] O'Casey goes on to give the literal translation, and the occasion was the week of annual tree planting.

To Seumas Scully

MS. SCULLY

28 APRIL 1955

Dear Seumas,

I'm glad you got a job. It isn't easy to get one, unless you have had technical training—building, engineering, or even laboring work. Clerical work is hardest to get anywhere—in Ireland [as] well as here. Certainly, you could do no better in the way of boarding, for £3.10.0 is very reasonable for what you say you get. London is pretty expensive, as everyone recognises; more so than the Provinces. My dear Seumas, it was very cold, damnably cold everywhere during the winter—even in glorious Devon. Indeed, only this week have I left off a muffler. When winds blow from the N. Pole or from Siberia—look out. You won't be able to save much in London. But can't you be satisfied with covering costs? Leave the rest to God. The English don't work as hard as the Americans; nor anything like so hard as Ireland's 500,000 "peasant proprietors." You simply can't get the hang of London; and, likely, you are a bit too old to ever get used to it. You know all who work in Dublin hadn't the quiet, steady job you had in Shell-Mex. You got into a bad habit; but of course, that wasn't your fault.—No one would fling himself from a cushy job for the enjoyment of working harder. But that is one reason why you feel the change so much. Most of those in middle-class Ireland are content to sink into mosey fossils, and die dumb.

I wouldn't venture to advise you about the "Book." That is a question concerning your Capital, & one for yourself only. Come now, Seumas, surely the theatres here aren't that bad! Poorer than Ireland's? Well, well, well! It's hard luck on you, right enough; but, at least, it's an experience.

Don't bother, dear lad, about the "T[imes]. Pictorial." I read the I. Times, & will soon have the I. Press; & these are more than enough, if I am to conjure time to do a little work. You aren't that old. Look at me—75 & still have to keep going; and with a wife & 3 children, none of whom yet bring in a penny. But I'm not down-hearted. I haven't read "Lift up your Gates."[1] Does she mean the Gates of Dublin?

Well, Seumas, on the whole, I'd say Dublin is your best mark. I never would have advised you to come to London. I don't think you will ever be comfortable here, bar during a holiday.

All good wishes
Sean

[1] Maura Laverty, *Lift Up Your Gates* (1947), a novel.

To Philip Rooney[1]

TC. O'CASEY

29 APRIL 1955

Dear Philip Rooney,

Thanks for letter. So one Broadcast has to be liquidated.[2] Well, honestly, I shouldnt mourn a lot if all of them were. I did them very reluctantly from the start, for, first I didn't want to provoke cries against letting O'Casey blow out of him over Radio Eireann; second, because it's a hard job for me. I have only one eye, and that is very much subnormal, so that I have to concentrate too much to guard against missing the right line on the MS. It would have been fine had I had enough time to commit the B's to memory. You know, I daresay, that I had to do two of them over again, which was a misery; but gave me a god-sent chance of making a few improvements; so it wasnt all ill. I cant remember which of the "essays" mentioned the *Standard*. I think it was that which ended with the song to the air of "Green Bushes." I'm sorry the song has to go; I rather prided myself on that effort; but it cant be helped. I'm sure R.E. has often a tough time guarding against the listening ears eager to catch anything detrimental to "nationality" or "religion." I have here a "religious" tract sent to me, which has the odd title of "Dead Men Tell No Tales." I, too, hope I may get into touch with R.E. while the broadcasts of the plays are on—particularly RED ROSES; but the reception is often bad, and it is sometimes maddening. The same way with the Third Programme; but the new transmission stations, it is said, will be a great improvement.

I hope Michael O hAodha is getting better. If you can, please give him my earnest wish for recovery.

And give my love to Frank McManus and to pretty Moire Cranwell; To R[obert Ó] Farachan, and, if you arent too proud, take a share of it yourself.

With all good wishes to The Little Dark Rose: may she widen her

---

[1] Philip Rooney (1907–1962), journalist, novelist, radio and TV scriptwriter; Head of Scriptwriting, Radio Eireann.

[2] Radio Eireann's "O'Casey Festival" ran on four successive Sunday nights, from 15 May to 5 June 1955, with performances of four plays by the Radio Eireann Players and the Abbey Theatre Players, each play followed by a recorded talk by O'Casey, except the last one about *Red Roses For Me*, which was "liquidated" because of his references to *The Standard*, the Catholic weekly newspaper in Dublin which had consistently attacked O'Casey and all his plays, especially *Red Roses*. See Gabriel Fallon's "Roses With Thorns," *The Standard*, 28 June 1946; and his "Calling Mr. O'Casey," *The Standard*, 9 August 1946, Vol. II. The schedule of performances for the "O'Casey Festival": *The Shadow of a Gunman*, 15 May, R. E. Players; *Juno and the Paycock*, 22 May, R. E. Players; *The Plough and the Stars*, 29 May, Abbey Theatre Players; *Red Roses For Me*, 5 June, R. E. Players.

roots, strengthen her stem, add to her foliage, and bloom fresh and strong in the coming times.

Yours very sincerely,
Sean O'Casey.

To Plays and Players

MAY 1955

SEAN O'CASEY COMPLAINS

In your valuable theatrical journal for the month of April, Bourke MacWilliam in his review of my play, says, "The priest is no longer a power in the land (Ireland). . . . Joseph Tomelty's play shows that the people are no longer priest-ridden, it is the priest who is people-ridden!"

Is that so? Bourke MacWilliam and Joseph Tomelty must be blind and bothered. They have banished from their minds the recent fiat of the Hierarchy on the "Mother and Child Bill," a fiat that made the Irish Government shiver in its skin, and drove the Irish Minister of Health out of office; they have hidden away the recent affair that took place during the Debates organised by the Students' Debating Society; and they have not read, or if they have, they have murmured "hush," the very recent declaration by the Catholic Bishop of Cork that the Clerics (not the Church, mind you) "were the final arbiters of right and wrong even in political matters. . . . You have a right to provide for your own health and that of your dependents; you have no right if you are a Minister of State or a Deputy to inaugurate a so-called free health service, and make medicine in effect a State monopoly. A socialised health service, therefore, is at once a wrong to the average person and a wrong for the person introducing it." This is the real McCoy.

Keep in step with ME, said this clerical Johnny from Cork, and the Ministers change accordingly. This pronunciation was made on April 12 at the Congress of Christus Rex, in Killarney, the lordly Bishop forgetting that Christus Rex, according to all accounts, went about healing all who came to Him for nix.

Later on, this same Bourke MacWilliam says about the play, "Foor-awn Reiligan is shot by her lover, but manages to write a long 'confession' of suicide before she passes on." The "long" confession consists of nine words. Before this, she speaks 25 words.

In the play, *The Plough and the Stars,* Bessie Burgess is shot, too; before she "passes on," she speaks over a hundred words, plus part of the verse of a hymn.

Now I ask Bourke MacWilliam why is the very long record regarded as short, and the short record regarded as long? Why is the very long transition from life to death in one play not only forgiven but admired; while the short one in the other is condemned?

Why does this reviewer deliberately call a short "confession" of nine words a long one? Not to take up your valuable space, maybe he would let me know why through a personal letter?

Sean O'Casey

40 Trumlands Road, St. Marychurch, Torquay, Devon.

Bourke MacWilliam will reply to Sean O'Casey in the next issue.[1]

[1] See MacWilliam's "Reply to Sean O'Casey," *Plays and Players,* June 1955, reprinted below.

To R. L. De Wilton

TS. DE WILTON

1 MAY 1955

Dear Mr. De Wilton:

Thank you for sending me the Review by V. S. Pritchett which appeared in THE NEW YORKER.[1]

A very clever fellow who understands little about Ireland, less about the Catholic Church (I have bowled over many by asking them what they mean by the term of "The Catholic Church." I find that they don't know anything about it; don't even know what the term means; they associate criticism of Catholic practice with Catholic theory, making them one and indivisible, which, of course, they are not); and, I'm afraid, little about his own country, bar the narrow circle of reviewers among which he goes.

But I've noticed that all was well while I wrote about Ireland; not well at all when England is mentioned. The English are just as touchy about themselves as we Irish are; they hiss at criticism while we shout and bawl, going mad, while they remain cunning.

I like Pritchett's writing, and I often wondered why he never offered

[1] V. S. Pritchett, "Within the Gates," *New Yorker,* 16 April 1955, a long essay-review of *Sunset and Evening Star,* with many references to the previous five books of the autobiography. It is a lively review of mixed censure and praise. Pritchett scolds O'Casey for his voluble contentiousness: "When people disagree with Mr. O'Casey, he starts a band playing outside their meeting." Nevertheless he admires his vitality and eloquence: "What he has got is vitality and the 'fine talk' of the Playboy in him, so that one will always remember a phrase when one forgets the page or even the book itself."

to come to see me. He came, as he says, to see me in the Dublin tene-ment;[2] but never since; never heard a word from him during my long living in London. Once, during an exhibition of British Books in London, the Committee wrote to ask if they could exhibit a copy of JUNO AND THE PAYCOCK. In my reply, refusing, I asked to be remembered very kindly to Mr. Pritchett, who was one of the Committee; and reminded him of his visit to me in Dublin; but never a word came back; never one word. Curious.

Well, it doesn't matter. I have to go on in my own way; but I don't understand why Americans should so wish to get closer, while the English critics and reviewers strive to keep so far away. Well toiling, rejoicing, sorrowing, onward through life I go, whether the Pritchetts turn their faces to, or turn their backs on, O'Casey's Corner.

With all good wishes,
Yours very sincerely,
Sean O'Casey

[2] Pritchett ends his review with the following remarks: "When I went once to see him, over thirty years ago, in the room in the Dublin tenement where he then lived, I found a kind, peering man looking shrewdly from under the peak of his work-man's cap and pointing to a piece of paper pinned over the fireplace. 'To remind me,' he said. It read, 'Get On with the Bloody Play.' He has never stopped haranguing himself and others."

To Brooks Atkinson

MS. ATKINSON

3 MAY 1955

My dear Brooks:

Come in the evenin', come in the mornin'
Come when you're asked, or come without warnin',[1]

Come this week-end, a mhic. It's a long trip—for England's topography—it takes over four hours to get to Torquay. There are good trains and bad trains. You'd have to get the Savoy people to separate the sheep from the goats for you. Eileen is writing to you. She'll book a room for you in a hotel here—it won't be as lavish as the Savoy.

By all means, bring Alan [Dent] along with you. What matter that he was once Secretary to Jimmy [Agate]; he is still a son of man. So was Jimmy, &, if there be a heaven for critics, I hope he's there.

[1] From Joxer Daly's speech in *Juno and the Paycock*, Act III.

I hope the Irish weather may be kind for Oriana. If it is she'll have a great time (or should have) watching the hurried & hustling activity of An Tostal. Radio Eireann are broadcasting four of my plays this month, three of them preceded by a quarter-of-an-hour's chatter and blather and blow from me. A kinda O'Casey Festival: and after all the fiercely-massed denunciations of the "Bishop's Bonfire."

> *Till I see you, my love; as ever.*
> *Sean*

To Mrs. R——

MS. PRIVATE

9 MAY 1955

Dear R——,

Glad the old Abbey still seemed to be alive, all alive O! Wish it was as spiritually alive in its plays as the old building is. Ria [Mooney] probably exaggerates a lot, but the plays she has to produce, are, on the whole, pretty dull things: safe and commonplace. Besides, she had rather a sorrowful love affair—her lover succeeded Yeats as manager of the Theatre; a young & very good poet; married to an exacting wife. He got a sudden stroke, rallied for a day or two; got another, & was found dead: a great loss to the Abbey, & a big trial for Ria. She never married, & lives in the belief that she "will walk with her love again." Don't know why you chose Greystones—it is grey as its name. If you had gone farther, you'd have fared better; the Dargle, or Delgany, or Glen of Imaal; but, anyway, you saw the Glendalough—the Glen of the two lakes, &, I suppose, Kevin's Bed, away out in the middle of the waters; but, maybe, you didn't get a boat to take you there. Ah, yes, Lipton's isnt what it was when I was a kid in Dublin; not the same anywhere now. International, Universal Stores, & the Maypole have done Lipton's in. You should have gone to the "Summit" of Howth—there you would have got one of the finest views in the world; or on the top of the Dublin Mountains, with the city & the Bay away down below, & all around. I'd like to have met the chap who was a friend of Labour—as if the rich didn't serve their own interests. The Lord this & the Lord that still owns most of England's towns, & Ireland's, too. The aldermen of London own Londonderry—that's why it got the prefix of "London." We always call it "Derry": its full name is Derry. Colmcille's Derry. "Derry" means an oaktree; like the Dart, here in Devon.

I'm sending you a photo done by Jane Cown of "The Observer"— for you & A. It's copyright, & mustn't of course, be published anywhere without J.'s consent; & she couldn't give it till the Observer chooses the one they want. All she took are the Observer's till they finally make their selection. I am sending under another cover. I hope you may like it.

All the best to you & A., with my love.
Sean

To Marianne Roney[1]

TS. CAEDMON

11 MAY 1955

Dear Marianne,

Thanks for your letter. Oh, I have been busy, right enough, too much so to be pleasant or exhilarating. The Bonfire was mainly the cause, though, while I remain on my feet, I am busy with things abroad and things at home. The Bonfire caused a stir in Dublin not experienced for the last thirty years. Mrs. O'C. and our daughter, Shivaun, went over, while I remained where I was—too old now to bother much about fuss and fury. The first night was a scene of frenzied excitement, for the theater had been booked out a fortnight before it; so packed that your Ambassador here and Mrs Pandit Nehru couldnt be provided with seats; which wasnt good management, for, had they known, Mrs. O'C. and Shivaun would gladly have given up their places to them. I worried for a week over this example of Dublin's bad management manners. The traffic was held up outside the theater; hundreds couldnt get in, and they spent the time around bonfires in the streets, singing songs. The Dublin critics to a man—bar one only—denounced the play as worthless, mean, feeble, wretched, a thing that should never have been noticed. The play had been booked for three weeks, and a lot thought it wouldnt run two on account of the critics' deep damnation of its taking off, but it ran for five to packed houses, and the last night was like the first one; and during Lent, too, in Catholic Ireland. Then a great Press controversy began, and its echoes are going about yet; some still saying that the play should never have been produced. Now the PLOUGH AND THE STARS is playing to packed houses in the Queen's Theatre, Dublin (the Abbey substitute for the burnt-out Abbey); and it goes to France end of this month for the Paris Theater Festival. Those are the main items of news.

If at all possible, I shall be glad to see you. But there is a difficulty. The period you chose—July—is the "height of the season" here, with all hotels and houses filled with guests, paying ones of course. Our flat isn't

---

[1] Miss Marianne Roney, Caedmon Publishers, New York.

anything like the old "Tingrith," and we cant put anyone up. It may be possible, of course, to find you a room for a night or two in some of the minor hotels or hotel-pubs here; and, if you come to London, and let us know, we can try, and if we succeed, we can tell you to come. Where we are is outside of Torquay, but it gets an immense overflow of visitors. Totnes was ten miles from the sea; here, we are on its border, and so crowded with visitors in the months of June, July and August. From what you say, I gather you are trying to get into touch with business in England. Apropos, this coming Saturday, Mr. Brooks Atkinson and Alan Dent, drama critic of NEWS CHRONICLE, are coming down here to see me; Brooks for friendship's sake; Alan Dent, Brooks says in a letter, to "discuss plans for making records of JUNO AND THE PAYCOCK for Columbia here and Angel Records in America. This will mean a bit of money for you, I'm glad to say." This is the first I've heard of this. An Irish Agency of some English Firm, H.M.V., I think, if I remember right—havent got the letter before me—suggesting this play with others, with an offer of a percentage on records sold; but I declined the suggestion. Now Alan Dent, apparently, is on the move for the same purpose. However, I shant know till he comes and tells me.

The broadcasts for Ireland's Radio have been spoken, 4 of them, but one, which answered a few things said by the critics, has been set aside, for, they say, the controversy having died down, there's little use in bringing it back again. The first is to be broadcast on May 15 at 8 o'c, before the broadcasting of a play of mine, the other two on the Sundays following, 22 and 29, at the same hour. You couldnt possibly hear them in New York, for I find it next to impossible to get Radio Eireann here; so, almost certainly, I wont hear them either, which wont be much of a loss; except a song of mine, which I'd like to hear sung by myself.

Well, that's it, and I hope it doesnt bore you.

My love to Barbara [Cohen], Peter [Bartok], Gordon [Rogoff]—if he's within reach—and to you.

Yours very sincerely,
Sean

To John Beary[1]

MS. BEARY

12 MAY 1955

Dear John,

Thank you so much for sending me "Feasta," and the reference in the "Irish Workers' Voice." I am a subscriber to the "Voice," and a friend of M[ichael]. O'Riardain & his wife. I wish it could become a louder voice, now that the voice of the Labour Unions has been stricken dumb, except to murmur frightened Paternosters—whenever a cleric hoves in sight. Glad that you are trying to earn a living. I do hope you may succeed in earning a good one. I have read the article in the "New Yorker," by Pritchett. No D.D. (Doctor of Drama) degree there for me![2] Oh, is Dame Sitwell writing about the Drama now?[3] What style is Shakespeare's? He has a hundred styles; sometimes different styles in the same play.

What are you trying to earn a living at? (bad English, but it will be plain to an Irishman) I hope it isn't the theater. There isn't much scope in the theater anywhere—least of all in Ireland; and an article in "Irish Times" tells us of the death in Ulster of the infant voice of literature that gave a few squeaks, and then went to heaven.

Don't worry about the "Bonfire." After all, a good many seemed to have warmed their hands at it, and the Irish Critics burned their arses, so that something was attempted & something was done by its flame & its sparks.

Not a bit "cheeky" in writing about it. If you don't start giving your opinions now, in after life—when you are older, or in heaven, you won't have any opinions to give. So leather away with the wattle of opinion while a tongue wags in your head; for it is the one way one learns how to state things; &, later on, one may have very important things to say. So it is important to gain experience, & so know how when the time comes to say real things.

Good fortune to you in your effort to earn a living. Must end now, for we're waiting for Brooks Atkinson's arrival on a visit from New York. He'll arrive any moment now; so au revoyer for present.

Sean

[1] John Beary, 7 Merrion Square, Dublin. He worked as a production assistant to Cyril Cusack and Tyrone Guthrie on *The Bishop's Bonfire.*

[2] See O'Casey's letter to R. L. De Wilton, 1 May 1955, notes 1 and 2.

[3] Edith Sitwell, *A Notebook on Shakespeare* (1948).

To Anthony Harvey

TC. O'CASEY

17 MAY 1955

My dear Anthony,

Ay, I have been busy, and am busier now, today, and expect to be busier still tomorrow. But I snatch a second to say a word to you. Of course, there is but one race—the human race, and we are all brothers and sisters. The Gaels saw this unconsciously, when they allowed a son to call his father a son: A son can say to his father, A Athair, a mhic, meaning, father, me son. But there are, thank God, many varieties of race; varieties among the one people, varieties in the states forming one people; varieties among communities in the State, and varieties among families within the community. I agree it is difficult to accept, dramatically, a negro among the characters of JUNO,[1] but the play is universal, and it needs but time and a closer union with our colored brothers to render the experience a common one. I hope that one day the characters will be all Chinese, Negroes, Indonesians, or any other race interested in the work; and that, indeed, would be Glory for Me.

I sympathise with you about your difficulties with essays and the subject of preaching. I dont quite get the idea that a sermon should be the holding up of the one redemptive act—meaning, I suppose, the last Act of Jesus, laurelled with the Phrase "It Is Finished," or it is consummated. But, if we be Christian, we have this redemptive act held up in a way more forcibly, and canonically, in the Mass of the Roman Catholics, in the Communion Service of the Anglican and Lutheran Churches, than any sermon can hope to do. Besides, as Emerson pointed out, we all preach in what we say, in what we do, and every day is a holy day. The churches tend too much to exalt the cleric by separation, and forget that the laity form every part of the church, for a priest is but a layman with a special duty and responsibility to his brothers and sisters, to wait upon them through the sacraments, and to be supported by them in return for his labours. The anglican priest is still a Clerk in Holy Orders; in the early ages, those who could read and write were few; they were the clerks, and all were VIP's; and a priest was a clerk who had taken Orders, and had the power of the Levite in dealing with the things of the Church. I daresay you have learned all about the differences attached to the memorial of the Redemptive Act— Transubstantiation in the R.C. Church; Consubstantiation in the Lutheran; the Eucharist, or Holy Communion, in the Anglican; and the Last Supper or The Breaking of Bread, in the various Nonconformist and the Quakers respectively. Anthropologists tell us that this rite goes back to very primi-

---

[1] A Negro actor, Clark Morgan, played the role of Bentham in a revival of *Juno and the Paycock,* directed by Frank Silvera, which opened in New York at the Greenwich Mews Theatre on 22 February 1955.

tive times, the Priest-King, the Corn God, etc; assimilating the qualities and virtues of the slain god. Respecting the theory of Redemption, the buying back, the ransom, an interesting Shavian conception is given in the Preface to ANDROCLES AND THE LION, a theory B. Shaw calls "Crosstianity."

As for preaching, which we all do, in pulpit, on platform, by the fireside, if you asked me personally, what I think it should be like, how it should be formed, then I'd say it should connect up with all the activities of man, his work, thoughts, poetry, art, science, and literature; for in my opinion all these things are concerned with God just as much as man; and, if we read aright, the Bible shows it. To be influential, we must be interesting, and to be interesting, we must know something about all these things; not knowing them, however, just to show off, or to convert persons, but because we know them and love them, for they have become an essential part of our life, woven into the web and framework of our being; always natural, and never forced. I fear though that theological preachers will never come to look upon the rose, and call it fair. But, unless you have decided to become pastors of the Episcopal Church, I dont see why you should trouble too much about theological theories. If it is a thing you have to take, then take it as an interesting subject—which theology really is—; but dont try yourself too much with its many unsolved and unsolvable complexity of problems.

Dont worry either if a friend has swallowed T. S. Eliot; many have you know, and Eliot is worth a lot of thought and respect, even from those who dont believe in his solution of the spiritual of the Universe around us; or worry much about whether St. Thomas sought (he didnt, according to T.S.E.) martyrdom for the wrong reason; it would be hard even for a theologian to decide from what the poet has said about the reason: it remains the old story of clash between church and state; between reason and faith—as is happening now even in R. Catholic Argentina. M[urder] in the C[athedral]. is, first and last a lovely play, and let us take it as such, asking no questions.

About the reader—I couldnt give an opinion without personal contact with the problem. Thanks for the picture of you and George by the fireside. That's the best way to learn and live—by interchange of ideas, of argument, of listening for awhile, of talking for awhile, of listening again: we learn little by little. I am ashamed when I stop to think of how much there is still to learn. There's a prolific weed growing in our patch of a garden, and I dont know what it is; neither does the man who comes once a week to trim the place. But, sooner or later, I shall know; know its name, and the family to which it belongs.

Wish I could have been with you in New York, for it is a city I love.

Brooks Atkinson was with us here on Sunday last, and Alan Dent, Drama Critic of the News-Chronicle, joined him and us a few hours later; and we all, me and me wife, with our girl, Shivaun, Brooks, and Alan, had a fine time talking about many things, and telling stories.

Take care of yourself, and go out into the air often as you can. My love to Dr. Simpson, and my earnest sympathy with his Wife. I do hope her mother may get better shortly.

Affectionate regards to George, my love to you, and good wishes to you both.

As ever,
[Sean O'Casey]

To Peter Newmark

MS. NEWMARK

18 MAY 1955

My dear Peter,

I've read your article, and a thoughtful and good one it is. But it is to the bigger ones in the world's Knowledge, whereas I know things only about the beginnings; I see but the light from the day of small things. I send, or try to, my voice sounding out among the Proletariat, & their leaders. Education, to me, has its most important time in the Primary Schools, where the great crowds are; and few there to guide them. But from these, eventually, will come the kind of students you are looking for; & these will have the secular spiritual qualities which will give us a new heaven & a new earth. However, lad, you peg away, & don't lose heart— one student even may grow into a crowd: here a little & there a little, for the time being; what you do in your essay. Some of the seed will fall on good ground.

No Editor now will bother with longhand; & no one can blame them. Handwriting is a terror, most times.

The "Bonfire" ran its 5 weeks to crowded houses, crushing the critics into silence; & ended in a blaze of glory. The Theater it was in closes for some months for alterations. It has an old-fashioned entrance which is to be changed to a wide-spreading foyer, & stage & dressing-rooms are to be changed out of recognition. I shouldn't be surprised if it re-opened with the "Bonfire."

Don't know where the MS of talks are now; but, anyway, not worth reading. I did them very reluctantly; but the first, on Sunday, we heard here, and it didn't sound too bad.

I think, too, the Election will be a dull one. No one seems a bit excited.

I return the magazine with this letter. Brooks Atkinson & Alan Dent, of the "News-Chronicle" were here with us Saturday & Sunday. Had a very pleasant time with them. Niall is still in Germany. All well.

My love to Monica & to you
As ever,
Sean

To Stephen White and Carl Trost[1]

TC. O'CASEY

19 MAY 1955

Stephen White,
Carl Trost.

Dear friends,

I am too old to render service now, but I send a whisper that joins with fervor in the song you sing, the song that all brave men and women must sing; of belief in man and in all that man can do.

I mingle myself with your tribute to the artists, poets, dancers, painters, architects, actors, actresses, composers and them who play all instruments, who have, and who are, given to the name of man a great, great glory.

Says an Elizabethan,

> Man is his own star; and the soul that can   x20.6
> Render an honest and a perfect man,
> Commands all light, all influence, all fate;
> Nothing to him fall early or too late.[2]

We have had too many great minds to enchant us, to urge us on, a great cloud of witnesses, to go cap in hand, or crook a knee to any [Senator Joseph] McCarthy in Europe, Africa, America, or Australia, or in my own little country of Ireland. God damn it, what do these fellows think men and women are? A few mice among men dont make all men mice. There are tens of thousands of George Nidivers in our world today, and

---

[1] Stephen White and Carl Trost, of the American Labor Party, had asked O'Casey for a message to be read at the Cultural Tribute to America's People's Artists, held at the Manhattan Center, New York.

[2] John Fletcher's *The Honest Man's Fortune* (c. 1613), the Epilogue. Nathan Field and Philip Massinger collaborated with Fletcher on this play.

to those in the United States, I send my greeting; those who face front, and fear little; who, though they may fear, still face front; who realise that man has had a great past, and that man will have a greater future.

Yours sincerely,
Sean O'Casey.

To Cyril Cusack

TS. CUSACK

20 MAY 1955

Dear Cyril,

Thanks for your letter which I'm answering from dense clouds of business; a lot of things to think about and do; most of the hours are devoted to the god of Do. I hope the two girls are free from the mumps by now—a nasty illness and very painful.

I dont envy you speaking for two hours about the Irish theatre, or any other theatre, including the land of the Noh. It must have been a test of endurance, and I hope the Germans took a lot of it in; for it [is] largely in this way that Ireland will come before the Nations; the more important Ireland, more so than any representative on the Board of the United Nations; and, I sometimes surmise, that is why the politicians dont care for the artist: while the politician gets into the limelight, the artist is wandering about in the sun. Yes, Germany seems to be interested in me. Indeed, they are to translate the six biographical books into their language. How happy and busy we can be without war.

The Theater of France is away ahead of the English one, with its combines, and its flowers garlanding the box-office. Did you read that the B. Arts Council wouldn't let [Henry] Sherek send over a play by Shaw; wouldn't help, that is, because Shaw was Irish, and criticised the English. I'm beginning to believe that Shakespeare was really born in Cork.

I hope, of course, that THE BONFIRE will eventually come over here; Macmillan's tell me that the book of the plays has been recommended as a book for June; though why they took this, and passed over COCKADOODLE DANDY is nobody's business. I suppose the production has a lot to do with it; and all the publicity that followed; and the tears shed by the Standard Eagle. Poor Seumas Byrne seems to be having a terrible time of it. A great unconscious comedian; but then, all the Irish drama critics, or almost all of them, are comics; black and white ones; none of them good enough to be colored. Graham Greene has, it appears, now become Standard Enemy No. 1. Nothing like keeping these cods busy.

2 queries about the suggested Third Prog. Broadcast of the play [*The Bishop's Bonfire*]: Wouldn't any broadcast hurt a possible London production? Doesn't the Third pay rather badly? If both of these were satisfactory, I shouldn't object.

Brooks Atkinson was here with us last Saturday, and Alan Dent joined us on Sunday. I have agreed to the Recording [of *Juno and the Paycock*] with the Cast listed by Alan—the main parts, anyway.[1] I am expecting a letter from Columbia re the business end, and, if this is good, I'll confirm agreement.

The lady who wanted to see you was a remarkable Englishwoman, with a daughter, Anne. Both intensely interested in Ireland. Mrs. R____ wants to get O'Grady's romantic Irish stories of the past, with a lot more, and says she wants to learn Irish, too! Pity you couldn't see her. Hope the Abbey will do well in Paris. Heard officially of the visit for the first time day before yesterday. All good wishes for recovery of the two little girls. Oh, so glad to hear that Maureen is running around—so long as she takes care of herself.

As ever,
Sean

Shall be glad to see you anytime you have time to come down.

   [1] For details about this recording of *Juno,* see O'Casey's letters to Cusack, 9 June 1955, note 3; 25 May 1956, note 2.

To Dr. Frank Morrell

MS. MORRELL

22 MAY 1955

My dear Frank,

Well, well, I was harsh, was I? I didn't mean to be, for I hold you in affection, & resented you wasting your energy on matters that threatened to become an obsession that would throw aside your possibility of giving new understanding to the Science of neurology. I was shocked to see you didn't seem to realise the tremendous importance of what you had set out to do for Science & for man.[1]

   [1] See O'Casey's letter to Dr. Morrell, 17 January 1955, note 2. When I met Dr. Morrell on 12 November 1970, he told me that in these two letters, 17 January and 22 May 1955, O'Casey had convinced him that he must dedicate himself to the science of neurology instead of the fanaticism of politics: "Sean really saved me then, he helped me get my values straight so that I could excel in neuro-physiology rather

That is the great & maddening weakness of many Communists—they can't or won't see the terrible necessity & divine importance of other things, outside their own unripe imagining & conceit. I am delighted to hear of the success of your Research Work, for this is what you can do best; and it is just as important as any (a lot more) speech, however eloquent, any Harry Pollitt could give. What, in the name of God or man, would Communism be like (if we had it), if the Scientists weren't there to help us in our living; to make life safer, saner, healthier, and more adapted to the problems we have to face & solve? All who contribute to life, in whatsoever way, are Communists; & not only those who so often pester a soul with theses they themselves hardly understand; thinking themselves local Lenins, whereas they are but human tom-tits that aren't able to twitter properly.

The play "The Bishop's Bonfire" went on in Dublin; it was to run for 3 weeks; the Irish critics—bar one—shouted it down to a man as feeble, stupid, unworthy of a dramatist, boring, & in every detail, & as a whole, a poor downright bad play. It started a tremendous controversy; ran to packed houses for 5 weeks, & is still discussed & argued on in Ireland & here in England, too. Eileen & Shivaun went over, & had an exciting time of it. I have done 4 talks which Radio Eireann will broadcast, & then will come more talk & more rows. Dublin hadn't experienced anything like the "Bonfire" since the "Plough," 30 years ago. The winter is with us still—hail, snow, frost, & bitther winds, so I still wear a muffler.

Now take care of yourself, & go quiet.

All good wishes & affectionate regards to you.

As ever,
Sean

We live in a flat now 2 miles from Torquay. Very pleasant, but the sea-winds are strong.

---

than flounder in political idealism. It was those letters, and it was the sword of Sean's spirit that did it."

To Eugene Weintraub[1]

MS. WEINTRAUB

22 MAY 1955

Dear Mr. Weintraub:

Thank you very much for your kind letter. I'm glad you found something in my work.

Believe me, G. B. Shaw was a most generous man. No one, or few, know the many generous things this great & good man did. For instance, in a school a poor earnest man started—our elder son went there 'till we left for Devon—, Shaw handed out 1000 pounds—at so much percent, knowing he'd never get interest or capital—for he had a kink to make good business contracts. Few know how often the generosity of this good and great man was taken advantage of. Only those who were very intimate know. I could have got as much as I asked from him, but I am a proud lad; & rather do without than get what I needed through favor from anyone. Besides, how could those who sought money from him honestly put in mind or heart that their reverence for his work & greatness was a genuine feeling?

I managed allright; & the few years back haven't been so bad. Prudence kept us free; and now, I hope I may be able to give our younger lad—at present a Lance Bombardier in the Royal Artillery in Germany—& our girl, a better education than I got. Our elder lad is a painter, & hasn't earned anything yet, but, if he turns out to be a good artist, that doesn't matter much. Brooks Atkinson was here with us Saturday and Sunday—a grand man as well as a good critic.

Well, thanks again, & I hope you may like "Sunset & Evening Star" as well as the other books.

Yours sincerely,
Sean O'Casey

Remember, Shaw was as kind as he was great, & that's saying something.

---

[1] Eugene Weintraub, 240 West 55th Street, New York 19, N.Y.

To William Honan[1]

MS. HONAN

25 MAY 1955

Dear Mr. Honan,

Thank you for your kind letter, and for the photographs, which are fine, and look like what I remember seeing in the Abbey Theater 30 golden years ago; and for the singular Poster, delightful & original, reminding me of the tumult that lightened up the gold of the golden time of 30 years ago. Thanks, very much for them all.

I am glad the audiences were so pleased with the production & the play.

The playing of the last act in Clitheroe's flat is a very trivial change; & couldn't alter very much the punch of the play—provided, of course, if the acting was good, as it certainly seems to have been in your performance. You were right to cut the "Woman" out of the 3rd scene—it was a very false note. I hope it has been cut in "Collected Plays," for I intended to do this; & I hope to God I haven't forgotten.[2]

I don't think there was any necessity for a realistic sign of Nora's pregnancy; leaving it to the imagination of the audience. As for using pregnancy as a means of keeping Jack with her, this condition wasn't considered a very serious thing in the tenements; it happens so often. The pride of Jack as Capt. is a feeling that no coming baby could conquer. Besides, I had enough on my hands without bringing on another reason for a hateful shout from Ireland's unco'gude.

Thanks again, and all good wishes to you.

Yours very sincerely,
Sean O'Casey

---

[1] William Honan, University of Virginia, Charlottesville, Virginia. The University Theatre had performed *The Plough and the Stars*.
[2] He forgot. See his letter to John Bell, 30 June 1956, note 2.

To Rex MacGall

TS. MacGall

25 MAY 1955

Dear Rex,

Thanks for your kind letter. Why do you refer to yourself as a "duine gan tabhachtas"?[1] Is there anyone of intelligence—even without any education—without some power, some deep influence? The man with the one talent is terribly important as well as the one with the five. The best of us, in another light, is, relative to life, insignificant; but in the life around us, at home, in the street, each has an important influence, and woe to him or her who does not use it usefully. I hope your Wife is safely back with you once again, for a man is a poor substitute for a good woman. A house is a cold place without a woman, be the sky never so blue, the weather never so balmy.

By God, you have a handful—rather your Wife has a handful—with four sons; it would, of course, be just as much a handful with four girls. And all called after the pagan Fianna! A friend opposite to us, has two sons, Peter and Andrew—a good protestant, and he calls his sons after the apostle brothers. I have three—Breon 25, Niall 20, and Shivaun 15: one in London trying to be a painter, the other in Germany, a lance bombardier in the Royal Artillery, and the girl still at school. I sympathise with you in the struggle to make both ends meet. I have often had this strain myself, and will again, and often, I'm sure. The "middle-class" is feeling the sharp winds of sociological change, and no longer lie in the sun. But dont let any curious and false idea of "snobbery" prevent you from giving your children the best education your means can give; nothing can make up to them for this, if they lose it. It is the salt of life. I dont know about the Gaeilge:[2] looks like a forlorn hope. The people no longer bother about it; and it was [Dr. Douglas] Hyde and the middle-class of the time that neglected the one power that could make it the power of the natural language of the land. I remember writing an article about the problem many years ago, over forty, I think, in Ryan's *The Irish Nation;*[3] and I remember being rebuked for its impudence by Mrs. De V[alera]. then Siobhan Ni Flannigain. They turned from the people; now the people have turned from them: a melancholy business. Of course, the loom of language mingles them all together; and, ours goes back to the Sanscrit. Our word "Or" gold, is a word in S. meaning bright and shining, a word which has directly or indirectly a similar meaning in many languages; and sex words

[1] "person without importance."

[2] The Gaelic language. MacGall's letter of five typed pages to O'Casey was written in Gaelic.

[3] "Sound the Loud Trumpet," *The Peasant and Irish Ireland,* 25 May 1907, by "An Gall Fada" (The Tall Foreigner or Protestant), O'Casey's first pseudonym and first published article; reprinted in *Feathers From the Green Crow* (1962).

must, of course, have had a very early prominence. Your word "bod," is evidently related to the word "bud," from an Indo-European root, "to inflate, to swell up." But Ireland needs badly a good dictionary of the origins of words; indeed, we need a good dictionary of any sort; Dinneen's[4] is very unsatisfactory. I got a copy of *Feasta,* and from what I've read, it seems to be much better than *Inniu.* As for a Certain Party [Gabriel Fallon], holidays or no holidays, he wont come to see me. I hope not, anyway. I'm afraid I'll not be comin' back again. You chaps seem to think one has but to pack but a bag (given the desire), and move from one place to another. Believe me, there is a lot of nonsense talked and thought about "Exiles." They arent so unhappy as some think; and the picture seen by a Certain Party of O'Casey's desire for Ireland gnawing at his vitals, is only pathetically amusing. O'Casey is too busy to mourn. . . .[5]

[4] *Irish-English Dictionary* (1927, revised 1934), compiled and edited by Rev. Patrick S. Dinneen.
[5] Page missing.

From Bourke MacWilliam, Plays and Players

JUNE 1955

REPLY TO SEAN O'CASEY[1]

Last month Sean O'Casey wrote a letter about the criticism of his play, THE BISHOP'S BONFIRE. *The critic, Bourke MacWilliam, replies.*

Alas, the fairy drums still beat beneath Sean O'Casey's window. Like myself, he has been singing *The Song of the Dawn* (or, rather, his own more vividly worded version of it) too long. He remains one of our greatest singers. His song, unfortunately, is no longer in the Top Twenty.

That is what I implied when I wrote—and I hope he will pardon the correction: ". . . Ireland is no longer a deeply spiritual nation. The priest is no longer a power in the land and the O'Casey tirades against him no longer rouse the 'heretics' to rebellion, or the angelic to anger."

It is what I stressed when I explained: "The Ireland of the young O'Casey is dead. In its place stands a new Ireland, an Irish-American Ireland, stamped with the indelible stigmas of Hollywood and the political machinations of Tammany Hall. There is room for sorrow. There is no longer any room for anger: and O'Casey is essentially a man of anger and righteousness."

The most influential priest in Ireland of recent years was Barry Fitz-

[1] See O'Casey's letter to *Plays and Players,* May 1955.

gerald. And that only because he was canonised according to Hollywood rites in *Going My Way*. Sean O'Casey has been an exile too long. A new power and a new people have arisen in the land. The power is represented by Sean O'Casey's own generation: the heroes and idealists—the men who began by doing good and ended by doing well.

The people are represented by the new generation: the film fans and Tin Pan Alley "cats"—the young women who mob crooners and the young men who ape East End Edwardians. Does he suggest that the swirl of the clerical cassock strikes terror into such hearts?

Clerical power in Ireland was born out of necessity in his own generation. The remnants of it that so annoy him today are still political, carried down by contact and conceit from his generation to ours. The young priest of *The Bishop's Bonfire* is closer to the Irish cleric today than is his old canon.

This is not to deny that Sean O'Casey's bishop, his canon or his count exist. It is to deny that they are (or ever have been) anything more than the political and ambitious representatives of personal power. Ibsen found them in a Norwegian seaside resort; Shaw found them in a London mission-house; Arthur Miller found them in a wartime American garden city.

Bishop Bill Mullarkey may make the Kelleys, the Burkes and the Sheas hop and hesitate and hide. But the chances are that they will be found in Bill Mullarkey's uncle's pub in Ballyoonagh, drinking pints and saying what they think, without benefit of clergy or Sean O'Casey.

On the technical issue of Foorawn's fade-out, he would appear to be parrying with the wrong rapier. He is measuring his thrust in folio inches—confusing length with depth. And depth—emotional depth—is surely the test of time in the theatre?

Comparing the poetic passion of the dying Bessie Burgess with the Church Hall charade of Foorawn's farewell is like comparing the climactic keen of *Riders to the Sea* with the barbaric bathos of a Hollywood horse opera in which the perforated protagonist pleads with his weeping Horatio: "Hold my hand, kid. I . . . I'm . . . going . . . places!" (Eyes roll skywards and head sags on chest as camera pans upwards into a patch of clear blue sky and music rises to a crescendo.)

It is true, of course, that Synge's grief-stricken Maurya is as grandly garrulous as Sean O'Casey's own Bessie Burgess. It is true, too, that there are fewer words in the celluloid saga. The difference is that one makes shorter listening and the other takes shorter saying.

Bessie Burgess in *The Plough and the Stars* was (and is) a living and breathing woman of real flesh-and-blood. We watch her grow to greatness and we share that greatness with her. We *expect* her to die with greatness. And we lean forward to listen to her passion and poetry, not only for its own emotional beauty and truth, but because in listening to it we are holding to her.

Does one count words at the death-bed of a friend? Can one measure such moments in terms of time?

Let Sean O'Casey apply that test to his beloved Foorawn—that chilled child in black whom even *The Bishop's Bonfire* couldn't warm. Foorawn died slowly because you cannot kill a corpse. You can only mutilate it. And Foorawn was a corpse before the curtain went up. Watching her culminating contortions was about as soul-searing as watching the two-part samba of a separated worm.

Her voice was a voice from the dead, and her thirty-four farewell words were to Bessie Burgess's one hundred what a U.S. Congressman's marathon is to the urgency of a child's cry for help.

But in graciousness to his greatness let the last word be Sean O'Casey's. In a recent interview with Laurence Thompson of the *News Chronicle* he is quoted as saying: "I am still interested in melodrama. I don't see why there shouldn't be a little bit of melodrama. It's a play, you see, the theatre's make-believe." And, again: "I don't give a damn what a man says, or what he believes, or what he thinks, as long as he writes well." Against such standards there can be no argument. So humbly backing out of the presence of a master—I still more humbly bow.

Bourke MacWilliam

Dublin

To Mrs. R——

MS. PRIVATE

8 JUNE 1955

My dear R——,

The Lord deliver you, woman! Learn Irish, is it? What's come over you? Years & years work, for the Gaelic is a hard one to learn, and differs from all languages known, & a lot unknown. Standish O'Grady's books are out of print years ago; years before I could afford to buy one. I never read one in my life; tho' I've read the tales in other places, & have heard some of them told. The life of Parnell was written by Barry O'Brien in 1910, published by Nelson & Son; but must be long out of print. This is the book I have. St. John Ervine wrote a Life more recently; but I never saw it.[1] Most of my knowledge of, & love for, Parnell was gained from the talk of the people; & a friend, an old friend, a Meath man who fought for him; sold his business thro' bankruptcy because of boycott from clergy &

[1] St. John Ervine, *Parnell* (1925).

laity, in the fight. He could never mention Parnell's name, or hear it spoken, without tears. He bared his teeth whenever a word was said against the Chief. Did you ever read the episode around Parnell in Joyce's "Portrait of An Artist as a Young Man"? Most of the translations of the Legendary Stories were issued by the Irish Texts Society years ago; now unobtainable. They were beyond my reach. I have but two smaller ones: Keating's "Forus Feasa Ar Eirinn"[2] & A. O'Rahilly's poems.[3] Eleanor Hull's books are interesting but untrustworthy, too romantic.[4] She really didn't know much about them. Lady Gregory wrote some, too,—"Gods & Fighting Men" [1904] & "Cuchullain of Muirthemene" [1902]—all out of print. Just now, a book has been published that might interest you. I enclose a review of it; as cold, dull review by the poet, Austin Clarke.[5] Always cold, tho' not cold enough to enjoy a shiver to shake some of the cold away.

Pity the weather was too bad for the top of Howth-Hill. I've seen the dew glitter on the grass, & the dawn rise over the sea there; & I've worked on the Hill when all the Tel. poles were down; the waves lashing halfway up the cliff; over the wall at Howth station, high over the waiting train, & surging into the booking offices; & three feet of snow on every path.

What an extraordinary letter from [Henry] Sherek! I'll keep it—it will give me something to say later on, when I've more time—oh, God, if we had but more time!

This letter had to be hastily written, for I have fifty more to write; write, too, & directions & remarks for a Columbia recording of "Juno"; and amend essays & articles for a book a New York Publisher wants to print. We had Brooks Atkinson & Alan Dent, of *News Chronicle*—he's in charge of the record—here last Saturday & Sunday week. Busy time. The comments & denunciations of O'Casey are still flowing into Irish Papers, with answers defiant from others, and a Journal in Gaelic alone saying I'm a "true patriot," & should be a member of Ireland's Board of Education. Aha!

My love to A. & to you.

As ever,
Sean

Believe "Legends of Ireland" published by Batsford—not sure.

    [2] Geoffrey Keating (1570–1650), *Foras Feasa ar Éirinn*, The History of Ireland, vol. 1 (Irish Texts Society, 1902), edited by David Comyn; vols. 2, 3, 4 (Irish Texts Society, 1908–1914), edited by Rev. Patrick S. Dinneen.
    [3] *The Poems of Aodhagán O'Rahilly* (Irish Texts Society, 1900), edited by Rev. Patrick S. Dinneen.
    [4] Eleanor Hull (1860–1935), Irish scholar and journalist; founder of the Irish Texts Society in 1899; author of *The Cuchulain Saga in Irish Literature* (1898); *Pagan Ireland* (1904); *A Textbook of Irish Literature*, 2 vols. (1906, 1908).
    [5] Austin Clarke, "On Lough Neagh's Banks," *Irish Times*, 14 May 1955, a review of J. J. Campbell's *Legends of Ireland*.

To Cyril Cusack

TS. Cusack

9 June 1955

Dear Cyril,

Thanks for your letter dated 26 Bealt [May]. It was a pity about A SLIPPER FOR THE MOON,[1] but those things often happen in the theater, and Mairin mustn't let it get her down. A prodigious lot must be left to chance with a play, with a theatre, a producer, an audience. Indeed, those who make the theatre, dont often get a bunch of red roses presented to them. When we lose, we must just go at it again.

Quite a lot of persons hate Brooks, but I hope [Henry] Sherek isn't one of them. But the theatre is a notorious place for hatred. Brooks has written a notice about THE DEVIL CAME TO DUBLIN[2] that will prompt P.V.C. to dislike him, too. But Brooks remains a very lovable man. He has said a good many wild things about my work—opinions with which I am in violent disagreement with him; but he still remains a very lovable man. I've read things he said about part of my work that made me exclaim Jaysus! but he still remains a very lovable man; and I've known him now for many years; and, most important of all, he is a fine Critic. I know there is a grain or two of truth in what he said about me, which I dont like, and he has made me more cautious.

I'll think over the idea of THE BONFIRE being broadcast, though thought wouldn't be of use, for damn all I know, one way or the other.

---

[1] Micheál MacLiammoir's *A Slipper For the Moon* opened in Belfast at the Grand Opera House on 16 May 1955. The reviews were unfavorable and it closed after a week.

[2] Brooks Atkinson, "Dublin Talk: Of a Carroll Play and O'Casey in Exile," *New York Times,* 3 June 1955; a review of Paul Vincent Carroll's *The Devil Came From Dublin,* which opened in Dublin at the Olympia Theatre on 2 May 1955, and ran for a month; and an account of Atkinson's visit to O'Casey in Torquay. He dismissed Carroll's play as a "stock-company farce, directed mechanically and acted in a style that matches." About his meeting with O'Casey he wrote in part:

"But nothing in the world interests him as passionately as Ireland. Living about half an hour from Dublin as the plane flies, he reads everything about Ireland he can lay hands on. He talks about Ireland continually—the literature, politics, history, legends and individual people, as though he were still in the midst of them.

"The tone of his voice is more Irish than many Dublin voices; and if the conversation lapses for a moment he still sings Irish songs, with more gusto than elegance. If there was ever an Irishman body and soul, Mr. O'Casey is one. His heart is smack-dab in the middle of Ireland. . . . Wearing a beanie to protect his head from drafts, he looks like a venerable archbishop. He is warm-hearted, gentle, affectionate in manner and humorous."

I'd have to leave it to you; but I cant see the comedy coming over in the broadcast. I have agreed to the recording of JUNO, so you should be working on that soon.[3]

Glad you liked the broadcasts;[4] but had I known they would have aroused such interest, they might have been sharper. I did them very reluctantly, pointing out that I didn't wish it to be imagined I was taking up space and time from younger aspirers. The R.E. Officials assured me that there would be no interference whatever; and that the Younger got a very fair chance. Personal reasons, too, counted: it's a job to have to keep close to the MS with one eye only, and still allow the microphone to hear my bladher. To make matters worse, two of the four when made, were technically wrong—the ribbon wasn't the right one, and so I had to do these over again; one of the four had a technical breach of the rules and had to be dropped—not much loss anyhow. I haven't a copy, but, far as I can remember, it merely said in an O'Casey way things about war and the A. Bomb that were far more effectively said at the Kilkenny Debate by O.S-S. General D.G. and Dr. N.B.[5] In the record I indulged in my propensity to chant a few old war ballads, or bits of them—a vice which I hear is getting on the nerves of a Certain Party. This kitchen poker[6] of the theatre knows little about it if he condemns the singing of songs in a play, for the Elizabethans rarely wrote one without some song or other, and Shakespeare seems to have been always humming a ditty. Never mind the French notices,[7] Tom Curtiss, critic for the "Herald-Tribune" sent them to me, with a letter mentioning that he thought too much of the comedy was under-played. Is the Abbey becoming respectable? Has the kitchen poker raked out the flaming embers? A nice, soft, wee, respectable glow. I heard the Broadcast, and it wasn't good at all. Whoever played "Peter Flynn" lost the part entirely. It seemed to be all confused. The others were much better; and, in spite of the kitchen poker, it was RED ROSES FOR

[3] *Juno and the Paycock,* Angel Records, 3540 B, recorded by Cyril Cusack Productions, June 1955, in Ireland, supervised by Alan Dent; with a "Preamble" spoken by O'Casey, and the following cast: Seamus Kavanagh as "Captain" Boyle, Siobhán McKenna as Juno Boyle, Cyril Cusack as Joxer Daly, Maureen Cusack as Mary Boyle, Leo Leyden as Johnny Boyle, Maire Kean as Maisie Madigan, May Craig as Mrs. Tancred, Milo O'Shea as Jerry Devine, Gerard Fay as Charlie Bentham, Godfrey Quigley as Irregular Mobilizer. Dent decided to eliminate the final scene between Boyle and Joxer, and for O'Casey's first knowledge of this, see his reaction in his letter to Cusack, 25 May 1956.

[4] For details on Radio Eireann's "O'Casey Festival," see O'Casey's letter to Philip Rooney, 29 April 1955, note 1.

[5] On 20 May 1955 in Kilkenny, the Kilkenny Arts Society sponsored a debate on the topic, "In the Atomic Age, Can Small Nations Stand Alone?" in which the participants were Dr. Owen Sheehy-Skeffington, General Dorman O'Gowan, and Dr. Noel Browne.

[6] O'Casey referred to Gabriel Fallon as "a Certain Party" and "the kitchen poker."

[7] The Abbey Theatre Company took part in the second Paris Festival of Dramatic Art, opening at the Sarah Bernhardt Theatre on 18 May 1955 with O'Casey's *The Plough and the Stars* and Dr. Douglas Hyde's *An Posaidh* (The Marriage).

ME that came over the best—songs and all. It was very well acted indeed. And, wonderful news—the kitchen poker has fallen in love with "Naturalism," and he has an arm around her waist, for now he is the only boy in the drama world, and she is the only girl. And he scorns away "sentimentality," he does, so he does. But Nathan says "Heroes of the stage must think with their hearts and feel with their minds." Oh, boys! I have a lovely secret in my heart about the Kitchen Poker and G. J. Nathan. Some day, I'll reveal it.

By the way, me lad, I've wandered through Mairin's Home and yours, and know a lot about it now, from the article that was in INNIU;[8] very charming. And doesn't herself look lovely! What a pretty, buoyant face, with a touch of roguishness. But she must take care not to do too much.

Well, me blessing on Máirín agus a Muirin[9] and on the old man, too, for he is one of them as well.

> *As ever,*
> *Sean*
> *Alias Mr. O'Casey*

[8] Eilis, "Maírín Ui Chiosoig is a muirean" (Maureen Wife of Cusack and Family, by Eilis), *Inniu,* 8 April 1955.
[9] Maureen and her family.

To Christopher Murray Grieve[1]
(*Hugh MacDiarmid*)

MS. GRIEVE

11 JUNE 1955

My dear Chris,
Thanks, a chara chroidhe, for Glór na hAlbon.[2] I had it already— I'm a subscriber to the Voice & to Goodsir's Poetry Magazine—& love them both.

Your Hymn to Lenin[3] could only be written by you. I've read more than a few Russian (translations) tributes to Lenin—and Stalin—, & all

[1] Christopher Murray Grieve (1892–1978), the Scottish poet, Communist, and nationalist who wrote under the pseudonym of Hugh MacDiarmid; a good friend of the O'Caseys. *Sunset and Evening Star* (1954) was dedicated "To My dear Friend, Hugh MacDiarmid, Alba's Poet and one of Alba's first men." For MacDiarmid's remembrances of O'Casey, see the poet's autobiography, *The Company I've Kept* (1966). See letters to MacDiarmid in Vol II.
[2] Thanks, dear friend, for the *Voice of Scotland.*
[3] Hugh MacDiarmid, *First Hymn to Lenin and Other Poems* (1931); *Second Hymn to Lenin and Other Poems* (1935).

of them seemed damned poor to me: tributes to Tom, to Dick, or Harry, written in evening papers as death notices, or carved on headstones: no life in them; no death in them even: nothing. Your Hymns are flames that spring from & light up Lenin's ideals, and all he did. Torches on the Proletarian Shore. Well, Chris, a gradh, you are one of our Banners, a silken one, & shining. Dia go deo leat![4]

I do hope you may be able to go to Prague. Would a guinea or two help?

Let me know. The visit would be an honor both ways: to you as our Banner; to them to welcome a grand poet & singer of great songs. My love, my love to Valda, to Michael, & to you.

As ever,
Sean

[4] God be with you always!

To Richard Coulson[1]

TC. O'CASEY

20 JUNE 1955

Dear Richard Coulson,

You present me with a poser! I know little about America, and less about "Catholic" authors. No one can learn creative writing from a College, however great the college may be: that is a gift from God, and comes not from a College. Long ago, when Learning was the prerogative of the clerics, time of Abelard, and for many years after, when all University Dons had to have Holy Orders, here in England and elsewhere, scholarship and a good deal else was confined to the Clerks in Holy Orders. But times have changed; education has widened; there is great competition, and the clerics havent got it their own way, or in any other way, except to pit themselves against others as good as themselves, and, in thousands of instances, a great deal better. Read the Pastorals of the Bishops, and you'll read the last and least things in composition, in thought, and in imagination. Rag tag and bobtail, all of them. Read the dreadful things published by the Catholic Truth Society with you, here, and everywhere else. Read the Roman Catholic Press, blessed by the Pope, and see what passes even for Journalism. Is it any wonder that the Catholic world is rising up against this waste wilderness of commonplace and ignorance and

[1] Richard Coulson, 5212 Castor Avenue, Philadelphia, 24, Pa.

deliberate cult of silly superstitions—Fatima, Lourdes, and here in Ireland, Knock? Have you ever heard of a Cardinal or a Bishop seeking favour of a cure from Lourdes? When Car. Griffin was ill here, he didnt go to L. but ran to the best doctor he could find; and recuperating, he didnt go either, but came down here to Torquay to sit down beside a quiet sea, and breathe in God's good gift of sea breezes so that he could take up life again, and go about his business. Timidity and cowardice are the two vices common in Catholic writing, and these can but destroy any imagination a gifted writer may have. Read REMINISCENCES OF A MAYNOOTH PROFESSOR, by Dr. Walter McDonald, for 40 years Professor of Theology in Maynooth College, especially pages 217–18–19, and learn a little. Here's a quote: "There must be large allowance for the writers—the self-sacrificing men who will take the risks. If you pull a man up, by a public letter of condemnation, for every departure from the tradition,—well, you can have no development and no virile thought. Where would the science of biology be if it had been left to the Catholic schools? . . . Bind our publicists down hard and fast to tradition, and you hand our people over wholesale to the secular Press. Look at the periodicals we have: the AMERICAN CATHOLIC QUARTERLY, for instance—what lead does it give the diocesan journals?" Read what McDonald says about the grip of the clerics on the schools—page 300, when he challenges the claim of these, almost a divine right, over education. ". . . the claim of something like divine right of the clergy to oust not only the State but the children's parents from any share in the management of the State-endowed schools. Is this, I asked myself, the law of God or of the Church? Is it the teaching of the Canonists?" Professor McDonald protested against this clerical attitude of mind regarding education in the schools. Read the Professor about the financial expenditure of the Vatican, page 232. Here he speaks again about Catholic schools in America: "The intermediate schools, or colleges for boys, seemed to be doing well, or if they showed weakness, it was not inherent in themselves, so much as due to the lack of support from the universities. Where the teachers have not themselves been properly taught, how can one hope to make the schools efficient?"

I have no time to write a book, or a thesis about all this; I have a host of things to do, and this is a hurried reply. The teachers in most Catholic schools are a flabby timid lot, and how can such souls give courage to the young? But it isnt Catholicism that makes Catholic writers inferior; it is their own lack of courage and terror of free thought on the things they see, hear, and feel around them.

Card. Newman was a great writer, but he was a brave man. And the greatest writer of this age (to me) was a Catholic—James Joyce; but he broke away from, and laughed at, the tradition. To keep to tradition, Mauriac and Greene have to cling to a certain style and meaning of Catholic writing; and will never stand forth as Proust did, as Joyce did, as Goethe, Tolstoy, and Balzac did.

Read Spellman's book THE FOUNDLING [1951], read his book, war-book—on freedom[2]—my God!

This is certain: there's no Catholic American of intelligence, who, if he gets the chance, will not prefer Yale or Harvard to any R.C. College that claims an equal status.

I know of no training course, college or corner, that can give, or teach, a creative faculty into a soul: God still reserves this grant of a gift as His very own prerogative, thank God.

Well, there you are, unanswered and bewildered; but it is all that I can do within the time allowed me by domestic chores, creative work, and by God.

Yours very sincerely, with all good wishes to whatever you may try to write.

Sean O'Casey.

[2] Francis Cardinal Spellman, *The Road to Victory* (1942).

To Cyril Cusack

TS. CUSACK

20 JUNE 1955

Dear Cyril,

Hope all goes well with you and yours. I daresay you are busy with the recording of JUNO. Alan [Dent] rang me up for a blessing before he left of St. Patrick's and St. Gabriel's isle.

This to say that I got a letter from a Mr. Peter Haddon, Resident Actor-Manager, Wimbledon Theatre, Wimbledon, London, S.W.19., asking me for permission so that his Company might do BISHOP'S BON-FIRE.

I replied saying you had the Licence, and would have it for some time; that you thought you might bring the play to London yourself; and I couldnt give permission; and, however, I would write to you to tell you the request made by him.

If my answer was the right one, there's no need to write to Mr. Haddon. I dont think, myself, that it would be good for the play—if there's any chance of a London show.

Didja see how the Kitchen Poker gilds itself in STUDIES?[1] And goes back on what it so often said before? It's a little self-conscious in

[1] Gabriel Fallon, "The Future of the Irish Theatre," *Studies,* Spring 1955.

such dignified company. It speaks in a mincing manner, quite refined for the time being, as if among superiors. Quite a dandy, a pur Mister.

All the best,
As ever.
Sean

To Tarlach Ó hUid[1]

TS. O hUid

25 June 1955

Dear friend,

Thanks very much for sending me the copies of INNIU with the references to me in them.[2] All very interesting—these and the other articles. It was pleasant to wander through Maureen and Cyril Cusack's home,[3] and get to know it a little; for I look on that family now as close to me, having met Cyril and Maureen here, and finding them what Irish Catholics ought to be.

By the way, there was an article in the IRISH PRESS the other day giving a list of Patron Saints for almost all trades and professions; but devil an Irish name among the lot. All damned foreigners! Even the poets got St. David—a worthy lad, able to sing, and brave in a fight, too. But what about our own Columbkille?[4] He could sing too; was a poet himself, and loved art. Didnt he fight like hell to keep a book illuminated with bright colours, skilled ornament, and fine print? If I thought of a patron saint for Irish art, literature, and poetry, I'd lay a hand on St. Columbkille's head without thinking of going farther and faring no better. We're going down the hill.

I'm sure you never heard a Railway Porter talk as the one did in THE BONFIRE—though I knew one, a Louis Blad of Dublin, who could talk, and knew Shakespeare and Shelley quite well; and who was an eloquent blatherer when he had drink taken. But did you ever hear a British prince talk like Hamlet? Or a spiv talk like Pistol? Or a Cardinal talk like

[1] Tarlach Ó hUid, assistant editor, *Inniu,* Dublin. He wrote to O'Casey in Irish.
[2] Micheál Ó Ciosoig, "Sean O'Casey agus aigne an tSasanaigh," (Sean O'Casey and the Mind of the Englishman), *Inniu,* 18 March 1955.
[3] See O'Casey's letter to Cyril Cusack, 9 June 1955, note 8.
[4] St. Colmcille or Columba (521–597), Ireland's great missionary monk and poet, who fought the bloody battle of Cooldrevny in 561 to save an illuminated gospel book, and later went into exile on the island of Iona, off the west coast of Scotland, where he established a monastery from which he and his monks evangelized Scotland.

Wolsey in Henry the VIII? Indeed, are they able to talk any way at all? Read their Pastorals—Spellman's specially. Card. Newman did know how to speak and write like a Cardinal and a Scholar; but damn few others. But I'd better not raise your ire.

I'd like to get INNIU, so I enclose a check for a guinea which, according to my reckoning, will go near covering a year's sending.

Thanks again for your kindness, and with all good wishes to you and Rex MacGall. By the way, one reference to me is wrong—I am no patriot; I am simply an Irishman.

Yours sincerely,
Sean O'Casey.

To Alan Dent[1]

MS. DENT

28 JUNE 1955

Dear Alan,
Thanks very much for your letter & for the list of the Caste in the Recording.[2] I daresay, you're glad to be quit of the Harp & Shamrock for the quilted cosiness of the Rose & Crown, failing the Target & Thistle. Well, that's over, and, as you don't complain, the venture seems to have gone quietly.

Thanks, too, for the two Everyman volumes; they are fine, & the print is much more suitable to my eyes than that of the vol I had—so small I could read but a line in a day's time. It was good of you to send them.

Your other suggestion about Stage Directions is very valuable indeed. I was worrying about them, not wisting how to go about it. You have mapped it out fine. I had done—typed—the directions for first act, & second act, wistfully hoping they'd do. I may have to type it all out, for the italics in the book are small, & I might have to look so close that the voice would sound like a badly-muffled drum; & it would sound like a mobled king speaking.

I go close by your directions, and I thank you very much for them: a fine relief.

I'm glad you got safe away from the Friars Minor. Their church—if

---

[1] Alan Dent (1905–   ), drama critic of the *News Chronicle*.
[2] Dent supervised the recording of *Juno and the Paycock* for Angel Records. See O'Casey's letter to Cyril Cusack, 9 June 1955, note 3.

I mistake not—is that of Adam & Eve, the place from where Finnegan starts to dream in Finnegans Wake.[3]

We shall be glad to see you anytime you are within hailing distance of St. Marychurch.

The Caste seems a fine one, & the Record should be good.

> *Warm regards to you,*
> *Yours very sincerely,*
> *Sean*

[3] Adam and Eve's, a Franciscan church (Order of Friars Minor) on Merchant's Quay, Dublin. The opening words of *Finnegans Wake*, "riverrun, past Eve and Adams . . . ," refer to the River Liffey flowing past the church.

To Ken Coates[1]

TS. COATES[2]

1 JULY 1955

Dear Ken Coates,

You are a young miner, a Communist, and you want to write. Well, you couldnt want to do a worse thing. It is the most precarious of employments, without any chance of a dole. If you persist, then hold on to your job, and write in your hour of leisure; unless you can get another job that may be more suitable under the circumstances; but till you are sure of an alternative job, stick to the one you have. I couldnt say for certain that I could see you if you came down to Devon. That would all depend on the circumstances of the time; I have a lot to do between work and family affairs, and cant make definite arrangements to meet all who wish to

[1] Ken Coates, a young British miner; now a Tutor in Sociology at Nottingham University.

[2] This letter appears in "Two Letters of Sean O'Casey," *The Socialist Register* (1965), edited by Ralph Miliband and John Saville, pp. 237–40. See also the letter to Coates of 17 July 1955. In his Introductory Note to the letters, Coates wrote: "I originally wrote to O'Casey to ask him his views on socialist realism, because I had been reading his work systematically, and had been led on from it to read Joyce. This had led me to the conclusion that O'Casey himself had nothing to do with socialist realism, and that if socialist realism had anything to do with art, it was purely accidental. His first reply clearly confirmed that he shared these views, so I wrote to him again, asking him why he did not express such opinions publicly, since if he and other great Communist artists like Brecht, Guttuso and Picasso were to speak up, the whole cramping, debilitating nonsense would be completely discredited. His second letter did not directly answer this question; but I read it as implying an answer, that if we 'first removed the beam from our own eye' we should see that the enemy of art in Britain was not Zdanov but the liberal establishment."

come to see me. There has been a lot of "Socialist" blather about "socialist realism," without any who wrote about it having an idea of what it is
or what it meant. What is it, anyhow? Remember that Life comes first,
even before socialism; and that socialism must be adapted to life, not life
to socialism. A writer must write of the life around him; what he sees,
feels, and hears, corresponding with life through his senses; there is no
other way. And the life of England, of Ireland, Scotland, Wales, the Chan-
nel Islands, and the Isle of Man is a complex one, bewildering, lively, dull,
selfish, generous, and so on. And what a complex thing is one human life
alone! All it has to deal with, within himself, without from the life of
others. Zdanov[3]—of whom you have heard, I daresay—didnt know what
he was talking about; and all who echoed him in the "Daily Worker," and
elsewhere, knew a damned sight less. Read Harry Pollitt's writing, his
"diary" while he toured India,[4] his biography,[5] and, however good a lad
he is—and he is clever, sincere, and good-hearted—he hasnt the faintest
idea of how to do it, or anything but the faintest idea about literature in
general. James Joyce would but irritate him; and the same can be said for
90% of the Communists of England. They are shamefully and shamelessly
ignorant of their own greatness in the achievements of the English people. The Soviet Writers are realising all this now. The other week, a prominent Soviet Writer came here to discuss with me a proposal to publish in
the USSR all my biographical books, which, alone, shows the change that
has or is taking place there in literary thought and desire. I wonder how
many "communists" have read Strindberg's DREAM PLAY? Yet in this
play, in a few lines, integral part of the drama, the dramatist, proclaims the
whole gospel of socialism. Again, Keats, who is never mentioned in the
"Worker," lets us know in fourteen lines the implication of all that Marx
and Engels ever wrote.[6]

The worst formalism that I know of is the formalism of the chattering
phrases uttered and muttered by the Communists themselves.

The Communist must be interested in everything, must know something about everything; he must talk to the shepherd about sheep, the
farmer about crops! I listen to the talk about farming problems on the
B.B.C. and Radio Eireann, whenever I get a chance—to the doctor about
surgery and medicine, to the priest about religion, and to the worker
about work. So, instead of going about always teaching, the Communist
should be always going about learning. The Communists I have met, and
I've met many, know too damned much, without knowing anything at all;

---

[3] Andrey A. Zhdanov (1896–1948), secretary of the Central Committee of the
U.S.S.R. since 1934 and in charge of ideological affairs. He introduced the obligatory
school of "Socialist Realism" and directed the ruthless campaign against Western
"Formalism."

[4] Harry Pollitt, *Indian Diary* (1954).

[5] Harry Pollitt, *Serving My Time* (1940), An Apprenticeship to Politics.

[6] See O'Casey's letter to David Krause, 12 April 1955, note 2.

a lot of them are the dullest humans imaginable; and do a tremendous lot of harm to the Communist cause.

And, because of this ignorance, they do the most stupid things. They dont know how to talk about anything outside of a socialist pamphlet. They make me sick.

Robbie Burns was a communist of his day, but he had time and the desire to sing "My love is like a red, red rose."

THE FLYING WASP [1937] has been long out of print. The critics didnt like it, and no wonder. At the moment, oddly enough, I am going over it again, for it is to be published—or so the prospect goes—with other articles of mine, in a volume to be issued by a New York publisher. So one day—if your desires hold out—you may be able to get it after all.

Finally, for I am very busy, dont attempt to write, unless you feel an irresistible and insufferable desire to do so. Fight against the desire; but if it conquers, well, then, go ahead, in the name of God and Man; but hold on to a job till you KNOW that your work will bring in enough to keep you.

All good wishes to the young miner.
Yours very sincerely,
Sean O'Casey.

To John Gassner[1]

MS. GASSNER

3 JULY 1955

My dear John,

Thanks for your letter. It was fine to hear from you again. About your talk with George B[raziller]; I don't know how things may go, for present publishing is complicated. You know, of course, that the Macmillan Companies have separated, & have established rival branches: The Macmillan Co. of N. York, one in London; and the Macmillan's here, one in New York called "St. Martin's Press"; a condition of affairs that embarrass authors who have been so long within unity while the two Companies worked together. G. Braziller, too, has now become a publisher—apart from Book Find Club—and naturally, is anxious to do all he can. He certainly has already published beautiful books on various subjects. Most of my autobiographical vols can't be gotten, & G.B. is eager to

---

[1] John Gassner (1903–67), drama critic, anthologist, teacher; Sterling Professor of Playwriting and Dramatic Literature at Yale University.

republish them, if he can arrange an agreement with The Macmillan Co. I've written to Macmillans about it, & await a reply. Since we wrote about it to each other, I've heard nothing from Macmillans, except an early letter saying they approved in principle of the two-vol. edition,[2] but nothing else since. G.B. also wants to publish "The Flying Wasp" [1937]—a book out of print for years & years—, with articles I've written from here & there, & the stories in "Windfalls" [1934]—still banned in Ireland. I wrote to Macmillans about this in January 1955, but heard nothing from them; so I concentrated on the idea of publication that came to G.B. in June, however, Macmillans wrote saying they were interested; but I had committed myself to G.B. Their letter came too late. I had assumed that they hadn't been interested in the idea. However, there's no reason why—if the series be done by G.B.—the two-vol edition shouldn't appear later. Of course, if The Macmillans did the series, I would probably get more royalties; for if G.B. did them, I'd have to give a big share to Macmillan. On the other hand, G.B. has a fine circle of clients thro' the B. Find Club, & the Seven Arts Club; & the books might sell better; but on the otherest hand, it isn't altogether a question of royalties. If I had always thought only of royalties, I'd have been a far richer man today. I'm trying to think of what may be best for the books. "Red Roses For Me" is to come to New York in the Fall, beginning, I'm told, in Philadelphia. Arnold Perl has written a work, on the style of Scholem Aleichem, of "I Knock at the Door,"[3] & it reads fine to me; simple & moving. Mrs. O'C. thinks it lovely, & our elder boy, Breon, says it is very good indeed; so my own judgement—a hard thing when its one's own work—doesn't stand alone. A. Perl thinks of doing it in the Fall. I've asked the Macmillan Co. to send you a copy of "The Bishop's Bonfire"—please accept it with my love. Columbia-Angel recording Co's are making a long-playing record of "Juno," & I am reciting the directions & description of characters. The "Bonfire" caused a stir in Dublin not felt for 30 years. Critics denounced it; audiences flocked to see it; bonfires were lighted in the streets; traffic was held up; great crowds gathered the first night; & one risked a limb trying to get in. Mrs. Pandit Nehru & the American Ambassador were two of the eminent persons who couldn't get in. This worried me, for the business arrangements lacked courtesy. I do hope you will have a grand vacation, & that

---

[2] Gassner had proposed that he edit a two-volume edition of selections from O'Casey's six-volume autobiography.

[3] Arnold Perl, who had adapted and produced *The World of Sholom Aleichem* in New York on 1 May 1953, had written a dramatization of the first volume of O'Casey's autobiography, *I Knock at the Door*, but it was never performed. Paul Shyre later adapted and presented the first three volumes of the autobiography in a series of successful dramatic readings; see O'Casey's letters to Shyre, 6 May 1956, note 1; and 17 July 1959, note 2. Patrick Funge and David Krause presented dramatizations of three volumes of the autobiography at the Lantern Theatre in Dublin: *Pictures in the Hallway*, 4 August 1965; *Drums Under the Windows*, 21 July 1970; *Inishfallen, Fare Thee Well*, 24 July 1972.

you may write a lot. God, how I wish Ireland had a one one could call a Drama Critic!

Pity, you didn't write the Introduction to the Letters from Shaw to Golding Bright;[4] but it is better not, if one has, or feels one has, nothing to say.

Daniel Macmillan has written me asking for a story (short) to go with a Collection they are to publish—offering a fee of £50; but, like you, I have no story to tell. I have many to tell, but not yet: I don't feel the desire strongly enough; so I shall have to refuse.

It is odd, but often, oh, so often, almost always, when I'm asked to write something, my mind becomes a blank.

It is rather sad about L[ennox] Robinson. It was he who should have taken the place of Yeats; but Yeats preferred F. [R.] O'Higgins, a young poet & a grand lad; but soon he got a stroke & died, leaving E[rnest]. Blythe to take over. Blythe doesn't really know the Theater, &, tho' clever & cute, has no sense of the art at all. There's few in Ireland, if any, who has this sense so finely as Robinson; yet he is idle, just writing old very tepid articles & work of that kind; a very inactive Abbey Theater Director. A great loss to the Theater. He does a bit of adjudicating at Amateur Festivals, & that is all. His History of the Abbey[5] is very dull to my thinking.

The Irish Theater, once so vigorous, stands still.

My affectionate regards to you, John.

Yours very sincerely,
Sean

[4] Bernard Shaw, *Advice To a Young Critic* (1956), edited by E. J. West, a collection of Shaw's letters to Reginald Golding Bright.
[5] Lennox Robinson, *Ireland's Abbey Theatre, A History, 1899–1951* (1951).

To Eric Gorman[1]

TS. GORMAN

9 JULY 1955

Dear Eric,

Thank you very much for your letter telling me of the Royalties due on the performances of the PLOUGH AND THE STARS in Paris.[2]

[1] Eric Gorman (1886–1971), secretary of the Abbey Theatre and an actor in the company.
[2] The Abbey Players performed *The Plough and the Stars,* followed by Douglas

Needless to say, I am very glad that the Company was a fine success there. But I imagine it wasnt quite a fair choice—a play by a younger playwright should, I think, have been chosen to show the Abbey Theater as she is today. For better or worse, you cant stand to attention in Paris with a play more than thirty years of age.

As for the royalties, I am a member of the French Society of Authors, and, doubtless, will receive them in due course through the London League of Dramatists.

By the way, from the broadcast of THE PLOUGH, I thought that your old part in it was very bad; indeed, has altogether ceased to exist in the person of whomsoever played it.[3]

I read the Press notices—they were sent to me by my friend, Tom Curtiss who is the Paris drama critic for the New York HERALD-TRIBUNE; and, by the way, he did not quite agree with the Dublin critic (I forget whom) who said of it that it "was the best ever."

I do hope you may have a great many visitors this Summer. Brooks Atkinson was there, with Oriana, his wife, some little while ago; and I'm waiting to hear from them what they thought of their visit. He was with us here just before he hopped over to Dublin. I see that Father O'Murthuile in the I. Press, in Bearnacha Baoil na Deoraiochta,[4] lays it down that Communism and the Connolly Clubs are mainly responsible for the decline in the Faith among our Irish Emigrants. He's a long, long way off the mark. He makes Communism a far more powerful Movement than it is here. If it were, as he thinks, there would be fifty of them (I wish there were) in parliament. They are at sea in leadership (no Jim Larkin) as Father O'M. is in his leadership of the I. Emigrant. Well, never mind; all the best to you and Mrs Gorman.

As I was before I left you,
Sean.

Hyde's *An Posaidh* (The Marriage), for three nights at the Sarah Bernhardt Theatre, beginning 16 May 1955.

[3] Eric Gorman played the part of Peter Flynn in the original production of *The Plough* at the Abbey, as he did often in revivals thereafter, but he did not play the part in the performance broadcast by the Abbey Players on Radio Eireann, 29 May 1955, during the O'Casey Festival.

[4] An tAth. Seosamh Ó Murthuile, C.I. (Father Joseph Hurley, S.J.), "Bearnacha Baoil na Deoraiochta" (The Hazards of Exile), *Irish Press,* 5 July 1955.

                              To Ken Coates

                                                              TS. COATES[1]

                                                            17 JULY 1955

Dear Ken,

   You are an insistent lad. Sorry, I didnt make my opinion clear in my
last letter. Still, I'm not sure of what you want to know. First, I havent
the faintest idea of what "Socialist Realism" is, and I dont think anyone
else has either. I've read miles of opinions about it, from Zdanov down
to Howard Fast, and cant yet get the swing of it. I dont bother anyway to
make sure, since I know something about the Realism and the Fantasy of
life, which are more important than any theory. Yes, I agree that a lot of
Communists are as dogmatic as any cleric; stupidly so; and I have had
many a dose of boredom from them. But you have this ritualistic formu-
lism or formalism among the liberal leaders of thought and literature here,
just as many as in any other place. For instance, the Drama Critic of the
TIMES LITERARY SUPPLEMENT said not long ago that "the British
People had decided to ignore O'Casey because of his lamentable judgements."[2] There's one for you. And, Indeed, so they have, for it's little I
get from them, three times more from Ireland, and as much from Israel
and Germany; but 95% of what I get comes from the USA. What in hell
have you got to do with Zdanovism? Is England not big enough for You?
The USSR has her own way of walking, thinking, and hoping, and the
Soviet People must evolve from their own environment and activities;
England from Her's, of which you are part. Communism will come, sooner
or later, to all countries, but not necessarily in the same way everywhere.
It hasnt come to the USSR yet; but, I believe, it is on its good way. What
remains for all is to live in peace, and for each to work out its own salvation in its own way; and that is the way things will have to go now, for
force no longer can be used without wiping out everything—Communism
included. Zdanov is dead. Out of date now; and always was. But remember,
the artist everywhere will have a hard task to get a living; good even if he
gets a loaf, a flask of wine, and a girl. I myself have been condemned by

---

   [1] This letter appears in "Two Letters of Sean O'Casey," *The Socialist Register*
(1965), edited by Ralph Miliband and John Saville, pp. 237–40. See also the letter
to Coates of 1 July 1955, note 2.
   [2] "The Paradox of Mr. O'Casey," *TLS*, 21 September 1951, a review of *Collected Plays* (1951), Vols. III, IV: "He uses then the language of the English Bible,
the language of the Dublin streets and the language of the Irish literary tradition to
comic or to tragic ends, compelling his audience to acceptance, now by sheer bewitch-
ment of phrase, now by an onslaught of rhetoric. Yet for all these natural affinities
with the theatrical trends of his day the fact remains that he has been out of fashion
for the best part of two decades. If, seeking to explain the fact, we re-examine the
plays in the light of his autobiography, it is unlikely that we shall deny his genius,
which appears in even his worst plays, but studying the course it has taken we may
well conclude that it has been ridden with lamentably false judgment. It is his judgment, not his genius, that has separated him from the intelligent playgoing public."

most; after JUNO, the Sunday "Worker" in a letter referred me to a Judas; Mike Gold a prominent Left-winger in USA, after WITHIN THE GATES appeared in New York, wrote a whole seething column of abuse;[3] the other day, 20 years after, he wrote another one bubbling with praise.[4] What do I care whether he praises or blames? He doesnt know a damn thing about literature or art. Read what Worsley said about SUNSET AND EVENING STAR.[5] If these lads had the power that Zdanov had, what would happen to us? Let us remove the beam from our own eye before we busy ourselves with the mote in our brother's. The USSR is now beginning to prepare for the translation of my work—after 30 years of friendship. I've never asked them to do it; or have I ever asked anyone to take an interest in me—bar once when more than 40 years ago I sent an effort to G.B.S. for his opinion, and got a reply![6] This I acted on—"depend on yourself, and be published for your own sake"—I suggested he should write a preface! By the way, the finest collection of Picassos is in the USSR, whose collection of Modern Art—got when they hardly had a red rex (a penny)—is second to none. Brecht is, I think, now in Moscow. I had his manager here the other day, who told me his "Ma Courage" is to be done there. The USSR has respect for Hauptman.

If you are going to write, write then, and dont bother about the gibbering Marx-theorists, who can prate like Poll, but dont understand in their minds what their mouths are spouting. This is the one and only way I suggest. You do as I do—if you write, write, and to hell with all opinions as to how you do it.

Are you doing N. Service in the mines? Must end now. The God of Marx, Lenin, and Stalin (three geniuses) be with you.

Sean O'C.

[3] Michael Gold (1893–1967), the left-wing novelist, playwright, and journalist, did not review *Within the Gates*. The play was attacked in a review by Leon Alexander, "Sean O'Casey Tilts a Dull Lance Against Puritanism in Play 'Within the Gates,'" *Daily Worker,* 27 October 1934, New York. This review appeared next to Gold's regular column, "Change the World," which ran in the *Daily Worker* for 32 years, and O'Casey probably made the mistake of associating the attack with Gold.

[4] Michael Gold, "The Flame in O'Casey," *National Guardian,* 9 May 1955.

[5] See O'Casey's letter, "Sean and Mr. Worsley," *New Statesman and Nation,* 6 November 1954, Vol. II; see also his letter to Peter Newmark, 10 November 1954, note 1, Vol. II.

[6] See Bernard Shaw's letter to O'Casey, 3 December 1919, Vol. I.

To Otto Brandstädter

TC. O'CASEY

18 JULY 1955

Dear Otto,

Thanks a hundred for sending me the book illustrated with the lovely pictures of the architectural beauties of Naumburg. It was a good thing that this fine and historic City escaped the bombing madness of the late war. What a blessed miracle that neither side had the atom bomb at the beginning, and that, I hope, and feel sure, that its flame, dastardly flame, rose and died down forever over the unfortunate city of Hiroshima.

Thanks too for the Brochure on the English and American authors. What one takes in through one's senses isnt an "excuse" for what is written; far more importantly it is the Reason why what is written is written; since only by our senses do we live, move, and have our being. What is called "Socialist Realism" is itself becoming a formula, and those who ever and always practise it dwell in a tower, too, though one not made with ivory; but of rougher material, but a seclusive tower just the same. Remember the variety of nature—no single leaf of a tree is identically the same as another; no human faces exactly alike; no finger-print of this man is precisely the same as another's; life is to be served by Communism, not Communism by life. We must interfere little as we can with a brother's vision whose eyes see not in quite the same way as our own; nor should we hate and condemn those who are not, as we may think, so close to the truth as we are. Orwell, to my thinking, was just a bitter raging disappointed man; riddled with disease, and one who, instead of fighting his ailment, wasted his life railing at those healthier than himself; and most of those who laud and adore him are ones who fear to do else, because their pay-packets are dependent on what they say and how they behave. O'Neill was in a very different class. He was a dear friend of mine, a very charming man, hating humbug, cruelty, and hypocrisy, who did not fully understand life—which of us can?—one who was always seeking the truth, and never even thinking of yielding his integrity for anyone or any reward. Look a little deeper into THE ICEMAN COMETH, and see what he says, implicitly, about the informer, who, alone of all the characters, if I remember right, commits suicide. And all written before the McCarthy came to glorify shame and the meanest of crimes—betrayal of a comrade. This theme is elaborated in Ring Lardner, Junr's ECSTASY OF OWEN MUIR [1954].

By the way, Paul List Verlag of Leipzig, has undertaken the translation of my biographical books into the German language; and I understand the USSR is about to commence the same work.

I'll write again about THE BISHOP'S BONFIRE. Great stir in Dublin. I have been, and am, terribly busy, so au revoir for the moment.

My love to you.
O'Casey.

To George Braziller

TC. O'CASEY

19 JULY 1955

Dear George,

I enclose GOING TO THE FAIR,[1] and also some changes in parts of THE FLYING WASP. I enclose a List from that book which shows all that I wish to retain in any publication you do. Mr. G[eorge] Brantl when he was here, told me you had a copy of THE FLYING WASP, so you can see that some of the chapters have been omitted—as shown in the re-arranged List—and a few of them have been amended. As well, there are headings to a few chapters, saying when and why they were written, which I imagine might be helpful if placed at the top of the chapters they indicate.

I have also written anew an article about Shaw written for the English Ministry of Information during the last war.[2] Without my knowledge, the Official Editor of the M. of I. sent it to G.B.S. who amended a short passage on Brahms, and wrote to the Editor saying "It was the finest article he had read about himself, and that it should be sindicated." I wrote to the Editor remarking that G.B.S. must have been joking, but the Editor assured me that Shaw was in dead earnest, and was enthusiastic about it. Reading it, I cant see myself why Shaw should be so enthusiastic, except that it does, I think, give a concise account of Shaw's many gifts as thinker, preacher, and playwright.

I have also an article somewhere called FLUTTER OF FLAGS,[3] another titled POWER OF LAUGHTER[4] (I think), one written for the Magazine part of HERALD-TRIBUNE, called St. Patrick's Day,[5] and one,

---

[1] Sean O'Casey, "Philosophy of Despair: A Modern Sickness," *Saturday Night,* 25 December 1954; now changed to "Come to the Fair."

[2] Rewritten as "A Whisper About Bernard Shaw."

[3] Sean O'Casey, "The Flutter of Flags: A Healthy Pride," *Saturday Night,* 24 July 1954.

[4] Sean O'Casey, "The Power of Laughter: Weapon Against Evil," *Saturday Night,* 3 October 1953.

[5] Sean O'Casey, "St. Patrick's Day in the Morning," *New York Times Magazine,* 15 March 1953.

somewhere, that appeared in the New York Paper-covered book, called THE SEVEN ARTS.[6] I will try to think of anything else I may have done; oh, yes, an article, critical of the Irish critics (a damned good one), which appeared in IRISH WRITING,[7] a monthly founded and subsidised by an Irish Jew [David Marcus], a very clever lad, and a rather fine poet, who against my advice, succeeded in losing a lot of money trying to afford a chance to young Irish writers to show what they could do; which wasnt enough to justify the lad's hope in them.

As for sending stuff to you as I sent them to the Macmillan Co., that isnt possible, for I have never sent anything to them. The Macmillan's here sent the fully printed matter to the American House (they did this even with the latest THE BISHOP'S BONFIRE), and I had nothing to do after doing the proofs for the London Firm. So we shall have to work our own way, and you will have to let me have the proofs to examine and correction, if correction be needed. My love to Marsha and to you.

As ever,
[Sean O'Casey]

[6] Sean O'Casey, "The Arts Among the Multitude," *7 Arts No. 2* (1954), edited by Fernando Puma.
[7] Sean O'Casey, "Tender Tears For Poor O'Casey," *Irish Writing No. 2*, June 1947. See the letters to David Marcus in Vol. II.

To Mrs. Elizabeth Kelly[1]

TS. KELLY

20 JULY 1955

Dear Mrs Kelly,

I am very sorry to hear of your great loss.[2] I knew Frank very well when he was very young, and I was much younger than I am now. I remember him as a lad of fifteen years or so, whose parents were respectable and poor, doing what they could to give him a good education, and fit him for the Civil Service. He was clever and had talent, though I fear the education and political situation of the times kept him from properly developing—as it did most of us. It must be forty-five years since he and I were together in the same branch of the Gaelic League. Years after, I met him in Drumcondra, near where I lived in N.C.R., and we had a brief chat about Samuel Butler for whom he had a great admiration; but

[1] Mrs. Elizabeth Kelly, 20 Oakley Road, Ranelagh, Dublin.
[2] Her husband, Francis J. Kelly, died of TB on 27 January 1955, at the age of 66. See O'Casey's letter to Kelly, 15 August 1954, Vol. II.

he was too busy wheeling a babe in a pram to stay long talking—probably his first. I never met him after, though I read a series of articles of his about the stars in the night-sky and one about flowers which ran in the EVENING HERALD—I think.

It was an added sorrow, indeed, to lose your younger son so unexpectedly. It is a pity, it is a shame when a life goes too soon. Indeed, Frank couldnt himself have been more than sixty—if he were so old.

Accept my sincere sympathy.
Yours sincerely,
Sean O'Casey

To David Krause

MS. KRAUSE

27 JULY 1955

My dear Dave:

I have gotten the tin of Tobacco you were so kind to send me—American tobacco, too, which I like well; but—and listen to this—you mustn't be doing these things; you should husband what you have, for life may become harder before many months have passed; and your wallet isn't richly lined. So be careful, for this American splendor of giving worries me when it comes from those who have little to spare, & whose life is yet before them.

I daresay, you have heard of Dave [Greene] coming along over the sea to Ireland next September, his head and hands full of a big book about J. M. Synge.[1] He wrote the other day to tell me; also, that you are working away on your own book; and that he had given you a lot of advice about revision. Be careful about this; & don't let it stun or stint your style. Davé G. is a very wise lad, with a good deal of experience; but doesn't, & can't, see things as you do; no one else can either. If mistakes can be made—& they can with all of us—it is far better to be responsible for one's own rather than another's.

I'm alone here till the week-end: Eileen & Shivaun have gone to Stratford-on-Avon to see Macbeth; Breon's in London doing a picture; & Niall's still in Germany.

Columbia-Angel have done a long-playing record of Juno, & I'm to read the directions and description. Bob Ginna—he who was here to do the story for LIFE—threatens me with the job of a family film & talkie—chat with him—that—he says—the NBC wants for Television; & I'm busy

---

[1] David H. Greene and Edward M. Stephens, *J. M. Synge* (1959).

gathering articles, etc, to go along with a lot from the "Flying Wasp" into a book to be published by George Braziller—if George finally decides it's worthwhile.

I do hope he may do yours. I've asked Macmillan's to send you a copy of "The Bishop's Bonfire." There are still echoes of the controversy floating round Ireland.

Hopes are rising high for Peace, me son. It will be odd—but grand— if Moscow & Washington embrace each other. What else can they do? Go on, say Good: don't be afraid.

My love to you.
As ever,
Sean

To Miss Joan McAlevey

MS. MCALEVEY

28 JULY 1955

My dear Joan,

Never mind about the prejudice—we all have personal leanings to this or that. "Persons are no more numerous than opinions," says a Gaelic proverb; &, on the whole, it is good so; for it would be a sad, & maybe, a bad world, if each thought as the other. New life, change, bring new thoughts to all: we are constantly adapting ourselves to life; or we become oldfashioned and close to death.

It is the first I heard about Warner's buying my plays. There is no truth in the statement. A long-playing record of "Juno" has been made— I have yet to do the comments on characters, etc—by Columbia-Angel Co. for USA, Canada, & England; & that is all I know of so far, except that there is a good chance of "Red Roses For Me" being done in Broadway this Fall.

I am very glad you have passed your exams, & so will get your Degree next year. That is fine. Our home has been full of an exam these few weeks. Shivaun, our daughter of 15, has been revising & writing, & asking me questions; she thinks she has passed—General Certificate, but won't know for a month. Except for her sake alone, I don't care a damn whether she has or not. I don't measure a mind by the certificates the hand holds.

As for my "favourite play" the one I like best is that which I may be trying to write at the moment. When a work is finished, written twice, typed twice or three times, changed, amended, proofs examined & corrected, it becomes old, and no longer interests me much. Grand news about Peace. I have been in the center of the fight for Peace, & was one of the twelve British Writers—the 12 apostles!—who first signed a declaration for peace a good many years ago[1]—a risky thing then; but from the nettle danger, we pluck the flower safety—or others may: the young who—heaven grant it—may never go to war again.

If you like, Joan, you may regard me as anything you like, provided you remember me as a friend.

My love to all you love, & to you.

> *As ever,*
> *Sean*

[1] See the letter, "World Peace," *Irish Times,* 26 April 1951, Vol. II, signed by O'Casey and eleven other "British" writers. See also the Declaration for Peace, " 'Stop the Drift to War,' Irish Writers Call For Peace," *Irish Democrat,* June 1952, Vol. II, signed by O'Casey and seventeen other Irish writers.

To John Beary

MS. BEARY

29 JULY 1955

Dear John,

Glad to hear from you. It must be an odd change to be on the roads, under the Circus Tent,[1] from a life in Merrion Square, working for the "Bishop's Bonfire." Yet not so great a change when one looks into it, for the Circus is [as much] a part of the Theater as is the Shakespeare Memorial Theatre in Stratford-upon-Avon: a different, but just as much art, kind of theatrical talent. Bread and Circuses! Never shall we be able to do without either.

It is hard work before the lights come on, & the colored costumes are donned; but so indeed is the life of the Theater; we all have to work hard before we can put on a golden sash.

My love & good wishes to you on the roads from Donegal to God knows where.

> *Yours very sincerely,*
> *Sean*

[1] When his work as a production assistant for *The Bishop's Bonfire* ended, Beary took a job as a groom for Fossett's Famous Circus in Ireland.

To Miss Sheila ———[1]

TC. O'CASEY

30 JULY 1955

Dear Sheila,

Under another cover, I send you the book, signed as requested. Where does Lady Winnie get the money to allow so many relatives to idle their time? And the money to let them go in for the priesthood? From the poor mutts—you and I included—who work hard, and hand over part of what we get to the noble ones, privileged by God to possess a big share of the world's goods—so they say; but, of course, God had nothing to do with it. However, their receipts are shrinking, and God may have something to do with that. Why, allanna, do you bother your head so much about sex? Why dont you take it as you take the other necessities of life? It is as natural to man as is hunger, which he satisfies with food.

Your priest who wrote about India[2] must have been a particularly ignorant fellow—as a good many of them are, even though they rise to be bishops. Many and many a Bill Mullarkey among them. It is comical to hear of a Maynooth-taught lad, raw in experience, going out to civilise the Indians! They could teach him something about the grace of civilization, if he had but the humility to hear what they say, see what they do. Just think what we might be like if we had an Irish Nehru associated with an Irish Gandhi. There's nothing "impure" in sex, lass. It's nature's—God's way, if you like—way of getting things done, of renewal, of energy, of change, of advance, of making life grander. Your view is actually heresy. The priest you mention simply didnt understand the implication of the symbols he saw; there is no shame in any part of the human body; nature—God, if you like—made it all. There is as much sex in the Bible as there is in an Indian Temple; and, more, the original Hebrew has been

---

[1] Miss Sheila ——, a young Irish Catholic girl, who had connections with some highly placed Catholic families in England, and maintained a long letter-friendship with O'Casey. See many letters to her in Vol. II, especially her first letter to O'Casey, 9 April 1945. See also his letter to Brooks Atkinson, 17 October 1946, where he describes Sheila as being "too wild to be educated," and mentions her father, an Irish major in the British army who was killed fighting in India. I met her in London in 1963, and after a considerable time she kindly allowed me to make copies of O'Casey's letters to her, only after I agreed to maintain her anonymity. Her preoccupation with sex is probably linked to the fact that her priest had convinced her to take a vow of chastity, although she never became a nun. Eileen O'Casey believes that the character of Foorawn in *The Bishop's Bonfire* is based upon Sheila.

[2] In her letter of 15 July she had written: "A priest out there years ago (now dead? God rest his soul) used to correspond and tell me how difficult it was to convert, or civilize them. Their peculiar beliefs in their Gods. Old Indian temples, their extreme beliefs in indelicate things, impure like sex. Enormous statues, emphasising the sexual organs studded with precious jewels, amethyst, ruby, turquoise. Where women, expectant Mothers would go to pray, and worship the various Gods, bringing exotic flowers and spices, and going into extasies. Ah, well, Please God—all that silly nonsense will be stopped." Sheila was born in India of Irish parents.

softened down to meet the requirements of the respectable, the unco' good, the cods that demean the courageous mind of man. Dont you know that the Cross was originally a sex symbol? These things in Pagan times, instead of being impure, obscene—as we blather about them now—were held much more honorably and sacredly than we hold them now. It isnt we who are fitted to teach—as per account of your priest—but unwilling to learn what we ought to know. So dont bother, or try not to bother, your head about sex so much. Oh, the self-righteousness and foolish pride of these christians!

Well, that's enough for one day, agradh [my dear]. I am terribly busy, and have more work than I can do; but a lot of it must be done. I hope you have had, or are having a nice time in Wiltshire. That you have had no ill effects from your bicycle accident, and that you keep in good health and good spirits. And, remember, the poor heathen isnt quite so forlorn as you and the clerics seem to think. All good wishes to you, and take care of yourself.

As ever,
[*Sean*]

To Cyril Cusack

MS. CUSACK

1 AUGUST 1955

Dear Cyril,
Received this morning the enclosed letter from Peter Haddon of the Wimbledon Theater. You may remember I wrote to you before, making a request for "Bonfire." I wrote to him, saying I'd write to you; but added that there was small chance of him getting permission from you. Now, he's written again; &, as I got no reply from you before, I imagine it might be good if you wrote a formal note (to me or to him), saying something like that you intended, or hoped, to bring the play to London, & so couldn't give your consent. We might be glad of Peter some future time.

I envy you (not uncharitably, though) carrying Epstein's Bronze head of Shaw home under your arm. Your Household is a lovely one, but this will add to its dignity. And, when Maureen's—& yours—young ones grow up, it will be a lovely introduction to the great Irishman. There should be a bronze or a marble one in Synge St;[1] or in Dublin somewhere.

What a pity Siobhan [McKenna] isn't to do St. Joan in New York;

---

[1] Bernard Shaw was born at 3 Upper Synge Street, Dublin, in 1856.

but, I daresay, it is but a postponement. I hope you liked the result of the Recording of "Juno."

My love to Maureen, to the little ones, & to you.

As before,
Sean

Damnably busy.

To Helen Kiok[1]

PC. *O'Casey Review*[2]

3 AUGUST 1955

Dear Helen Kiok,

Well, dear lass, thanks for your kind letter, and for the banner of praise you wave over my head. I only hope my work may be really worth half of it.

Sorry you didn't like poor *Juno.* Forgive her for nagging. She had a hard time of it, &, needing help, she got none. It is very hard to be brave (as she was) in the stress of poverty. Lord, after a day's work, to come home & start on regulating & replenishing the home. I know what this is like, having worked for years after my mother's death, then, having come home, had to set about cleaning up, lighting a fire, cooking the meal, before I could say my work was done. To give a lasting sunny disposition in poverty is not possible; the whole damned, rotten system must go, before the good word always comes to the tongue, & the smile shines forth from the eye. The play doesn't "end on a note of despair." Read Juno's last fine words to Mary as she & her daughter go forth to begin again. As for the other two—Joxer and Capt.—they are past praying for. "Ephraim is joined to idols: leave idols alone."[3]

Thanks again for your good wishes to myself & family. I reciprocate them earnestly.

Yours very sincerely,
Sean O'Casey

[1] Mrs. Helen Kiok, 82–48 229th Street, Queens Village, 27, New York.
[2] This letter was printed in the *Sean O'Casey Review,* Fall 1976.
[3] "Ephraim is joined to idols: let him alone." *Hosea,* 4:17.

To A. J. Leventhal[1]

TS. LEVENTHAL

4 AUGUST 1955

Dear Mr. Leventhal,

Macmillan's have sent me a cutting from the DUBLIN MAGAZINE of your "Dramatic Commentary,"[2] which came as a surprise, for I had thought the Magazine to be out of existence long, long ago. I have never seen it mentioned in any Irish paper, nor has any Irish visitor mentioned it to me. Are you one of the surviving "Dark Brothers," so often mentioned long ago in the old "Leader"? I thought it had gone as so many went before—The Bell, Envoy, Irish, Irish Statesman, Banba, The Gael, and, I daresay, others I have forgotten. I'm afraid, my lad, that the criticism of "The Bishop's Bonfire" was a concentrated attack, not on the play, but on the playwright. It stuck out two miles. And it was the only safe thing they could do; they darent take up the implications of the play. They were doing a term of torment in a critics' Patrick's Purgatory. Most amusing is the fact that the Old Codger goes on talking—in the "Irish Press's" column of references to agriculture, in Brother Gerard's wailing over the sponsored students sent to Galway to polish their Irish; the way they go to dances, streeling home at twelve, and after twelve, even—a dangerous deviation from the party line of purity; and the Bishop of Kilmore's outcry that his diocese is becoming a desolation with the departure of lads and lasses, and the consolidation of the place by men and women of forty-five, fifty, and even sixty, all on the way to death, but none of them on the way to the altar. Caoineadh of Cille Cais[3] is loud in the land: no trees; no childer. By the way, who in THE IRISH TIMES wrote the criticism of "Blood's Thicker than Water"?[4] Is he afraid to show us his name? Not even an initial. Listen to this sentence: "The more preposterous the happenings of the play may be, the more essential it is to deck them with the trappings of real life"! Oh, Jasus, help us! I hear the Dublin drums are muffled on account of the departure of one of the critics into a better job, and a different one: the laddo who cant abide the smell of turf; the one with the pouncet box beside the pen.

I dont know how often the DUBLIN MAGAZINE comes out in a year, whether weekly or monthly, or its price; but a quid should get me a

[1] Dr. A. J. Leventhal (1896–1979), Trinity College, Dublin; drama critic of the *Dublin Magazine;* author and friend of Samuel Beckett.

[2] A. J. Leventhal, "Dramatic Commentary," *Dublin Magazine,* April–June 1955, a favorable review of *The Bishop's Bonfire.* Founded in 1923 by Seumas O'Sullivan, the *Dublin Magazine* ceased publication with the issue of April–June 1958.

[3] The Keen of Kilcash. See O'Casey's letter to Cyril Cusack, 19 February 1955, note 4.

[4] John McCann's *Blood's Thicker Than Water* opened at the Abbey Theatre on 25 July 1955, and an unsigned review of it appeared the following day in the *Irish Times.*

few copies; so I'd be glad if you sent the enclosed to whomsoever pub-
lishes it with my request that the Magazine be sent for and up to the value
of enclosed check. Thank you. I dont know the address of the Magazine,
nor yours neither, so I send this to Dublin.

With all good wishes,
Yours very sincerely,
Sean O'Casey.

To Gordon W. Pollock[1]

TC. O'CASEY

5 AUGUST 1955

Dear Mr. Pollock,

It is of course very gratifying to me to hear from you that RED
ROSES FOR ME is to show itself off on the American Stage during the
coming Fall and—I hope—throughout the winter, spring, and summer
too; I hope it may be a long time before the Roses fade.

I take the opportunity to venture on a few remarks, which may (or
may not) be useful. First about the character of "Sheila Moorneen": In
the first production of the play a young girl gave a fine performance, but
at times, she put just a little too much harshness into her appeals, or reproaches, to Ayamonn. A little after, there was a broadcast over Radio
Eireann, and there the young lass gave a lovely interpretation of the part;
reproachful, but always gentle and sympathetic; understanding Ayamonn,
but trying to win him over to "commonsense" against her own understanding and his. Of course, it is much easier to give a reading (over the wireless) than it is to stand forth on the open stage, and do it well there, facing
a living audience visible, listening, staring, and throwing their reactions up
on to the stage at the feet of the actor; or, if they dont respond, striking
her or him sharp in the breast. For instance, on pages 170–172, and the
like, Sheila's remarks should always be draped in a pleading and tender
way, so that the reproaches she makes are, for all the sting there may be in
them to Ayamonn, always graceful and loving.

If you should have any questions to ask me, I shall, of course, do my
best to answer them.

Again, may I venture to suggest that the Scene in the Third Act, the
choreography, etc., should be as simple as possible. I have always thought

---

[1] Gordon W. Pollock, theatre producer, 250 West 52nd Street, New York. His
production of *Red Roses For Me* opened in New York on 28 December 1955. For
details of the production see O'Casey's letter to David Krause, 3 January 1956, note 1.

that the Theater should be a combination of all the arts; but each of them modified so as to suit a drama; none fully expressed as painting in a painter's picture; music to go with the play, not to dominate it; dancing suggestive of the ballet—or movement—not the ballet itself; not to strive to make actors expert ballet-dancers, for, as you know, actors have to speak and act as they move about the stage. We Irish can naturally break into a song, sung badly (as I sing) or sung well; the English actor always becomes embarrassed when he is asked to sing, or even to lilt a tune. But you Americans, with your tremendous variety of men and women, should be able to do these things "on your ears"—as we Irish say.

Thanks so much for letting me know of your plans. Naturally I shall look forward to the day when the play begins; and I pray that everything may go much more than well. With all good personal wishes.

Yours very sincerely,
Sean O'Casey.

To Dr. Gilbert Ross[1]

MS. ROSS

11 AUGUST 1955

My dear Gil,

Congratulations, my lad. I am so glad that you have started on "the next phase of your medical career." May it be a long and grand one! Congratulations, too, to your mother & your dad. Now, take things easier, & don't let yourself be anxious, for a doctor is an heir to ills as are we laymen. Take care of yourself, reasonable care, in hospital, & don't needlessly present yourself to any infection. A minute or two spared to Providence often means a week or more of regret saved. Doctors—and I know a lot of them—are apt, at times, to be careless, or casual: They should never be so; but quietly & cunningly on the alert. A doctor has to use his wits to defend himself as well as to defend his patients. Don't mind me acting the part of a Polonius—it is because I have a very great affection for you.

Your friend Herb. Rosen and a friend of his, Michael Seigal, came to see me; & we had tea together. I was alone, for all the family had gone out for the day. We talked of many things; tho' I don't think I was very bright, for I wasn't feeling too fine. At my age, we go up & we go down, & we go up again.

---

[1] Dr. Gilbert Ross, Montefiore Hospital, New York; son of Paul and Nan Ross.

Since I got your last letter, Peace has come from the horizon, & is in the midst of us; & I hope she will dwell forever with us now.

My love to your mother, father, & my love to you.

As ever,
Sean

To Irish Press

13 AUGUST 1955

"RICHES OF THE DEEP BLUE SEA"

Dear Sir,—In an article titled the RICHES OF THE SEA, Mr. P. O'Donnell is of the opinion that however valuable the resources Ireland gets from Agriculture, the Tourist Traffic, or reaforestation (he doesnt mention The Irish Sweep), the riches lying unharvested within Ireland's seas are more valuable than any of the above mentioned producers of income.

He tells us of the Donegal fishermen gathering the herring harvest for merchants who want to supply the Chechoslovaks with 80,000 barrels of the fish. Night after night out went the fishermen, but however hard they might work, however long they might live, they had no chance of fulfilling the demands of the merchants. Why? The writer tells us simply that their boats werent good enough. To make things worse, the weather got bad, and these poor boats couldnt risk a fishing effort only on a few evenings in the week.

The merchants were in a quandary: often they had a great catch of fish, but no market; now they had a fine market, but few fish. If they could get Scottish boats, those would have done fine, for they were seaworthy, and they had radar; but the boats of the Scots werent entitled to fish in Irish coastal waters.

However, the merchants heard of two boats held by a Dublin merchant which could go and come as they listed. So they came, within a week these boats landed as many fish as all the Irish boats put together. Why? Because they were seaworthy, more powerful, and had radar fitted into them. The writer calculates that if the men of the Rosses had boats as good and as clever as the Scots, they would be able within a year to gather in a revenue of half a million pounds.

From what the writer says, it would seem that the Rosses men couldnt venture out in such poor boats if any strong wind blew high waves over the top of the sea; while the boats of the Scots could ride them well and cheerily, while the Scottish fishermen chorused Bonnie Dundee.

If these statements made by Mr. O'Donnell are facts, and it is quite obvious that he is splendidly sincere, then these facts are a shame and a disgrace to any Irish Government. Maybe, it's because they dont want the Czechs to be fed? Enemies, enemies! But it might be advisable to have a Czech Representative in Dublin or the Rosses, for, like herrings as they do (and the Russians, too), their Government would probably be willing to help the Fishermen of the Rosses to build better boats and fit them out with eyes—the Radar.

But it might be, on the other hand, that a death wish is hovering over the land; and so it doesn't matter a damn whether the Fishermen of Donegal have sea-worthy boats or not, and that Radar might be a dangerous way of pampering them with the things of this world.

Well, O'Casey is all for the fishermen of Donegal having good boats, with radar astern or on the bow, even though the fisher folk may earn more money than they would know what to do with. Mr. Norton going to Germany for help, and the fish swarming the Irish seas. It doesn't make anything more than nonsense.

> *Yours sincerely,*
> *Sean O'Casey.*

To Cyril Cusack

MS. CUSACK

15 AUGUST 1955

My dear Cyril,

It's O.K. about Peter Haddon. I don't wish him to do the Bonfire. I told him you had the Licence, & just thought confirmation of this by you would show him I was telling him the truth. I am a little tired of having to refuse requests for production of plays by those unable to give even a tidy show: not only "Bonfire," but "Cockadoodle" "Red Roses," & "Purple Dust," all of which are under bond in the U.S.A. Peter H. has done "Juno," &, I fear, done it badly—a play that has been shown so often, that, one would think, no mistake could be made in production—apart from the acting, which, of course, is a God-gift, & not to be created by any Producer. I should be very glad to wait, & am, if you could lead a company to London some day, while the sun shines, or the frost is out.

I wish I had been with you & Willy, going through Connemara & Donegal; but them days is over for me—the blinds is half-down. By the way, I hear the Codger[1] talking still: Kilmore's Bishop bewailing his vanishing flock; an agricultural expert stressing the fact that Irish grasslands are rarely ploughed, but left to God's care; Donegal's fishing boats unseaworthy, & without radar—see my letter in Saturday's "I. Press"; &, in the same paper the lamentable story of loneliness in Glen Colmcille, Donegal; with a young "Boheroe" trying to keep life going there.[2] Do your Irish critics never see or hear aught other than stage-plays? Do they never look down at life? from their pillars—or pillows? Or even read the articles in *Inniu*? There, a writer said "soon it's not the low marriage-rate we'll be bothering about; but where shall we find the women to marry?" Yes, the wise Old Codger keeps on talking!

I'm very busy going over articles, etc. for a book to be published in New York. How does Siobhan [McKenna] sound in the Record as "Juno"?

Remember me to Maurín; give my love to her Clann; & my best wishes to you. Don't overdo the work: money isn't all—I've just refused an Amer. magazine a 6000 word story or non-fictional article, & $1000.00— tho' God knows, I regret the loss of the dollars; but I didn't like the Magazine. I am still waiting for Godot; & I still believe Tigeann gac maith le cáirde.[3]

As ever
Sean

[1] Cusack played the role of the humorous and philosophical Codger in *The Bishop's Bonfire*.
[2] Conallach, "Gleann Cholm Cille," *Irish Press,* 13 August 1955, an article in Irish on the hard conditions of life in the north at Glen Colmcille, Donegal, and the difficulties encountered by a young priest (Father Boheroe is the young liberal priest in *The Bishop's Bonfire*).
[3] Everything comes to him who waits.

To Seumas Scully

MS. SCULLY

17 AUGUST 1955

Dear Seumas,

I was glad to hear from you again. I mislaid your address—a bank, I think—& so waited till you wrote again.

I am glad, too, you are going back to Dublin—somehow your letters showed you wouldn't ripen well in London so long as you had Dublin in your mind. You hadn't enough interests in London to hold you there.

You should be able to do well after a little time and experience in coach-building, etc. I had, when I was young, a friend who served Hutton's, Summerhill, for 30 years as a clerk & head of estimate depart. That was the trickiest part—measuring time job will take, cost of materials used, and then adding the profit percentage of profit: needs a good quick understanding; but one has to get used to it; & then it comes naturally. I once could tell with a good glance the amount of cement, bricks, etc. & the time a job would take—a small job, of course; not a United Nations building.

Don't bother about the papers, Seumas—I haven't time to look at one: too busy.

I will sign & send the book to your friend, Sean Hurley, with pleasure.

Now keep quiet, & go back quiet; & don't let the boss—or don't let yourself—hunt you to death.

All good wishes to you
As ever.
Sean.

To George Devine[1]

TS. DEVINE

18 AUGUST 1955

Dear Mr. Devine,
    I dont think Oscar [Lewenstein] told Mrs. O'Casey (when he telephoned) explicitly what you wanted to see me about; and I wondered myself till I received your letter. Before you venture down here—it is a long journey, and, maybe will be a hot one, if the sun stays brazen in the heavens; so I'd like to set out my views before you set out on the journey. First, I cant see how I can or could help with the "plans for the Kingsway Theater." That is a problem far beyond me; so I couldnt be any help to you or to him in any way.

If—as it may be—Oscar thinks of putting on some of my plays there, that is a difficulty too. Most of my attention is given to the U.S.A., which gives me 90% of my income. At the moment, I am gathering together material for a book to be published by a New York publisher; there is a chance of a dramatised version of I KNOCK AT THE DOOR being done in New York; my play, RED ROSES FOR ME is planned to open in Philadelphia next October; COCKADOODLE DANDY is under option, so is PURPLE DUST and WITHIN THE GATES; and, as Oscar knows, THE BISHOP'S BONFIRE is held by Mr. Cyril Cusack who hopes to

---

[1] George Devine (1911–1966), English actor and director; artistic director of the English Stage Company at the Royal Court Theatre, 1955–65.

show it in London this year or next. So you see, from the play point of
view, there is no chance of my giving any help to the Kingsway. Besides,
I have had such shocking experiences in England in the matter of "productions" that I am never excited when I get an English proposal. The one
and only Production, worthy of that name (and well worthy, too) was
that given by Ray Massey, under C. B. Cochran's managership, to THE
SILVER TASSIE twenty-five golden years ago.[2] Another difficulty is that
most of our Irish actors are so busily engaged in adding ten pounds to one
in film work that they dont care more than a passing damn for the
Theater; only the third-rate among them pine to be in a play. It is almost
impossible to get a first-class company together; and if this becomes possible, as Cyril Cusack hopes it may be one day soon, then the cost of such
a company makes it imperative upon him to seek a theater where the returns would be satisfactory, a matter outside the power of the Kingsway.

There's how it stands with me roughly. If you still wish to come
down, I shall be delighted to see you. If you do decide to come, let us
know by phone or telegram tomorrow, Friday, so that Mrs. O'C. may get
you a room somewhere, because it is a bit difficult to find accommodation
here during the holiday season.

> *With all good wishes,*
> *Yours very sincerely,*
> *Sean O'Casey.*

[2] *The Silver Tassie* opened in London on 11 October 1929. For details of the
production, see Lady Gregory's letter to O'Casey, 11 October 1929, note 2, Vol. I.

To Cyril Cusack

MS. CUSACK

19 AUGUST 1955

Dear Cyril,

Forgot to say in last letter that there would be no chance of a play,
a new one, that is, by the time the Gaiety re-opens. Thought it well to
mention this for fear you might get thinking things. If my memory serves,
I think I remember you mentioning a play you had from Donagh Mac-
Donagh, when you first wrote to ask me if I had a play I could let you
read. So with one, too, from D[enis]. Johnson, you're well-armed; & I do
hope they may be successful whenever they are put on the stage.

George Devine is coming down here on Sunday to talk about the
plans Oscar Lewenstein has for the Kingsway Theater. I see Siobhan has

joined up with Gladys Cooper and Enid Bagnold.[1] I hope this is a wise move, tho' I doubt it. I see, too, a Gaelic Column in I. Press bewails the poverty of Gaelic plays; one Gael saying if they don't improve, Gaelic drama is doomed. But G. plays are no worse than those in the Béarla.[2] Look back thro' the years, & how many good ones graced the Abbey? Good playwriting, no more than good acting, doesn't come easy.

I hope Maureen & her little flock have managed to settle in somewhere comfortably. It will be a big change for the children.

Seumas Scully wrote & said he had been talking to you. I'm glad he's going back to Dub: he isn't one who could satisfy himself in England. An odd chap; but a very good-natured one.

All the best.
As ever,
Sean

[1] Enid Bagnold's *The Chalk Garden* opened in New York on 26 October 1955, starring Gladys Cooper and Siobhan McKenna.
[2] the English language.

To Elizabeth Gurley Flynn[1]

MS. FLYNN

20 AUGUST 1955

Dear comrade, Irish, and, at least, not ashamed of it. I understand that you reached your 65 Birthday on August the 7th of this year. I—one who is on his way to a 76th Birthday—sending you a sincere greeting, wherever you may be—in jail or out of it. It is, in my opinion, nonsense to think of you as any but a brave and a noble woman, who, like most of the artists & poets and thinkers who gave new resolution to life, stood by the principle that all men are born equal; & so should have equal opportunities to live a full life. It is not this man or that woman who owns the world; but all men & all women who own the right to make the most of what the world can give them, that life, however hard, may have a golden light around it.

Even where you are at the moment, in whatever kind of what is

[1] Elizabeth Gurley Flynn (1890–1964), union leader and Communist, American-born daughter of a Galway man; organizer for the I.W.W. early in the twentieth century; joined the Communist Party in 1937, and served as Chairman of the American Communist Party, 1961–1964. Miss Flynn was in jail when O'Casey wrote to her, for she had been convicted in 1953 under the Smith Act of conspiring to teach and advocate the forcible overthrow of the United States government, and was serving three years in the Women's Federal Reformatory, Alderson, West Virginia.

called a cell, this light steals through, & lingers round the head of the brave & good woman, Elizabeth Gurley Flynn.

My dear greeting to you, an Irish one, & my love, too.

Yours very sincerely,
Sean O'Casey

To Sir Gerald Barry[1]

TC. O'CASEY

26 AUGUST 1955

Dear Sir Gerald,

Thank you very much for asking me to say something about some old book which may happen to be a favourite of mine.

Among the many books I have read, old and new, I have no favourite; ne'er a one; and, even if I had, I shouldnt be the one to write about it, for the quiet skill of criticism eludes me.

The one book that I am continually trying to read, without attempting to understand it, is God's own book—no, not the bible; but God's own book of life, watching the buds bloom and the blooms fade, as I move among those with whom I live and have my being.

All books which gather vitality and colour, life, and form from this book of books are my favourites, and none other—so help me God.

All good wishes to you and your Journal, and I hope many may compete for the sunny chance of hurrying off to Moscow.

Yours sincerely,
Sean O'Casey.

[1] Sir Gerald Barry, *News Chronicle,* London.

To John O'Shaughnessy[1]

TC. O'CASEY

8 SEPTEMBER 1955

John O'Shaughnessy, Esq. Greeting to you.
Concerning RED ROSES:
Got your letter and script safely. Am busy going through it as requested. So far:

I-5   "Will Shakespeare," O.K.
I-8/9 Dont care a lot for the phrase used by Mrs Breydon; suggest the following:
    Good-lookin' girls have to live, an' Sheila's no exception. When she looks behind, or looks before, an' sees Inspector Finglas flyin' his plume of power, in his gay uniform, its pockets lined with coins all ripe for spendin', she forgets the lad who has nothin' to offer but an empty pocket an' a whistlin' song.
I-16   Cut in Sheila's speech O.K.
I-24   Change from "Christ's sake" to "God's sake" O.K.
I-30   Both changes O.K.

II-7   O.K.
II-8   Leave out the "Fairy story." "Paudrig" is the right name—not "Peter."
II-9   The typed insert should, of course, be left in.
II-11 Sheila's line is in the book of the play—"Collected Plays."
II-13 O.K.
II-18 O.K.
II-24 "All the power of the law . . ." etc. Dont quite care for this; much rather it should run, as under:

Sheila
(Vehemently, but appealingly—to the Rector) You talk to him; you are his friend. Get him to stay away, man!

Rector
It's right for me to warn you, Ayamonn, and you, men, that the Authorities are determined to prevent the meeting. You run a grave risk in defying them. All the power of the law will be against you.

Ayamonn
All the law against us, sir, but not the prophets. We are a poor, ragged

1 John O'Shaughnessy (1907–), director and actor; directed the American premiere of *Red Roses For Me* in Houston, Texas, on 25 April 1951; see O'Casey's letter to George Jean Nathan, 26 May 1951, note 2, Vol. II; and he was preparing to direct the New York premiere on 28 December 1955; see O'Casey's letter to David Krause, 3 January 1956, note 1.

army, but we have a few banners flying; and we shall fight to bring the law down to serve the people.

1st Railwayman

We'll fight, right enough. The little we ask of them is a measure of life to us an' our families.

2nd Railwayman

We'll stand up to them. We'll open another little window in a darken'd room.

Rector

I've warned you, Ayamonn . . .

1st Railwayman

(a little impatiently) We've been warned often enough sir; we're sick of warnins; let them who come out to fight us, now, be warned too!

Sheila

(Vehemently and appealingly—to Rector) Warning's not enough; warning's not enough forbid him to go—show him God's against it! etc.

The above covers the first two acts. I am trying to think out the problems of the next two acts, and will forward them on to you as soon as possible. The above changes are sent on at once in case you might be rehearsing the acts. One warning: dont let any exclamation of "be japers" creep into the text. No Irishman ever uses the phrase, now; and I greatly doubt if any Irishman ever did. So, if you decide to use the dialogue you have set down (I do hope you may use mine), knock out the "be japers" at all costs.

I see your point about Ayamonn's entrance in the next act; I agree with what you say about its "casualness," and will try to think out something other than what you suggest, which seems to be vague; and I shall try to insert a few phrases into the third act which, I hope, may make Ayamonn hold a place within the dialogue till he goes out. I have already thought of a piece which gives him emphasis just before he leaves for the meeting.

Thanks so much for your continued interest in the play, which, though the mood that first conceived it is gone from me, seems to read well, and should take up an interesting stand on the stage, with the sets you speak of, and through your production.

SECOND INSTALMENT
Inspector and Rector

III-3/4/5 Suggest the following slight alterations:

Inspector

A great wedding, sir, fittingly ended, too by the organ with THE VOICE THAT BREATH'D O'ER EDEN.

Rector

Oh, yes, quite, though I sometimes wonder, Inspector Finglas, if any thought, even a stray one, comes from our vain pride and glory towards the undistinguished congregations that lounge around these mean and desperate streets.

Inspector

(interrogatively)—These people, sir?

Rector

These and those like them. This strike is a terrible thing, Inspector. I am troubled to think it may come from our poor concern about the needs of these poor people; sad today, desperate tomorrow.

Inspector

Dont bother your head, about them, sir. Leave them to us. We'll not let them get the upper hand. They must be kept in the place where God has put them.

Rector

Our hands, and not God's may have driven them here, Inspector, into an outer darkness. That is what troubles me. The sun shines on the evil and the good, but there is no sun in these streets. And this strike will make things worse; make dark hearts darker.

Inspector

Well, that wont effect us, sir.

Rector

It may. Look up, Inspector: the heavens an earth seem very close together. The Scripture says in the beginning, God created all things very close together; yet sometimes they seem a hell of a way asunder.

Inspector

Dont be bothering, sir. Never fear, we wont let the scum rise to the top!

Rector

Inspector, is there no way of preventing this desperate strike?

Inspector

Dont bother, sir; we'll deal with them, never fear.

Rector

God grant it may not be that such as we gather grapes from thorns and figs from thistles.

Eeada

(whining towards them) On'ny a penny each, th' rosy apples, etc.

III-7/8/9   This is a difficult problem. I dont altogether like the dialogue that goes with Ayamonn and the Men. I agree that the spirit of decision and excitement should be carried on, and the following is what I suggest might be done:

Eeada

(nudging Dympna) That was some time ago, if y'ask me. (A cheer is heard in the distance; it has a defiant and confident sound though its echo only reaches the Bridge.)

Dympna

(drowsily, but lifting her head a little to listen) Wha' was that? A cheer? (Her head droops again) I hate the sound o' cheerin'.

(A Group of workingmen come on to the Bridge. They are excited, and they speak loudly to each other.)

1st Workman

(exultingly) The dockers are with us to a man; and the lorry-drivers, too. They'll all be at our meetin'.

2nd Man

With their bands an' banners.

3rd Man

(timidly) I wonder will they call the soldiers out?

1st Man

(loud and defiant) Let them; we'll stand up to them!

3rd Man

(doubtfully) What? Stand up against infanthry an' th' bang of their bullets?

2nd Man

Ay; or against horse, fut, an' artillery—what does it matther!

3rd Man

If the soldiers are out, the police'll get tougher, knowing the power that's behind them.

2nd Man

If they do aself, what does it matther?

3rd Man

(Irritably—in a half shout) Nothin' seems to matter wth yous two!

1st Man

Didnt you hear what Ayamonn said? Even if theyre against us, the prophets are for us.

3rd Man

(dubiously) What prophets? What prophets!

2nd Man

(shouting) All th' prophets, man!

(the echo of a rousing cheer is heard from the left in the distance)

1st Man

(exultantly) Hear that! Ayamonn rousin' the disthrict west from where we're standin'!

(the echo of another cheer comes from a distance beyond the bridge)

2nd Man

(exultantly) Hear that! Mick rousin' them up in the streets around the upper bridge!

1st Man

(excitedly) Come on lads—we've work to do before the real meetin'
begins!

3rd Man

(anxiously) If the soldiers come out, d'ye think they'll fire on us?

2nd Man

(hurrying out with rest of the men) Let them! All that matthers now is th'
meetin'!

(They hurry out)

In your change, Ayamonn, coming in with the men, seems to have to
hang about too long; so I've brought him in as before with Roory. From
above dialogue, the play joins up to "Brennan has come slowly over the
bridge from the far side," etc; and goes on to the entry of Ayamonn with
Roory—Brennan having sung his song, and is going away. This relieves
Ayamonn, I think, from the embarrassment of too long a time looking over
the bridge.

From Roory's sentence, beginning "Why didnt yous stop him before
he began" I'd recommend cutting "Watchman o' Tara he was" . . . down
to "star-lit Bethlehem." It is too long. The first phrase is enough to give
the cue to Eeada's reply.

But to Ayamonn's mild rebuke to Roory "Let him be, man; he sang
a merry song well, and should have got a fairer greeting." I'd add "Dont
worry us now with little things, and a savage fight before us!"

THIRD INSTALMENT

IV-7

IV-9   It is hard to change the mood and form of this part. However, I
suggest the following:

Following Mrs Breydon's "Stay here, my son, where safety is a green
tree with a kindly growth."

Ayamonn

I go, mother, to fight for the dark places, where there is no green tree and
no kindly growth; where we shall yet plant roses of Sharon and lilies of
the valley. (indicating men and women) I go with them.

Men and Women

(in chorus—above) He goes with us.

Sheila

(to Ayamonn) Stay here where time goes by in sandals soft, where days
fall gently as petals from a flower, where dark hair, growing grey, is never
noticed.

Ayamonn

(to Sheila) Sweetheart, I go, God helping me, to fight for them who know
no peace from poverty; I am of them, with them, and no fear of a threat,
no offer of love, can pluck me out of their hands.

Men and Women

(in chorus—above) He comes with us!

Ayamonn

(turning towards them) I go with you! etc.

IV-8

Ayamonn

(fiercely) Now!

Mrs Breydon

(angrily—to the Inspector) Look at the round world, man, an' all its
wonders, etc . . .

and after the Inspector half shouts

IV-4/9

Inspector

Bear back, my boyo, when you see the horsemen charging!

Ayamonn (to say)

Let the horses snort as you snort now: the people's rebuke will one day
cast your galloping horses into a deep sleep!

Note

III-9 B

To Ayamonn's reply to Roory

Let him be, man; he sang a merry song well, and should have got a fairer
greeting. Dont worry us now with little things, and a savage fight before
us—add "Damn it, man, we have to coax these into life before we can
win them for Ireland!"

Dear Sean [O'Shaughnessy]

Enclosed ends, I think, all that I can do to meet your wishes, in
answer to your sensible suggestions. I do hope they may improve the
aspect of the play in rehearsal and in official production for all our sakes.
I am hopeful that the play may make a fine impression. If there be anything else troubling you, let me know; I shall do all I can to answer any
query. At times I feel as Yeats did, when he exclaimed "Damn these plays

that have to be conceived in fifty ways!"[2] One thing more—do you think the play may be too long?

All good wishes, and thanks again for the trouble you are taking with my work. Yours very sincerely,

[*Sean O'Casey*]

[2] W. B. Yeats, "The Fascination of What's Difficult":

. . . My curse on plays
That have to be set up in fifty ways,
On the day's war with every knave and dolt,
Theatre business, management of men.

To Oriana and Brooks Atkinson

MS. ATKINSON

16 SEPTEMBER 1955

Dear Oriana & Brooks:

It was a relief to hear that you both came safely out of the storm and the flood. I've read about its dread & dire in "Time," and a fellow Irishman, there at the time, wrote vividly of the disaster in "The Irish Times." He crossed, in his car, the last bridge left, on his way to N. York. The place I went thro'—the Lehigh Valley?—in Penn., must have suffered a lot. I went thro' it on my way up to the Penn. Hills; coming back, I got on the train at Maw Chonk to return to N. York. In the car, going, we raced along the side of a very turbulent river—the Delaware?—; &, I daresay, this river joined in the devastation. John Tuerk and Bushar Markell, who were with me in the car, were so occupied with the coming show of "Within The Gates," that they wouldn't pay attention to a single question. On the other hand, I was so occupied with the flashing by me of the U.S.A., that I couldn't give a damn about the play—we were good company, neither paying court to the other's needs! Oh, God! how little I saw of it all! This is one reason why I welcomed "Once Round the Sun"[1] and "Manhattan & Me."[2] Recently, a panel of experts on Radio Eireann were asked about the Statue of Liberty, & the verses carved on it. None of them knew how it came there; one knew the last 4 lines; but none knew who wrote them. I wrote in to tell them all about it, adding they should be ashamed to know so little about a Land with which Ireland had so many links. I crowed out my knowledge; but, at the end of the letter mentioned I shouldn't have known myself but for your Book, "Once Round the Sun";

[1] Brooks Atkinson, *Once Around the Sun* (1951), illustrated by Don Freeman.
[2] Oriana Atkinson, *Manhattan and Me* (1954), illustrated by Al Hirschfeld.

saying, too, if they wished to see another side of N. York, they should read "Manhattan & Me"; ending with a recommendation that they be added to the R. Eireann Library. Atta boy!

You are right about the "B.'s Bonfire." Compared with "Cockadoodle Dandy," it is as a flute is to a tin whistle. Still, I think, I have managed to pipe an interesting air on the whistle. I hope so. Anyhow, it caused a furore of controversy in Ireland; and it is astonishing how many factual truths are in the play dealing with life as it is lived in Ireland today. Too many to be pleasant. Every Irish drama critic—bar two—denounced it; some before it was shown; but the audiences took to it, & it played to houses, packed with Catholics—during Lent! I thought myself that it wouldn't go for more than two weeks.

I've been reading a lot about Thomas Jefferson last few weeks. By God, yous started well with your first men—Washington, Jefferson, even Madison! Tho' Jefferson composed the Declaration, it is fine to think an Irishman printed it. Columbia scratched her head with lightning!

I hope you are both fit and well.

My love, dear Brooks, to you & to dear Oriana.

As ever,
Sean

To Seamus Kavanagh[1]

MS. KAVANAGH

27 SEPTEMBER 1955

Dear Seamus:

I share your sorrow centered by Dublin's Defeat in The All Ireland;[2] and add that it would take a helluva big win in a sweep to give me compensating consolation. Dublin, however, made a grand fight of it, & there is our comfort and hope for the future.

It was fine to read that the Lorcan O'Toole Pipers led the teams in— the Band I was interested in throughout many Dublin years; the time the O'Toole Footballers feared little that ran or jumped or risked a ball within the Four Beautiful Fields of Eireann. I'm glad Wexford won the all Ire.

[1] Seamus Kavanagh (1911–1964), radio and stage actor; Director of Children's Programs at Radio Eireann. He played the role of Dick Carranaun, the Prodigal, in *The Bishop's Bonfire;* see O'Casey's letter to Cyril Cusack, 5 March 1955, note 1. And he played the role of "Captain" Boyle in the Angel Recording of *Juno and the Paycock;* see O'Casey's letter to Cyril Cusack, 9 June 1955, note 3.

[2] Kerry defeated Dublin in the All-Ireland Gaelic Football championship game at Croke Park in Dublin on 24 September 1955.

Final in Hurling. When I was a laddo, I had a great liking for the Wexford Caman.

I'm just gathering up articles, etc, for a book to be published in
America; and within it will be an account of some of the flares from the
Bonfire you helped to light in Dublin.

All good wishes.
Yours very sincerely,
Sean O'Casey

To George Jean Nathan

MS. CORNELL

[? OCTOBER 1955]

My very dear George:
It's fine to hear that you are once more on the old battleground of
the Theater; & from here, I can hear the snort of the warhorse, ready to
charge. Thank you very much for the article from "Esquire":[1] a fine one,
and, naturally, very acceptable to me.

The reference to a production of "Cockadoodle Dandy" puzzles me
a bit. The only one I know of is that which is to be done in Yale.[2] Perhaps, something may come from it. John O'Shaughnessy, however, is to
do this Fall—December, I think—"Red Roses For Me."[3] The actor to do
"Brennan," [E. G.] Marshall, is coming down here this month. The one
thing holding them up is, I understand, the difficulty of getting an actor to
play Ayamonn, the "hero" of the play.

Columbia, here, & the Angel Co., in the USA, have made a recording
of "Juno"; the organiser, Alan Dent, drama critic of the "News-Chronicle," is to come here to supervise—and keep, I hope—me to read out the
descriptions of the scenes, etc. Braziller is to publisher a book holding a
lot of the articles in "The Flying Wasp," the 3 short stories in "Wind
Falls," & various articles I've written on & off, here & there. I hope it may
be worth publication. So I've been pretty busy.

Eileen & Shivaun spent a week in Paris, and had a pleasant encounter
with our friend, Tom Curtiss. I'm getting too old to go places.

---

[1] "From the Journal or George Jean Nathan," *Esquire,* October 1955. Nathan
writes about the impending New York productions of *Purple Dust* and *Cock-a-Doodle
Dandy,* praises the plays for their "satire, humor, poetry, and indignation," and con-
cludes that O'Casey is "not only the best of living Irish playwrights but the most vital
lyric dramatist anywhere writing in the English language."
[2] See O'Casey's letter to Nathan, 15 November 1955, note 1.
[3] See O'Casey's letter to David Krause, 3 January 1956, note 1.

I hope you had a good time in Venezuela, & that it has given you a lift-up for the winter. We have had the best summer for ten years, & I spent a good deal of time loafing about in the river. I know now every blade of grass, every leaf of every tree in St. Marychurch, and we all like the district well, in spite of the fierce winds of the winter blowing on to the sea today, & blowing off it tomorrow.

My love to Julie & to you.
As ever,
Sean

To R. L. De Wilton

TS. DE WILTON

17 OCTOBER 1955

Dear Mr. De Wilton,

I have been very busy for some weeks doing a Television feature, me and the family; with shots of Torquay and St. Marychurch; also doing a preamble or an introduction to a recording of *Juno and the Paycock* for Columbia Recording Co here and Angel Recording Co, U.S.A.; so hadnt time to reply to your recent letter.

I am dubious about the presentation, not liking very much the idea of having my [auto]biographies wrapped up like a prize for a Sunday School.[1] As well, a book of some 900 pages might be a bit cumbersome to handle.

As for the sending overseas, I havent the slightest idea of what a tube or a slide mailing carton may be. Does it mean that the books sent this way are not bound, and will get their covers when they reach where they are to be sold?

It isnt the royalty that bothers me—which I would be willing to accept; but the dread I have that the books may be presented somewhat like they were glittering pieces of literature, instead of what they are—simple and sad and jaunty chronicles of the life of a simple laddo, when he was young, and as he grew old.

Before deciding, I should like to have an opinion or two from you about the comments I have made about your kind and interesting proposal.

Yours sincerely,
Sean O'Casey

---

[1] The proposal by Macmillan of New York to bring out a two-volume edition of the six volumes of the autobiography, eventually published as *Mirror in My House*, 2 vols. (1956).

To Joseph W. Donohue, Jr.[1]

MS. DONOHUE

18 OCTOBER 1955

Dear Joseph Donohue:

Greeting, and may it go well with your Thesis. I've been busy with a recording of "Juno," and a Television feature of family and myself, which prevented me writing to you. "The Bishop's Bonfire" has been published by the Macmillan Company, 60 5th Ave., New York, 11.; came out end of August. You should be able to get it in your College Library. It is in the style of "Cockadoodle Dandy"; but not near so good; good enough, in its own way, all the same: caused a furor in Dublin. Popular success: ran for 6 weeks, instead of expected 3.

"The Robe of Roseen"[2] was written in a pathetic effort to prevent, or modify the Irish Civil War. I sent it to a Republican paper, then being printed, called "The Plain People." Hadn't the penny a week to buy the paper at the time; unemployed; no one acknowledged receipt of it; & it was five or six years later—after I had come to London—that a priest, Father Behan, C.C. in Killorglin, visiting me in London, told me it had been published. "Cathleen Listens In" was a satirical one-acter, showing the silliness & danger of the then divided Ireland—Free State—Republican—Labour—Northern Catholic & Northern Protestant. We are almost a' the same way still. Sinn Fein & I.R.A. & Fianna Fail & Eire Gaedheal; North divided from South. "Crimson in the Tri-Color" was the last play—kept for nearly 2 years—rejected by Abbey, before acceptance of "Shadow of a Gunman." "Nannie's Night Out" was a one-acter about a handsome woman, who, thro' adversity & unfortunate circumstances, took to drinking "Red Biddy"—diluted Methylated spirits; & her adventure during the night of the day she had been released from prison, till the police had taken her away again to jail, after a holiday of a few hours.

Well, my young friend, that's all I can think of telling you now. I do hope it may be a help.

With all good wishes.
Yours sincerely,
Sean O'Casey

[1] Joseph W. Donohue, Jr., P.O. Box 563, The Johns Hopkins University, Charles and 33rd Streets, Baltimore 18, Maryland.
[2] Apparently only a prose version has survived, "The Seamless Coat of Kathleen," *Poblacht Na h-Eireann* (Republic of Ireland), 29 March 1922; reprinted in *Feathers From the Green Crow* (1962).

To Robert Emmett Ginna

MS. GINNA

18 OCTOBER 1955

My dear Bob,

Enclosed is a note for the First Secretary of the Soviet Embassy. But do you think, or are you sure, that Oct. is a good time to go there? The Weather, for instance; may be very cold, &, far as I know, you have no furs. Were I you, I'd ask the Secretary's advice about this; &, anyway, don't go till your cold is completely gone.

A strain & all, as the televising work was, it was a delightful time with you & t'other Bob [Graff]. We were all sorry when the time came for you both to go. Give my love & Eileen's to Bob; & look after yourself. As you should know, Eileen forwarded the expected letter on to you.

Yours affectionately
Sean

To The First Secretary, Soviet Embassy

MS. GINNA

18 OCTOBER 1955

Mr. The First Secretary,
Soviet Embassy, London.

Dear friend,

An old and dear friend of mine, Robert Emmett Ginna, a young American, wants to visit your great country. He is one of the Editors of "The Scientific American," and was for quite a time one of "Life's" editors, too. He superintended the feature-articles about me which appeared in that American weekly. He has just taken part as an old friend chatting to me about various things here for a future Television broadcast of the "O'Casey family" for the National Broadcasting Co. of the USA.

He isn't a Socialist; but he is a charming, broadminded, & cultured young American; a dear friend of mine.

He wishes to get a Visa, and I shall be grateful if you would see him, and give him any help he may need in obtaining one.

All good wishes to you. Please give my love to the Editor of "Ogon-yek." My love to the Soviet Peoples.

Yours very sincerely,
Sean O'Casey

To Mrs. Kay O'Riordan

MS. O'RIORDAN

31 OCTOBER 1955

Dear Kay:

Thank you for your letter—as much of it as I could make out; for my eyes are not now like the eyes of an eagle. Don't know where the melody of "Bless'd be the Day" came from—heard something like it somewhere, & put it to the song that I meant for "The Bonfire"; but decided to put only a snatch of it in in the end. I heard the plays, but not well: Radio Eireann doesn't come down to Devon clearly; nor does even the Eng. 3rd programme. Expect it to be better next year when the B.B.C. puts up a high post on Heasary Tor, somewhere on the moor. Curious that anyone should think the Curate was like a Protestant Minister. Where's the one would speak out like Father Boheroe? Not now anyway since the Viceroy left Phoenix Park. They realise they are alone now, and give a half-hearted, lip service to Irish ideals so that they may continue to get a share of the loaves & fishes. The land has chilled for them, & they keep as close as they can to the little fire that's left—& say nothing. You see, Kay, I know both: I mixed freely with all. Yes, in Clonakilty [Cork], the protestants would be pretty secure—all of them. It is in Dublin where you would find most of the Protestant poor; those who had to damn well work for a living. To the worker, there's no differ between a P. or a C. Two of my pals in the old days were Bob Harvey, Prot. ex-Grenadier Guardsman, & a grand navvy: I've worked with him drunk & sober, & many a tuppence I gave him to get a "curer"; and Paddy Walsh, a Cath. red-bearded, strong as a horse, a permanent-way ganger; grand man & sterling follower of Jim Larkin. A worker's 3 leaved Shamrock: a decided Protestant—Bob Harvey; a decided Catholic—Paddy Walsh; a neither one nor the other—O'Casey; & yet we were three in one. They were both older than I, & dead now—the Lord be good to them. I'm afraid, that by & large, the Gaelic League is a rendezvous for snobs; it is still far away from the common people; as it was fifty or so years ago when I wrote an article about it in the old "Nation & Irish Peasant"[1] then edited by W. P. O'Ryan. God, how comic the Judges look on their way to Votive Mass in their morning-dress & toppers! They have won back "their own again." I couldn't make out the name of your first tune, but got the one "Lonely." The fact is that Ireland is still in the musical middle-ages. It is a god-damn shame you haven't a piano of your own on which to tinkle out a tune; or batter away to sadden or jollify a spare moment. Like you; less like you, rather, I never learned anything bar that Clef meant "Key," & then I was left there. It is maddening to see—as I often did & do— workers & workers' children with talent & talent's longing, light distances away from the means of practicing them. So much potential talent gone to waste. The blasphemy in the idea that a prayer to God should satisfy every need!

I shouldn't think that "Clare's Dragoons" is an Irish air. Good luck to Michael in his effort to bring sense to Ireland in the matter of her relationship with the USSR. It's pathetic to think of Ireland slicing off her nose in an effort to disfigure the smiling countenance of the Soviet Union! All just to pacify the vanity of the clerics. My love to you. I enclose a sub. for "The Worker's Voice." Please give it to Michael, with my love.

As ever,
Sean

[1] "Sound the Loud Trumpet," *The Peasant and Irish Ireland*, 25 May 1907; reprinted in *Feathers From the Green Crow* (1962).

To W. Suschitzky[1]

MS. SUSCHITZSKY

4 NOVEMBER 1955

My dear Su,

It was very kind and thoughtful of you to send us so many beautiful photographs. As Eileen has told you already, it was very hard to choose the ones we liked best: we put them down, we took them up; put them down & took them up, looked at them long, and, finally, with some sighs, chose what we thought we liked the most.

We might as well have shut our eyes & picked some up by random; for all were so lovely, any picked up would be good for keeping.

Yes we have all recovered from the televising: it was really made

[1] W. Suschitzky, 28 Willifield Way, London.

very easy with such a grand crew, the members of which I shall always remember as my friends.

My love to Mrs. Su, to your children, & to you, me son.

And many thanks again.
Yours very sincerely,
Sean.

To Seumas Scully

MS. SCULLY

5 NOVEMBER 1955

My dear Seumas,

I'm glad you are safe in Dublin again. I guessed from the first, you wouldn't find rest in London—the dove has returned to the Ark. Good thing you didn't go to New York. You have a job in front of you now, and it won't be easy; for however honest—& you are that—or intelligent—& you are that, too—, you will have to have practice & experience before you become easily proficient. So don't worry if things don't fit at first. Thanks, a lot, for the cuttings, specially the criticisms of the "Stop the Clock."[1] How quaintly deferential they all are before her ladyship's standing on the stage! The old Irish bowing & scraping to the Gentry. The Yugo-Slav Football affair was a foolish mistake on the part of the Archb.[2] Nothing will ever intimidate football enthusiasts, or the woman from following fashion.

Yes, [Anouilh's] "The Lark" can't hold a candle to Shaw's "St Joan." There are many who wish it could, & hoped it might; but they will wait a long time before a man like Shaw comes to laugh at them again.

I am, as you surmise, very busy. I'm writing a chapter about "The Bonfire" (including the critics trying to douse it)[3] for a book of mine to be published next Spring in New York; & they are in a hurry to get my stuff; but, as I don't do work in a hurry, they will have to wait.

The critics will be delighted when they read it: world revelation for

[1] Lady Christine Longford's *Stop the Clock* opened at the Dublin Gate Theatre on 20 September 1955.

[2] The Most Rev. Dr. John Charles McQuaid, Archbishop of Dublin, made a public statement urging the Irish people not to attend an international soccer match between Ireland and Yugoslavia in Dublin on 19 October 1955, and though Irish officials and politicians were intimidated into staying away from Dalymount Park, 21,400 Irish people turned out to see the match, ignoring the Archbishop's plea to boycott the Communist team. The Yugoslavians won 4-1, but the common feeling was that the Archbishop had lost.

[3] Sean O'Casey, "Bonfire Under a Black Sun," *The Green Crow* (1956).

their views! Remember me to them all, the Ks,[4] the N.C.s,[5] the T.C.M's;[6] what happened to "Thersites"? or is it Nolan, or is it Woods?[7]

However venomous he was, at least he could write, & said some unusual things; tho' I couldn't comprehend his bitter intelligence looking down on Joyce.

By the way, isn't Donat O'Donnell a double-barrelled son of a gun, too? Isn't O'Connor Cruise O'Brien the second tube from which he fires wisdom on behalf of the Cultural Committee of Dept. Ex. Affairs? He's an Attache now, isn't he?[8]

By the way, Seumas, are you wise to grudge a few more pounds to be comfortable? Your health is worth more than a quid or two. Forget about Shell's £14. You really are fortunate.

> *My best wishes to you, a mhic,*
> *As ever*
> *Sean*

[4] Seamus Kelly, drama critic of the *Irish Times*.
[5] Niall Carroll, drama critic of the *Irish Press*.
[6] T. C. Murray, the playwright and book reviewer of the *Irish Independent*.
[7] Thomas Woods's full-time duties as an official in the Department of External Affairs forced him to give up his regular "Thersites" column in the *Irish Times*. See O'Casey's letter to David Krause, 5 January 1955, note 3.
[8] See O'Casey's letter to Peter Newmark, 20 March 1955, note 1.

To George Braziller

TC. O'CASEY

9 NOVEMBER 1955

Dear George,

I'm allright once more. As I told you, I've been busy as a bee with many things. A wee bit tired, that's all. I have just finished a long article on the play, THE BISHOP'S BONFIRE for the book—9000 words or so. I think it good, and I hope I'm right. I just have to go over it once more, settle any mistakes that may be there; and then I'll send it on.

As well, I have already done some of the INTRODUCTION built on the chosen title of THE GREEN CROW. I still dont like the title of SELECTED PROSE. It isnt true, for a start. The Prose is mostly in the Biographical books; and again, I AM NOT AN ESSAYIST. Hazlitt, Lamb, and Emerson were, and fine ones, but not O'Casey—neither an Emerson nor an Addison. Not even a Steele. SELECTED PLAYS is all right, for it is a fact, and a play is a play; and there they are; but to me SELECTED PROSE would sound pompous. Essay writing is a high art, and I have never practised it; and dont know enough about it. I'll still think about the title, however. I'm fond of titles—you'll see how I changed the title on the article about the Bonfire, when you get it.

The Television I did was for NBC of Radio Center, New York;[1] those done before included Bertrand Russell, De Valera, and Nehru; so I'm in the company of the mighty.

I do hope Miller's plays may be a great success.[2] He's a lad with a vision; and a very powerful dramatist: I send him a lay Bishop's blessing.

I will forward the Bonfire chapter on within a week, and the INTRO. a little later on.

Have you ever thought of getting out a volume of Giaradoux's[3] plays—dont know if I've spelled the name right? The French playwright, alas! dead now; he had the newer vision of the theater. No new playwright of any value has appeared yet in Ireland: it is lamentable.

My love to Marsha and to you.

As ever,

[Sean]

[1] "A Conversation with Sean O'Casey and Robert Emmett Ginna," presented on 22 January 1956 on NBC-TV in its Wisdom Series, "interviews with elder wise men." The program was filmed at the O'Casey home in St. Marychurch, produced and directed by Robert D. Graff, photography by W. Suschitzky. Ginna conducted the interview with O'Casey and his family. In a review of the program in the *New York Times,* 23 January 1956, Jack Gould wrote in part: "Mr. O'Casey was an absorbing and warm figure on the home screen. He wore a turtle-neck sweater and covered his head with his favorite beanie. Strands of white hair fell over his ears, sparkling eyes peered through tin-rimmed glasses and his lean, esthetic face became absorbingly animated as he spoke. Not many moments had to lapse before it was clear why his study is famed as a haven for invigorating talk. . . . Some elder wise men may enjoy veneration, but Mr. O'Casey obviously still has relish for the fray. The N.B.C. film suffered a little from an apparent assumption that the playwright already had retired to a pedestal. That is hardly the place to find an Irishman with a beanie."

[2] Arthur Miller's *A View From the Bridge* and *A Memory of Two Mondays* opened in New York on 29 September 1955.

[3] Jean Giraudoux (1882–1944).

To Barrows Dunham

MS. DUNHAM

11 NOVEMBER 1955

My dear Barrows:

It was fine to get your letter and to hear that the Giant had broken his chains & was a free man, legally;[1] for he was always a free man, & it

[1] On 19 October 1955, Dr. Dunham, former professor and chairman of the

was because of this the chains had been fixed on his movements; in an effort to stay his thoughts. How odd it is to think a chain can bind a thought. This time, the judge was not a "rotten judge," but a quietly-true & just one. I congratulate—not so much on the freedom you have won as on the fight you made. This wasn't only a fight for Barrows Dunham, but a fight for all—and they are legion—who have minds and desire to use them to make life safer, brighter, & more sensible, thus justifying the ways of man to God.

Sure, you felt proud when you came from the Court House to stand on Constitution Avenue; so should I have felt, by God! All of us share your pride, not in yourself, but in the brave justification of all free-minded women & men. Bravo Barrows! A true son of Jefferson.

I am very glad that you are so happy with the newer Mr. & Mrs. Barrows (Clark) Dunham. I'm sure Alice will be glad of a companion of her own sex, & so near to her as the wife of her dear son.

My love to the new bride & to the bridegroom (my young friend, Clarke), to Alice & to you. Bravo again!

Yours as ever,
Sean

---

philosophy department at Temple University, who was charged with contempt of Congress by the House Un-American Activities Committee on 27 February 1953, and dismissed by the University, was acquitted in Federal District Court. For the background of the case, and the allusion to Dunham's book, *Giant in Chains* (1953), see O'Casey's letter to Dunham, 22 September 1953, notes 1, 2, Vol. II.

To David Krause

MS. KRAUSE

11 NOVEMBER 1955

My dear Dave:

I retreated for a week or so from the battalion of questions doing the goosestep as they went by me; but here I am, now, trying to face them out, & answer a few, as they come in a quick march on top of me—like the troops on Review that come flooding in on Pickwick and his frightened companions. No, I didn't deliberately intend the plays to form groups of trilogies—they must have formed "forms" themselves in a natural way; for, as you say, they do seem to group themselves together, tho' I never noticed it before. I notice it, now that you have put it in front of my mind. The question of the "Bishop's Bonfire's" ending is a difficult one; but I think the rest of the play explains it, if it doesn't, as you say, prepare us for it. "It gave me a big jolt," said Breon, when he first read the play in MS. "I never expected it." I'm afraid it was meant to be a jolt. Foorawn was dead as the play began; she began to live only when she was dying. Cold & dead: Fuar—pronounced Foor; Irish for cold. Manus was close behind her. He was marked as "dead" when he left the clerical college: all students for the priesthood who go are marked down as "dead." The environment & the psychology of these places give a touch of death to those who go. The Church hates and dreads courage. She downs all who show it; if she can't, she bides her time till she can; & meanwhile, loudly or silently hunts them down—as she did in Jefferson's day: Wolfe Tone, Emmet, Parnell, Larkin, Connolly, Yeats, the Republicans; & her own priests—Dr. McDonald, Fathers Flanagan, Sheedy, O'Hickey, & Sullivan, to mention a few. Keelin Knows. What should I do? Can't fight it; odds too great; so get out of it; but Danny fails her: he wants to live on in it; it is a dope, & he is content to die among the weeds thinking them good enough as blossoms. They are—for him. There's no Union among the thinkers in Ireland, & so there is no power. They are content to live on in an "atmosphere of genteel terror," & so they die—like Manus—in their youth. The gunshot isn't heard, but it sounds in an open ear. As for the stealing of the money, why should that trouble you? Why not take the few pounds, which, if left, would but provide more geese & plover for Bill Mullarkey, or the Monsignor? And what are these few notes, stolen by Manus, to what was stolen from him? Is the treasure of a bank more than the treasure of a man's soul? Or the soul of Ballyoonagh? or soul of Ireland, from whom all courage of free-thinking has been robbed? Foorwan makes a row over what is of no earthly or heavenly concern—just like what all Ireland has done & is doing today. Ireland has her humor, her reckless jollity, which are all very delightful—till the shot rings out in the darkness; & the Codger & the Prodical are left to talk it over a couple of drinks by a lonely fire, with wonder in their hearts, and a lot of silent fear. I do hope your book may finally pass the Censors. Have the Magazines taken the articles? Anyway, be patient—you have the talent.

Yes, Dave [Greene],—the big one—was here for two days. I don't envy him his job. It was a cruel blow that little Candy[1] should have been stricken with polio. I pray God, she may get allright again.

I've been, & am, very busy. Columbia here, & Angel Gramaphone Co. in U.S.A., have made a Record of "Juno," & I did the Introduction. As well, N.B.C. USA—Radio Center—made a half-hour film of the family & me; which gave us a hectic two weeks; and I'm now writing a chapter about Dublin & the Bonfire for George B[raziller]. to put in the new book of Collected stories & articles. So, I've no time to brood on the shot in the last act of the play.

Breon is with us here, for Niall has taken his place in the London

---

[1] David H. Greene's daughter.

ramshackle flat. He is going to London University seeking a degree in Biology. Breon has done another picture of me—full length, sitting on a chair, & wearing a beanie that Shivaun made for me. Shivaun is still at school.

"Red Roses" is to open in New York on December 17;[2] and it's me who hopes it may bloom there for some time.

Don't worry about the atom bomb. I've sung of it in the film for NBC as a "jolly" good fellow, for it has frightened us all away from war. No, Dave, a mhic, not "chassis," now; but an awakening.

My love & Eileen's love, Shivaun's & Breon's go to you.

As ever,
Sean

[2] The opening of *Red Roses For Me* in New York was delayed until 29 December 1955.

To George Jean Nathan

MS. CORNELL

15 NOVEMBER 1955

My very dear George:

I haven't heard from you for some time, and assume that you are busy. I have been hard at it myself; in spite of a few bitter attacks of muscular rheumatism in a hip that forces a few curses from tightened lips—the muscles aren't so flexible as they used to be when I ran along a hurling field. A few weeks ago, NBC did a Television-film here of me & the family, which ran through a fortnight of cameras and lights. The Leaders, Bob Graff & Robert Ginna were grand lads, & we were sorry when they had to go. I am now just finishing an Introduction to a book—chapters from the "Flying Wasp," the 4 short stories from "Windfalls," & various articles written from time to time—which George Braziller is to publish. He favours the Title of "Selected Prose"—Essays of O'Casey; but I don't. I'm not an Essayist, & don't want to pose as that which I never once was. I am calling the book "The Green Crow," & think the title far more suitable. I daresay you have heard of Yale's production of "Cockadoodle Dandy."[1] "Red Roses" is to open, I'm told, on Dec. 17, and I hope it may be in

[1] *Cock-a-doodle Dandy* was produced by the Yale School of Drama, directed by Frank McMullan, at the University Theatre, New Haven, on 1 November 1955, for a one-week run. See Brooks Atkinson's review of the production, "O'Casey at Yale," *New York Times*, 4 November 1955.

Broadway for some little time. I have acted as model for Breon for another picture—a full-length one; so I have filled up the hours busily, & God
help me, I hope, usefully.

No changes in Ireland—still writing very poor plays. Odd how the
going of Yeats & Lady G. brought such loneliness to the Abbey. It is a
pity that Lennox Robinson didn't (or doesn't) step in to do something.
He knows the Theater, is a very clever playwright, a fine Producer, yet he
contents himself with writing a weekly trivial article in "The Irish Press."[2]
It is a great pity.

I hope you are keeping fit & that you will soon give us another book.
My love to Julie & to you, my very dear George.

As ever,
Sean

[2] Lennox Robinson wrote a series of articles titled "I Sometimes Think" for the
Saturday *Irish Press* during 1955; they were collected and published as a book under
that title by the Talbot Press, Dublin, in 1956.

To Cyril Cusack

MS. CUSACK

18 NOVEMBER 1955

Dear Cyril,
Couldn't reply sooner, for I have been very busy, and am so still.
Glad you got out of the Film work safely. It must be rather a stifling job,
mixing the Blessed Virgin with the fairies—and Carroll's fairies, too!
Surely, he should know that the Irish fairies of today are fake ones. It is
odd that the English fairies—Shakespeare—should be more beautiful &
real & musical than ours, where, for so long, we thought they had their
home—bar our Bean Shidhe[1] who reminds us that life never lasts forever.
The fairies of Alba—a la Barrie's Tinker Bell—are appalling. They are
embedded in the folk-lore of most countries, & the anglo-saxon word
aelf-siden meant "fairy art or power." It is generally believed that "fairy"
comes from the Latin word meaning "fate" thro' long times & many
changes. They aren't at all an "Irish" clan; they are a world-wide family.
Racehorses & Fairies! Curious connection. What will the Scottish pech,
the Cornish pixie, & the Irish Pooka (a spirit) think of it all!

I couldn't go over to Dublin—the effort would have been too much;

[1] Bean Shidhe (banshee), literally Fairy Woman, in folklore a woman figure
who appears combing her hair and is heard keening on an impending death in certain
families.

& our commitments don't allow of much thoughtless expenditure. I don't think Shivaun will go to Dublin, for the advantages here are more than those of Dublin. Niall is now at London University studying biology; Breon is here painting; & Shivaun has two more years at school before she can think of anything else; Eileen is busy with many things about the family as well as going to a French class—she knew French well when she was a young lass—like me with the Irish. I am very glad you think well of "Juno's" Recording—you should know.

A question: Hasn't Doṇat O'Donnell a second name—not the one got thro' Confirmation? Some tongue told me he was O'Connor Cruise O'Brien, & one of Ireland's Art Council, or a chap in the Dept. of Ex. Affairs; now some kind of Charge See affairs. I'm gathering together a book of articles, short stories, etc, to be published Spring in N. York; & one of the newer chapters is about the recent production of "Bonfire," with many curious & comic quotations from the Irish Drama Critics; including one or two from the Parlour Poker [Gabriel Fallon]. By the way, which of the new Irish playwrights, in your opinion, show promise? I've mentioned Molloy[2] & Byrne—"Design for a Headstone,"[3] & MacGlaisne [Risteárd Ó Glaisne] mentions [Richard] Power who wrote a one-act play in Irish. To me, [Paul Vincent] Carroll has baptised, confirmed himself, & nourishes his spirit now on the false sacraments of Hollywood—tho', I remember the Parlour Poker went into ecstacies over "The Strings, My Lord, are False."[4] I wonder what does he think of it now?

I've read Macken's "Mungo"[5] & Nathan has written me about "Home is the Hero,"[6] &, in my opinion, so far, Macken doesn't ring a bell. I hope his new play may be something worth while.

I hope Maureen is taking care of herself. Give her my love; & my love to the children, & to you.

As ever

Sean

[2] Michael J. Molloy, whose best-known play, *The King of Friday's Men,* opened at the Abbey Theatre on 18 October 1948.

[3] Seamus Byrne's *Design For a Headstone* opened at the Abbey Theatre on 8 April 1950.

[4] See O'Casey's letter to Gabriel Fallon, 23 May 1942, note 1, Vol. II.

[5] Walter Macken's *Mungo's Mansion* opened at the Abbey Theatre on 11 February 1946.

[6] Walter Macken's *Home is the Hero* opened at the Abbey Theatre on 28 July 1952. It opened in New York on 22 September 1954, and closed after 30 performances.

To J. P. R. Budlong[1]

TS. BUDLONG

20 NOVEMBER 1955

Dear Mr. Budlong,

What with recording for a Record of a play, and the same for a Television feature for the NBC, it wasnt possible to see you, which I regret very much; but at my age, one can do enough in a short time, and then mind and body strike for a rest. Since I got your letter, I have been half-handicapped with what the doctor says in fibrositis; so I'm writing now to say that I agree to the terms in the agreement (Returned, signed, herewith) sent to me by Mr. De Wilton; plus the clause in your letter of $2500 Advance, payable at my own demand, that is at whatever time I may ask for it.[2]

I still am a little dubious about the boxed books, but agree that you should know a lot more about this than I do; so go ahead, and may God bless the work—as we say in Irish.

I am very busy with many letters to write about strange things embedded in questions asked of me on Theology and Nuclear Science!

However, though I don't know much, I take an interest in everything, and so am always too damn willing to give an opinion.

All good wishes,
Yours sincerely,
Sean O'Casey

[1] J.P.R. Budlong, Macmillan Company, New York.
[2] The advance for *Mirror in My House* (1956), the two-volume edition of O'Casey's autobiography, originally published in six volumes.

To Anthony Harvey

TC. O'CASEY

20 NOVEMBER 1955

Dear Anthony,

This must be a brief letter, for I have many more to answer, and, God knows when I'll get to the end of them; as well, I am busy writing an Introduction and some additional things for a book of Short Stories, etc., to be published by George Braziller next Spring. I am glad to hear that you and George are still going strong, and I hope you are minding your health, and not overdoing it with reading and study. My God, you are immersed in abstruse things! Theology alone is enough for one poor human being. Dont forget man in your studies about God. Of course there is more than One Way; they are narrow ways, but there are many of them: there is no final answer, except to the individual who must decide for himself how to go; the way that best suits him—by being a teacher, a Professor, a writer, a carpenter, a politician, or whatever state to which it shall please God to call him. On the whole, I think Brooks' review wasnt a bad one, indeed, a good one.[1] I dont agree about the idea of my being out of Ireland weakens the characters I draw; but, of course, I'd hardly believe anything else, and I'm not infallible. But I've some reasons for believing this: Yeats began it when he said at the rejection of THE SIL-VER TASSIE that O'Casey's absence from Ireland had done him harm—though I was then but a year from Ireland. Yeats conveniently forgot that he himself was educated in his youth in Hammersmith, London; that he lived as a young man there for twenty-five years—they've just put a plaque on the house he lived in; and that if one adds the later times he spent out of Ireland (when he married, he took a house in Oxford), in Italy, in France, and in the USA, well, we'll find that he was far oftener out of Ireland than he was in it. Why am I alone in this matter? Why not say the same thing of P. V. Carroll and of Denis Johnston? Both are clever dramatists; both have written fine plays; and both have spent as much time as they could out of Ireland. Carroll permanently so, and Johnston nearly the same; yet I have never seen any remark in any review about them or have I heard a single remark implying that they have lost something by living away from Ireland's shore. And what about the hundreds of actors and actresses who have gone from Ireland—most of them, past and present, forever? Every character comes from the playwright's mind; none of them—bar the dull ones—are as God made them, but as the playwright conceived them. Falstaff isnt made up from one person; he is too great to be but one. God, if you like, created Shakespeare, but Shakespeare created Falstaff. However, in my next book, the one I have mentioned, I have a long article dealing with the production of THE BISHOP'S BONFIRE in Dublin, and in this article, I go into this question more fully. Most characters in plays are composite—for instance, one of the characteristics of "Sailor Mahan" is taken from a person, not found in Dublin, nor in London, even, but in New York! Dont bother about sending me the COCKADOODLE SET, me son; save your money, for I'm sure to get it from Yale.

I hope your article will find a corner in the Divinity Magazine. Yes, Maid Marion and Robin Adair are meant to be what you suggest, as well as being lovely names. They are legendary figures in folklore, and dont go as the world goes. Your theological friend should remember Him who pointed out the Lilies of the Field. The humanism of the young, the gay,

[1] Brooks Atkinson, "O'Casey at Yale," *New York Times,* 4 November 1955, a review of the Yale School of Drama's production of *Cock-a-doodle Dandy.*

and the beautiful do not leave things empty, for they are everlasting; they are always with us, or should be always with us; and are, if we have but eyes to see and ears to hear. All of us have eyes and ears, but many of us fail to use them. Your theological friend when he said this was just de-crying the world of God; for, according to Christian belief, as announced in the Gospel, "Everything was made by God, and without Him was not anything made that was made." The oaks, the beeches, the poplars, the sycamores, the rhododendrons, the lilies of the valley and the roses of Sharon, of humanism are all the works of God; as much so as the Apos-tles, the angels and archangels, and all the spirits around the throne of God. All the poets saw this, and all the artists; it seems that it is only the theologians (who should know better) who are blind and deaf and bothered. And that is one big reason why humanity everywhere is rising up against them. Sorry, I havent the MS of the chat called "The Holy Ghost Leaves England"; they were just notes from which I blathered.[2] Far as I remember, the chat went on the lines that the Spirit of loveliness and truth was gone from the British Press, from British sport, from British theater, from British politics, and from the British religion. You seem to have had an exciting time in the Theater. [Arthur] Miller, to me, is Amer-ica's finest dramatist, since the death of O'Neill. What did you think of S. McKenna?[3]

Breon is still painting; he has done me several times; lastly, a full-length portrait. At the moment, he is doing a wall-piece (mural) for a children's ward in an hospital here. Niall is now in London University studying biology; Shivaun is studying for her Certificate in Higher Maths and History. Mrs. O'C. is fine, but very busy. I got the book by Dr. Shrader safely.[4] I've read a good deal of it—when I can slip a few minutes into leisure time—and I think it to be very caustic, but very true; if it isnt a two-edged sword, it is certainly a one-edged one. Give him my warm re-gards. I hope he may win the faculty, for he would hardly be comfortable where he was before he came north. We dont like to be told the truth.

My best regards to George; I hope he does well. My love to Mrs. Harvey and to your brother and sister, and, of course, to you.

As ever,

[Sean O'Casey]

[2] See O'Casey's rough draft of a letter to Alfred A. K. Arnold ("The Holy Ghost Leaves England"), 18 January 1936, Vol. I.

[3] Siobhan McKenna in Enid Bagnold's The Chalk Garden. See O'Casey's letter to Cyril Cusack, 19 August 1955, note 1.

[4] Wesley Shrader, Dear Charles: Letters to a Young Minister (1954).

*To Proinnsias Mac an Bheatha*¹

MS. MAC AN BHEATHA

20 NOVEMBER 1955

Dear Mr. Mac an Bheatha,

Enclosed is a refusal to do what you ask. Certainly, it is a good one to expect me to write in Irish when it is 30 years since I heard a word of it spoken; &, moreover, after all that has been done to it by T[homas]. Page & his assistants; so that it looks, at times, a perfect stranger in its New Look. Yes, "P. O'C." and Sean O'C. are one.² The Story was the first "book" I had published, so I knew little about "Proofs." I got the pages to do, but not the Title-Page. I imagined this wasn't sent, because it was so simple that no error could occur. It was on the T-Page that the big mistake appeared.

That is how it happened. May I give you my warm regards.

Yours very sincerely,
Sean O'Casey

Enclosures
Please note new address.

¹ Proinnsias Mac an Bheatha, 110 Vernon Avenue, Clontarf, Dublin; chairman of the editorial board, *Inniu,* Dublin.
² A reference to O'Casey's *The Story of the Irish Citizen Army* (1919), by "P. O'Cathasaigh." The "P." was a printer's error.

To Proinnsias Mac an Bheatha

TS. MAC AN BHEATHA

20 NOVEMBER 1955

Dear friend, So I'm a "duine uasal"¹ now! Has Gaelic Ireland conferred some Ordher upon me? Indeed, friend, I am the same kind of Mac Ui Cathasaigh² (without the Gaelic enthusiasm) that I was more than fifty years ago on the streets of Dublin. I can still hear Dr. [Douglas] Hyde— the most voiceful yet most timid man I ever met—addressing me as "A Mhic Ui Cathasaigh,"³ many, many years ago in the St. Laurence O'Toole Christian Brothers' School, Seville Place, the time the banner of the

¹ gentleman.
² Mr. O'Casey.
³ Mr. O'Casey, vocative case.

O'Toole Pipers was unrolled publicly before a packed house, with Father Jimmy Breen, C.C. in the chair, and Father Cantell in the audience. But Mac Ui Cathasaigh was but a worker, and Hyde was soon done with him, though if he only had known it, here was the answer to the problem of lifting the Irish Tongue into the hearts and minds of the people. Before saying anything else, I'd better say that I have neither the time nor the energy—I am 75—to do what you ask. I am writing some chapters and an Introduction for a book of mine that New York is to publish next spring; and I have fifty more letters to write, before I can sleep in peace— before that time comes, I shall have fifty more. So you can see. I've read, and I like, your comments upon the great Jim Larkin—the "greatest Irish- man since Parnell" as Shaw said of him. But who in Ireland now cares a damn about the great Labor Leader? No more than they care about Padruig Pearse—in spite of the commemoration of his name and his work. Your Archbishop McQuaid saw Larkin safely to his last rest, and the British Government made sure of the Pearse eag.[4] I have said almost all I wanted to say about Jim in my biography. He was here with me, and his son, Fintan, a short time before he died. This man was a man. Have you read Niall O'Donnell's lecture given in the current number of *Inniu*?[5] They are slashing words, and all to the point. At the base of anything to be done is the economic core. You may build colleges in every rood of the Gaeltacht [Irish-speaking district], but if the people there havent a secure livelihood, they will scamper off to where they think they will find it. Make it pleasant for them to live, and then you may expect it will be pleasant for them to speak: before all else, a man must have the wherewithal to live. Most of them who are now in high places think more of their grand cars than they do of a Gaeltacht soul. Gentility, in my opinion, killed the Language. As it is now, so it was then: If you look up some number of W. P. Ryan's THE NATION, you may find an article of mine on this matter.[6] That plan was put before the then Coisde Ceanntear, B'Cliath [Dublin District Committee], with Sean T. O'Kelly in the chair, in Irish and English; the delegates listened politely and attentively, then solidly voted against it. One item was that those Gaels who lived in the district should, perforce, be members of the Branch that worked in it. But all the genteel members insisted on flocking into either the Ard Craobh [High or Central Branch] or into the Keating Branch. Mind you, there were grand lads and lasses in both—M. O'Foley, M. O'Loinsigh, Donal O'Murachu, poor Peadar O'Nuallain, and others; specially Donal O'M. who was with us through most of the Lock-Out in 1913, a grand lad from Ballyvourney,

---

4 Pearse's death.

5 Liam Ó Domhnaill, "Sean O'Casey Is An Ghaeilge" (Sean O'Casey and the Irish Language), *Inniu*, 2 December 1955. O'Casey must have seen an advance copy.

6 "Sound the Loud Trumpet," by "An Gall Fada" (The Tall Foreigner or Protestant), O'Casey's first article and first pseudonym, *The Peasant and Irish Ireland*, 25 May 1907; edited by W. P. Ryan; reprinted in *Feathers From the Green Crow* (1962).

who spoke in his lovely Irish at Citizen Army gatherings; and a Doyle, from Wexford, who had a revolver, and sent a few shots through the windows of scab-trams as they whizzed by us. But, all in all, the gentility couldnt, or wouldnt, rub shoulders with a laborer or a docker; they were too "grand." Now, you force the language on to the children, mostly workers' children, so that they hate to see *Inniu*. Well and good then; but why not force it on the Dail members too? I remember trying to get it settled to allow five years to them in which to get the Language, and if not with them by then, then no entry into the Dail for them. Well and good, then why dont you force it on the priests, the Monsignors, and the Bishops? Couldnt a bishop give a sermon once a month in Irish, the Monsignor once in a fortnight, and the priest once a week? Force it on the sparrow but leave the cockatoo alone!

You are always talking about foreign games, foreign music, foreign customs, but what about foreign saints? It makes me laugh at the way some talk about being Irish, when for one plea to an Irish saint, there are a thousand to some foreign one. Read in *Inniu* what is said about the plays done by the Drama Club. These plays seem to be no better, indeed, not quite so good, as those I saw in the old days—Sean na Scuab, Duchas, by a Miss Kennedy, Tadhg Saor, by Dinneen, I think, and Seabhac na Ceithre Caoile, whose authorship I cant remember. All pretty bad, but as good apparently as what you are displaying now.

Read the article on Thomas Page. It isnt a secure revelation. It isnt the searcher nor the scholar that will give to the language its peculiar life in Literature, but the poet and the writer immersed in the living language of the people. Like Father O'Leary; you seem to have gone away from him. I've read nothing so vivid as his "Aesop a haunig go hEirinn."[7] You need a poet like Shakespeare or like Dante who both added many gems to their own languages. You need, too, in my opinion, a deep and good dictionary of etymology, so that poet and writer may build new words from the roots of the Gaelic.

My hour is over: I never could go down to any Irish-speaking district like the gentility; I never had enough to get even the Gaelic Journal published in my day; I used to get the "Sword of Light" when I was working, but had to give it up when I was idle. "Banba" and such magazines were above my means, and few indeed were the books I could buy; so I concentrated on O'Leary, and the song-books called *Fuinn na Smol* edited by Father Walsh. I have these songs still. The other day, I looked over the songs, searching for one I wanted, THE LITTLE RED LARK, but it wasnt there. I wanted it for a Television show—American. I found the air, however, in a Community Songbook, with terrible words added to it by P[erceval]. Graves.

Well, I've blathered enough, and now I must get on with my work.

---

[7] Canon Peter O'Leary, *Aesop a haunig go hEirinn* (1900), Aesop Who Came to Ireland.

The above are, you know, but opinions that may be either wise or foolish—I don't know; though I believe them to be wise.

Yours sincerely
Sean O'Casey

To Mrs. R ——

MS. PRIVATE

24 NOVEMBER 1955

Dear R——,

Salud! I am still busy, & the years, like great black oxen, tread me down a little, & make me feel tired oftener. I hope you liked the Coast of Mullaghmore, & Knocknarea. No, not much use in going to Drumcliffe to see where they put Yeats. He is not there, he is risen, & shines in his books. I hope J. made a good picture of A. I've heard his name; but one sees few things here, bar the natural beauties. Torquay has a Museum; a fine Library, a Pavilion where they play plays of vast nonsense. There's no exhibition of Art ever here. There is a local Society of Artists. I saw an exhibition of theirs—pleasant, but nothing original. Do you know they showed Soviet Films at a Festival in—of all places—Wexford! And gave them the palm! Wexford seems to be alive.

I went nowhere this Summer—it was too hot for me; &, anyway, I like moving about no longer. Eileen & Shivaun went to Paris, partly on business for me—I believe they owe me a lot of Francs this many a day; but poor France is in a bad way. [St. John] Ervine says odd things right enough; but he never remembers the terrible 700 years of Captivity we went thro', & the poverty that downed us body, soul, & spirit. He should have read what General Gordon said of what he saw in Ireland when he travelled thro' it. [Michael] Davitt was a peasant's son. He lost an arm in a Manchester mill; he was a Lancashire postman for years, & educated himself. Ervine is wrong about him. Davitt was a Revolutionary—witness what he said to the Bishop of Limerick; he was a Socialist long before his time. Parnell didn't hate England: to hate English "law" & to despise those who made them, isn't hatred of England. He fell in love with an Englishwoman; or so I imagine her to have been one. The trouble with Ervine— & he is a verile writer—is that he cannot make up his mind about anything; any policy, any opinion other than his own. "Red Roses For Me" is opening in New Haven, [Connecticut] on December 7; then Boston; then New York—if all goes well. The Television film I and the family did recently was for National Broadcasting Co. of New York.

Thanks for the verses about the "Bonfire." I am glad you liked it well enough to write such charming & encouraging things about it. I pray your poetic prophesy may come true. Anyway, a few sparks from it still fly about Dublin. The Archbishop of Dublin didn't get his way to stop the football match between Eire & Yugo-Slavia; tho' all who were for it this week, went against it the next; but football fans went in their tens of thousands; & gave the Y.Slavia men a Banquet afterwards—the Archbishop made a blunder.[1]

My love to A. & to you.

As ever,
Sean

I think Sinn Fein—DeValera's Party, is turning to the left—a little anyway.

[1] See O'Casey's letter to Seumas Scully, 5 November 1955, note 2.

To George Braziller

TC. O'CASEY

26 NOVEMBER 1955

Dear George,

Thanks for your letter and cutting. Thanks a lot for what you say about COCKADOODLE DANDY, but Publishing is your line, and a difficult one too, needing big intelligence and great skill to do it even at all, let alone to do it well. So you stay put among the books, and dont come into the delusive limelight of the Theater.

I packed the MS for the book—the article on the BISHOP'S BONFIRE carefully, and registered it. I remember the Girl in the Post Office here asking me if it was a "gift"; so, probably, other officials wouldnt believe that it was merely MS, and opened it to make sure. There is passionate competition between the West and the further West. However, since it was intact, it's all O.K.

I imagine that Anouilh cant hold a candle to Giraudoux, though he is a greater favorite. We've been flooded with Anouilhs over here (and but one Giraudoux), they arent worthy of him. To come back to the book: No, not WINDFALLS neither. THE GREEN CROW is the best title. WINDFALLS suited the book that was then published; it wouldnt suit this one. And, as I said, the other name ["Profiles By O'Casey"] doesnt suit me at all; not typical of O'Casey. I forgive the "select" in the gathering of the plays; but if it were used to suggest the stuff in this book, I'd never hold up my head again. This isnt obstinacy: I asked the opinion of George

Jean Nathan as to the choice between the two, and, in a letter to me, he says "I await your newest book the title for which seems to me infinitely better than the one chosen advocated by the publisher." Again, talking yesterday over the phone to Thomas Quinn Curtiss, Paris drama critic for THE HERALD-TRIBUNE, I told him of the book, and mentioned the two titles. He, too, was in favor of THE GREEN CROW, saying that it was a very "intriguing title." My anxiety, George, is that the book mightnt be worthy of the title. If it is, that will be fine. So, we are three to one.

I am enclosing the Foreword Caw Caw Caw, which, as you will see, is built up on the title (and cunningly, too, tho' it's I shouldnt say so—but why not?); some songs, and a sub-description of what the book is to be, to help compromise on your title-suggestion, which I hope you may find acceptable and pleasing. I dont think pleasantly about placing some of the articles or stories in magazines, as you suggest. Wouldnt it be better for both of us that they should come fresh into the book? Seems a bit egoistic to be spreading myself in that way. I should like to see [Frank] O'Connor's PROFILE of me.[1] Cant understand why he's doing it. I've never met him; never even saw him passing in a street; he has never had a letter, even, from me, nor I one from him. So I cant see how he can do a Profile of me, except that "he may have heard somethin." However, know me or not know me, O'Connor is a very fine writer, and a courageous one too.

I enclose also another sketch; the following songs:

The Ruin'd Rowan Tree (with music)
We're ready for Anything Now
I Grieve for the Time
Down by the Green Bushes (with music)

and a "Poem" called CAW CAW CAW, which you may or may not like.

I think these are all, and closes the book finally. I might, later on, send a dedication.

I am delighted to hear that you are going to Press with another 3000 of the plays.[2] Be God, that's good news! I am teasing my mind with the suggestion of a book of PROFILES, and will write about it when I have thought the idea over. It would be a big and a long job.

Meanwhile my love to Marsha and to you.

As ever,
[Sean]

---

[1] Frank O'Connor, "O'Casey and the Ghosts," *Holiday,* January 1956.
[2] *Selected Plays of Sean O'Casey* (1954), Selected with a Foreword by the Author, and an Introduction by John Gassner.

To George Jean Nathan

MS. CORNELL

26 NOVEMBER 1955

My very dear George:

I guessed something had happened to you—I often say to Eileen, "Odd, I haven't heard from George. I hope to God nothing is wrong with him." Well, now you are over the worst of it; & with rest and care, you should soon feel more comfortable.

These operations are nightmares indeed; the whole experience of pain, preparation, the undergoing of the ordeal, take a lot out of one; but we have to endure these things from time to time, till we become more sensible, & cease to hack at each other in Conferences, & more realistically, with sword and gun and high explosives. Then we can brood over what we can do, & what we ought to do, to make ourselves more remote from pain and physical trials.

You were very fortunate to have Julie with you. She must have been a great & colorful companion; for no man has that mysterious quality of comfort and courage which flows from a woman's presence. And, God knows, they have to stick things, too, with that contributing comfort & courage; for few men have it to give; & most women have to suffer alone, & bear up in their own hearts.

Tom Q. C[urtiss]. rang me up from Paris the other day, & was distressed to hear of your illness. I shouldn't have told him had I know known of your fondness for him, & his deep fondness & reverence for you.

I am fairly good, after a spell of fibrositus in the right lumbar muscle—damnably painful while it lasted, but saved from fainting by large swallows of Hennessey's 3 star Brandy—a gift from the Americans who did the Film of family.

We grow old, Master Shallow. So we do, George; but we shall make the best of it, & kick out while there's a spot of go in us.

Now, put aside everything for awhile, & rest.

My love to Julie and to you, my dear lad.

As ever,
Sean

However old we grow, I don't believe either of us can ever become an old fogey. Thank God!—

To Miss Joan McAlevey

MS. McALEVEY

28 NOVEMBER 1955

Dear Joan,

Glad you are near the end of your Thesis, & I hope it may win you what you want. You needn't tell me about typing—I know it all, and more. It is great drudgery, but it has to be done; harder on those who do not learn the craft blindfold. But there's drudgery in all things—from washing things to saying one's prayers—if we do say any. I am only sorry that I have been the cause of your toil. It isn't quite right that poetry and plays should be associated with drudgery of any kind; and that is why I'm against the use of them for "Study." The minute one feels weary of a play or a poem, it should be flung away for the time being; but this can't be done in school or College. We have many weary years to go before a sensible way of education comes to live with the very young. It is only when we grow too old that we can make a choice. Shaw's resentful remark wasn't meant for teachers; but for those critics who maddened him with so many silly sayings; & those who think they can teach art. Indeed, one can't teach teaching, Joan; that, too, is a gift; & if the teacher hasn't it, the teacher can't teach: that is, can't be an inspiration. Of course, we can learn, if we be diligent; develop the gift we have; & that, too, is difficult; & one grows weary at times. But it is all well worth it in the end. I'm glad you like your comrade-teachers, even the teacher from Dublin.

I hope your Brooklyn Dodgers have done better by now. Like my Dublin footballers who should have won the All-Ireland Final, but were beaten by one point by Kerry. Oh! the disappointment! However, I'm consoled by the fact that they made a gallant fight of it.

My love to your eleven little ones; your mother, daddy, & John; and to you, Joan.

Yours very Sincerely
Sean

To Stanley Levenson[1]

TC. O'CASEY

I DECEMBER 1955

Dear Stanley,

Glad you are expanding; growth is a thing we expect from the young; physical and growth of the mind, and the growth of the mind is halted for two years that the army swallows up: gulp! and down the two years go, never to [be] recovered again. I am against 2 years of it; against a year of it, against a single minute of it: it is waste, a woe, and a wandering off from better and more useful things that the young are so eager to do. Let them be free to do it, and do away with the tramp tramp tramp the boys are marching. The one march now worthwhile is a march to the tractors, to a factory, to a sports field, to a concert, to a library, where God is, and not a little puffing non-commissioned officer giving orders to those a damn sight better than himself. To hell with all but what brothers and sisters, the world over, can do together. And tell me this: why dont you fight for the VOTE to be given at eighteen years of age? Why doesnt the Labor Party fight for it? And, above all, why doesnt the Communist Party put it in the front of their programme? Christ Almighty, if a young man is fit to go out to fight for his country, fit to die for it, he is fit to have a vote. Surely a young lass who may be running a home, may be indeed, a mother, is fit to have a vote. Are Eden and Atlee afraid to give them one? Let the young demand one, then, for the more afraid these are to give one, the more necessary it is for the young man and the young lass to have it. Then we'd hear what they thought of two years service in the armed forces. I'll go bail that ninety out of every hundred would declare for dungarees before the battle-dress.

Needless to say, you have my blessing on all you are trying to do. If the young had more power, we'd hear some wild things; but we'd hear some true things, too; and that is what's needed—the outspoken phrases of enthusiasm and resolution and of hope from the young and the brave.

I enclose a subscription.
Yours sincerely,
Sean O'Casey

[1] Stanley Levenson, British Youth Festival Committee, London.

To John O'Shaughnessy

TC. O'CASEY

1 DECEMBER 1955

Dear John O'S.,

Fine to hear from you, and to hear within the hearing that so far all is going well. You seem to have gathered a good Cast together.[1] It seems a fine bit of good fortune that Kevin McCarthy is to be in the part of Ayamonn; finished his film in the nick of time. I agree with you about having, if possible, one with a rich experience, especially for a difficult part, a part on which so much depends; though I am very sorry for Patrick O'Neal. Oh, so many who just dont come up to what is needed! The little less and what miles away. It is coming close to the crucial day now, and we can but hope for the best, plus the knowledge that you have done your best with the play; and, I'm sure, the Direction will be fine; I hope the play may respond to it.

I'm glad the old veteran W[hitford]. Kane is to do "Sammy"; he should be very good in it. He should know something about the Orange Lily O! Eileen [Crowe] should be very good in the part of Mrs. Breydon; she is a clever actress. Give her my best wishes, and say I hope her children are doing well. Like my own, they must be quite grown up by now.

Yes of course, put in the words quoted. They arent too many, though I prefer the word "Rising" to that of "Rebellion." We did not, do not, look upon it as a rebellion, but a "Rising Out" for restoration of what another held which belonged to us—Nationhood. Anything that helps the American audience to understand the play is to the good. I have had a letter from Robert Downing who, he tells me, saw a rehearsal, and he adds that the play was making excellent progress in Rehearsal. Well, on the day, I hope many bells may ring.

With all good wishes,
Yours sincerely,
Sean O'Casey.

[1] For the production of *Red Roses For Me,* opening in New York on 28 December 1955.

To Brooks Atkinson

MS. ATKINSON

3 DECEMBER 1955

My dear Brooks and Oriana,

Greetings to you from the heart out. I hope both of you are well. I've been very busy with "The Bishop's Bonfire." Dublin was very excited for days before, and at night for the first performance, the crowds blocked the street, & more police had to come to regulate the traffic around bonfires, singing, till the play ended. Many distinguished men & women couldn't get seats, which was bad management, but the bookings were overwhelming, & confusion came, for nothing like it had been known before. Eileen, and Shivaun were there; but the snow & fierce winds were too much for me to risk the journey. The Irish critics to a man condemned the play, lock, stock, and barrel, & the R. Catholic Standard denounced me & the play by, bell, book, and candle. The surprising thing is that the people are going to the play—two weeks of packed houses, & the booking promises another for the third week. They revel in the comedy, & listen tense to the serious moments, and many are afraid to applaud at the end of the play, & so give any sign of agreement with its sentiments. The impact of the play on the minds of the audience seems to be a big one, & many are saying that it expresses what is in the minds of many, many Irish people. Cyril Cusack is very fine as "The Codger," and most others are fine too, so papers say, & Eileen & Shivaun agree. Certainly, be the play good or bad, O'Casey has returned to Dublin with a bang. It has provoked a great competition between the boo and the cheer. I guessed there'd be a stir, but didn't expect one quite so big. I've just recorded four fifteen-minute talks on tape for Radio Eireann, to be broadcast in May, with four plays of mine—an "O'Casey Festival," they call it! They wanted the talks to be prefaces to these plays, but I couldn't talk about my work; so they gave me, more or less, what they called "carte blanche," & I talked of various things; sang snatches of old songs & two new ones of my own making. And I'm answering shoals of letters; but, by God, I'm tired! The English Critics were there, too, & even some American critics, who were much, much kinder than our Irish boys. A Representative from *Time* was there, & took photos of the Cast & the scenes. Altogether, an hour of glory in a first performance. 30 years after the last first production of mine in Dublin—"The Plough & the Stars."

Well, Brooks & Oriana, you must be tired of this news; so I'll continue only by the blessed hope that you are both well, and all that belongs to you are safe and sound.

My sincere love, dear Oriana & Brooks, to you.

As ever,
Sean

I enclose a few clippings which may interest, dealing as they do, with an old friend.

To George Jean Nathan

MS. CORNELL

6 DECEMBER 1955

My very dear George:
    You send me bad news indeed; but maybe not so bad. This obstacle of surgery[1] once passed, you will probably be a lot easier, with a chance for more work. But anything surgical is painful, and much of an ordeal; one can only clinch one's teeth, and go thro' with it when it has to be endured. Don't, for heaven's sake, worry about work for the time being. You have already projected yourself so splendidly, not only into the Theatre of America, but into the Theater of the world, that you can afford, well afford, to keep quiet for a little while.
    God has been good in giving you Julie, and that is a blessing right in the center of your illness. I've known what it is to be ill, very ill, and alone; &, by God, it wasn't agreeable. My hope, wish, and prayers will go with you, my dear, very dear friend.
    My love to Julie, and my love, deep love, to you, George.

As ever,
Sean

1 Nathan underwent prostate surgery.

To Ivor Montagu[1]

TC. O'CASEY

9 DECEMBER 1955

Dear Ivor,
    I amnt in the least anxious about GBS. He had a full life, and his influence has been tremendous, and is still spreading away over the world. Let him alone. Let them rave about Atlee today, Churchill tomorrow,

1 Ivor Montagu, English writer and socialist.

much as they like; but it was such as Shaw who salted the world with wisdom, with courage, and with commonsense, and so freed India, Burma, Ceylon, and will give them fuller freedom in the years to come. Who are the "they"—besides Lady Astor? L. Astor was a great friend of his, and they went to the USSR together. If she thinks he's outdated, then let her. She has a right to think so, if she wants to. She is probably mistaken; indeed, I'm certain she is—if what you say be right; and I can hear GBS laughing. Who then are the "they"? Are these the Muggeridges, the Worsleys, the Koestlers, et al? Well, if they want to "belittle" GBS, let them. D'ye think I'm going to waste time or thought on what they say or think of him?

You seem to think little yourself of Shaw as a playwright; as if playwrighting was but small beer. It isnt, you know. It's a damn sight harder to write a play than it is to make a speech, political, or one praising some name at some Anniversary. Ivor, have sense. "A chance to rescue him from all these false flatterers"! Rescue Shaw! Cant you see that the very fact that some interested fools are trying to belittle him shows the man's power? He doesnt need you or I to rescue him; he is well able to take care of himself.

As for helping the way you suggest in any "Anniversary"[2] that may be held—I am to be counted out. I am too old now to join in such festivities, as well as not allowing myself to attach much importance to them. It is the quiet reading of Shaw, the performance of his plays (as with Shakespeare) that matter; and that is the way his influence spreads. Never fear, Shaw will be a long time living. As for your "millions in Asia, Indonesia," they seem to be doing fairly well by themselves; and China and India are a damned sight more alive than we are. So think rather about the millions in England—and Atlee going into the House of Lords. A new book of mine, coming out in the Spring, published in New York, has an article on Shaw; one of which he himself said "was superb"—he may have been joking. That is the best way I can think of to center Shaw before the world as the great man he was. So.

My best wishes to Mrs Montagu and to you.

Yours very sincerely,
Sean O'Casey.

---

[2] On the occasion of Shaw's 100th birthday, 26 July 1956. He died in 1950 at the age of 94.

To Augustus John[1]

MS. JOHN

10 DECEMBER 1955

My dear Augustus,

It's grand to know that your grand head of Yeats will be in Dublin. The Abbey Theater has a treasure. I've seen the photograph, and it looks lovely and it looks strong; a poet's head.

I was delighted to read that you were painting the Kabacka [Kabaka of Buganda], & doing a drawing of [Albert] Schweitzer. By God, you are a man!

We, of course, have our Johns in Parade on our best wall, in our best room; and lovely they look still; & will forever.

It is fine to think of you still working, and the head of Yeats shows the old hands have lost none of their cunning.

Many years of such work to you.

My love to Mrs. John and to you.

As ever,
Sean

[1] Augustus John (1878–1961), British portrait and mural painter, etcher and lithographer, born in Wales. He painted a portrait of O'Casey in 1926. See letters to him in Vol. I.

To A. J. Leventhal

TS. LEVENTHAL

10 DECEMBER 1955

Dear Mr. Leventhal,

It's only now that I have found time to say a few words of reply to your letter of the long ago. Thanks so much for putting me in touch with THE DUBLIN MAGAZINE, which I like very much, for it has the old dignity of Dublin in its pages. It is a long time since we last met, a long time indeed more than twenty golden years ago; far more. It was in the Fortune Theater, if I dont mistake; you wanted me to go to have lunch with you, and I flatly—and, I fear, rudely refused. Never mind. I was then bewildered and annoyed by the ballyhoo raised about me, because of JUNO and the fact that I was a tenement-house dweller. I hated the publicity—almost all of it humbug and false—and wanted to get away from as much of it as I could. Besides, I was damned ignorant then; just unaware of many things; but proud and resentful: I had a lot to learn. I have learned a lot, and I thank England for a good deal of it. I still dislike publicity—like S.O'S[1]—but when one is a professional writer, and has to earn a living, one has to submit quietly to some.

I'm glad you burned that savage attack on my work. I assure you I didnt deserve it, for, however bad a critic may think of what I do, I am conscious of always having done my best; and no man can do more than that same.

I liked your remarks about the BISHOP'S BONFIRE.[2] There was no "spleen" there; and so all's well. It was really a kind tribute, and I thank you for it. But, my dear, A.J., the Irish critics, as a whole, are pretty poor, and more's the pity. I laughed at a saying of N. Carroll's recently in the "Irish Press." He was grieving (rightly) over the Abbey refusing to put on a new play by Giltinan.[3] But what he said: "Would you like, if you had used herculean efforts to compose a Masterpiece for the theater." No playwright uses herculean efforts to write a Masterpiece for the theater. He makes a great effort to write an effective play for the stage; if it turns out to be a masterpiece—hurrah! Is N.C. a young lad? By the way, I've heard good reports of THE IRON HARP written by Joseph O'Connor; done by Rep. in Brighton. I wonder does the Abbey know about it? Looks like, from a friend's letter, that it might be a very good play. Give my best wishes to S.O'S and to Miss Solomons—Estelle, if my memory serves me still. I wonder does she remember the way she shook Shaw Desmond in discussion, the night he brought me to meet her? All the best to yourself, with regrets that I didnt have that lunch with you in the days of long ago.

Yours very sincerely,
Sean O'Casey

[1] Seumas O'Sullivan (1879–1958), pen name of James Sullivan Starkey, poet and editor, who founded *The Dublin Magazine* in 1923.

[2] A. J. Leventhal, "Dramatic Commentary," *The Dublin Magazine,* April–June, 1955.

[3] Niall Carroll, *Irish Press,* 28 November 1955. The Abbey Theatre had rejected a new play by Donal Giltinan.

To Frank McCarthy

MS. McCARTHY

11 DECEMBER 1955

Dear Frank,

Thanks for the "Messenger."[1] A fine Sermon; but all who reject the Gospel Stories aren't "cynics." But that's a big question, & we won't go into it here.

I hope you do well in your new post. I daresay you have thought it out, after you "jumped at it." No job is as good as one thinks it will be at first. In a place like a Mission, you may have to work more hours. There is a strong point in your getting too old to be bumping about boxes, especially if your health isn't too good. I do hope you may be happy.

I got one Dublin letter from [Seumas] Scully, which I answered; but haven't heard since. He'll find Dublin hard to manage now. An odd lad.

Yes, I heard St. John. He was, in my opinion, very good. I've no doubt of Ervine's honesty. He blurts out a lot at times about us "Eireans"; but he is forthright about it anyway. I've spoken to him twice only in my life—once at the Critics Circle Dinner, 1926—they never asked me a second time; and once at a Charlie Cochran lunch! He lives quite near here— East Devon; but I never hear from him; or him from me. Belfast & Dublin a long way from each other. I'm afraid Beckett (Waiting for Godot) wouldn't suit the fervent souls of your Mission, Frank.

Except for what the doctor called "fibrositis," I'm fairly good; and very very busy.

Good fortune to you, and my affectionate regards.

As ever,
Sean.

[1] *Kingsway Messenger,* the Methodist magazine of Dr. Donald O. Soper's West London Mission.

To Sean O'Rourke[1]

TS. O'ROURKE

12 DECEMBER 1955

My dear Sean,

Well, that was kind and thoughtful of you to send me the music of "An Fuiseoigin Ruadh,"[2] and I thank you very much for it. I got it a long

[1] Sean O'Rourke, 2 Seville Place, North Strand, Dublin; one of O'Casey's friends in the St. Laurence O'Toole Club during the first decade of the century. See letters to him in Vol. II.
[2] "The Little Red Lark."

time ago, with many others, from Dublin's Government Office; and, having all the rest, couldnt, and cant, find my copy of "The Little Red Lark." I wanted it for an introduction to an O'Casey family Television film, done for the American National Broadcasting Co. They suggested "The Bard of Armagh," but I wanted something more typical of Ireland; so we compromised by using the air (a lovely one), and I sang a verse of the song, "The Bard of Armagh" for them. Fortunately I got the air from an English Community Song Book. Why, though, did INNIU put my name on a poster? I read INNIU, and like it very much—brings one more close to Ireland than the three National Dailies put together. But as it was a letter I sent to them, they shouldnt have published it without permission;[3] for letters are copyright as well as poem, play, or story. Not that I mind a bit; but I must warn them for possibly, some day or another, they might get into a row for publishing something they had no right to. It is always safer to write for permission.

Yes, the unfurling of the banner was a great night for the O'Toole Pipers. I wonder is the lass who made it—Mrs Patrick Cabalan—living still? What changes have taken place since that night—with me, anyhow! You still live in the old spot by the five lamps; and I have lived in many different places. I met Father Jimmy Breen once in Webb's bookshop, after he had been made a Canon, and P.P. of Arklow; but it was the same Jimmy. He wouldnt talk; wouldnt wait for me to even congratulate him, but slipped off, nose in the air, unwilling to remember the older times. I'm glad you sent me the air with the Irish words. I have the English ones by [A. P.] Graves, and pretty terrible they are, too. The Irish ones are charming—evidently a Jacobite song. God, we did sacrifice a lot for the unworthy Stuarts!

Well, Sean, a mhic, my love to you. Give my best wishes to F[rank]. Cahill, and tell him I hope Ireland may soon—for her own benefit—start up diplomatic Relations with the USSR.

All the best, and thanks again.
Yours very sincerely,
Sean

You say damn little about yourself. Did you marry, & have you any children?

---

[3] In his article, "Sean O'Casey Is An Ghaeilge" (Sean O'Casey and the Irish Language), *Inniu*, 2 December 1955, Liam Ó Domhnaill quotes a letter O'Casey had written in Irish to Proinnsias Mac an Bheatha. See O'Casey's letter to Liam Ó Domhnaill, 20 December 1955; and his letter to *Inniu*, 25 December 1955.

To Anthony Harvey

TC. O'CASEY

14 DECEMBER 1955

Dear Anthony,

A hasty line or two just to hope that you have passed the examination on the [9th] and that you will come out of the last one with honor; though I have never thought that any examination is, or can be, a true test of ability and intelligence. They are a makeshift arranged by man to suggest that he has done something good and effective. I daresay there must be some kind of a test in organised educational matters, but the real test is Life; what we do in life rather than what we do in school. To do well for school or college is pleasant; but to do things well in life is important.

I'm very glad that Dr. Dittes[1] found something to praise in the psychology of COCKADOODLE DANDY. I am interested in psychology—which like all sciences is built on common sense as well as experiment—but couldnt say I know anything about it, bar reading a few books, in addition to those written by Jung and Freud. I daresay there is unconscious psychology in the play, for I watch characters keenly, and mark a lot of what they do and why they do it.

I have neither read nor seen THE RIGHTEOUS ARE BOLD.[2] It hasnt been published, and it has never been done in London. It was performed in the Abbey where it ran for nearly a year. All I know about it is what I heard, something about a girl who is possessed, and who smashes a statue of the blessed Virgin into smithereens. If you go to it you'll have to tell me about it. Long ago, the Abbey plays used to be published in paper-back editions, at sixpence or a shilling; but that practise stopped long ago. A pity. I have some of the old copies still. They used to be sold in the foyer of the theater.

I'm very glad Siobhan [McKenna, in "The Chalk Garden"] was so good. No, I didnt see her in ST JOAN, but Eileen did (Mrs O'C.), and liked her very much in it. A clever lass. I knew E[nid]. Bagnold slightly as Lady Jones. She was a great friend of the doctor head of a child clinic to which we used to bring our first two children; and the doctor—a son of the clergyman Wallace, a great friend of Livingstone's—was a friend of ours. I was in her house once at a lecture, but I really dont know her. She was the author of NATIONAL VELVET a best-seller, and of other books.

I was amused by what you quoted from the opinions of the Board of the I.C.[3] Opinions are as many as people, so we cant complain that some

[1] Dr. Dittes, Professor of Psychology, Yale Divinity School.
[2] Frank Carney's *The Righteous Are Bold* opened at the Abbey Theatre on 29 July 1946. For O'Casey's reaction to the play, see his letter to George Jean Nathan, 14 November 1946, note 8, Vol. II.
[3] *In Context,* student literary magazine at Yale Divinity School.

differ from our own. If you think writing the article will add to your confidence in writing and thinking, write it; but, if you arent interested, dont. Dont waste—or rather USE—energy unless you think strongly you should. I think [Arthur] Miller a very fine playwright, but havent read enough of T[ennessee]. W[illiams].'s work to venture an opinion as which is the better one. As for Giraudoux—ah, he is charming and lovable, and sturdy within the grace of his writing. George wasnt a bit "sacreligious" for making a joke about the laddo saying his long grace. The laddo isnt such a sacred vessel as all that. Your other friend who says he "must feel over-arched by God" is serious of course; but, surely, if there is a God, we are all over-arched by Him. The Universe is His, and all the lily in the pond, the lily in the field, Anthony Harvey in New Haven or Lynchburg, and O'Casey in Devon, are part of that Universe, and so over-arched by his power. The point is that we cant be always thinking of God; even the best of Christians cant be always worshipping. We all have work to do, and this work, so necessary, cant be done fully and effectively if we are thinking of God as we do it. Here we are, and here we must do as the life on earth demands, not what the life in heaven may command; but doesnt, for a lot of the personal and public homilies spring not from God, but from the pride of the preachers, and their resolute determination to project their own ego into the minds of others.

Your sister shouldnt be too much troubled about her boy "flunking his grade in school." With an arm in a steel brace, grades are of little importance. His arm is the grade he has to think of till it recovers. Mrs O'C. once a few years ago, fractured a wrist badly, and while the arm was fixed in thick plaster, she didnt think much about anything other than getting it well; thought as little as she could, for the first thing we must do is to get rid of whatever may be troubling us: if we can. Your other sister will have to hope for the best; the future alone can tell, and worrying wont alter it. Thank Mr. Pearson for me.[4] It was kind of him to think of me; but imagine me lecturing at Yale! Lecturing is as much an art as playwrighting; and I amnt one to venture gayly into things about which I know little. But thank him for his good thought about me. Now, my best wishes to George; and my love to your Mother, to all the family, and to you.

As ever,

[Sean O'Casey]

[4] Professor Norman Holmes Pearson, English Department, Yale University.

To Liam Ó Domhnaill[1]

TC. O'CASEY

20 DECEMBER 1955

Dear Sir,

You have a hold of the wrong end of the stick. I am not responsible for my letter appearing in INNIU.[2] Mr. Mac an Bheatha wrote to me asking me if I would write something about Jim Larkin for his Journal. This I refused to do, and gave reasons for the refusal, with a few opinions added to it. The letter was not written for publication; but just a courteous reply to one from Mr. Mac an Bheatha. By the way, criticism and statements of facts cannot be classified, tabulated, or construed into any kind of "boast" or "brag." As for your "drantanai cungarach,"[3] if you look within the columns of INNIU itself, you'll find plenty of them. Read this very week's column on An Radio, "Ar gha na hOlluin uilig?"[4] concerning the lectures on Thomas Davis. Or "Cogadh ar Mhuir"[5] in Saturday's issue of THE IRISH PRESS (17 Dec. 1955). As for the gentility of Gaelic Leaguers, see Hyde's "Mise agus an Connradh," or his "Turas go America."[6] There the Leaguers were reckoned up among Earls, Barons, Baronets, Knights, and American tycoons; not a mention of a docker, a laborer, a shop-assistant, or anyone of that class; and, to my knowledge, there was [not] one of these in either the Ard Craobh [Chief Branch] or in the Keating Branch either. Indeed, when speaking at a lecture in the Ard Craobh, given by Dr. McHenry on "The Soldiers of the Irish Brigade," I myself afterwards was rebuked for wearing a muffler instead of a collar and tie; my first and last visit to the Branch. I am not a rich laddo, and dont wish to be one. Thanks for your kind wish that I may be seven times richer this time next year, or, if no richer, then no poorer. I have no desire to be seven times richer, though I do not wish to be any poorer. It is odd that you should associate authorship with riches. Had I used the talents I have towards that end, I should have been rich long ago; but talent is too sacred a thing to be consecrated to worldly wealth—or so I think, though I may be wrong. You mention those who "gave health and life for the Gaelic without hope of any reward." So many of them did; and so did I. Let me say, too, that many of the patriots surviving made more of this world through their patriotism than I did out of my authorship. As for making it through the use of English, there was, there is, no other way. Next number of IRISH WRITING is to consist of Gaelic stories done into

[1] Liam Ó Domhnaill (O'Donnell), staff writer of *Inniu,* Dublin.
[2] See O'Casey's letter to Sean O'Rourke, 12 December 1955, note 2.
[3] "witty growling"
[4] "Were all the Professors necessary?"
[5] "War at Sea"
[6] Douglas Hyde, *Mise agus an Connradh* (1905), Myself and the League; *Mo Thurus go A hAmerice* (1905), My Journey to America.

English. Did you know? Why is this? A wider audience? We just have to face the facts. When Irish story, play, or poem is done into English in England or America, then we can say the Irish is doing well. Paradox, but a fact. P. H. Pearse, you know, did a lot of writing in Eng. De Valera speaks almost always in English, so why blame O'Casey. Of course, there were many noble lads and lasses in the Keating and Chief Branch of the League. I mentioned a number of them in my letters; but they did not understand, nor try—as far as I could see—that the masses alone could save the language. It is so now. If the "Sovereign People" dont want it, or wont have it, the language is dead. How many of them read INNIU? How many even of your Gaelic speakers go to an Irish play?

As for me, I am still what I was—a man of the masses; an "evil Communist," if you like; and I have fought and striven for them and with them. I am glad that they now have a power, the power, which we—Larkin, Connolly, and many others—labored to bring to them. Today eighty of them can threaten Dublin with darkness by simply withdrawing their labor. It is time that the Gaels should realise their power and their influence.

Finally, please remember that my letter to Mr. Mac an Bheatha was a private one, and never meant by me for publication.

With all good wishes,
Yours sincerely,
Sean O'Casey

To Anthony Perry[1]

TC. O'CASEY

21 DECEMBER 1955

Dear Anthony Perry,

If your Magazine be seen and READ by 500 students, then you have a very important audience, for I hope none of them is a greybeard. What would my old racous voice be doing among your young, shrill, eager ones? It is you who have, or ought to have, the say in the world now. My world's gone, gone in the winds of yesterday, and I dont intend to run back after it, like a man running after his hat. You will have to write for yourselves—a Magazine of the students, by the students, for the students.

[1] Anthony Perry, Central School of Speech and Drama, Students' Union, Royal Albert Hall, London. One of the editors of *Encore,* Perry published this letter as an article, Sean O'Casey, "Not Waiting For Godot," *Encore* VI, Easter 1956; reprinted in *Blasts and Benedictions* (1967). This issue also contained an editorial on O'Casey by "Osric"; an article on O'Casey by Gordon Rogoff, "Wasp Against the Criticonians"; and a reproduction of Breon O'Casey's portrait of his father.

Beckett? I have nothing to do with Beckett. He isnt in me nor am I in him. I amnt waiting for Godot to bring me life; I am out after life myself, even at the age I've reached. What have any of you to do with Godot? There is more life than Godot can give in the life of the least of us. That Beckett is a clever writer, and that he has written a rotting and remarkable play, there is no doubt; but his philosophy isnt my philosophy, for within him there is no hazard of hope; no desire for it; nothing in it but a lust for despair, and a crying of woe, not in a wilderness, but a garden. The earth isnt either a graveyard or a roaring camp—save in a war, when it is both; but today war is a non est, for with the new nuclear explosive power, all are within range of death; the rich and the poor, the ones who go out to fight, the ones who remain at home; the catholic pope and the catholic peasant share its shivers, and so arent ready to nod the head in favor of strife. And there is life and energy even in decay (not Beckett's, but nature's), for dead leaves turn to loam, and dry bones to phosphates.

What witnesses does this Beckett call? A dowdy and a doleful few: Camus, Kafka, Orwell, Graham Greene, Huxley, with T. S. Eliot a wan follower, cross on breast and hands clenched in an obscure prayer. And what witness have we? A cloud of them: Copernicus, Newton, Beethoven, Angelo, Shelley, Whitman, Balzac, Faraday, Titian, and, yes, by God, and Shakespeare, too, with ten thousand others close up to the greatest!

As for the English Theater, it is but a ghostly memory, with the Irish Theater a runner-up. There is, of course, Joan Littlewood's Theater Workshop in East London—a cinderella without a fairy godot-mother; a theater that should get what is given to the Old Vic, for it is adventurous as the other is timid and tired and lazy. There is the People's Theater in Newcastle, a venture that is spreading into what may become a sanctuary for the drama, the film, and chamber quartette. A nest of amateurs who have kept the rose of Lancaster, rose of York, and Tudor rose in a state worthy of wearing: colour and scent are in them still. But what are these among so many? The rest is silence; or a mutter and a mouse, hurting a silence that would be a finer honor. Today, bar the Musicals, WAITING FOR GODOT and THE WILD DUCK, there isnt a play worth a penny on the London Stage; and these are by an Irishman and a Norwegian. No, sir, English Drama is the bird in the golden cage, and it is safe in the vaults of the Bank of England.

Yours sincerely,
Sean O'Casey

To Tarlach Ó hUid

TC. O'CASEY

24 DECEMBER 1955

Dear Tarlach,

I am still reading your AN DÁTHRÁ,[1] for I am a slow reader, as well as having many an interruption with work of my own and work with the home and the children.

I havent grasped it as a whole yet, not having come to the end; but there's a lot in it. I dont quite get the exact translation—is it "The Two Strands"? But, of course, I get the sad and sometimes terrible implication. Oh, these dividing religions! It is simply written, at times, homely, but very effective. I am beginning to get used to the Roman type and the "simplified spelling," but it was hard going at first.

I have just read your story—THE OFFERING, in IRISH WRIT-ING,[2] and it is fine—even in the Beurla.[3] The best in the book. Oddly enough, I refer to this "custom" in an article for a book of mine to come out in New York next spring. I knew it under the name of "Canting the Corpse."[4]

Thanks for sending me your book. I have written my name in it; but wish it could have been given a far better format.

With all good wishes,
Yours sincerely,
Sean O'Casey.

[1] Tarlach Ó hUid, *An Dá Thrá* (The Two Strands), 1952.

[2] Tarlach Ó hUid, "The Offering," *Irish Writing No. 33*, Winter 1955, Gaelic Writers Issue: A representative selection of the modern Gaelic revival presented in translation; guest editors Seamus O'Neill and Valentin Iremonger.

[3] The English language.

[4] See "Bonfire Under a Black Sun," *The Green Crow* (1956): "This is the cultural custom of collecting money to show respect to a dead neighbor. At the ceremony, the priest, or the official collector, sings out the name of the donor and the amount given as the tribute is put on the plate resting on or beside the coffin; all making desperate assaults on themselves to give as much as they can so as to preserve a high standing within the community. In my young days, it was known as 'canting the corpse,' from the Irish word *cantail*, selling by auction." (p. 151)

To Inniu

TC. O'CASEY

25 DECEMBER 1955

Dear Editor,

Are ye all drunk? Were these five PUNT[1] meant really for me? On Christmas Day in the morning too! I nearly decided to keep it. What are they for? Has Mhic Ui Domhnaill [Mr. O'Donnell] shown you the letter I sent him?[2] Another private exposure? Listen lad: When I sent Mac an Bheatha the letter he showed to you, I didnt think it would be published; it wasnt meant for publication; only for Mac an Bheatha's enlightenment. But its publication doesnt matter a damn to me. It was I who wrote it, but all the world can read it, if the world is so inclined.

I intended to write to you to warn you—not against the publication of my letter—that a letter is copyright, of which fact INNIU doesnt seem to be aware. It's allright by me; but some other time, someone may write a letter which if published by you, might cause a row. In future, for your own sake, I'd advise you to get permission to publish first.

Fees arent given for letters, far as I know—anywhere; so you lads must have a lot of money to throw away. If anyone got anything, it should be the lad that put Irish on the letter.

When I became a subscriber, I merely wished to help INNIU; not to get money out of it (by the way, I like it very much. It comes closer to Ireland than all the nationals put together); so I return your check with thanks for the unkind thought of sending it to me.

With all good wishes for the New Year.

Yours sincerely,
Sean O'Casey

1 Five pounds, payment for the use of a letter in Irish that O'Casey wrote to Proinnsias Mac an Bheatha of *Inniu*, which was printed in Liam Ó Domhnaill's "Sean O'Casey Is An Ghaeilge" (Sean O'Casey and the Irish Language), *Inniu*, 2 December 1955.

2 See O'Casey's letter to Liam Ó Domhnaill, 20 December 1955.

II

"WE CANNOT ALWAYS SUFFER ECSTASY"

1956

I KNOW what a housewife has to face & has to do. I've scrubbed bare floors—no oil cloth for the poorer slums—kindled poor fires, washed my own & my mother's poor shirt & shift; but it was no treadmill task to do what we could to keep ourselves alive, & go about; at least, dishonestly clean; for no tenement dweller could keep honestly clean under the conditions, around, about, & above them. I did chores before I became ill, to help my wife; & am beginning again—washing up, peeling spuds, carrying down the garbage, etc. It is partly good for us, for it is routine, & this checks the excitement of the mind, & gives us rest. We cannot always suffer ecstasy."

"I was anxious about 'Purple Dust'; but a sad circumstance has put it out of my mind: our younger boy of 21 years died on us on Saturday night, the 29th Dec. He came home on holidays on the 14th tired, & on Monday we knew, & he knew, that he had that fell thing Leukaemia. He had a brilliant mind, a de-

lightful, if somewhat sardonic sense of humor, & was thoughtful & unselfish; a great talker.

Well, just another Golden Lad gone to Dust."

This was to be O'Casey's year of lingering pain and sudden grief,
when he had to endure two consecutive major operations early in 1956—
prostate and kidney stone—then an attack of bronchial pneumonia, a long
post-operation infection, and finally the late December shock of the death
from leukemia of his 21-year-old son Niall. It was an extended and finally
grim ordeal for the half-blind 76-year-old playwright who, nevertheless,
like Teiresias, seemed in his suffering to have taken on prophetic visions
in the letters that provided his necessary catharsis of words. He became
more eloquent in adversity. At the beginning of the year, even before the
blows struck, he seems to have anticipated the dark journey ahead when
he told a despairing and "perplexed" young editor in London that there
must be some redemption through suffering, "for out of the decay a new
life will rise, like as in Strindberg's DREAM PLAY, when the Castle, with
its foundations deep in the mud of the earth, goes on fire, the flower-bud
on its roof bursts into a giant chrysanthemum. There can be no resurrection without a grave. You young people are this resurrection."

O'Casey's concept of the resurrection sometimes sounds like a Communist vision perceived in various letters through Christian symbols, where
he invokes the "Holy Ghost" or "God's throne" or "Praise God," or cries
out for his homeland, "Oh, God, this grip that Ireland gives!" Meanwhile
he can urge his London friend to "Get hold of some idea for the common
good. Transfix your mind with the Communistic ideal of 'From all according to their means, to all according to their needs'; and 'An injury to
one is the concern of all.' " He expands his eclectic dream in an early
letter to a class of American students: "Let the vision live within you. If
you be poor, don't let the hardness of poverty petrify the vision in disillusionment; if you be well-off, don't let the vision be silked and softened;
for to do either is to sin against the Holy Ghost."

O'Casey might have been tempted to succumb to that sin himself
early in the year when confronted by the failure of the New York production of *Red Roses For Me,* which had opened to mixed reviews and might
have survived, but ironically it had to close after 29 performances because
the theatre owner demanded capacity houses or an arbitrary closing. Perhaps chastened by this disappointment, O'Casey took a modest view of
himself as an itinerant minstrel when he wrote to another American student
in early April: "I am but a wandering road-minstrel, singing an odd song at
any cross-roads where a few people may be gathered together; an odd song
in the form of a play, a few thoughts set out in the form of an article, or a

song in the form of a song itself." Nevertheless, he picked up the challenge in early September by making a detailed reply to a cruel attack on his life and work by an Irish Catholic critic who called him a bigoted Protestant and failed dramatist. He left the judgment of his writing to posterity, but insisted that as a poor Protestant he was always closer in experience and sympathy to the Catholic workers than he could possibly have been to the Protestant establishment.

O'Casey wrote two of his most poetic and prophetic letters to a Brooklyn woman in June and to John Gassner in August. The ailing and despairing woman had written to tell him about her sorrow and lost hope, and he replied in his "We cannot always suffer ecstasy" letter with a prose poem of stoical and enduring faith: "It is not for me to say nay to your sad letter; but surely it is the lot of all of us to know the feverish brow, and the body hot with illness, or cold with the many hopes vanished, a voice lost, & no light, apparently, before us. Only apparently, for the light is there always, tho' we often keep our eyes shut so that we cannot see. I am aware of all you say about underpaid workers, of many a funeral; thro' many strikes, & have eaten dry bread & bitter waters, with my half-famished comrades; but never lost the will to keep fighting."

Although he was still weak from his operations, from bronchial pneumonia and a prolonged infection—it was mid-July before "the wound across the belly decided to close"—he was still fighting and singing, as his epistolary voice took on a tone of biblical incantation and wisdom in his comments on a despondent friend of Gassner's who wanted to be an artist: "I, when I was young, fiercely wanted to be a painter, but, even in employment, when bare necessities were pacified, I had not the means to buy brush or paint, or canvas. God can't always be in attendance on us. It would be glorious if the seed of talent within brought forth fruit a hundredfold; grand if it brought forth fruit sixtyfold; but who is he or so who am I to be dissatisfied with a yield of thirtyfold? Considering the dangers of the wayside, the stony ground, the thorns of triviality, a tenfold fruiting is a thing by which to Praise God. We mustn't rail so that the ripening grape sours again; but rather allow the still sour grape of life to ripen." There is something quite remarkable in O'Casey's ability to create the informal and spontaneous flow of this parable for a friend.

He was also capable of a Dickensian rage against injustice when in a September letter to an MP he pleads for clemency for an unfortunate and incompetent house-breaker who has served six years of a harsh ten-year sentence: "It was a Judge Fingleton or Jingleton, gave the savage sentence. Some years ago, this judge went west, and Christ only knows how long a sentence of detention he is now doing himself somewhere else."

In January O'Casey rings a bell for some of his American heroes, Washington and Lincoln and Whitman; in May he is defending Shaw's plays from foolish clerical attack by the Bishop of Galway; in July he recalls meeting the "shy" T. E. Lawrence with G.B.S., and receiving a friendly "nod" from Sir Roger Casement; in November he praises President Eisenhower, "for tho' his politics aren't mine, he is a good man and true and gentle-hearted—soldier an all as he was."

Politics and art continue to occupy O'Casey's mind, particularly the misleading approach to art made by Communists. In April he tells a young American woman that he rejects the Communist dogma that explains the artistic process as an inevitable reflection of the class-struggle: "There is no 'class-consciousness' in art; there is but bad painting and fine painting. It is the mind of the artist that creates the art." And he proceeds to defend the abstract art of Picasso and Braque. In a December letter to a Bulgarian Communist, he repeats one of his frequent charges: "Communists should not be so dogmatic about Literature and Art, about which most of them know little or nothing. The artists should be free to picture life in paintings, music, and words, as they see and feel it." When Brooks Atkinson teasingly draws him out about his eclectic and aesthetic "Shelleyan and Dickensian and Byronic and Whitmanian Communism," and confronts him with some yes-or-no questions, O'Casey gives his friend this direct reply: "Am I a Communist? Yes; as deep a one as I was more than fifty years ago. Am I of the Party? No, for, like Shaw, I wished first to be a good playwright before anything else. That is the thing that many Communists seemed unable to learn—that a man must be first excellent at what his hand findeth to do before he could be a Communist at all." He remains therefore his own kind of instinctive and non-party Communist, but he goes on stubbornly and unconvincingly to defend Stalin on the dubious grounds that "He was not infallible."

It was Communist politics, not aesthetics, that prompted O'Casey to tell a Dublin woman in late November that the Soviet army's invasion that crushed the Hungarian Rising was a tragic necessity. The woman's husband, an Irish Communist, agreed with O'Casey, but she was a Catholic who saw the invasion as an outrageous act of Russian tyranny. Here is the key passage of O'Casey's reply:

> "I'm afraid I agree with Michael. To me, there isn't a shadow of a doubt that those who hate, and always hated, Communism (Socialism, if you like) tried to seize hold of the popular discontent in Hungary, and use it to overthrow all signs of Socialism there, and set up the old regime of landlord, clerical and lay, and fascist boss."

A generation later the noted British historian, A. J. P. Taylor, no apologist for Russian aggression, in an interview by Duncan Fallowell, "Historian at Home," in the *Irish Times*, 21 June 1983, made the following comment, which closely parallels and apparently supports O'Casey's 1956 interpretation:

> The Hungarian Rising of 1956 was a rising by all the most reactionary forces against the socialism taking place and if victorious would have led to a full restitution of the power of the Roman Catholic Church and a

restoration of the great landowners. So I think in every way what happened to Hungary in 1956 was fortunate.

This difficult year closed with several tragic ironies for O'Casey. His young son Niall, home for the Christmas holiday from London University, agreed with the Dublin woman's view of Russian tyranny in Hungary. This led to a painful father-and-son confrontation, which was fortunately resolved by an emotional reconciliation and agreement to disagree. On the 27th of December *Purple Dust* opened successfully in New York and was to continue for a whole year, becoming the longest running O'Casey play ever. Two days later Niall died of leukemia.

To Anthony Perry

TC. O'CASEY

1 JANUARY 1956

Dear Young friend,
I wonder why you say that "after all, we are only students"? Arent we all only students? Are we not, or shouldnt we be, investigators, seekers after an explanation of all the wonderful and amazing phenomena around us? Wasnt Rutherford, Einstein, Faraday, Shelley, Byron, Yeats—each in his own way, and all of them—students till the day they died? So was Marx, so was Lenin—peering out into the future from where they stood in the present; as we are now, and as those who come after will be too. It is reported that God once said "Speak to the Children of Israel that they go forward"; and the Bible is full of "Go forth." Are we to hearken unto them who are forever mumbling "Speak to the people of the world that go backward"! The people of the world dont even hear them. Pity that some of the students lap it up, or seem to lap it up; in England anyway. The other night, over the wireless, Mr. Malcolm Muggeridge, in the program, "Frankly Speaking," gave us all his flippant misereries on mankind (how reverent and full of awe were Margaret Lane, John Betjeman, and Mr. Morpurgo, the inquisitors, to him, before him, and round about him!). He told his sorrowful questioners that our civilization was in its decline; that it was going, that it would soon be gone. Begone, dull cur! Well, this was hardly hot news, for many knew it years and years ago. Nothing to worry about, he added; but many are worrying about it, and see in its death the end of God and the end of man. The moaners think that when they die, life and all will die with them. It wont, for out of the decay a new life will rise, like as in Strindberg's DREAM PLAY, when the Castle, with its foundations deep in the mud of the earth, goes on fire, the flower-bud on its roof bursts into a giant chrysanthemum. There can be no resur-

rection without a grave. You young people are this resurrection, taking over the burnt-out Castle, and building a bigger life around the giant chrysanthemum, leaving the dead to bury their dead, and the mourners to cry alone.

You say your young are "a bit perplexed." Well, dont be perplexed any longer. Get hold of some idea for the common good. Transfix your mind with the Communistic ideal of "From all according to their means, to all according to their needs"; and "An injury to one is the concern of all"; or, if this be too grand for you, then join the Labor Movement; or, if you think this too dangerous, then the Young Conservatives; for even they have to go forward sometime or another.

A question: I see by the papers that the Students are having a Drama Festival. Good; but why dont you get a panel of judges from your own young flock instead of getting an adjudicator from among the critics outworn and slop-soiled from the commercial theater?

I enclose a cutting showing the state of the English theater today. Read, too, K. Tynan's article in OBSERVER 1st. 1. '56. In 1946 a million granted for a National Theater; then one stone was laid on the site; today, it is but the one pebble on the british drama beach. And we go on singing carols in the church and in the street!

You can publish what you like in these letters,[1] if you think your students would be interested. One thing only as a condition: By all means get your fee from the Perfumier in exchange for an Ad; but dont send it to me. No paper or magazine pays a fee for letters.

All good wishes from the heart out to all your students for the present year of important time.

Yours sincerely,
Sean O'Casey.

[1] See O'Casey's letter to Perry, 21 December 1955, note 1.

To David Krause

TS. KRAUSE

3 JANUARY 1956

My dear Dave:
Many thanks for your letter, for the cuttings, and for your comments on the production of RED ROSES FOR ME.[1] The play has gone

[1] I had seen the play in mid-December during its two-week run at the Wilbur Theatre in Boston, prior to the opening at the Booth Theatre in New York on 28 December 1955, directed by John O'Shaughnessy, settings and lighting by Howard

on to the New York stage, with the result of two to one against. Brooks Atkinson of the *N.Y. Times* writes glowing of it; Walter Kerr, of HERALD-TRIBUNE says it worse than no good,[2] and so flung us into a faint—tho' it didn't last long; and the blood is once again flowing regularly to the brain. I do hope it may run long enough to give the actors some reward for their strenuous work, and cover the cost of production so that no one may lose from it. What a trip—R.I. to Boston—to see a play! Just as Wilde said, it takes the audience to make a play before it can be a success. Personally, Dave, down deep in me, I am quiet-souled about either success or failure. To be in harmony with oneself, one must set honor in the one eye and death in the other, and look on both indifferently; but I hope it may run long enough to give me say a year's pay, enough to reward the actors reasonably, and cover the backers' costs. Apart from these, I am interested only in the possibility of a newer and fresher shape being brought to the Drama. I've just read Miller's two new plays in the vol A VIEW FROM THE BRIDGE[3]—fine drama, in my opinion—and I was glad to see the signs of change in each of them; touches that bring the Drama away from the out-worn method of composition.

As for your comments, they are well taken; and I feel sure you are right. It is hard for actors, practiced in other methods of acting, to come suddenly and clearly into a new and strange style—though even in commonplace plays, it is hard to win perfection of Caste, for it is almost impossible now to get the actors a Director might desire. The Rake on the stage[4] had nothing to do with either Producer or Director—I think. There is a movement abroad for such a stage, in the belief that it will facilitate movement and grouping—not so successful, apparently, as was hoped, if your reaction is a good one. I get this idea from a letter I read in the N.Y. Times which congratulates the theatres—four or five—who have adopted it. I'd like to see it, before I venture an opinion; though, on the other hand, I've never seen the Arena Stage, but decidedly reject the idea. RED ROSES was done on one in Houston, Texas—or was it COCKA-DOODLE DANDY?[5] The Grey beard was my suggestion:[6] that was how

---

Bay, music by Edwin Finckel, costumes by Ballou, choreography by Anna Sokolow, presented by Gordon W. Pollock, with the following cast: Eileen Crowe as Mrs. Breydon, Kevin McCarthy as Ayamonn Breydon, Ann Dere as Eeada, Katherine Hynes as Dympna, Virginia Bosler as Finnoola, Joyce Sullivan as Sheila Moorneen, E. G. Marshall as Brennan o' the Moor, David McDaniel as A Singer, Eamon Flynn as Roory O'Balacaun, Casey Walters as Mullcanny, Michael Clarke Laurence as Rev. E. Clinton, Shamus Locke as Inspector Finglas, Whitford Kane as Samuel, Barry Maccollum as Foster, Jock McGraw as Dowzard, David Ryan as Lamplighter.

[2] See O'Casey's letter to Brooks Atkinson, 4 January 1956, notes 1, 2, 3.

[3] Arthur Miller, *A View From the Bridge* and *A Memory of Two Mondays* (1955).

[4] A raked stage was used, so that the actors had to move carefully up and down on a surface sharply inclined toward the audience.

[5] O'Shaughnessy had previously directed the American premiere of *Red Roses For Me*, on an arena stage, at The Playhouse, Houston, Texas, on 25 April 1951, with Kevin McCarthy and Joyce Sullivan in the same roles they played in the New

I saw the character in my mind and in reality; for the part was built on
a man who had a graceful white beard who earned a part living by singing
in front of middle-class houses in the afternoons of Saturday whenever the
weather allowed, playing a melodeon in a quiet way as an accompaniment
to his quavering sentences.

I'm glad that you think the play a lyrical one—though that remains
a matter of opinion; see what Walter Kerr says about it. One thing—I can't
grow conceited; for one bell rings rejoicing, another tolls a knell. The
Mulcanny and Roory with you couldn't be worse than the Irish ones we
had long ago in London. I smile when I hear it said that all the Irish are
natural actors. And, as for myself, and what Dick W[atts]. said about me—
well, I don't feel any religious core in either play or man. If anything, I
forever feel as Peter must ha' felt in the midst of his hot profanity; or as
a convent-novice would feel in her worst hours.

I'm so glad to hear that Candy [Greene] is improving. It was a blow
to the little one, a hard blow; and I do hope she may come out of it only
with the stain of a bruise or two.

Eileen is writing to you to thank you for the Christmas Gift; and I
thank you, too—tho' wishing you'd set aside your money for a future
need. Should what I get now, and what I've gotten, for the last couple of
years, I shan't growl. I hope the play may run long enough to give the
actors a reasonable return for the hard work they put into it; and long
enough to pay back the money that has been put into it. You see, Dave,
I'm always worried by the knowledge of what the actors have to do before
a play comes to the stage; and how miserable it is when a play packs up
before they have had a chance to get a return for their work. This thought
comes to me even when I'm starting to write one. That is a torment in the
Theater. With a novel one just writes it, and, if it be any good at all, the
Publisher will at least cover the cost; the author after the proofs have been
read, has no worry save about how much he himself is going to get out of
it. That is why I am all for, and all out for, the Municipal Theater that
employs a permanent company, and meets the loss—if there be a loss—
out of public funds.

Just got a letter, a short one, from Dave [Greene], who seems to have
been glad to get out of Ireland, and back to the old townland. I think he
is wise to do the work at home: Ireland isn't a fine place to work in today.
He has a big job in front of him, too; one I shouldn't like to tackle. I wish
him all success; for Synge is, indeed, worth more than a mention.

We all send our love to you. My hand is tight in yours.

As ever,
Sean

York production. For details on the Texas production, see O'Casey's letter to George
Jean Nathan, 26 May 1951, note 2, Vol. II. *Cock-a-Doodle Dandy* had its American
premiere at the Arena Theatre, Dallas, Texas, on 30 January 1950, directed by Margo
Jones.

⁶ The beard worn by E. G. Marshall in the role of Brennan.

To Brooks Atkinson

TS. ATKINSON

4 JANUARY 1956

My dear Brooks:

My hundred thanks to you for your glowing review of RED ROSES.[1] I hope I deserve it; or, rather, that the play deserves it. All I am sure of is that the play doesn't altogether deserve the one given by Walter Kerr.[2] Though it may not be as good as you think, I'm sure it isn't as bad as he says it is. There is no doubt in my mind that John O'Shaughnessy did all he could with it, and did what he did well and that Mr. Pollock was a brave man to put it on: and these two facts, plus what the actors have put into it, are what worries me. In my time, I have been to many rehearsals, and I know the hard work it is for the actors, the strain and the anxiety within them of how they will do their parts, and how the play will go. And that goes, too, for the Director, who, woe is me! put money into it, too. I don't like, either, anyone to lose their money on it. As for myself, I honestly don't care a damn so long as I manage to forge a fair and decent living for the family; and this I have managed to do—with help from American friends—up to today. Considering all I have no reason to say a mumblin word. All I pray for is that it may run long enough to give the actors a reasonable return for their hard work, and that neither O'Shaughnessy nor Pollock may lose any money over it. To me, there is no loss of prestige whatever in a "failure." At the moment, I am busy writing letters to the Editor of a Students' magazine, who asked for an article, promising the fee given by a seller of perfumes for an Ad. in the magazine, in return for an article. I have let meself go in the letters which they are to publish; and I've pointed out that no Fee is given for correspondence, so that the Students can keep what they get from the Perfumier, and use it for development of their magazine. Just now, I hear Shivaun playing the piano and Niall playing his trombone, so the Island is full of Noises; pleasant ones associated with contented life.

So don't you let yourself worry, or our dear Oriana either, for there is life and fight and joy in our hearts still. To me, three For and four Against is good going.[3] A disturbed psyche is alive. Yes, I know about

[1] Brooks Atkinson, "Theatre: Sean O'Casey," *New York Times,* 29 December 1955.

[2] Walter Kerr, "Theatre: 'Red Roses For Me,'" *New York Herald Tribune,* 29 December 1955.

[3] The three reviewers "For" the play: Brooks Atkinson in the *New York Times;* William Hawkins in the *New York World-Telegram;* Richard Watts Jr. in the *New York Post.* The four reviewers "Against" the play: John Chapman in the *New York*

George's severe trials, and I hope he won't go to the Theater till he is really fit to go. I am writing Julie to keep him in bed. George made a mistake in not always having a woman near him. The great complexity of life is that one must look after oneself as well as thinking of others—a very sensible complexity. I shall be writing to Oriana next time. In the meanwhile, here are a few suggestions for a title for her book—though it is difficult to do anything outside of a guess when one hasn't read the MS:[4]

Twisting Shamrocks.	Green Smoke.
Dust Shamrock.	Aging Furniture.
Shabby Discontents.	Threadbare Torments.
Green Commentary.	Take Me Home From Ireland.
Round Tower Roofless.	Keltic Conundrum.

The above may give Oriana a suggestion for a title that would be better, and more suitable for what she may have written. The book should rouse a noisy stir where the river Shannon flows. Would that make a title? "Where the River Shannon Flows"? It's the title of a song well known a few years ago.

And, last, but, by God, not least, thanks a hundred again for Oriana's and your Christmas Gift to us.

> *My love to Oriana and to you.*
> *As ever and ever,*
> *Sean*

PS. To make title shorter, it could run "Where the Shannon Flows."

Daily News; Robert Coleman in the *New York Daily Mirror;* Walter Kerr in the *New York Herald Tribune;* John McClain in the *New York Journal American.* For the account of the play's closing after 29 performances, see O'Casey's letter to Whitford Kane, ? January 1956, note 1.

[4] Oriana Atkinson's book on Ireland was published later in the year under the title, *South and the West of It: Ireland and Me* (1956).

To Mrs. Oriana Atkinson

MS. ATKINSON

4 JANUARY 1956

My dear Oriana:

Thanks for your kind letter. I'm so glad you had, at least, an interesting evening—at the play. On the stage, one rarely gets all one wills or wishes. I'm afraid you're right about the Rector[1]—he was indeed a warm-hearted man. He was a real friend of mine. Tho' he wasn't rich, he had a large family of six, & it took him all his time to meet their needs. He couldn't afford a maid, & his wife, a grand lass, did most of the housework. They had a woman in for an hour a day or so; & they had a big parochial house (The Rectory) to keep in order—a dreadful job. He was the one Protestant priest I met of whom I could honestly say he was a man, Human, withal; for once with him, I saw him fling a book at the eldest son because the boy hadn't learned a Greek lesson correctly. I withstood him then with a hot rebuke that he took quietly; tho' he didn't excuse himself. But, maybe, the part in the play wasn't written well enough.

And the dancer! Oh, I've met her (or him) before. It has always been a trial to me that no one seems to be able to do this spontaneously as it should be in a play. Such must always have been done as a perfect ballet performance. Brooks probably remembers a lot of it in the rehearsal he saw of "Purple Dust." If I have time, and God spares me, I intend to write something about this: First aid to Directors of choreographers.

I hope you got a title for your book. May I add these 3 as suggestions? "A Yankee on the Shannon Shore," or "Manhattan on Shannon Shore." "Under an Irish Moon."

If this writing seems a bit shaky, put it down to this: today I got a tangled knot of fibres burned from the sole of a foot by Electricity; and the plastered foot seems to be burning away still.

By the way, why not try to get an English publisher to do your book in alliance with your American one?

My sincere love to you, my lass, my good lass.

As ever,
Sean

[1] Rev. E. Clinton of St. Burnupus Church, in *Red Roses For Me,* the character based upon O'Casey's dear friend, Rev. Edward Morgan Griffin (1852–1923), of St. Barnabas Church, Dublin. The second volume of the autobiography, *Pictures in the Hallway* (1942), is dedicated "To the memory of The Rev. E. M. Griffin, B.D., M.A., one-time Rector of St. Barnabas, Dublin. A fine scholar; a man of many-branched kindness, whose sensitive hand was the first to give the clasp of friendship to the author." His picture is the frontispiece of the third volume, *Drums Under the Windows* (1946).

To Whitford Kane[1]

MS. BERG COLLECTION

5 JANUARY 1956

Dear friend,

Thank you so much for the Cuttings and your kind (or unkind?) re-marks. I wish I could have been with you to take a few of the knocks; but, still, they travel far enough to bang the old head here; tho' the old banged head still sings and shouts. Unfortunately, you actors & we playwrights have to stew, too, in the juice of the Theater—be it bad or be it good. It was fine to hear from an Ulsterman—Ultach [Ulster]—one "beautiful field," detached from the other three.

I have quite a few friends in Ulster.

All good wishes to you, & thanks again.

Yours very sincerely,
Sean O'Casey

---

[1] Whitford Kane (1881–1956), Irish actor, born in Larne, Northern Ireland, played the role of Samuel in the New York production of *Red Roses For Me*. He died on 17 December 1956.

To Miss Joan McAlevey

MS. MCALEVEY

14 JANUARY 1956

Dear Joan,

176 Pages![1] I can hardly imagine it; but it is amazing what one little head and one little hand can do! I'm glad you've put the Thesis well be-hind you. It is a relief to be able to cry Finis.

The rumor you heard about "daughter of an Irish playwright in a film" has very slender foundations. NBC recently did a half-hour Televi-sion of the family—to be shown on the 22nd of this month, Jan.[2]—, and, of course Shivaun appears in it, as do we all. She is still at school, & will be there for another two years at least. At the moment, she's studying "Janet" in Fry's "Lady's Not for Burning," for a public school perfor-mance. When she & her mother were in Paris, the two of them, with Thomas Quinn Curtiss, Paris drama critic, for the Herald-Tribune, did

---

[1] Joan G. McAlevey, "Sean O'Casey: Three Decades of Criticism," M.A. thesis, Columbia University.
[2] See O'Casey's letter to George Braziller, 9 November 1955, note 1.

"extras" in some film or other, & earned a few hundred francs: that is all the truth there is in the story.

I'm so glad your mother & you liked the Play [*Red Roses For Me*]. Yes, I'd like to meet your Reverend Mother, who doesn't want the young to hear anything that hasn't been said by an Anglican. What a hope she has! Won't be long till many of them are reading "The New Yorker"; & they could do a lot worse.

Is she herself an Anglican or a Roman Catholic Reverend Mother? Like all other classes & groups, some R. mothers are clever and kind, some cruel & stupid.

I do hope you may have a fine time when you go a roving over Europe.

And I hope your father isn't seriously ill, & that he will soon be better, so giving relief to your mother—to whom, my love, to all yours, & to yourself.

Yours as ever.
Sean

To Eugene Weintraub

TS. WEINTRAUB

14 JANUARY 1956

Dear Mr. Weintraub:

Thank you very much for your kind letter. I shouldn't for a moment say "Red Roses" was a "great play." It isn't, but I believe it to be a play worthy of production on any stage—and that's saying a lot you know. The "break" isn't so terrible: it is the vision filling the mind of Ayamonn. There have been many "breaks" in Drama: Shakespeare from the Classical way; Ibsen from the Romantic way; and so on. Such breaks are bound to be controversial. Voltaire thought Shakespeare a barbarian.

I, too, hope, the Producer may find another theatre to act as a vase for my bunch of Red Roses.

Sorry Eddie Marshall's singing sounds rasping. I'm afraid I'm to blame. He was here with me in the summer, & I sang the songs to him. I have the raucous voice of a crow, & poor Eddie may have been affected. But, I, too, have—if not a "musical ear," at least an ear for music. Last night I listened to Mozart who is being celebrated here by the B.C.C., he is my favorite Composer; tho' I've no real or even fanciful knowledge of music—not like G.B.S., who had.

That was denied me. I had to go to work too soon. But my lads and my daughter know music, thank God. Thank you heartily for your kind interest in the play.

> *Yours very Sincerely,*
> *Sean O'Casey*

To Mrs. Oriana Atkinson

MS. ATKINSON

16 JANUARY 1956

My dear Oriana:

I think "Oh, oh, the Dear Little Isle" or, "Oh, oh, the dear little Isle," is fine: better than the others, I imagine.

You've got the words a little wrong—tho' I can't remember them myself—bar the chorus. The song's title is "Our Dear Little Isle," & it goes to the air of "The Caravet Jig." I've often sung it in the years now so hazily behind me. One verse goes—omitting the first line which I can't, for the life of me, bring back into my mind:

> . . . .
> When with O'Neill, and O'Donnell Abu,
> Sassanacks everywhere rank in the slaughter o—
> Vengeance on tyrants, dear Eire, for you!

and the chorus:

> Oh, yes, we've a sweet little spot of it,
> Oh, yes, a dear little Isle;—
> Yes, yes, if Irishmen thought of it,
> 'Twould be a sweet little, dear little Isle!

Oddly enough, dear, the song Brennan sings is attached to it, for I adapted the air "I walked with a fine maid far out in the country" from "The Caravat Jig."

It is a lively, & in a way, a fine tune.

I think your title is as good as any of the others; & I believe it to be better. I'd advise you to decide on it.

Give Brooks my dear little thanks for his kind letter and his dear big reviews which have lifted up my heart—I hope and believe deservedly. But reviews apart, Brooks is a grand American and, deeper still, a grand man. I will be writing to him one day.

I took a walk today—the first for a fortnight, and saw the Catholic

& the Protestant churches of St. Marychurch, facing each other fiercely, and chiming out their differing messages of love.

> *To Brooks & to you, sweet lass.*
> *My deep love.*
> *Sean*

To Cedric Belfrage[1]

TS. ROSE RUSSELL[2]

16 JANUARY 1956

Dear Mr. Belfrage:

Thanks for your letter. Leaving me alone doesn't leave me at peace, but at war; at war with those things with which I can most effectively deal; and with which I have a close personal connection. For instance, I've just sent a message to the Irish Workers' League who are to hold a meeting to remember Jim Larkin, the great Irish Labor Leader—he was jailed in the USA for five years—with whom I went through the great Lock-out in 1913.

You should see that I cannot hope to interfere in the cause you mention in the natural way which comes to me when dealing with things and affairs in my own country. If the USA is to be delivered from this lousy spying persecution, the incentive to fight must arise and remain within the USA herself. We must fight on our own home fronts.

Aside from this reason, to make such a record as you mention would be to do something altogether outside my nature, character, and inclination.[3] I couldn't think of doing it. It would be an impudent, pompous, and arrogant act of exhibitionism; and I'll have none of it. God knows America has her own prophets; let the Americans hear them. There are—to mention but three—Jefferson, Lincoln, and Whitman; two of them American Presidents, the other America's great poet. Beside them, O'Casey's voice

[1] Cedric Belfrage, British-born journalist who lived in the United States after 1937; founded *The National Guardian,* a left-wing weekly newspaper in 1948 in New York, with James Aronson and John T. McManus. For an account of his difficulties with the House Un-American Activities Committee in 1953–55, see his book, *The Frightened Giant: My Unfinished Affair With America* (1957). See O'Casey's letter to him, 22 July 1939, Vol. I.

[2] This letter was in the possession of Rose Russell, legislative representative of the Teachers Union of New York. Extracts of the letter, as "A Message to the New York Teachers Union," were printed in *The National Guardian,* 2 April 1956.

[3] Belfrage asked O'Casey to send a recorded message against McCarthyism to Rose Russell for the Annual Meeting of the Teachers Union of New York.

would be but the chirrup of a sparrow to the Eagle's whistle, and she in full fight, fearless facing the sun.

Of course, my sympathy and good wishes go with Rose Russell and the Members of her Union; and I could wish that the Teachers' Union of Ireland had half the fighting-spirit of their American brothers and sisters; for they are facing finely the informers who would be ready to swear that a prayer to God threatens His throne; while my Irish comrades wouldn't dare to say boo to a Roman Catholic school-manager on the one hand, or a Protestant school-manager on the other.

In a way, it's amusing to think of the manner innocent people are harried while the greatest sub-versionist has to go free forever; for the greatest sub-versionist is life itself, changing everything as she goes through Time, even, turning things all tapsalteerie O!

The record you ask for is out of the question. When India was fighting the exploitation of the British Gov., I sent many a message to the Indian People; but now that India is free, I shouldn't venture any message— except one of goodwill to all—for India's People, led by their great leader, Nehru, alone, can make what I'm sure She will be in the years to come; a colorful People with a strenuous and safe and happy social life.

Life in Time will pull the McCarthies and the stooges into forgotten graves; as she has carried the Great into the grave too; but these are about us still; Jefferson and Lincoln speak still within the minds and hearts of America's People, and Whitman sings his songs still in Manhattan, and not only there, but everywhere all the world over.

Please give my love to Rose Russell, and my good wishes to the Members of her Union.

Yours sincerely,
Sean O'Casey

To John Beary

MS. BEARY

17 JANUARY 1956

Dear John,

Very glad to hear that you have some kind of a decent job, instead of barking your way through an Irish Circus group.[1] And don't rush out of it [into] the theater or the B.B.C. for an hour of sunning yourself before oth-

[1] After working for a season as a groom for Fossett's Famous Circus in Ireland, Beary went to London and took a temporary job "packing things" at the Pakistan Embassy.

ers. Think long before you let the bird in your hand go before you go to catch in a bush a bird that, most likely, isn't there. You won't find hedges in London alive with blackberries; but one can't live alone on blackberries,[2] without an occasional dish of egg and bacon. So mind your job. Ay, "Pal" is a Gypsy word, coming from "Bral," a continental dialect word for "brother or mate, or chum"; it goes back to Sanscrit for "brother," "bratr." I'm glad you typed your letter—any writing other than my own, is a great strain on my eyes. Glad you know Charlotte & Sam [Wanamaker]—two excellent and very charming souls. I do hope Sam may have a success with Brecht, tho', I fear, even a success won't bring him in much money; & he has three children now.

Sometime, in the summer—if you hold on to your job, and have saved a little for a holiday—if you come west, maybe we could see each other—the young Chal & the old Codger.[3]

My warm regards to you,
a chroidhe,[4]

Sean

[2] Beary explained the blackberry reference to me in a 1984 letter: "I must have described my circus life to Sean, on the road with the horses and blackberries. Riding on a bicycle, I drove the nine or ten ponies of the circus from town to town. We didn't have trucks in those days. We had a new town to go to every day, and on the road I would collect and eat the blackberries, hundreds of them every day."

[3] The Old Codger is a colorful character in *The Bishop's Bonfire,* partially modelled after O'Casey himself.

[4] my dear friend.

To Stanley Richards[1]

TS. RICHARDS

17 JANUARY 1956

Dear Mr. Richards,

The plays you mention, Robe of Rosheen, etc., are buried God knows where. The R of Rosheen was written in an effort to stay the Irish Civil War—poor wan hope—and was published in a Republican weekly called THE PLAIN PEOPLE.[2] It was written in ink with a poor pen; I hadnt, at the time, the penny needed to buy the paper; the play was never acknowledged, so I assumed it had gone in the WPB. It was seven years after, when I had come to London, when I had married, that a visitor to

[1] Stanley Richards, Library Publishers, New York.
[2] See O'Casey's letter to Joseph W. Donohue, Jr., 18 October 1955, note 2.

us, the Rev. Father Behan of Killorglan, Kerry, spoke about the play, and told me he had read it in the Journal mentioned above. I doubt if there be a copy of the journal anywhere, and less likely that a copy holding the play should survive.

Far as I know, there isnt any MS of the other plays extant. NANNIE'S NIGHT OUT and CATHLEEN LISTENS IN were done by the Abbey Theater, but since the fire there, it is almost certain that they have gone, even if they ever kept them. Anyway, I've no wish to have them published.

So there you are.

Yours sincerely,
Sean O'Casey

To Whitford Kane

MS. BERG COLLECTION

[?] JANUARY 1956

Dear Whitford,

Many thanks for your kind letter & the clippings. I understand that "business" is growing, and Brooks Atkinson—my good friend—tells me that "word of mouth" is very favorable. A Director of the Macmillan Company writes about a Matinee—a matinee, mind you—that it "would warm my heart to hear the clapping for 7 curtains, & the shouts of bravo." Well, these are for the Actors, Designer, & Director, and right glad I am they get them, after the toil & tumult of the rehearsals; for I have gone thro' this mill myself, & know what a wearisome work it all is. This is what worried me most—that you (the company) wouldn't get what you deserved to get. I feel much more at ease now. I pray you may be able to get another theatre.[1] As for Reviews—you should have read the Irish Critics' reviews of "The Bishop's Bonfire"! Bar one, a united chorus of denunciation. I refer to a lot of them in a chapter "Bonfire Under a Black Sun" in a book—The Green Crow—to come out in New York sometime in the Spring. "Word of Mouth," however, spoiled the reviewers, & the play was a great success to my very great surprise. I hope you are taking care of yourself, & getting plenty of sleep in the day after the late hour of the theater. Neither you nor I can prance as we once did.

---

[1] *Red Roses For Me* had played to good but not full houses; however, according to contractual agreement, it had to play to capacity in order to remain at the Booth Theatre. Since no other theatre was available for a transfer, the play was forced to close on 21 January 1956, after 29 performances.

By the way, Whitford, St. Marychurch, tho' in the Borough, isn't Torquay, it is five miles off from it; & the local people still call it "The Village." Torquay is a parvenu, an upstart; for when Marychurch was chief Priory of Tor Abbey, Torquay was an insignificant fishing-village.

All the best to you an all, & to Ulaidh [Ulster].

Sean

To Brooks Atkinson

MS. ATKINSON

31 MARCH 1956

My dear Brooks and my dear Oriana,

Here I am again, but only able to squeak like Petrouska's ghost. Thanks a thousand (mo mhile buidheacheas) to you for your generous review of "The Green Crow."[1] I'm glad it didn't overwhelm you—God forbid it should, for you wouldn't be the Critic I know you to be if it had. All my minor efforts; no notes from the bar here; only tunes pushed & pulled out of an aging concertina: Still, I think—God forgive, if I be boasting—that my articles on Shakespeare helped to shame away the neglect of the great Poet-Dramatist.[2] Now, they're going to the other extreme, thinking of no one else, other than the usual trivial things that glitter for an hour, & then fade forever.

I have had a tough time. I was ill for a year before my resistant will broke, and I had to yell for help. I spent fourteen weeks in hospital, underwent two major operations,[3] & in between had to fight off (with help from doctors & nurses) a nasty bout of bronchial-pneumonia; plus inflammation of the kidney, which still is under observation—a whole anthology of ailments. I've been home for a few days. I thought I would enter into its appearance & its life at once; but the dream faded. I was far away from most of it, separated from it by all that had happened, & it will be some time before I again absorb its color & its activity: all but Eileen. She came to see me three times a day; day by day, week by week month by month, & was to me what Julie was to George—a Godsend. Out of the misery & pain, however, I managed to pull a song for her—the only thanks I had to

[1] Brooks Atkinson, "Feudist With a Song in His Heart," *New York Times Book Review,* 18 March, 1956.
[2] See "The Public Death of Shakespeare," "National Theatre Bunkum," "England, Say When," "Shakespeare Lives in London Lads," in *The Green Crow.*
[3] During the first week of February 1956 O'Casey underwent a prostate operation at Torbay Hospital, Torquay; and a month later on 1 March 1956 he underwent a kidney stone operation.

give. Well, I'm back looking out of the window anyway, tho' chained by orders that I must lie easy, & do no work, not even lick a stamp for an envelope; with a Masseuse coming 3 times a week to rub life into me, instead of rubbing life out of me.

I'm so glad Oriana is writing about Ireland. I'm sure she will see us as we aren't able to see ourselves. Of course the Irish literary chaps will either condemn it, or mock at it as another American fulfilling a fancied mission; the way they mock Americans trying to find material for an essay on Yeats, Joyce, or Shaw; all mocking at any praise given to any other than the praise each of them gives himself. But, I'm sure, Oriana will bite deep, & is bound to rouse into reflection some young writer, for we are not wholly lost to our own sterility, & our need.

My deep love to you, Oriana, & my deep love to you, Brooks.

As ever,
Sean

To David Krause

MS. KRAUSE

31 MARCH 1956

My dear Dave:

A few lines to acknowledge the Birthday telegram from 125 of your Students. It was kind of them to remember me, & kinder still to tell me so. The few lines only is because of Doctor's orders to stay quiet, for a pen feels like I had the lance of Milton's Lucifer between my fingers. Why? Well, I've just come home from a fourteen weeks' stay in hospital where I underwent two major operations, & in between had to fight away (helped by doctors & nurses) a nasty bout of bronchial-pneumonia, plus inflammation of a kidney, which is still under observation. I'd been ill for a year before, but, a resentful will kept me fighting till the pain at last made me yell for help. Months of misery & pain, but it was (and is) an experience that joined me to what so many, many young soldiers, wounded in the war, had gone through (I have a wound still stretching across my belly that is still being treated, and still hurts); and so my hatred of what war brings is more intense, solid, and satisfying than ever—God's & Man's curse on it.

Eileen was a godsend. Day after day, week after week, month after month, she came three times a day to press my hand, & give a kiss that kept me linked to home and life. However, in it all, by an only way of thanks, I culled a song to her—"The Scent of the Blossoming May," & so made the experience a better memento than all the pain.

That's why your last letter remained unanswered; & I'll have to wait till Lucifer's lance feels more like a pen, before I can reply to it. I'm still something of a shadow among substances, but the shadow is beginning to feel for the substance of life again.

So give my deep love & earnest thanks to your students for their telegram to the "Green Crow," which has lost some of its feathers & vigor from its wings, is still in the battle, & hopes before the daffodils are done dancing, to be in flight again.

And my deep love, Dave, to you.

As ever,
Sean

To G. W. Head

MS. HEAD

[?] APRIL 1956

Dear Mr. Head,

I am indeed sorry to hear from you of the death of Capt. Monteith[1]— a very brave man gone. I should have written to him when you wrote to say he was ill, only that I was ill myself. I've just returned from over fourteen weeks in hospital, two major operations, &, in between, an attack of bronchial-pneumonia. So I was battling myself, & still am, for I am still under observation, & ordered to go easy about even writing letters.

I hope you have got over the bout of intestinal flu—a rotten ailment.

Poor Monteith was a disappointed man. I'm afraid Ireland today isn't the Ireland he saw in a dream. Like all countries, Ireland must go thro' the mill.

All good wishes to your wife, two sons, & yourself.

Yours very sincerely,
Sean O'Casey

[1] Captain Robert Monteith (1878–1956) had just died in Detroit, Michigan. See O'Casey's letters to Head, 12 August 1954, note 2; and to Monteith, 31 December 1954, Vol. II.

To Robert Hogan[1]

MS. HOGAN

2 APRIL 1956

Dear Mr. Hogan,

Can't answer your questions, even had I the knowledge of a scholar, which I'm far from being. I'm but a wandering road-minstrel, singing an odd song at any cross-roads where a few people may be gathered together; an odd song in the form of a play, a few thoughts set out in the form of an article, or a song in the form of a song itself. Don't know what Catastasis, etc, mean. Never met them. "The golden rule" said Shaw, "is that there is no rule." Amen, say I. I do know a little about "Catastrophe," which I've met, & am meeting still. Just arrived home from 14 weeks in hospital, where I went under 2 major operations, with a lusty bout of bronchial-pneumonia between them; & with another possible operation looming before me. All this has left me low, & I am under strict orders not to write even a letter. Anyway, give your own opinions—wrong or right—& don't bother to seek those of others. As for "Within the Gates," I have touched it up—the version in "Collected Plays" is different from the original.

I must rest now; so I send you my good wishes, my thanks for your kind letter, & regret I can't reply more expansively.

Yours sincerely.
Sean O'Casey

[1] Robert Hogan, teacher, writer, editor; author of *The Experiments of Sean O'Casey* (1960), and editor of *Feathers From the Green Crow* (1962).

To George Jean Nathan

MS. CORNELL

2 APRIL 1956

My very dear George & dear Julie:

Home again; in it, but not of it yet. I am a distance away from making use of it & enjoying its life. I've been more than 14 weeks in hospital, undergoing two major operations, with a nasty attack of bronchial-pneumonia in between, plus inflammation of a kidney which hasn't cleared altogether away yet; but the watching surgeon thinks it may. The wound is slow to heal, & the surgeon still visits to examine & dress it. But I feel myself gradually getting familiar with old & loved things; & hope to be half myself in a few weeks' time. I have, however, to keep a mile from work, & even letter-writing is forbidden.

Brooks in his last letter tells me you have picked up finally; of which I rejoice, and give a lot of thanks to Julie. Don't overdo anything now for months, & not until George Jean is fully himself again. Many thanks, dear George, for advice about the Cockadoodle. I've written Miss [Jane] Rubin setting down the conditions to be kept, if the [Theatre] Guild takes the play; & she has sent them, "verbatim" to Mr. [Lawrence] Langner.

Eric Bentley has sent me "Dramatic Events"[1]—I wish he hadn't—. Clever, but I can't help feeling that E.B. knows too much. Seems to be settling the affairs of the Theater for all time. No humor. Very cold writing which (to me) carries no love, not even liking, for the Theater. Every, or, almost every article on a play, seems too fixed in a deep freeze.

Well, George a vic, keep yourself well.

My deep love to you & to Julie.

> *As ever,*
> *Sean*

[1] Eric Bentley, *The Dramatic Event* (1954).

To David Krause

TS. KRAUSE

6 APRIL 1956

To Dr. Krause's 125 Drama Students
working in Brown University:

O'Casey's greetings enfolded in many thanks for their kind and thoughtful Cable.[1] It is grand to get a brave message from the Young; to an old man who still dreams a dream from the Young who have a vision within them; a vision of a newer life; a vision of a Theater that has life, even if it hasn't learning. Let the vision live within you. If you be poor, don't let the hardness of poverty petrify the vision in disillusionment; if you be well-off, don't let the vision be silked and softened into conformity; for to do either is to sin against the Holy Ghost. And, by God, you won't find this an easy thing to do! There can be no vision without life, and life has to have its needs satisfied; not only on Christmas Day, on Thanksgiving Day, or St. Patrick's Day (if you be Irish), but on every day of the blessed or damned year. That takes some doing. Then, you have

[1] On the occasion of his 76th birthday, 30 March 1956.

your health to guard, for the vision is within a body, the body is vulnerable, and if the body fails, the mind has to think of the body, and, till health returns, forget the vision. I have had a number of these experiences, but none so sharp and so deep as the one that lasted through our recent year; an experience that has left me in a condition so that I shouldn't be writing these few words to you. But the Green Crow couldn't but send a few thankful caws to his student friends. Listen—can't you hear them? Caw caw caw caw! He flutters the good wing gayly, and flutters the injured one as bravely as he dare, as he caws his thanks, before he sinks into the painful quietness of his nest.

My love to each and every one of you!

As ever,
Sean
Alias "The Green Crow."

To Paddy McLaughlin[1]

MS. MCLAUGHLIN

14 APRIL 1956

Dear Paddy,

Thanks a lot for your kind letter. I've just come back from 14 weeks in hospital, two major operations, with an attack of pneumonia in between—the reason why I couldn't reply sooner. Indeed, I'm under orders still to write no letters; but feel I should send at least a word or two to you. You have had a full and an adventurous life; &, I hope, from now on, you may have peace with your Kathleen, as I look for peace with my Eileen. Frank Ryan was a friend of mine. He spent a day with us in London, resting his wounded arm, just before he returned to Spain for the last time. What men Ireland has lost!

You tell a shocking story about your mother. It is my experience that clerics will spill out any tale to satisfy themselves; but surely the ones in Moville must have known your mother, &, even out of charity, should have told her personally & publicly they knew her son would never stand for such outrages. But looka what they said about the Fenians & about the Irish Republicans!

P[atrick]. Galvin should have written to you; but, maybe, he is too busy knocking out a living—a hard job for a young writer. Don't be too hard on him. I myself get so many letters, that I can't answer the half of them.

---

1 Patrick McLaughlin, 62 Waterloo Road, Liverpool 22.

Thanks again for your good opinion of "Sunset & Evening Star" (and Kathleen's too).

My warm regards & good wishes to both of you.

Yours very sincerely
Sean O'Casey

Hope you'll make this out—hand a bit shaky still.

To Robert D. Graff[1]

MS. GRAFF

18 APRIL 1956

My dear Bob,

This is O'C. plus "The Green Crow" trying to flutter broken wings in greeting to you; trying, anyway, which is the near next thing to fluttering them fully. I'm home again after more than 3 months in hospital, going thro' a tough time with two big operations, &, in between, an attack of bronchial pneumonia. Something of a shadow still among substances, but getting more solid as the days go by.

The check came safely, and was very welcome, & needed, too. Thanks, young son, for the safe custody of the dollars. You're going to have a busy time with psycho-analysis, painting, and politics. I hope you may be very successful with all three. I know now how difficult a job it is for you to make everything interesting to such a throng of differing minds watching what you did. The best way is to satisfy yourself—as, I believe, you do.

We got the Film[2] safely, & it is snug in one of my private corners, waiting for the family to come together, so that all can applaud each as the other appears. [Donald] Aldous—the man who is always winning— will bring his apparatus, & show it to us.

We had our share of frost here, & all the gardens show it, for ne'er a thing—bar the big trees—survived; & crops—early ones—were ruined, so that now we have even a famine of spuds.

If you come to London, & if you can come so far, come to St. Mary-church—the door is always unlatched for you.

> Come in the evening, come in the morning
> Come when you're asked, or come without warning—

---

[1] Robert D. Graff (1919–   ), New York, film producer and director.
[2] A film copy of the interview with O'Casey and his family, conducted by Robert Emmett Ginna, produced and directed by Graff, and shown on the NBC–TV Wisdom Series on 22 January 1956. For details see O'Casey's letter to George Braziller, 9 November 1955, note 1.

You'll always be welcome; you & your buddie, Bob the Second [Robert Emmett Ginna].

All our good wishes, wrapped in our love, to you.

As ever,
Sean

To Norman Myles Sudbury[1]

PC. *Irish Times*

20 APRIL 1956

Dear Myles Sudbury,

Thank you for your kind letter. I am home since the 20th, but under orders to write no letters—I've written bunches of them, but rather less quickly. I've had a tough time, for I was ill a year or so before the hospital swallowed me up for three months—Jonah in Whale's belly. My feet are beginning to feel the earth solid under me—hurrah! There's a lot in being a B.A., if one has taken in things learned during the studies to win the honor; and the experience gained by association with other students.

Indeed, yes—what does a young fellow, like you, know about plays? Or what does an oul' fella, like me, know about them either? Damn little, if you ask God. Is "Big Jim"[2] in print? Heard of it, of course, but haven't read it. Plunkett is a clever laddo, with undoubted talent. Have read some of his short stories. I've answered, in "The Green Crow," some of the funny Irish "critiques" of "The Bishop's Bonfire." Sorry you found the going heavy. I thought there was some fun in it. You're right—I'd be afraid of my life to go back to Erin while the Dread Drood of Drumcondra's there.[3]

So thanks again for kind wishes,

Yours sincerely,
Sean O'Casey

[1] Norman Myles Sudbury, a young Dubliner studying economics at Trinity College, Dublin. His letter was printed in Quidnunc's column, "An Irishman's Diary," *Irish Times*, 2 August 1969.

[2] *Big Jim,* a radio play by James Plunkett, based on the 1913 strike and lock-out in Dublin and the career of Jim Larkin, performed by Radio Eireann and published in Dublin in 1955. It formed the basis of Plunkett's stage play, *The Risen People,* first performed at the Abbey Theatre on 23 September 1958, and his novel, *Strumpet City* (1969).

[3] An allusion to the Most Rev. Dr. John Charles McQuaid, Archbishop of Dublin, whose palace is in Drumcondra.

To New York Times

20 APRIL 1956

Thanks From Sean O'Casey

[*Dear Sir,*] I should indeed be grateful if you would allow me, through your widely read journal, to thank from my breast out the many letters of goodwill and cards, telling me of sympathy and giving good wishes during the time I was in hospital ill.

Even were I fully recovered, it would be impossible for me to answer all, or even many, so I appeal to these dear friends to take this grateful acknowledgement of their kindness and to give it the shape of a personal reply.

Thanks to all, and a blessing on the kindnesses that flow out from the kindness of Americans.

Sean O'Casey.

Torquay, England, April 16, 1956.

To Dr. Frank Morrell

MS. MORRELL

25 APRIL 1956

My dear Frank,

Glad to get your glad letter, telling me about the colors & loveliness of Provence. God musta been in a gay mood when he made it. This time, your letter has no mention of Politics, & is all the better for it. All active life is political, for it alters things, and makes life greater, giving us more knowledge of ourselves, which so many English and American Communists lack. Augustus John often spoke to me about the charm and colorful joy of Provence. You united business with pleasure; as it should be always. I have been studying physiology myself for the past 6 months—my own, & under duress. I've been very ill; in hospital for 14 weeks, 2 major operations, & in between, an attack of bronchial pneumonia. I came home a few weeks ago, but am still under observation for a suspicious kidney—had a big boulder in it! and for the wide wound that hasn't healed yet. As well, when I go thro' any illness for any length of time, a fifty-year-ago-attack of Beriberi (brought on by hunger, as no one would employ me after the lock-out battle of 1913 with Jim Larkin) brings me numbness of the nerves from knee to ankle & the little finger of the right hand; but I'm fighting them all, & am much stronger than when I first came home. I'll sound a few more taps on the Drum of Life before I go.

I end now, for I'm not supposed to be doing this sort of labor. All the best—good health & fine achievement.

As ever,
Sean

To Mrs. R——

MS. PRIVATE

25 APRIL 1956

My dear R——,

Thanks for all—your letters, flowers, and press-cuttings. This must be short, for I'm under orders to write no letters; just to stay still, & listen to the clock's ticking. It is interesting to hear of A.'s decision to marry— the quick way the young go! But (very diffidently) I imagine, she should wait a little longer, for she is still very, very young. Marriage is a big leap with the eyes half closed; but, like all ventures in life, it isn't possible to advise infallibly. If she does marry, I hope she may be blessed with a life-long companionship. [Richard] Findlater's articles on the National Theatre seem to echo mine, written many years ago—the 30's—first in "Time & Tide"[1] (after begging me to write about the Theatre, coming personally to see me, & persuade), they closed down on me—I was too outspoken; afterwards in "The Flying Wasp," the MS of which brought Harold Macmillan to see me & beg me not to publish it.[2] Now, most of them are (Resurgam) living again in a book "The Green Crow" just published in New York. Curious, how Ulick O'Connor (*The Listener*) looks back longingly at the Georgian houses of Dublin.[3] He apparently never read what Shaw said about them. I'll go bail, he never lived in one. I did when they became slums; but even in the grandee's day they were hell for the poor servants who toiled in the basement & slept in the attic for 2/—a week! It is in these that Dublin's basement dwellers (Cave-dwellers, the Dubliners call them) live; but Ulick O'Connor never mentions these; doesn't know they exist probably. And "*W. for Godot* is a denial of materialism"! As if materialism can be denied, & Ulick going about in a material body. I wonder how he'd feel without it! Read enclosed letter for Civil Liberty Committee. They're

[1] See the first four chapters of *The Flying Wasp* (1937); reprinted in *The Green Crow* (1956).

[2] See O'Casey's letter to Harold Macmillan, 25 September 1936, Vol. I.

[3] Ulick O'Connor, "Dublin: Decline and Fall," *The Listener*, 19 April 1956, from a B.B.C. Third Programme broadcast.

asking only for a Modified Censorship law, on the strength of a Bishop's remark that it may be too strict; & yet they are afraid to disclose their names. Why? For fear of their material livelihood. Waiting for Godot!

Hope you may make this out: hand a bit shaky. Let me have Civil Liberty letter back. I signed the Petition boldly & they, if they like, can hang it out on Nelson's Pillar.

My love to A. & you.

As ever,
Sean

To Mrs. Stanley J. Hochdorf[1]

TS. HOCHDORF

29 APRIL 1956

Dear Mrs. Hochdorf:

Your kind letter finds me better, but far from well. I've roamed away from the bed, and am able to look out of a window, and do a little about the house.

The question you pose would take more than a letter; it would take a big book to answer it, and even then, the answer would fade away as it was being read. There is no "class-consciousness" in art; there is but bad paint-ing and fine painting. It is the mind of the artist that creates the art; color, line, and form make the picture; and however near to the present a picture may be, if it hasn't these aspects within it in shining excellence, then the picture won't live: if it has, however near to the present it may be, it will last forever. For instance, I can't see any class-consciousness (bar that of beauty) in a Ming vase; or in Robbie Burns' MY LOVE IS LIKE A RED RED ROSE; or in Van Gough's CHAIR, or in his THE CYPRESS; but there is beauty in the song, and a curious great wistfulness mingled with strength in the Chair and the cypress tree. You say "I will think only of the universal truths: sky, flowers, green things." But these aren't the only universal truths. Man is another, and the most important of them all. The painter is a universal truth—whether he paints realistically or abstrac-tions; and, if it be first-rate, then the picture he paints will be one too. I don't care myself for Abstract work, for I belong to a past generation; but many of Picasso's abstract paintings are very beautiful, as are Braque's, because these two artists are first-class—class-conscious or not. A body

---

[1] Mrs. Stanley J. Hochdorf, 1719 Capitol Avenue N.E., Washington 2, District of Columbia. Later Mrs. Stanley J. Howard. See O'Casey's letter to Clare and Stan Howard, 10 July 1956.

isn't a "traitor to the struggle around him" if he paints a lovely bunch of roses, a kid aswing on a gate, a cow in a meadow, or a house on a hill. Cezanne's many pictures of Mt. Victoire are treasures for all men to see, though Cezanne when he painted them didn't bother about the struggles around him. A lot of Communists, tipsy with ignorance, prate a lot of what they think to be Marxian philosophy, but it is simply the stuttering of their own foolish fancies (I am, and have been, a Communist for well over 40 years, so I speak with some experience). Let your husband cease to bother about being a "traitor," or about "class-consciousness" when he's trying to paint a picture.

Well, I must end now, for I'm under orders to go easy; and so, for the time, good wishes to you and him, and farewell.

Yours sincerely,
Sean O'Casey

To George Jean Nathan

MS. CORNELL

[?] MAY 1956

My very dear George:

Thank you, amhic, for the Press-clipping.[1] It was very acceptable, for the reason that it showed you up as your own self; humorous, but none the less critical, & eager as ever to salute anything that gives a glow to the Theater. I'm so glad you are at work again. I won't thank you for the gift-award of the George, but I thank you from the heart out for letting me know I was awarded one, & for the way you presented it: it gives a glow to this old heart when I get a good word from you, feeling, somehow, that it is deserved; & I can tell you, your cheer was echoed by one I gave for myself.

I've heard no more about the Guild suggestion of doing "Cocka-doodle." I mentioned provisos that would have to be put into any contract offered (on your & Brooks' advice), which, I daresay, annoyed Mr. [Lawrence] Langner; & which he probably sets down to O'Casey impudence & conceit.

---

[1] George Jean Nathan, "Theatre Week," *Journal American*, 5 May 1956: "The time for the annual award of the chocolate Georgies, the only edible and hence most desirable of all the various prizes for conspicuous theatrical achievement, has again rolled around and I herewith accordingly pass them out with low bows to their deserving recipients. For the most beautiful lyric dramatic speech the Georgie goes with a cheer to the finest living Irish playwright, Sean O'Casey, in this specific case as represented by 'Red Roses For Me.' "

It is odd how the Theater Guild & the Abbey seem to be sinking down together. It's a sad thing that Lennox Robinson hasn't done something to check the Abbey's decline. He is a fine Director; he knows a great deal about Drama; & he has great talents; but he doesn't now venture even to bite his thumb at poverty in plays. A Lost Leader. It is a great pity.

I hope you are taking care of yourself, & that Julie is always near you. My love to her, & to you, my dear George.

> *As ever,*
> *Sean*

To Paul Shyre[1]

TS. SHYRE

6 MAY 1956

Dear Mr. Shyre,

Yes, indeed, we'd like a tape of the performance;[2] for, tho' we have neither a recording machine, or long-playing phonograph, neighbours near have both.

Regarding the snatches of song in P. in the Hallway, that presents a difficulty: "Caanan, sweet Caanan" is a crude hymn formed in Sankey & Moody Hymnbook. Any Irishman or Woman would lilt you "The Peeler & the Goat" P. 79; "A Sober Black Shawl" is the music that goes with "Red Roses For Me"; "We'll hang oul' Parnell on a sour apple Tree" to the "Battle Hymn" or "Marching thro' Georgia"; the rest are, far as I know, to be gotten nowhere, bar an old man's mind. I could get a neighbour—for a fee—to take these snatches down on a recording tape, or, perhaps, a phonograph record. Is this a good idea? I don't think it could reach you in time, for the Customs would probably hold it up.

> *Yours sincerely,*
> *Sean O'Casey*

---

[1] Paul Shyre (1929–), theatre director, actor, writer.

[2] *I Knock at the Door*, adapted by Paul Shyre and directed by Stuart Vaughan, was performed as "A Concert Reading" for two Sunday performances on 18 March 1956, under the auspices of the Y.M.–Y.W.H.A. Poetry Center, Kaufmann Auditorium, New York. *Pictures in the Hallway* was in rehearsal for two similar performances on 27 May 1956. Both productions were highly successful and were subsequently presented on Broadway for limited engagements, *Pictures* opening at the Playhouse Theatre on 16 September 1956, and *I Knock* at the Belasco Theatre on 29 September 1957.

To Paul Shyre

TS. SHYRE

16 MAY 1956

Dear Paul Shyre:

On the night of the 14th, this month, in spite of feeling rotten, with a temperature, I got the "neighbour" to come here with a tape-recording machine to take down the singing manner of the snatches of song in PICTURES IN THE HALLWAY.

I managed in a way to stagger through them. They will sound a bit husky, but I'm sure the airs will come through in a way that you'll get the hang of them. The "Neighbour" was to send them off to you yesterday— the 15th—and, if all goes well, you should have them by the time you get this note. He sent them via AIR MAIL. The song A SOBER BLACK SHAWL, is of course to be found in the published RED ROSES FOR ME, air and all.

It seems a shame, after all your work on I KNOCK AT THE DOOR, that you couldn't have given many more Readings.

Fine that Macmillan's should be setting up a Display in the Lobby; I hope it will look good, and that the book may sell well.

With all good wishes,
Yours sincerely,
Sean O'Casey

To John Gassner

MS. GASSNER

21 MAY 1956

Dear John,

It's a long time since I heard from you, & this is, at least, a warm hello to you. A theater in Hanover, Germany, is doing a play of mine— "The Bishop's Bonfire"—odd choice—, & the Director in a letter asked me for a few critical references to my work. The chief one I suggested was the article on them by you in "The Theater of Our Times";[1] which, I think, is one of the best reviews of what I have done, and what I have tried to do. I hope you don't mind. If Hanover (British Zone) can't supply the book, I'll give them the loan of the one I have.

I hope you are well and busy with the Theater, for New York seems

[1] John Gassner, *The Theatre in Our Times* (1954).

to have had a fine time of it in play-writing & play-acting. I've been ill for near a year, with more than three months in hospital; but, I imagine, am slowly getting back into myself. I did a tape recording of snatches of songs appearing in "Pictures in the Hallway" which, I understand, is to be given a Reading soon in New York. The Director didn't know the airs; & what with the raucous voice of me singing them, God only knows if he knows them now.

My warm wishes to you, a mhic o.

As ever,
Sean

To Cyril Cusack

TS. CUSACK

25 MAY 1956

Dear Cyril,
I've written to New York telling them what you said, and am waiting a reply. I certainly would like you to do THE BISHOP'S BONFIRE in London, with most of the original caste—if it could be gotten. If you added JUNO to the event, it would be finer still. I agree about Ireland being a good place for Film production—I argued this thirty years ago with Brunel of Elstree, with Ivor Montagu of Educational films, and with Hitchcock; but they listened and didnt hear. I do hope THREE LEAVES OF A SHAMROCK[1] will be good, and go well. Now I know why I got no record of JUNO. They didnt wish me to realise that the epilogue had been cut out.[2] I was *not* "informed" of the cut, and it never crossed my mind that such a god-damned stupid thing could be done to spoil a play. God damn these bastards who think they know more about a play than he who wrote it; or, even if they do, they have no right to make amends without the knowledge and consent of the author. Well, from this out, in any contract I'll set down a clause saying that it is null and void if any part is taken out without my written agreement. The cut from JUNO is in my opinion the comic highlight (and tragical highlight too) of the play.

I've read his highness of Galway's remarks about Shaw, and, for a start, there is a lie in it, namely, "Shaw devoted all his energy to mocking

[1] This was a proposed film to be made in Ireland, directed by John Huston, with Cusack in the cast, but it was later abandoned.
[2] In the Angel recording of *Juno and the Paycock,* made in Dublin in June 1955 and supervised by Alan Dent, the final scene between Boyle and Joxer was eliminated. See O'Casey's letter to Cusack, 9 June 1955, note 3.

at Christian faith."[3] He didnt; he devoted a tremendous lot of his energy to a hell of a lot of things besides the "mocking of the christian faith." It is the christians themselves who spend their time mocking the "christian faith." Take his highness, the Bishop of Galway's own saying: "The fundamental idea of a festival of welcome to all visitors to our land was in itself good, and worthy of a Christian and free people. An Tostal was intended to attract visitors, not to be a time of merry-making for our own" (people, I suppose, he means). Well, the "welcome" is good in God's sight only if the motive be good too. Is it? If it be for "merry-making" and for national stimulation, it is good, and so good in God's sight. But is it? It is not; it is not for "merry-making," but for money-making—a very different thing, and hardly a glorious thing in God's sight. Money-making—that is the fundamental idea of the Tostal, as the Bishop himself implies when he says it is "a festival of welcome to all visitors." All? Even to those who havent a red? Do we welcome the visitors out of pure love (christian) for themselves, or welcome them for the money they bring? Ha, ha, the spirit of Shaw is using its "energy to mock the christian faith"! The Almighty dollar is getting in front of Almighty God.

The visitors "for the most part, are children of Irish exiles"; right, but hear what follows: "They value every church, abbey, high cross, and castle as memorials of Irish greatness. They will not come to Ireland to listen to Italian Opera or Shaw's plays." "They value every church, every abbey" etc. Why, I have a volume of THE DUBLIN JOURNAL of more than a hundred years ago, and in it articles bewail the destruction of many historic buildings, sacred and profane—depleted, not by "our Protestant invaders," but by the Irish Catholic farmers, robbed stone by stone to build barns, the old walls used to shelter their cattle. And the children of the Irish exiles would hardly know one high cross from another; all they would recognise is a Round Tower, and damn little they could tell you about them. No, the spirit of An Tostal is materialism; not the higher philosophical materialism or the higher still historic-materialism, but the materialism that adds pound to pound in the till or the bank. No harm, I

---

[3] In a news story, "The Bishop of Galway Criticises Tostal," *The Standard*, 11 May 1956, it was reported that the Most Rev. Dr. Michael J. Browne, Bishop of Galway, when presiding at a Solemn High Mass to mark the opening of the Tostal in Galway, stated that he saw no trace of deep religious feeling in the national Tostal program, and he particularly objected to the plan to perform foreign works and the plays of Shaw: "There is mention of a display of Italian opera and of Bernard Shaw plays . . . but if they do not want to give place to Christian things, why give place to an anti-Christian like Shaw, who devoted all his energy to mocking at the Christian faith."

As an ironic parallel it might be noted that in 1958 the Most Rev. Dr. John Charles McQuaid, Archbishop of Dublin, canceled the High Mass that traditionally opened the national Tostal because he did not approve of the performance of O'Casey's *The Drums of Father Ned* and a dramatization of Joyce's *Ulysses*, which led to the rejection of both works. See O'Casey's letters to George Jean Nathan, 11 January 1958, note 1; to Paul Shyre, 14 February 1958, note 1; and to Kay Carney, 15 February 1958, note 2.

daresay in "spoiling the Egyptians" even though they be the children of our Irish exiles. I love the dollar myself; I'd have been down and out long ago, would be now, if it werent for the dollar, and so I bow my head to it; bow myself in the house of Rimmon; and any needy Irishman or woman who wouldnt is a bit of a fool; but, all the same, the dollar comes from the U.S.A.; it doesnt come from heaven. I'm sure the Bishop wouldnt mind having a wallet (like Card. Spellman) full of them.

At the moment, I cant think of writing about Shaw, for my mind isnt yet settled, due to the after effects of two operations, with a wide wound across the belly that has so far refused to heal, and stings spitefully when I move; but time will heal it, and the uncommon bug that settled under the skin is hard to kill. I've just sung all snatches of songs in PICTURES IN THE HALLWAY for New Y. (Dollars again!), and have to sing those in I KNOCK AT THE DOOR, when I get me breath. Moscow has asked me to do a tape-recording about Shaw, and Eileen was asked to do one, too; but I'm doubtful that I will have the will and the breath to do it; so forgive me for not having the energy to say something about Ireland's great, good, truly christian genius. My love to Maureen, to your little ones, and to you; and success to A. And The Lion.

As ever,
Sean

P.S. Isnt the Browne we know, anti-shavian—the Bishop who thought Galway's councillors, who differed from him over site for a school, to be anticlerical?

To Franklin D. Murphy[1]

MS. MURPHY

25 MAY 1956

Dear Mr. Murphy:

This slow-moving letter in reply to yours of February last carries the bad reason that illness shoved me away from replying sooner. I am still consecrated to care from the effects of a year's tough time; but holding my own now, & able to realise how lovely lilac & laburnum are: bushes of both grow in our little garden. Thanks for your kind words. It would be

---

[1] Dr. Franklin Delano Murphy (1916–), Chancellor of the University of Kansas, Lawrence, Kansas; in 1960 became Chancellor of the University of California, Los Angeles; owner of a private collection of Sean O'Casey manuscripts, papers, and memorabilia, which he later donated to the library of the University of California, Los Angeles.

dishonest to deny the pleasure it gives me to hear praise from a distance; those close to me, praise embarrassing, & I try to change the talk whenever a visitor speaks it; for, to me, the spite of dissatisfaction remains in a lot of what I have written. Certainly, I never thought of any University thinking of giving any sort of honor to my work, & I feel shy of sending any MS to you. Indeed, I've made few efforts to preserve any except the letters written to me by friends (mostly American), &, at times, the replies I may have sent to them.

Under another cover, I am venturing to send you a few items. I believe Mrs. O'C. has some buried in a deep chest we bought when we were first married; but to search among what may be hidden there would be a job for which I have neither energy nor heart.

Well, my friend—from what you write to me, I feel assured the title will not offend you—I hope the few slips I send may be of some interest to you.

> *With all good wishes,*
> *Yours very sincerely,*
> *Sean O'Casey*

To Dr. Frank Morrell

TS. MORRELL

31 MAY 1956.

Dr. Frank Morrell.

What a buzz your letter makes in mine ears, Frank! A very kind buzz, and one that touched me much, and is very much appreciated. The "wide wound" hasn't completely closed, but it is getting tighter, and I hope it may be shut tight in a short time.

Since you are kindly interested, the ailments were a stone in the kidney, causing inflammation, and provoking spasms of intense pain; a case of prostate gland. These meant two big operations, and, in between, an attack of bronchial-pneumonia—so I had a lot to think about. The legs are much better, and I can walk swift as a young swallow can fly, but get tired and a little breathless after a short while. But I'm venturing farther each day, and am counting the lilacs and laburnums spreading their crowding blossoms over the garden walls.

As for food, I've plenty, but have to go canny, for I've always had a delicate stomach, and the multitude of drugs swallowed while in hospital seem to have left a legacy of weakness. You neednt worry about me, my dear Frank, for I have all I need. Indeed, for the past few years, my income has been so satisfactory that we are—or Eileen is—laying up a little for any eventuality of the future—all thanks to the USA, and this year, too, to the USSR which has begun to be interested in what I've written.

So there you are, Frank—far as material things go, I'm more than O.K. But that doesnt take in any way from your very kind offer to help. Now, me lad, you must think of yourself, and look after yourself, instead of worrying about me. You're a young lad, and have a long life before you, and, to make it effective, you must think of yourself without worrying much about the concern of others. I have been very fortunate, for a lad of 76 to go through such a lot and come out able to walk swift, is more than one thing to be thankful for; aha, yes. Eileen stood to me bravely, and every day, while in hospital (more than 3 months) she came three times a day, which was no mean achievement. Hers was the hand that really pulled me out of a de profundis. I have handed over all financial affairs to her, for I havent the energy to deal with these now, though I have re-sumed household chores—washing up, etc., that I used to do before I was knocked baw-ways by the sudden illness. You'd love St. Marychurch for it is prettier than Totnes; something like an Utrillo aspect in the "vil-lage," and it is a good way from Torquay and all its bourgeois fuss. All well here. Breon painting, Niall at London University, and Shivaun going there soon to join an Art school.

My love to you, dear friend.

As ever,
Sean

To Eve Salisbury[1]

TS. HAROLD D. JONES

31 MAY 1956

Dear Eve Salisbury,

Thanks very much for your kind words. The rumor you mention was no rumor, but a long fact. I have been very ill, and am still striving to get back to where I was before I started. My dear, I'm sorry to read that you "are lonely among the lonely." Why? Surely, if you seek, there is a friend waiting somewhere; that is, if you forget yourself, and think of others. It isnt self-assurance which wins friends, but the awareness in others of the interest one takes in what they say and do; a sympathetic interest, if what they do be interesting, and they dont happen to be bores. I have self-assurance only in my own integrity; aside from that I am as

---

[1] Eve Salisbury, 50 West 96th Street, New York City.

shy as Shaw was shy. Even when I work, all or any new thing I set down to do, article or play, I feel as if I were but a half-numbed beginner; but I always try to do my best, and when the best that can be done is done, then I let all things pass by, enjoying what is enjoyable, enduring what has to be endured. It may be that you think a little too much about yourself. Try not to do so. It is vain and futile; and breeds loneliness. As for "creeping into a corner," well, the best of us can occupy only a corner in the world. And what more than a corner does a sensible soul want? Shaw was a very great man, and he was content to live his life in a corner. Indeed, that was carved in Iron Letters on the gateway of his home in Ayot St. Lawrence—"Shaw's Corner." If he was satisfied with a corner, who are we who pine for a square? Fools who know not the glory of life's simplicity. And as for what is called Fame, let it come, if it will; but seek it not; for if we seek it, and it comes, unhappiness comes with it: the fame that comes breeds an appetite for further fame, and that often destroys the soul who pursues it. And we must be content to use the one talent to the full, just as he who has five must use them all to the full, too. Let us not pine because we havent more than a single talent—if we use it well, we'll satisfy God and pacify man; dont let us wither because we imagine we've been shoved into a corner: even the Queen of England, with all her palaces, can live but in one room at a time; and the corner of life which we cheerfully choose (as Shaw did), if we live can carry us, through imagination, to the ends of the earth. I agree with you heartily about the theater. I too wish I could see the vigorous imagination of Leonardo de Vinci showing us what hell and heaven looked like. And, last, but not least, all good wishes, Eve, to you, now and always.

Sean O'Casey

To Miss Joan McAlevey

MS. McALEVEY

1 JUNE 1956

Dear Joan,

1st June, 1st June, with the sky clouded grey and a cold nor'east wind blowing about one's ears here. Summer is a goin' out! I hope it's better where you are.

It will, I'm sure, be grand to come to Europe, with a week in Paris. Make it two, if you can, for Paris is a lovely city.

As for a visit to me, Joan, don't waste the time, for Devon is a long way down, & the old chap somewhat silenced—for a while only—by a very tough time. Let the hands you shake be young hands; young and firm and active, with a Thrill in the handclasp; hands of your own generation; not hands wrinkled, each like a sere and yellow leaf.

Congratulations on leaving St. Hilda's behind you, and that Reverend Mother, who should be clapped close to old ones, & not allowed to be a nuisance to young teachers & younger children. "Waiting for Godot" has baffled a lot, & most are afraid to say what they think about it. It is laughable, the way the wise heads nod over it! Well, instead of waiting for Godot, there's nothing to keep us from going to him by sense & laughter and a good life. He, maybe, is waiting for us.

My best wishes for your enjoyment during the tour; may it be a joy, halo'd by good weather. What about your boy?

My love, as ever
Sean

To Mrs. Marie Strong[1]

MS. T. W. ALLEN

3 JUNE 1956

My dear Marie;

It is not for me to say nay to your sad letter; but surely it is the lot of all of us to know the feverish brow, and the body hot with illness, or cold with the many hopes vanished, a voice lost, & no light, apparently, before us. Only apparently, for the light is there always, tho' we often keep our eyes shut so that we cannot see. I am aware of all you say about underpaid workers, of many a funeral; thro' many strikes, & have eaten dry bread & bitter waters, with my half-famished comrades; but never lost the will to keep fighting. Ireland misses [Jim] Larkin just as the USA misses [Eugene V.] Debs, for such flames are rarely kindled; but they, in the work of others, will flame again, if not in America or Ireland, then somewhere else to lighten & warm the whole family of man.

I know what a housewife has to face & has to do. I've scrubbed bare floors—no oil cloth for the poorer slums—kindled poor fires, washed my own & my mother's poor shirt & shift; but it was no treadmill task to do what we could to keep ourselves alive, & go about; at least, dishonestly clean; for no tenement dweller could keep honestly clean under the con-

[1] Mrs. Marie Strong, a housewife in Brooklyn, N.Y., of Irish-Italian stock, whose father had worked for the socialist Eugene V. Debs, died in March 1962. Michael Strong was her son by a previous marriage, and her husband, T. W. Allen, was unable to find two more letters O'Casey had written to his wife.

ditions, around, about, & above them. I did chores before I became ill, to help my wife; & am beginning again—washing up, peeling spuds, carrying down the garbage, etc. It is partly good for us, for it is routine, & this checks the excitement of the mind, & gives us a rest. We cannot always suffer ecstasy. There must always be a lot of "petty service," if not for others, then for ourselves. Each has to go thro' the routine of petty life day by day, year in & year out; there is no escape, nor should there be, for we are civilized animals that must accept civilization's laws.

I wish I could write you a long letter, but I'm still away from normal activity, & soon grow tired.

You have my sympathy, and a faraway touch of a hand that wishes you well, and Michael, too. I still have the same view of life; I love it, even in the midst of pain, when the candle of activity gutters.

Shake Michael's hand for me, and give me your own.

Yours very sincerely,
Sean O'Casey

To Helen Kiok

PC. *O'Casey Review*[1]

4 JUNE 1956

Dear Helen,

Thanks for the letter you sent to Breon, & for the many kind things you said in it. And thanks, too, for the clippings. I hope you have since gotten "The Green Crow," and that it has interested you.

As for George B.[2] I have met him, and found him a very charming man. It isn't easy to stand up straight always when confronted with power and malicious souls armed cap-a-pie against all opinions outside of their own. The world is getting more tolerant, and progressive minds must lead the way, bar those lost souls who use hysteria to lift themselves to power, or use hysteria to heighten an account in the Bank. The ghost of Joe McC[arthy]. still walks, but its shadow grows less, & the beckoning finger grows weaker. America is still alive, & beginning to kick. More power to her blows.

With all good wishes,
Yrs very sincerely,
Sean

Had a tough time, but am slowly getting back to form.

[1] This letter was printed in the *Sean O'Casey Review,* Fall 1976.
[2] George Braziller, American publisher of *The Green Crow* (1956).

To Mrs. Alice Kornbluth[1]

MS. KORNBLUTH

7 JUNE 1956

Dear Alice Kornbluth,

I'm sorry I've been so long in replying to you, caused by a very serious & tedious ill time, from which I am just now coming away. The friend in Dublin is altogether wrong about the name of "Joxer." There is no special significance in it. It is common with us (Irish) to add "er" to diminutive names. For instance—"Mollser," "Nedser," "Mickser," "Patser"; but only to names that take the addition well; and mostly the names of men. It has the significance of an added familiarity over plain Pat, Ned, Jock, or Mick; &, in a few instances, according to the tone in which the added "er" is sounded, it also gives a touch of implied affection.

Now, you have it, my dear. No, the name of "Bentham" was used after the Economist; it just occurred to me as a name signifying a more dignified aspect—even in name—to the "commoner" Boyles. And thanks, my dear, for your very kind words.

Yours very sincerely,
Sean O'Casey

[1] Mrs. Alice Kornbluth was a graduate student in English at the University of Tennessee.

To Frank McCarthy

MS. McCARTHY

8 JUNE 1956

My dear Frank,

No! Dont phone. It means an effort, & I am anxious to avoid all activities I can—for some time. I have had a bad, tough time with 2 major operations, & in between them, for good measure, a bout of bronco-pneumonia; so I am still fighting a kind of rear-guard action against all that happened; and, so far doing it well.

I'm not surprised that Dr. [Donald O.] Soper didn't like what he saw in Poland. You see, the Doctor lives in a world of his own creation, within (as he thinks) the Christian Community; "he enthuses all he sees, and sees only what he enthuses"; and so cannot fully enter into another world. He is, in my opinion, a great, good, brave man, and is—tho' he doesn't realise it—helping to strengthen & expand the activities of mind & hand now happening in Poland, USSR, China, Ceylon, & other lands. Christianity—spite of Billy Graham and his yodelling comrades—is at the Cross-Roads. Which way? There, then, remains the question.

Forgive me for asking you not to phone: I'm very busy, and have to meet & talk to, many people, mostly Americans. I had six here the other week, & two come on Tuesday.

Eileen (Mrs. O'C.) saw "The Quare Fella,"[1] and has told me it is fine. I do hope that Brendan Behan will prove to be the new young Irish Playwright—we need one badly.

Put Anna Magnani outa your mind—she'd cost a fortune, and, if she be what you say, would need very good actors around her (with a Boyle good as herself), to keep the balance of the play. Norah is wise: it's expensive to live in London; & a writer's job rarely covers the cost. It is a dog's life. Pity to see such as Cyril C[usack]. wasted in such rubbish. Haven't heard from [Seumas] Scully myself; but neither you nor I can do aught about it: we have problems of our own, God knows. Seumas has some cash in the Bank, & couldn't be "Hard up" for a few years. Long life to the famous Aunt of yours. She must be a great skin.

Now, my love to you & Dr. Soper, & Mrs. Soper too. She looks a handsome lass in the [Kingsway] Messenger Picture; & I like handsome lasses.

As ever,
Sean.

[1] Brendan Behan's *The Quare Fellow* was first presented by the Theatre Workshop at the Theatre Royal, Stratford East, London, on 24 May 1956, directed by Joan Littlewood.

To R. Heatley[1]

TC. O'CASEY

11 JUNE 1956

Dear Mr. Heatley,
If you imagine me to be a suitable Sponsor, go ahead and make me one.
Of course, my hope and pride are in the young who carry the torch of life, in full flame.

[1] R. Heatley, 71 Upper Meadow Street, Belfast; Northern Ireland Committee,

Looks like the present-day generation of youth will fan it into a new light of the world, if—as Shaw's last words said—"If they are not wasted in another war." The young should themselves make another war impossible. They should get to know, not what death is like—they have known this long enough, Christ knows—but what life is like, so that when they, too, grow old, they will know more of what life can give than the preservative misery of an old-age pension. Let the young say Let there be Light, and there will be Light.

My blessing on your Committee and on all the eager hopes of the young, wherever they may go, whatever they may do, wherever they may be. I enclose a sub. of £3.3.0. to help.

Yours very sincerely,
Sean O'Casey.

6th World Youth Peace Conference. Mr. Heatley had asked O'Casey to be a sponsor of the World Youth Peace Festival to be held in Moscow.

To Seumas Scully

TS. SCULLY

20 JUNE 1956

My dear Seumas,

Thanks for your letter and for the most interesting press-cuttings. Glad to hear from you and to know that you are working away. Dont you worry as to the kind of man the boss is; while he pays you your wages, he's a friend. I think you would never have been happy in England; you arent a cosmopolitan lad, and Dublin is the surest way to heaven for you. It's not an easy way, but it's the way you know, and the way you like. I heard from David [Krause] the other week, when he read a letter from me to 150 of his students. Of course, there was a long spell, one of five months or more when I didnt bother about hearing from anyone; and all the whispers of the world were faint ones. Eileen was the only one I wanted to see, the one voice I wanted to hear. I can walk at a good speed now, but havent yet swung back into work. Often hear from Bob Ginna who is now working in California for the National Broadcasting Co. His girl-friend has just been with us (she returned to London yesterday) for the last five days, so we talked a lot about Bob. But David and he are very busy in different ways, and dont spend much time in writing letters. Who is "JJF"?[1] I see he reminds the world that a CRITIC in the old IRISH

---

[1] J. J. Finegan, drama critic of the Dublin *Evening Herald* who also wrote a

STATESMAN declared in 1924 that the drunken epilogue between Joxer and Boyle "was a disaster," and that the play should end with Juno's prayer.[2] JJF says "That is what actually happens in the gramaphone recording; there is no 'epilogue.'" JJF goes on, "Sean O'Casey obviously must have approved of the cut. Is this another instance of one of the first critics being strangely right." On the contrary, it is another instance of one of the first critics being strangely wrong. I wonder how his wonderful mind fostered the idea that O'Casey "obviously had approved of the cut"? O'Casey didnt approve of it; doesnt; never imagined that anyone would be so blasted stupid as to make such a cut. He will, however, from this out, see that a contract has a declaration that no cut must be made without O'Casey's written consent.

RMF has a waily waily letter in the same clipping.[3] He does take himself seriously, doesnt he. He implies that on a certain day in a certain year, he became a drama critic—Feb. 1st, 1939, to be precise. On that day, he received his critico-baptismal cert. Before that day, he was but a rover, dropping an article here, and article there, wherever he could find a local habitation for one. Neither he nor the rest will ever realise that O'Casey just likes to have a bit of fun out of what they so pompously say—the pompous lads. They are all funny. RMF actually sent me his review of THE BISHOP'S BONFIRE,[4] thinking, I daresay, that I'd think it important. He "plumped" for it as being the "best play of the Irish year," and didnt me poor heart jump when I read this! He fails to see that the reasons he gives for thinking it the "best play" arent dramatic criticisms at all. A play might cause excitement, stir, anticipation, and controversy, without being even a good one. But these skibereen eagle[5] critics are just a joke.

I hope the book arrived all right for your friend, Miss Butler. The first step towards Moral Rearmament, I think, would be to immediately

---

regular "Show Talk" column in that paper under the initials "J.J.F.," had commented on the Angel Recording of *Juno and the Paycock* in his column of 9 June 1956, praising the cut of the "epilogue." See O'Casey's letter to Cyril Cusack, 25 May 1956, note 2.

[2] Finegan quotes this opinion from W. J. Lawrence's review of the original production of *Juno* at the Abbey, *Irish Statesman*, 15 March 1924.

[3] In the same issue of the *Evening Herald*, 9 June 1956, a letter appeared from R. M. Fox, "Has Sean O'Casey a Persecution Complex?" in which Fox, drama critic of the Dublin *Evening Mail*, commented on a review of O'Casey's *The Green Crow* by J. J. Finegan, "Sean O'Casey Throws Down a Challenge," *Evening Herald*, 2 June 1956.

[4] R. M. Fox, "'Bonfire'—Kindled on Comedy, Quenched by Melodrama," *Evening Mail*, 1 March 1955.

[5] The Rev. Francis S. Mahony, S.J., in his *Reliques of Father Prout* (1836), wrote that Jack Montesquieu, editor of the *Cork Chronicle*, "kept an eye on Russia, an eye of vigilant observation, which considerably annoyed the czar." Later in the 1880s the *West Cork Eagle*, published in Skibereen and known as the "Skibereen Eagle," had on its masthead a drawing of a large eagle peering over a globe of the world—hence, the well-known comic saying in Ireland, "The Skibereen Eagle has its eye on Russia," or "on You." See some references to the "Skibereen Eagle" in Vol. I.

open (split infinitive) diplomatic and cordial relations with the USSR. Shaw has done a lot, and I have done a little to open an Irish way to the generous Russian heart. Keep an eye on your health, oul' son: you'd lose a lot if you lost that.

Eileen & Breon send their best wishes. Shivaun goes to London's Central Art Center in September; Niall is at London University; and I am here among the flowers.

All good wishes from O'Casey.

As ever.
Sean

To John Beary

MS. BEARY

30 JUNE 1956

Dear John,

Glad to hear you are in the old nest again, away from the elephants & the lions. Thanks for Van Gogh's—one of my dear friends—"Gipsy Caravan."

I hope you all have a very successful time with "The Golden Cuckoo" and with "Androcles & the Lion"[1]—with a lion again! Will you ever get away from them. I hope his honor, the Bishop of Galway,[2] may go to see the Shaw play; it might stir him up to tell us more about Shaw, and the dread danger he is to Galltacht & Gaeltacht.[3] Don't forget to number among the Irish Giants of Literature the statues of James Joyce and George Moore: we have had giants in all walks of life as well as Literature—none in Music yet, or in Painting, or in Sculpture; but the day will come—

Give my love to Cyril & his sweet wife, Maureen. Me Dublinman's blessin' to Seumas Kavanagh, & my good wishes to all the other artists.

My love to you
as ever,
Sean

---

[1] Beary had returned to Dublin to work again as a production assistant and actor for Cyril Cusack, who was presenting a season of revivals at the Gaiety Theatre, Denis Johnston's *The Golden Cuckoo* (1948) and Bernard Shaw's *Androcles and the Lion* (1911). Beary played a minor role in the Shaw play.

[2] The Most Rev. Michael John Browne (1895–1980), Bishop of Galway.

[3] The Protestants and the Gaels.

To John Bell[1]

MS. BELL

30 JUNE 1956

Dear Mr. Bell,

"The Lady from Rathmines" is of no value to the play, & the inclusion of the part means trouble for nothing.[2] I removed her myself from the play: go thou and do likewise.

I am very glad to hear of your Company's activities & of their success in performances. May you go from good to better, and from better to best.

With all good wishes to you all.

Yours very sincerely,
Sean O'Casey

[1] John Bell, Newry Abbey Players, Cloughrea, Newry, Co. Down. The Newry Abbey Players were preparing to present *The Plough and the Stars* on the occasion of their 15th Anniversary.
[2] The character of the Woman from Rathmines appears in Act III of *The Plough.* O'Casey forgot to cut her from the text of the play that appears in his *Collected Plays* (1949), Vol. I.

To J. J. O'Leary

MS. O'LEARY

1 JULY 1956

My dear J.J.

Thanks so much for your kind letter. Glad you had an enjoyable holiday up North, tho' I wondered why you didn't go South so early in the season of the Summer. Maybe, it was warmer where the ice is than here where the sea winds blow.

I don't think there's any fear of me going over to Ireland ever again— I'd be shamed to death what with Coole Park dust and Killarney up for sale. Don't let any thought of me possibly arriving in Dublin keep you away from where you think of going. I'm quite content to sit and see things from where I am. I get the Weekly Bulletin, "Eire," issued by Roinne Gnothai Eachtracha [Department of External Affairs], so I know who's who & what's what in Ireland, even the reputation & pedigree of the Irish Greyhounds who help to keep the old green flag flying, "all Irish dogs, Irish bred" said the Announcer of Television last night. By God, we're in the News still!

Eileen talks at times of going again to Dublin; but she & I have so much to do with the affairs of the children—Niall is in London University, and Shivaun goes to Central Arts School next October—that we hardly have time for an evening stroll. By the way, is C. Cusack the one lone bird to whistle a tune in favor of Shaw? Perhaps, R.E. will do some of his plays: introduced, produced, & traduced by the Bishop of Galway, Ireland's Great Atlantic Port. I wish to God it were.

Glad to hear the name of Will Shields [Barry Fitzgerald] again. If he be anywhere near, give him my love. It's a long time since he had Breon on his lap, & presented him with the toy dog "Bunser."

All good wishes & warm regards to you, &, if ever you be within sight of Torquay, come a little farther on to St. Marychurch, & take a cuppa tea with us.

> *Yours very sincerely,*
> *Sean*

To Martin Browne[1]

TC. O'CASEY

3 JULY 1956

Dear Martin,

No, oh no, John: heard a Russian soldier singing this delightfully on Sunday night; and I sing these words for you now. Let someone else, better than I, review Ervine's book on Shaw.[2] I've just read a book on the Master by Eric Bentley,[3] and I dont want to read another one for some time to come. Besides, I've just sent an article on the great man, by request, to the New York Times,[4] and there still remains a hundred letters to write; so I have to say hail and farewell to your kind offer.

I understand that, so far, thirty books have been written about Shaw along with millions of articles, so we should know all there is to be known about him by now; though the only Shaw is to be found all over what he has written himself. Too many were acquainted with Shaw; too few knew him. The very first article in DRAMA[5] shows this plain. Murray thinks of him only as a comedian, a comedy writer, but hardly a play of his

---

[1] Martin Browne, editor, *Drama,* London.
[2] St. John Ervine, *Bernard Shaw: His Life, Work and Friends* (1956).
[3] Eric Bentley, *Bernard Shaw* (1947).
[4] Sean O'Casey, "G. B. Shaw: The Lord of a Century," *New York Times,* 22 July 1956, an article on the occasion of the centenary of Shaw's birth, 26 July 1956.
[5] "Bernard Shaw to Gilbert Murray," *Drama,* Autumn 1956; six letters from Shaw to Murray.

that doesnt contain something of life's sorrows. He knew the deeps of life far further down than did Smuts, going from man to animals (the pig in J. Bull's Other Island) to plants (the daisy in the same play). Murray seems to think that because a soul can laugh, it cannot weep, though a soul that can laugh the merriest can often weep the bitterest way. His last words were, "If the young are not wasted in another war," while Smuts wore the Sam Brown Belt to the last.

Well, I didnt set out to write another article, so this is the end.

Thanks a lot for your offer, and please accept regrets that it doesnt appeal to me.

With all good wishes,

Yours very sincerely,
Sean O'Casey.

To Claire and Stan Howard[1]

MS. HOWARD

10 JULY 1956

Dear Claire and Stan:

Thanks for your letter. I've been very busy recovering from illness, hard & long. I wish I had seen Washington; but it would take a long, long time to see everything worth seeing in the U.S.A. Nature is a fine study; but everything in life is part of Nature, even the "fads" that flood "religion" & the "fads" that help or horrify painting. All our time is limited, & earning a living takes a lot of time away from us; but this we must do—earn our bread by the sweat of our face—and nothing can be done about it. We must live before we can enjoy life; even before we find time to look at the fairer features of her wonderful face.

I know only too well of the "Left's" indifference to, and ignorance of, art; the whole movement is full of tiny popes, fierce and futile; so few of them know enough even of their own philosophy to measure and use the circumstances of our times. It's true that the people, Massmensch, alone can fight the inevitable fight, but their leaders should see to it that when the last fight is faced, the people will have knowledge as well as power.

Never heard of [Jackson] Pollock; &, if what you say of him be true, don't want to hear of him—tho' I'd like to see a few of his pictures to see for myself. These seem to think too much of the soul, & forget that the soul forms a substantial part of the Body—Council of Vienna.

1 See O'Casey's letter to Mrs. Stanley J. Hochdorf, 29 April 1956, note 1.

Don't call your baby "Sean," give him a name of his own. If your husband gets joy or pleasure from Painting, I think he should go on; if he doesn't, then he should abandon it.

My love to you both.
Yours very sincerely,
Sean O'Casey

To Frank McCarthy

TS. McCarthy

14 July 1956

My dear Frank,

Thanks for your letter. Eileen and Niall saw THE QUARE FELLA and pronounced it very good indeed. Seems to be no doubt that Behan has something in him. I do hope it may be a fine success in the Comedy,[1] which will give Behan time to think, and arrange his psychology to his new environment. Experience should teach him to do this quite safely. As for me writing to him and spreading advice before him—it wouldnt do, Frank. You dont know Irish writers as I do, though I dont know Behan. He might consider my interference to be an impudent thing, or sign of a "swelled head." He has never made any effort to come into touch with me; and, besides, his circumstances are different from mine, so that advice would be of little use. Anyway, it's damned hard to give advice, and damned harder to take it. I didnt see the Television interview of B, with Muggeridge, though I heard that B. was a little over the edge,[2] and that Muggeridge teased him, which was no credit to Mister Muggeridge— a sophisticated cynic tackling an excited Irishman fresh from a very limited experience of such things as interviews over Television. Wish I had been one of the interviewers, for then Mister M. shouldnt have had it his own way. However, if there's something in Behan, this experience will do him good; and if it does, I shouldnt recommend Muggeridge to tackle him a year or two from now.

There was little reason for either you or Dr. [Donald O.] Soper to argue bitterly about such a trivial thing. I hope Nora will have a happy time of it in Wicklow—and a cheaper time too. I dont see why the pub-

---

[1] Brendan Behan's *The Quare Fellow* was transferred to the Comedy Theatre in the West End on 24 July 1956. See O'Casey's letter to McCarthy, 8 June 1956, note 1.

[2] Malcolm Muggeridge interviewed Brendan Behan on the "Panorama" program of B.B.C. TV on 18 June 1956. Behan apparently "had some drink taken" at the time.

lisher should refuse to publish her book, if she wishes to do it; but if she thinks it would [hurt] her sales (not her soul), then it is a problem to be considered, for one has to live. I am going along fairly well; the wound across the belly has, I think, decided to close, so that's one thing done. I am beginning my old habit of going at a good pace through the village, looking at the roses in the gardens, and the trees topping their walls. What about you? Are you minding yourself, and keeping far from the frying pan and fats? I hope you are.

My blessing follows you to Ireland, and may you have a fine time there, and a good rest. Enclosed a poem by B.B. appearing in the I. Times. English a very free translation of the Irish.[3]

As ever,
Sean.

[3] Brendan Behan, "Ceadunas Nua Kruger" ("Kruger's New License"), *Irish Times*, 30 June 1956, a comic poem in Irish with an English translation. Kruger Kavanagh was a well-known publican and popular personality in the Dingle peninsula.

To Macmillan, London

TS. MACMILLAN, LONDON

16 JULY 1956

Dear Sirs,
I have this morning received a letter from Braziller Inc., of New York City, saying that my book, THE GREEN CROW, published in the U.S.A., hasnt interested you, and that you have declined to enter into an English publication of the book. You may remember that part of it is taken from THE FLYING WASP, and the short stories from WINDFALLS, both published by you many years ago. Another publisher, [W.H.] Allen and Company, are very much interested in an English edition, and, I assume that you have no objection to such an issue by this publisher; though I regret very much that your Firm werent interested enough to take on the publication (the book got many and excellent notices in the American Press); and I should be very interested to know the reason why you wouldnt agree to sponsor an edition in England. Some time ago, Mr. Braziller wrote saying he was very hopeful that you would take over the distribution of an English edition. I'm not trying now to imply that you should change your mind now, just expressing a sigh of disappointment.

Another point of complaint: Three Professors of the University of Michigan are compiling an Anthology of plays in which they wish to include JUNO AND THE PAYCOCK. I am told that this anthology isnt competitive, and will be used only as a text book for colleges, and that the effect upon the sales of the regular editions would be nil. The Authors (the 3 Professors) wish the anthology to be circulated to colleges on a world-wide basis. In response to a request to print the text, I understand, the St. Martin's Press [said no] on a ruling from Macmillan & Co. Here I would like you to change your mind, for, not being a popular writer, I get great sustenance by the interest taken in my work by the American students in the American colleges everywhere. For instance, this morning I got a letter from an American who is lecturing in the Belgian college of Louvain; so a change of mind or of heart on this matter might mean a lot to me and my work. Of course, if you cant see your way to do this, it cant be helped, and it must be met with the expression of one more sigh.

Yours sincerely,
Sean O'Casey.

To John Allen[1]

TS. ALLEN

18 JULY 1956

Dear John,

It was fine to hear from you after so many years—the last I heard of you was a flying visit you paid to Dartington Hall, but you hadnt time then to run in and see us at Tingrith. Yes, indeed, the production of THE STAR TURNS RED in Unity by you was a fine event; though it isnt a *Communist* play. Shaw saw the kind of a work it was when he wrote to say that he "was delighted that I had given them the Authorized Version";[2] it is the democracy of the prophets they couldnt and cant stick. Not that I care much one way or the other, for I get a living allright, mostly from the USA, Ireland, and, lately from the USSR. But your production was spoiled, or the memory of it, by a later shocking one by a conceited lad named Ted Willis,[3] author of *Buster;* and now doing a series of half-hour plays for the BBC Television. Why dont you try for a job there?

We left Tingrith more than two years ago; the landlord wanted the house, so he gave us notice to quit; and we live in above address now.

I have been very ill since, in hospital for four months, and am now

[1] John Allen, 21 Lydford Road, London, N.W.2. Allen directed the premiere of *The Star Turns Red* at Unity Theatre on 12 March 1940.

[2] See O'Casey's letter to Bernard Shaw, 29 April 1940, note 2, Vol. I.

[3] Ted Willis directed a revival of *The Star Turns Red* at Unity Theatre on 31 July 1946.

getting something like myself again; but not yet able to do very much work. I'm glad you did your letter out in typescript, for it is far easier on my eyes than the close formation of most handwriting. I am too tired still to set myself to read your essay; but think it a mistake to leave out Yeats, L. Gregory, Synge, and Robinson; but, of course, a lot depends on the size of the book.

You have indeed a task to find enough for seven children—one for every day of the week. I know a little about it, for we have three; and quite enough to care for.

I wish I could help you, but I cant see any way to do it. From what I know of you, I feel, as I felt at first, that you should go far in any theater worth a damn. Pity, you didnt keep in touch with me. Eileen and I often thought of you, and we both send our best wishes to you and yours.

Yours sincerely,
Sean

To Mrs. R——

MS. PRIVATE

18 JULY 1956

Dear R——,
Thanks for your letter and the cuttings. All the talk and the tales about what a play should be on the stage, over the wireless, & how it should flicker its way home across the Television Screen! And the right way on any of them will never be known; not to man, though, maybe, to God. And the other cuttings telling us why the Irish are stampeding out of Ireland. Not a word about the export of thousands of young men & women as priests and nuns to this far land, that one, & God knows where; all hoping to be reverend mothers & all hoping to be Bishops. Now skedaddling out of China, where the Red Flag flies, & soon to be skedaddling out of Africa where the shadow of the Red Flag falls over veldt, koppie, waterfall, and jungle, to lose its shadow & become a substance when the bad time comes. Greenland's icy mountains, India's coral strands, & Africa's sunny fountains darkened by the shadow of the Red Flag—the thought is terrible!

I'm glad A.'s wedding went well, and hope it may have many & many a happy remembrance thro' the years to come.

Yes, yes, [T. E.] Lawrence died too young. I met him once, in Bernard S.'s company: very shy, so was I, so was Shaw—the three shy men; yet three in one and one in three. I was too busy at the time with many problems to have a chance to get into closer touch with this remarkable man.

Casement I met once in Tom Clarke's tiny tobacconist shop; introduced snappily by Tom, and got a nod from Sir Roger. I was unemployed then, and too ragged to be admitted to the finer society of the Republican & the Gaelic Leaguers. Easter Week & all that led to it was essentially a middle-class revolution. [James] Connolly's tiny band was swallowed down and smothered up by it.

With all their memorial Theaters and Old Vics, Shakespeare is still outside his English home, & getting a little tired of knocking at the door.

I hope you may have a fine holiday in Ireland, if you go; and A., too, with J.

Torquay is all agog about Marilyn's possible visit to Torquay.[1] If she rings up to say she'll come, I'll do what I can to advise her how to come like a thief in the night; for I don't want a crowd bellowing about within my quietness.

My blessing on A. & J.; my love, too, to them, & to you, joined to Eileen's.

As ever,
Sean

---

[1] Marilyn Monroe stated as she was leaving America on a trip to England that the one man she wanted to meet there was Sean O'Casey. They never met.

To Brooks Atkinson

MS. ATKINSON

20 JULY 1956

My dear Brooks & my dear Oriana,

My love to you both as a preface. Thanks, Brooks for mentioning me to Mr. [Lewis] Funke. I sent him an article on G.B.S.—too long—but he wrote to say that it was "a magnificent piece." Who says we Irish are the greatest at exaggeration! I didn't feel any guilt over it after it had been written; but the Drama Editor's opinion has comforted me with an idea that it might be better than I thought. Heaven grant that he and I be right. I'm grateful that you stopped the proof of the letter from Miss Davis. It certainly saved me a lot of agony of inwit over the non-response to kind inquiries. I've too many already to feel safe or settled. Miss Davis sent us wine and canned goods; but left out any sign of where she lived, so that thanks could be sent, and a warning to send no more. For the past four years or so, our income has been enough for most of our needs (thanks mainly to the U.S.A.). We as a household are mightily beholden to American generosity, and God forbid we should abuse it.

I am grieved to hear your news about George Jean. It is hard to get rid of anything you get at the age of seventy. I hesitate to write to him, not knowing what to say to give a little comfort and a little hope. Last I heard from him was when he sent me his article distributing his chocolate Georgies, for which I wrote my thanks for article & the Georgie he gave to me.

I daresay, you are now busy as a carpenter & mason in Durham, and I hope you aren't overdoing it. Last time, after removing an old Dutch oven, you wrote to say you were pooped. Keep the pooping out of it this time, Brooks, & go steady; for, although you are young and lithe, you weren't made of dressed steel. America can do without its mason or her carpenter, but heaven forbid she should lose her Drama Critic.

It's a pity Oriana didn't get the Title she wanted. A Title is a hard thing to come by; but better to have a bad title & a good book than a bad book with a good title. What you say about it, & what others say, shows a good book. Oriana must send me a copy of it. If she writes as brilliantly, as critically, & lovingly about our S. & West as she did about Manhattan, I'll widen the green band I wear all round me hat. You're a lucky lad to have such a gay and good companion. I do hope dear Oriana's book may have a fine sale in Ireland, for we need to look at a view from another's eye; and Oriana's is a bright one, and a fair one too.

My love again to her and to you.

As ever,
Sean

I send this to the office, not knowing address in Durham.

To Mikhail Apletin[1]

TC. O'CASEY

25 JULY 1956

Dear friend,

You may remember asking me to do a tape recording of opinions about Bernard Shaw. I was too ill then to think of it, and too tired still from the illness to do it now.

A week ago, the Drama Editor of THE NEW YORK TIMES asked

---

[1] Mikhail Apletin, secretary, Foreign Commission, Union of Soviet Writers, Moscow. See letters to him in Vol. II.

me to write an article on the great Man in honor of his anniversary. This I did, and it has been published by that Journal.[2]

I am sending the article on to you, venturing to think that you might be interested, and find it good enough to merit publishing in a Soviet Gazette or Magazine.

The N.Y. Times Drama Editor said it was "magnificent," but I dont go with his opinion by a very long way, though I do think it worthy of appearing in any magazine whose readers may be interested in Shaw's place in the world of man.

I do hope you are fit and well for I look upon you as a very old friend indeed, both of us having weathered a lot of storms together, you there in Moscow, and I here in England. We have come out of them safe, and the sky over us is brighter than it has been for a long long time.

I am getting stronger, but had had to make a big battle to get out of the illness, but I am used to struggle, and am still alive and kicking and hoping for renewed advances by the Soviet Union in the affairs of Man.

I send my love to the Soviet People and to you.

As ever,
Sean O'Casey.

[2] Sean O'Casey, "G. B. Shaw: The Lord of a Century," *New York Times,* 22 July 1956; reprinted in the British edition of *The Green Crow* (W. H. Allen, 1957).

To John Gassner

MS. GASSNER

1 AUGUST 1956

My dear John,
Thank you, and thanks, many of them—a thousand, as we give in Ireland—for the *The Theater in Our Times* [1954] and for the book, *Form & Idea in Modern Theater* [1956]. Both are very welcome additions to my shelves. I shall soon be entering into the pleasure of reading the "Form & Idea," which—as you can guess—interests me greatly. Thanks, too, for the Review of "The Green Crow" by Max Cosman.[1] When you see him, remember my name, & hand him my thanks for his kind words. Yes, John, we're all captors of one thing or another; deluding ourselves by thinking we have led captivity captive. The artist, playwright, Painter, Critic, poet, even, are not only captives—they become slaves; but slaves wearing a pentecostal crown. I sympathise with Max; but I think we shouldn't be too

[1] Max Cosman, "Embattled Irishman," *Theatre Arts,* July 1956.

resentful when we find we cannot do the things that we would. I, when I was young, fiercely wanted to be a painter, but, even in employment, when bare necessities were pacified, I had not the means to buy brush or paint, or canvas. God can't always be in attendance on us. It would be glorious if the seed of talent within brought forth fruit a hundredfold; grand if it brought forth fruit sixtyfold; but who is he or so who am I to be dissatisfied with a yield of thirtyfold? Considering the dangers of the wayside, the stony ground, the thorns of triviality, a tenfold fruiting is a thing by which to Praise God. We mustn't rail so that the ripening grape sours again; but rather allow the still sour grape of life to ripen. You have done more than well, John, in all your tasks, and so should thank God feasting.

I join you in betting on Strindberg: a northern star, sulphurous at times, like a glow from hell-fire, but anon brilliant with a ray of light straight from God's throne. After *Easter* the *Dance of Death,* when the lily festered and became a smoking weed, but even in this terrible play, the evil budded into a beautiful flower that shone in the *Dream Play's* ending. Although, like his hollyhocks, Strindberg was ever mounting higher, he was ever close to Satan. Well, so was Jesus, on the Mount of temptation, during the betrayal by Judas, when Peter denied; all along, down along, all along lea. And we, too, for there can be no rise without a fall.

To me, Strindberg is away ahead of Ibsen; a man he was who is very close to Shakespeare. We can but follow, limping behind; but we follow, and that is what matters.

My warm regards to Max, and the same, with affection to you.

Sean

To Paul Shyre

MS. SHYRE

3 AUGUST 1956

Dear Paul:

Yes, I got the Bird Book allright, and a very charming book it is, too. Thank you very much for it. I love birds, and watch them quietly, as often & as well as I can. An irritating thing is that I can't see them clear till they come close; and that they are wary of me, tho' a blackbird here comes to where I sit, & cocks an eye at me but a foot or two away. I give him an odd scrap of fat & a crumb or two, placed a little distance away from me. It was funny how first he hesitated, looking at me with a questioning eye, till desire gave him courage to come and take his fill.

I do hope the Readings in The Playhouse[1] may be a good success for all our sakes; & will give you & your comrades something in return for the hard work you all must have put into the learning.

Bette Henritze wrote me some time ago from the London American Express, asking to come to see me, but I was feeling too down at the time to even reply to her kind note. I am still under surgical inspection; kind of house arrest. Bette gave no address in New York, so I couldn't write to tell her this when I felt good enough to bawl hiya! Please tell her, and give her my regrets whenever you see her.

All good wishes to your comrades & to you, a mhic.

As ever,
Sean

[1] See O'Casey's letter to Shyre, 6 May 1956, note 1.

To Brooks Atkinson

TS. ATKINSON

4 AUGUST 1956

My dear Brooks:

Miss [Jane] Rubin wrote to say that the proposed production of THE GUNMAN had been abandoned, adding she enclosed the letter she got from Mr. [Jack] Garfein; but she forgot to put his letter in, or, maybe, she didn't like me to know what had happened. However, I knew soon enough, for the doctor attending me brought the news. It appears that the cutting you enclosed had been reprinted in the London DAILY EXPRESS.

I never thought the play would go through, so was disappointed when I heard the news, though I never imagined it wouldn't be put on for the reason given in the papers.

Regarding your questions about my Communism, let me say first, as a prelude, that I should be indeed sorry if you got into any bother on my account, and I have assumed now that you will be sensible, so that in anything you may write about me, you don't hurt yourself. That would grieve me greatly, and do me no good: let all my work be banned in the U.S.A. rather than any of my friends there should suffer.

Am I a Communist? Yes; as deep a one as I was more than fifty years ago. Am I of the Party? No, for, like Shaw, I wished first to be a good playwright before anything else. That is a thing that many Communists seemed unable to learn—that a man must be first excellent at what his hand findeth to do before he could be a Communist at all. The doctor watching me, for instance, is a very conscientious Catholic, but a very clever doctor; a friend as well as a doctor, calling me Sean as I call him Hugh [Varian]. A bad doctor, tho' a good Communist, would be of no use to me. An American young fellow who is a nerve specialist, came to see me in Tingrith some time ago. He thought of nothing but Communism, lived for it so ardently that he was nearly dying for it, his nerves were in such a state of trembling. I gave him some sharp advice, following it up with letters when he got back to the USA; one letter giving him great grieving, for, he said, it was harsh and merciless. It did him good, for he realised at last, as I commended that he began to be a Communist when he became a valuable and trusted Nerve Specialist. He is a new lad now, and his letters are bright with resolution and certitude. I am never moved meeting one who can go on quoting almost verbatim, some Comm. pamphlet, for Communism is not to be found in a booklet, but springs to life within, as does the Kingdom of heaven. So I am a Communist, but not a talking comm. pamphlet.

I have never tried to put my beliefs into the minds of anyone by any other method than pleasant argument; and I've never tried to interfere with the opinions of my own children. I've read to them when they were young, Dickens, Scott, Hardy, Melville's MOBY DICK, and M. Twain's HUCKLEBERRY FINN and his LIFE ON THE MISSISSIPPI; but never even the Communistic Manifesto, though it was there for them to read if they so desired. They, however, chose the COMICS, and neither Eileen or I tried to interfere with them. My books were there for them whenever they got interested in them; all sorts from all kinds of great minds. I and Eileen agreed that they must grow up with minds of their own.

Communism isn't what you lay it out to be, my dear Brooks. It has no reason to be "godless, treacherous, despotic, anti-art, cruel, or barbaric." To me, the "godless" seem to be those gathered together in the Christian churches. No power was more ruthless, more barbaric, more cruel than these when they ruled the world.

All the various types of Comm. you mention—of the Pilgrim Fathers, Jamestown Colony, etc, were largely emotional, and were bound to fail; but Marxism is scientific Socialism, as philosophical as any other philosophy, but keeping well away from any kind of emotional mysticism. But scientific Socialism was hammered out through the passage of centuries, and Marx did no more than gather up the many pieces, and set them out in logical order. It is in the nature of life to change, and this evolutionary restlessness in life will, I believe, bring about Communism as the natural and orderly way of life in the future. It is rather ironic that it was the U.S.A. herself who started the more modern aspect of social advance when she fired the first shot at Bunker Hill, a shot—as Carlyle saw and said— that went echoing all round the world; one man making music, soul-stirring music—out of the echo in the mighty march of The Marseillaise. Its virile seed is in your Declaration of Independence. And in the American Constitution, too. May the United States live forever!

As for Stalin, I don't accept the reported versions of speeches said to have been made by Bulganin and K[hrushchev]. The denunciations made of the man's mistakes are, to me, but an implied idea that he should have been infallible. He wasn't infallible, as no man is. To connect his name with that of Hitler is wrong, for Hitler, for instance, when he died, left his land a desolation, while Stalin, when he died, left his land one of the strongest in the world. As for "cult of personality," Stalin was not the founder of this practice. It flourished everywhere, and flourishes still. Everybody's doing it. No more than Parnell was Stalin responsible for having a picture of himself on every banner, in every home. Each of us is trying, one way or another, to project a personality. As for cruelty, all revolutions are cruel. Ireland's Free State executed 77 Republicans, and God only knows how many Irish were executed by England's various governments. It was England created Concentrated Camps. I could list (as you know yourself well) a host of horrors with which Communism had nothing to do. We have all sinned, Brooks, and fallen short of the glory of God.

As for being "anti-art," that isn't Communism, but ignorance. There was plenty of it in the Western World. Even George Russell (A.E.) opposed any idea of Cezanne or Picasso entering the Dublin Art Gallery. I had a "quarrel" with him about it, and, indeed, a letter of mine appeared in the *New York Times* about the dispute.[1] Look at the way Joyce was honored. His works are still banned in Christian Eire.[2] Anyway, there is a wholesome change appearing in the Soviet attitude towards art and literature. It is passing out of the childish age.

Communists should aim at knowing something, and being interested in, all things which pulse with life; and must be amiable and broadminded with all who can't see things through communistic eyes—including art and literature. I'm saying this, not only to you, dear Brooks, but I've said it more than once to the writers in the Soviet Union. I have defended Eliot and Joyce when they were denounced by the Soviet Union. And God help me, Brooks, I'm conceited enough to think that my writings had some influence on them. Influence again!

I can't understand the American fear that Communism can destroy the American Way of Life. Under Communism your way of life would still be the American Way of Life; its manner would have changed, but it would remain American. It just couldn't be anything else. Oriana would be Oriana and Brooks would still be Brooks.

I am still all the kinds of Communist that you quoted from a letter of

---

[1] See his letter, "Sean O'Casey and George Russell," *New York Times,* 20 March 1930, Vol. I.

[2] James Joyce's works were given the silent or unofficial ban in bookshops and libraries in Ireland until the 1960s, but officially the government Censorship of Publications Board banned only *Stephen Hero* on 10 November 1944; and the prohibition was removed on 13 April 1951.

mine;[3] and a Keatsian one too. You may remember that Bernard Shaw somewhere said that Keats in 13 lines of poetry uttered all that Lenin and Marx ever stated and implied.[4]

I am not trying to Argue with you, Brooks—only setting down a few of the opinions I hold with conviction and regard; and remember, in them all and through them all, I wear upon my breast the glittering order of human fallibility.

Of course, I do look upon life from the workers' point of view; but they have a multitude of grades. You Oriana, and Mr. [Lewis] Funke are workers just as the docker, the factory worker, the railway-man, and the rest, are workers. Workers of the world!

I am, naturally, very glad that you thought the article about Shaw[5] to be a "corker." I wasn't quite happy about it myself. You and Mr. Funke are generous, and very encouraging. There's no fear of me developing conceit, for a friend has sent me a copy of COMMONWEAL, in which an Irish critic tells me that all I've written after the PLOUGH AND THE STARS, is "rubbish."[6]

If America thinks my plays shouldn't be put on because I happen to be a Communist, well and bad. I have no wish to interfere with these or this decision, even though it makes life harder. Nevertheless, I can't help hoping a change of mind may come, knowing that if it does, the American way of life will continue to be American still.

Yes, indeed, I've heard of Marie Doro, and please give her my regards. And let Oriana and you let up a little from the hard work of Prink Hill. For God's sake, don't overdo it.

My deep love to Oriana and to you.
As ever,
Sean

[3] The quoted passage is from O'Casey's letter to Atkinson, 11 April 1949, Vol. II: "Of course, I am a Shelleyan Communist, and a Dickensian one, & a Byronic one, and a Whitmanian one, & one like all those who thought big & beautifully, & who cared for others, as I am a Marxian one, too. We can really move about & play and embrace, when we are tired on a wide, wide space of common ground."

[4] See O'Casey's letter to David Krause, 12 April 1955, note 2.

[5] See O'Casey's letter to Martin Browne, 3 July 1956, note 4.

[6] Vivian Mercier, "The Riddle of Sean O'Casey: Decline of a Playwright," *Commonweal*, 13 July 1956. See also the letter of reply by Robert Hogan, 24 August 1956.

To Mrs. John T. Cooper[1]

MS. CSU FULLERTON LIB

10 AUGUST 1956

Dear Georgie,

Oh many many thanks for your kind letter, and for the lovely Sonnet; delightful to me—God forgive me for liking the jewel of praise. However, I shall strive to mitigate the sin by trying to be a little like what you think me to be. Indeed, my lass, you have a poet's strain in you: and wit, too.

All good wishes to your husband & to you.

With affectionate regards,
Yours very sincerely,
Sean O'Casey

P.S. Didn't write sooner because of illness. Am still under medical inspection, and tire more quickly than of yore; but still defiant.

[1] Mrs. John T. "Georgie" Cooper, 415 No. 12th Street, Fort Dodge, Iowa. Many years ago Mrs. Cooper sent me copies of 10 of her 25 O'Casey letters, and in 1984 copies of the remaining 15 were very kindly sent to me by the California State University at Fullerton Library, where all the letters are in the Special Collections. In 1984 a student at the university, JoAnn Byrne Todd, sent me a copy of her Independent Study Project on the letters, in which she wrote that the correspondence began when "Georgie Cooper was a young woman who had read O'Casey's work during an attempt to alleviate the cabin-fever of a long winter in snowy Iowa." Georgie wrote a sonnet of praise for O'Casey and enclosed it in this first letter.

To Seamus Locke[1]

TC. O'CASEY

16 AUGUST 1956

Dear Seamus,

Thanks for your letter. About Rowan Tree: I dont think I'll change the line.[2] It is typical of what Ireland has to suffer. There is an outcry be-

[1] Seamus Locke, Irish actor and singer, 1250 Hilldale Avenue, Los Angeles, California. As Shamus Locke he played the role of O'Killigain opposite Siobhan McKenna's Avril in Sam Wanamaker's 1953 production of *Purple Dust;* see O'Casey's letter to Wanamaker, 28 April 1953, note 1, Vol. II. He also played Inspector Finglas in the New York premiere of *Red Roses For Me;* see O'Casey's letter to David Krause, 3 January 1956, note 1.

[2] Locke had planned to make a record of O'Casey's songs, but he objected to the opening line of "The Rowan Tree," an extra song that O'Casey wrote for Wanamaker's production of *Purple Dust,* the opening stanza of which reads:

A sour-soul'd cleric, passing near,
Saw lovers by a rowan-tree;

ginning against the rigid way the clerics (not all of course) regard sex. Many are pointing out that it comes close to Jansenism, and is responsible for the lowest marriage rate in the world. You should read the book recently published in USA—THE VANISHING IRISH [1954], edited by Dr. [John A.] O'Brien, Professor in the Pauline Society, and one of the heads of Notre Dame College, Notre Dame, Indiana, run, I think, by the Pauline Fathers: even I am quoted in the book. Father O'B. himself sent it to me.

I enclose a copy of "Bless'd be the Day," the air of which is to be had in the book of the play—THE BISHOP'S BONFIRE—by the way, this play played to packed houses in the Dublin Gaiety, and all actors were Catholics, headed by Cyril Cusack who sponsored the play.[3] The air to the song isnt a very good one; but many of the folk airs are pretty repetitious.

I enclose copy of "Oh, When Shall I Hear." The air is that which Siobhan [McKenna] sang on her entrance in the first act of P. DUST— "The Maid of Bunclody." I wrote it for the play and for Siobhan, but seeing how the play was going, I said nothing about it; it would have been just a waste of time. As for recording an Introduction, I will think over it, but it all depends on my condition, how I may feel when the time comes, for I'm still under doctor's care. However, when you write again, send me a list of the songs you think of including—I havent the faintest recollection of what they are. By the way, dont do much about the idea till you are sure of a possible result; that it will be acceptable to Columbia, for there's no use of spending time on what mightnt happen. I hope S. will do well in "St. Joan."[4]

Filming the biography is a big order—couldnt even try to think about it at the moment. There are Readings of PICTURES IN THE HALLWAY to be given a run next month in The Playhouse, New York, and I hope they will go well. Produced before, they got a wonderful reception. So much for the present. Eileen's and my love to you.

[Sean]

He curs'd its branches, berries, bloom,
Through time and through eternity.
Now evil things are waiting where
Fond lovers once found joy,
And dread of love now crowns th' thoughts
Of frighten'd girl, of frighten'd boy.

[3] See O'Casey's letter to Cyril Cusack, 5 March 1955, note 1.
[4] Bernard Shaw's *Saint Joan* opened in New York on 11 September 1956, with Siobhan McKenna in the title role.

To Cyril Cusack

TS. CUSACK

21 AUSUST 1956

Dear Cyril,

Belated thanks to you for your letter written to me long, long ago. I have since heard the Recording of JUNO, and to all of us who heard, it went splendidly, bar the cutting of the last scene between J[oxer] and B[oyle]. I had, of course, nothing to do with this extravagant foolishness; never conceived for a moment that such a stupid cancellation could even be thought of.[1] But there you are—one can never tell. I have just agreed to a contract of JUNO for America, but took care to issue a clause prohibiting this particular part from being removed. Well, the rest of the Record was fine; far better than I expected it might be. All the Artists did, in my opinion, splendidly. What a lovely voice your Maureen has! She made a very winsome Mary. I do hope you did well with ANDROCLES and THE G. CUCKOO;[2] or, at least, that you lost nothing on them.

Did you read Niall O'Carroll's giant jot of a thought in last Saturday's I.PRESS? "What a pity that he (D.Johnston) persists in this looking back when the Irish Theatre so badly needs a keen mind like his to turn its attention to some of the many problems facing us today and which are just calling for the pen of the playwright." I hear her calling me! Ireland's Eye has her eye on Denis J. I remember a play that did try to face some of the problems facing Ireland today, and I remember the welcome the Irish drama critics gave it. What processed pretenders the Irish critics are! Waiting for a playwright who will face the problems Eire is facing today! Waiting for Godot. Not Niall O'Carroll, of course. He's a forthright critic. No hypocritic-critic he. Always courageous, and always expectant. The problems of Ireland calling for the penance of the playwright. So they have sold Killarney again![3] When a kid, I remember often singing a song that went

> Why didja sell Killarney,
> All for the sake of gold;
> Why didja sell her lakes an fells,
> Her mossy banks an her flowry dells;
> Where the girls all love to wander,
> An the boys they speak their blarney?

[1] See O'Casey's letter to Cusack, 25 May 1956, note 2.

[2] Cyril Cusack Productions presented these two plays in Dublin at the Gaiety Theatre: Denis Johnston's *The Golden Cuckoo* (1939) on 25 June 1956; Bernard Shaw's *Androcles and the Lion* (1912) on 2 July 1956.

[3] With a banner headline, "AMERICAN BUYS KILLARNEY," *Irish Press,* 11 August 1956, it was announced that Mr. J. Stuart Robertson, an American, had bought the Kenmare Estate in Killarney for £100,000, which includes the lower and middle lakes and the historic Ross Castle, an 8,820 acre property.

> Ireland may be poor, but still,
> Why did she sell Killarney!

'ja ever hear it? And it has all happened again. By God, it is a humiliating thing that our Killarney should be put up for sale in an English auction-room!

My love to Maureen, to your children, and to you.

Sean

To David Krause

TS. KRAUSE

23 AUGUST 1956

My dear Dave,

I haven't been too good, or I should have sent a message earlier to thank you for the tobacco; and with the message, a warning to send no more. You must put by whatever you can for another day that may not be so fine as those you may be enjoying now: you must think of yourself.

Dave Greene was here for a night recently, before he went to Ireland for some more details about John M. Synge and his stay on Inish Meadhon of the Aran Islands. I daresay, he has got back to his own country by now; and I hope he did well, and that the biggest part of his work is over. He looked well, and was in great spirits—he and his comrade [Emmet] Larkin, busy with another life—that of the big Jim Larkin, the Irish Labor Leader.[1]

A great many thanks for the article in BROWNNONIA;[2] a fine and flattering tribute to what I have tried to do. By the same post, a very different article came; one that appeared in THE COMMONWEAL, and was written by the Irishman, Vivian Mercier, colleague of Dave G. He called it THE RIDDLE OF SEAN O'CASEY, with a s-title of "Decline of a playwright." "People often ask" he says, "What happened to O'Casey?" meaning what caused him to start writing rubbish "after those three plays of genius?" Dunno, meself. Dublin, he says, explains it by believing that "Sure, Lady Gregory wrote all the early plays for him." or, "He was going with a teacher, and she helped him till they fell out." The poor tachure! I'm afraid it was O'Casey who taught the teacher, and not the teacher O'Casey. It was I brought her to Shakespeare, to Keats, Shelley, even to

---

[1] Emmet Larkin, *James Larkin, Irish Labour Leader, 1876–1947* (1965).
[2] David Krause, "A Portrait of the Artist as a Green Crow," *Brunonia*, Summer 1956, the literary magazine of Brown University, Providence, R.I.

Dickens and Jack London; not to mention G.B.S. Well, let the lie lie. He stresses that "The poor Protestant can never be at home with his Catholic fellow-workers." I wonder how he knows this? If he had said that the poor protestants were never quite at home with their better-off co-religionists, he would have been closer to the mark. On the other hand, I remember Lady G. being very upset and grieved that Yeats never mentioned her co-operation with him when he was thinking out Cathleen Ni Houlihan; for she told me once, when I was in Coole, that she had practically written the play, and was the author of its construction. I've never mentioned this before, for, though she believed what she said, I had no idea whatever or no she was right in her contention. It doesn't matter, for take away the play, and Yeats stands out, big as ever.

I'm glad that you have built a little corner for yourself. Each of us needs a little loneliness occasionally; to look out of a window on the world, and see for oneself; to watch the rhythm of the dance and see the color of the clothes, and enjoy or judge for oneself, without any intruding opinion from another. Good news of the rise in the wage, for each of us could do with a little more: "the little more, and much it is"! Success to you in your new venture in the graduate Seminar in Irish Drama and Irish eye Literature. Shivaun is to go to a London Art School next October; Niall will be two more years in London University; and Brian—Breon—is busy painting. Eileen slipped on the steps going down from the flat, and hurt her back a little. Just now, I'm waiting for a call to go and rub her back with embrocation; while I am fairly fit, with our doctor keeping an Irish on me. I've seen a number of your fellow-countrymen this summer—a shockingly bad summer—, and Henry Hewes is coming down next month for a chat. He's the Drama Critic of THE SATURDAY REVIEW. Bob Graff of NBC is to try to come down when he returns from a Television Commission in S. East Asia. He tells me they are planning a longer Television show of the one he made of me, adding material that they took, but didn't include.

Mind, you, no more tobacco. You'll have a lot to add to your flat, and a lot of these will cost money. Remember!

We all, dear Dave, send our love to you.

As ever,
Sean

Love, too, to all your Students

To Arvid Paulson[1]

MS. UPPSALA UNIVERSITY

31 AUGUST 1956

Dear Arvid Paulson,

I hope your eyes are better by now. Anything wrong with them is a great hindrance, even to the sage Teiresias or the minstrel, Demodocus. I constantly am in trouble with my eyes, so know how unhappy one can be when the eyes fail us. How interesting to know Harriet Bosse![2] I have a picture of her as she appeared in "Easter," & a handsome young lass she was. I liked your translation of Indra's daughter's farewell, [it] read well; though I'm no judge of these things. It must be very difficult indeed to put English on poetry that is written in its own way and its own peculiar idiom. To me, I imagine the one way to do it is to write it down, thro' a recreation of its spirit, in one's own way and in one's own idiom; but then it would cease to be Strindberg. Certainly, we owe a lot to many patient translators for the chance they give us to enjoy the work of great minds writing in another tongue.

All the best to you.
Sean O'Casey

[1] Arvid Paulson, actor and translator; born in Sweden, went to America in 1904, acted on the New York stage until 1947, when he retired as the result of a near fatal automobile accident in which he lost his sight, and had it restored after a number of operations. Translated the works of Strindberg, Ibsen, Bjornson, and others; awarded the first Gold Medal of the Swedish Academy of Letters in 1964 for his translations of Strindberg.

[2] Harriet Bosse, the Norwegian actress who was Strindberg's third wife and acted in many of his plays, notably *Easter* (1901).

To Arvid Paulson

MS. UPPSALA UNIVERSITY

3 SEPTEMBER 1956

Dear Arvid Paulson,

Many thanks for the book of Strindberg's "The Great Highway,"[1] and for the very kind Inscription. The translation is a fine English-speaking Memorial to the great playwright and passionate lover of man. It is a brave play, a sad play, but, at least, near the end, we hear a child's voice in the

[1] August Strindberg's *The Great Highway*, translated by Arvid Paulson, in *Modern Scandinavian Plays* (1954).

darkness; and (we are told) "of such is the Kingdom of Heaven." He had a lot of the child in him, yet his ambition was "to be a constantly performed dramatist." Yet, that was part of the child, too—constantly performing in his own mind; dancing from Darkness to Light, & back again from light to darkness. One sad thing about him: God nor time seems to have given him no chance for a laugh: a great sorrow and deprivation.

I would write longer only that I am not too well, and get tired quick. I have never read "The Great Highway," & am very glad to get it. We all go along the great highway, thro' desert, up hill, down thro' donkeyville, &, sometime, find ourselves in the arbour—waiting. S. was too anxious about the meaning of life: to make the best of it is its one meaning. He made a good deal of it, & left behind a rich collection of drama. Sometime, he will be constantly performed, when the chrysanthemum breaks into bloom over the castle of the commercial Theater.

Thanks again. With warm regards & best wishes.

Yours very sincerely,
Sean O'Casey

To George Elliott Sweet[1]

TC. O'CASEY

5 SEPTEMBER 1956

Dear Mr. Sweet,

For God's sake have a little pity for, and mercy upon, a poor old fellow of 76 whose one eye has but half a normal vision; who has recently spent many months in hospital and has had two major operations, leaving him with less than a sense of adventure in life. Besides, I have on my table many books, plays, and verses sent to me for admiration; many more than I can ever hope to read, plus a pile of letters calling for early—some immediate—replies. I declare to God I wish I had the power and the time to reply to even half of them, but God, not I, made the day to last but twenty-four hours, and a year but a thing of 365 days.

I read slowly, and it will take me a month or more to read your book properly, for the squint I've given it shows me that it is worth reading, and so taken seriously, and not gulped down in a second or two—even had I two eyes, and both of them good ones. I have never troubled myself over

---

[1] George Elliott Sweet, c/o Stanford University Press, California, publisher of Sweet's *Shake-Speare the Mystery* (1956), a book that sets out to prove that Queen Elizabeth wrote the works of Shakespeare. Sweet made mimeograph copies of O'Casey's letter and enclosed one in each copy of the second printing of his book.

the Baconian question, or any other one questioning the right of Shakespeare's name to go with play and poem; but have simply used both for
my profound delight and enjoyment. I have read Shaw's remarks, and
have enjoyed them too, and a few other books dealing with Shakespeare's
allegories, his reference to flowers, his similes, and so on; but none questioning his right to authorship of the works called by his name. I have also
read what I think is a very fine book called "The Sense of Shakespeare's
Sonnets" [1952] by Edward Hubler of Princeton University, a treasure of
a book to me, one that always lies near to my hand. From the little I have
read of yours so far tells me that it will go beside Hubler's, for it is original and doesnt fear saying what it thinks, and saying it in a very interesting
way which is so important—as important as accuracy. I am very glad to
have it, and it was very kind of you to send it to me. The folder you enclose fair glitters with good opinions, and mine cannot add but a poor,
spluttering spark, for I'm no scholar, though I've met scholars coming
home from school, and used their knowledge for my own development.
I'll use yours now, and give you a hasty word of thanks for sending me a
book that I like to have near to my hand, and close to Shakespeare's Works.

With all good wishes,
Yours very sincerely,
Sean O'Casey.

To Mrs. John T. Cooper

TS. COOPER

6 SEPTEMBER 1956

Dear Georgie:
    Thanks for your kind letter; and for the photos of Georgie and John.
I shall keep them in my wallet. None of us is only a doer or a thinker; like
it or no, we all have to do and we all have to think. We have to think little or more about listening when we do a concert, and about listening and
seeing when we do a theater. Indeed, thought was first given or developed
to enable us to do anything at all, and thought itself was developed more
so that we could do the things we did better than we'd done them before.
Thought and action are as near allied as are genius and lunacy. I'm afraid
that the brotherhood of man isn't always invested with nobility, but, noble
or vile, it remains brotherhood. It wasn't noble during the last war; but
though nobility was lost, brotherhood remained. Cain was always brother
to Abel, no less so even when he was knocking him into death. He couldn't
escape by shouting out that he wasn't his brother's keeper. Never mind

that others say "you are a snob," "you are rich," "you are poor," "you are a pioneer," "you are depraved." We all flood ourselves with opinions, but if we knew everything, we'd find most of them were wrong. We, in various ways, are poor, rich, pioneers, depraves, and are snobs. There is a poverty other than being without many of the world's goods; a depravity other than that of sex; riches other than having a big balance in a bank. Anyway and anyhow, if we are wise, we can find a laugh lurking in the moods of others and in our own. That will save us from every ill. There is often a laugh in death itself. Like the dying Cuchullain, Ireland's half-mythical hero, having tied himself to a stone pillar by his belt so that he might face his enemies on his feet, laughing loud at the antics of a raven, waiting for him to die, stumbling about in the hero's blood, unable to maintain a dignified balance. The crow never eats till its prey is dead. It will follow a wounded rabbit for days, waiting, waiting, perching when the dying rabbit rests to get renewed breath before it hurries on to hide, then following after when the wounded animal moves on again. So Cuchullain laughed as he died watching the antics of the waiting raven. If nobility is to be more than a creamy word, we ourselves must make it noble, as we must too with honor by making it honest, and justice by making it just in our life with a community or family. The above aren't dogmas, of course; only my opinions, and may all be nonsense.

Marilyn M[onroe]. is a pretty lass, and, since she said before leaving the USA for Eng., "One I'd like to meet is Sean O'Casey," she can be no fool. You yourself look to be a very pretty lass, and, certainly, you are no fool. It is splendid when loveliness and intelligence go hand in hand together.

As for me, I'm still well below par in body, but near to par, I think, in mind. I got an infection in hospital, and find it hard to shake it off; but it is being attended to by a doctor, whom I don't wish to "curse," for he has become a very dear friend, and his wife, too.

It is charming to have two Mississippi friends. All I know about the Mississippi State and River, comes from Twain's inimitable story and the song of Ol' Man River that don't say nothin, but jus' goes on rollin' along, and that the State's geological Period coincides with the first appearance of the reptiles into life.

Well, to end this written garrulity, my love to Georgie and to John, with the wish that I could hear that Southern drawl.

All good wishes to you both; amen from an ol' man of 76 to two young buds of life.

Yours very sincerely,
Sean O'Casey

To David H. Greene[1]

TC. O'CASEY

11 SEPTEMBER 1956

My dear Dave,

Fine to hear from you again and that you are safe at home. The hunter home from the hill; thought you might have been astray on the hill o' Connemara. Dont agree about the "impressiveness" of unkempt ruins. Clonmacnois[2] has just been taken over by the State, and just in time, for the jungle around it was destroying it completely; eating it away to the very marrow. When the monastery was alive, it wasnt unkempt, and order and cleanliness but brings it back closer to what it was when it flourished. Look you, Dave, you have had a bit of running about! Now, take care, lad, and dont overdo it. It's good, though, to have Catherine with you this time, for, speaking for myself, I'm lost when Eileen isnt with me, or, at least, on the near horizon. I assume that all the family is well, or you'd ha' said something. That's the main thing, for a man's history is largely written in his health.

Curious to think of L. Robinson going to Pekin.[3] He's the last one I'd expect to see there, though, of course, he is quite capable of delivering a fine talk about Shaw. The Chinese Embassy asked me to go, but I was too old and too ill to even think of it.

Yes, I read Vivian Mercier's article.[4] It was sent to me by some American scout. I didnt bother to answer it. He leaves himself open to many assaults, if one wanted to make an assay. He says "no play since the original trio has won unambiguous success on the world stage—not even, I think, in Moscow." He doesnt choose his words well. What is "unambiguous success"? What is "the world's stage"? Bar that "all the world's a stage," there's no such thing as the "world's stage." As for "not even in Moscow," I can tell him that no play of mine, not even one of "the original trio," has been done, far as I know, in Moscow; but, he would find it odd to know, O'Casey isnt in any way the least bit worried about it. More, some time ago, D. P. Pritt wrote to say that the USSR had asked him about O'Casey plays, and he (Pritt) had suggested THE STAR TURNS RED. They asked for the MS, and Pritt asked for the book of the play. I said I had but one copy, and couldnt part with it. He then asked if he

---

[1] David H. Greene, Professor of English, New York University. He had been in Ireland to begin research for his biography of Synge, in collaboration with Edward M. Stephens, *J. M. Synge, 1871–1909* (1959). He directed David Krause's doctoral dissertation on O'Casey. He was also a friend of Vivian Mercier.

[2] Clonmacnois, one of Ireland's foremost early monastic settlements and educational centers, on the Shannon below Athlone, founded in 545 by St. Ciaran.

[3] On 10 July 1956 Lennox Robinson left for Peking, China, to give a lecture on Bernard Shaw.

[4] Vivian Mercier, "The Riddle of Sean O'Casey: Decline of a Playwright," *Commonweal*, 13 July 1956.

might send the Typescript of the play held by Unity Theater London (they were doing it then, or had done it). I wrote back refusing permission, saying I didnt want any play of mine to be forced on the attention of any one; and that my friendship for the USSR didnt depend on how many (or none) plays of mine that saw the light in Moscow. I wonder how many Irish playwrights would have been indifferent to such an offer? Not one, if you ask me. I'm afraid this criticism of his isnt criticism at all. He says "O'Casey finds it harder than his Catholic comrades to distinguish between respectability and a state of grace." Did ja ever! Can he, I wonder? Doesnt he know that the pursuit of (not happiness) respectability was as keen among Catholics as among Protestants? "Srón i náirde" (nose on high) was a feature of the C. middle-class no less than the middle-class of the Protestants. Has he never even heard in America of "the lace-curtain Irish"? He can take it from me that thousands of Catholics think more of being in a state of respectability than they do of being in a state of grace. The trouble with V.M. is that he touches the skin and thinks he has thumped the heart. The genteel poverty of the Joyces was just as genteel as that of the Shaws. Has he never read "A bhean na trimbo"?[5] "Oh, dont be saucy, dont be proud, great woman of three cows!" Did Mangan sing this of a Protestant? Ah, Is fuatha liom bard gan eolas.[6] And does he know all there is to be known about the condition of being free from mortal sin, and pleasing to God? What is this state of being free from mortal sin? So that we may "distinguish it from respectability"? Can he tell us? Now, where does the supernatural begin in the roots of faith? Can faith be lost without formal mortal sin? What is mortal sin, indeed? How does it stand in regard to charity—in its commission and its remission? Questions asked, not by O.C., but by Dr. MacDonald, Professor of Theology for 40 years in Maynooth College. So you see, Dave that these questions have nothing to do with criticism of my plays, old or new. A playwright can write a fine play without knowing the distinction between respectability (ridiculous) and a state of grace (sublime).

Again, he calls OAKLEAVES AND LAVENDER "Surely the most blood-thirsty play ever written by a congenital pacifist (sic)," two critical erroneous opinions: I am not a c. pacificist, nor am I a pacificist of any kind; no Communist is. I hate war; so did Sherman—"war is hell!" but he was no pacificist. Again, V.M. doesnt take the trouble (as a critic should) to link a play with its time and theme. The expression in it represents those of the time, from Churchill down to the worker in field, factory, and workshop: it was a Blood-thirsty time; the gods were athirst.

Ireland and I: the burden of guilt—if guilt there be—is on Ireland not on me; on her for her scurvy treatment, in youth and in age, of a valiant and an intelligent son. O'Casey lost most of his comrades—not in the

[5] "Oh Woman of Three Cows," a traditional Gaelic song against jealousy, translated by the poet James Clarence Mangan.

[6] I hate a poet without knowledge.

streets of Dublin—during the Easter Rising, but in Suvla Bay in the battle for the Dardenelles. There most of the Irish Citizen Army—and the
best of them—died. The Irish Ireland comrades I had—a lot of them—
fell in the later Civil War—another blood-thirsty time, too, tho' V.M.
doesnt seem to mind that little shower of blood. Most of the Gaelic
Leaguers—fine fellows that they were—were hidden from O'C. by an
iron curtain of respectability. I was never in the home of one of them. The
sedate collar and tie didnt like the muffler; but I bore no grudge because
my natural bent was the comradeship of the many thousand Catholics in
Jim Larkin's Union; and my Union, too; and it was our fight in 1913 that
lit the first fire that predicated Easter Week. His "He was brought up to
regard much of the practice of their religion as barbarous superstition . . .
and back of his mind the idea that the Catholics (Irish) are lazy, dirty,
drunken, lying spendthrifts," is, Dave, frankly a libel. I never have regarded the Catholic Faith in such a way; to do so would be to assign oneself as an ignorant and stupid fool, and I am neither. If this critic would
read Dr. MacDonald, he'd soon larn that many ideas held by Catholics,
and "by many priests, too," were not essential to the C. Faith. If he reads
Shaw he'd find out what an Irishman is capable of—he can be any of these
things mentioned by V.M.; but P. Irish as well as C. Irish; as my plays
show: Grigson in GUNMAN and the Mason in the B.'s Bonfire. I brought
myself up—on Tone, Mitchel, Fintan Lalor, and Parnell, as well as Raftery and M. Davitt; primary lessons; the Gaedhilghe [Irish language] followed after. Never at ease with Catholics! Well, you know to the differ
about that libellous statement. And his Marxianism! Maybe, I should use
the Freudian method on him: is he frustrated; is he envious?

He doesnt seem to know (not arf!) that the "three originals" were
denounced in the same way that the later ones are denounced now. I have
put this query to the I. critics several times, but the pharasees pass by on
the other side. They refuse to take the challenge. So, Dave, since the earlier poets, writers, and critics thought those to be rubbish, and the present
literary ones think the same of these, what can I do but sit down and wait
for the wending and wailing. So let V.M. think, if he likes, that Lady G.
wrote a line or wrote the lot; men cant live without killusions.

Pity, tho', he didnt read Ernest Newman's criticism in the SUNDAY
TIMES of Feb. 5, 1956. He writes about Strauss and his change from one
method to another, which led to the critics saying about the composer
what they are saying about the playwright. He says, "I freely admit that at
one time, too, I regarded 'Die Frau ohne Schatten' as a falling back; but
after subjecting myself, as every critic ought to do now and again, to a
ruthless psychological overhaul, I think I have discovered the cause of that
sad abberation. In the early 1920s, with nothing to go upon but the vocal
score of the new work of Strauss, I made the common mistake of looking
at it, from force of habit, for the wrong thing. I came to it expecting a con-
tinuation in another form of the idiom of 'Elektra' and 'Der Rosenkavalier.'

When I happened to alight on a page of that sort, and found it unequal in quality to the thing it reminded me of, in one of the earlier works, I was disappointed; and I condemned the new work as a lapse from grace on the composer's part. It was only long afterwards that I discovered that the proper line of approach to the Strauss of this middle period was not through the first period but through his last. Then, but not till then, did I realise what a remarkable work this 'Frau ohne Schatten' is. . . . Far from being the work of a talent well on the way to exhaustion, 'Die Frau ohne Schatten' is for me now the work of a genius reaching out boldly and successfully into a musical country previously unexplored." Aha, what's good for the music-critic goose may be good for the irish-critic gander.

Dave, achroidhe [dear friend], this has developed into a long O'Casey encyclical, and it is going to end now. Finis.

Dave the II [Krause] has left apartments in College, and has taken a flat of his very own. He tells me he is busy painting, putting up shelves, etc; and may be too busy to write to you. May God prosper the work, for I love Dave II as I love Dave the 1st.

I hope Little Candie is fine; a big kiss for her from the old Lad; and a kiss for Katherine through a kiss from you; and for all the other lads and lasses. May God be with you all.

As for me, I'm alive, but still under doctor's care. Just now I'm having daily injections (five of them) for a "post-operative infection," a bug which is hard to kill; but even though these Inj. make my legs stiff, I swing along on the great highway with a song in my heart and a few new ideas trickling into my old napper. You must start on Synge some day, why not now. I always dread the start of any thing—article or play. We have no freedom, Dave, from the way of life. By the way, I shouldnt have written the encyclical had not your reference to COMMONWEAL set me something of a challenge. I hope V.M. is a better critic than his art. shows him to be. I've read a lot by him, and I thought that here was a lad that might give Ireland a new and courageous critic—illusion, I fear.

All here send their love to you, and all means all, for all are home just now.

A thought came to me like a full-blown rose:

Says V.M. "O'Casey's unwise decision to settle permanently in England, away from his true material" (many another has said the same). The material I left behind wasnt mine. I hadnt bought it as others bought the Lakes of Killarney; it isnt locked up; it is there for all to use. Now, explain, V.M. why dont they use it? There are many playwrights in Ireland, in every county, with material outside of their doors, as plentiful as peat in the bogs of Connemara; but why dont they make use of it, and turn it into flaming plays?

Notice the decorations that went with V.M.'s article? A New York scene, or town scene: A bakery, a delicatessan store, a speciality shoppe, a crowd, busy people busy with themselves, a man standing atop of a motor-

car, urging support for an election candidate, through a loud-speaker—
Life. The other, a round tower, a little church, a spruce tree (I think),
all set down in the midst of a graveyard; so graceful so quiet; not a soul
about—quietude of death. So symbolic of Ireland; even COMMONWEAL
couldnt but unconsciously give the contrasting symbols. By the way (I
think I should settle this fact), the row over THE SILVER TASSIE had
nothing to do with my settling permanently in Eng; though V.M. states
that it "undoubtedly had." Why is he so sure of all these things about me,
tho' he never met me; I certainly never saw him, never even heard his
voice. The day I got the rejection was the morn of Breon's birth, and we
had taken a lease of a little house for five years months before.

This quarter's IRISH WRITING has a review by V. M. on Hugh
Kenner's book about Joyce.[7] Like me to send it to you?

All the best again to all.
As ever,
Sean

[7] Vivian Mercier's review of Hugh Kenner's *Dublin's Joyce* appeared in *Irish Writing* No. 35, Summer 1956.

To Robert Hogan

MS. HOGAN

14 SEPTEMBER 1956

Dear Robert Hogan,
A right good Irish name—O'Hogan. I wonder did you ever hear of
"Galloping O'Hogan"? Thanks for the Dissertation.[1] I've read many
parts of it—always interested in what intelligent minds try to make of
me—the one way we have of seeing ourselves as others see us. It is vigorous, and, mostly, your own opinion, which is well. I don't agree with some
of what you say—that the dialogue in "Within the Gates" is "banal." Of
course, tho', you may be right. Anyhow, it is to you, & that settles it, &
I won't argue "to the differ." I like the term "uncontrolled explosion." It
is something, at least, to cause an explosion, even an "uncontrolled" one.
I hope every play I write may have an explosion as its kernel: the bigger
& louder bang the better; or, at least, strong enough to shake down the
dust. By the way, wasn't "Wake up & Sing" written by Odets & not by
Rice?[2] Or am I wrong, & the memory grown old?

[1] Robert Hogan, "Sean O'Casey's Experiments in Dramatic Form," Ph.D. dissertation, University of Missouri, 1956.
[2] Clifford Odets' *Awake and Sing!* opened in New York on 19 February 1935.

Well, with four children and a hulk of a house, you have important things to deal with besides a Dissertation. I have had some experience of new homes, & a burden they were getting things to settle down safely. Your wife has her own dissertations—four of them—& harder ones than that you have finished—I hope you give her a good hand.

I've been ill, & am now getting daily injections against a post-operation infection, so amn't able to read for long without a rest & a quiet song to myself.

All blessings on Sean óg (young) & the other three children; on your wife, & on you.

Yours very sincerely,
Sean O'Casey

To Major Gwilym Lloyd-George

TC. O'CASEY

14 SEPTEMBER 1956

Dear Major Lloyd-George,

I am venturing to lay before you a letter from a friend of mine[1] asking me to use my influence (God help her innocence) to bring about the release of her husband from jail after six years of detention. I tried to help him during the trial, and Mr. Harold Macmillan gave us some sympathetic help at the time, especially when the Bumbles of Coventry tried to take her children away on the pretence that, as the wife of a housebreaker, she wasnt fit to mind them. We succeeded in preventing the panic-stricken children from being whipped away from a good mother, anyway. John Howard is a poor house-breaker, invariably caught before he has managed to get farther than the back garden. I myself would be a far more proficient one, and, at least, would put a day or two between what I'd done and the police who might be after me. John Howard has the proficiency of safely breaking open a box of matches. The sentence of ten years detention was to me a savage one; and I appeal to you to allow his case to be reviewed after six years of confinement.

He had previous convictions, but, as I said, never made the shadow of success of it. I do wish this might be done for the sake of the brave woman. John was a good husband and father out of jail, and will, I guess, be as good, if he manages to get a sympathetic hearing towards his release.

It was a Judge Fingleton or Jingleton, who gave the savage sentence.

[1] Mrs. Elizabeth Howard, 32 Links Road, Radford, Coventry.

Some years ago, this Judge went west, and Christ only knows how long a sentence of detention he is now doing himself somewhere else.

Pray be kind enough to allow this case to be reconsidered with some mercy, for John's sake, for the mother's sake, and for the sake of the children.

With all respect and good wishes,

Yours sincerely,
Sean O'Casey.

To Cyril Cusack

TS. CUSACK

16 SEPTEMBER 1956

Dear Cyril,

Thanks for your letter of the 10 Sept, to which this is an answer; also a sort of a one to a letter from you—just found—written from THE IRISH CLUB—no date fixed to it.

First, the first. You mention a request from France, saying you would send cuttings, etc, if I agreed; and that inquirer collaborated with another who had translated THE BONFIRE for a French production. If you havent sent them, dont; I havent heard anything from him or them, and amnt interested anyhow, for this sort of business is done for me thro' the Dramatists League here, and thro' the French Society of Autheurs there; so here and there we are. If you have sent, doesn't matter a damn.

Now the second letter—I put away the first, and forgot about it. Havent been too spry, having got what is called "post-operation infection," meaning entry of a bug hard to kill, so that letters have been, on the whole, but thin snowflakes falling on very distant hills. Now for the second—

Your contract for BONFIRE ends on Feb. 28 Feb. next ("Two years from first performance, Feb. 28, 1955"), and this was told to Miss Rubin when the question of T. Guthrie's proposal for a N. York production came before me. Now, I'm afraid that any agreement made with America will have an option on the English rights; that there is almost a certainty that Miss R. will have offers for an option (Amer. and Eng.); and that she wont wait till June, 1956.

And very good, too, considering the terms demanded by our friend, Mr. Oscar Lewenstein. £600! A week! Well, he can keep his theater! And plus a per cent. He goes about with the sound of a band playing in his

ears. It is a question and a gamble for an Eng. play to get on in an English
Theater, much more a gamble and risk for an Irish play. If Mr. Lewenstein thinks O'Casey's dying for a show-off in his theater, or any other
London theater, he's very much mistaken. And I've no desire, either, to
be beholden to Mrs Gottlieb—kind of her to be interested—for a week
or two or three in the Court. So we can cry it off, for, added to other considerations, is the fact that O'Casey wont have Cyril Cusack risking what's
left to him in a venture to enhance my point of departure or arrival in
the Eng. theater. See what Gordon Craig says of it in the latest number
of DRAMA.[1] Let it go to hell by itself.

I am sorry to hear about the Gaiety venture.[2] That is a blow to the
whole family of Cusacks. You'll have to be more cautious, Cyril. Bishop
Browne has a big influence on an old play; not a new one which no one
has seen, and which may be exciting—like the BONFIRE. "J.B's Other
Island" would have been a better choice, I think. These, tho' are the risks
of the theater, and you must guard yourself from taking too many of them.

As against Bishop Browne, we have Dr. Stanton, Bishop of Ferns
(I presume he is the Catholic Bishop; if so, what is the Protestant one
doing? No guts, no guts!), standing out as the Patron of the Wexford Festival. Why doesnt Bishop Browne do the same for Galway? Or is it that
he isnt "the man for Galway"? I wager a fiver that not more than ten
of his flock ever saw Gheon's MARVELLOUS HISTORY OF ST. BER-
NARD. Why doesnt he get his one done—for a start—if he doesnt like,
or is afraid of Shaw? Indeed, was this play ever done in Dublin or Cork?
I can understand Belfast refusing it; but maybe they wouldnt, if it were
done there; it would be better for the B. of Galway to do something in
this way than to stay barking on the sideline.

All well here, bar myself, tho' stirring about a bit. Just finished a
course of Streptomycin injections to kill the bug, leaving my legs feeling
as if they had been hit hard by Miles the Slasher's sledge; but that'll soon
go, and I'll be doing my twenty miles an hour walk round the village
streets and roads, eyeing the yellowing leaves in autumn, reminding me
that we are mortals, but not all fools as Ariel thought us to be.

So, so long or slan leat, libh.[3]

Word eile:[4] Some day or another, Cyril, you'll have to think about
running over and back again; it's trying and it's wasteful. Where most of
the money is is the place to be as a rule. Dont over do it, ould son. Think

---

[1] Gordon Craig, "The English Theatre Today," *Drama,* Summer 1956: "The
poor English theatre is not yet dead, but it is being mutilated."
[2] Cusack's production of Shaw's *Androcles and the Lion* (see O'Casey's letter
to Cusack, 21 August 1956, note 2) played to poor houses and lost a lot of money,
mainly, Cusack felt, because of the attack on Shaw by the Most Rev. Dr. Michael J.
Browne, Bishop of Galway (see O'Casey's letter to Cusack, 25 May 1956, note 3).
[3] good-bye, to you.
[4] another word:

well before you tire yourself too much; and again, there's the frequent separation from the family. Well, Tá fuasgladh gach ceiste innti féin.[5]

My love with a kiss to Maureen, the children, and, without the kiss, to you, a mhic ma chroidhe.[6]

Sean

Prefer reading typescript—easier on the old eyes.

[5] Every question contains its own answer.
[6] oh, son of my heart.

To Frank McCarthy

MS. MCCARTHY

27 SEPTEMBER 1956

My Dear Frank,

Glad you had a good time in Dalkey—Dublin, & I hope it did your health good. I do read the "New Statesman," & I read Raymond's article. I have too much to do to point out to Mr. Raymond's rather presumptuous remark that "O'Casey loathes contemporary Eire." If he thinks that Eire consists of the "smooth-expense account, the striped trouser-pressed world," he is bloody well wrong. It focuses an insignificant tittle of Eirinn. I dont loathe the farmer, railway-worker, nurse, lorry-men, docker, building-worker, factory-worker, shop-assistant, dustmen, waiters, busmen, et al; who form Ireland's soul & Ireland's body, too.

Of course, Dr. [Donald O.] Soper is genuine; but he can do little. No single ego can these days when life en masse is awake. One must have a horde of helpers, organised—not flotsam and jetsam of the Christian Church—to get things done. The days of Utopianism, even in dreams, are over. The dream must go with the mass to come true. That is why Communism is shoving the Church aside everywhere—see what Father Huddleston said about it in "News-Chronicle"—& he's genuine, too.

By God, you look brave with the St. Bernard! I'll keep it in my museum.

I return the photo of the charming little lass whose name is "Mary": God be with her wherever she be.

How about your health? I hope you keep fit.

With all the good wishes of my heart.

As ever,

Sean

To Joseph Stein[1]

TS. STEIN

8 OCTOBER 1956

Dear Joe,

Thanks for your letter. Yes, I have had a lot of thoughts flowing thro' my [mind] about a musical JUNO; so have all of us had; but I find it very difficult—almost impossible—to get my mind back to the mood of the play, written more than thirty years ago. I have read your notes a number of times, and can't find anything better to suggest, for, as I said, I have never had any experience of musical plays, per se, and so dont really know how to go about thinking how one might be done. However, to prove that I have been thinking of it, I enclose two examples of words for songs—the one on the MA, and the other about J[oxer] and B[oyle]'s discussion about the moon and the stars—and they took me a long time to sort them out, even to the shapes in which they are now. I'm afraid, I've little talent for this special work, but I present them to you as (I think) the best I could do; and if, as is likely, they aren't any good, I'd be obliged if you would let me have them back as a souvenir of what I tried to do to make a musical of JUNO! We got the colored photos all-right, and liked them very much. One was a bit dusky, but the rest looked fine, and my old velvet coat (one that got too small for Breon) shone out like the sun herself. Thanks very much for them. I daresay Sadie is glad to be back with the children—one rarely gets used to them out of sight— till they're married, and have a home of their own. Shivaun is away in London at an Art School, and Niall back at the College, so there's but three of us here now.

My love to Sadie, to the children, and to you. I've been busy fighting a post-operation infection, which flared up a little, but, I think, is de-clining under control now, and I feel livelier, and the world's frown is changing into a caress. All the best to you.

Ys very sincerely
Sean

2 words of songs enclosed

---

[1] Joseph Stein (1912–   ), playwright and librettist, wrote the book for the musical *Juno,* which opened in New York on 9 March 1959. For details of the pro-duction, see O'Casey's letter to Richard Watts Jr., 13 March 1959, note 1, Vol. IV.

What is the stars.

Boyle

There's questions galore to be answer'd, I say,
To be answer'd today or tomorrow;
Questions of livin', honest work and fair pay,

Joxer

An' why do we dance within seasons of sorra?

Boyle

We're bother'd be there, which is which, what is where,
For here can be there, which can be why, and what is what's
found everywhere?

2.
Boyle

First question, me man, while you kneel for a pray'r,
Or when you lower stout at a bar,
Afther tighten'n your belt, set your mind at a dare,
To find out—   Joxer: to find out—
Together: The odd goins on of a star!
Boyle: A star!   Joxer: a Star—
Away in the distance, though ever so far,
We'll find out— Joxer: We'll find out,
Together: The odd goins on of a star!

3.
Boyle

While we ponder th' question about stars, very soon
Another pops up—Joxer, what is th' moon?

Joxer

That question of question's a question to me
That cannot be properly solv'd dhrinkin' tea;
For its which an' its why an' its what that is queer,
Can be answer'd at best as we swally our beer.
Boyle: The Stars—   Joxer: An' the moon—
Together: Be it late, be it soon,
    While th' silly world goes its way whistlin' its tune,
    We'll find out what's stirrin' the stars an' the moon!
Joxer: Bring curse or a boon; Boyle; Bring fame or bring ruin,
Joxer: We'll find out about—Boyle: the ins and out of
Together: The stars and the moon!

Page 2

MA

A Ma is a woman of burdens small,
Growin bigger an bigger as kids grow tall,
While th Ma grows smaller n smaller, till
There's hardly anything left at all.
I'd love to give th gob a smack,
That's hangin a mink coat on a rack,
While tellin to Jill and th wife of Jack,
God fits th burden to the back!

When I hear voices call Ma, Ma, Ma!
An I'm not dull of hearin—
I wish I had the pow'r to do
An act of disappearin!

Some can lie in a meada green,
With daisies growin round them;
With never a trouble that's dull or keen
To tickle, or tease, or pound them.
I'm sick of voices callin Ma,
Some plaintive, some with swearin,
I sometimes think that God is lost,
An a Ma is just past carin!

When I hear voices call Ma Ma!
I'm often weak with fearin
That God'll make me do an act
Of suddenly disappearin!

To Boris Izakov[1]

TC. O'CASEY

9 OCTOBER 1956

My dear Boris,

It was charming to get your letter, bringing you back close to us all
again. We have often thought of you, and wondered how you were, and
how you were getting on in the world. We always remembered you with
affection, for during your visit here, you won your way into our Irish
hearts.

[1] Boris Izakov, Union of Soviet Writers, ul. Vorovskogo, 52, Moscow, U.S.S.R.

I am very pleased to hear that my biography is to appear shortly in your Russian Language—a great honor and a decided pleasure; though I sympathise with him or her who translated. My Irish manner, added to the O'Casey manner, isnt easy to change from one language to another; much more difficult, I think, than G. B. Shaw, whom we miss badly. I got the clippings of your article allright, and I thank you for them.

Regarding THE STAR TURNS RED, I'm not surprised that it isnt in your Libraries—I dont think it is to be found in any library here either. It got me many a cold look, and many turned away because of "O'Casey's lamentable political judgements." It has been out of print for many years; but it is included in the volumes of COLLECTED PLAYS, and I am sending to you the volume that holds the play to its breast— under another cover; also a copy of THE GREEN CROW, recently published in New York. The play, S. TURNS RED was written some years before the last World War, and wasnt liked very much by the Publisher. It was done by Unity Theater, London, directed by a very clever lad, done well; but later on this Director who didnt see eye to eye with Unity opinions, and who couldnt stand their rigidity, left the Movement altogether, and I, for one, couldnt blame him. I remember, years ago, a group of Plymouth Communists came to see me in Totnes, and during the chat, I found that of all only one had ever read Dickens; and he was accused of being a "Bourgeois"! I told the group what I thought of Dickens and them; and, I fear, made them feel a little unhappy. I have marked out some of the parts of the play that I think might be dull. The third scene, I think, is the best one. With the play, I send a photo that you might like to have as a memento of our friendship. It would be a delightful thing, dear Boris, if I could visit your great country, but I am too old now to take the Journey. I have been very ill, and am still fighting a post-operation infection; but better and full of a finer fire than the fierce one within me during the days of my youth. However, some day, I hope, the younger members of the family will be able to go on a visit to the Soviet Union which the old man heralded from the year, 1917, when he added his young voice then to the shout of "Hands off Russia!"

Niall and Shivaun, whom you saw, our elder boy, Breon, whom you didnt see, Eileen (Mrs. O'C.), and I, dear Boris, send their love to you; to all the Writers in your Union of Writers, and to the great people of your great Country.

Ever yours,
Sean O'Casey.

To Richard Magat[1]

TS. MAGAT

10 OCTOBER 1956

Dear Mr. Magat,

Welcome for your letter, a warm one, for it was all very kind and charming. As for exhibiting an ego by writing to an author, well, an author exhibits his by writing his books; and it is, very often, a damned big and pompous one.

What better work could you do, could anyone do, than that of telling people more about what Scientists are doing in New York University, or anywhere, and everywhere, else? I myself am an Associate Member of the Atomic Scientists Association; have been for years, and we get your THE SCIENTIFIC AMERICAN every month; so you see we take a keen interest in what science knows and what the Scientists do—I and the boys. For many years to come, Science will be, I think, the most fruitful activity of man.

It must have been interesting to listen to the talk in the Faculty Club, and the discussion that went on there; but, after all, a Scientist, if he is to know all he can about his subject, has little room in a small head for anything else. Our younger boy, Niall, is away studying biology, and he has a lot to learn, though he does like music, and very often, in the holidays, anyhow, reads a book. But what about those laymen who love music, art, and literature; who can talk sensibly about each of them, who dont know a thing about Science? After all, there's no use of blaming a Scientist for having a scant interest in literature when the writer himself doesnt know, or care, about what the Scientist is trying to do, or trying to find out—unless the matter is spread sensationally over the pages of the popular press. Science ought, at least, to have as important a place in our reading, newspaper or book, as art, literature, or music, of which, to life, it is the most important. If we arent able to sit down in the lounge of Science's home, at least we should be knocking at the door.

It is indeed very pleasant to me to know that your wife and you were pleased with the Readings, but, of course, this pleasure came mainly from the clever adaptation and production crowned by the splendid way it was beamed by the clever artists taking part in the work.

My good wishes and warm regards to your wife and to you.

Yours very sincerely,
Sean O'Casey.

---

[1] Richard Magat, 85–44, 53rd Avenue, Elmhurst, New York.

To H. Jeremy Wintersteen[1]

TC. O'CASEY

10 OCTOBER 1956

Dear Jeremy,

What another! I get a lot of letters from the young people making their senior plunge into the world, the whirling world, of Thesis Writing. Yesterday, I got one from a young lass studying in another College, choosing me, though, oddly enough, I gave her the suggestion that your Advisor has given you—to write about Jefferson, Emerson, Whitman, or Hemingway. Is this an example of great minds thinking alike? I imagine it to be easier to write about Americans who are nearer (and, surely dearer) to scholars than an Irishman living, if not long ago, then far away.

Of course, my dear Lad, I have no objection to your getting a photostat copy of The Plough and the Stars from the Dublin Historical Museum; though this is a print of the design made by a Galway artist, and isnt a good one. The actual flag was more stylised in pattern, and more lovely, and had as a spear-point a Red Hand (the then badge of Ireland's powerful and militant Trades Union) grasping and strangling a green dragon of Capitalism. I hope you like the Reading of PICTURES IN THE HALLWAY.

As for suggesting one who had met me, so that you may meet him or her, that is too dangerous a commission. Brooks Atkinson is too busy a man to be bothered by anyone bothering about me. So, indeed, are all I know: Richard Watts, John Gassner, etc., all busy with work of their own. The one nearest to you—David Krause, Teacher in Brown University, lives in New Jersey. He teaches in Van Wickle Hall, B[rown]. University, Providence 12, Rhode Island; but he, too, is a terribly busy man, and might tell you to go to hell, for which he couldnt be blamed.

Well, there you are, and I can do no more for you, so help me God. But think over changing to a subject nearer to your ear, eye, and all other senses, before you decide to immerse yourself in the yeasty morass of O'Casey's writings.

My warm regards and good wishes go to you.

Yours very sincerely,
Sean O'Casey.

[1] H. Jeremy Wintersteen, 7–9 Blair Tower, Princeton University, Princeton, New Jersey.

To Robert Hogan

TS. HOGAN

14 OCTOBER 1956

Dear Bob:

None of your work has "grieved" me in any way.[1] The only thing that has bothered me is that such a fine copy of your Thesis must have cost you money that you can ill spare. I am always a little distressed when young people spend impulsively, forgetting that self-preservation is nature's first law. I have read your Thesis with great interest, I assure you, and though I don't agree with all you say, I remember that I can't expect others to agree with all (or anything) I say either. Of course, you may be right in what you say about the plays; all I claim is that each was the best I could do at the time.

Thanks for the cuttings of the article by Vivian Mercier, and for your letter in reply[2]—a fine one, and I am grateful to you for your defence of my work. I had already read the article, and had sent a detailed reply to a friend of mine[3] (a colleague of V. Mercier's) who had sent it to me. I didn't bother to say a word in THE COMMONWEAL. I fear that V.M. is mistaken in a lot of things—for instance, when he says I was "always at unease with Catholics." If he had said with Protestants (who weren't workers), he would be close to a fact. In work, the bosses were usually Protestants, the workers Catholics, and I was always with the workers, for I was one myself. I knew them from the bone out, and from the heart out too; and was one with them in the Labor Movement, the Gaelic League, the Irish Republican Brotherhood, and one with many, many of them in their poor private lives. I knew them all, and worked with all, from the lapsed Catholic to the Catholic who went to weekly Communion. And I am not, and never was, a Pacificist. I really don't think that V.M. understands the spirit of drama at all.

I do hope that by this you have managed to repair the ceiling, and that the house is becoming a ship-shaped home. It is a job, a wearing job, to get a house into order, and to settle down into it comfortably. So much is learned in School and College about the arts, and so little learned about a house! Yet, before all else, we have to live, and must have a home in which to shelter. I give my pagan blessing to all you and your wife are trying to do to make the family safe and satisfied. I hope some of the apples you pick may be like unto the apples of the Hesperides.

---

[1] See O'Casey's letter to Hogan, 14 September 1956, note 1.

[2] Vivian Mercier, "The Riddle of Sean O'Casey: Decline of a Playwright," *Commonweal,* 13 July 1956; Robert Hogan's letter of reply to Mercier, *Commonweal,* 24 August 1956.

[3] See O'Casey's letter to David H. Greene, 11 September 1956.

With warm regards to your wife and family and to you.

> *Yours very sincerely,*
> *Sean O'Casey*

To Mrs. Oriana Atkinson

MS. ATKINSON

15 OCTOBER 1956

My very dear Oriana:

I've read your book on Ireland's South & West,[1] & am a little sorry I did so, for it brought back to me memories that I thought I had forgotten, & a catch in the breath I didn't wish to feel. Oh, God, this grip that Ireland gives! And I never imagined an American lass would invoke the grip on me again; ay, and tighten it, too. I've read it slowly, pausing in memory often, & never getting away from it, even when the book was closed. You need not say, you don't understand Ireland, for you do, well as she can be understood, well as I do; well as any mind and heart can; for I sometimes think even God can't understand her fully. It is—apart from its memories to me—a delightful book, full of the wit you never found there; & a lovely sense of humor that flickers and tumbles like the waterfall of Gougane Barra. It is a kindly book, kindlier, perhaps, than we deserve. I never tired of it, and, by God, that's saying something. You have a keen eye, even if it be a kindly one; and your swift descriptions of man & his place are sure and vivid. You are right about places more beautiful than Killarney—lots of them—Loch Derg in the Shannon, for one; tho' no legend there, far as I know, tells a sad tale of a girl thinking of a lover, forgets to cover a fairy well, so that it bursts forth, enveloping the girl, her lover, & all the villages round to form the sheets of water now known & honored as the Lakes of Killarney. It was a strange experience in Muckross Abbey—the singing of the Mass by a Choir; but you must be psychic, & this, added to a vivid imagination, would easily bring the past to the present. Sceptic as I am, I'd rather have company in these places. I sympathise with you & Miss Witton about heat. It's the same here, even in the house we live in: on a certain date in April, even if the snow be falling, off comes the heat; & had a bad time of it just out of hospital, trying to get some warmth into my old bones from an icy flat. The American system for me. The West, of course, has a mystery significance: it is the place of departed spirits ("going west"), where the sun

---

[1] Oriana Atkinson, *South And the West of It: Ireland and Me* (1956).

sets; the Land under the Sea; land of the ever-young; the Keltic fields of Asphadel. Today, even, most farm houses have the parlor—the "west room," where, when a married son or daughter takes over, the old couple go; it is their sanctuary, where they wait before the time comes to go west.

Yours is a very kindly book; kindlier than we deserve; but, most important, it is well & charmingly written. May God bless the book. I'm reading just now a book by an Irishman, farmer, article-writer, broadcaster on "All Ireland," and I find it heavy going. I may be wrong, but it is a dull work to me; & I don't like to say this; for I'd prefer an Irishman to write a better book, any day, than one written by an American lass—much as I love her. But there you are: to me, an American girl, a few weeks in Ireland, writes a better book about Ireland than an Irishman who has lived all his life there. God forgive you, Oriana.

My love to Brooks & to you, a chroidhe [my friend].

As ever,
Sean

To Paul Shyre

TS. SHYRE

17 OCTOBER 1956

Dear Paul:

We are all very glad here about the good news of PICTURES IN THE HALLWAY doing so well I hope it may be good news for a long time.[1] It has rather amazed me that the Readings should have been so successful; but the artists taking part have infused the pictures with a new and strange life—the Pictures have come out of the frames!

Thank the Artists (and yourself) for my sake, and for the O'Caseys' sake, too.

As for PURPLE DUST, it is a long story.[2] During the Rehearsals continuous changes were made, and, later on, these, or some of them, changes were changed again. I enclose some of them, most of which, I think, would do no harm, and might be good. The Director, a very lovable man, and a dear friend of mine, as is his whole family, had the idea that the play called for some more songs, and these were written by me. The song THE RUIN'D ROWAN TREE was very fine, and was sung by Avril and O'Killigan as a kind of duet—I enclose a copy of the words which

---

[1] See O'Casey's letter to Shyre, 6 May 1956, note 1.
[2] For the details of Sam Wanamaker's 1953 production of *Purple Dust,* see O'Casey's letter to Wanamaker, 28 April 1953, note 1, Vol. II.

appeared in a Magazine done by the School where our daughter used
to go; it has a charming old Irish air. It might be included with advantage. Another one was sung by Avril, Souhaun, and Stoke, just before he
and Avril went for a horse-ride; it was called THE OLD DAYS (OLD
WAYS) ARE COMING AGAIN; and another sung by Poges after, in
first act, I think, says "We're ready for anything now." That was the name
given to the song he sang. There are a good many cuts, particularly that
of the display of the bases, and the alarm over the rats, a scene which
seemed to drag too much. The chief change, I think is found on page 4
of the Corrections and Additions, and on pages 74-5-6 of the printed
play which happen to be the same in the Vol of COLLECTED PLAYS
as in the original printing. I suggest you use the one as printed in Vol III
of COLLECTED PLAYS. You can get this from ST. MARTIN'S PRESS,
103 Park Avenue, New York, 17; but if they have no Vol III in stock,
I'll be glad to send a copy to you. In the above scene—changed from
Souhaun and O'Kill. to Souhaun and the Workman, O'Dempsey, Souhaun
sang a song, which, if you like, I can send to you—if I have kept it. I
also have a verse of a song to be sung by Avril as she comes in, according
to the Play Direction, "singing a verse from THE MAID OF BUN-
CLODY." The new verse is my own, though the air is that of the original
song.

As for the efforts here, it didn't go too well on tour, and by the time
it came to within a few miles of London, there was no money left, no
more could be gotten, and it was withdrawn. I understand there was a
difference between the D. and some of the actors. A letter I have says
"M . . . . . . and D . . . . . . were defeated and defeatist about the
whole thing after Glasgow, and of course it affected their performances
badly. They were the only ones relieved by the fact that the play wouldn't
open in London." What really caused this, I don't know, for I was kept
in the dark. Whether the actors named got cold feet, or had a row with
the D. (I think they had), or if it were some inherent faults in the play,
I don't know. So I am frankly telling you this, so that you may consider
the whole venture very carefully before you decide to try it out. It tor-
ments me when any one I know is tangled into a failure with a work of
mine. For myself, failure doesn't affect me. I never, even from the start,
ran after "success." Long as I can knock out a decent living for mine
and me, I don't concern myself with what is called "success." But I have
to think of others, and it is this anxiety that suggests my warning for you.

With many thanks for all you & your comrades-artists have done,
and warm wishes to you an' all.

Sean

Enclosures
"Corrections & additions"
Copy of song. "Ruin'd Rowan Tree"

Warning 2: Don't spend money nights in a **Pub**, even in the good & charming Company of dear Bob C. & dear Kathy F.; and don't drink much of Irish Whiskey (or any other brand), for none of these things, done often, are wise for the mind, or uplift for the soul, or good for the body.

S.

To Dr. Claus Helmut Drese[1]

TC. O'CASEY

20 OCTOBER 1956

Dear Dr. Drese,

Good and warm greeting to you, my German friend. And may success shine upon your resurrected Theater;[2] and may no more bombs fall again on church or theater, on castle or cottage within the wide and warm boundaries encircling the human family.

I have read a good deal by your great Schiller, in English translations, and all good men revere his name. Most poets had a revolutionary spirit within them, even the Biblical ones; and even the Blessed Virgin sang "He hath put down the mighty from their seat, and hath exalted the humble and meek"; though revolutionaries, though they may be humble, are rarely meek.

Your questions are tremendous ones, and are beyond the smartness of my mind to answer. One needs to be a scholar as well as a playwright to answer them. All I have to present to you are a few opinions, not well thought out, but well within me, and uttered with sincerity and conviction.

Will drama go back to its religious origin? I take this to be a return to the worship through dramatic ritual the worship of a god-concept. My answer is No. Never. The god-concept was always man's god-concept, and is now old-fashioned and futile, and man can never return to it. But man does not, and never will, reject the poetic beauties woven around the earlier god-concept. For instance, he will listen to, and love, the lovely music of a Bach Mass without accepting the dogma of Christ's Sacrifice, symbolised or realised here, for the redemption of the world; or Handel's Messiah, without believing the dogma of Christ's divinity; but as long as man has ears to hear, minds to understand, and hearts to love, he will

[1] Dr. Claus Helmut Drese, Nationaltheater, Mannheim, Germany.
[2] The Nationaltheater at Mannheim, destroyed by an air attack in 1943, had been rebuilt and was to reopen in January 1957. See O'Casey's letter to Dr. Horst Scharschuch, 16 April 1957.

continue to enjoy and love the beautiful poetic music of both works. The same is happening to the lovely ritualistic dances of the Hindu and the Balinese; their intrinsic beauty will remain a joy forever. But as for worship, for the future, man shall sing hymns to himself rather than to a god. Worship in life and on the stage will be the man-created achievements of man himself; "all that man has done but earnest of the things that man shall do." The church of the future will be that predicted by Bernard Shaw through the vision he gave to the inhibited priest, Peter Keegan, in the play JOHN BULL'S OTHER ISLAND.

Will the Theater be an instrument of enlightening, and contribute to the improvement of human conditions?

It may, or it may not. My answer is No, but I'd hardly say Never. Poets and playwrights may be—one in more than ten thousand—a trumpet-call to battle, may legislate new thoughts into the life of humanity; but surely, we look for enlightenment from the Scholar and the Scientist—I do, anyhow.

Your second question of Do I prefer the appeal to reason over or before the representation of irrational destinies tending to religiousness hardly allows a direct reply.

Reason marches triumphant through the plays of Bernard Shaw, and nothing could be more splendid; but Shaw had a lot of room for emotion, too. If there be a God, emotion comes from Him as readily as the colder thoughts of reason; and so emotion is not to be, cannot be, banished from the stage; for emotion is an inherent quick quality of the human nature of man. Shakespeare is full of it; Goethe full of it; Strindberg is full of it; and all the poets (save those who live in despair today) serve under its wide, enfolding human banner. By the way, religiousness is very different from religion. There is a vast and dangerous lot of pretence and humbug in religiousness which a reasonable mind detests. Its hypocrisy is being discovered and is being hunted out of life. If there be a God, He cannot be but scornful of His whimpering self-centered slaves. Not the despairing resignation of sinking down, but the resolute determination of rising up is the ideal and accepted destiny of man today.

Your third question[3] is that both shall be shown on the stage: a call to the people towards moral *and* political activity; its power, its fortitude, its determination to make the world greater, and life within the world livelier, more secure, and much more joyful. I dont believe that Feebleness is inherent in human nature; rather is it strength and astonishing determination that man has shown through the ages of his life. Feebleness seems to be attached to the christian (particularly the catholic aspect) idea of Original Sin, in which I dont believe. I know the Psalmist is reported as saying, or singing, I was born in iniquity, and in sin hath my mother conceived me. A pleasant character to give the mother and her

---

[3] "Will you call up the public to moral or political activity or will you help to understand human feebleness by giving instances on the stage?"

child. A medieval mixture that has poisoned us for centuries, and which many poets and writers today are trying to bring back as the only possible pleasant drink man can lower. Not for me; and not for the advancing ranks of man the world over. The great men and women of the human race, the many known, the countless unknown heroes, testified to by Whitman, have fashioned us into a race worthy to live forever. Feebleness is to be shown on the stage to show what a stupid and unnatural thing it is.

Your last question—the most pernicious enemy of mankind in our times?

Well, the reply, my reply, to this question is one that I shouldnt ask to face the world. Regarding my own country, I should say that the most dull-damning enemy of the Irish writers was moral cowardice; the fear of acting as they felt, the fear of speaking out what they thought to be true. Courage is what we most need; courage to shove away the fear of being one's self; the habit of hiding our mind from the minds of others: the priest hiding behind his ambition to be a bishop; the politician hiding his honest opinion behind that of his party; the author hiding what he feels to be the truth behind the desire or need of sales; the artist hiding his art behind his passion for applause. In my country, Ireland, it is as if Shakespeare had never written To thine ownself be true, and it must follow, as the night the day, thou canst not then be false to any man. I would have it that everyman should fearlessly set his thoughts and beliefs, right or wrong, freely before all men; pin them on the world's breast as Luther pinned his ninety-five propositions to the church door of Wittenberg Castle.

Again, my best wishes for the inauguration of your Nationaltheater, and my sincere regards to you.

Yours very sincerely,
Sean O'Casey.

To Miss Joan McAlevey

MS. MCALEVEY

22 OCTOBER 1956

My dear Joan,

I'm glad you're back in your own townland, safe after all your travels. I'm sorry I wasn't quite fit, at the time of your visit to us, to give you a livelier welcome; fitter now, but not quite over it all yet. Well, Joan, unfit as I was, I was fit enough to see what a handsome lass you are—much more so than the photo-snapshot shows—, and how lovely you looked sitting opposite to me in the O'Casey room; and what good taste you showed in the way you dressed: a lovely and charming American girl. Had I been a young man, I'm sure my arms would have hovered around you. You did go places! Where Burns lived, and Scott, and Wordsworth, and Chaucer (Canterbury), and Dublin, too, which is known to O'Casey. You are a vigorous lass as well as a lovely one. I sympathise with you in your hard work among 86 Compositions, & little talent in them. Have patience. If you'd only seen the first futile efforts of an O'Casey article, and he 26 or 27 years old! I don't like to encourage anyone into a literary adventure on my work; but you could do one on Shaw; or, if you do one on both of us—Bernard, the Saint; Sean, the Sinner—then you know quite a lot about me from play, book, and a personal visit. I'm sorry to hear of the adjournment of your love experience; but, my dear Joan, 23 is very young; you are but a Spring bud, tho' a very charming one. You have time on your hands yet. A wife & the care of a home is harder work than teaching; for it takes time, some years, at least, to build a Home. Never fear, you'll be married one of these days; but it is better to wait till you are as sure as mortal can be of the right mate. An hour in a Restaurant, at a dance, or in a theater is very different from a life in a home. Yes, I remember Dr. George Dowell well—that was when I had just finished writing "The Bishop's Bonfire," amended a little since. The damp climate here doesn't give us an autumn glow, but I've seen one often. I don't think it sad: every fallen leaf will produce a new stem next Spring. It is the bud of the new stem that pushes off the leaf. The new, young life making room for itself. Niall is at London University; Shivaun at a London Art School; Breon, our elder boy, is here. Eileen sends her love to you; and so do I. I've read a little by Frost, a fine poet, tho' I don't always agree with his poetical philosophy. Everything bold does last throughout time; maybe eternity, too.

My love again.
Sean

To Mrs. John T. Cooper

TS. COOPER

25 OCTOBER 1956

Dear Georgie:

You weren't any more surprised, dear lass, when you heard my voice than I was when I first heard it myself: I never imagined I had such a pronounced Irish accent; surprised then, rather proud of it now. English hasn't altogether wiped away the Gaelic tone of it. By the way,

well you got away from the Garfish in a backwater of the Mississippi—
for gar comes from the word a spear, and, far as I know, the snout of
this ganoid isn't a pleasant thing to be near. Tell John that we (the Irish)
are getting busy with Gypsum. Big deposits have been found in Ireland,
and many hundreds are busy turning out various slabs of it for building
purposes. God be good to them, for we have the highest ration of un-
employment in Europe.

As for being an "Author," what is he more than any other soul?
Why especially try to reach an author's heart? Why not try to reach the
heart of everyone that comes across our path, and stays there for any
length of time? There is a man even in the ape, whether the "ape" shows
the man or no; it is ours to see the better shape, like Caliban, who, in the
end, says he will seek grace; and how finer he was than many of the
nobles, or, at least, as fine, and much more so than Trinculo or Stephano,
who revelled in the glittering gewgaws that Caliban despised, tho' even
Prospero seemed to think something of them for he decked himself out
to meet the unhappy nobles stranded on the Island. It is generally accepted now that there are lower forms of life than the Amoeba, which
for so long was reckoned the lowest life of all, but is recognized now to
have a complex, comparatively, being; so what are we to think of the
highly and magnificent complexity of an ape!

I'm sorry you had so much trouble over the biographical books. Since
your bookseller was something of a fool in the book sense, you should
have written to Macmillan yourself, and mentioned me. The Sales Director,
Mr. Budlong is a friend of mine, and would do a lot for me—if I let him,
for I have a conscience, even towards a publisher.

The Record came safely, without a scratch, and I have listened to it
a number of times. It is here close to me now. Though no authority on
music (nor on anything else), I see no reason to throw it into any ocean,
for I found it charming, particularly the Toccata by Khachaturian, whose
music I like—the little I've heard of it. In spite of the poor studio, the
low-temperature piano, the music flowed sweetly and softly through the
listening ear, and left a memory of delightful sound, many, many, in a
harmony of a lovely unity. And don't develop the bad habit of dispraising
yourself. My wife had that till I forced her by many admonitions to abandon it. We mustn't think too much of ourselves, but we must avoid the
greater sin of thinking too little of what we do well. This modesty is
mainly caused by fear of what others may think. We must guard against
this, so long as we don't set out deliberately to hurt others. The important
thing in what we do is what it does to ourselves rather than what it may
do to others. If we be honest, and do our best under all circumstances, we
do well, and we vindicate man, and so have no cause for shame. I shall
often play the Khachaturian Toccata, and the Seixas too, tho' it doesn't
move me as much as the first.

I sympathise with the South in the problem of Negro integration;

I'm afraid it will not blossom into fullness suddenly; but the world of men comes closer together daily, and we must have patience. The economic foolishness of two schools where one would do is obvious. We have it here, and in a worse way, for there are schools for Roman Catholics, for Episcopalians, for Methodists, and the schools of the State. A confusion of stupidity. In the north of Ireland where the Government organised a common dining-room for Catholic and Protestant children, the Catholics wouldn't let their children take a meal with the others, preferring them to eat a cold sandwich than that they should "risk the loss of the faith." In the schools of S. Ireland, catholic children aren't permitted to sit down to a warm meal, for fear "it would mean the thin edge of the wedge of communism"! So you see, we have problems too. Any way, the Negro problem can be settled only by the Americans—views of foreigners, tho' interesting, cannot remove the difficulty.

And thanks, the thanks of the O'Caseys, for your kind and affectionate greeting on the Record. It startled me at first, and touched me deeply before it ended.

You shouldn't have bothered about your accent! I've heard almost every American accent from n. to s., and from e. to w. during the last war when thousands of Americans passed thro' and camped in the Devon town where we then lived; chatted to a lot of them, and understood them all. The Readings have been done by a splendid band of Artists, and it is they who have given the writing an added glory—may God be with them. I, too, am dubious about a musical JUNO, but Joe Stein who is organising the venture is very enthusiastic, and very clever. He and his wife were here with us last Summer, and he convinced me that it would be worth trying, and, last, but not least, it gave me some of America's valuable dollars; but I'm still a little dubious, for I have no desire to enter into the adventure in any helpful way, preferring to go on with something new.

Well, agradh [my dear], my love to you and to your husband, John.

> *Yours affectionately (if this word is*
> *allowable to you both) and with all*
> *good wishes.*
> Sean O'Casey

To Mrs. Helen Kiok

MS. KIOK[1]

31 OCTOBER 1956

My dear Helen:

Of course, I agree with all you say about the Film medium. The medium is allright; and a new Art form. The Camera can't sin; it is those who exploit it who are the culprits; turning a mechanical goddess into a mechanical whore. And I don't mean the camera-man, or the scenario writers—these must make a living; & have to do as they are ordered. I've often worked on a building that I knew was badly done, away from specifications, so that the contractor could make a bigger profit; I burned to expose it—& did in the "Irish Worker"[2]—but no important paper would print it, & the only result was that O'Casey lost a job; & found it damned hard to get another. One must keep his job, and work with others to change the things affronting us.

I've seen many of the Russian films—The Mother, Potemkin, Storm Over Asia, Chapayilov, Lost Days of Petersburg, & the Modern Babylon; and fine examples of film art they were. Chaplin, a genius, in all he did, showed, not the art of the film, but the art of Charlie Chaplin; and great art it is. Parts of Eisenstein's Storm Over Mexico were very beautiful— potters of people, horses, houses, cactuses, & Mexican hats & cloaks. As for Wolfe's "L. Homeward Angel," if I had taken the offer,[3] all that would have been to it would have been O'Casey's name—Hollywood's rich amadouns [fools], USA's holy Joes & Biddies would have done the rest. No thanks; I've enough reverence for God yet to deny these Art hooligans the use of an honest name.

As for all that [Senator Joseph] McCarthy did, I fear the stupid activities of many Communists brought about suffering to themselves & others, with their rigid, negative idea of Marxism, which wasn't Marxism at all; for the finest thing in Marxism is its flexibility, to fit itself without loss into things as they happen to be at the time; needing cleverer women & men than Communists have in the USA.

What a whining wail Howard Fast had in the "Daily Worker" recently! And here, in a weekly, too. Well, Helen, agrah, my good wishes to you.

Thine,
Sean

---

[1] This letter was printed in the *Sean O'Casey Review*, Fall 1976.
[2] See O'Casey's letter to the *Irish Worker*, 9 March 1912, Vol. I.
[3] For O'Casey's refusal of the offer of $50,000 to $100,000 to write the screenplay for Thomas Wolfe's *Look Homeward, Angel*, see his letter to William Herndon, 17 January 1945, Vol. II.

Feeling good, tho' I had an X Ray yesterday; but running around, and lively.

S.

To Paul Shyre

TS. SHYRE

1 NOVEMBER 1956

Dear Paul:

Very sorry I wasn't quite able to talk to you over the long distance from here to there the other night. Eileen however did well for me. I had had a big booming X Ray, after a special injection, and I was giving myself a rest. Anyway, I always find it difficult to talk sensibly and clearly over a telephone.

About your questions regarding the changes I made in PURPLE DUST: The added dialogue I should retain, and, I think the change that eliminates O'Killigan flirting with Souhaun so that her ultimate union with the Workman, O'Dempsey, is made clear, I should retain. I am a little dubious about the songs; but I'd like to keep the RUIN'D ROWAN TREE, and the verses written (my own) for the entrance of Avril in the 1st act to the air of The Maid of Bunclody, the air given in the book. I think the others might go, bar that I have a sneaking liking for the song that Souhaun sings just before O'Dempsey makes up to her—How I long for the Day when my Heart was Mine Own.

Otherwise, I'd like the play to be done as it is written, tho' I shouldn't recommend any elaborate musical arrangement. In my plays, as done in Dublin, there is never an orchestral accompaniment; the actors just lilt them as they would in actual life, along a road, or in a room at home.

However, at rehearsals, I found that the Scene between the Postmaster and Poges didn't seem to go well, but the man who acted the part of the P-Master was very bad, and this might have caused the doubt. A number of the actors weren't tip top either, so one could never be sure whether it was play or actors that made me doubt. Frankly, I must say that I don't think the part of Avril suited Siobhan McKenna. I believe that you mentioned something that that was your opinion too. She is a splendid actress, vigorous and forthright, but hardly soft-hearted enough for Avril. Liam Redmond was fine; so was Joseph O'Connor in the part of O'Dempsey; Seumas Locke so so as O'Killigan; Poges was done grandly by Miles Malleson, but some quarrel that I have mentioned before, put him out, and he played half-heartedly; Walter Mudd as Stokes was good, but he, too, was concerned with some dispute—of which to this day I know really nothing, having been told nothing—and fell away, too. Souhaun was good, but physically didn't look the part at all. Well, there it is: I'd like you to study the play well before deciding anything.

If you have any questions to ask, ask away; I'll do my best to answer them. I hope the Readings are going well; tho' the other week seemed to be a bad one; but, even were they to end today, you and your comrade-artists have done splendidly, and have given a bolder life to the books.

Am feeling fine again. Remember me to all the artists, and give them my love; and to Bob Ginna and to Kathy, if you see them. We all send you our love and fine wishes.

As ever,
Sean

To Mrs. Alice Kornbluth

MS. KORNBLUTH

3 NOVEMBER 1956

Dear Mrs. Kornbluth,

Thanks for your letter, & more thanks for pointing out the mistake in the book, "The Green Crow."[1] Our elder boy told me of it, but neither of us could find it when we looked for it. Along came your letter, which enabled me to correct the mistake for an English edition of the book. It was a very bad error to make.

Thanks, too, for the picture of your little girls—may God be with them always. I rather love children, &, even now, old as I am, & full of wrinkles, give me five minutes with a shy child, and he or she & I are friends forever. We have three—two boys & a girl. They are grown up now, but young enough still to be new to the world; & we (meself & herself—my wife) are one with them in the way they want to go.

My love to your little ones, & my love to you.

Yours very sincerely,
Sean

[1] In the introductory chapter, "Overture," of the American edition of *The Green Crow* (New York: Braziller, 1956), O'Casey had written about "the frolic drunkenness of Joxer and Captain Boyle in the ending of *The Plough and the Stars*" (p. 9), instead of *Juno and the Paycock*.

To David H. Greene

TC. O'CASEY

4 NOVEMBER 1956

My dear Dave,

Of course, the letter was meant for you alone, and I'd rather you didnt show it to Mer. [Vivian Mercier]; though, if you have already done so, dont be troubled, neither let your heart be afraid; if you havent shown it, dont, for I've no desire to give second aid to my Irish critics. They are all hostile, so let them go to hell. This quarter's IRISH READING or WRITING has another on the lines of V.M., and a similar criticism blossoms into the center of this quarter's DUBLIN MAGAZINE.[1] It is a strange unanimity, all played on the same few notes. Oddly, the one criticism of the recent BISHOP'S BONFIRE that faced the play and what it aimed at was THE LEADER, a weekly I knew well when I was a young fella, and with whose then Editor, I had a dispute.[2] He denounced the plays JUNO and THE PLOUGH as anti-Irish, accusing the author of being one of the Garrison, hating everything Irish. I challenged him to a debate on the question, the debate to be in Irish alone, and to be judged by the officers of the Irish-speaking FAINNE: so I never heard another word from him. This Journal had two reviews of the play, written by one signing himself or herself X;[3] and both gave a good account of the play, not failing in critical remarks, but castigating the other critics for failing to see the value and worth of the effort: and, oddest of all, the Journal is an intensely Catholic one, not pietistic, but deep and thoughtful, expressing Catholic thought that one had to respect and value. But the rest of the critics present a solid, invincible phalanx of hostility, similar to that shown by the earlier critics to the earlier plays. It is odd that none of them ever rebuke D. Johnston or P. V. Carroll, or Frank O'Connor for living outside of Ireland; it does, apparently, no damage to them. Or even Yeats who was educated in Eng., who lived in London for, I think, 20 years, and who set out to live in Oxford after his marriage, and who ran out of Ireland as often as he could. Well, Dave, amhic, there's more important things in the world than their criticism and my plays; and further work to do, for it behoves us to work while it is yet day, for the night cometh when no man can work. So I am to get along with my work in progress, and you are to get along with yours. There goes the bell for the next round!

[1] Patricia Baggett, "Sean O'Casey's Development of a Basic Theme," *Dublin Magazine*, October–December 1956. There was no comment on O'Casey in the current *Irish Writing No. 36*.

[2] For O'Casey's dispute with D. P. Moran, editor of *The Leader*, see O'Casey's letter to *The Leader*, 20 December 1924, Vol. I.

[3] Valentin Iremonger, writing under the initial "X," wrote a favorable review of *The Bishop's Bonfire* in *The Leader*, 12 March 1955; and he wrote again attacking the Dublin critics for their attitude toward O'Casey, "Sean O'Casey: A Postscript," *The Leader*, 9 April 1955.

You have a work in front of you: a thousand letters and 70 or eighty note-books! A pyramid of paper! You will be relieved when the last word's written. You are quite right about the dialect—Synge didnt learn it in Wicklow; it comes from the West. Yeats didnt know Synge, nor did he know Shaw or anyone else: all living things he met where phantoms to him; but I'm surprised to hear that Synge whined so much about himself in his letters to Molly [O'Neill]. But to whom could he go for sympathy, if not to her? She had the words of life for Synge; as so many women have for so many men. Too, there was something of the wildness in Molly that Synge longed for in himself but couldnt achieve more than the gaze he gave to the Aran men and women. So he tried to link his weakness with her strength, as so many of us actually do with our wives and sweethearts; for women can bear trouble and pain more stoically than most men. These, Dave, arent O'Casey dogmas, but just a few opinions. Am I right or am I wrong, Misther Gallogher?

I hope you, Mrs. Greene—Catherine, of course—and the family are well. Catherine has her hands full with all she must have to do with the children, not forgettin' the bigger one—Dave. And Candie—how is she? My blessing on her and on all of you. I hope the twins are rushing around again.

Give my good wishes to V. M. though I'd rather you wouldnt say I was writing about him. And, if you have the address of Horace Reynolds, I'd like to have it. He changed his place of living some time ago, sent me the new address, I mislaid it, searched for it, couldnt find it; and I'd like to say hello to him, to Kay, to Peggy, and to John.

I feel fairly good; had an X ray some few days ago, but only some damage done; and nothing to be sad about. I find myself much more able now to think of work, and can walk at a great speed for quarter of an hour or so; tho at 76, sure one should be feelin like one of them rosy cities, half as ould as time.

My love again, and all good wishes to you and yours.

Very, very glad you liked the Reading.[4]

As ever,
[Sean]

---

[4] Paul Shyre's adapted concert reading of *Pictures in the Hallway*.

To Franklin D. Murphy

MS. MURPHY

17 NOVEMBER 1956

My dear Mr. Murphy:

Thank you for your letter. Never mind the delay in answering. God made time, &, some Irish say, He made plenty of it.

Your Catalog was a fine one, and I congratulate you. I'm so glad your Exhibit & Catalog had such an effect thro' the Mid-West, & all the other states.[1] It is fine to have a University getting a hold of the people; shaking their hands & saying look what we're doing; not keeping their achievements to themselves, nor hiding their light under a bushel. Of course, the American Universities & Colleges are closer to the common man than the Universities here, which hide in a valley of study & learning, & blind their windows to keep their light from shining out on other men & women.

Well, I'm glad to have a share in Kansas, with its university & with its people by a chance with a Kansas soldier, recorded in one of my books,[2] & with Kansas University, tho', I believe both soldier & University are of Kansas City which lies in Missouri—if I mistake not—but not very far away. As well, I have two young friends, now in Iowa, who are born & bred of the State of Mississippi; so I come closer to the Middle West, & don't spend all my time in New York.

My warm regards and good wishes.

Sean O'Casey

[1] Dr. Murphy had organized an exhibition of his private O'Casey Collection.
[2] See O'Casey's conversation with an American soldier from Kansas City during World II, in "Red Laugh of War," *Sunset and Evening Star* (1954), *Autobiographies II,* pp. 577–78.

To Joseph Stein

MS. STEIN

17 NOVEMBER 1956

Dear Mr. Stein.

Thank God your boy, Joshua, came out of the accident safely. Our love for our children is a great persecution. Our girl, when very young, got a bad fall from a bicycle, & was severely hurt, bruised badly & cut badly on head and face; but it all healed quickly; tho' we felt the fright for a long time. It must have been a very painful time for Sadie. It is almost impossible to guard children these days. No proper road-planning leaves the children in perpetual danger. They have to be constantly warned, &, in cities, trained to look all ways before they cross a road; but children think never of danger. However, since it is allright now with little Joshua, the sun shines again.

My love to Sadie, the children, & to you.

Yours very sincerely,
Sean O'Casey

To Seumas Scully

TS. SCULLY

19 NOVEMBER 1956

Dear Seumas,

I mislaid your last letter, couldnt remember your new address, and so couldnt write to you. Thank you very much for the past and the present clippings; all very interesting. Glad you are hanging on to your job so as to be able to keep a reserve untouched in the holding. You are better where you are. Now the London fogs begin to pack the sky, and that wouldnt be good for you. I'm glad THE QUARE FELLA is doing so well, but I hope Brendan Behan wont try to become a quare fella himself—that is, deliberately. What he has to do now is to concentrate on playwriting, and, if he does that, he wont have time for much else: I hope he does. No one seems to know why the UCD banned his appearance there. Probably this banning business is becoming a habit: everyone's doing it! "Monserrat"[1] isnt, I fear, a "wonderful play," but maybe you are right. Perhaps Dev. is, at least, a little more left than Costello; not much, but a tiny way. Dave G.—Professor Greene now—is busy at the Life of Synge, and he has no easy job, wading thro' eighty notebooks and a mountain of letters. He is very busy, and has had a lot of anxiety: three of his children went down with Polio, two slightly and one badly; but the little one is allright again, with a slight mark left in the shape of a very slight limp. God be thanked it was no worse, for Dave is a grand lad, and I'm very fond of him, as I am of his buttie, Dave Krause. And a warning! Dont show my letters to you to anyone; they are private, and meant only for you to see; unless something in one of them might strike you as being

---

[1] *Montseratt* (1949), a play by Emanuel Robles, translated and adapted from the French by Lillian Hellman in 1950, was produced by the Globe Theatre Company in Dun Laoghaire on 12 October 1955.

something someone ought to know, and then, even, only with my permission. No harm done, however, Seamus; only one does like to feel sure that his letters will be regarded as something personal, and not for all to see. Dont bother about Miss Barrett's article.[2] I've read it, for I get the DUBLIN MAGAZINE every quarter. There was another in the American COMMONWEAL by Vivian Mercier, on the same lines, so, bar THE LEADER, all the Irish "critics" are at one in their opinion of me. At Swim All the Birds. Youre right about him whom you mention: he [Gabriel Fallon] has a neurosis about me; O'C. is to him what K. Charles's head was to Mr. Dick in "David Copperfield." Amusing how he thinks the old boy grumbled as he read Mrs B.'s article. Well, let him think away; it'll do him bad. Thanks again, and all good wishes. As ever,

Sean.

---

[2] Miss Patricia Baggett. See O'Casey's letter to David H. Greene, 4 November 1956, note 1.

To Miss Mai McCarthy[1]

TC. O'CASEY

21 NOVEMBER 1956

My dear Mai,

Here's a hurried word or two, in reply to your letter from Mamaroneck and New York City. Odd that you should have been at one time depressed by the Fall—perhaps it reminded you of the first Fall, sub-consciously; for this idea of Original sin oppresses a great many persons, and often keeps them from a glimpse of God. But I'm glad that you see the beauty of autumn now. Odd, I had a letter from a young girl living in Iowa, born Mississippi, who, too, writes about how lovely the autumn looks in her part of the USA. We havent many autumn tints here; few brilliant ones, for the Devon County lingers green nearly the whole year through; a thing that greatly struck the Americans who come here in Winter, and see so many trees green as in summer, and grass green as Ireland's green sod. But I miss the autumn tints which I knew so well when we lived in Buckinghamshire. As I look from my window, I see but one tree golden and red-tinted—a beech (rare here); the rest are conifers and cypresses, gloomy and dark, but the leafage shelters the birds from frost and rain, and they give life to the still trees. There is one white poplar, but it sheds

---

[1] Miss Mai McCarthy, 227 East 72nd Street, New York City.

its leaves before they've time to turn to autumn tints. There's a red hawthorn, too, but its hidden away behind tall shrubbery of laurel. We have a
lilac bush, hidden too by the crowding laurel, and a very beautiful laburnum tree, a great cascade of golden bloom in the spring. No nest there, possibly because the whole thing is poisonous— leaf, bark, and pod. I daresay
your Irish loafer worker is interesting, but I have scant time for them,
unless the loafer has a gift like Whitman's, the Prince of loafers—but what
a loafer! This is common in Ireland, two kinds of life: one working always, and too hard; the other declining to work at all. And those who
wont work seem to live a hell of a long time; God seems to be good to
them. I'm afraid I agree with you about the Irish trying to be either Saxon
or Italian; when they cease to be themselves, they become pitiful nobodies.
A few specially gifted can do it—like [John] McCormack or Peggy Sheridan; but the most of us would do better to remain as we were born.

I was surprised to hear of R[andolph]. Churchill. Imagine an ex-prime
minister's son—and of England, too—standing a quiz for American dollars. How have the mighty fallen! If every dollar in $64,000 were in six
parts, and every part a dollar, I wouldnt do it, and I'm as fond of dollars
as Mr. Churchill; and need them more.

As for the sad tale of your brother, you must remember one thing—
you owe a lot to yourself; the first call of life is to mind the life one has
herself; that musnt be thrown away to help another, who, as often as
not, refuses, or neglects, to help himself. I had a very dear friend, a Scot,
a business-man, something of a rascal, which, I fear most businessmen
must be to survive; but he had a rare intelligence, a glorious sense of humor, and was a born story-teller; but he drank and drank whiskey, and
finally contracted consumption. While the going was good, or even fair,
I labored to convince him of his foolishness. He spent many weekends
with us, and I used all the power and influence I had to get him off the
drink. But he got so bad that for fear of infection, I would let him come
to see us no more. He died a year or so after. If you knew the facts, you'd
find that your brother had a hand in giving the disease to himself; or neglected it when he got it; or didnt use his intelligence to throw it off. One
has to fight these things, even under unfavorable conditions. I have many
scars on my own lungs which took a big battle to heal in my younger days,
and had to fight when conditions were terrible; I never entered a Sana-
torium, never had much to eat, sometimes nothing at all; but I fought it
all; fought hard, and am fighting now against another ailment. Your
brother's life depended, not on you, agradh, but on himself. No one can
wage a fight for a sick body unless the body, or the soul within the body,
or that is part of the body, fights for itself. As for your father being a
"germ-carrier," I dont think that can be so. As a matter of fact, the
whole of Ireland's a germ-carrier, and, indeed, all the world, too. We
have to fight these ills nationally as well as individually; and those who

are afflicted are often irresponsible about the possible infection to others. Dr. Noel Browne tried to carry on a national fight in Ireland—he was Minister of Health, and had had the disease himself, in the Mother and Child Bill;[2] but, as you probably know, the Bishops put the caidpbais[3] on the best parts of it; so that Browne had to resign, though before he had to do this, he did a tremendous amount of work for the co-ordinated attack on this terrible ailment. Today, even, the Bishops wont let the children have a hot meal in school hours, because, they say, it would be the thin edge of the wedge of communism! The schools are overcrowded, and 600 of them are declared to be unfit for human habitation; so you see, there are many things contributing to the incidence of this disease in the 26 counties. However, things are much better now; and your brother will have first-class skill to help him, and, if it hasnt gone too far, he will get out of it; but he, too, must help this medical and surgical skill by fighting it in his own body and own soul. This germ lives in the air, and in the dust of the roads, and all are in danger. We are, of course, our brother's keeper, but this doesnt mean that we are to carry him on our back, or coddle a sister on our lap. Your first letter shows that you are trying to do too much, and I warn you to take a little more thought for YOURSELF. No one else can do this for you. Spend as much time as you can resting on a roof, and dont be afraid of bees or wasps—they dont want to sting, and, anyway, only half the wasps have stings to use. And dont worry about your brother—you can do nothing about it. All one can do is to try to make the world a more sensible and sane and safe place to live in. I think you are very wise in deciding not to go to Ireland: it would do you harm. It isnt a pleasant place now. Joyce's terrible picture that Ireland was "The old sow that eats her litter"[4] is a terrible truth. You have had enough. So have I had: my family, bar one brother, is buried there, and a hard and unprofitable life they had—no outlet for whatever gifts any of them had, and each had a few. Now, you take things easier; dont try to want to do too many things. Your body has its claims, and cant stand too much mental exertion. Glad you flung away Tanizaky[5]—sounded very high-flown to me—making art and culture a torment instead of an enjoyment. Breon is with us here. He's just found a little studio at a cheap rent, and is busy fixing it up. Shivaun is trying to get into London Drama School (God help her!), and Niall's at London University. Eileen very busy and bright; the old fella fighting domestic puzzles, with her, of

---

[2] For the background of Dr. Noel Browne's unsuccessful Mother and Child Health Scheme in 1951, see O'Casey's letter to Robert Smyllie, 22 April 1951, note 3, Vol. II.

[3] *caidhbpbais,* cap of death (pronounced ky-bosh).

[4] "Ireland is the old sow that eats her farrow," Stephen Dedalus says in James Joyce's *A Portrait of the Artist as a Young Man* (1916), Ch. V; and in *Ulysses* (1922), the Circe or Nighttown chapter.

[5] Junichiro Tanizaki, *Some Prefer Nettles* (1955), a novel translated from the Japanese by Edward G. Seidensticker.

course, and fighting the lingering post-operation infection with vim and vigor. Trying to think out a play, and jotting down a few thoughts for a possible book—title, so far, WORDS, WORDS, WORDS.

My love, dear Mai, to you, as ever.

[*Sean*]

To Dr. Frank Morrell

MS. MORRELL

24 NOVEMBER 1956

My dear Frank,

I got the book allright, but had no time (or strength) to reply at once. Still fighting a post-operation infection which takes time up and keeps energy down; but doing a lot. I've a pile of letters to answer (if I manage one in 5, I'll be elated); am trying to think out a play, & am jotting down thoughts for a new book, as well as dealing with domestic affairs; so I'm not in bed. You shouldn't think too much of your visit to Tingrith. The magazine founded by our friend didn't last long. He & I wrote each other for a while; but he didn't reply to my last letter, written 2 years ago; so Mr. Cox has gone from my life. There's no such thing as "Socialist reality," except in the getting of daily bread (a terribly important thing); the wine of this land or that vintage will taste different (tho' all is wine), & the book of verse will be as the poet sees & feels the personal & natural life surrounding him.

I wish I were on the banks of the Mississippi with you, looking at the lovely flare-up of the Autumn trees before they stand stark for the Winter. I haven't seen the letters of Kaethe Kollwitz.[1] Her pictures are very interesting, very grim, very sad; but so was her life; & so were all things in Germany then; & sad & grim enough here, too. As an artist, she can't come up to Daumier, or Van Gogh, or Goya, or, indeed, even Millet. There's no lyrical quality in her pictures; & they haven't the curious power of unconscious stoicism of Van Gogh's peasants or prisoners; or the terrifying sarcasm of Daumier, or the pitilessness of war & its savagery depicted by Goya. But they are pictures of a life that no one should be called on to go through. I hope your patient got rid of the tumor, tho' I doubt even an operation could permanently remove all the tumor's tentacles from a brain. [W.] Suschitzky, the photographer, is away televising for N.B.C. in

[1] Käthe Kollwitz, *Diary and Letters* (1955), edited by Hans Kollwitz, translated by Richard and Clara Winston.

S.E. Asia. When he comes back, I'll get a photo, a Socialistic realism one—& send it on to you with pleasure. Why should I disapprove?

My love.
As ever,
Sean

To E. J. West[1]

TC. O'CASEY

25 NOVEMBER 1956

Dear Ed,

Thank you many times for your kind letter and very kind Review of THE GREEN CROW—too kind, maybe? However, it was very gratifying to me. I like praise, but only when it comes from minds I think are competent to give it; though adverse criticism amuses me, and I like to have a fight with it, if it, in slating me, reveals an ignorance of dramatic experiment, or is founded on sectarian or political venom: that is why I wrote about the Irish critics in BONFIRE UNDER A BLACK SUN.

On the other hand, I am very shy about praise, and I have rarely quoted it; and the one thing I most avoid is any chat or talk about my work. It makes me embarrassingly self-conscious, and I always shy away from it. Far as I can judge, your Review is a fine one, and hits the man it is all about in the heart and on the head. But even if it raged against me, I should not suggest the cutting of a word of it. I am always telling young people who write to me that they should say what they honestly feel to be the true thing, be it right or wrong: it is the one way by which we can inch a little nearer to the truth of things; that way we are always, if not before the light of truth, then well within her shadow.

I think that it is a grand thing to belong to "the group of scholars." Many of them have given me great pleasure and most of them not a little profit. They are all searchers—over the land, under the sea, through the skies, and, hardest search of all, into the mind of man. Look at your own Thanksgiving Day that commemorates the first American Harvest from which all the American harvests grew, the handful of corn that increased into great abundance, and settled the United States into a teeming life. When there is pride in what we do, we must be proud of what we are.

I am sorry to hear that you were on your back when my last letter came to you—a bad way to be. I know, for I was that way myself for

---

[1] E. J. West (1903–1958), teacher, critic, editor, stage director, University of Colorado.

six months—though, now and again, I slid from the bed, and tip-toed round the room for five minutes or so, twice daily, so as to keep my limbs from betraying me. I'm glad to hear you have forsworn alcohol— third attempt. It's a bad habit, and particularly for a man of mental stirring; he cannot shake it off as a navvy can, for his work is not with the muscle, but with the mind, the first thing that alcohol goes for, and loves to confuse. Many thanks for Siobhain's letter,[2] a very kind deed on her part. I shall await the Shaw letters[3] with interest. Meanwhile, my love and best wishes.

[Sean O'Casey]

[2] Siobhan McKenna wrote a letter to the *New York Times,* 25 March 1956, praising O'Casey and Paul Shyre's Concert Reading of *I Knock at the Door,* which she had seen at the Belasco Theatre in New York. See O'Casey's letter to Shyre, 6 May 1956, note 1.
[3] Bernard Shaw, *Advice to a Young Critic* (1955), edited by E. J. West.

To Joan McAlevey

MS. MCALEVEY

26 NOVEMBER 1956

My dear Joan,

I hope the music of "My Fair Lady" pleased the fair lady who was listening to it. I have the records of the music, & we all like it, though I can't guess what Bernard Shaw would think of it were he alive. I am far from being a sage, my dear. Thousands of things puzzle me as they do everyone else, even here at home. We puzzle over our children as your own parents probably puzzle over you; for mother & father—if they be natural—can't help anxiety about their children. But take it quietly, Joan, & don't rush into a married life. You are young enough to spend a few more years in your own company. Further experience will help you to face more faithfully the additional problems of a home; & these are not very easy these days.

I'm very glad you have had an enjoyable birthday—a thing I never knowingly had, for every day was such a struggle that we never had time or chance to make any day special; tho' my mother used to try her best at Christmas.

Yes, the world is disturbed, but, in one way or another, in this place or that one, it was always disturbed, for change is always taking place. I've heard, often & often, gunfire & crossfire in the towns & streets of our holy Ireland, with bullets whistling by, first in the fight with England, then in the fight between ourselves; but in it all, and through it all, life goes on changing here and changing there; always evolving out a pattern of eventual goodness and unity. Well, Joan, your Eisenhower is back in the White House, & heaven grant he may have the health to stay there till his term is up, & long, long afterwards; for tho' his politics aren't mine, he is a good man and true and gentle-hearted—soldier an all as he was. Yes, Paul Shyre is thinking out "Purple Dust" for production. The camera-man, [W.] Suschitzky, working for NBC. here, when they televised the family took one. He's away just now; but when he comes back, I'll get one from him and send the photograph to you.

My dear, I am always writing, but just now only thoughts & ideas, which may—or may not—blossom into a play or book.

Now, dear lass, take care of yourself, for, like my own daughter, you have a long way to go; & it needs thought and prudence and courage. May God be with you all the way.

With my love
Sean

To Robert D. Graff

TS. GRAFF

27 NOVEMBER 1956

My dear Bob,

I am very glad you are safely back in New York again, away from all the Has-beens in S.E. Asia: Back from Borobodur and Angkor Vat leaving the people there to cut away the jungle just to show the world what they once were. Well, Bob, this has happened in a lot of places when invaders came carrying God with them to civilise the natives and save their souls. It happened in India, in Africa, in Ireland, Burma, and Ceylon when the British came with their god-given skill to make the savages god-fearing, the natives showing their belief in Christ by lying prone before their masters, and working for them while the sun was out, and then, when the sun was gone, working while the stars were visible. The Spanish, too, did a lot for God among the Aztecs and the Incas, and all brought the world of men wonderfully close to God. It was your country that first put the growing cap of death (Kybosh) on this good and glorious practice when your countrymen let fly those damned shots at Bunker Hill. Looka the way things are now! All because Washington and his gang (including some Irish, I'm sorry to say) went away from God, and thought they should think their own thoughts, do their own work, and issue taxes only under the hand and seal of an American-elected government. Yous destroyed the world, and prevented the Kingdom of God from appearing on the earth as it is in heaven.

I signed the vol of MIRROR IN MY HOUSE,[1] Breon packed it up, and posted it to you, yesterday. I hope it may get to you safely, but it takes some time now for a package to get from here where I am to there where you are.

We all hope to see the s. Asian film, and again enjoy Su's wonderful photography; we shall be looking forward to it, and we hope the British Television wont be shy or resentful over the rift that has appeared between the USA and the bumptious british bumpire, now, perhaps, more fitly styled British Rumpire.

All well here, with a reunion in the offing, when Niall and Shivaun come back from London to spend the Christmas holidays at home.

When you meet Bob (G[inna]), give him our love. We got Su's [W. Suschitzky] post-card allright, and I wondered how far you had all got into the jungle; but everywhere has its own jungle nowadays. I shall be very pleased if the NBC does the film again; but DONT you try to worry them into doing it; it isnt all that important, and those who saw it once may not wish to see it again. We all send our love to you. Le 'cuile deagh-Ghuidhe. With every good prayer—in Irish. as ever,

Sean

[1] Sean O'Casey, *Mirror in My House* (1956), the two-volume edition of the six-volume autobiography.

To Mrs Kay O'Riordan

TS. O'RIORDAN

27 NOVEMBER 1956

My dear Kay,

Thanks for your two letters and enclosed clippings. Very interesting, and very true. I didnt write before this because I amnt able to write so long or so often now—getting on to 77 is just a little tiring; but, never mind—the heart's young yet. I'm afraid that I agree with Michael. To me, there isnt a shadow of a doubt that those who hate, and always hated, Communism (Socialism, if you like) tried to seize hold of the popular discontent in Hungary,[1] and use it to overthrow all signs of Socialism there, and set up the old regime of landlord, clerical and lay, and fascist

[1] For further comment on the Hungarian Rising, see the Introduction to this year, and O'Casey's letter to Brooks Atkinson, 12 January 1957, note 1.

boss, so that in the future Hungary might be changed from a socialist country into an armed camp and arsenal for a possible attack on the USSR,
if ever the glorious chance came. If you read all accounts, written by
biased reporters, you can see that it tried to go too far; that bitter revenge
was meted out to any communist captured—no holy protests against this!
It is ridiculous to think that the revolt was one of the whole people, and
the people's army. If it had been, it couldn't have been crushed in a few
days—even with the help of Soviet tank and Soviet soldier. When in
Easter Week, with a hostile people, and the might of Britain against them,
a few hundred badly-armed lads held back the British power for a week.
How much longer would they have held out if they had had a well-armed
force say of 10,000, backed by a united people? No; after a few days, the
workers saw what was happening, so did the Hungarian soldiers, and they
drew back—a lot of them, puzzled, not knowing what to do, till a strong
party government, headed by Kardar [Jan Kadar], did what was terribly
necessary to save Socialism for the Hungarian People, with the aid of the
Red Army. That is how I see it, and saw it, though members of the family
saw it differently. But I have had too long an experience of the workers'
Revolutionary Movement to be deceived. Even here, I saw it in 1926, when
the mercenary labor leaders sold the workers in the General Strike—the
[Imre] Nagys of the Eng. Labor Movement. As Shaw has said, "It cannot
be too widely known that Socialism is not loving-kindness, or compassion,
or pity, or philanthropy; it is a struggle by the workers and enlightened
minds for a way of life that will give the people control and ownership
of the means of life—the instruments of production and distribution to
be used for the common good." That is what Socialism is, and it isn't the
Muggeridges, the Crankshaws, the Atlees, or the Orwells who are going
to save it, and make it the life of the people, but you and I and all the
others who are constricted physically, mentally, and spiritually, by the
system of Capitalism, loving rent, profit, and interest, above men, women,
and children; and even—spite of what clerics say—above God. So to
save Soc. in Hun. the Hungarian workers and people called upon the Red
Army to give them a hand in the essential task of preventing ten years of
Socialism to be swallowed away by the enemies of everything that has been
done, and is doing [sic], to bring Socialism into active vitality and work
the world over.

As for what is called "the moral aspect," let those who hate socialism,
who hate with their outer and inner guts all that the USSR has done, who
have surrounded the USSR with implacable hatred and animosity, who have
tried, time and time again, to destroy her, and whose latest effort was shown
by this revolt in Hungary; a revolt—when it seemed, because the thought
was father to the big wish, that it would succeed, caused the pean of delight which rang out in every British newspaper and British platform, thinking that this was the beginning of the end of the USSR. It didn't last long,
and they are already sinking into silence. Even Muggeridge last night spent

an evening talking to three Anglican clerics—one a well-known cricketer, the second an ex-Guards' officer, the third an ex-naval officer—about the best way of bringing the Eng. people (the workers of course) back to God! The four of them scholars from Cambridge or Oxford, with hardly a word to say or any original way to say what they tried to say; with Mugg. suggesting that the Eng. People were "Pagans"; ignorant that a baptised soul cannot be a pagan, and that every baptised soul is made a child of God, a member of Christ, an inheritor of the K. of heaven. Well, well, here I am writing a thesis! I understand your mind about the children; but children in our own country and in this have been suffering torture, not for a few days, but for years and years in our prisons of schools; and are still there, deprived of a hot meal daily in our country (tho they get it here), while the mouthers run round yelling out against the bad deeds of the USSR and the Communists. Well, my dear, you must use your own judgement to form your own opinions about all the things that happen, and far be it from me to try to change them.

I send you a little token to get a little something for the two children (I think they are two—cant find your earlier letter), and my blessing. Good wishes to Michael, and to you.

As ever,
Sean

In any note or letter you may write, please, Kay, don't mention a word of thanks—I hate these expressions.

Workers of All Lands, Unite!

To Mrs. John T. Cooper

TS. COOPER

29 NOVEMBER 1956

Dear Georgie:
You are quite right—there's no place in the Church for the colossal nightingale. She is well content with the chirruping of the sparrow; well enough in its little way, often charming, but the sensitive ear gets tired of it, and at times longs for the soaring and sustained song of the colossal lark. It seems odd that the lesser music is to be for God, and the greater music for man; but the church prelates are jealous of Berlioz and Beethoven; their greatness tends to distract the mind from God; so the monks go on sweetly chanting the Plainsong sounds of the psalms and canticles; and lovely it is, but not so lovely when it goes on, like Tennyson's brook,

forever. By this ever-stated assurance that there is a special music which is sacred to be used only in church, the church separates God from man more effectively than the music of Berlioz or Beethoven could separate man from God.

The bawdy song, if it be human and witty, is as much a part of God's life in the world as the Vatican quoir singing Edeste Fideles with trumpet accompaniment. This whole world's temple, whether soiled by war or sanctified by peace, though it is still a third full with moneychangers and with thieves.

I am as dubious as yourself about the musical "Juno." It is a bow shot at a venture, in addition to the fact that it may bring dollars into the purse for five people. I know that it won't be a "Don Giovanni" or a "Boris," but there's room for things interesting as well as things magnificent: a seed pearl has its loveliness as well as a Kohinoor diamond; but I hope it may have the gentle sparkle even of a seed pearl. Anyway, whatever it may be, even should it be but a dull pebble of limestone, the play remains, and will remain for whatever the play is. If it wasn't turned into a musical now, it might be some day—as Shaw's *Pygmalion* has been, voiced as a fine show by thousands. But I haven't much interest now in *Juno*; it belongs to a different man for better or for worse.

You shouldn't "dispraise" yourself, for you'll find plenty of others to do that for you; though we shouldn't think too highly of our own judgements; it is so hard to be fair. Shaw says somewhere that "There are many who couldn't write a line of dramatic dialogue to save their souls who had a far better knowledge of the world's dramatic literature than he had." And somewhere else that when Moliere wanted to try out opinion on a new comedy, he didn't ask the ones high in the literary world, but tried it out on his cook. And Caliban had a lot in him; he at least worshipped beauty in the shape of a lovely girl, and resented the shape that prevented him from winning her; he was discontented, the first sign of grace; and, too, he was shocked at the appearance of Western civilization in the shapes of the drunkard and the fool; and had he known the hearts and minds of the grandees, he'd have been shocked more, for when the nobles were such as Shakespeare shows them to be, how could the proletariat show signs of grace, of good manners, of civilization?

I should have liked to have listened to Bishop [Fulton J.] Sheen, and heard him chatting about Lenin. There wasn't much of the "saint" in Lenin for the R.C. clerics while Lenin was alive. They said of him then what they say of Stalin now. It is hard to understand what the bishop means by "hating." Christ himself had an occasional mouthful for his enemies—Oh, generation of vipers! Whited sepulcres, it will be better for Sodom and Gomorrah in the day of judgement than for you! And this, not of the common or the vulgar, but of the educated, the leaders, the priests of his day. These prelatical christians are damned cute when propagating their own importance; so gently plausible where they have little or no power. Of course, they just can't get rid of Lenin, and so must semi-canonise him some way; as they do in my own country with Wolfe Tone, Larkin, and Connolly, now that they are dead and silent. I don't think Lenin hated anything or anybody. Marxism has nothing to do with loving-kindness, charity, or philanthrophy; it is a scientific social philosophy. To a communist, a capitalist can no more help being a capitalist than another can help being a proletarian. Capitalists may be, and often are, very kind lads, and very enjoyable company. One of our greatest Irish friends, is also one of Ireland's biggest business-men, and he is most generous, kind, with a fine sense of humor.

Our two boys have already done their military service in the artillery; but should a war begin, they'd be summoned at once. It wouldn't signify much, for in the next war, everyone will be in the front line. We were there almost all the time in the last one. We had our windows blown out, our roof shattered, and our ceilings down during bomb raids, so, in one way, we are seasoned so much that we never want another one.

I was shocked to read what the priest said of the word "agradh." What a mind must be his! It is a word used often in Irish, a father to his son, a mother to her child, a friend even to another friend. It means literally O love. It is what we know as the vocative as in the old days visitors and messengers said O king, live forever. We often say in English, "he or she has a great gradh for this or that"—a food or a drink, for instance. "He has a great gra for sherry; she has a great gra for roses." It is entirely innocent, though of course, a lad could (and does) say it of his sweetheart. Well, Georgie, agradh, you have a very pretty face and a charming figure, capped with an intelligent and poetic mind. You have many gifts, and I am delighted to think of you and of John—if he doesn't mind—as my friends. I guessed from your letter, the first one, that you had a fine mind, and, by God, I wasn't wrong. And now I see you have many natural charms enveloping it. A gift from God! Thanks for the fine verses which touched me very much. In my next book, if ever there be one, and I hope there may, you should let me print them as a preface. You have a poetic gift as well as the other ones, and I should be glad if you would let me include them in the next thing I do, acknowledging, of course, the gifted girl who composed them.

Tell John that there seems to be only Irish doing the Gypsum, according to a Gaelic article in "INNIU" "Cloch luachmhar ata fairsing againn." "A valuable stone that we have in plenty." Indeed, the article says some of the slabs are sent to the USA! So beannacht libh—a blessing with you—with my love to John and to you.

Sean

To Horace Reynolds[1]

MS. REYNOLDS

I DECEMBER 1956

Dear Horace,

I've wondered often how you, Kay, Peggy, & John are? I know you shifted from 422, but couldn't find your letter, with its new address, anywhere. I wrote to Dave Greene, but he didn't know your new abiding place either. So I chance a hello to you all at the door & through the Windows of the auld house.

I hope you are all well. You, Kay, Peggy, & John, with the little Kays, Peggies, Johns, & Horaces.

Very busy, but not able to keep it up as I used to do. Warm regards & vivid remembrance of the dinner in Boston, the drive in the old grey motor to Cambridge, the "lecture," the evening with you, Kay, & the family, & the departure—not forgetting the tea & sherry in the Harvard Club. Oh, Boys! Them was the days!

As ever
Sean

[1] Horace Reynolds (1896–1965), writer and teacher, taught at Harvard and Brown universities. He invited O'Casey to Harvard in 1934 to give the Morris Gray Poetry Talk, "The Old Drama and the New," on 16 November. At the time O'Casey was in America for the production of *Within the Gates*. See letters to Reynolds in Vols. I and II.

To George Braziller

TC. O'CASEY

5 DECEMBER 1956

My dear George,

Many thanks for your letter and for the Check of $1431,13., received today. It was welcomed by Eileen, Breon, Niall, Shivaun, and Sean, and will do a lot more than just put Christmas over.

I am, needless, to say, [pleased] that you think that my books continue to do nicely—certainly, the Check shows that the GREEN CROW is still sailing through the American skies—long life to the flight!

I have been very busy, mostly answering letters, many from young people who read my books, and ask many questions. I reply to as many as I can, though my energy isnt quite what it was, but is, I think, coming back nicely. I am still battling with a "post-operation infection," but it doesnt trouble me too much now. Though I couldnt shine in the Olympic Games, I can go along for half an hour or so through the streets of Mary-church with a fine swing, watching all that passes me by, and marking houses and gardens along the way.

You do indeed seem to be busy with publication of 40 books behind you, and 16 planned for the coming year. I am trying out a play and jotting down thoughts for a book that I may call, "Words, Words, Idle Words," but it will take a long time to finish either, and longer to finish both.

No, neither things in Egypt nor in Hungary are "getting me down." Both were, in the nature of political and economic things, inevitable. There is hardly any wonder in England putting up a last waning fight for the remnants of her Empire. I, personally, havent a doubt that the old elements seized what they thought to be a chance to get on top again in Hungary, led by the Prince-Primate, Mindszenty. The October Revolution has been surrounded by enemies since its birth, and Socialism had a bitter fight to establish itself; it is still surrounded and beset, but it is powerful enough now to give a blow for a blow. Let them, the others, cast the beam out of their own eye before they complain of the mote in the eye of their brother. My warm wishes to Marsha and to you. Should Marsha come to England, we shall be delighted to see her. My love to you both.

As ever,
[Sean]

To Arvid Paulson

MS. PAULSON

7 DECEMBER 1956

Dear Arvid,

Greeting again. I was sorry to hear that Harriet Bosse had been ill; but, then, at 78, one can't expect to be among the runners, fencers, & swimmers of the Olympic Games. It isn't always Easter with anyone: the lily of Easter changes into the hard holly of December, beautiful, too, withal, clad in its glossy green and brave red berries. I hope you are keeping fit, tho' winning ne'er a gold medal for the USA; and your friend—our friend, John G[assner]. Wexford had a great time unveiling the statue of C[ommodore John] Barry, "founder of the American Navy"— tho' I seem to remember that a [John] P. Jones had something to do with this too. However, Ireland is proud of Barry, & has issued a special stamp, showing the statue of the naval officer, anchor at his feet and sword in his hand. A warlike hero is always sure of remembrance. "They will be remembered forever."[1] No fear of a statue to Shaw or Joyce—yet; perhaps more heroic than the greatest of Irish heroes known. I wonder is there one of Strindberg in his own land, in his own townland? I'm not fully well yet, but I'm very busy, & haven't time to think of myself, and have no desire to do so; except, of course, to join still in the activity, the gaiety, and the pain of life.

My warm regards to you.

As ever,
Sean

1 "They shall be remembered for ever," a reference to the patriots who died for Ireland, in W. B. Yeats's early nationalistic play, *Cathleen Ni Houlihan* (1902).

To Paul Shyre

MS. SHYRE

12 DECEMBER 1956

Dear Paul:
Thanks for the letter telling me that the Rehearsals are going ahead. I thought you were going to direct it, but, maybe, this would have been unwise since you are playing in it.

I have sent a few words—around 800—to Mr. [Otis] Guernsey about "P. Dust," & I hope it may be good enough to print.[1] It was posted today. By all means knock out any "improvement" I've made, if you don't think it goes well. How do you think the "Postmaster" goes? It seemed a little tedious to me during the abortive effort in London. I sent you the music for "The Ruin'd Rowan Tree"—an old Irish air "Owenabwee." I daresay you got it though you didn't mention it in your letter. I think you should try to keep the comedy to the fore—very hard to act comedy; &, if you can, keep the "Bringing in the Quatro-Centro Bureau" to the front, so's to be well seen. It can be very funny, and, again, if not well acted—It was very funny done by the actors in our London misadventure.

All good wishes.
Yours very sincerely,
Sean

1 Sean O'Casey, "Symbol, Prophecy, Slapstick," *New York Herald Tribune*, 23 December 1956.

To Anna Seghers and Bernhard Seeger

TC. O'Casey

15 December 1956

Anna Seghers and Bernhard Seeger and Friends.
German Writers' Association,
Berlin.

Dear friends,

I whole-heartedly agree with all you say—except for one qualification: I have deep and wide sympathy with the sturdy Israeli. I think it is time that the Jews should have a national place on which to rest the soles of their feet; and that they have been threatened and tormented by the surrounding Arab Governments; and that they were justified, or, at least, had a good reason for pushing their dangers a little further from their border. I cannot forget the dreadful holocaust of Jewish people blasted and burned by the savage fascist powers, who were driven back only by the world's united forces, and particularly by the almost miraculous valor of the Soviet Army.

In all other sayings I agree, and realise only too well that many of these Fascists are now out of their quiet, hidden dens, and are barking at Socialism, and eager, if they get a chance, to destroy all that has been done, and all that cooperative Socialist Peoples hope to do.

When we remember that Governments and politicians make mistakes, writers can make a hell of a lot of mistakes too.

My greeting to the German People, East and West, and I hope all will soon realise that it is a blessed thing to dwell together in unity.

Though my eyes are often on Europe and the world, you, my friends, will understand that they are oftenest tensed to peer out over my own country, Ireland.

Here's hoping, not only for co-existence, but for all peoples' co-operation in the building of Socialism everywhere so that we may come nearer to the gentler, safer, and more natural life of Communism.

Yours very sincerely,
Sean O'Casey.

To L. Rosenstein[1]

TC. O'CASEY

17 DECEMBER 1956

Dear Mr. Rosenstein,

I am not a prophet, a scholar, or a statesman, but simply a citizen of the Irish Republic venturing to put a few opinions before my comrades of the People's Republic of Bulgaria. What is to be done during 1957 to disperse the clouds of war on the horizon is a problem which no mind of one man, or ten men, can solve; we must all adapt our resistance to war according to the conditions and the circumstances of the time. The peoples of the world have set their face against war, and that is a damned fine beginning. A thermonuclear war with hydrogen bombs and devastating rockets dropped on, and fired against, the fellows who differed from us, would solve no problem for the living, but would solve all problems for the dead. One solves no problem by killing the man who differs from us, politically or religiously, when that same man whose opinion differs has the identical chance and power of killing the attacker. In that way—the simultaneous killing of the two opponents—is, of course, a way out of the problem, but it is the way of death, leaving nothing behind but a smoking world, and a few things, maybe, crawling about among the dust and the ashes. The leadership of the world in the various countries know this well; know it as well as we the common people do, and dare not even enter the thought of it. This way we could destroy all differing beliefs, political and religious, destroy even fear, but nothing would be left, not even a bird singing from a tree; so this method wont do. There is no use, nothing to be gained, by violence towards those who profess a different faith, or hold a different political opinion. Their error to us is our error to them; so enemies must, whether they like it or not, must become friends if we are all to go on living. If we can but get into close touch with one another, these things wont matter much: the touches of nature in us all makes the whole world kin.

The absence of war, though, isnt good enough—we should have an active peace; socialism to be developed and strengthened where it has been established, and encouraged forward in those countries which have no official Socialist Government yet. Communists shouldnt worry too much about those countries which have differing social and public systems. These social systems are gradually changing, and all of them seem to take the change towards a deeper and sensible Socialism. Each country has its own way of thinking and acting, and cannot be forced away from its own road without causing confusion. England, for instance, has her own way; it is often a clumsy way, slow and involved, but it is her own way, the one way she knows, and so, slow as it may be, it is the only way for

---

[1] L. Rosenstein, Radiodiffusion Bulgare, Sofia.

her. My country, Ireland, is at present in the grip of control by the Roman Catholic Church, but even she is beginning to put forth the slender stalk of thought on Social questions, and, though slower, even than England, the way of Socialism is becoming plain before her. Let every plant blossom in its own way, says a Chinese poet, and he is right, for to interfere is to deprive the flower of its full form, and check the vigor of the plant.

Communists should not be so dogmatic about Literature and Art, about which most of them know little or nothing. The artists should be free to picture life in painting, music, and words, as they see and feel it. The great artists of our race, the human race, have fully justified through the ages all that they have done.

As for what we should do in 1957 to keep the peace, we must do all we can, for only within peace shall all other things be added unto us. The peoples of the world should aim at forcing away all atomic tests, save those made to give a livelier and safer use of life for us all. All nuclear weapons of war should be sent down to hang on a christmas tree in hell. The armies of East and West should be separated as far as is possible from each other; those in the East sent back to their own countries, those of the West withdrawn from Europe, Air-bases, and all, and sent back to where they first came from. Only when this is done can the West expect the Socialist countries to breathe more freely. Always and ever a ring of insistent hostility has surrounded them; time and time again, efforts have been made to destroy the Socialist conception of life within them and without; and these should cease if the world of peoples is to [go] along and march ahead without fear to a fuller and a grander understanding, and a more active co-operation in the things that belong unto our peace. Anything less than these things may bring war, and war will do away with both East and West and everything else with them.

So we must aim at bringing these things to pass so that it may become a criminal offence for anyone to mention the word WAR. These things done, we shall find how easy it is, not only to co-exist, but to work and play actively together, learning as we work and play that it is a blessed thing for the peoples to dwell together in unity.

Sean O'Casey.

To Miss Elena Kornilova[1]

TC. O'CASEY

21 DECEMBER 1956

My dear friend,

Thank you so much for your very kind letter and for the kind and generous article,[2] and all the many things said in it, which you so kindly sent to me. It is very gratifying to think that the Soviet People, or some of them, think of me in a kindly way, and I am very proud that they do so. I have followed the fortunes of your People since 1917, the great things accomplished by your great Lenin, and, afterwards, by your great Stalin; for whatever may be said in the West, to me Stalin remains a great man, and did a tremendous lot to make the Soviet Republic the great power she is today.

I should have written to thank you before this for your good opinion of me and for your article, but for the fact that our younger boy of 21 years was suddenly stricken with leucaemia, and had to be taken to hospital, where he is now undergoing treatment, and we hope—though it is a very serious ailment—that he will eventually come safely out of it.

Please give my warm regards to your fellow-writers, and say I wish most heartily that they and your great Country may have a prosperous New Year, and that the world may come to know a true and brotherly peace; and so be able to work together for the good of all.

Again thanks, and all good wishes and warm regards to you.

Yours very sincerely,
Sean O'Casey.

[1] Miss Elena Kornilova, Union of Soviet Writers, Moscow, U.S.S.R.
[2] Miss Kornilova's review of *The Green Crow* appeared in the Soviet magazine, *News*, Moscow, 22 November 1956.

To Tyrone Guthrie

TS. GUTHRIE

23 DECEMBER 1956

Dear Tyrone,

Thanks for your letter and for the curious news that you have added business on to art—for God knows youve enough to do with the art of the theater without sitting on a Board.[1]

[1] Guthrie was on the board of a film company that was interested in making a film of O'Casey's one-act play, *Bedtime Story*.

But, on the other hand, all artists, in a way a circumlocutory way, an anxious way, are all up to the neck in business—however they may exclaim against it—to get all they can; to sell in the dearest market. And another thing, it might be a good thing if an artist or two were on every business Board so's to bring a little imagination into the machine.

I cant go on with the argument, for my mind isnt settled just now into thinking: our lad, Niall, is very ill with the cursed leucaemia, and we are all anxious, though he has improved, and is so vital that we have hope he'll be with us again soon.

I, of course, am willing to sell anything—bar meself—if the price be good and the conditions satisfactory.

I am writing to Miss Rubin of 522 Fifth Avenue, New York 18., enclosing your letter, for she takes charge of all my American business.

I have heard a rumor that Cyril C[usack]. is going to get a theater in Dublin, for his own use, which, to me, seems not to be good business even on the part of a bad business-man. However, Ireland's the mother of rumors, and the Island is full of sour noises always so we cant say what might happen there, with fire and smoke on the Border. When shall we ever sober down into sense!

> *My warm regards and all good wishes.*
> *Yours very sincerely,*
> *Sean O'Casey.*

To David Krause

TS. KRAUSE

26 DECEMBER 1956

My dear Dave,

Thank you, dear friend for the parcel of fine goods that came on Christmas Eve. I've warned you more 'n once, God knows I have, not to send these things to us. You really must think more of your own needs; you aren't a one with a hoard of cash in the bank, and have to earn what you get in the hard way. You must put aside whatever you can spare for future needs, or for making the place you live in redolent of the picture and the book; and these cost money; more 'n they did a little while ago. So, Dave, a mhic [my son], do think of yourself, now, and for the future, for our affection for you, dear lad, isn't registered with what you so generously send us: we all respect and love Dave Krause for what he is, and we shall always hold him in dear affection.

I am trying to write a kind of a play, and I'm jotting down a few notes for a possible book as well; but it is hard going, for I haven't yet gotten back the old fiery energy I had some little time ago; but one can do but his best; and, anyway, I have to try to write something while the spirit breathes.

We are having a troubled Christmas, a week or some ago—when he came back home for the holidays—Niall was stricken down with leucaemia, and had to be hurried to The Royal Devon and Exeter Hospital, Elizabethan Wing, where he is now lying. He is seriously ill, of course, but cheerful, tho' not resigned to the risk, for he is but 21 years old. I find it hard to write, for he is never out of my mind, and I feel myself everything, or a lot of the things, he feels. He belongs to an uncommon bloodgroup, and this is a bit difficult to get for the blood transfusions he has to have; but, thank God, they have had enough so far, and enough for some little time still. Eileen, of course, is hardest hit, having had me down for nine months, and, tho' home now for nine months, not quite recovered yet. She stays with him as long and as often as she can get permission, and is with him now—Christmas Eve—. She stays at the Clarence Hotel, Cathedral Close, Exeter, Devon. He looks forward to her visits, for she has a peculiar way of encouraging and soothing him, as indeed, she did with me, too. She is a brave lass. Niall may be moving on to St. Bartholomew's Hospital, W. Smithfield, London, on Thursday, and Eileen and Breon will take up quarters in London so as to be near him till we know definitely what will happen. As for me, I feel that the lad will get allright again; but it will be a long time before he's fit again. Such a grand lad, such an analytic mind, such a sense of humor—it is a great misfortune; but we must bear up, and will that he may soon be with us again.

Dave [Greene], our pal, has written to me, and told me he wrote to you, but got no reply, which made me a little anxious about you being well and working. I assume now that you are well and fit, and pegging away with what you have to do.

28? December.

Breon, Shivaun, and I go up to Exeter tomorrow, Christmas Day, to spend an hour or two with Niall, gathering round his bed, giving him his C. Cards and the few presents we got for him. If he be as well as I hope, he can chat away, and it is as good a way to spend an hour, under the circumstances, as to sit by the fire, and moodily think about the sudden and unexpected misfortunes in life. I have seen so many of these things happen among the poor in the slums, "natural causes," they said; and, later on in the fight with the British, and later on still, during our Civil War; so I should by now be hardened; but I'm not. I feel these things within the family, within the community, as much and as keenly as ever.

Went up to join Eileen and spend the christmas hour with Niall. He was too ill to bother about us; only Eileen was needed to bathe the sweat from him, change him into dry pyjamas and encourage him to swallow down as much of the milk and jelly as he could within the quarter of an hour's ease to his throat after taking a drug; a great woman is Eileen. Well, we set out back in the evening through slashing rain and roaring winds, but half way on, we plunged into swirling waters up to the car's bonnet, and had to turn best we could, and crawl back again to London to St. Bartholomew's Hospital, where he lies now. Eileen went with him in the ambulance, then the train, then ambulance, and she is in London now, lodging near as she can get to him. Breon is with her in his little flat, and joins her often as he can; Shivaun and I are mucking in here at home; but it's a painful period, for Niall is ever in my mind. However, Niall has a chance; he is under the Doctor who knows all that is known about the fell disease; and we all hope for the best.

> *God be with you.*
> *My love.*
> *As ever,*
> *Sean*

To J. J. O'Leary

MS. O'LEARY

28 DECEMBER 1956

Dear J.J.

I am relieved that you couldn't come to Torquay during Christmas, & hope you won't have to come early in January, for it mayn't be possible or happy to see you.

Why? Well, just a few days before Christmas, Niall felt unwell, & an examination showed he was stricken with that fell thing—Leucaemia. He was hurried away to Exeter & Devon Hospital, where he had a number of blood-transfusions. Today, at 3.30, an ambulance brought him to the London train, & I'm waiting now for Eileen to ring up (she went with him) to tell me he has reached St. Bartholomew's Hospital, where he will be under the care of Dr. Scott. It has been a harsh time—harshest for Niall, who knows he is dangerously ill. Well, that's the reason, & you will understand it. Please tell Ria [Mooney]; but ask her to [say] nothing about it to anyone: we don't want all sorts of letters coming here; &, maybe, the Press ringing up about it.

I hope you are fit & well. Eileen sends her love, & so do I.

> *Yours very sincerely,*
> *Sean*

To Paul Shyre

MS. SHYRE

28 DECEMBER 1956

My dear Paul,

Hope things go well with you and all.[1]

I had no time to send even a Cable wishing success, for our younger boy aged 21 was smitten with Leucaemia just before Christmas, & we were all upset. He was taken first to Exeter Hospital, & then to St. Bartholomew's Hospital, London, where he is now, dangerously ill. We are hoping for the best.

Don't tell any of the Company, for each has his or her own worries. So have you; but I wanted to let you know why no cable came.

By the way, Paul, if you can, I'd like you to send me a typescript of the Play as you do it, according to the changes I suggested, so that I could have it against any future printing of the play, when the changes could be included. If it gives you too much trouble, please don't bother.

Warm regards & all good wishes.

As ever,
Sean

[1] O'Casey's *Purple Dust* opened in New York at the Cherry Lane Theatre on 27 December 1956, presented by Paul Shyre, Howard Gottfried, Noel Behn, and Lewis Manilow, directed by Philip Burton, with setting, lighting, and costumes by Lester Polakov, and the following cast: Mike Kellin as 1st Workman, Stephen Elliott as 2nd Workman, Robert Geiringer as 3rd Workman, Harry Bannister as Cyril Poges, Paul Shyre as Basil Stoke, Kathleen Murray as Avril, Mary Welch as Souhaun, James Kenny as Barney, Bette Henritze as Cloyne, Alvin Epstein as O'Killigain, Sandy Kenyon as A Yellow-bearded Man, P. J. Kelly as Canon Creehewel, Stefan Gierasch as Postmaster, Alan Bergmann as The Figure.

The play ran for just over a year at the small 189-seat Cherry Lane Theatre in Greenwich Village, the longest run ever for an O'Casey play, closing on 5 January 1958.

To John Gassner

MS. GASSNER

31 DECEMBER 1956

My dear John,

Thanks, indeed, for your kind letter and the article on productions of "St. Joan" and "Pictures in the Hallway."[1] Aside from the Review of the Reading, the comments on the Production of "St. Joan," in the Phoenix, were intensely interesting. I know S. McK. very well, and I was anxious she should do well; tho' I imagine she made a mistake in not insisting on a first-class Caste; possibly thinking that the character of "Joan" alone mattered. But G.B.S. in most of his plays, in my opinion, makes all the characters very important; few of them slip in & slip out again without saying & doing something of value to the play as B. Posnet & the Sergeant in "Devil's Disciple." Your comments are very wise, very fair (wish I could be as wise, as fair), and, in my imaginative opinion, gave a true picture of what was seen and heard in the Phoenix. Your comments on the Reading was, naturally, another pleasant Reading for me; for I know what you say was how you felt about the magic in the actors' work. You give a fine account of Yale, & I hope your talented young student will grow in grace, & be a fine playwright; for God knows the Theater needs him. As for your very fine collection of books, MS, & Photos, I'm afraid any of mine would be useless for they were written in all ways, on all sorts of papers, various old books; & a lot of them destroyed. Don't think I have one example of S. of a Gun. Juno, or P. & the Strs. I must have a look some day when I've time.

I was anxious about "Purple Dust"; but a sad circumstance has put it out of my mind: our younger boy of 21 years died on us on Saturday night, the 29th Dec. He came home on holidays on the 14th tired, & on Monday we knew, & he knew, that he had that fell thing Leukaemia. He had a brilliant mind, a delightful, if somewhat sardonic sense of humor, & was thoughtful & unselfish; a great talker.

Well, just another Golden Lad gone to Dust.

It has been a swift & savage blow to his mother who fought gallantly to save him staying with him many hours each day, nursing him, washing him, & feeding him when the drug opened his throat for a few moments; by God, a gallant fight that failed. We can but bear the blow.

Arvid [Paulson] has had pneumonia. I hope he is quite well again. I shall answer his letter when things are settled.

My love to you, my friend.
As ever
Sean

---

[1] Bernard Shaw's *Saint Joan,* starring Siobhan McKenna, opened at the Phoenix Theatre, New York, on 11 September 1956; O'Casey's *Pictures in the Hallway,* a Stage Reading, adapted by Paul Shyre, opened at the Playhouse Theatre, New York, on 16 September 1956.

To Dr. Frank Morrell

MS. MORRELL

31 DECEMBER 1956

My dear Frank,

Thanks, dear lad, for your kind Christmas Card. I'm not sure if I owe you a letter, for my old mind's a little astray at the moment.

We have just lost our younger boy, Niall, age 21. (He died of Leucaemia on Saturday night at 9 o'c. the 29th Dec. What a dreadful disease is this Leucaemia.) It came as a sudden blow. He came home for the holidays on Friday the 14th, feeling tired, but gay & ignorant of course, of what was wrong with him. Our Doctor on Monday pronounced Leucaemia, & he was hurried to Exeter, & after a few days, to Bartholomew's in London, where he died. Eileen fought gallantly to save him, staying by him, nursing & feeding him—when he could swallow; but it failed on her, as I guessed it would.

Well, it can't be helped, & we must face it bravely as it may be within us to do.

Love. As ever,
Sean

He had a brilliant mind, a good sense of humor, a good, brave nature; & he took his death sentence quietly, tho' no one can know his thoughts. He was well on his way at London University to be a fine Biologist; but the end came too soon for him.

SEAN O'CASEY, 1955

NIALL O'CASEY, 1955

III

THE SACRAMENTS OF
SORROW AND SEX

1957

NIALL's death was a bitter blow, and the heart is bruised. He was a dear lad, handsome, gay, honest, and he and I were very close friends as well as being father and son. We all loved him very dearly, and his end came so swift and so unexpectedly that we still stay stunned. Well, you see, lass, there's no one who hasnt had a sorrow, and sorrow is the one sacrament that binds us together, all men and women the world over; you with yours, me with mine, and ours with others—an endless chain of a bond of sisterhood and brotherhood."

"A word or an action is obscene only when the mind thinks it to be so; and, odd enough, this obscenity in Ireland seems to be exclusively connected with sex. But sex laughs at cleric and censor. When it comes, a physiological upsurge, the robin sports a redder breast, the lapwing gets himself another crest,

a livelier iris changes on the dove, and dodging into secret
places go the lover and his lass."

Throughout this year of mourning for his dead son, O'Casey tries to
endure what he calls "the sacrament of sorrow" by writing about it in
his elegiac letters, sharing his grief with many friends and strangers. After
three months, in early April, he confesses that the pain of his lost son is
always there: "He still keeps very close to me, though I try to bury
myself in work; but, without any conscious cause, memory of him sweeps
over me, tears come, and I hear myself crying out his dear name." But the
written word gradually functions as an essential part of his catharsis. He
starts a new comedy in the hope of easing the burden of personal tragedy,
as he tells George Jean Nathan in July: "I wrote it, I suppose, to help me
keep from thinking of things that can never be forgotten." His art was
always an act of faith and transfiguration for him, more than ever now.
Meanwhile, he was also sustained by the continuing good news from New
York, where *Purple Dust* was well launched on its successful run for the
rest of the year.

It was that New York success which apparently revived the malice of
the Dublin drama critics, who now took pleasure in reporting, errone-
ously, in two of the major Irish newspapers, that the O'Casey play had
failed in America. In several February letters to Dublin friends, O'Casey
takes even greater pleasure in exposing this backbiting, as well as a number of misrepresentations in the press about him, and temporarily his gratifying corrections help him forget his sorrow as he assumes his old fighting
manner. O'Casey is nothing if he is not a richly comic writer, and he is
more amused than outraged when he quotes one critical judgment against
himself by a malicious Dubliner: "O'Casey probably thinks he is a devil of
a fellow at the writing of comedy. This he is not, as the medium is alien to
him as a writer." He is not amused when he contradicts a dear friend, a
devout Irish Catholic, who had tried to assure him that man cannot understand the ways of God, who must have had a mysterious and divine reason for taking Niall away from life. Momentarily O'Casey comes to terms
with his sorrow by replying with this typical example of what might be
called his pragmatic skepticism: "Why do you think God's ways are ununderstandable? It wasn't God who killed Niall, it was Leucaemia—unless
God created the bug or the virus, or whatever causes it; and, if a God exists, I'd hardly say he had any hand in it. As Shaw says, 'It isnt we who
are in God's hands, it is God who is in ours.' And if we wont deal with the
things that plague us and destroy us, then we damn well have to suffer."

God and religion are common concerns in the letters, and O'Casey
tries to be pragmatic when he links them to the creative arts or to what he

broadly describes as his visionary Communism. When the Yale Divinity School student asks him about T. S. Eliot's religious beliefs, he thinks of Eliot primarily as a poet and says in early February, "There's more in his poetry than merely religious belief." In a similar way he might have claimed that there is much more in his own plays than merely Communist belief. And later in February he is still trying to convince a reluctant Brooks Atkinson that the drama critic of the capitalist *New York Times* is really an ideal Communist because he performs his writing task to the best of his ability: "Your best brief is Criticism; and the best Communist is he who uses his best faculty for the added knowledge and surety of man—a truth ignored by many of them." And good Communist that he is himself, O'Casey tells an American friend in late March that he must work on his new play, even if he is not enthusiastic about it, because "it wouldn't be good just to stay idly looking out of a window. It is said God never ceases working out His way, so why the hell should I?"

He continued to work out his own way by refusing to remain idle, by writing his play, by starting a new book of essays, and by becoming involved in public as well as private matters in his correspondence. In a series of letters to the *Irish Times* he takes a stand on the controversial issues of civil war, censorship, and sex in Ireland. In March he calls for an end of violence in Northern Ireland by total tolerance on both sides, because "gunfire will never make friends." In May he gets into an argument with a priest who demanded that writers in Ireland must reject "obscenity" and adhere to the morality of the Catholic faith; to which O'Casey replies: "Literature demands excellent writing, not caring a damn what religion the writer may be." In June he takes on "another Richmond in the field" who denounces the terrible sin of "sexual corruption," which prompts O'Casey to declare: "It is near time that these banning boobies realise that God made the bottom as well as the top of the body." In all of these instances he defends views that he presents in his later plays, through a comic and satiric dramatization of political and religious and sexual enlightenment. Nevertheless, his running argument with Ireland remains in large part a lover's quarrel, for in spite of his complaints, he tells a Russian editor in May, "Ireland takes the first place in my heart, and will until the end comes."

O'Casey also has room in his heart for a host of loyal friends, many of them women in Ireland, England, and America, who instinctively trust him and share their lives with him. In June he writes to one of these special women, Georgie Cooper, moving away from large issues to more mundane matters, and he tells her about some new friends he has discovered in his garden: "I have made friends with a blackbird, a robin, and a cock and hen bullfinch, all of whom I feed with scraps of fat and biscuit-crumb as well as supplying them with water. The robin comes to my knee, the hen bullfinch on to the toe of my boot, the cock watching her, and the blackbird stays a few feet away, cocking an eye at me, and piping a tune; so I have a happy hour or two with the lot of them. Tonight I listen on the wireless to a Concert of French Composers." It was a day of simple pleasures, with an anticipation of fine music. His favorite was Mozart, but in September the experimental playwright tells Georgie he has heard the experimental music of Anton Webren: "A curious, new, spare music of strange rhythms. I couldn't enjoy most of it; but a Dead March was strangely beautiful."

In literature he concentrates on the classics, as he tells a Yale graduate student in November, remembering how as a young man he educated himself by buying second-hand copies of Shakespeare and the Elizabethans, and "Shelley, Byron, Keats, Burns, Dickens, Thackeray, Milton, Whitman, and Emerson . . . Jane Austen and Charlotte Bronte. But I dont try to imitate any of them; I sit down with them, talk to them, drink with them, have even whored with some of them, S, for instance; just for the holy and happy joy of it all." Emerson, as well as Shakespeare and Whitman, was always one of his special literary deities, he reminds Atkinson in November. Himself a devout Emersonian, the Yankee Atkinson must have been surprised to hear again about O'Casey's conversion to Communism, but this time how it was hastened when as a young man he bought a used copy of Emerson's works—"what I read there helped to open my mind to Communism." Ralph Waldo Emerson, transcendentalist and Communist!

Several days after his agreement with Atkinson that in a non-dogmatic and non-institutional way "all Art is religious, and is part of man's transfiguration," O'Casey makes a similar point to another of his regular women friends; but this time he adds that the religious aspect of art includes "the laughter of the clown as well as the prayer of the sorrowful or the saint. Falstaff is as religious a character as Hamlet, & more so than Wolsey." In a June letter to a sixteen-year-old "Welsh-speaking Welshman," he draws a similar parallel in claiming that the aim of drama is entertainment, not instruction: "Hamlet is as entertaining as Falstaff."

O'Casey strikes another blow for the art of entertainment in a September letter to Harold Macmillan, his old publisher-friend and now Prime Minister, by calling for proper recognition of Gordon Craig, the pioneer of theatrical design who was a sadly neglected octogenarian: "You are very apt to dilate upon the hide-bound attitude toward Art in the USSR, but, at least, they gave Stanislavsky a Theatre. Did you do that much for Gordon Craig? No, by God, you didn't!" Several days later the septuagenarian O'Casey shifts from amusing indignation to amusing humility when he confesses to the wife of his doctor that he is somewhat weary of his own entertaining plays: "In the 'Hereafter,' Mary, I hope God may not penalise me by making me watch, & listen to, the performances of my own plays: I am well tired of most of them already."

Nevertheless, as the year draws to a close, his new play, *The Drums of Father Ned,* has been accepted by the Dublin Drama Festival for performance during the Tostal celebration in May 1958. There is some hope in this news, though O'Casey and his wife dread the thought of Christmas and the anniversary of Niall's death.

To J. J. O'Leary

MS. O'LEARY

4 JANUARY 1957

My dear J.J.

Our Niall died last Saturday night, 29th Dec., and was cremated today, 3rd Jan.[1] It was a swift death—he was a gay soul at a Party just a week or so before, & when he came down on holiday here, no one imagined he'd be dead in a few days. Rather ironical that it wasn't I, an old codger of 76, who didn't lead the way out of the world; but there the mystery begins & there the mystery ends.

I'm doubtful about your idea of a book about Larkin; there are few now living who were in close touch with Larkin—bar William O'Brien & Cathal O'Shannon, who stood in his way when he came back from the American Jail; & Barney Conway, who couldn't write, tho' a grand old soul, who loved Larkin for Larkin's own sake; for what the great man was.

Do you know there's a Life of Larkin, by R. M. Fox,[2] coming out soon? Some one sent it to me for Review, but I'm not a reviewer, & besides, the book is a dull one. A Jim Larkin[3] of New York has written a thesis on Jim, & told me he hoped to get it, finally, into book-form to be published. So, for awhile, anyway, unless for collecting items from old friends—if there be any alive—for a future publication, I don't think anything would go just now.

> *All good wishes,*
> *Yours very sincerely,*
> *Sean.*

[1] Niall O'Casey's ashes were dispersed on 3 January 1957 at the Garden of Remembrance, Golders Green Crematorium, London, where Sean O'Casey's ashes were eventually to be dispersed on 3 October 1964.

[2] R. M. Fox, *Jim Larkin: The Rise of the Underman* (1957).

[3] This should be Emmet Larkin (no relation), who wrote a doctoral dissertation on Jim Larkin at Columbia University in 1956, and it was later expanded and published as *James Larkin, Labour Leader, 1876–1947* (1965).

To J. J. O'Leary

MS. O'LEARY

4 JANUARY 1957

My dear J.J.

Enclosed is a little Booklet issued monthly by an Iowan Gypsum Co. John Cooper is a manager there, & he and his wife are friends of mine. She has poetry in her, a very sensitive, pretty, & clever girl; a very good player of the piano, and a wide knowledge of literature. Both are Mississippians, & now are in Iowa.

It struck me the Director of our Irish Gypsum Co. might be interested to see the magazine. Some time ago, there was a fine article on this Industry in "Inniu," but it didn't give the names of the management—just, far as I remember, gave a description of the process, & how everything was done.

You're a big business man—I saw you in a recent "Irish Times"—& probably know the Company, or, maybe, have something to do with it. John asked me if it had (the Company) any American connections. I said I didn't think so; but I don't know.

Niall was cremated yesterday: a gallant lad gone.

All the best to you,
Sean.

To Boris Polevoy[1]

TC. O'CASEY

5 JANUARY 1957

My dear friend,

Thank you so much for your kind letter and your fine and good wishes for the year that is with us all, with you in Moscow, and with me in Devon. For all the miles away, we are not very distant, the one from the other. My Irish love and my Irish good wishes to you, to the work you do, to your friends, and to your great People.

The year has started for us. We lost our lad of 21 years a few days before the New Year began. He was a fine lad of six feet, a sharp analytical mind that promised to make him a first-class biologist; he had a lovely sense of humor; loved Mozart, Beethoven, Haydn, and your Chaikovsky, and also had a love for New Orleans Jazz. He had a keen sense of what

[1] Boris Polevoy, Union of Soviet Writers, Moscow, U.S.S.R.

was fair to others, and followed the progress of your Country with insistent interest. He was saving up to go to the Youth Festival in Moscow in July of this year, and looked forward to this visit to Russia; but the damned disease of Leucaemia struck him suddenly in the bloom of his youth and activity—he loved football—and within a few days he was dead.

Now, we can but carry on, always remembering him with deep love, and live and care for, our other two children; and fight on for peace so that all time and attention may be given to save men from these terrible diseases, and so make life a happier and more secure adventure. Our lad loved life up to the last, and so shall we, and work to make it free from the evil of war, fear, and illness.

Please give my love to your colleagues, and take a good share in it yourself.

By the way, my dear Boris, I am no teacher, but one making a way through life, facing many problems, knowing that sorrow and loss is part of life, and determined to face these things too, trying to make the least of them, while making the most of the happiness and the joy which life shares out to all.

Yours very sincerely,
Sean O'Casey.

To Thomas Quinn Curtiss[1]

TS. CURTISS

9 JANUARY 1957

My dear Tom,

A happy New Year to you, too, a mhic!

I am sorry to hear about our George,[2] but I'm afraid he wont be able again to be what he was; it is, eventually, the lot of us all. George wont miss seeing a lot of people, for he was never a one for welcoming crowds, and was always careful, as far as I knew him, about whom he allowed over his threshold. One thing should be a comfort to him—he can look back on a full and active life; can look back over all he has done for the Theater, in his own country, and in many other lands too. His writings live, and are as lively and as effective as ever. He should be able to face his present dis-

---

[1] Thomas Quinn Curtiss, drama critic of the *New York Herald Tribune,* International Edition, in Paris.

[2] In early 1956 George Jean Nathan had to undergo prostate surgery for a second time.

ability with the remembrance that there was but one Nathan and will never be another, as there will never be another Shaw: Nathan is unique. When you see him, give him my full love.

Thanks for your kind article which I had not read. There's one little error—we live here in a flat, not cottage. It seems a long, long time since I had the controversy with J. Agate.

As for my "projects," Tom, they must wait awhile, for at the moment, I'm not in a state to think bravely or decently about life and all it has, and all it may mean; for a great blow has struck the family into a curious, quiet sorrow: Our dear Niall of 21 years, died on us on December the 29th, after little more than a week's illness with Leucaemia. Less than a fortnight before, he was dancing, he was gay, though feeling a little tired, when he was stricken down, and the doctors gave him his death sentence. He was a gallant lad, and died gallantly; but it was a great loss to us, and, maybe, to others, for he gave a fine promise of becoming a first-class biologist. He was cremated on Jan. the 4th, and is now but a handful of purple dust scattered over the Garden of Remembrance. Eileen was with him almost all the time in hospital, and she and Breon were with him when he died. She seems to be bearing it well, but it must be a shocking blow to her. So you will understand, dear Tom, that definite work with me is at a standstill. I did jot down some notes for possible play, and more for another book of Comments, to be called "Words, Idle Words," but these must rest where they are till I get accustomed to the curious and still incomprehensible vacancy left in the family by our dear Niall's death. I feel ashamed that I, a one of 76, who went through so much in a recent illness, should be left living, while such a young, gay, and active lad should be taken away. It is a bitter reflection. But we must try to face it all, and try to face it bravely.

It's grand that George has Julie with him, and that he is able to write some things, even though he is handicapped. Alas, we all have to meet this semi-retirement sometime or another. Time goes so damned quick that it is on top of us before we are ready for it; but George has a galaxy of books behind him, all fine ones, and that should give him some satisfaction: his life has been a full day with a lot of overtime. There isnt a speck of rust on George's whole nature; it is well-worn, but it shines brilliantly from constant use; he has fulfilled a great mission. At the end, he is bound to hear "Well done, good and faithful servant." I hope all of us may do as well.

Eileen and Breon send their love to you, and so do I.

Yours as ever,
Sean

To Hilda Pollak

TC. O'CASEY

11 JANUARY 1957

Dear Hilda,

I got your letter which illuminated your past and your present, and I see you, though as through a glass, darkly. It would seem to me that you tend to undervalue yourself more than a wee bit. It is obvious that you have a keen intelligence, and tell me what greater gift could God or nature bestow upon a being than an intelligent and active mind? Why with this gift should a body be depressed, or grieve as one without hope? I understand how your father, maybe, thought too much of the "cause" than he thought of his children; there are a lot who do this; and in Ireland, too, I've seen it often; giving up all, not for any social cause, but for an abstract devotion for Ireland under the abstract symbol of "Kathleen ni Houlihan"; even Yeats was immured within the symbol for a while when he wrote the play of the same name; and so was I. I remember a play in Russia some years ago which depicted a man who was so good a Communist that he neglected his family, and only at times knew they existed. A common sin with idealists. I've had them with me, even from America, and at time lost patience; for, say a doctor or lawyer, may be a damned fine Communist, but if the one be a poor doctor what good is he to his patient, and, if the other be a poor lawyer, what good is he to his client? If one be either, he (or she) must first be a good doctor or a good lawyer before he can be a good and useful Communist. It doesnt follow that because one is good at this or at that, that he or she loses a high dedication; on the contrary, the high dedication is strengthened, and made more effective. To me, the best psychiatrist is oneself; no remedy is of much use without one's own resolution and effort. After all, in spite of politics, or war, of stupidities, we are surrounded by beautiful things, and in spite of television, radio, and theater, the world is full of sweet noises. Art, literature, and music are with us, and science too. Man is moving, and man is more than Hilda Pollak or Sean O'Casey. Of course, you were disorganised when your sister, whom you loved, died: death always does this, materially, and when a loved one goes, psychologically too, and deeply so. But life must go on, and we must, if we're wise, make it as effective and as bright as we can in another way and to another rhythm. It cant be done quick and smoothly; and persistent effort is needed. I'm not just preaching now, for a cloud of sorrow has covered me, and covers me still: on December the 29th, last, our younger boy of just over 21 years died of Leucaemia, and on Jan. the 3rd his body was cremated, leaving but a tiny handful of purple dust. He was a grand lad, six feet tall, lithe and active and handsome. He loved life, and was dancing and delightful less than a fortnight before he was dead; he had a lovely sense of humor, and was a lover of Beethoven and Mozart and Jazz, and could play well on the trombone. He was an ardent progressive, and cherished the ideal of a finer and a better world for men. He was studying biology at London University, and gave good promise of becoming a first-class biologist, for he had an intense and probing mind. And all are gone now, and as I loved him dearly, it was a great blow to me; and a worse one to his mother who loved him as I did, and, perhaps more deeply. Indeed, all who knew him had a deep affection for him. So you sorrow for a sister while I sorrow for a son. At the age of 76, it is hard to get used to such a swift and unexpected change in family life; but an effort must be made, even through a way of tears.

So, Hilda, you arent alone in missing one you loved. When I got your letter on the 21 of December last, I little thought that eight days after our boy would have gone from us. That is why we should feel for others, for we can never tell when a sorrow may fall upon ourselves. So, Hilda, be brave as I am trying to be brave, though it is far from easy when I remember all the dear associations I had with our Niall.

But two more children, one old, one younger than he, and we must think of them, and do what we can to make their lives as secure and as happy as we can; though these trials leave a bitter scar upon the heart. That is why I asked you to tell me something about your life, so that I might know you better, and feel the association—even though it be but by letter—more sensibly.

All good wishes and warm regards to you,

Yours very sincerely,
[Sean O'Casey]

To Paul and Nan Ross

MS. ROSS

11 JANUARY 1957

My dear Paul & my dear Nan,

Thanks a great many for your kind sympathy with Eileen and me at the loss of our very dear son. It is, of course, a heavy & bitter blow. It came very swift, & was utterly unexpected—the way these things often come. A fortnight before, he was dancing, and full of confidence, and suddenly, within a few days, was mingling his dust with the golden lads & lasses who had gone before him. He died bravely, talking to Eileen earnestly about keeping an ideal at all costs. He was a dear friend of mine, & we often and often had long discussions about Socialism & the ways of the world. He added a lovely sense of humor to a keen probing mind and gave good promise of becoming a first-class biologist. Well, at least, it has joined us in a link of sorrow with those brothers and sisters who have suffered a like loss—with you, closely, for Merrill and Niall were spiritual comrades.[1] I have one thought of comfort—that for so many years, I have hated & always fought against, the waste of young life in war or by illness; for I verily believe that both can be banished from life; and have always detested the hateful heresy that excused the death of our young in the poem of "They will not grow old as we grow old." That is youth's first heritage—that they will live to grow old as we have lived to grow old: if this isn't God's law it is nature's law; & this law must be strengthened so as to shelter & protect all our young.

My love to you both, and special love to Gil & Joyce, whom may God preserve to you & to the world of man.

As ever,
Sean

---

[1] The Rosses' son, Dr. Merrill Ross, had died of Hodgkin's Disease in 1951 at the age of 26. See O'Casey's letter to Paul and Nan Ross, 1 October 1953, note 1, Vol. II.

To Brooks Atkinson

MS. ATKINSON

12 JANUARY 1957

My very dear Brooks & my very dear Oriana,
Thank you both from our hearts for your cable and your letters of sympathy. It is a comfort to feel sympathy flowing from very dear friends into our hearts. Niall was a gallant lad, & died bravely. In his delirium, half an hour before he died, he babbled of our going to America (meaning of course, the U.S.A.), & there we would see "Purple Dust"; a little later, he was a handful of purple dust himself. He had been deeply troubled by the tragedy in Hungary, & couldn't agree with me that it was a sad necessity.[1] He vehemently opposed my view, &, seeing him so earnest, I embraced him, kissed him, & urged him not to bother about my view, but to hold on to his own. Curious, I embraced him, for none of us then had the faintest idea of what was waiting for him. Two weeks later, he was

---

[1] For a moving account of his disagreement with his son over the "sad necessity" of Russia's suppression of the Hungarian Rising, see his essay on his son's death, "Under a Greenwood Tree He Died," *Under a Colored Cap* (1963), especially pp. 122–23. See also his letter to Kay O'Riordan, 27 November 1956, note 1, and the Introduction to 1956.

dead. It is a bitter blow, but we must bear it, even though tears go with the bearing. We miss him in the home, but we miss him, too, in our hearts, which is harder to bear.

I'm glad, dear Brooks, you let your article about me stand.[2] As a Critic, you are concerned with no one's personal troubles. As a very dear friend, of course, you are concerned with ours. There was nothing in the article that could in any way worry or bother me: it was very kind, and very true.

I am glad "P. Dust" promises to go well, for dollars can ease the way one has to live.

Death has done all Death can and we must go on without our lad, though it will be harder going.

Eileen sends her love to you both, and, dear Brooks, dear Oriana, so do I.

As ever,
Sean

[2] Brooks Atkinson, "Comic Exuberance," *New York Times,* 6 January 1957. Atkinson praised the production of *Purple Dust,* though he did not rank it among O'Casey's best work; but he also commented on O'Casey's penchant for controversy, and he had thought of eliminating these remarks out of respect for his friend, who was in mourning for his dead son. Here is the passage which he "let stand," which begins with a calculation on why O'Casey's plays are so seldom performed: "Perhaps the fact that like Shaw, whom he revered, Mr. O'Casey professes to be a Communist has congealed the pocketbooks of backers. Mr. O'Casey is a turrible man on paper. At home with his family and friends he is a mild and lovable old codger disarmingly humble about his talent. But put a piece of paper in front of him and he starts hurling thunderbolts over the landscape. He has more feuds up his sweater sleeve than the Hatfields and McCoys. 'The Green Crow,' as he calls himself in his last book, is a turrible cawer."

To Christopher M. Grieve
(Hugh MacDiarmid)

MS. EDINBURGH UNIV LIB

12 JANUARY 1957

My very dear Chris,

Thanks for your sympathy, and for Valda's[1] & Michael's good sympathy, too. We've suffered a bitter blow, and my heart is bruised. Niall was 21, a gallant lad, grand sense of humor, gay, and reliable. He bid fair to become a first-class biologist. He was deeply troubled over the tragedy of Hungary, & couldn't find a reason for the Soviet action. He came from

[1] Valda Trevlyn, MacDiarmid's second wife.

London to talk with me about it, but couldn't agree with my view that it was a sad necessity. I insisted he should have his own opinion, while I held on to mine. We shook hands and embraced, thank God, deciding that each opinion was sacred. He came down with his sister, Shivaun, for the holidays, driving a small van, and a few days later he was dead.

I listened to "Drunk Man"[2] on the Third, and enjoyed it immensely. I have your Tribute to Joyce,[3] but haven't read it yet. I was in hospital for 5 months; two big operations, &, in between, an attack of bronchial-pneumonia; so I was left pretty low after it all; but after 6 months, I began to pull out, & am now fairly fit, and trying to get away from the recent shock of losing a lad I dearly loved. Eileen was with him all the time, & gave him great comfort, so that he died a brave boy.

My deep love to you, Chris, to Valda, & to your Michael.

As ever,
Sean

[2] *A Drunk Man Looks at the Thistle* (1926), a book of poems.
[3] *In Memoriam James Joyce* (1955), a book of poems.

Rex MacGall[1]

TS. MacGall

12 January 1957

Dear Rex MacGall,

I'm afraid, I shall be disappointing. I cannot advise you for or against what you propose to do. You have a wife and four children, and these must, of course, be your first concern; or ought to be, in my opinion. Looks like your clann is a young one, too, since Oisin is but a year old, or was when you went to Arann, which makes things more complicated. I am sorry that your wife isnt so well, nidh nach ionagh [no wonder], having four boys, all in a row, apparently. What a time Irish women have! Now, are you sure that, if you go on with the PLOUGH[2] you will hold the jobs you have already? What you get from the three of them—Radio Eireann, Irish Independent, and The Farmer's Journal, isnt a lot on which to keep so many lives going; and you cant afford to lose them. Can you hold them if you are connected with the PLOUGH? Would you, then, become "redundant" as you became with The Irish Press? You see, there are many things to be considered, and you are the one to do this, and not I. All this

[1] MacGall wrote his letter in Gaelic.
[2] *The Plough,* a new socialist weekly newspaper in Dublin.

is apart from the possibility—not a remote one, in my opinion—that the PLOUGH will find it hard to push a furrow long and fruitful enough to keep the work in action.

As for the loss of job in the I.P., you say that Ben Kiely (Benedict?) will do the work along with his own. Is he a member of the Union you think so much of; and, if he is, why should he take up the work of another member who has been sacked? As for being hesitant about working for the Independent, those who called for [James] Connolly's death are, I daresay, gone, and you cant blame others who had nothing to do with the then policy of the paper, so long as they dont want you to write something that is against the conscience of an honest man. You have some good names for your adventure: [Máirtín Ó] Cadhain who, I think is he who writes for the Irish Times, [Prof. David] Greene who lectured recently in memory of T[homas]. Davis, May Keating who has written to me long ago, and B. Behan, whose play I like—I've read it, and Mrs. O'C. my daughter Shivaun, and Niall, saw it—they paid for their seats, tell B.B.; the others I dont know. Pity P.OD [Peadar O'Donnell] didn't join you, but I'm sure he had a good reason for refusing. I wish I could tell you to go ahead, but I wouldnt dare take on this big responsibility of putting anyone into the danger of losing his living: it is for you yourself to decide.

As for writing an article—it will be some time, indeed, before I am in a vein for writing: the loss of our Niall who was 21 has bruised the heart and has made the mind slow to think of a thing other than what the memory brings back of our boy. Besides, anything from me would go to damn all your hopes, and nullify all your efforts. There is but one thing I can do—this: If you let me know to whom a check is to be made out, I'll send one for five guineas as, at least, a token of good will.

Such a Journal is sharply needed in Ireland, and there should be men and women enough to give it a hearing; if not, then Ireland is a vain thing and a shadow of life only.

I hope your wife is better, and that you are managing fairly well with the three children.

All good wishes to you and your comrades.
Yours very sincerely,
Sean O'Casey.

To George Jean Nathan

TS. CORNELL

26 JANUARY 1957

My very very dear George:

Many thanks for your letter.[1] I am sorry that you are still ill, but these things are hard to shake off, but we can, at least, battle against them. It is more than a year since I fell ill, and I am still, like you, under the doctor's care, and am unable to go into the full swing of work as I used to do, for tiredness comes on, and one has to surrender to it with some sighing. It is very gratifying to me that PURPLE DUST got such good notices from the New York Critics, and, from what I hear, the play is likely to have something of a run. Not that I am very concerned personally, for I'm too old now to throw up my cap, and go out to cheer in the streets; but it is very useful to Eileen and to the children, and gives them a chance of living safely that they very much needed. Of course, a lot of good praise is to go to the Director and the actors, and the Designer, too, who all seem to have done extremely well with a small stage and limited funds. Paul Shyre who organised the Readings of the Biography seems to have the gift of the Theater in him, and it was very fortunate for me that he has, and that he interested himself in my work.

As for your kind interest in my receiving the Nobel Prize, please, my son, don't bother yourself about this again; nevermore. Really, I don't care a damn, and, indeed, it might be a nuisance, for it would mean the descent upon me of a horde of reporters, the constant ringing of the telephone, and a fuss that I am no longer interested in—if I ever was. Believe me, your awards are more important to me than a dozen from the various Academies of the world. I have always been sceptical of Academic awards, and I've so often seen the crowning of clowns (poor clowns, too, for the great clown is a great artist too), that I often give a hoot when I hear of another literary coronation; and, anyway, what good is an Academy if they have to be told what to do? Such an award would have no honor in it. As for the money, well, that's allright; but your country has helped me so much for the past few years that I have been able to sit back, smile, and murmur God's blessing on the U.S.A.; and you, me dear lad, have had a lot to do with that blessing. So rest as much as you can, take things as easy as you can, and be sure I am never very far away from you in my admiration for you and my deep love for you too.

> *My hand in yours,*
> *As ever,*
> *Sean*

Now, don't trouble to reply.

[1] Nathan was too ill and weak to write himself and dictated the letter to his wife, Julie Haydon.

To Louis Sheaffer[1]

MS. SHEAFFER

28 JANUARY 1957

Dear friend, (all lovers of O'Neill are friends)

No one's a stranger to me, tho' all strangers aren't friends. I haven't answered your first letter because a bruising blow just borne by the death of a young beloved son kept me careless about other things. As you say, I, too, have to try to deal with a few requests out of hundreds. I'm afraid this letter may be disappointing to you, for I have little to say; but what I have, here I say it: I first heard his name from the great Irish Labor Leader, Jim Larkin—not unlike O'Neill in stature, & one, too, who once went down to the sea in ships. Larkin was a beloved friend of mine, knew I was interested in the theater, saw "The Hairy Ape" in New York;[2] told me about it, & said, "You should get this play, Sean; O'Neill has a great gift, and will be heard of in days to come." A good prophecy, by God! Long afterwards, I got the play, with others, & immediately entered into understanding of the greatness of the man who wrote them. Like the towers of Illium, he was topless. Dramatic glory shows round about him. Of course, he wore a mask at times; he didn't appear naked before every Tom, Dick & Harry; but in his plays, he revealed himself, body, soul, and spirit; and in his last play, "Long Journey,"[3] he holds up a flaming torch showing the nooks & crannies of a younger life, and transcends it with a poetic vision. Oh, Eugene, Eugene, your going is a great loss to the Theater. There was a giant in the American Theater in his day.

O'Neill wasn't a ready correspondent. He concentrated on his plays in a wise way. He wasted little time. So I got few letters from him[4]— three or four; but where they are now, God only knows, so I can't send them to you, for it might mean a hunt of weeks among the MS. letters, etc., I have in a big chest; and I haven't the heart or energy for a search. The friend of his youth & riper years—a very dear friend—is G. Jean Nathan, and he must have many, if he has kept them. He mentions Eugene many times in his books. G.J. is now very ill, & shouldn't be disturbed; but Mrs. Julie Nathan might help you. If I remember right, Eugene wrote to

---

[1] Louis Sheaffer, author of *O'Neill, Son and Playwright* (1968).

[2] Eugene O'Neill's *The Hairy Ape* opened in New York at the Playwrights' Theatre on 9 March 1922.

[3] Eugene O'Neill's *Long Day's Journey Into Night* opened in New York on 7 November 1956.

[4] See O'Neill's letters to O'Casey, 15 December 1933, Vol. I; and 5 August 1943, Vol. II.

me from California & from Georgia. His publishers got out a Brochure about him years ago and I wrote a few comments for this booklet. I met Eugene in New York, and was with him several times. I can honestly say I was a friend of his. The first visit was with Mr. Nathan, when Eug. feeling lonely in Calif. came to N. York, and was staying in a hotel in Madison Avenue—the Madison Hotel? On the way, Mr. Nathan—a soul-friend (anam-cara, we call this in Irish) of Eugene's, bought a few little toys for his friend—it was Eug.'s birthday, I think—, & this, meant as a joke, was none, for Eug. was a child as well as a great man to the end. Eugene wore a new pair of Daks—present from Carlotta, and was very proud of them in a child-like way. The moment we met, we got close together, & were at once Eugene, Sean, and George. Carlotta was there, of course, and presented herself as a very beautiful woman, devoted to Eug. She, too, became a friend, & I was Sean to her & she was Carlotta to me. We spoke of many things from Daks to the Drama. When I told Eug. what I thought of him, he was pleased, but took the praise like a shy child. He wasn't really conscious of his greatness: he took this in his stride, & was concerned only in the work he had done & that which he thought of doing. The last time, when I was going, we embraced, & realised that our feelings for one another came close to love. Of course, Eug. was of Irish extraction, but he was thorough American; tho', on the strength of this extraction he accepted association with the Irish Academy of Letters founded by W. B. Yeats, the Irish Poet.

O'Neill is one of the most famous Gaelic names Ireland has; a great Ulster name given to Ireland's greatest Clan Chiefs, and many Septs branch from this prime O'Neill clan name; so certainly Eugene was of Irish extraction, & a famous one, too.

I can't see a reason why Carlotta should put any obstacle in the way of a Life of O'Neill. His life, in my opinion, should be recorded, however hard the work may be. It was a full life, an adventurous life in many more ways than one; and a great man should have mention made of him, how-ever inadequate the mention may be. We can never get to know the whole man, for that wasn't known even to himself; but we should set out to get to know as much as we can of one who took such a great and influential part, not only in the American theater, but in American life.

I do hope Carlotta may see this to be so. If you ever see her, give her the love of O'Casey.

I'm sorry I can't do more than this; but, unfortunately fate put many thousands of miles of space between him & me. "An' seas between us braid ha' roared."

All good wishes to the big work you set yourself to do.

Yours sincerely,
Sean O'Casey

To Boris Polevoy

TC. O'CASEY

[? FEBRUARY 1957]

Boris Polevoy of Kalinin and the USSR.

My dear young friend,

I put my hand in yours with a strong and an earnest clasp, with esteem for you as a Russian, as a fine Author, and as a family man; and, too, as a Citizen of a country that has given so much hope and so much leadership to the world of men.

I know something of what the Peoples of the USSR suffered in the recent terrible war, for I have read many accounts of what was done there, of the frightful destruction done by the monstrous Nazis, and of the heroic stand the Red Army made against a destroying and terrible foe; a stand that finally gave the Red Army and the dauntless People, the bright banner of victory. I suffered real grief during your Army's retreat, and at the destruction of so many fair and happy places; then, afterwards, I passed into a great joy at the mighty resistance of Moscow, of Leningrad, and of Stalingrad; a joy that swelled into a shout when the Red Army surrounded the Nazi Army under Paulus, and captured the enemy hosts on the banks of the Volga. May it be the last time that war soils and harrows the peaceful soul of humanity. My sympathy with, and my love for, you and all your People who still feel the stings of their wounding.[1] The two garlands of sorrow and joy bind us all together. "I will bear it like a man, but I must also feel it like a man," said Macduff in Shakespeare's MACBETH, when he heard of the loss of his "wife and all his chicks." So must we, too: feel our loss keenly, but bear it like a man, a "real man," for there is many a problem to be faced, many fights to be waged in the future before us.

I read your book[2] a long time ago, and I have just read it again—I read slowly, but after awhile, I have to give my old eyes a rest. Yours is a grand story of heroism, of a gallent success in overcoming a terrible physical handicap; of facing life shortened of limbs, and entering fully into active life again. The story is finely written, even in translation, and I followed your Hero through his agony, his despair, and out of it all into resolute courage, and final victory into joy and activity again. Thank you for the volume. It will, indeed, be a welcome addition to the books I have.

I was grieved to read of the loss of your Scientist Manuilsky by the fell disease that killed our own boy. This is one of your present-day fights—to save the worthy from a too early departure from us; the noble

---

[1] Polevoy and his wife each lost two brothers in World War II.

[2] Boris Polevoi, *The Story of a Real Man* (1947), translated from the Russian by Eve Manning.

spirits who strive for others even before themselves. Give my deep love to your family. May they never know the dreadful waste and woe of war again; and my love to all your comrade-writers and to the People who gave birth to so many women and men who added honor to the name of man; and for those two great souls, Lenin and Stalin, who led their People in the way of Socialism, and gave courage to so many other peoples to go the same way, towards a brotherhood of all men, the world over.

As for my own country, Ireland, she is in the grip of clericalism today, and there is very little freedom of thought, but signs are showing that there are men and women there who are gaining the courage to stand up and sing, and speak their minds against the tyranny of bishop and priest; but it is a hard fight, but hard as it may be, it is being fought, and if it werent for the bitter feeling between the southern Catholic and the northern Protestant, the fight would be a merry one, and victory would come sooner than we can expect it today. In Scotland, too, the fight goes on. The other day, the Supreme Judge, a Lord Clyde, gave judgement that a Communist and Atheist could not be left in charge of his own child, though, in every other respect, the father was an exemplary man; an illegal judgement, for Communism here is not illegal, nor does atheism come under the law; but, as usual, this insolent Judge has the support of the wealthy and the clerics of the various churches. There is growing a vigorous opposition to this judgement, led by Scotland's greatest poet, Hugh MacDiarmuid, a very dear friend of mine.

Thank you, dear young friend, and thanks to your family for their sympathy in the loss of our beloved son, who was preparing to take part in the coming Festival of Youth to be held in Moscow during the coming July, and I was looking forward to his meeting your People, and returning to tell me a lot about your great City; but we must bear these sad things till we can bring about a state of life when such mishaps will be rare, and, I believe, will be ultimately unknown.

My love to you, and an old Irishman's blessing on you and your family.

Yours very sincerely,
Sean O'Casey

To Seumas Scully

TS. SCULLY

4 FEBRUARY 1957

Dear Seumas,

Thanks a lot for the cuttings, only a few of which I have read already. I'm sorry you didnt like the new play,[1] though the Irish "critics" seemed to write well of it. Was it a failure? Why didnt they give it a longer chance, or are they still afraid of an empty till? I dont altogether like a play of mine[2] following a new one that hasnt run, for it looks like I was laughing at the effort of another, which of course isnt so; for I know only too well what it is to have a play that the audiences dont like a lot. I remember the time of the first showing of KATHLEEN LISTENS IN,[3] when, after curtain-fall, every mother's son and daughter in the theater kept a dead silence, got up from their seats, and filed out of the theater without a single handclap or a word—the only instance in the Abbey I know of when the audience took the celebrated and tremendous advice of B[rinsley]. Macnamara to receive a play they didnt fall for in dead silence, till "the merciful fall of the curtain." Well, we all go through it some time or another; though not like me, in dead silence. But it didnt take more than a pin feather outa me. By the way, one of the critics says that the present production of the P. and the S's. "beats the 'old days' to a frazzle." I wonder how, and I wonder why. Is there a secret reason for this lovely exaltation? It is nonsense to say that [Arthur] Sinclair, Molly O'Neill, Sally Allgood, or Barry Fitzgerald could possibly be beaten to a frazzle, for they were superb in their roles, and one cannot find ascension over that fact—however good the present actors may be. And, surely, this critic [Gabriel Fallon] has forgotten what he says about F.J. [McCormick] in one of the *Capuchin Annuals*. No; at least, the old ones in the older days were as good as those who are flourishing now. They are even conscientious about their facts, as even a village critic should be. The same chap writing about PURPLE DUST says "It was produced twice in England: once by the Glascow Unity Theater (Glascow, by the way, isnt in England), and once under the direction of Sam Wanamaker. The play opened in Brighton, and died that night."[4] Every item wrong. It wasnt done by Unity, far as I know; it was done in Liverpool by The Old Vic,

1 Hugh Leonard's *A Leap in the Dark* opened at the Abbey Theatre on 21 January 1957.
    2 Sean O'Casey's *The Plough and the Stars* was revived at the Abbey Theatre on 8 January 1957; it was replaced on 21 January by Hugh Leonard's play, but resumed on 4 February for three more weeks.
    3 Sean O'Casey's *Cathleen Listens In* opened at the Abbey Theatre on 1 October 1923.
    4 Gabriel Fallon, "How To Write a Play," *Evening Press,* 19 January 1957.

and ran for two weeks.[5] It did not OPEN in Brighton; it opened in Glascow, then went on to Edinburgh—where I and Eileen spent over a week, mingling with Highland friends, and Seamus Ennis; then came down to Blackpool (or Bolton), and then down to Brighton, where it ran its full week.[6] I wonder is this admirable inaccuracy deliberate? The same chap says that I dont care a damn, or near a damn, for money. I do care, and welcome American dollars with open hands, though the love of, or need for, money doesnt form my plays. Again, there was a big splash in IRISH TIMES and I. PRESS which implied clearly that PURPLE DUST— N. York production—was a poor thing, and a failure. Funny, though I shouldnt have been astonished if it had failed; but surprisingly—surprises in the theatre happen often—it has been a success, with almost every drama critic praising it—N. York Times, Herald Tribune, N. York Post, etc; so that the latest announcement in the Press is that the "Mailing Orders have been filled for the next sixteen weeks," and that the theater is bulging every night with laughter. The I. critics wouldnt like to hear that, so I took no notice of the accounts in the I.T. or I. Press, not wishing to hurt their feelings.

I knew Louie Bennet in the old days. She was an active and useful woman among the women workers, but never a revolutionary; she always held back her punches, and seemed to side later on with Jim Larkin's enemies. But dont forget that it was JIM and not Louie Bennet who put the spirit of discontent first into the heart of the Irish girl-worker, while Louie, I'm afraid, did something to damp the fire whenever it flamed up too hotly. She was a trades unionist, and contented to go no farther, which, in its way was good, but left a lot undone, and paved the way to hold JIM down to an ordinary flight.

I dont think, either, that H[ilton]. Edwards or [Micheal] Macliamore were the pioneers in continental drama. You forget the Dublin Drama League who did a lot to bring the continent to the Abbey stage. Yeats was President, but Lennox Robinson was then the pivot on which the League worked, and fine work was done long before H.E. or Macl came on the scene. Everyone seems to have forgotten this Drama League, but I havent.

I am glad youre holding on to your job. I dont think an English city would be good for your health. For you, the air of Dublin is far, far better. So hold on to the job.

[5] Sean O'Casey's *Purple Dust* received its premiere performance in Liverpool at the Liverpool Old Vic on 31 October 1945. For details of the production see O'Casey's letter to Beatrix Lehmann, 30 September 1945, note 1, Vol. II. The play was later performed by the Glasgow Unity Theatre on 9 April 1946; see O'Casey's letter to George Jean Nathan, 5 May 1946, note 3, Vol. II.

[6] San Wanamaker's production of *Purple Dust* opened at the Theatre Royal in Glasgow on 27 April 1953. After a one-week tour of four cities it closed in Brighton on 23 May 1953, due to a lack of funds, without going on to London. See O'Casey's letters to Sam Wanamaker, 28 April 1953, note 1; and to George Jean Nathan, 11 May 1953, note 1, Vol. II.

Canada is a tough place for a tenderfoot to go to; N. Zealand is better for your health, but there there's not much besides sheep-farming or a trade. You see, clerical work is not in demand in many places, and with the newest compiling machines they will be less in demand, so dont leave Ireland, unless you have to.

You are really fortunate you know to have a job that at least keeps you going. By the way, Seumas, a mhic O [my dear friend], why do you think God's ways are ununderstandable? It wasnt God who killed Niall, it was Leucaemia—unless God created the bug or the virus, or whatever causes it; and, if a God exists, I'd hardly say he had any hand in it. As Shaw says "It isnt we who are in God's hands, it is God who is in ours." And, if we wont deal with the things that plague and destroy us, then we damn well have to suffer.

All the best to you.
As ever,
Sean

To John Allen

TS. ALLEN

5 FEBRUARY 1957

Dear John,

Thanks, my lad, for your kind words. I am fairly indifferent whether or no I'll live to see appreciation of my work in England or in Ireland either. I would give all I have ever done, adding all I may do, if I could have saved the life of our son, Niall, of twenty-one, who died at Christmas time last year.

The answer to your query as to whether I'll give permission to Unity Theater to do COCKADOODLE DANDY is no. I have already refused this play to George Devine for production in the Court Theater, after many appeals, or despite of them rather. I hope for an American production of this play, and amnt anxious or eager about any offer to do it here. It is like Unity to hanker after the most difficult play—far as production is concerned—I have written; but they cant have it. I have no quarrel with Unity, but am always offended when anyone tries to do what they are obviously incapable of doing, as was the case with production of STAR TURNS RED by Ted Willis, a lad they boosted when he wrote that piece of hokum called BUSTER. They even had it printed. He has a talent for writing hokum, so let him stick to it—as he is doing now with his Police Constable Dixon. I watched two of them to see if I was right (though I knew I was) about him, and he has confirmed my faith in him most brilliantly. My dear John, a "most earnest and conscientious manner" isnt enough in the production of drama; a fella without either might do a splendid job, having the imagination and ability, yet without the conscience of a louse. That is what Unity and those who go with them have never understood. When one has to call a doctor, we dont expect him to help us with communism, but with his skill, and his political opinions dont matter a damn till he cures us; and so it is with Producer (or Director, as the Americans say). Well, there you are: the answer is no; and when you transmit this reply to Unity, tell them there's no use in any appeal, or a deluge of appeals either.

I hope you and your family are doing well, and that you have had some chance with your talents, far and away above those of T.W., though you'll hardly make as much out of them. I hope you may. My best wishes to you all.

As ever,
Sean

To David Krause

TS. KRAUSE

6 FEBRUARY 1957

My dear Dave,

Thanks for your kind letter of sympathy. The utterly unexpected death of Niall has been a bitter, bitter blow to us all. It all occurred so swiftly that it left us all stunned. Indeed, Eileen went physically numb after he had gone for she was with him almost all the time, from when he went from us here in the ambulance till he gave his last sigh in Barts Hospital in London. Although I wasn't there, Niall's last sigh will always sound sadly in my ears. My beloved Niall was very close to me, and we had a habit of discussing everything together when he was here; the last talk was all about Hungary. Indeed, he came down especially a week or so before the University holiday recess, to talk it over, for he was sorely troubled by what had happened. Then on the 14 of December, he came down with Shivaun for the Christmas holidays, feeling tired, but as gay and as talkative as ever. For a holiday, and we assumed that all he needed was a good rest, for he had been active through demonstrations in London against the invasion of Egypt, and we thought he had just overdone it a little. Well, he has had his holiday and his rest, a long rest, God knows, and one neither he nor we desired. Two days after he had come home, he went with Eileen to the doctor, and two later he was told he had little chance of further life. He took it very bravely; all he said when I went in and took his hand in mine was It's hellish, dad; and said no more. He was a few days in Exeter hospital, treated to fit him for the journey to London. When he got to Barts, the doctors there had good hope that he would be with us for a few months longer, but the third day, day before New Year's Eve, he died with Eileen and Breon beside him. Among our children, the center link has vanished. It is the severest blow my life has known, but it must be borne, even though it be through many tears.

My love to you, my dear friend.
As ever,
Sean

The shock has jolted me far away from what I was trying to do. All I've done since has been an account of Niall's death, and of what happened, & how we felt.

To Mai McCarthy

TC. O'CASEY

6 FEBRUARY 1957

My dear Mai,

Thank you, dear, for your very kind letter of sympathy. Niall's death was a bitter blow, and the heart is bruised. He was a dear lad, handsome, gay, honest, and he and I were very close friends as well as being father and son. We all loved him very dearly, and his end came so swift and so unexpectedly that we still stay stunned. Well, you see, lass, there's no one who hasnt had a sorrow, and sorrow is the one sacrament that binds us together, all men and women the world over; you with yours, me with mine, and ours with others—an endless chain of a bond of sisterhood and brotherhood.

Eileen has had the hardest blow, and has had a physical shock; has had to have special treatment, but, brave lass as she is, she is rallying out of it, which is well, for our two other children need her very much still.

I cannot realise it yet, and I find it hard to believe that our boy is now but a memory; but I have tried to realise it by settting down an account of what happened, and, very poorly, the thoughts I had during the tense time we had before the end came. He lived a brave lad and died a brave lad too. Please thank Judy[1] for her kind words about me and mine. My love to her.

---

[1] Judith Brayer, Mai's teacher at Hunter College, N.Y.

So for the present, dear lass, no more just now, for I have a lot to do, many letters to answer that were set aside, not having the thought or energy to attend to them. My love to you.

As ever,
[*Sean*]

To Anthony Harvey

TC. O'CASEY

9 FEBRUARY 1957

Dear Anthony,
I am very glad you had such an enjoyable time at Christmas. Take all the fun from life you can while you are young. I hope you have settled by now where you go for the rest of the educational work. I imagine a teaching post would be the most suitable for you, though, I hear, they arent very well paid; but neither are the preachers, though, I think, we have too many preachers and far too few teachers. You and George seem to have had a gorgeous theatrical time in New York. Glad you liked P. Dust—if it be that you arent just saying so because you happen to like me: friends arent good critics. I think P. Shyre a good clever lad—that's why I gave him P.D., and he did the Readings splendidly, and seems to have done well with P.D. too, though he had an all-American Cast. I never met him, but possibly may this summer if he comes to Europe; but I seem to have known him a long time. No, I didnt see the lovely Marilyn Monroe nor her famous husband. I got an invitation from T. Rattigan and Laurence Olivier to go to an At Home in Olivier's place, but didnt go. I'm rather glad Marilyn didnt come here; it would have meant a lot of damned pressmen hovering around, and I dont like this kind of publicity. I have refused an interview by Ronald Duncan for THE DAILY MAIL, and a Television interview by Richard Attenborough. They even wanted me here to sit in a bookshop and autograph any book of mine bought from a display in a great window. I've never liked this kind of self-exhibition. It would take me a long time to comment on T. S. Eliot's "religious beliefs" (what are religious beliefs?). He declared himself to be an Anglican, and therefore, presumably accepts the Anglican Creed and the Church's 39 Articles. There's more in his poetry than merely religious belief. I have no religious beliefs myself, bar a love of life and a belief that all the young should have time to enjoy it; and that life lived is the most important thing in our universe; and to get our fill of it till we grow old, to secure peace, to devote all thought to the things that belong to peace, and to give first thought

to the health and vigor of the community. I dont mind very much what
D[enis]. Johnston said about me or my plays, except that I dont intend to
do as he advises, unless it should please me to do so; and I hardly think
it will. He goes about saying these things often as he can, and he and
others in Ireland seem to have a curious obsession to lead O'Casey on the
way wherein they think he should go. But none of them ever wait to
answer a question. I have asked them many in book and newspaper, but
they have been far away, and didnt see and didnt hear. They have their
reward. And many thanks for the charming little photographs of yourself.
You look fine, and I hope you will take care of yourself. We have had a
very sad Christmas for our beloved younger son, Niall, 21 years, was
dying that day, though he kept chatting away to his mother, and he gave
his last sigh on the evening of the 29 December, last year. He had Leucaemia, a malady before which up to now the greatest doctors must just
stand helpless, for little is known about it.

He was a grand lad, lived bravely and died bravely from the day he
heard his death sentence, for the malady is invariably fatal, and he knew
all about it; but it must have been hard on him to know over the days that
he was saying farewell to all the joys and thrills of life. So ironical that
I who am 76 should come out of a very serious time after a ten months
struggle, while he a grand lad physically should go down to death within
a few swift days. He was very close to me, and I loved him very dearly,
and I shall miss him gravely all the days that may remain to me; and so
will poor Eileen, his mother.

My sincere love to your mother and family, to George, and to you.

As ever,
[*Sean*]

To Paul Shyre

TS. SHYRE

12 FEBRUARY 1957

Dear Paul,

Thanks for your letter and script which arrived this morning. You
shouldn't have bothered sending it by air mail—I could have waited.

Regarding the London production of the Readings, I amn't at all in
favor of them. I don't think they would be successful, for the London
patrons of the theater don't like O'Casey, and the literary critics, I fear,
don't like him very much either. It is a matter of indifference to me, for
over many years now, I have fixed mine eyes on the hills—that is to say,

the theater patrons of New York. As for Sam Wanamaker and P. DUST, it is hard to say what happened. Linked to the aforementioned opinions—dislike of my work—there was the spirit of the play which could hardly appeal to the English who rule the roost here; then there was the violent attack made on the play by the late James Agate[1] when he read it; roaring that it was striking England when she was helpless, etc; and then again the fact that at the time of Sam's production, the English were in a state of patriotic ecstasy about the Coronation of the present young Queen, to whom may God give good health and a long life, whether England goes on wanting a royal house or not. Sam W., his wife, Charlotte, and their children are very dear friends of ours, and I don't like to have very dear friends implicated in any production of mine; it might become embarrassing; as it did with P. DUST., for poor Sam lost a lot of money on it. But, apart from all the considerations above, I think Sam tried to change it too much, and change it too often. I was constantly taking out dialogue, and putting in new speeches as suggested by Sam; but in fairness to Sam, he was, I think, right in changing the play so that Souhaun's affection was changed from O'Kill. to the 2nd Workman, and it was his suggestion that made me write the RUIN'D ROWAN TREE. (By the way, the word in last verse is "nestling" and not "nesting," as it appears in the script. And "ken" is an old English word meaning "within my knowledge," I know, to know, etc., in the script it is given a Capital K, and I thought maybe, Americans mightn't know this clearly. (It is the root of "can.") Well, I would rather that the London Readings were not given; but I leave the final decision to you. Sam did the stories called Scholem Aleicim here,[2] and they were splendidly done; but then they were written by a poet-Jew, Sam is a Jew, and he was in his own element, and responded beautifully; but I don't think he is quite as much at home with our Irish idiom. At any rate, I think you should hold away from the idea till such time as you may be over here, or they will be willing to bring you over. Anyway, I personally am against the idea.

I sympathise with you about interviews—they are very trying, and I am all against them. GBS advised me NEVER to grant one; rather ask for written questions to be sent, and answered in a quiet and serious way, saving any danger of an interviewer giving a wrong impression of an answer.

In the matter of advertising my book THE GREEN CROW here, they wanted me to sit in a book-sellers and sign books as they were bought! Then an interview by Ronald Duncan (he wrote libretto for Benjamin

[1] See James Agate, "Mr. O'Casey: A Reply," *Sunday Times,* 3 May 1942; reprinted in Vol. II. Writing about *Purple Dust,* Agate stated "that this is not the moment to produce a witless lampoon at the expense of the English, too busy fighting for freedom to answer back."

[2] Sam Wanamaker's production of *The World of Sholem Aleichem* opened in London on 11 January 1955.

Britten) for THE DAILY MAIL; then an interview by Richard Attenborough—he does a lot of acting and broadcasting—on a television quarter
of an hour; he to come here with equipment, and do it quietly in my flat:
all three refused. I'm a little sick of this publicity; I always hated it; and
can't see why I should have to sell the book as well as write it. I appreciate the Publisher's position, and anxiety to sell the book, which touches
me, too; but I'm in no way so anxious to sell it as he is.

I am struggling along, but will never forget our beloved boy who
was very close to me in all things, politics, literature, science, modern
thought, music, humor and football. Part of my life left with him.

I am, naturally, glad to hear that P. DUST is still going well. All this
was a suprise to me. A great lot of the success's reasons go to you, to
Director, to Designer, and Caste; and to think it is an American company,
with no big Irish actor's name to prop it up!

My warm regards to all of them, and to you.

As ever,
Sean

To G. A. M. Wilkinson[1]

TC. O'CASEY

13 FEBRUARY 1957

Dear Mr. Wilkinson,
Thank you very much for your kind invitation to lecture during the
coming Cheltenham Festival, and for the honor implied in the invitation.

I am indeed sorry that it wont be possible for me to take advantage
of your kind offer for various reasons.

First, I am no lecturer which is an art in itself, and an important
one, and one which I have never practised, though I have, in my time,
spoken from many platforms, at times peaceful, at other times surrounded
by turbulence and police. The last lecture I gave—though I called it a
chat with the students—was given more than twenty years ago at Cambridge, and since then, I have kept silent, though the "lecture" I gave at
Cambridge (I have described the incident fully in a book of mine) was
enjoyed by those who heard it (I was told).[2]

---

[1] G.A.M. Wilkinson, M.B.E., Cheltenham Festival of Contemporary Literature.
[2] See the rough notes for his talk at Cambridge University, "The Holy Ghost
Leaves England," 18 January 1936, Vol. I. See also the chapter "Cambridge" in
Sunset and Evening Star (1954).

Second, I am now bordering on seventy-seven, and prefer to sit quiet, think a little, do a little, and then sleep a little, and write a lot.

Third, we lost a lad of twenty-one a few brief weeks ago, and my mind is full of what he was and what he might have become, had death not taken him from us.

So, my friend, all I can do is to wish, most heartily, that your worthy festival, very worthy Festival, may be the success it undoubtedly deserves to be.

I enclose a small subscription to endorse my good wishes to the gallant citizens of Cheltenham and Gloucestershire in their gallant efforts to show the world and England that we do not live by bread alone.

Yours very sincerely,
Sean O'Casey.

To J. J. O'Leary

TS. O'LEARY

14 FEBRUARY 1957

Dear J.J.

Many thanks for the tobacco and for the press-cuttings and for kindness to Eileen and Shivaun when they were in London, and you were there too. The cuttings show again how miserable in thoughts the Irish critics are. In one the critic giving an account of the viscissitudes of PURPLE DUST gives every item of information wrongly. Two I got from I. TIMES and I. Press about the production of the play in New York labour to show that it was as big and as fancy a failure there as it was in London; or rather, England, for it never got to London. On the contrary, it has been a surprising success in New York, and a letter this morning from Brooks Atkinson, Drama Critic of the New York Times tells me it is going strong, that many fine references to it in Press frequently occur, and that everyone who speaks to him about it says they were delighted with the play—and it's a 100% American Caste! Who, anyway, is the critic of U.P. I.N.A. which I take it means United Press—Irish News Agency. He says "O'Casey probably thinks he is a devil of a fellow at the writing of comedy. This he is not, as the medium is alien to him as a writer." "is not as" is funny. Are these chaps even semi-literate? I did think I had at least an element of humor in me. However, the New York papers say that every night the walls of the theatre bulge with laughter, so they, the audiences, must be aliens too. But the laughter is o k by me,

for it's the best humor I could think of, and, indeed, what I've met with—
I was part of the "bureau scene" myself, and a viewer of the gentleman
trying to manipulate the "big roller." All the humor, poor or rich, is, at
least, founded on fact. By the way, my friend, I have something which
makes me uneasy: Eileen told me you had put money into the enterprise
showing SHADOW OF A GUNMAN. This not only makes me uneasy,
but displeases me. I dont wish or want any friend to risk a make for my
sake. I never have, and I still feel the same way. It seems to me to cut
across friendship, taking from it its purity and its full satisfaction. I beg
you not to do this any more. I like you from your letters and for your
kindness to Eileen and Shivaun in Dublin and in London, and dont want
this friendship to be embarrassed in any way, for I'm a proud devil, even
if humor be an alien medium to me.

And by the way, be careful how you pour money into film and
play—both are dangerous insecurities.

Now I'll leave you in the throes of your Election. I see, if I remember right, Dev mentioned about some meeting of the great powers, USA,
France, Britain, The USSR, and—Nationalist China! A nation about as
big and as important as Ireland's Eye. Why the hell doesnt Dev or Costello do an original and sensible act for once, and (if they wont recognise
the USSR) admit the Republic of China on to their list of friends? What
a fine thing it would be to see the red flag with its five gold stars flying
beside the green one with the gold harp in its center!

Well, thanks again for the cuttings and for all else—bar putting
money into any play of mine; tho' I'll forgive you this time if you never
do it again.

Just refused an interview by Ronald Duncan for the DAILY MAIL,
and a television interview by Richard Attenborough to make known my
book, THE GREEN CROW, to millions and millions of people. I never
liked publicity; now I hate it, and hope they will let me rest in peace for
the rest of me days.

All the best from Eileen and from me.
Sean

To Rex MacGall

My dear friend,

I understood you well enough.[1] How could I give advice about running a Journal, never having had the slightest experience of doing such a thing, not even a parish magazine. All I can think of is that those who do in Ireland are going to have an unhappy time of it. Poor puzzled Ireland. Ad ardua non astra.[2] You may find it hard to get a publisher, for possibly a silent word from a bishop will frighten a printer away.

I'm sorry I cant write an article for you, for my mind is restless, and it will be so for many a day to come; the death of our boy will take a long time to forget even for a short time, and possibly, with me, it will never go till my ashes mingle with his. I have refused to let Ronald Duncan come here for an interview about THE GREEN CROW, for the Daily Mail, and I've refused a television by Richard Attenborough about the book, too, and I've declined to write an article for Theater Arts, America, even though they offered $200.00 for it; so, you see, you arent alone; though I've done a short and prosaic review for the TRIBUNE on a book by a Sean O'Callaghan, titled THE EASTER LILY;[3] just because I thought the book deserved to be read.

Yes, I'm afraid INNIU is a little timid. An article last week told us—in an effort to make the great Jim Larkin respectable—that the Archbishop of Dublin visited him when he lay dying. So he did; but I never saw a bishop, or a monsignor, or a Canon, or a humble priest (bar Father O'Flannagan) visit him while he was well and fighting. On the contrary, they did all they could to down him, and us with him.

Enough, my friend. I really hope your Journal may be a fine and lasting success, and will send you another fiver at the end of a six months' printing.

That's as much as I can do.
All good wishes to your friends and to you.
Yours very sincerely,
Sean O'Casey.

[1] MacGall had written his letter in Gaelic, asking O'Casey to write an article in English for the new socialist paper in Dublin, *The Plough.*
[2] A reverse pun on the R.A.F. motto, *Per ardua ad astra,* The way to the stars is hard.
[3] Sean O'Casey, "Poor Puzzled Ireland," *Tribune,* 22 February 1957, a review of Sean O'Callaghan's *The Easter Lily* (1957), a book about the Easter Rising of 1916.

To Miss Joan McAlevey

MS. MCALEVEY

18 FEBRUARY 1957

My dear Joan,

Thank you, dear girl, for your very kind sympathy in our grief. There is little to be said for the same kind of sorrow has come to many others too. The lad was a lovable one, and had a fine & penetrating mind, a lovely sense of humor, & we miss him grievously, & all the qualities that were within him. I have always resented any interference by death in a young life; but never thought that I might feel the blow personally. Even tho' it came swift, & he died within a few days, leaving us stunned, we must go on, & live the rest of the time—for Eileen, Breon, & Shivaun—bravely; for me best as I can.

I hope by now, the harder weather is gone from Saratoga Springs, & the temperature more easy to bear. Only now, with us, are the winds coming from the north bringing the bite of frost with them, and the snow over hills & the moor. I'm very glad you and Frank enjoyed "Purple Dust."

It is, I know [difficult]—I taught the Gaelic Language, not as a Professional teacher, but as a labor of love, for some years; and it wearied me that so few could grasp the idioms of the Language. Reading Theses is a tiring thing; but we never know the results of what we may do; never in this world anyway. All things are important—even reading dull Theses; for we cannot say what will eventually blossom within the nature of those who write them: not great writers, I fear; but, more valuable, maybe, good women and good men. We cannot afford to despise the day of small things.

By the way, Joan, some time ago, I received a lovely grey woollen jumper, & I think it came from you. I have been so bewildered the last seven weeks (and am a little still) that I have forgotten many things, & have mislaid letters. If you sent it, forgive me for forgetting, and take my many thanks now for a delightful & useful present (now that cold winds blow & snows fall).

My love to your family, to Frank, & to you, my dear.

Yours as ever,
Sean

Money is not in itself an evil thing: nothing is; it is only evil by the way we think of it, & how we use it. So take more care of the little you have, dear Joan.

To Frank McCarthy

MS. MCCARTHY

18 FEBRUARY 1957

My dear Frank,

Here's the book, signed as requested. You must have looked swell in your Groomsman's suit. I'm glad you had a holiday. I don't like you having "a hell of a good feed." Take care of that duodenal ulcer, & don't go in too much for these feeds. [Seumas] Scully would do ill to come to London. I've advised him against it. You see, he has a tendency to T.B., & Dublin has clearer air than London. I don't mention T.B. to him, but suggest Dublin's better than London in the way of general health. Besides, Jim Scully, as far as experience goes, is a Primitive, and he is advancing into middle-age now; so don't encourage him. I hope "Green Crow" goes well. They wanted me to give an interview to Ronald Duncan—he did libretto for B. Britten—for the "Daily Mail," & another television interview with R. Attenborough about the book; he to come here, with equipment, & do it as I sat be me own fireside; But I declined both offers. I have always avoided publicity as much as I can. I don't want to persuade anyone to buy my book. I hope they may buy it of their own accord; but not by a push from me into a bookseller's.

I enclose a cheque for £2.2.0., for Magazine "Kingsway [Messenger]." I can't go on cadging it from the good Dr. [Donald O.] Soper, who, God knows, has his hands full keeping Christ's flag flying. I like the idea of your new sign. Never mind the "gaudy" colors, for most ordinary folk like them, and I like them too. Near time we tried to get away from the Drab. I wear an Indian house cap, crimson and black, speckled with spangles. I've a number of differing ones with differing colors, & wear them as I feel for the colors they show. So you wear a bright tie—it'll do you good.

My love.
As ever,
Sean.

To Arvid Paulson

TC. O'CASEY

19 FEBRUARY 1957

My dear Arvid,

Just sit down before you read this letter, and listen to me. You should take more care of yourself, and give the back of your hand to cocktail parties. You should get your share of sleep, even if you have to let us wait till you wake. After a spell of pneumonia (I had this in hospital, so I know what it is like), you should go cautious; go through life like an Indian scout prowling out enemies, watchful, careful how he puts his foot down. Healing is a slow process, and nature takes her time. So should you. Do nothing over easy-going work for at least six months. Even steel tires, and you arent made of iron.

I'm glad you typed your letter, for my eyes now find it hard to read writing, and they tire after a moment of strain; though I write myself which I can do without using them much, and much more rapidly than I can set down words by typing.

Dont do any more about trying to get me the Nobel Prize, or you'll have me worrying about you. I assure you, Arvid, I wont go crying into the arms of death if I dont get it. What does worry me is thinking of you hunting after it for me. Looking back over my life, I can honestly say I never sought publicity or prize, and I never shall; bar, of course, the publicity of friendship; the talking to a friend, or the writing to him or her, if talking is separated by territory or broad seas flowing between us. The laurel fades—not so quick as the rose; but it fades; and the Captain, Strindberg's Captain, in his stately regimentals and his medals, doesnt last long before he becomes a barrowful of dust. It was very good of you to think of me, and I look up with affectionate feeling at your kind interest in me and my work.

I'm sorry the Critics didnt like Miss [Elizabeth] Sprigge's effort to show forth the tenderness of Strindberg's EASTER, for in any translation almost, this is a very lovely play. But it is very hard to get within the soul of a fine writer who uses a language not that of his translator; and even were it so, then the language he changes it into is a different one too; both languages must be almost native to him. With the great Strindberg, it is terribly difficult, for his was a soul that stormed after the truth; yet there were beautiful and strangely tender hours, and loving moments in his saddest plays which stood out like lily ponds in a whirlpool. I'm glad you had a laugh or two out of PURPLE DUST.

Now, take care of yourself.
With affectionate regards,
[Sean]

To John Gassner

TS. GASSNER

20 FEBRUARY 1957

My dear John,

Thank you very much indeed for your kind letter and words of sympathy. I am still bewildered by the swift and utterly unexpected death of our boy. He was a fine lad, tall, strong, full of laughter, and a mind that was always trying to see away from himself into the problems facing man and the questions posed by the universe around us. He came down from his London College for the Christmas holidays, and felt a little tired but we imagined that he had overdone it a little by activities demonstrating against the British invasion of Egypt. Three days later, he heard his death sentence; but took it quietly and very bravely, still interested in the problems of politics and of life. We thought, and so did the doctors, that he could be kept with us for a month or two, but within little more than a week, he died. All my thoughts of what work I had in hand vanished, and all I could do was to write down what had happened, and how I felt about it. He was very close to me in ideas about the theater, about literature, about science, about football, about politics, except that he had been deeply troubled by the tragedy in Hungary, and couldn't agree with me about it. He had taken a swift run down for a day from London a week before the term ended to talk about, and though he heard great argument, he went back as he had come down, puzzled and distressed. I gave him a last kiss at Christmas while he was in Exeter hospital waiting to be brought to Barts hosp. in London, and I never saw him again; and never will now. But life must go on, and personal grief can't be allowed to hinder its march. I am so glad to hear that you would soon be a grandfather. I often wondered if you were married and had children, but dont like to intrude such questions into correspondence. I hope and pray that your daughter may have a happy and a safe birth. Please give her my sincere good wishes for welfare and happiness. I get the Literary Supplement (Times), but dont often read it; for I must limit the use of my eyes to a certain amount of time and effort; so I missed the reference to your book, and haven't been able to find the issue in which it appeared. You are, of course, a fine writer about the drama, past and present, and yesterday I lent your book to a friend of mine who had taken it from the shelf, read a little of it, and had immediately asked for a loan of it.

All good and affectionate wishes,

As ever,
Sean

To Brooks Atkinson

TS. ATKINSON

21 FEBRUARY 1957

My dear Brooks,

Thanks a lot for your letter. It is good of you to go to see George, and to have a chat with him. It must be a trying thing for him to find that his hand has lost its power to carry a pencil; and, I'm sure, your visits must be very welcome to him. I know what it is myself, for during seven or eight long months, I couldn't write a word—my hands staggered over the paper, and left just signs that belonged to some pre-historical hieroglyphical alphabet, unknown even to the writer himself. I didn't want him to know about Niall, and I and Julie arranged he wasn't to be told, but I'm afraid Tom Curtiss phoning from Paris told him of the loss to the O'Caseys.

You are a busy man! But a lot depends on the genuine and sincere ones who are trying to mould the world nearer to the heart's desire; and we can't afford to despise the day of small things. The little more, and how much it is; the little less, and what miles away! We never know, Brooks, how the little today may mean so much tomorrow. But don't overdo it. Your best brief is Criticism; and the best Communist is he who uses his best faculty for the added knowledge and surety of man—a truth ignored by many of them. So take care of yourself, my dear liberal-minded man—one of the kindest and most broadly-minded men I know—and don't forget that you are a Critic first, whatever you may be afterwards.

I am still full of thoughts about our Niall; he was so well-balanced, for fair-minded, so gay, and his was the shrewdest voice that used to advise on all our family problems. It has proved a deep wound, and one that will never heal, but we must still engage in the activities of life.

I hope to resume some kind of work again soon and have filled in the sad space by an article on Niall, feeling such a lad should have a brief memorial within the chronicle of my time; now, and forever, a dear son of memory. We all, at least have a sorrow to share; it is the one great sacrament that unites all men together.

I heartily wish Oriana every success with the next book, and am glad she has so much mail about her gentle, laughing book about Ireland; poor, puzzled Ireland.

Give dear Oriana my love, and, when you next see George, give him my love, and to Julie as well, and as you know, you yourself are in its center.

As ever,
Sean

To Mrs. John T. Cooper

TS. COOPER

22 FEBRUARY 1957

Dear Georgie,

You are surely right about music; the simple soul can search for God in the folk tune as the greater spirit, like Mozart or Beethoven, can search for him in Symphony or sonata; though, I'm afraid, that many who compose popular tunes today seek, not God, but their own temporal advantage, and sling an insult at Him. As far as listening is concerned, I have gone beyond the folk tune. Shaw says somewhere that it is all right to hear a simple tune once or twice, but to hear it repeated many times over is maddening; and I've found out now that Shaw was right.

[Bishop Fulton J.] Sheen is a wily one in demonstrating that having read every word Lenin wrote, he still remains a Most Reverend, as if it were Lenin who spoke for the first time; that before him all was silence. There are a helluva lot of footsteps leading up to Lenin's footmarksism. Go back along the way, and we can see them stretching back to the prophets, to China and Peru. There's Piers Plowman and his own Saint, More, with his Utopia in his right hand; Shelley, even Keats, even Tennyson—to mention but a few among the crowds of footmarks leading on to Lenin; without even mentioning the prophets in Lenin's own great country.

Thanks for the Gypsum Factory Magazine. I have sent it on to Ireland's factory, and have received a letter of thanks from the Manager. I hope they will follow suit with a magazine of their own—some day. I liked Charlie Robinson's "Spirit of Giving," and, indeed, how could we live without it? In one way or another, we are always giving something to life. "Silver and gold have I none, but what I have give I unto thee"; a glass of wine or a glass of water shines out in the same way. My good wishes to Mike Zaskalicky, quarryman, and may he be long able to fill where he lives with many sweet noises. Your [William] Faulkner is, in my opinion, a first-class artist, but, to me, he seems to always weep coal-black tears; each tear has lost the glint of sunshine that gleams out of human sorrow. Unlike poor Timon who did it from a cave, Faulkner flays life from the top of a well-grassed hill; and does it all the more bitterly. Or so it seems to me. No one could be bitterer than Shakespeare, but however far down he went, he always rose again to the gusto of life.

It is very interesting to hear about John. I had a son, Niall, who, too, took an intense interest in social and political activities; who brought me first to Mozart, so that whilst before I knew him a little, now I know him well; who was, too, a fan of Jazz, and who played the trombone in a jazz band oh, so often. He was just over 21, a tall lad, fine footballer and badminton player, a gay sense of humor, and bid fair to become a first-class biologist. The day before New Year's Eve, he died from leucaemia; had a swift end, and met it bravely and with quietness. The trombone hidden in its case, is here, but our boy is gone.

I sang several old Victorian songs for him which he took down, and then had a lot of fun improvising on them, and turning the phrases into odd rhythms that gave him and the other members of the band a lot of fun. He was just as lusty at the singing of carols on Christmas Eve night and Christmas evening with friends; singing them heartily, and, I imagine, believing in all they said while he sang them. Next Christmas will be a dark one for us all.

May John have a long life of enjoyment with life, with you, and with the clarinet and saxaphone.

I will make inquiries about the book, or a book, of Gaelic pronunciation, though I fear there isn't much to be had in this way, for Gaelic is hard set to show its sounds by phonetic symbols; and its grammar is unlike, I fear, any other living tongue.

> *My love to John and to you.*
> *As ever,*
> Sean

To Oscar De Liso[1]

TC. O'CASEY

25 FEBRUARY 1957

Dear Mr. De Liso,

Thank you for your request to write an article about what I think of America. I am very interested, but wont attempt it, for I know next to nothing about the U.S.A., beyond the little timid glance I gave at the little I saw and heard during a brief visit to your great country in 1934. All this has been recorded in my biographical book, ROSE AND CROWN, and I have nothing to add; I dont know even yet how the People elect their Government. I have listened, and I've listened to why and how and where this is done, but I'm still puzzled. Indeed, I have a cinch that the People themselves dont know very much about their own country, but could tell one far more about ruined abbeys in Ireland and ruined castles in Spain than they could about the things that belong to themselves.

Well, there you are; ask someone else who knows less than I do, but is well prepared to say more; for me, it is silence.

---

[1] Oscar De Liso, Ballantine Books, Inc., N.Y.

One thing I may say that happened since my visit (Roosevelt was President then), I Like Ike, but disagree with him about his opinion that sanctions should be put upon Israel. I think he is mistaken here, as is the USSR too. The Jews have had a terrible time for centuries, and it's near time they had a fair do; they have gone submissive through the other peoples long enough, God knows, and it is time they stood up, and gave an answer for the hope that is in them. There is no doubt in my mind that they have been subjected to many attacks, and are being constantly threatened, and it isnt surprising that they wish to defend themselves. It has been said of them that they couldnt make good farmers or good fighters, but they have proved the world wrong. They are bonnie fighters; they are a generous race, they are tremendously industrious, and they have a right to the place they now hold in the sun; and I, for one, hope they will fight to keep there.

Aha, so all good wishes to you; but there wont be any use in asking me again to do what I am incompetent to do; so there is the end, with more good wishes to you.

Yours sincerely,
Sean O'Casey.

To Moe Fishman[1]

PC. ABRAHAM LINCOLN BRIGADE[2]

8 MARCH 1957

Dear Moe,

I'm sorry I can't hurry or haltingly go to the Reunion of the Veterans of the Lincoln Brigade. I should love to be among those friends who were the first to face and first to fight the murderous host of Fascism; a host we all had to face and fight later on, after allowing them to gain and gather the power to destroy half a world. The twenty years that have passed since the Lincoln Brigade fought in Spain have brought many changes; changes that have vindicated all the Brigade fought for; and for all Franco and his Falange did, the world is alive today, and the world is kicking, ay, and Spain is beginning to kick too. And Africa, ay, and even Ireland.

[1] Moe Fishman, Executive Secretary, Abraham Lincoln Brigade. In February 1957 the Veterans of the Abraham Lincoln Brigade, the American volunteers who first went into action against fascism in the Spanish Civil War in February 1937, held their 20th Anniversary Dinner and invited O'Casey to attend.

[2] This letter was printed in the Brigade's 20th Anniversary program, and was sent to me by Irving Weissman, 711 Amsterdam Avenue, New York City 10025.

I daresay all of us now have grey hairs, but they are but symbols of an honorable age that hasn't yet finished the fight for the Brotherhood of man.

My Irish blessing on you all.

Yours very sincerely,
Sean O'Casey

To Clara Rotter[1]

MS. ROTTER

8 MARCH 1957

Dear Clara,

Thank you very much for the Press-clippings. They were very acceptable, particularly the one telling of the interview with the shy Paul Shyre.

It was good of you to take the trouble to send them to me.

DeValera's in the saddle again; on the old rocking-horse that jingles many bells, but goes nowhere. But Dr. Noel Browne, whom the clerics & he tried to demolish, is in for Dublin. A very sincere Catholic, but a very brave one. There's hope for Ireland yet.

All the best to you.
Sean O'Casey

[1] Clara Rotter, secretary to Brooks Atkinson at the *New York Times.*

To Paul Shyre

TS. SHYRE

11 MARCH 1957

Dear Paul,

Thanks for your letter of March the 8's date. Very glad to hear of the onward march of PURPLE DUST; may it blow about for a good while to come.

I know about the request from Hilton Edwards. The managing Director of the Gaiety Theater in Dublin, wrote to me asking me to give per-

mission to perform the Readings, to be produced by H. Edwards. He suggested that I make my own adaptation. I replied by saying that a young
American had made the Adaptation in a whole manner, without any help
or even a suggestion from me; that I should never have thought of doing
it; and "the young American" had the licence, and had also an option on
British and Irish productions. I didn't, and don't, want to have anything
to do with Edwards; and, of course, wouldn't consent to any performances
without your guidance; for I can guess how bad the Readings could be, if
not done in the best way. The Managing Director didn't mention in his
first letter anything whatsoever about the request made to you. It was not
till he replied to my refusal that I heard he had written to you about it. A
rather lousy way of doing business it seems to me. A representative of
United Press, Irish Agency, wrote in the Irish papers about P. DUST,
saying the play got a poor reception; that it was a corny exhibition of
slapdash that wouldn't be allowed in any 2nd class music-hall; that it was
boring and tedious; and that "it was clear that O'Casey's medium wasn't
comedy." Not a word has appeared in the Papers about the play's success.
I had a young Irish actor here yesterday, and he was astonished that the
play was still on. Now, having heard of what you did with the Reading,
they are out to exploit O'Casey, not because of any love for him, but
simply they want to make money (so they think) on the courage and
initiation of another lad—the young American! They haven't said a word
to me about doing it in Paris or during the Irish Festival. Last time they
brought the P. AND THE STARS to Paris, I heard no word till I saw it
mentioned in the papers, and had no word from the Abbey about it till
the Company had come back to Dublin. So you see the scant courtesy
they show to me in these things; so why should I be anxious to oblige
them to do with my work what I do not wish them to do; or give it to
those in whom I have no confidence. Don't give the Readings, unless you
can be in charge; and, if P. Dust be on then, don't give it to anyone else.
It is but fair that I should desire the best possible production. And that I
should get it too. As you say, rather than that it should be done badly,
better to wait and see; far better, say I.

I take it that the Package Tour will be by another Company, and
that you won't go yourself. I'm a bit doubtful about running "I Knock at
the Door" each night of the week but you know best.

If you visit England in the Summer—or in Spring, Winter, or the
Fall—there is, or will be, I hope—every chance of seeing me. If I'm on
me feet, I'll be delighted to see you. Inevitably, I've suffered a lot from
the death of a beloved life; one who was not only a son, but an equal and
delightful friend as well. I shall never forget him; and feel ashamed that
I so old (by the way I am 77, not 73) should have gone through such a
long and serious illness, should have come out of it (and he was so
anxious about me at the time), while Niall, only 21, should have been
been swept away in a week of days. However, we must struggle on while

life is allowed to last, and I am still working (sometimes with tears of which I am in no way ashamed), and can talk anyway; so

> come in the evening, come in the morning,
> come when you're asked, or come without warning,

and you'll be very welcome.

Give my love and my continued thanks to the Director, the Designer, and to the Caste.

I hope the Recording may be a great success.

I read your Interview,[1] and liked it very much; but go on being shy; but don't be too damned shy.

> *My best wishes and thanks to you.*
> *Yours very sincerely,*
> *Sean O'Casey*

[1] Richard W. Nason, "Shyre Batting For O'Casey," *New York Times,* 3 March 1957.

To Mrs. Isabella Murphy[1]

MS. MURPHY

12 MARCH 1957

Dear Babsie,

Thanks for your kind sympathy.

Enclosed are a few pounds to buy something for Easter—and don't bother thanking me.

All good wishes to you and all and "Kit" Casey.

> *Yours,*
> *Sean or "Jack"*

Enclosure

You will have to write your name in on top line of cheque, after the word "PAY." I couldn't remember it—was it "Mooney"? Your Grocer will cash it for you.

[1] Mrs. Isabella "Babsie" Murphy, O'Casey's niece in Dublin, the daughter of his sister, Isabella Casey Beaver.

To Seamus Kelly[1]

Irish Times[2]

19 MARCH 1957

AN IRISHMAN'S DIARY

It was both seasonable and appropriate to receive, on the day when the country was officially enjoying St. Patrick's Day, the following letter:

"Dear Quidnunc—Regarding your paragraph, 'Old Times,' I knew the song, a verse of which you quote.[3] I've forgotten it now, but some of the events which evoked it are vivid in my memory. There is a bit of history surrounding that old time which doesn't seem to have been recorded anywhere. A lath and canvas castle, representing one of the city's gates (it was said) was erected by Baggot Street Bridge (I think that was the place), and here the Queen of England was to halt and receive the Keys of the Kingdom of Dublin from the hands of the Lord Mayor, then Alderman Pile, Protestant Home Ruler, Fish and Ice Merchant.

"The Nationalist groups were in a state of angry agitation about the Royal Visit, and the then I.R.B. determined to show that Ireland wasn't conquered yet; so it was arranged that this paper castle should be blown up while the Lord Mayor was presenting Dublin's keys to the Queen. A big official of the then Corporation, the Lord Mayor's Secretary (I think) and head of the Electricity of the Dublin Council was a member of the Supreme Council of the I.R.B. and was a party to the plan. But the plan miscarried for one reason or another; probably because the less militant members of the I.R.B. became frightened; and so everything passed off as arranged by the Dublin Corporation and the Castle.

"Afterwards, the I.R.B. split from top to bottom; the timid ones were eventually ousted by those more militant, led by Tom Clarke and his followers. I knew the man who stood with the Lord Mayor to receive the Queen, but don't want to mention his name for fear that he might be still living and remember the event as well as I do myself. For some time, two separate Irish Freedoms (the I.R.B. Journal) were issued, but finally the one controlled by the militants, with B[ulmer]. Hobson as Editor, and S[ean]. MacDermott as Manager, won the fight, and the journal of the timid ones perished.

[1] Seamus Kelly (1912–79), born in Belfast, drama critic of the *Irish Times,* 1945–1979; also wrote the "An Irishman's Diary" column in the paper under the pseudonym of "Quidnunc," 1949–1979.
[2] This letter was printed in Quidnunc's "An Irishman's Diary," *Irish Times,* 19 March 1957.
[3] Quidnunc, "An Irishman's Diary: 'Old Timers,' " *Irish Times,* 9 and 12 March 1957. On the 9th he asked his readers if they knew anything about a Dublin street ballad about the Dublin Fusiliers and the late Lord Mayor Pile which mocked a state visit to Ireland by Queen Victoria at the turn of the century. On the 12th he printed a version of the ballad.

"Many able men then left the Organisation, one of whom was a Mr. Cowley (MacAmhlaidh) manager of Mackey's, the Seed Merchant in O'Connell street. Him I knew well, for he was the Centre of the Circle that received me when I first joined the I.R.B. I wonder who has, or where are, the records of that exciting time?

"By the way, I have read all the multitude of letters written to the Irish Times about the possibilities and impossibilities of a union between the North and the South; many calm, some furious, and all, it would seem, futile. What a heaven-bent thing it would be if all the North were as of the South—all Catholics; or if all the South were as of the North—all Protestants! Then one damned problem would be solved anyhow. But it isn't so, and so we are where we were.

"How then could we bring the Northern Protestant and the Southern Catholic together, if not in a bond of faith, then in a little closer companionship? You can well ask me! Let us think a minute. How can we make a good start? Any suggestions? Yes, I have one. Catholic theology teaches and maintains that the Catholic Church is the one, true, and only Church of God; that this Church is the one way through her ministration by which man can receive the grace promised and given freely by God. Well, then, the members of this Church should be the most charitable, loving, and kindest-hearted people in the Christian world. I have lived with them most of my life, and can say that they are, by persons and in family groups, all these fine things; but in collective array, in a crowd, they can be as intolerant as any group of Orangemen excited about some declaration of the Pope.

"Well, having the privilege of being in the true Church, with its added responsibilities of showing a light to the world, why not start by showing this gracious light of good-will and charity to the Irish folk in the North? Easy enough. The Irish Government, President, Senate and Dail, should by an unanimous vote invite the Orange Order to hold its celebration of the Twelfth of July, not in Belfast, but in Dublin; should ask the Orangemen to come to the capital as the guests of the Republic, march through the chief streets of Dublin, and hold their meetings in the green glades of the Phoenix Park.

"The procession would give a new colour and a new glow to our Dublin streets, and Dubliners would get to know what sort of persons were those who formed the Orange Order, the Purple Division, and the Knights of the Grand Black Chapter. On the whole, they would find them to be very little different from themselves, excluding the Northern accent. It would be a grand occasion, with the Lambegs beating their loudest, with the northern iron and the steel passing us by.

"Certainly, there will be no union till an Orange sash can walk the streets of Dublin without protest, and the Green sash can walk the ways of Belfast, with many a look, maybe, but without a murmur. Another thing is certain—gunfire will never make friends. So let Dublin start on the fight for fraternity, between the North and South.

> " 'And let the Orange lily be
> Thy badge, my patriot brother—
> The everlasting Green for me;
> And we for one another.' "

"All good wishes. Yours sincerely, Sean O'Casey."

To Conor O'Brien[1]

MS. O'BRIEN

28 MARCH 1957

Dear Conor O'Brien,

Thanks for your letter, and the good advice not to bother my head about the Irish drama critics. I'll think over what you say; though I doubt those cheers you mention. Anyway, I dont want cheers, and I dont think I ever did.

I know that a new generation has grown up since 1916, but they seem to have less courage and less say than the generation that joined in the Rising. By the way, there is nothing wrong or foolish about being proud of Easter Week: the sorrowful thing is that those who followed have betrayed the ideals of the men who fought for Ireland then. The "terrible beauty" that then flamed died as soon as it had been born; died with the men who died then.

And the Irish Language—what's wrong with it? It may not be "glorious," but it is an old tongue and a very beautiful one; though one wouldnt know this when listening to Dev or the President speaking it.

[1] Writing to me from his home in Dun Laoghaire in 1978, Conor O'Brien stated: "At the risk of adding to your Fund of Useless Information, I toss you the following O'Casey morsel. I was in my twenties when I saw the first night of 'The Bishop's Bonfire.' Because of the disproportionate noises by the lunatic few, and the publicity they got, I became passionately concerned to let O'Casey know that a new generation was about to take charge of things in Ireland. We were rejecting the lay-tyrants of the Catholic Church, the double-think nationalism, the enforced imposition of the Irish language and the various forms of censorship of Irish and other writers. (As I write that, it strikes me that we didn't do too badly!) But as you can see, Sean wasn't too optimistic about us. You can deduce that I had told him how funny I had found the first two acts, but was forced to admit I thought the last act was daft. He sent me, and inscribed, a copy of Cock-a-Doodle etc which, of course, I still greatly treasure. Well, amen! Conor O'Brien. PS.–I'm *not* Cruise O'Brien!"

As for the "daft ending" of THE B'S BONFIRE, you may remember Wilde's verse from Ballad of Reading Jail, "each man kills the thing he loves"; and Ophelia, and many other instances of daft endings. Besides, it is symbolical of Ireland today, when so many seem to be killing the thing they love. Well, I'm very busy, and cant go on arguing with you, only to add that I'm glad you enjoyed the fun in the play. An Irish critic writing from New York, said about PURPLE DUST, that it was plain that humor wasnt O'Casey's medium; but the N. York people are finding it the funniest play I have written. I sent you, under another cover, a copy of COCKADOODLEDANDY—hope you'll like it. Well, amen.

Yours sincerely,
Sean O'Casey

To Robert Emmet Ginna

MS. GINNA

29 MARCH 1957

My dear Bob,

It was very pleasant to hear your voice speaking the other evening, after travelling for such a distance under the waves, & bringing a good kind message from friends in the United States. It was good to hear, too, that "P.Dust" was still as bright as ever, and giving a laugh or two to many. Curious you should say you thought it was the funniest play of all; for when it first showed itself within the Cherry Tree [Cherry Lane Theatre], an Irish Critic of the Irish Newsagency in New York wrote home to the Irish Papers that "P. Dust" showed plainly humor wasn't O'Casey's medium. So you must be mistaken, Bob, for this Irish Press agency genius evidently [knows] where & how humor is born, and where humor dies.

By the way, Bob, when you were here, you took some fine photos of meself and of Niall as we stood on Totnes Station waiting for a train; also a lovely one of me & you together, tho' who took this I can't remember—musta been Niall.

Well, if you still have the plate, could you do one or two of Niall? We have but one copy of him, & would like one or two more. He is bare-headed, wears a duffle-coat, & is standing by himself. It is a lovely picture, the best we have of him, for in it, he stands out alone in all his young glory. If the plate isn't handy, please don't go to search for it, for you've enough to do without looking for things past, &, having taken so many pictures, a particular one would be hard to find.

I am trying to mold a play into being, but am not very enthusiastic about it; but it wouldn't be good just to stay idly looking out of a window. It is said God never ceases working out His way, so why the hell should I? In my mind's eye, I often see you still wearing that grand crimson cap when you came to us with Gjon [Mili]; & I envied it. If you ever see Gjon, give him my love, who wouldn't listen to anyone but himself.

My love to all my friends, and, of course, Bob, to you 'specially. Eileen, Breon, & Shivaun, join their love to mine.

As ever,
Sean

Our eyes to the West when the Fall comes, and the Petunias are still in bloom, looking for you.

To Oscar De Liso

TC. O'CASEY

31 MARCH 1957

Dear Mr. De Liso,

Brrrrm brrrrrm—that's the beat of the O'Casey drum against an enemy trying to persuade him to do what he isnt fit or able to do. Brrrrm brrrrrm—there it is again! So beware!

My friend, my countrymen (or countrywomen) at the moment arent thinking of America (bar those who hope to get there one day). They have many other and more terrible things to think of. We're all nearly down and out, and the guns are shooting along the Ulster Border. The Irish are just thinking of themselves, for they have no time to think of others if Ireland is to last. They are up against a diminishing population, the slowest marriage-rate in the world, a trade deficit that threatens bankruptcy if not taken in hand and by foot, and, proportionate to population, the highest unemployed list in the world. Since the Irish Government was established near a million people have emigrated, mostly, of course, the young and the active.

So you see, the Irish dont care a damn about America now, except to coax dollars from her. The bald-headed eagle looks like a golden one to us now, and dollar bills are more important than the prayers of St. Patrick.

However, if you insist, I suggest you ask Sean O'Faolain to write something for you—he would be far better at the task than I could be. He lives somewhere in Wicklow, but am not certain of the precise spot.

A letter to him as Chairman of the Irish Arts Council, addressed to Dublin, Ireland, is sure to find him.

I am very busy trying to get ideas for a new play and another book of opinions, as well as having to deal with a mountain of letters; so this note is written in haste.

All good wishes,
Yours sincerely,
Sean O'Casey.

To David H. Greene

TC. O'CASEY

2 APRIL 1957

Dear Dave,

Your article in COMMONWEAL[1] was fair and fine, and I doubt if I disagree with any of it. Thanks for sending it to me. I have been very busy, trying to find thoughts for another play and a book of words. Eileen hasnt been too well, for watching Niall die gave her a great shock that numbed her nerves, and stopped digestion from working; but she seems better now. She has had some X rays, and goes to see her doctor today; so I hope the result will be satisfactory.

Niall died very swiftly. There are two kinds of Leucaemia, one chronic, the other acute. When he went into Barts Hosp. London, the doctors thought they could keep him with us for a few months, but, suddenly, after two days there, massive bleeding occurred (said to be rare, but it happens at times), and he died in an hour or two; but retained his fine physical form and his clear and penetrating mind up to a half hour before he died. It was just as well, for what would a few months have meant to him but constant pain, blood transfusions and the shrinking away of the handsome body. He still keeps very close to me, though I try to bury myself in work; but, without any conscious cause, memory of him sweeps over me, tears come, and I hear myself crying out his dear name. But life has to go on, and we have the fond knowledge that he had a happy and a gleeful life, for all his serious thoughts about things, while he was with us.

PURPLE DUST still goes along under full sail and remains a surprise to me that an all-American Caste should have done it all so well.

---

[1] David H. Greene, "A Great Dramatist's Approach to Autobiography," *Commonweal*, 25 January 1957, a review of *Mirror in My House*, the two-volume edition of O'Casey's autobiography.

Sorry to hear about your mother has had a knock, but at 80, one realises that the life is well nigh spent; and there can be naught but a feeling of fulfilment after such a long life. I do hope Catherine is better, for she needs all the energy life can give her to look after her family. Of course the attack on little Candie, and the lesser one on the other children, must have taken toll of her, and the anxiety of it all upset her very much indeed, having so much to think of, so many things to do. May she be as strong as ever soon; BUT she must take care of how and what she eats, and tell her that from me, advice given with the assurance of affection and regard.

I hope you had a lively time at Columbia University, [with] our pal, Emmet [Larkin] on Jim L[arkin]. and the Socialist Party; for Socialism is not only the hope of the workers (Professors are workers just as are field laborers), but also the one hope of the world. You have heard of course that Dev is in again, jumping about like a kid; but Ireland is in a shocking state, economically, spiritually, and culturally, though the Tostal is helping to bring to us a livelier sense of art, if not of literature. I enclose cutting that may interest you; and also my love to the children, to Catherine, and to you.

As ever,
[Sean]

To Seamus Kelly

TC. O'CASEY

3 APRIL 1957

Dear Quidnunc,

The chorus of THE MAN WHO STRUCK O'HARA, sent in by correspondents, was incomplete.[1] They left out two important lines. The word "mopped" was the correct one. The whole chorus, oddly, is sung by a dazed sargeant in the C. Guard, in my play, TIME TO GO, shown within the IV vol of COLLECTED PLAYS.

No one seems to have noticed it, possibly because no one has read the play. It is mentioned, too, in the description of Nuncio O'Hara's flight from the famous meeting held by the Vocational Debating Society, or the students of the Technical Schools[2]—I forget which.

[1] Quidnunc (Seamus Kelly), "An Irishman's Diary: 'O'Hara and the Stick,'" *Irish Times,* 1 April 1957.
[2] See O'Casey's letter to Seumas Scully, 22 November 1952, note 3, Vol. II, for the background of the "insult" to the Papal Nuncio, the Most Rev. Gerald Patrick O'Hara at the inaugural meeting of the Technical Students Literary and Debating Society in Dublin.

So a Belfast Correspondent thinks that an Orange Procession passing through O'Connell Street (Dan wore the Orange and Green) would "be unthinkable at any time." I wonder why. Has the saying changed to "North is North and South is South, and never the twain will meet."

Well, so be it, if God wills it so; but does he?

All the best.
Sean O'Casey

Confidential.
Private.

To R. D. Dougan[1]

TC. O'CASEY

16 APRIL 1957

Dear Mr. Dougan,

Not a chance. I'm not aware that I have any original MS of THE PLOUGH, THE SHADOW, JUNO, or even RED ROSES.

They were written here and there, and never straight out in a fair hand within a tidy copy book; parts appear in books, but sudden ideas were often jotted down on slips of paper, and when transferred to type-script, were flung away; and the books themselves contain other material mixed among the MS of the plays. Where these books may be, I dont know, and I amnt terribly interested; certainly not enough to go on a search after them.

At the moment, while busy with many home problems, I am trying to draft out another play—here and there again—and another book, under a brightly-colored cap. So I am too much engaged with new work— I hope it may be new—to think of far unhappy things and battles long ago.

However, there is an MS in the possession of Mr. Lennox Robinson— he has had it for a long time—of an older play even than the SHADOW— THE CRIMSON IN THE TRI-COLOR, and, if you could persuade him to give it to you, I should be glad, when youve finished with it, to send it back to me.[2] Mrs. O'Casey wrote to him for it (he had mentioned it to her during the production of THE BISHOP'S BONFIRE in Dublin, and had promised to return it, but, evidently forgot all about it).

I should very much like to see the MS of this play myself—it was

[1] R. D. Dougan, Deputy Librarian, Trinity College, Dublin.
[2] See O'Casey's letter to Dougan, 11 May 1957, note 1.

written out in longhand—to see what kind of a thing the play was. The Abbey almost decided to do it, but finally decided against production. It was followed by the Shadow.

All good wishes to you and to all who read in the Library under your care.

Yours sincerely,
Sean O'Casey.

To Dr. Horst Scharschuch[1]

TC. O'CASEY

16 APRIL 1957

Dear Dr. Scharschuch,

Thank you for your letter.

Little as you may know about foreign writers, I assure you that I know less about foreign composers. Not altogether my fault, for the world I lived in as a boy and youth did not look upon music as even an unconsidered trifle.

However, my children know a vast amount more than I do, and I have learned much from them; and am still learning. Yesterday evening my son and I listened to a performance of Wagner's PARSIVAL; and, of course, I know something of Beethoven, Mozart, and Bach; but not half enough, not half enough.

The quotation you mention wasnt taken from either Shakespeare or Milton; nor was it mine. It was written by Alfred Tennyson, a great Victorian poet; one who is now somewhat decried, but, to me, a poet of the first rank.

It was taken from Tennyson's LOCKSLEY HALL,[2] a poem which contains curious prophecies, foretelling the ghastly bombing from the air—which we all have since experienced—please God, never again—; though this poet died in 1865, long before an aeroplane was thought of.

I hope your Theater may be a great success, and I wait with great interest the arrival of the Festival publication.

---

[1] Dr. Horst Scharschuch, Musikbucherei Herschelbad, Mannheim, Germany. O'Casey's letter of 20 October 1956 to Dr. Claus Helmut Drese was translated into German by Dr. Scharschuch, a musician, and printed in the festival magazine commemorating the reopening of the Mannheimer Nationaltheatre.

[2] The lines from Tennyson's poem quoted in the 20 October 1956 letter are: "all that man has done but earnest of the things that man shall do."

With all good wishes to the German people, to German Music, and to you.

Yours very sincerely,
Sean O'Casey.

To J. J. O'Leary

TS. O'LEARY

17 APRIL 1957

Dear J. J.,

A favor or two I'm asking of you; rather is it an asking for information—like Rose Dartle.

Could you find out for me from a friend in the TIMBER business—T. C. Martin or Brooks, Thomas—the weight of a Standard of timber and how many planks would be in one; also the approximate cost of a Standard as supplied to builders from wholesale builders' providers. This request is not wanted for any business matter, but just information to be used in a play that I am at present trying to write.[1] I used to know what was in a standard of timber—many a time with the canvas-covered pad on shoulder, I carried the planks—but I have forgotten weight and number of planks, and never knew the cost. Favor No. 2: Could you let me have a picture—from a poster, or from an advertisement—of the TOSTAL HARP? I've seen it, but don't remember it quite well enough to make an accurate sketch; and no picture of it appears, apparently, in any Ad. here. This too I want for the fore-mentioned play. I have just sent a big ad. of the Dub. and Cork Festival that I cut from the NEW STATESMAN to a friend, Thomas Quinn Curtiss, Paris Drama Critic for the New York "Herald-Tribune," who had never heard of the Tostal. Tom is an American and should be told. He knows about it now, anyhow. By the way, I was seeking a hymn, and got Eileen to search for a Westminster Hymnal when she was in London; but could get no copy save in Westminster headquarters, costing 30/-; and the hymn wasn't in it! A friend of mine in the BBC searched, but found that the hymn hadnt been used for a long time here. However, he found a Hymnal (after I had suggested that it might be used as a Mission hymn), and there it was, large as life, in a Redemptorist Hymnal, the book printed by a Firm called the Cahill Printing Works[2] of Park Lane—no, Park Street, of course, its cost 3/6. Looks like a

---

[1] *The Drums of Father Ned* (1958).
[2] O'Leary was managing director of Cahill Printing Works, 43 Parkgate Street, Dublin.

photostat printing. If the above give bother, never mind. Just let them slip by unnoticed. Very busy at work at a book under a gay-colored cap.[3] I do hope you are well. Eileen sends her love; so do I.

As before & as ever,
Sean

[3] *Under a Colored Cap* (1963).

To Seumas Scully

MS. SCULLY

18 APRIL 1957

Dear Seumas,

Thanks for all the clippings—no improvement in the critics: they still write like those of the "Totnes Times" or a reporter on the "Skibereen Eagle." How respectful they all are to Lady Longford! Never mind about showing what I said about "P. Dust" to the critics—they probably know it's still running; & anyway, their criticisms or opinions are really of no value either to a bad dramatist or a good one. This "modern dress" is an old stunt now: Barry Jackson did it more than 20 years ago. It adds nothing whatever to any newness or experimental advance in the Drama.

I haven't had time to read "Threshold."[1] I get so many magazines myself that I haven't time to read half of them: about 10 a week: American, Canadian, English, Russian, Chinese, Irish, Bulgarian, & Scotland: so I'm full up, & can't crowd another one into my reading. Besides, I'm very busy at new work; have many letters to answer; & I've to find time for Eileen, for eating, & for sleep. I'm writing this note at 1 o'c. in the morning.

If you decide to go in for the Civil Service—good fortune go with you; but won't Dev do something to bring Ireland back on the right way; or is it utterly hopeless? I read somewhere that the Abbey's going to do a play by Niall Carroll. So you see. I don't see this lad doing anything Startling; but one never knows; God does not always appear in expected places.

All good wishes & thanks.
Yrs ever,
Sean.

[1] *Threshold,* a quarterly magazine published by the Lyric Players, Belfast, edited by Mary O'Malley, began publication in February 1957.

To Mrs. John T. Cooper

TS. COOPER

23 APRIL 1957

My dear Georgie,

Thanks very much for your letter and for the fine little photographs of you and John and your friends; photographs that open the door to me, and let me in to join in a family life living in the State of Iowa; a curious sensation; and all young, very young people making a nook in the home for an old veteran of 77 years. And another generation appearing there too—the baby with the nut-brown hair. You are a graceful and fine-looking lass, Georgie, with a delightful figure. Don't mind me saying these things, for an intelligent Irishman always has an eye for a pretty girl; and however ancient he may be, the fine faculty never goes from him. Thanks, too, for the very remarkable article about Ireland in "Foreign Affairs." I have sent it on to the IRISH TIMES, and the "Features Editor" writing says "Thank you very much for sending us the article. It is very interesting indeed. I have a notion that we might ask permission to reprint it in THE IRISH TIMES, but I want to discuss it with the Editor first."

It is a most interesting article, and should be reprinted so that many of us Irish could read it, for it tells almost to a T the way Ireland is today. I've just heard from an Irish Agent who acts for booksellers that every copy of THE GREEN CROW coming into Ireland was seized by the Customs Officials, and held by them.[1] The official Censorship Board isn't in session, because of a resignation, and so, in the meantime, the Customs Officers can seize any book they think may be either indecent or obscene. Very annoying for the persons who have ordered the book, have paid the cost, yet have to wait till God knows when, to get the book they sent for. However, there is a stir going on, through the Tostal, bringing into Ireland many foreigners who are sure to have a good influence upon us Irish by scattering thoughts and ideas that would shock us if they came from our own minds. Indeed, I am just now trying to write a Comedy touching on the activities and ideas of the Tostal (and other things), and hope it may come to a good conclusion. You are indeed right, I fear, about the Christian Church. I who am not a Christian, regret deeply that She hasn't more courage, more understanding, even more faith. But I can't see any reason—from the Christian view, and not from mine—why there should be any objection to doing MURDER IN THE CATHEDRAL within a Church. If I mistake not, it got its first production in Canterbury Cathedral; certainly some Cathedral. So also, did his (Eliot's) THE ROCK. It is curious that the Followers of Jesus should be always running away, and that their

---

[1] All copies of *The Green Crow* were mysteriously seized by the Irish Customs Officials and banned for a year, from February 1957 to March 1958. For further information see O'Casey's letter to Jeffrey Simmons, 14 March 1958, note 1.

Master, should always be on His way to execution. Shaw knew this when he wrote the Epilogue to his ST. JOAN. Let us decorate the statue of the Saint with fresh and sweet flowers, let her shine forth upon us from gorgeous stained-glass windows; but let her not come among us in the flesh, or in the spirit to disturb and to dismay.

Your John Taylor is, I fear, unique. We, I mean life, has a brave fellow, Dr. Soper, head of the West London Mission, a Methodist, who stands firm against all that he thinks to be evil; against war, against hatred of others, whatever politics they may choose, whatever may be the color of their skin; the one cleric in London, far as I know, who fearlessly seeks the truth of life. So we must not despise the day of small things; and God often appears in unexpected places, and doesn't always pop up in a pulpit.

I can't understand why the clerics should be afraid of the drama—or is it embedded in envy and the fear that their thunder might be stolen? Is the dramatist a better preacher than the cleric? And, indeed, isn't the whole Life of Christ, as recorded in the Gospels, and in the Gospel of Nicodemus, a drama from beginning to the end that never is? The church has passed away from the Bishops, and has set her candlestick down in the midst of the militant workers, of whom the Hierarchy are fearfully afraid—witness what happened to the Worker Priests in France.

As for our few words about Faulkner, I enclose a curious reference to him—and to me, in which I am bracketed with the Mississipian Author, with Whitman linked between us. An odd coincidence. Sean O'Faolain is a very clever fellow, and a very fine writer himself of novels and short stories, as well as being a keen-minded critic. He is now Chairman of the Irish Arts Council—the cleverest and most liberal-minded the Council has ever had.

And many thanks for your kind remembrance of my birthday, and for the charming song that came with it. I am sure about the song, but not so sure about the music. Breon played it for me—after a practice, but found it difficult; then Shivaun played it for me, and as she plays much better, it sounded fairer than when Breon assayed it; but I found it hard to lilt the words to the music. However, that's nothing, for I have not yet gone beyond the power to lilt a folk-song; though I can manage a little of Verdi. Thank you, Georgie, for *When the Hand of Spring,* and you, Kenneth Haxton, for the Music that goes with it. The hand of Spring has touched our little garden, and the twigs have ravelled into the green leaves. The polyanthuses are out, and the lilac, too, and the laburnum has thousands of yellowing buds upon it, that will soon be a golden cascade of bloom. And, yet, there is one who will never again see this sight, this wonderful sight, or sit serenely beneath them.

Give my thanks to John for the book on America's Heritage; I have looked at the pictures, and will, when I have a moment, read what the book says about them. I shall write to John when I get a second moment (Shivaun is home with us, and takes a lot of my time) to spare.

Meanwhile my love to him and to you, Georgie; and to your friends in the photographs, and to the dear little one with the Nut-Brown Hair.

As ever,
Sean

To Mrs R——

MS. PRIVATE

23 APRIL 1957

Dear R——,

That was an unexpected announcement in your last letter, tho' by no means a surprising one, for falling in love is a common thing in this life, tho' it's always uncommon indeed to the one who suffers in the fall. And there is no advice or council to be given; for in this condition the ear is closed, & the poor one hears only her own heart-beats. But I should advise you to refuse to feel pity for the lone soul in Connemara. He is not lonely, for he is among thousands; thousands of souls there & elsewhere are as frustrated as his seems to be. Ireland is one long drawn-out sigh. The people have the burden, not only of original sin, but also of unoriginal sin, and aboriginal sin as well. I doubt if their multitude of prayers have the buoyancy to lift them out of the Purgatory they have created for themselves. There is a sign of a stir there now; several in fact, and, I think, the Tostal is one of them; but this won't reach the lonely soul in Connemara: he seems to be past praying for. But take care of yourself: don't let your sympathy betray you. I imagine you to be a rather impulsive woman, ever ready—&, at times, too eager—to shed forth that sympathy regardless for the time of your own needs & your own importance; and many there be who are only too inclined to take advantage of it, ay, and abuse it as long as it may last. I can think of no more to say, for in such an emotional experience, words from others are as the idle wind; pleasant to feel, but having no possible power to help or modify the passion. The sufferer can be his own physician; no one else can give a remedy. So, R., my dear, think over it all quietly—if you can—, and see if there be enough reason & sense in the emotion to allow it to remain in your heart. I am so glad to hear that A. & her husband are happy & busy together.

And thank you so much for the lovely flowers which always look so lovely and so calm in full bloom, & stay so calm when the bloom is over, & their petals fade.

I am very busy trying to write another comedy—"The Night is Whispering"[1]—touching on the Tostal; & another book of passing thoughts & comments.

My love to A. & her man, & to you.

As ever,
Sean

[1] The tentative title of *The Drums of Father Ned.*

To Miss Jane Rubin[1]

TS. RUBIN

26 APRIL 1957

Dear Miss Rubin,

Mr. [Philip] Burton was here with us on Tuesday, and gave us a graphic account of the production of PURPLE DUST; very interesting and encouraging. I am inclined to the idea of Paul Shyre taking charge of COCKADOODLE DANDY; but should like to see and speak with him first before deciding. The question of a Director comes into my mind. I think we can set aside the thought that Robert Lewis will ever be in a position to do this; and we have waited a long time. I am in some doubt about a Broadway Production—it would be so costly; but will talk to Paul about all this when he comes to England.

I havent got the Contract for the Film of JUNO. I remember sending it on to Mr. Madden who had gotten an inquiry. There was a proposal from a John Heuston (I think) years ago that I should agree to a Film of JUNO, starring Barry Fitzgerald, minimising the part of Juno; and Barry's brother, Arthur Shields, wrote me a long letter appealing for my consent; but I refused to have anything to do with it. It may have been for this; but I'm sure it was for an earlier inquiry. Anyhow, to make assurance double sure, I searched, and Breon searched, and Mrs O'Casey searched, but, as I foresaw, there was no contract to be found. The Film was done—if I remember right—by a Co. called "The International Film Co.,"[2] but it ceased to exist years and years ago. Hitchcock was their

[1] Miss Jane Rubin, The Richard Madden Play Company, New York, O'Casey's American agent.

[2] British International Pictures made the film of *Juno and the Paycock,* released in 1930, directed by Alfred Hitchcock. Barry Fitzgerald, who created the role of "Captain" Boyle on the Abbey stage, played an extra in the film. For the cast, see O'Casey's letter to Gabriel Fallon, 28 February 1929, note 4, Vol. I. For objections to the film version, see his letter to Charles Rosenberg and Martin Kesselman, 23 March 1955.

Director, and a Mr. Mycroft—who came to see me to arrange terms—was Manager.

That's all I can do about it; except to say I have an offer from Television Diffusion Co. Dublin, for the rights of this play and for "The Plough and the Stars." This Co. has the sole right (they say) to the services of the Abbey Theater Company, and have already done a Film of George Shiels "Professor Tim." I wont take this up, however. I have had an offer for THE GUNMAN from Independent Television here—one or two performances—but am waiting till I hear something about the terms submitted by me to the English Co. who asked about it, and about which I told you in a previous letter. Sorry to hear the three short plays cant come to Broadway. I share your hope that PURPLE DUST will pull up again now that Lent and the Jewish Feast is over. By the way, I wonder are those who wished the musical JUNO now wishing it no longer? I shouldnt mind a bit, if it didnt go forward, though it would be hard on Joe Stein. All the best and thanks for checks received safely. As ever,

Sean O'Casey

P.S. I'm inclined to think Philip Burton would be a good Director for Cockadoodle Dandy.

To Frank McCarthy

TC. O'CASEY

28 APRIL 1957

Dear Frank,

Enclosed is your typescript, DEATH OF ONE MOTHER'S SON— better D. of a Mother's son. I have read it, and there is enough in it to make a book: the Waiting; the stay in the dark basement; the march to the wharf; the tramp steamer; the torpedoing; the Island; the final barracks or camp, and Lew's death.[1] It is written very simply and straightforwardly, and, in my opinion, deserves publication; but hardly in JOHN BULL. THE ARGOSY, on the other hand, dont want these simple, honest-to-God stories. Not a nice thing to read on a train journey, for it would remind many mothers (and fathers too) of how their sons left life.

Again, it isnt concerned with the big ones; Churchill can write about the war, publishers war to get the rights, C. makes a fortune; but then he

---

[1] This autobiographical short story was based upon McCarthy's military experiences during World War II, when his troopship was torpedoed, and he was rescued after floating in the sea for twenty-six hours. See O'Casey's first letter to him, 27 October 1946, note 1, Vol. II.

doesnt discuss the ordinary inarticulate Tommie or Jack Tar. So can Alanbroke, and others can make a big sum in other books about these books written by generals or by admirals, who just pass-by with shut eyes to the millions of poor damned souls who had to suffer to make their histories. I think your story very interesting; anyhow I read it through; without stopping, and not a line of it bored me. You might chance the Statesman with it, though it might be too long for them; or IRISH WRITING, whose address I've forgotten; but I get their quarterly, and when the next comes, I will let you have it.

Well, there you are—that's my opinion; but shouldnt have read it, even opened it if you hadnt been Frank, for if I dealt with what comes, I'd do nothing night and day but read MS. of others; mostly terrible.

By the way, dont make a mistake about R. Catholicism and their filled churches here. 50,000 leave the Church every year in England alone; or so they themselves say; and they are in a way about this "leakage." And what with the state in other C. countries—seven per cent go to Church in France, and as few in Italy. Ireland's (with Portugal) is the outpost of the West. Remember what happened to The Priest Workers in France? Must end now; trying to think out another play, and another book, so have little time to meself; and hundreds of letters to answer. All the best to you, and I hope you are minding your health.

As ever,
[Sean]

To Miss Mary Doyle[1]

MS. O'LEARY

29 APRIL 1957

Dear Miss Doyle,

Thank you very much for your information about the Timber.[2] So now, I know. It was very kind of you to take all the trouble to find out, & then to write to tell me. I never guessed 4 tons would cost £185; but, then, in my time—more'n 50 years ago—timber wasn't quite so dear; tho' less of it was used: funny that.

By the way, please tell Mr. O'Leary not to bother about the Tostal Poster—I've gotten a design of a somewhat similar kind of a Harp, with

---

[1] Miss Mary Doyle, secretary of J. J. O'Leary at Cahill Printing Works, Dublin.
[2] She sent the following information in a letter of 26 April: "On Timber, One standard: 270 cubic feet; Weight: 4 tons approximately; Price: £185; No. of planks: 120—size 12 ft. x 9 ins. x 3 ins."

the addition of the head of Oengus & one of his Beautiful Birds, the former placed among the strings; the latter placed at the butt where the Harp rests.[3]

Thanks again to you, and all good wishes to you.

Yours sincerely,
Sean O'Casey

[3] Below he drew two rough sketches of the strings and butt of a harp.

To Konstantin Simonov[1]

TC. O'CASEY

[? MAY 1957]

My dear Friend,

Enclosed is an attempt to write a few words for your *Novy Mir,* which may be or may not be suitable for your Magazine.[2] However, if it isnt suitable, the good wishes and the blessing at the end of my say will, I am sure, find a welcome in the bosom of *Novy Mir.*

The coming [Youth] Festival has a special interest for me, for our younger lad of 21, who died swiftly as the New Year came our way, was eagerly looking forward to be one of the students at the Festival. He had been preparing for it, putting up money to pay his way, and eagerly talking about it to me when we happened to be together. He died from the same horrible thing that killed one of your famous scientists but a short time ago—another problem for the young to solve, and deliver themselves from this danger.

Well, if there be any survival after death of the spirit, then Niall will be in the midst of the young and gallant and gay in Moscow during the Festival on July next.

In a few days, I shall write to Pavel Chuvikov to try to answer the questions he has put to me. Please tell him so, and give him my warm regards; and to Mr. Apletin, and all my friends and fellow-writers of the Soviet Union.

Yours very sincerely, with my love and regards.

Sean O'Casey.

[1] Konstantin Simonov (1915–   ), Russian poet, novelist, playwright, on the editorial staff of *Novy Mir.*

[2] The accompanying article, "The Rose of Youth," appeared in translation as "Roza Yunosti," *Novy Mir,* Moscow, July 1957.

The Rose of Youth

The Rose of Youth will be a big one—far bigger than the glorious chrysanthemum budding out from the top of the burning castle in Strindberg's *The Dream Play,* and bigger than the huge thistle, its barbs pointing everywhere, its handsome purple plume touching the clouds, in Hugh McDiarmuid's great poem, *A Drunk Man Looks at the Thistle;* the Rose of Youth will be greater than either of these, for its many-colored petals will cover the whole of Moscow's great City during the coming month of July; and the voices of youth will in many tongues proclaim its loveliness and its greatness to the living world; and to those parts of the world which have not risen from the deadness of old ideas, old customs, and out-worn creeds.

I am sure it will be a great sight to see the active, buoyant spirit of youth, serious and gay, moving melodiously about under the fluttering flags of almost all the Nations, they themselves under the broad and generous Banner of the Great Union of Socialist Soviet Republics. Though unable to be there, I shall be there in the spirit, singing with the young people, dancing with them, my old somewhat quivery voice adding a word or two to what their young and eager voices are saying, my hope as bright as theirs, my resolution to go on working and fighting for the newer and far more sensible way of life that Communism will eventually bring to the world of men.

Of course, we cannot be always dancing or always singing, or always playing games—these pleasant things would become an irritating monotony if we were to keep doing them always. We have to work as well, for by work alone can we win the leisure and energy and the health to [enjoy] these pleasant and often wonderful things. Not work, of course, that forces us to savage ourselves, to work from dawn to dark, so that leisure and enjoyment and power may be provided for the privileged few; those few who think they are favored by God because they have been born with a silver-spoon in their mouth, and who bribe so many of the brighter minds through the Press, the Radio, the Theater, and Television, to keep their plump arses safely seated on thick-piled plush seats. So we work to provide for our own needs and the needs of our neighbours, while others work to make leisure profitable, healthy, and pleasant; each using his gift of energy and intelligence and imagination for the benefit of all; for only in this way can work become a good rhythm keeping the body healthy and the heart young.

Every kind of work has some art in it: the smelting of steel; the serving in a co-op; the handling of food in a restaurant; the driving of a train, navigation and management of a ship; the making of everything as well as the recording of items in a ledger: there is art in all of these as well as in the writing of a story, the painting of a picture, the carving of a stone, the creation of a music-score; and so we welcome and we honor everything that man can do—the surgeon and the nurse, the soldier and the sailor, the tin-worker and the tailor, and the machinist who weaves the cloth and him or her who makes the shoes with which we tread the world.

All these young workers will be gathering together within the arms of the great city of Moscow during the coming month of July. They will come with banners and with much music, and will go about on dancing feet; and the young of all Nations, men and women, dear men and women, of all colors, and of many languages, and of differing creeds, will embrace and kiss each other, and cry comrade dear comrade, hail to you! Come sing with me, and dance with me, and eat with me, and drink the good wine to a safer and a happier world, which we are helping to bring within the happy and sensible management of man.

First of all, the young will wet their red lips with wine to drink to their Host, the great, throbbing Soviet Union, flying Her Red Banner, embossed with Hammer and Sickle, their Host's grand symbol; then the young lips will wet their mouths with wine, and drink to the Red Star, the shining symbol of Communism, the wide world over. Let me echo a line from a song in a play written eighteen years ago: "Aha, Red Star, arise, the wide world over!"

I send an old Irishman's warm wishes to all the young who will gather to make the Youth Festival of 1957 the great joy and activity it is bound to be; and I put my blessing on them, in the name of all those who in the Auld Lang Syne labored, consciously or unconsciously to bring this great gathering of the world's youth to life.

Yours As ucht mo chroidhe—from my heart's center.

Sean O'Casey.

To Clayton Garrison[1]

TC. O'CASEY

2 MAY 1957

Dear Clayton,

Yes, I got the book[2] allright, and have read a good deal of it, though my reading has to be limited these days, for the one eye left to me shows its age, and knows its age, and has to be guarded with many rests. I found your thesis very interesting indeed, but cant say whether you be right or wrong. I am always very reluctant to speak about my own work, reluctant even to think about it; and I could never recommend anyone to take on the task of writing a book of comments about what I have done in the way of drama. So you must decide this for yourself.

The reason why I didnt write before is that when your book came, we were all in a state of emotional upset, for our younger lad, a lad of twenty-one, was dying. He ended his life just as the first day of the present year was dawning. It was a great blow, and up to now, I not only cannot

---

[1] Clayton Garrison, a graduate student at Stanford University, California.

[2] Emery Clayton Garrison, "The Structure of Sean O'Casey's Plays," doctoral dissertation, Stanford University, 1956.

reconcile myself to his death, but am unable even to realise it. For a long time, Mrs. O'Casey was ill with the shock and is still under the doctor's care.

As for the structure of my plays, I havent much of a clear idea about it. I never make a "scenario," allowing the play—as I write it—to grow into fullness in its own way; for, like life, thought has odd ways of changing, circling about, coming back, and going away again; and of taking a multitude of shapes. The unexpected so often so suddenly. We, for instance, were expecting a happy, a very happy Christmas last year, with a few presents bought for each other, and all the family at home, two boys and our girl—to sing the usual carols, and spend the day with quiet hilarity. Our boy, Niall, had come home from University for the holidays, feeling a little tired, which we thought was due to his activities against the then invasion of Egypt by France and Eng. However, a test showed what was wrong, and Niall got a sentence of death. So, I spent Christmas Day motoring through a fierce wind and floods to get to the hospital where the boy was fighting bravely to be reconciled to death. So you see, life, and all it means, can change in the twinkling of an eye; and that is why—one reason, anyway—why I havent much favor for the "well-made play."

But dont ask me to encourage you to use your time on an "exhaustive study of my life and work." I, for one, couldnt say that the work would be worth it. I havent an exalted opinion of what I have tried to do; am far from satisfied with it; and couldnt for a moment wish or expect another to have one either.

Thank you, Clayton, for the book, a fine-looking work, and thank you for your criticisms, but dont ask me to say Amen when you praise me. My love to you and yours,

As ever,
[Sean O'Casey]

To J. J. O'Leary

MS. O'LEARY

8 MAY 1957

My dear J.J.

Thank you for the Tostal Poster, and a very graceful and charming Poster it is. It is now up on a wall in my room, and gives the space where it's placed the colorful look of a stained-glass window in a secular church. I'm glad it's so good. I've been trying to write a play touching the Tostal, a comedy—in the Tostal's favor, & all that this activity may bring to our sore Irish souls—"The Night is Whispering"; but God only knows whether or no I shall succeed in writing it; or, if I do, when it will be finished. I hope the Drama Festival may be a success, tho' I imagine the Abbey should have chosen newer plays—even if they had to leave Ireland to get them. All old stuff in Abbey, Gate, and Olympia, & indeed, in Gaiety, too.

Isn't it possible from the population of Ireland (or even from the companies of Abbey, Gate, Globe, & Pike) to do a Shakespeare play, full out, no word missing, so's to get the Censorship Board & Customs offices going to rid Eire of this shockingly indecent & blasphemous playwright?

I see some Waterford cleric says there's 700 or 800, or 900, or the round 1000 Communists in Dublin![1] And that some homes have taken down the picture of the Sacred Heart, & replaced it by a picture of Stalin. Wonders will never cease. Dublin is missing her Alfie Byrne.[2]

All good wishes to you.
Yours very sincerely,
Sean

P.S. I see, too, the Hungarians are giving trouble.[3] I'm afraid they aren't the dispossessed angels a lot thought them to be.

---

[1] "Irish Reds Still Active," *The Standard,* 10 May 1957, a report of a speech by the Rev. Father Harty, O.P., inaugurating the Rosary Crusade among the employees of the Irish Tanners Ltd., Portlaw, Co. Waterford. *The Standard,* a weekly newspaper published in Dublin; the issue for the week of the 10th appeared before the 8th, when O'Casey saw it and wrote his letter.

[2] Alderman Alfred "Alfie" Byrne, who died on 13 March 1956 at the age of 74, had been elected Lord Mayor of Dublin for the 10th time in 1954, and for years was known affectionately as the official hand-shaker of Dublin, the object of many good-humored jokes as well as the symbol of good fellowship.

[3] On 29 April 1957, 371 Hungarian refugees in Knockalisheen Camp, Co. Clare, staged a hunger strike as a protest against their "sit and rust" existence in Ireland, where 500 of them had come five months earlier after the Hungarian Revolt of 1956.

To George Jean Nathan

MS. CORNELL

9 MAY 1957

My very dear George,

Now that Spring has come again (badly here, for frost chills the ground o' mornings, rain is slashing down, and many hearts feel miserable), I hope you are holding your own, and writing an odd word about the Theater. I daresay, you've heard an attempt is being made to transmute "Juno" into a Musical; a venture that doesn't fill me with enthusiasm; but if the effort kills the Play, I won't wail, for I'm dead sick of this play; & would like to forget all about it.

To keep my mind from brooding about our boy, I have set out to try to write a comedy, with my head among the clouds rather than the stars; a play of common language, but, I hope with some humor in it. It's called "The Night is Whispering."

Speaking over the phone to our friend Tom C[urtiss]., he told me he was with you to celebrate your Birthday. How I wish I could have been with you.

Well, we are always pretty close together, in spite of the broad sea between.

My love to you, as ever, George; & to your Julie, too.

Sean

To Paul Shyre

MS. SHYRE

9 MAY 1957

Dear Paul,

Thanks for your letter. You sure do need a rest, & deserve one, too. Sorry to hear audiences are less, but it is inevitable that in the Spring thoughts should be of things other than purple dust; and all things come to an end: good or bad.

Fine for you getting the Drama Desk Award.[1]

We listened again a few evenings ago to "I. K. at the D." & to "Pictures in Hallway," and were astonished again at the vigor and humor of the acting. God's truth, I laughed a lot myself; ay, & was moved, too; so that I didn't recognize me own writings, the Life that was put into them!

Shall be glad to talk about "Cockadoodle" with you when you come here; & thanks for the honor of being in a Baseball Team, a game I often loved looking at when crowds of your boys were over here with us to help save the world.

All the best to you,
Sean

[1] On 6 May 1957 Shyre had received one of the Vernon Rice Memorial Awards given each year by the Drama Desk, an organization of stage reporters, for "outstanding achievement in the off-Broadway theatre."

To Pavel Chuvikov[1]

TS. INTER LIT, MOSCOW

10 MAY 1957

Dear Friend,

Yes, I safely received the Russian translations of my two plays,[2] and of the two volumes of my autobiographical books;[3] for which I thank the Translators and you.

I liked the format of all, especially of the biographical books—the figure of the lanky lad standing against a russianised background was charming, and, I hope, a harbinger of one-day closer attachment between the great USSR and the tiny Republic of Ireland.

Frankly, I cannot understand why my books should "arouse immense interest among Soviet Readers." They were written against a background of thought and activity, which, though intensely Nationalistic, was, and is, illiberal, at times frantically so; and the only time I can think of when the Soviet thought and action had any resemblance to ours was during the War of Intervention, when the Soviet People had to fight, not only against the nobles, clergy, and big business, but also had to fight for their National Independence. Your news [of] an Edition of 90 thousand amazes me, and, truth to tell, frightens me a little, for I never thought of such a reception for what I had written in the Soviet Union, or indeed, anywhere else. There is, too, the Irish idiom in which I write; the spirit that moves me to go from grave to gay (my own idiom), the references to Irish legend, myth, and the curious, tortuous incidents in our strange eventful history: all hard to understand, except by an Irish mind; and far, far harder to translate. So I can only attribute this (to me) fairy-tale reception of my writing to the Translators, and not to myself.

How different this from what is happening in my own country! Last month, I got a letter from an Irish Dublin Book Agency, who, after telling me of the fine sale of the first issue of my THE GREEN CROW, goes on, "Then as I began to [get] the repeat orders, the Customs commenced a campaign of stopping all copies at entry for submission to a censorship board for examination. This they are entitled to do under the Act, but in one instance, (my instance) without waiting for any examination or decision, they seem to have simply returned the copies without yea or nay of explanation to the publishers." Really a good sign, for it shows that my

[1] Pavel Chuvikov, Director, Publishing House For Foreign Literature, Moscow.

[2] *Ten' Strelka* (Moscow, 1956), a translation of *The Shadow of a Gunman*, by N. Treneva, with notes by A. Startseva. *Yunona I Pavlin* (Moscow, 1956), a translation of *Juno and the Paycock*, by N. Volzhina.

[3] *Ya Stuchus' V Dver'. Na Poroge* (Moscow, 1957), a translation of *I Knock at the Door* and *Pictures in the Hallway,* by N. Volzhina, N. Daruzes, E. Kalashnikov, I. Kashkin, M. Lorre, V. Toper, and O. Kholmskaya, with an Introduction by P. Balashov.

books are having an influence with many Irish readers. Indeed, I have many friends in Ireland, but they live in unsettling conditions, in which it is hard to speak one's mind about anything in the nature of thought beyond the accepted rule and order of the Roman Catholic Church.

Most of the Bishops there are of the Mintzenty type, arrogant, dominating, expecting instant obedience to every little thing they may say, even to the choosing of a site for a school.

But in Dublin, they have to fight for their power. A young doctor, who had been Minister of Health in a former government, and who had brought in a Mother And Child Bill, having within it something of the nature of Socialistic medicine, found that the Cabinet, first having approved of the Bill, had met with a firm demand from the Bishops, during a private meeting between them and the then Irish Prime Minister, that the Bill must be rejected. The young doctor resigned, and, subsequently, joined the Party bossed by De Valera, and in the recent election, during the preparations for the contest between the Parties, this Doctor Noel Browne, was unanimously chosen by the Dublin Branch of De Valera's Party, to stand for a Dublin seat. Immediately after, another prominent member of De Valera's Party, Sean McEntee, declared that if Browne was allowed to stand, he would resign; and, following the clergy's quiet demand that Browne should stand down, the Members of De Valera's potential Cabinet (it was generally expected that De Valera would win) ordered Browne to resign. This he refused to do, and was then formally rejected as a Party candidate. He stood as an Independent, and won a glorious victory, receiving by far more votes from all classes than the very man who had first opposed him—McEntee. So you see my friend, though it is a hard, even a bitter, fight, the fight goes on; and I, for one, will do all I can to forward it till the day I die; for, as you can guess, Ireland takes the first place in my heart, and will till the end comes.

Now, about the question of translating the remaining volumes: Of course, I shall readily do all I can to help in explaining the difficulties of legend, myth, and historical references; but seeing that the work presents so many difficulties to your translators, why go on with it? Why torment your Translators with so much research, so much thought about things, about men and women who are so far away from their ken and knowledge; and who are of so little concern to your Soviet People. Surely, your Publishing House has enough to do with Soviet and kindred literature, without bothering about me. Believe me, I shall not mind a bit if you and your helpers say, Oh, to hell with this chap: he's too hard to make head or tail of, and it would mean too much labor to make his books presentable to the Soviet People. I shall not mind, and I wouldnt be a bit surprised either.

My warm wishes to the Soviet Union and Her People, to your comrades (and mine, I hope), and to you.

Sean O'Casey

To R. D. Dougan

TC. O'CASEY

11 MAY 1957

Dear Mr. Dougan,

I am sorry you didnt manage to get the script of *Crimson in the Tri-Color* from Mr. Robinson.[1] It has a little history of its own. At the first going off, when I sent the MS. in, and was waiting for the decision of the A. Theater, I got word from Mr. Robinson that in his removal from Clare St. to a new residence in Foxrock, the script had been lost, and, in the same letter Mr. R. asked me for a copy. Since the script had been written out in long-hand, there was no copy, and I had to put up with the mishap. After a long time, near a year, if I remember right, I got word that the script had been found, and that it was under consideration. The Abbey got the script typed, but the long-hand one never came back, and this is the one that is still missing.[2] I should be very interested to see how I wrote then; but it seems that the script is gone forever.

But THE CRIMSON IN THE TRI-COLOR did not afterwards become THE PLOUGH AND THE STARS, for, of course, the next play was SHADOW OF A G., and, after that JUNO, to be followed by two one-acters—KATHLEEN LISTENS IN, a political skit; and THE COOING OF DOVES. The Abbey, oddly enough, took the skit, but rejected the other one. It is this play that is probably in Mr. Robinson's mind, for it was, practically, word for word, the present 2nd act of THE PLOUGH. It was far better than the skit, and I wondered why the Abbey didnt see that it was so. Well, a long time afterwards, it was turned into the 2nd act of THE PLOUGH, which Lady Gregory recognised, and spoke to me about how finely it fitted into the play.

The A. Theater must have the script of this play too, for I never got it back; but having a copy (I had a typewriter then), it didnt matter; and the script of the skit, and also a script of THE STAR TURNS RED, sent

---

[1] Lennox Robinson wrote to Dougan saying the script was misplaced or lost; and in his letter of 27 April to O'Casey, Dougan included the following extract from Robinson's letter of 26 April to Dougan: "Sean O'Casey is quite right, I have a very interesting m.s. of *The Crimson in the Tri-Colour* which became afterwards 'The Plough and the Stars,' with a very interesting letter from him: but where? An American searching last summer through all my papers couldn't find it; when Mrs. O'Casey was over last summer I said I would search again and send it to Sean because I know it is of value and he should have it. But it hasn't turned up."

[2] For the background of the above sequence of events see the letters between O'Casey and Robinson from 5 August 1921 to 9 October 1922, Vol. I.

to Fred O''Higgins at his request when he was Manager—his death was indeed a loss to the Theater.

Ah, well-a-day! All good wishes to you and Trinity and to you.

Sean O'Casey.

To Eric Gorman

TS. GORMAN

14 MAY 1957

Dear Eric,

Thank you for the cheque and your letter.

I enclose with this note a formal receipt for payment of royalties on performances of "Plough" last week.

I am not quite happy about the selection of JUNO for the Tostal week. When I heard of it first, I decided to write asking that another play should be performed; but thinking after that this might have caused inconvenience, I left things as they were.

I think the younger playwrights should have had the show during Tostal Week, say Behan or [Michael J.] Molloy; or the play called "Goldfish in the Sun"[1] or [Walter] Macken. Maybe, even, a play that hasnt been on, far as I know, for a long time—Mr. Robinson's WHITEHEADED BOY [1916]. Next Tostal Week, I hope a newer and younger dramatist may shine out among the shamrocks.

I see Tipperary's hurlers are off to America soon. Pity they arent going to the USSR. I do wish this great game should be shown in Moscow, and, later on, we might have all sorts of Nations at it, and fighting Tipperary or Kilkenny or Cork for the World Championship. Why isnt there a Television show of this game? The Soviet People are intensely interested to know more about Ireland; and, indeed, the world knows too little about what we do. I am sending a Tostal Poster to Moscow. Strasburg isnt enough—there they just blather, and we need to show how we live, rather than to let others hear how we talk.

Well, all the best to you and yours, and to the Tostal.

Yours very sincerely,
Sean O'Casey.

[1] Donal Giltinan, *Goldfish in the Sun* (1955).

To Miss Joan McAlevey

MS. MCALEVEY

16 MAY 1957

My dear Joan,

First, my blessing on your stay in Oxford; on all you may see, on all you may do there. You will be a busy lass. Yes, JUNO is to be made into a Musical, tho' I am doubtful about the result. However, no matter how the Musical may change the play, the play will always remain the same. Remember the French (I don't) Ca plus.....[1] And I'm trying to write another play—"The Night is Whispering"; but don't know how it may go. It won't be so good as Cockadoodle anyway; but I'll do my best to weave a comedy out of experiences of my own, of people I knew, and mingle some fancy with all that's said and some of the things done.

Fine to hear that the lilac is with you again; that "the praties is dug an' the frost is all over" in Saratoga Springs. We have had the lilac here, too—one in our little garden—come and gone with fierce cold winds, and frosts o' nights. Spring color is here; but no warmth in the sun; & to sit quiet needs a fire to do it.

I hope your College Pageant may be a great success. The difficulty with these is to portray all, and keep it from going on too long. I remember a Pageant in Totnes that went on & on, till all the watching people left, tho' the pageant went on for ever. But George Dowell won't do that damage to mortals, for he is clever, has a natural bent for the Theater, & has had a good deal of experience: tho' it won't be an easy job even for him. Nor for you, either, watching over the props. Success to both of you.

And please, Joan, dear, *don't* make any socks for me. It is kind of you to think of it; but you simply must reserve all your energies for yourself. Do you hear me? Well, heed, me, too.

My love to your Mother, Dad, and to yourself.

As ever.
Sean

[1] *Plus ça change, plus c'est la même chose,* the more things change, the more they remain the same.

To Irish Times

18 MAY 1957

IRISH WRITERS

Sir,—At the congress of the Christus Rex Society (April 26th) the Rev. Thomas Halton is reported to have said that "writers (Irish) who were loudest in refusing to take dictation from Rome were surprisingly meek in accepting dictation from their English and American publishers."[1]

Who are and who were these writers who accepted dictation from English and American publishers? Yeats, George Moore, Joyce, Synge, Shaw? Here are a few; they represent the great among us. Did these accept dictation from English or American publishers? Did they take dictation from anyone? God says No.

Father Halton says that "in writing for a world market, Irish writers might be forced to forsake the real Ireland and take to writing instead about an Ireland which existed only in the minds of outside publishers and readers." What is the "real Ireland"? Ireland, like all other lands, is a land, not of one, but of many realities; and the one pictured by Father Halton—one of "sex and savagery," and "mawkishly masquerading in shillelaghs and shamrocks," is as real as any of the others. He should read Bullai Mhartain[2] for a glimpse; and it's not long ago since our Civil War gave a big example of it, adding in the riot that opened Ireland's first Tostal.

If he looks at our Irish Christmas cards, he'll find them covered with designs ostensibly taken from the Book of Kells—a bad habit just as amusing and as irritating as one covered over with shamrocks. And, again, the caman [hurley stick] is just another very beautiful form of the old shillelagh. The "shamrocks and shillelaghs for the Americans" are fostered, displayed, showered over every card and memento, not by or for the American, but by and for the Irish-Americans themselves; and, apparently, they won't let go of them. I myself have received cards from many Americans, born and bred in Ireland, that have shown me houses made of shamrocks, lad and lassies swathed in them, round towers growing out of them; and, let me add, those who sent them me were far from being fools. Indeed, a number of them came from minds that any highly intelligent mind would be proud to know. I'm afraid that the shamrock, round tower and shillelagh Ireland is, in its own way, as real as any other

---

[1] From a news report in the *Irish Times,* 26 April 1957, quoting the Rev. Thomas Halton, of St. Patrick's College, Cavan, who had read a paper on "The Catholic Writer," at the 12th annual congress of the Christus Rex Society, at Rosslare.

[2] Síle ní Chéileachair and Donncha Ó Céileachair, *Bullaí Mhártain* (1955), a book of short stories in Irish.

aspect of our country. And there isn't a lot of harm in any of them; it all depends how they are used in a decorative sense.

As for present-day Irish writers "using the clergy as sitting targets for satire"—why not them as well as others? They form a stout part of the population, and are more numerous (and far more powerful) than the Irish politicians, who are hunted hither and thither by all; they even revel in hunting each other. Present-day satire is nothing to what it was once. He should hear the goings-on of Sir John, the priest, with Tyb, the wife,[3] played before a greater presence than Father Halton. Times are changing, if not in Ireland, then almost everywhere else. For good or bad, the cleric's word is no longer a law.

As for censorship, it doesn't stop with the Board. A week or so ago, I received a letter from a friend telling me that a recent book of mine was being held up by the Customs officers at the port, or at the P.O. Parcels Office, and that every copy sent to a customer was unceremoniously returned to the publisher. This has been done so often that the publisher has decided to forward no more of this book to any customer's order.

A short time ago, another letter from one who was, or had been, a student in the N.U.I. [National University of Ireland], asking me to come back to Eirinn, adding that I should be received, not with boos, but with cheers. Cheers, mind you! I challenged his statements, and back came a letter admitting that I "had called his bluff," and telling that some time before the Irish Arts Council had asked the Drama Club to do "Juno" in Cambridge; that the remarks I had been asked to write—called "Captains Courageous"—for the forefront of the programme had had chunks cut out of it; that protests were made, but the fight against this lousy censorship lasted but a few moments, and then died down dead. Not that I want anyone to fight for me, thank you, but it is a manifestation of bad manners, to say the least of it, to mutilate a solicited comment, without as much as a by-your-leave to the author. It is this kind of mean and stealthy censorship that is sapping away the virility and courage of Irish thought. The Board, at least, is open, and a body that is a laughing-stock to the outer world, though it is, of course, a stupefying menace to Irish writers dependent upon Irish appreciation of their work.

The idea that "what appeared necessary was more study, or criteria which might help the Board to assess obscenity," makes a fella laugh. A word or an action is obscene only when the mind thinks it to be so; and,

---

[3] John Heywood, *John John the Husband, Tyb his Wife, and Sir John the Priest*, a 16th-century anticlerical farce of uncertain date. Heywood (c.1497–c.1580), playwright and poet, first writer of English comedy, musician at the courts of Henry VIII, Edward VI, and Queen Mary, married to the niece of Sir Thomas More and one of his distinguished uncle's disciples, was eventually forced to leave England because of his Catholic faith. O'Casey obviously knew about Heywood's life and work. See O'Casey's letter to the *Irish Times*, 8 June 1957, note 2.

odd enough, this obscenity in Ireland seems to be exclusively connected with sex. But sex laughs at cleric and censor. When it comes, a physiological upsurge, the robin sports a redder breast, the lapwing gets himself another crest, a livelier iris changes on the dove, and dodging into secret places go the lover and his lass.—Yours, etc.,

Sean O'Casey

Devon, May 14, 1957

To Eric Gorman

TS. GORMAN

21 MAY 1957

Dear Eric,

Thank you for the cheque, the formal receipt for which I enclose with this note.

I am glad you had such a good week, and I do hope the PLAYBOY may have a better one.

I am still a little unhappy that a younger and a newer playwright wasnt chosen instead of me for the Tostal Week. Denis Johnston's MOON ON THE YELLOW RIVER [1931], for instance—a fine play from a younger dramatist than I am. I am always sensitive about younger ones feeling envious about my play being on instead of theirs—a very natural feeling. I applaud your hope that next time, a fine play from a young fella may be in your hands for the Tostal.

I am all for the Tostal—not for the delectation of visitors, but for the stir it makes among ourselves; and Ireland needs this stir. The only doubt I have about the Tostal is that one every year may be too much for us. Look at England with HER National Festival, a fine one, and then— looks like never again. She must have exhausted herself, and she with all her resources. It takes a lot of organization, and a hurried year's work— just after the celebration—for the coming Tostal seems a big pressure. There should be a Ministry for this work, for it is essential to Ireland's move forward into the living breathing world. Did you see the picture of the statue of the Blessed Virgin and Child, done by a French sculptor for a church in Southern France (in Irish Times)? Very graceful, and a harbinger, I hope, for a new spirit in the Art of the Church.

And the Tostal Poster was a fine one; graceful, colorful, and full of meaning. I'm sending it on to Moscow to show friends there something that Ireland has done. They are all very eager to know as much as possible about us; and my books have sent [them] studying other books about Ireland's past and Ireland's present.

Well, all the best to you and yours, and to the Tostal.

As ever,
Sean

To Philip Burton[1]

MS. BURTON

22 MAY 1957

Dear Philip,

For Christ's sake, man, don't bother your head about what you read in the TIMES. There was nothing objectionable in it that I could see. Rather, it was a kindly reference. Tho' you didn't act out the whole play, you did a good deal of it; & tho' I didn't laugh uproariously, I was amused. I was too intently interested to laugh a lot. And it is true to say that I wished I had had a rehearsal of P. Dust, such as yours, before I sent the original script to the publishers.

The one reference I didn't like was the reference, not to me, but to the Great O'Neill, who wasn't really a "cantankerous fellow"; rather was he a very charming man; & who did not scorn a tip or two, if it came from an intelligent commentator. O'Neill had a great respect for Nathan and B. Atkinson—to mention two critics—, tho' not necessarily agreeing with everything they said about his work.

My new play—if it ever come to life—was not inspired by the success of "P. Dust," but if anyone wants to believe it was, well, they are welcome to do so. On a lot of occasions (not on all), there's no harm in thinking wrongly. So ends my philosophy.

My good wishes to you in your hard & tedious work of keeping "P.D." going.

Warm regards
Sean

---

[1] Philip Burton (1904–   ), Welsh-born theatre director; foster-father of the actor Richard Burton. He directed the highly successful New York premiere of *Purple Dust,* which was still playing at the Cherry Lane Theatre. For production details see O'Casey's letter to Paul Shyre, 28 December 1956, note 1.

To Brooks Atkinson

TS. ATKINSON

25 MAY 1957

My very dear Brooks and Oriana,

It was very pleasant to hear from you, though I often do, indirectly—I have just been reading your Review of A MOON FOR THE MISBEGOTTEN.[1] A sad history of a self-lost brother. Eugene was inclined to be too compassionate, too inclined to torture himself by the sin of omission in others who were near and dear to him. Frailty thy name is man as well as woman, and all that Eugene could do about it was nothing; and so it was futile to grieve. I've seen over years great talents in my own brothers, not one, but three, wasted either through drink or vanity; but it availeth me nothing to go into perpetual mourning about it.

Well, Brooks, there's me for you! I thought I had told you about the play I was trying to write; but my memory fails me at times now since Niall went from us. I have written one out which has to be gone over, and a lot of work done on it, before it passes away from me; I have left the MS aside for a month or so, till I have forgotten a lot of it so that I can come fresh to it again, and so make a last effort to set it in form for a possible production. I hope I may succeed. It is to be titled, I think, THE NIGHT IS WHISPERING, and I'm calling it a comedy. There is no tragedy in it, anyway. The play does deal with the activities of the Tostal, and tries to urge the activity onward, with funny interludes—that is, I hope they may be funny. It takes place in a small town called Doonavale which is rough Irish for "Shut his mouth," and the hero, Father Ned, doesn't appear at all, but inspires all that is attempted, and blesses the something that has been done. I include the scene that took place in Yonkers,[2] told of in ROSE AND CROWN, but the Northerner in the play takes a bigger part in the various stirs, and is bewildered by Father Ned. The trouble is that I haven't been able to pack in all I should have liked, and though I haven't been able, it seems to be too long already. It is to open with a prologue (Prerumble, I calls it), showing Doonavale on fire, with the Black and Tans prominent in the picture; then opens when the present-day survivors have established themselves as the lords and masters of the people, the middle-class, who under the wing of Holy Church, dominate, and try to make themselves impressive. But, God only knows, whether or no I shall succeed in making a plausible play of it.

Paul Shyre rang me today from London. He is crossing to Dublin tomorrow to speak at a "symposium" upon the International Theater; and he will enter into a fine stir that has just happened. The Director of the

[1] Eugene O'Neill's *A Moon For the Misbegotten* opened in New York on 2 May 1957, and Atkinson's review appeared the next day in the *New York Times*.
[2] See "Wild Life in New Amsterdam," *Rose and Crown* (1952).

Pike Theater,[3] a small Club activity, brave and experimental—they were the first to do WAITING FOR GODOT—has been arrested for producing a lewd, indecent, and obscene play, calculated to corrupt the morals of those who go to see it; the name of the play is THE ROSE TATTOO, a name that you have heard before. Before allowing bail, they wanted him to go under bond not to do the play again, or to allow any other to do it under his name. This he refused, and, as the case was adjourned till July, he may be prison for quite a while. Just a week before, I had a letter in THE IRISH TIMES replying to a Catholic teacher in a Cavan College, who had lectured about the Catholic writer and the Censorship; a letter that is provoking yelping letters in the same paper. It is all very comic, but it has a dangerous effect on potential Irish writers, and we have neither a Shaw nor a Yeats in Ireland now. THE ROSE TATTOO was to be transferred from the Pike Theater to the Gate, but Lord Longford has timidly cancelled the arrangement.

I am very sad about George,[4] but, as you say, he will hardly be himself again. The old resilience isn't there when one reaches seventy—except on rare occasions. He tells me he still writes for ESQUIRE, and that he has managed to write another book on the theater. He's making a bonny fight of it. By the way, Brooks, how does he stand financially? I asked Tom Curtiss, and he told me he was still earning; but I have been anxious about him. If any effort is needed to help him, and is undertaken, I'd very much like to give a hundred dollars or so to the fund. I didn't like to ask Julie, but you may probably know how things are.

We are all well. I agree that I do write too many letters, but I find it hard to restrain myself from answering those who are good enough to write to me.

Oriana is, apparently, as busy as ever. I hope her novel may be a great success. I hope neither she nor you are overdoing it with the wallpapering, polishing, and the other domestic jobs. By the way, several hoopoes are nesting in Sussex—the first, and it is hoped that they may become nationals. I do hope they do, and that some of the clan may come to Devon.

Talking on the phone to Shivaun tonight—she is in Dublin—, she asked me to give you and Oriana her love, Eileen and Breon join her, and so, begod, do I.

As ever,
Sean

[3] Alan Simpson, director of the Dublin Pike Theatre, was arrested on 23 May 1957 for having "produced for gain an indecent and profane performance" of Tennessee Williams' *The Rose Tattoo* during the Dublin Tostal. See Alan Simpson's *Beckett and Behan and a Theatre in Dublin* (1962), Ch. V, "The Rose Tattoo." And for the relationship between *The Rose Tattoo* case and the "banning" of *The Drums of Father Ned* ("The Night is Whispering"), see David Krause's *Sean O'Casey: The Man and His Work* (1960), Ch. 5, Part 3: "Bonfires and Drums."

[4] George Jean Nathan continued to suffer from serious complications after his second prostate operation in 1956, and he never fully recovered. See O'Casey's letter to Atkinson, 16 April 1958, on the occasion of Nathan's death.

To Irish Times

30 MAY 1957

IRISH WRITERS

Sir,—The Rev. Thomas Halton hasn't answered any question of mine.[1] He hasn't said whether or no he thinks it right or wrong or foolish that power should be given to a Customs officer to seize a book and return it to the publisher without a word of explanation for his action. What sort of a life is that of an Irish writer, when, apparently, a book by one may be prevented from leaving Ireland, or a book from another writer may be prevented from coming into Ireland!

There is something of a suggestio falsi in the statement that "the Irish aren't at their best when they're angry, only when they are smilin'; smilin' through." These words are not the opinion of O'Casey, but ones spoken by a character in a play, one for whom O'Casey would have no reverence and little respect. Associating words of characters with my opinions is a common thing with Irish critics; but Dr. Halton isn't a critic, and should know better. By the way, in Ireland's present state, and her anxiety to get out of it, there'll be a lot of anger, but very little smilin', as she goes through with it.

I assure Dr. Halton that I wasn't angry when I wrote "The Bishop's Bonfire," or any other play either.

It is odd that when one writes, or tries to write with conciseness and vigour, one is immediately said to be angry, or to be giving vent to an "outburst." Nor was I angry about my book being seized by a Customs official. I am in the fortunate position of not caring a traithnin [a straw] whether a single book of mine is delivered to Ireland or not. But there are many Irish writers brave but budding, who are for ever harried by the thought of what an Irish censorship may say to what they try to do.

I'm afraid that the world in Ireland of St. Tremolo[2] is far more real than Father Halton allows himself to believe—that body of ignorant conviction that gives a yell whenever it thinks Ireland's virtue is being corrupted, or the Catholic Faith (about which it knows very little) undergoing an open or an insidious attack. Ironically, right under the reply given by

---

[1] A letter from the Rev. Thomas Halton, *Irish Times,* 21 May 1957, a reply to O'Casey's letter of 18 May.

[2] One of O'Casey's fictional and satirized Saints in *The Bishop's Bonfire,* famous for the miraculous powers of his horn or *buccina.* He is also called "the buckineeno boyo."

Father Halton, we hear the blast of its bookineeno[3] from the letter of Frank Cunningham of Loyola in St. Assam's avenue (who was St. Assam—was he Irish of the Irish?). An island of tremulos, full of sour noises; the body trembling with tension in its resolution to defend God's Kingdom from any nosey parker; and the Irish writers trembling in fear of writing anything that might start the bookineeno blaring.

This letter must be a little embarrassing to Father Halton's theory of Tremolo's unreality. How these souls revel in the buoyant use of such words as "obscene," "loathsome," "indecent," "profane," and "filthy"! The dull stars of their low-cast sky! Let me halt to say that a couple acting the "double-backed beast" is neither indecent nor obscene—though its aspect may be a comic one. It is the way nature or God ordained it, and neither Cunningham nor O'Casey can do anything about it.

Let Mr. Cunningham cease bothering about the Red Star in O'Casey's coat, and bend to the better job of getting his Government to give up their silly boycott of the Soviet Union, and induce them to invite the Red Army Assembly to display their gifts in the Theatre Royal in Dublin for the next Tostal; or, alternatively, to send to Moscow two of Ireland's first-class hurling teams, and let our brothers, the Russians, see what a grand game we Irishmen play. And a whisper to those unco guid ones who care nothing about money—there is Trade in Moscow, too.

As for being out of touch with Ireland, what I spoke about to farmers in Clare-Galway 33 years ago is still there—farmers forced to sell their produce to shops from which they had got their seeds or a loan of machines—see "Amharc Eireann" [The View of Ireland] in Inniu, May 24th, 1957. I wonder does Dr. Halton or Mr. Cunningham read this paper? If not, they should. Rotten schools and rotten dispensaries are still there, too.

With all respect to Father Halton, the world of literature doesn't recognise a writer as a Catholic per se. Literature demands excellent writing, not caring a damn what religion the writer may be.

I see the Pike [Theatre] has been blunted, whereas it should have been sharpened. The bookineeno boys are blowing fiercer than ever! Yours, etc.,

Sean O'Casey

Devon, May 27th, 1957

[3] O'Casey's pun on "buckineeno." See his letter to John O'Donovan, 30 March 1955, note 6.

To Ralph Ginzburg[1]

TC. O'CASEY

30 MAY 1957

Dear Mr. Ginsburg,

Thank you for your kind invitation to write about the Irish attitude to sex life as if the double-backed beast wasnt something that God hadnt ordained.

I am too busy with other things—a play, a book, and a controversy in the Irish papers about this very matter, coupled with the surging yell and fisty opposition to the performances of THE ROSE TATTOO by Tennessee Williams—to undertake an article about anything.

Besides, I'm not too good at writing articles, and, in my opinion, nothing better could be said than what has already been written by our friend, Sean O'Faolain.[2]

With all good wishes and thanks,
Yours sincerely,
Sean O'Casey.

[1] Ralph Ginzburg, *Esquire,* New York.
[2] Sean O'Faolain, "Love Among the Irish," *Life,* 16 March 1953. Ginzburg had sent a copy of O'Faolain's article to O'Casey, as an example of the kind of article he wanted him to write.

To New Statesman and Nation

1 JUNE 1957

ROSE TATTOO FUND

Sir,—Mr. Alan Simpson, producer-director of the 50-seater Pike Theatre in Dublin, is at present on bail on a charge of "producing for gain an indecent and profane performance"—to wit, *The Rose Tattoo,* by Tennessee Williams.

We have launched a fund to assist him to meet the cost of his defence. Offers of assistance will be welcomed if addressed to our offices, and gifts of money should be made payable to "*The Rose Tattoo* Fighting Fund."

Sean O'Casey, Peter Hall, John Osborne,
John Gielgud, Benn W. Levy, Wolf Mankovitz,
George Devine, Harold Hobson.

Encore. 25 Howland Street, W.1.

To Irish Times

8 JUNE 1957

IRISH WRITERS

Sir,—Now there's another Richmond in the field—a doctor this time.[1] I hadn't an idea that we were dealing with perversion or sexual irregularity, but with normal healthy sexual appetites, whose minds are, or may become, interested in the other worlds of literature, art, and music; the multitude that form Ireland's people, in field, factory, workshop, secondary school, and university. While Dr. Little (May 30th) is insistent on the harm over-indulgence in sex may do (which in normal people is not likely, for nature herself calls a halt, and bodily weakness overpowers the foolish), he never once mentions the positive harm that may be done to those men and women, who, because of differing circumstances, are deprived of this essential enjoyment altogether; Ireland suffering, too, from the restless minds and the barren bodies of those condemned to live a life alone.

And how eager and careful Dr. Little is to light the halo of innocence around his own peculiar surgical and medical textbooks. With all respect to Dr. Little and his authorities, there's very little known about even the physiological nature and functions of the nervous system, less about the configuration of the mind, and nothing at all about the wonderful mystery of thought. They are all still in the region of speculation and experiment; even in the day-to-day work of the general practitioner, there is still a good deal of guess-work. And, whisper, the flip of the doctorial hand, right or left, doesn't send Freud out of the realm of psychological thought and discovery. Freud has made the going damned hard for the fanatics.

Dr. Little thinks to stun us, it would seem, with his "indecent books were the greatest extra-familial collateral cause for sexual corruption." Does he think that an Irish writer has the time or the thought, when he is writing anything, to rush over to have a chat with Dr. Gillesby in order to ask him whether or no what he was writing might possibly be an extra-familial collateral cause of sexual corruption? All this high-faluting nonsense when we don't know even why those whom we call Teddy Boys dress and act as they do, though the inquiry is still going on!

Freud issued no "doctrines"; no one could be more humble than he was about what he thought of the human mind; so different from the dogmatic proclamations of Dr. Little and his extra-familial collaterals. As for His Holiness's declaration, he has to depend for his idea of psychiatry

[1] A letter by Dr. G. A. Little, *Irish Times,* 30 May 1957.

upon the opinions of others, and as this science is but in its infancy, neither one nor other of these opinions has any infallibility of fact. There is nothing new in them, for all know that over-indulgence in anything has unpleasant after-effects.

Dr. Little tells us gloriously that "censorship is a function of law designed to withhold matters (matters!) injurious to men's minds from being made available." Now we know. This insignificant bunch of censors, I suppose, have been designed by God to make no mistake in banning any book written by any man or woman with mind and imagination. If these miss any, there are others waiting in ambush, hordes of them. If not the Board, then a cardinal (Cardinal Logue banned Yeats's "Countess Cathleen" without reading it); the politicians (A. Griffith shouted down Synge's "Playboy of the Western World"); the Board shutting their eyes from modesty while they banned Shaw's "Black Girl in her Search for God." If the cardinal or the bishops miss one, there's the librarians (a lass among them burning a hundred books off her own bat); if the librarians miss, there's the confraternities, the Legion of Mary, the top-gallant ones of Maria Duce, and the readers who ban the books debanned by the Board of Appeal (at the librarians' congress, it was said that often books allowed by the Appeal Board were denounced by local readers, and so removed from the shelves). The banners are like the fleas—a big flea has a little flea on his back, and the little flea a lesser one, set there just to remind him to seize a writer's naughty word and knock it down, and bind him.

Dr. Little reports that His Holiness said: "The dangerous excitation that indecent books may produce resembles that of narcotics." Unfortunately, sex is a "narcotic" that every healthy man and woman needs, and, indeed, so does life itself; for sex is the one way through which life can come. But Ireland is safe from it all. But is she? Here we have bishops, priests, and deacons, a Censorship Board, vigilant librarians, confraternities and sodalities, Duce Maria, Legions of Mary, Knights of this Christian Order and Knights of that one, all surrounding the sinner's free-will in an embattled circle, the bookineeno blowing, and—the thing happens in the midst of them! Close the ranks! Tighten up and tighten round the ironical curtain!

It is near time that these banning boobies realised that God made the bottom as well as the top of the body, and not go running about roaring against human things, as a Boston cleric did when shouting down my own "Within the Gates," exclaiming that "God made the skin to cover the body so as to conceal the horrors lying beneath it"! God hiding His horrors! Horrors within and horrors without. The human form divine is getting a tough time of it in Banba [Ireland] of the Screams; but it would be well if the choir singing with the blare of the bookineeno gave up acting as if the love-affair between the legendary Adam and Eve brought about what a lot of Christians call Original Sin.

Other things besides "indecent" books excite excitation; there's the bicycle, television, films, great paintings, advertisements, and, above all, the nylon stockings! The stocking brought an esthetic touch to a girl's leg, and the fat was further in the fire; but no one can do anything about it. None has yet answered my questions: Should a Customs Officer be permitted to ban a book? Would the Civic Guard set about stopping production of "John the Husband, Tyb the Wife, and Sir John the Priest"? Oh, fie, fie, they would! Yet this lusty play was written by More's nephew for the More household, and it is certain that the shameful play—in which the priest carries on with Tyb the wife—gave amusement to Sir Thomas More himself.[2] But we thank God that we are not as they were. Amen!

We should be up against, not what brings life, but against all things that take it away, till old age sends us into a gentle sleep; for a start, up against the hydrogen bomb and all nuclear weapons, till, grown stronger, we strike against war everywhere. The banning of bombs is more to the point than the banning of books, and Christians should know this better than anyone else, instead of going into hysterics over the natural merry-making of a Jack and a Jill.—Yours, etc.,

Sean O'Casey

Devon, June 4th, 1957

[2] See O'Casey's letter to the *Irish Times,* 18 May 1957, note 3.

To Seumas Scully

MS. SCULLY

16 JUNE 1957

My dear Seumas,
Thanks a lot for the cuttings and the letter—some of it hard to make out. I am very glad to hear that your health is so good—the main thing in life, talk as they may about the soul.

About going out of Ireland, I would not venture advice, bar caution; it is a matter for you to decide entirely. I doubt if you could get leave to enter Canada. They want only professional men & artizans—Carpenters, fitters, bricklayers, etc.; & the climate is a rigorous one. England is nearer home, & a hop, step, & lep could bring you home; but Canada is a long way off.

This must be a short note, for eyes are bad, & doctor has ordered far less writing & reading. Plays in Abbey seem to be caught in a rut of commonplace writing—and acting too. I *am* sorry you have lost your job. Surely, among so many you know, someone ought to be able to place you somewhere. Why not some kind of laboring work? But with so many old, experienced men idle, you'd have a poor chance.

I have seen a notice in the Press that Irish Press has a new editor; one who has written a book on the "Lives of the Saints." Is the I. Press going to become another "Standard"?

All the best to you, & I do hope your troubles will soon become less by getting some job that will let you stay where you are.

As ever
Sean

To Mrs. John T. Cooper

TS. COOPER

18 JUNE 1957

My dear Georgie,

I agree with you that ROSE TATTOO isn't a marvel to fight for, but a principle of freedom lies in the core of a poor play, indeed. T. Williams never seems to see God smiling, nor a woman or man bending to admire a full-blown rose. Thanks, dear girl, for the check, but I am returning it to you with this note, for the fight is a purely "internal affair," to be fought out by ourselves; for if we don't do it alone, then no one outside can save us: just as Americans and Americans only (however foreigners wished to help) could battle with McCarthyism.

God forgive me, I have never heard of Kurt Weill's DOWN IN THE VALLEY, reminding me of how many, many things that are still hidden from me; but, thank God, me mind is still seeking things that lie beyond the horizon; all so important, for from the old generation, the new one must come, as, I think, Chaucer said "From the old fields the new corn must come." I wish you every success with the folk-opera.

I see that Monsignor Thomas Duffy has ordered the parents of Christ the King's School, in Nashville (Tennessee?) to change their children into a uniform, for "Children in the costume of manual laborers (children were wearing blue jeans) has a Communistic tendency and influence." I thought that Christ the King and Christ the Carpenter were one Person.

I have to limit my reading and writing for present; but the weather's very warm, the ground is hard and dry, so the birds find it hard to get food. I have made friends with a blackbird, a robin, and a cock and hen bullfinch, all of whom I feed with scraps of fat and biscuit-crumb as well as supplying them with water. The robin comes on to my knee, the hen bullfinch on to the toe of my boot, the cock watching her, and the blackbird stays a few feet away, cocking an eye at me, and piping a tune; so I have a happy hour or two with the lot of them. Tonight, I listen on the wireless to a Concert of French Composers.

My affectionate regards to Miss Snow of the Books, Lucille of the Violin; to Jane, Bill, and Raymond, with love entwined among the regards, and my love to the lad, John, and the lass Georgie.

As ever,
Sean

I return letter from Ron—you should keep it as a reminder of vigorous days. 500! When we ran our Drama Class in Dublin of the long ago, we could muster but twenty-five or so. 2 Enclosures

---

To Gareth W. Williams[1]

TC. O'CASEY

19 JUNE 1957

Dear Gareth Williams,
Dont set me down as "sir" so often; dont set me down as "sir" at all. I dont like it, for I am as one man is to another, of the same flesh and blood subsisting.

Remember, the Teacher has a right to his own opinions as you have to yours. Listen to his, but keep your own—if you are convinced of them.

I wasnt told that my play would be set down on an examination paper. Had I known, I should have done all I could to prevent it. I dont believe in studying plays, nor do I believe in examinations either; at best, they are a poor test. A play wasnt written to be studied. It is written to be performed on a stage in schoolroom or theater—not to become a lesson, but to give play to sight, hearing, and the imagination. A play, to me, is for entertainment, entertainment for educated and civilised human beings: Hamlet is as entertaining as Falstaff. A play is entertainment, whether it

---

[1] Gareth W. Williams, 9 Rosehill Road, Rhyl, Flints, N. Wales. A sixteen-year-old high school student and "Welsh-speaking Welshman," Gareth in a June letter to O'Casey says his class is studying "Juno and the Paycock" and the students had an argument with the teacher: "Our teacher, as is usual, has praised the play highly, and has, wrongly I feel, disected it, and read into it all kinds of meanings which I, for one, do not think you, sir, intended. In addition to this disection, we have to answer ridiculous questions such as 'How does Juno's character develop'? I am sure you, sir, will agree that such questions are heartless and pointless. However, although our teacher considers 'Juno' to be a masterpiece, I have myself preferred 'The Silver Tassie,' and agree with Shaw when he says 'What a hell of a play . . . etc.'" Seven times he refers to O'Casey as "sir."

quietens an audience into a sadness, or sends them into sounding laughter. It is the quickening of the spirit, either by tears or by laughter, that acts as "instruction" in a play; though there may be wise phrases in many, as in HAMLET, or the wonderful catechism of Falstaff.

Your questions now:

I cant say which is my best play: the great critic, Time, must decide that one. My choice as the best-written play of mine is COCKADOODLE DANDY, though I like THE SILVER TASSIE, too; but the best play of a playwright is the one chosen by him or her who sees them on the stage, or reads them in a book. Your Teacher thinks of JUNO, and he may be right; you THE TASSIE, and you may be right; I COCKADOODLE, and I may be right too.

2. My one aim in writing JUNO was to write a play, taking into my mind as I wrote the people whom I knew, and the circumstances of the life then around me; these were the materials from which I made a play. Your 3rd question[2] has already been answered—as well as I could do it—above.

So, Gareth of sixteen summers, all good wishes to you, and all success to you at school and in life afterwards. I am Irish as you are Welsh, and, like you, know my own language, the Gaelic.

Yours sincerely,
Sean O'Casey.

[2] "Do you think that the theatre should entertain first, and then instruct, or instruct primarily and entertain, provide enjoyment, secondarily?"

To Brendan Smith[1]

TC. O'CASEY

19 JULY 1957

Dear Mr. Brendan Smith,

Of course there's a chance of a reply to your kind and courteous letter. I had a painful infection of the eyes, and had to limit my letter-writing, and keep only to the play. Well, here is the answer: There's a lot to be considered. I am on the fourth draft, and when this is done, it must be sent to a professional Typist to get fair clean copies. This will take a month at least. I havent any objection to your reading it (when it's ready),

[1] Brendan Smith, Director, Festival of Dublin, 5 and 6 South Great Georges Street, Dublin. In a 1st of July letter Smith made the first move by asking O'Casey: "Presuming we could agree on producer, cast, and business details, would you consider giving the Festival the world premiere of your new play," for the 1958 Dublin Drama Festival, which coincided with the Tostal celebration.

if you promise to keep its contents to yourself. First, though, to prevent unnecessary trouble to me and to you, I'd like to hear from you about your ideas for its production (provided that the play be acceptable—which is unlikely); the possible Caste, the probable theater, and the probable Director (Producer); as well as what you would be likely to offer financially for a license to last only for the run of the play.

Another consideration: I amnt in any way eager for an Irish production, not being willing to provoke the Irish drama critics into another frenzy of making fools of themselves. Indeed, I have thought of refusing to allow a performance of any of my plays in the Republic. Another thing, too: I dont want to be one standing in the way of the younger or newer playwrights, who may have a play in hands for the Tostal. I've written to the Abbey already of how worried I was at them putting on JUNO for the last Tostal Week, instead of some play by a less known dramatist.

As for the play of mine, it is a little curious, a frolic, more or less, with an odd serious line here and there, and the Tostal as the background. I am of the opinion that this Festival could be a Bringer of new life and activity to Ireland, replacing the lost enthusiasm of the old National Movement, which, in many ways, is now old-fashioned, and outworn. Ireland, if she is to live, must create a new Ireland from the old one, and, I think, that this is the spirit of the play I have tried to write. Well, there's your answer, and, though it may not please you, be heavens, it's better than none.

With all good wishes and a dark blessing on the work you are trying to do.

Yours sincerely,
[Sean O'Casey]

To George Jean Nathan

MS. CORNELL

22 JULY 1957

My very dear George,

I have often wondered how you are, and if you had gone away for a while from New York, at least, during the great heat, which must be trying to anyone not well. We had a share of it here; but the cold has come back again, & I write this with the fire going. I have had a painful infection of the eyes for some weeks, & had to let letters pile up around me, without any hope of ever answering half of them now.

I have almost finished another play, called "The Night is Whispering," not one of my best; a comedy written against the background of the Irish Tostal; but not one that will foment a desire on anyone's part to hand out a laurel leaf. I wrote it, I suppose, to help me keep from thinking of things that can never be forgotten; but, I think there is some humor in it; and for this, God will forgive me. Anyway, it was the best I can do at my age, & in my present mood.

Funk & Wagnall wanted me to join their advisory Editorial Board; but I wouldn't take it on, feeling either [Sean] O'Faolain or [Frank] O'Connor would be far better than I for the job. Paul Shyre is coming here again in Aug. to talk about "Cockadoodle" for a possible Fall production. Talking of myself all the time!

My very dear George, I pray you to be better, & able by now to write more easily. All well here.

My dear love to Julie and to you.

As ever,
Sean

To J. J. O'Leary

TS. O'LEARY

24 JULY 1957

My dear J.J.

Thanks for your letter. I have already told your buttie, Brendan Smith, that I'd give him the play to READ, provided he didnt spread its contents over the map of Ireland; and so I will, when I have had fair copies typed by a professional.

There is a lot more, J.J., than negotiating. For a long time now, I have been uneasy about giving any play I do to be done in Dublin, because of the resentment it seems to arouse when such an event happens. Remember MacNamara's cry from the heart about them?[1] The personal abuse over the BONFIRE? Recently, too, a letter in the I. PRESS from one of the O'Brien clan complained about O'Casey being so prominent in Paris and during the last Tostal. As a matter of fact, I didnt know about Paris till the Company were already there; I have written to the Abbey saying how worried I was that JUNO was done at the last Tostal, and saying that a newer play from a younger writer should have been done. I had determined that no play of mine should appear in the Abbey during the coming

---

[1] See Brinsley Macnamara's statements attacking O'Casey and the Abbey Theatre for the decision to produce *The Silver Tassie* in 1935, *Irish Times,* 7 September and 7 October 1935, Vol. I.

Festival. Now, you, Brendan Smith, and Mr. [Louis] Elliman of the Gaiety, come battering at my door demanding the latest one written. As for the play—it's an odd one, I think, though it may really be a cod one, for my opinion goes no farther than meself. I think it may give rise to a lot of differential chatter, may even arouse resentment, though, as far as I can see, there's nothing in it to provoke animosity, secular or theologica. It is a comedy (I hope it is), no tragedy in it at all, and its motto could be Múscáil do Mhisneach, a Banba![2] It begins with a prologue, called by me "a prerumble," showing Tans in the center of a burning town. How about you reading it first? You are a "layman," one who doesnt write to the papers, has never written a play, never studied the drama, so you could give it a good judgement. If you like, I'll send it on to you (when the fair copy's ready), and you can hand it on to B.S. I dont know about Mr. Elliman. I dont believe I promised it to him anyhow. Well, there it is, with me loth to give it to Ireland at all, and if I do, demanding a guarantee that there will be no ballyhoo of publicity about it. It isnt anything so good as COCKADOODLE DANDY, or, I imagine, the BONFIRE, but just a play that may be worth doing.

Eileen tells me that Shivaun is going over to Ireland in September, and that she will join Shivaun when she is there; about the middle of the month. She, Shivaun, and Breon go to Cornwall on Friday, so for awhile, I will be alone with the multitudinous bees and birds. Eileen cracked a rib the other day, and had a painful time, but is much better now. I'd have written before, but had a painful eye infection, and limited my writing to an odd dab at the play. Beside me, is a huge pile of unanswered letters, and they frighten me to look at them.

I got some Mick McQuaid[3] from Shivaun when she came back, but didnt write because you had gone to some faraway chalet in Eilbis [Switzerland]—is that the right Gaelic?

I see be this morning's papers that the Gough Statue is gone,[4] an old friend of mine, for the Park was the one estate I ever owned, and I was proud of what could be seen there, a pleasure I shared with many many thousands. Many a time I passed by on my way to a hurling field. I am sorry it's gone—effigy of an Irishman done by the Irish too. And G's descendant, the one who led the Mutiny against Home Rule in Ulster, at the Curragh, is repentant now (or was), and advocates union. This isnt patriotism—it is barbarism. It was one of the finest open-air bronzes we had. Why the hell dont the IRA suddenly some day, seize the Lane Pictures and bring them back to Dublin? Now that would be something sensible, patriotic, and a challenge in the kisser of Philistine England.

---

[2] Arouse your courage, Oh Ireland!

[3] A brand of Irish pipe tobacco.

[4] On 23 July 1957 the I.R.A. blew up the Gough Monument in Phoenix Park, Dublin. It was a statue of a rider on horseback, honoring Field-Marshal Hugh Viscount Gough, sculpted by J. H. Foley and T. Brock in 1879.

Well, now—as the Radio Times says in the Television programme—
it is time for prayers, and I must go. Eileen sends her love; Shivaun would,
too, but she's in London; and I join Eileen in her affection and fine wishes
to you, and for you.

As ever,
Sean

To David H. Greene

TC. O'CASEY

25 JULY 1957

Dear Dave,

Thanks for your letter of June 27. Had a painful infection of the eyes,
and had to limit my writing; but better now.

You are right about Cyril C[usack].—he is a very talented actor, and
a fine lad to boot, ay and saddle too; a genuine Catholic, a grand sense of
humor, and one who isnt afraid of the opinions held by others. I like him
very much, and have a deep respect for him; and for his grand little wife,
Maureen; from the BLACK North, from Durry's ain toon.

[Herbert] Coston rang up, but I wasnt feeling too fit, had my eyes
bad, and so had to refuse for the present. However, he's gone away to
Italy, I think, and Dublin for awhile, and when he's back in London, and
I feel allright, I'll do my best to see him. I have had to refuse a number of
friends who rang up, and wanted to come down. At 77 one feels fine one
day, not so fine the next. Paul Shyre is coming down early next month to
talk about a possible production of COCKADOODLE DANDY, and of
course, I must see him about it, fit or unfit.

I hope you, Catherine, and the children had a good time in Mass[a-
chusetts]; I'm sure you all needed a holiday. Eileen, Shivaun, and Breon
set out for a fortnight's stay in Cornwall, and, like you, I will be alone with
my old pal, the typewriter.

I have almost finished the new play—THE NIGHT IS WHISPER-
ING, not half so good as the Cockadoodle theme, maybe not even as good
as the BONFIRE, but it has some amusing moments (I hope), and is
played against the background of Tostal activities, with a theme of courage
and the doing of things—"dispensing harvest, sowing the To-be" as Tennyson put it. Glad to hear about the good news regarding Emmett [Lar-
kin]. May he prosper as a Teacher. It's odd how few realise the tremendous
influence Teachers have on the shape of the To-be. We are inclined to
think all this depends on the politicians—important enough, God knows—

but teachers get closer to the individual, and so send out minds that must have some reflection of their own ideas in many things. I'm glad, too, that you are nearing the end of your pilgrimage through the life of Synge. How the Abbey misses him and his great colleagues! The Festival Council are eager to get my new play; but I'm worried over the resentment it may give to younger writers who should be represented instead of O'Casey. They put on JUNO at the last Tostal—the Abbey did—at Council's request; and I've written deploring the choice. I am determined that no play of mine shall be done by the Abbey next Tostal; they must show what they are doing now; not what was done 40 years ago. . . .[1]

[1] Page missing.

To Mrs. Kay O'Riordan

MS. O'RIORDAN

25 JULY 1957

Dear Kay,

Thanks for your letter. My eyes haven't been too good, so I had to be content to write a little. I'm afraid, the workers would wait a long time for what they're asking if they depended on the outcome of pious talks on Sociology. I read where Mr. [Wilfred] Sheed is reported as saying that to be sane one must be a Catholic, implying, I suppose, that Catholics as such never go balmy, never can go berserk. But Hitler was one; so was Goring, and, God help us, Catholics fought Catholics most bitterly in the Civil War; & in the first world war Polish Catholics slaughtered Galician Catholics by the hundreds, burned their church, & made whole districts heaps of ashes (like the Tans), or so Attwater, said to be an authority on the Eastern Churches, said in the Dublin-published "Studies."[1] There is nothing for the workers outside of what they can gain by their own discontent and constant battle.

Yes, I know these Labour Exchanges. I myself attended one in Gardiner St. (used to be a Protestant Church), when I was idle, & it was a shocking experience; such hard work to secure a half-a crown. Many a year I went hungry, even getting Beri-beri, from starvation; & battling out of it by living richly on fresh air.

I enclose a couple of quid for [Irish Workers'] League.

My love to you all,
As ever,
Sean

[1] Donald Attwater, "Russian Spirituality," *Studies,* March 1940.

To Peter MacManus[1]

TS. MacManus

26 July 1957

Dear Peter MacManus,

Thanks for your letter, but you ask questions that would fill a book. I have always, far as in me lay, supported the fight for freedom of Nationalities—differing from Nationalism—but am also a fighter for the preservation of the greater freedom of man; economic freedom—in other words, Socialism, and this great economic achievement has its bulwark, its spear-head (European) in the USSR; a Nation that all other Capitalists have persistently tried to destroy; and the recent disturbance in Hungary was one of the attempted ways to weaken, if not destroy the Socialist power in Europe. The natural and justifiable discontent of the workers was seized upon by those who hate and fear Socialism, particularly that Power which in Europe is a symbol of strength, courage, and realization for all men and women everywhere; the Power that gave hope and courage to the People of China. You know as much as I do what Krushchev said about Stalin— all we know appeared in the Capitalist papers, and no Communist would take these for gospel. Stalin was a great man. He brought his country from raggedness and starvation; from two wars that devastated Russia twice; into a Country second to none in the world, while England, a Protestant country, and France, a Catholic one, lie almost prostrate in political and economic chaos. Anyway, Ireland is beginning to know just what kind of beings these "heroic" Hungarian refugees are. See what Templemore Urban District Council thinks of having them near. So is England learning too. As for the Papal Sociology you mention,[2] if they cannot be applied in Catholic Ireland, then the sooner Ireland goes Communist the better. Read what Dr. Walter McDonald, Professor of Theology in Maynooth for 40 years, said about the Rerum Novarum. Read the chapter "Silence" in my book DRUMS UNDER THE WINDOWS. I dont agree with the methods of the present IRA. I never believed in Irishmen killing other Irishmen, for enough of that has been done already. Apropos of Hungary, remember that 77 were OFFICIALLY executed in Ireland in the Civil War, not counting all those who were executed "unofficially." The black kettle cant afford to call the pot black. Years ago, when I asked the Talbot Press to

---

[1] Peter MacManus, 8 Wainsfort Drive, Terenure, Dublin; a young medical school student.

[2] MacManus had said: "It is the failure to put Papal teaching into practice in Ireland, not its application, which is partly responsible for the exasperating state!"

publish my plays, they said it wouldnt be worth their while.[3] And, for that matter, do you think Irish publishers would be likely to risk publishing of books likely to be banned? God help your innocence.

I heartily return your Gaelic good wishes.

Yours very sincerely,
Sean O'Casey.

[3] MacManus had asked: "Why do you not have your books published in Ireland? Surely a man so prominent in the labour troubles, should support Irish workers!"

To Herbert Keppler[1]

TC. O'CASEY

29 JULY 1957

Dear Mr. Keppler,

Thanks for your kind letter asking if I should like to write an article on the art, science, and journalistic power of the camera.

I am sorry I cannot undertake the job, for I know next to nothing about the theory or the practice of the art. My only experience has been that of subject, and of the camera, my one experience of it is an odd moment or two looking through the lens at the figures standing in the manner of the world—upside down.

If Shaw were alive, he'd give you a rousing article, for he was fond of the art, and was an expert user of the camera himself. He says a lot about the art in his novel, THE UNSOCIAL SOCIALIST. I have a lovely picture someone took of him sitting by Coole Lake, and another charming one of the young Yeats, taken by G.B.S., standing against a leafy background in one of the Coole Woods.

I am ignorant of the art, and I amnt one who runs towards the chance of writing about, or speaking of, some art or activity about which I know little or nothing.

I'm sure you will understand this, and do me honor for being something other than a fool.

With all good wishes for the success of your project,

I remain,
Yours sincerely,
Sean O'Casey.

[1] Herbert Keppler, *Modern Photography,* 33 West 60th Street, New York.

To J. J. O'Leary

MS. O'LEARY

30 JULY 1957

My dear J.J.

Tobacco you mentioned came yesterday morning, & I thank you for the gift. Glad you find play-reading tedious—the most of them are. If when you read mind, you find it a little less than tedious, it will be fine. Moliere never gave a new play to a critic to read, but always to his cook, on whose inexperienced judgement he placed great reliance.

Glad to hear that "Capt. Boyle" [Barry Fitzgerald] is at last, as Bo'sun, earning his title. Give my love to him. I've read "Finian's Rainbow" and think it a charming childlike fantasy, in no way "Stage-Irish," if there be any meaning at all to such a term. What do you think of enclosed clipped from De Valera's IRISH PRESS? The Journal that is Gaelic of the Gaels showing a pixture that is stupid, vulgar, and "Stage-Irish" of the lowest type—even to the "dudheen" stuck in the caubeen,[1] and underneath "The Week's Good Cause."

Yes, Nehru is removing the British memento's, but he isn't blowing them to pieces. He's having them removed to less prominent places; but preserving them as memories of the past; a bad past, but a past, all the same.

I'll tell Eileen.

All the best to Will [Shields, ie., Barry Fitzgerald] & you.

Did you read the lassies expelled from a Tech. School because of larking with boys in a wood? And a C[hristian]. Brother doing a Peeping Tom. As if a private life had anything to do with Commerce, Art, Politics, or anything in the nature of public activities. And they wonder why the Young are flying away from the clerical lectures, & C. Brothers who use their eyes as binoculars.

My love,
Sean

---

[1] "Clay pipe" stuck in the hat.

To Manchester Guardian

31 JULY 1957

NUCLEAR TESTS

Sir,—If the Disarmament Subcommittee of the United Nations Disarmament Commission is unable to agree even on the limited problem of nuclear tests, millions of people all over the world hoping for at least this first step towards wider disarmament will be bitterly disappointed.

May we, speaking for countries unarmed with nuclear weapons, but subject to the same fears, appeal to the five Powers represented on the subcommittee not to allow differences of opinion on other issues to prevent agreement on the suspension of the tests? Russia has proposed a two to three year ban with the requisite controls. The Western Powers have proposed a shorter period. This is a question, surely, for negotiation, not a matter of principle. Sufficient agreement exists, we feel, for the first step to be made for which all the world is waiting.—Yours &c.,

> *Sean O'Casey (Ireland), H.K. Handoo (India),*
> *David Pitt (West Indies), Tefkros Anthias (Cyprus).*

London N.W.3.

To Miss Joan McAlevey

MS. McALEVEY

12 AUGUST 1957

My dear Joan,

I'm very glad you have arrived safely in Oxford, & glad you like it. Well, there you are, ensconced among the Colleges, which, for so long, have sent out those who misgoverned England—and Ireland, too. A jungle of Gothic spires. When I first came to England, I was ushered through them; in by one gate, out by another, and had breakfast with a group of students who were interested in the Drama, mixed with the members of the Oxford Players who were then doing a Vanbrugh play in the town. I liked the students a lot—they were young and eager and genuine. I never met a Don, so don't know what kind they were or are or will be. In Cambridge, I met two; liked one, and didn't like the other—not that it mattered a damn to them whether I liked them or no.

The weather here has been as bad, or worse, than that in Oxford:

thunder, lightning, great gales, lashing rain, and a stinging cold air when the evening steals over us.

For the past two months, I've been talking to visitors here till my voice has become a whisper. Paul Shyre—he who did the "Readings" and "Purple Dust"—, was here all the week discussing possible productions next season; so I am very tired by now, & forced to rest a little. You must forgive me, Joan, if I have to hide from you this time—anyway, the company of Frankie is far more congenial than mine could possibly be.

I have finished the play, and sent it off to have "fair copies" typed— my script is clouded with corrections; so when these come back, & are looked over, and further, corrections made, will receive the final (for the time being) O.K.

Do forgive me for being unable to see you this time, dear.

My love to your Mother, father, Frankie, and, Joan, to you.

As ever
Sean

To Richard Findlater[1]

TC. O'CASEY

23 AUGUST 1957

Dear Mr. Findlater,

I am sorry I have to say NO again, first because I am not desirous to fling myself into any further Irish growling about books and plays and persons; secondly because during the first 10 years of the Abbey I was far away from it, in the thick of the Gaelic Movement, and without the money to pay for admission to see what was going on there, even had I the wish to have a peep.

When the book comes out, I shall buy it and read it, think my own thoughts about it, and put it on the shelf with my other Irish books. Gerard Fay is, I think, a son of Frank Fay, not of William; but, like you, I'm not sure. Once while at F. Fay's flat in Dublin, I saw a lonely lad surrounded by books, learning lessons, and my heart went out to him. This lad, I think, was Gerard; and I am glad he has made a way in the world, for God knows poor Frank made little out of his love and devotion to the Theater.

On the other hand, I always thought that Mr. [Lennox] Robinson

---

[1] Richard Findlater, Editor, *Parade,* London. He had asked O'Casey to review Gerard Fay's *The Abbey Theatre: Cradle of Genius* (1958).

should have taken over the control of the Abbey when Yeats died, or before it; but apparently, there was a different opinion elsewhere. L.R. is a fine producer, a fine actor—when he likes to do it—, and knows all, or near all, there is to know about the Theater in Ireland, and other lands too; but, I fear, he lacked the "go" and self-confidence needed to follow Yeats, a damned hard one to succeed. I'm afraid the Abbey Swan has now turned into a wingless goose, with but a hiss instead of a song.

All good wishes to you.
Sean O'Casey.

By the way, you were hard on Passmore; and, I think, not quite right, and so not quite fair.

To Brendan Smith

TS. Smith

9 September 1957

Dear Mr. Brendan Smith,
I am sending the MS of my play to Mr. J. J. O'Leary, having completed it to my entire dissatisfaction.

He will give it to you after a preliminary reading of it—if he can find the time, and survives the reading.

I have changed the Name to THE DRUMS OF FATHER NED. I am sending it now because I assume that you will be anxious to arrange your program for the coming Festival as soon as you can; to make as many things as definite as you can as soon as possible. Of course, you will understand that the sending of the MS by me to you doesnt in any way commit me to finally deciding that the Festival can have it—provided of course that you might think it interesting enough. Now for a few remarks about what you say in your letter of the 10th of August last:

I am hesitant about giving the play, preferring that a newer Irish playwright should have all the chances of whatever honor and glory may be attached to the production of a play during the Festival; I am anxious to avoid anything that might arouse a natural envy, or a sense of frustration around any favor given to an older and, more or less, established dramatist; and I cannot—whatever you may say—forget the savage and ignorant reviews appearing when my last play was done by Cyril Cusack, from the lordly lad Dunno O Donnell Rory O Moore Cruise O Brien[1] to the laddo

---

[1] A reference to the review of *The Bishop's Bonfire* by Donat O'Donnell (Conor Cruise O'Brien), "No Bishop, No Bonfire," *New Statesman and Nation,* 5 March 1955.

writing in the English PLAYS AND PLAYERS:[2] it was all an attack on O'Casey rather than a criticism of a play. I am human, my dear Brendan, and, like Yeats, dont like to give a chance to ignorance and venom to provide publicity for themselves.

I dont wish to have to do with the Abbey—Theater or Players. The first have never bothered to ask me for anything since Fred O'Higgins died, so, since theyre not interested in me, I am not interested in them; and the Players are bad—even in the PLOUGH, spite of what you say. I heard them on Radio in this play, and, to me, it was very bad indeed. For a Theater, I prefer by far the Gaiety because, one, they did THE BONFIRE; and, more important, Mr. [Louis] Elliman paid me the courtesy, when he heard I was writing another play, asked me to let him consider it; wrote again when he read that I had almost finished it; and, far as I can remember, I promised. So, when you have read it, maybe you'd let him read it, too, under the proviso that no one may be told of what the play is about.

As for actors, there are in my mind C. Cusack, Eddie Byrne, S[eamus]. Kavanagh, a chap named [Godfrey] Quigley, I think, who played in the BONFIRE, Mairin Cusack, et al. The Producer? That's a question! I dont want to have H[ilton]. Edwards, between ourselves; F[rank]. McDermott (Dermody) has had little experience, and has been confined to the usual naturalistic efforts, plus plays in the Gaelic, which, unfortunately, arent much to talk about. I have never heard of Jim Fitzgerald, who, I assume, has no more experience than the others. You see, my play has something within it besides its "realism," and it is this odd breeze within a wind that worries me in direction. However, we can discuss this later, if you should think after reading the play that it is worthwhile considering. Of course, all this in confidence, for I dont want to read angry letters in the Press, or have any floating in on top of me here.

Royalties: I dont want any GUARANTEE. The royalties paid for the BONFIRE, a sliding scale on the gross receipts (Cusack could let you know what they were; I havent the energy to look up the contract), and an advance, say of £20 or £25 would be allright by me.

You say that "exciting new material is just not coming up at present"; I cant say that my play will be "exciting"; all I am personally sure of (and I may be wrong) is that if played and produced well, it will at least be exciting, with a lot of humor (I hope) and an overtone of seriousness threading it all together, touched by a fanciful imagination along the work's way.

By the way, I changed the name because I think the new one to be sturdier, and the play is, I believe, a sturdy one; and because I happened

[2] A reference to the review of *The Bishop's Bonfire* by Bourke MacWilliam, *Plays and Players*, April 1955. See O'Casey's letter of reply, "Sean O'Casey Complains," *Plays and Players*, May 1955; and MacWilliam's "Reply to Sean O'Casey," *Plays and Players*, June 1955, reprinted above.

to remember that Mr. Molloy had written a play entitled THE WOOD
OF WHISPERING[3]—is that the right title?—and didnt want to confuse
his with mine, a thing he might (rightly) resent. I hope your very fine program will come to pass, though I have my doubts about a play on [Sir
Roger] Casement. But beware! If [Alfred] Noyes hears you are doing
ULYSSES, he wont set a foot on Ireland's pleasant strand. I wont say a
word, of course, about the potential program. And by the way again, I
think, if you do all you hope to do, I can hear Pangur Ban[4] doing more
than giving a purr! The cat in a rage! Well, no more for the present; I'll
pack up the play and send it off to JJ. Now, I just want to thank you
very much for your interest in my play, and for asking me to let you read
it: this is, believe me, an encouragement, coaxing me away from some bitter feelings evoked by the abuse I have so often received for Play and
Biography from my fellow-countrymen. See what was said in I. Press
and I. Times about New York Product. of PURPLE DUST last year by
an I. Crit. of the Irish News Agency, and never a word since, because, of
course, the play was a great success, going on as strong as ever, and now
in its tenth month. All good wishes to what you are doing for Ireland,
and for the Tostal of the coming year. Amen.

Sean O'Casey

[3] Michael J. Molloy, *The Wood of the Whispering* (1953).
[4] "Pangur ban," (The Scholar and His Cat), an anonymous early 9th century
Irish poem. See *Early Irish Lyrics* (1956), edited with translations by Gerard Murphy,
pp. 2–3.

To J. J. O'Leary

MS. O'LEARY

10 SEPTEMBER 1957

My dear J.J.

Enclosed as you can see is the play. I've changed the name to "The
Drums of Father Ned."

Don't worry about reading it, if you have any reluctance about play
reading. I can understand, for I myself find it almost impossible to read
a novel.

Any way here it is for better or worse, for richer or poorer. I've written to Brendan Smith telling him it was on its way to you.

All well here, bar myself, who is feeling not too good these days; &
finding it hard to get away from an ache in the mind and heart. But facing
life all the same. By the way, who is Ulick O'Connor? He had an article

lately on the Edinburgh Festival in the "S. Times" or "Observer". And who is Jim Fitzgerald, the drama producer; & what has he done—if you know?[1]

Very bad and bitter weather here. Love to Barry, if he be in Dublin still.

All good wishes to you from Shivaun, Eileen, & me.

As before,
Sean.

[1] In a letter of 12 September to O'Casey, O'Leary made the following comments: "As regards Ulick O'Connor, he is one of our younger writers and in his articles is inclined to use the shillelagh, so there are mixed opinions about him. To my mind he has a good deal of initiative and is a young man who is going to get on in journalism. I think Jim Fitzgerald is probably one of our best young producers. He spent some time in the Theatre Workshop in London, and has done some good productions for the Globe. You will probably remember that he did the Juno production in Liverpool which was used afterwards as the basis of the T.V. production. I think a good deal more is going to be heard of him as the years go on."

To Brooks Atkinson

MS. ATKINSON

11 SEPTEMBER 1957

My very dear Brooks,

I've read your "Note on Art,"[1] and a brilliant & beautiful note it is. I read it with delight, and the simple way you told us all what art is, and its relationship to man is one of the finest things you have written, me laddo. I have asked Miss [Clara] Rotter to send me a few copies so that I may send them to friends. I'd like to send one of them to a friend, G. Kholopov, Editor-in-chief of the Magazine "Zvezda" (Star), if you have no objection.

In an early number, next year, they are publishing my play, "Bishop's Bonfire" in it[2] (I don't know how or where they got the play: I didn't send it to them); they have asked me to write an article about the play & the Theater; so I'd like them to read your article (a much grander one) as well as mine.

I've written another play, with the characters playing against the background of An Tostal;[3] good enough, I imagine, to warrant a production—

[1] Brooks Atkinson, "Note on Art," *New York Times*, 19 August 1957.
[2] *Koster Episkopa*, a translation of *The Bishop's Bonfire*, by M. Druzina, appeared in *Zvezda*, Leningrad, January 1958.
[3] A Gaelic pageant or festival.

at least, I hope it is. I called it "The Night is Whispering"; but it is, I think, a sturdier play than its title would suggest; & so I've called it "The Drums of Father Ned," who never appears, but is the spirit of all the activities.

I hope George Jean is better. I wrote to him during the summer; but assumed he had gone away to escape the heat of New York. I hope he did. We had little of the sun here, & it was a very disappointing summer to me.

By the way, Brooks, by an odd coincidence, I use the word "gusto" twice or three times in the new play.

Shivaun goes on Tour with the [Ronald] Ibbs Dublin Players, & will be in New York next month. God be with her thro' the journey. I've become a little apprehensive about what is left to us. Very stupid, for the lass must live out her own life, & die in her own way; but may it be when she is very old as I am.

And Oriana? How is she? As active as ever, I hope, God bless her.

My love to her, and to you: to you both together.

As ever,
Sean

To Harold Macmillan

TC. O'CASEY

11 SEPTEMBER 1957

The Right Hon. The Prime Minister,
House of Commons, London.

Dear Prime Minister,

I should like to suggest you should let your eyes glance at the article enclosed which appeared in THE NEW YORK TIMES.[1] It recounts the visit of a young American to Gordon Craig, living in Vence in the South of France. Craig is now nearing his ninetieth year; old and lonely, but brave and confident as ever. His name is rarely, if ever, mentioned in England, in the theater or out of it; all are too busy looking back in anger instead of looking forward with courage. His neglect is a disgrace to England; a disgrace to her governing-classes, Tory and Labor. He is the man who revolutionised the design in the Theater, whose imagination did honor to an Art with an Apostolic Succession far farther back than any Church. You are very apt to dilate upon the hide-bound attitude towards Art in

---

[1] Paul Shyre, "Talk With Two Titans," *New York Times,* 8 September, an account of Shyre's interviews with O'Casey in Torquay and Gordon Craig in France.

the USSR, but, at least, they gave Stanislavsky a Theater. Did you do that much for Gordon Craig? No, by God, you didnt! Well, now, the least you can do, the least you ought to do, is to honor the man in a way the finest imaginative mind in the English Theater of the century deserves to be honored; that is the highest you have to give, which, considering what the man has been, what he still is, is little enough. He is lonely and poor, and feels England's neglect very much. I happen to know that he would appreciate this honor, this bare recognition of a great and imaginative mind; and, if there be a slight conscious regard left in England for her great men and women, the Government will confer the Order of Merit on Gordon Craig.[2] Like Joyce, he has been shoved away, but Joyce, being an Irishman, didnt give a damn about English Orders. Craig, however, is an Englishman, and, I believe would welcome this recognition; but only the best is worthy of such a man. He has been nudged out of the Theater, nudged out of England, near nudged out of life; so the gesture I mention would be but some reparation for the long and disgraceful silence around this great name.

> *With respect,*
> *Yours very sincerely.*
> *Sean O'Casey*

[2] Unknown to Shyre and O'Casey, Craig had apparently been awarded the Companion of Honor in 1956, but he was too poor to receive it. When he died at 94 in 1966—Edward Gordon Craig, stage designer, producer, son of the actress Dame Ellen Terry—the following account of his award appeared in the obituary in the *New York Times*, 30 July 1966: "In the spring of 1956, Mr. Craig was made a Companion of Honor in the British honors list, but he was too poor to receive the award from Queen Elizabeth II. His only regular income at that time was the equivalent of $16.80 a week, from investments made by his mother. Friends later came to his rescue in a modest way." See also O'Casey's comments on the Prime Minister's reply, in 11 November 1957 letter to Paul Shyre.

To Mrs. Hugh Doran[1]

MS. DORAN

14 SEPTEMBER 1957

My dear Mary,

Thanks for your kind letter. I've been busy trimming scripts of the play "Purple Dust," two for the USA, and one for Czechoslovakia; writing a lot of necessary letters, & adding a few last points to my new play, "The Drums of Father Ned"; so I couldn't find time for friends.

[1] Mary Doran, wife of Dr. Hugh Doran, the O'Casey family doctor; Southover, Bronshill Road, Torquay, Devon.

My dear, I'm not one to try to give "enlightenment" to anyone; God knows, I need it badly myself. I'm afraid listeners or viewers, or both do not get proper enjoyment from work badly acted and badly produced. A recent article in "The Times" confirms all I've said about the Irish Players: they have lost the art of acting; and I don't want them to try to re-learn it from my plays. In the "Hereafter," Mary, I hope God may not penalise me by making me watch, & listen to, the performance of my own plays: I am well tired of most of them already.

There is talk in the USA of making a film of "Purple Dust," & I'm more interested in that than anything the B.B.C. can do with my work.

Don't worry your kind little head my dear, because I have delivered you from what would probably be a sorry Show.

Please give enclosed stamp to Tony or Hugh. Eileen tells me his Surgery was crowded yesterday. I do hope he isn't working too hard.

My love to him, to you, to all yours.

As ever,
Sean

To Ronald Ayling[1]

TS. AYLING

[23 SEPTEMBER 1957][2]

Dear Ron,
God Almighty! I couldnt answer your Essay: couldnt even read it; havent the sight, havent the patience, havent the energy. Depend yourself on what you say, and dont pine after, dont angle for, the opinions of others: your OWN is the one opinion that is important. And, For God's sake, card me no more cards!

Now your questions: *Roisin's Robe*:[3] a one-act play, circa 1922, sometime after the signing of the TREATY, when the row was on that became a Civil War. Printed in a weekly voicing the opinions of the Republicans against the Treaty; edited by one named Erskine Childers, afterwards executed by the Free State (set up by the opposite party, the one England supported), which DeValera and his followers opposed. Only last

---

[1] Ronald Ayling, a student at Nottingham University. He later became an important O'Casey scholar and critic.

[2] Postmarked date.

[3] The only extant version of this work is an allegorical short story, "The Seamless Coat of Kathleen," *Poblacht Na h-Eireann* (The Republic of Ireland), March 1922; reprinted in *Feathers From the Green Crow* (1962).

week, an American came here; he'd been in Dublin for a month, searching papers and files, but couldnt trace the copy containing the play. I myself didnt know it had been printed till a visiting Irish priest came to see us in London many years after and told me he had read it. You can read all about the C. War in Dorothy McArdle's *Irish Republic,*[4] which should be in Lon. Library.

I've read Ervine's book,[5] a fine one. Dont know why he never mentioned me; perhaps didnt know I knew Shaw. Of course, I am what St. J.E. hates, a Bolshie; a Communist; and I dont think he likes me as a Dramatist; or doesnt now (he did in the early days), for he sent a personal letter to G. J. Nathan reproaching him for thinking so highly of my work. Nathan wrote about this in a copy of the American *Newsweek,*[6] and added what he said there to a Preface to Five Famous Irish Plays, published by Random House, New York;[7] a Preface that gave a very sharp swipe to St. J.E. But I cant see how dislike of my politics or of my plays should prompt him to leave mention of me from his book. There was the close affinity between me and G.B.S. on Social problems (he was a Communist too) that never existed between the Sage and St. J. I suggest you should ask St. J. himself. His address is Honey Ditches, Seaton, Devon. I dont know if Shaw's letter re "The S. Tassie"[8] was ever published in full; certainly not by me. After his comments on the play to me, he added a rather ironical one on W. B. Yeats, saying that when the thing to do was clear, Yeats often acted with bewildering foolishness; and when the situation was subtle and difficult, he acted with extraordinary cleverness. I got permission from GBS to publish what he said about "The Silver Tassie," but said I shouldnt care to add what he had said about Yeats. I havent time to search out the letter from the heaps of others I have from all kinds of people. Similarity to Shakespeare: I have to leave this to yourself; I really cant guess; but I rather tremble to be set even a mile away from Shakespeare. The same applies to your comments on my later plays: you must follow your own way here, for I dont wish any words of mine to sway you from your course of thought. But, all the same, I hold fast to my belief in man. Toller (fine lad) centered too much on himself; his own tragedy became the world's woe in his own imagination. Shaw had heartbreaks, and I have had many; one very recently that left me an invisible and mysterious wound that only death can heal; but I am not man; nor was Toller. The tragedy of this or that man is no concern of Life; and it is the life of man that goes on forever; only this man or that man is faced with the tragedy of his own death; and, if he lives to be old, then death is often no more than a lullaby.

The individual is important, relatively, only to himself and a small

[4] Dorothy MacArdle, *The Irish Republic* (1937).

[5] St. John Ervine, *Bernard Shaw: His Life, Work and Friends* (1956).

[6] See George Jean Nathan, "The Best of the Irish," *Newsweek,* 29 January 1940, reprinted in Vol. I.

[7] See O'Casey's letter to Nathan, 22 September 1941, note 1, Vol. I.

[8] See Bernard Shaw's letter to O'Casey, 19 June 1928, Vol. I.

group around him. Whatever tragedy may happen to him or to her is a small thing to life, which goes on careless of, indifferent to, his "fate"; because life must go on, stretching itself from the present out into the future. The USSR had to go on without Lenin, without Stalin, as India has to go on without Gandhi. Keegan's "dream"[9] was, to Broadbent, and to Doyle, "the dream of a madman," and Keegan says so himself to disarm them; but Keegan knows that this dream of his, once it is born, can never die, and slowly, here a little, there a little, will grow in strength and wisdom, till the dream becomes a fact within the life of man; and it is manifesting itself everywhere today, from one side to the other, from one end to the other, of the world. Copernicus, Gallileo had the dreams of madmen, so had Darwin; so had Karl Marx; so had Lenin; so had Wolfe Tone and Robert Emmett: only Hitler's dream was the dream of a madman, and he was helped, encouraged, and prodded on by the children of this world, till they found out, almost too late, that they had created a monster who near destroyed them all. To the C[hildren]. of Light he was mad; to the capitalists, he was a wise, sane, sensible soul; though, he was so clever in his mad dream that he deceived many even of the C. of Light. No; the dream born of goodwill towards man issues out of its dream, and becomes, sooner or later, the common usage of civilised man. As you say, I picture the life of Ireland as that life is today; but there is always a following day: sorrow may endure for the night, but joy cometh in the morning. Keegan's dream is a vision (without a vision, the people perish), and when he reveals his vision, it is no longer his alone; even Larry Doyle is forced to think of it, and never can forget it, though he may oppose its realization; though his very opposition spreads it further, till it sinks deeper and more effectively into the souls of inquiring men and women.

Toller seemed to forget that man himself is a part of nature, and tho' he cant change its laws, he can use them for his own advantage and greater security; nuclear energy, aeronautics—the plane; now Moscow can speak to London, everybody's ear; the world is becoming one.

It is nonsense to say that there is no solution to suffering. There have been many already; and fitter education will eventually reduce it further. Today, there is no solution for the individual suffering from Leucaemia (a lovely and brilliant son of mine, aged 21, died swiftly in a few days from it); but the solution will come.

Keelin's "when we come out of our dream, we darent think of what it told us,"[10] will always be a dream till one dares to think of what it has told us, and tell the world, as all dreamers eventually do, tho' they themselves perish for it: St. Joan, Bruno, Savonarola, et al.

[9] See the "three in one and one in three" dream of the unfrocked Father Keegan in Shaw's *John Bull's Other Island* (1907).

[10] See *The Bishop's Bonfire* (1955), Keelin's speech to Father Boheroe in Act II: "It's nice to dream, an' it does us good; but when we come out of our dream, we daren't think of what it told us."

The "long sad sigh from God"[11] was, I believe, cut from the Dublin production; I think the Director thought it bad, but I amnt sure. I was very ill (unknowingly) at the time, and couldnt bother to argue. After, I spent many bad months in hospital. Perhaps, they didnt want God to seem to support F[ather]. B[oheroe]. It remains as the end of the II act in the book, and will stay so there. Boheroe means "red road"; Keelin is a diminutive for a "slender one"; Reiligan a "graveyard"; Burren a lovely but rather stony barony in Clare, historical too—the Kings of Burren. Foorawn means cold; Moanroe means the red peaty place, or mossy peaty place.

I changed the method of W[ithin]. T. Gates after New York production. Some of the play appeared to me to be very dull, due, I think, to the absence of the chief characters. I tried to adjust this by the newer version. In the "Silver Tassie," I found that the personal tragedy of the central figure was too much ingrained in the tragedy of society; that it was a tragedy that formed the center of a small group only; and that life left must swing into its own dance again, and go forward, scattering a few petals of pity over the broken men, and then leaving them to die their own way, just as life has to do. In the tragedy suffered by myself and wife, the mysterious wound inflicted upon us by the swift death of a brilliant and beloved boy, a wound we shall carry to our last day alive, was felt by us two alone—in a minor and passing way by our two other children; and that life, outside ourselves could not share this sorrow, and had to leave us to it, and go on living, as, indeed, we two had to do ourselves.

I daresay you are right about the ritual. I know the English prayer-book and its lovely prose well, and this, no doubt, influenced me, though not consciously. The R. in the S. Tassie just developed as the play was being written; at the outset, I had no idea that it would take such a form. I know nothing about any of the "isms" of drama, and dont care a damn about them. They never troubled me. Anyway, ritual is all around us, as well as in the prayer-book: the rhythm and ritual of the seasons; of the flowers, the michaelmas daisy in Sept. when the sun of summer has declined; the snowdrop when the snow is a carpet for country feet; the rhythm of the winds, the sun, the moon, the Fall, of the sea—they are all there; and we fit our own rhythm into theirs.

I say nothing about your essay. It might be right, it might be wrong; I might agree, I mightnt. This I say; it is good; I liked it, for it is interesting, bold, original, and a welcome reading from the welter of meaningless blather we have to read from the daily paper critics, and weekly ones as well. Right or wrong, it is breezily written, and that gives it a crown; from me, anyway.

[11] See *The Bishop's Bonfire,* Father Boheroe's curtain line at the end of Act II, explaining the symbolic cold wind that suddenly sweeps through the darkened room: "It was, my child, a long, sad sigh from God."

Well, there you are, and here am I. This letter of mine was a tremendous effort, and I'll no more of them! It is too much like work. By the way, you'll find it hard to get your stuff in print, for they dont want curious and original minds to be probing. And, meanwhile, how do you live? This is more important than the best of criticism, for without the means of life, you can do nothing. I hope you have a job.

All the best to you, and send no more cards. I return your essay and your letter: you want the one; you may want the other.

Addenda

Near forgot your inquiry about me and the Daily Worker. I never resigned the position of membership of the Board, nor had I ever any intention to do so.[12] I am a subscriber to the Funds, and a Shareholder in the Co. Each day, I read the D.W., or a great part of it, or some bit of it. I have sometimes been indignant at the things said in it; but one cant expect perfection or infallibility. Twice I was damned annoyed because of a change in title to an article of mine; or rather a number of comments on matters that concerned the paper. It wasnt meant (c. the title) badly; just an Editor thinking he knew better than the writer—a common occurence.

I'm glad you think so highly of H. McDiarmuid—a very fine poet and a very dear friend of mine.

Lastly I think you think and say too many good things of my work. Looking back over 78 years, I am humbled with the realization of so little done, so little achieved. A little heap of dust; not even purple, just grey.

S. O'C.

[12] See "O'Casey on Daily Worker," *Daily Worker,* 10 June 1940, note 1, Vol. I.

To Mrs. John T. Cooper

MS. COOPER

24 SEPTEMBER 1957

My dear Georgie,

Thank you very much for the press-clippings where Paul Shyre brings me to the side of Gordon Craig, both of us on the farther end of time. I got the music and words of "The Valley Below." Shivaun played it for me, but God forgive me, I didn't take fire. The theme song seemed to me to be gentle, & had charm, but the rest—to me—seemed to lack life—real or make-believe.

I have been reading "Ape, Angels, & Man";[1] all about the tremendous commotion caused by Darwin's "Origin of Species" and his "Descent of Man," with Huxley's championship of the amazing discovery of Evolution by Darwin and Wallace on the same day, within the same hour; giving man, if not a new heaven, at least a very new and astonishing earth. I read both of Darwin's books, oh, fifty years ago; but it was exciting to feel again, in a more sober way, the thrill of the lang sin' again.

I've been very busy finishing my new play whose name I have changed from "The Night is Whispering" to "The Drums of Father Ned," a striking change of title. I've written something for Literary Gazette, Moscow, and the Leningrad "Zverda" Star, who, they tell me are printing "The Bishop's Bonfire" in an early number next year. An odd choice. I don't know where they came by the play, for I didn't send it to them. I have had to jib away from all the letters, theses, plays, stories I get to judge; many asking me if I should or shouldnt commend them to stop or go on. As if I could tell!

I do hope you, your John, your auburn-haired friend & her man & their little ruddy-headed babe are all well; all thriving, enjoying life as well as living it. I fear most of those, who ask me for a judgement (nearer an opinion) on what they write, are out, not to try to do things, but to persuade others to notice what they do, & sing its praise out. How little that may be, and is, when all is done, & the time comes to go. I should have readily (almost joyously) have given all I ever had, or ever might have, and life itself, could this denial have meant the saving of my beloved boy.

By the way, Georgie, have you ever listened to [Anton] Webren? A curious, new, spare music of strange rhythms. I couldn't enjoy most of it; but a Dead March was strangely beautiful.

My blessing on you, Georgie & John, and upon all you love and respect.

As ever,
Sean

---

[1] William Irvine, *Apes, Angels, and Victorians* (1955), The Story of Darwin, Huxley, and Evolution.

To Ronald Ayling

TS. AYLING

29 SEPTEMBER 1957

Dear Ron,

Under another cover, I've sent you your Essay—which I read after all, and thought it good, very good; your list of queries, with replies. My poor eye missed your question asking if I had read the references to me in *Encore*.[1] I read them. I am a subscriber to the Magazine, and have done what I could to help it; but I fear it wont last, which is a pity, for it is more redolent of the fighting theater than *Plays and Players,* or even *Drama,* attached to the Amateur Movement. I didnt reply to what Amis or Wilson said of me, for the same things have been said before here and in Ireland; so I'm used to them; and am too old now to mould myself into the shape of one looking back in anger. I rather prefer to look forward in anger at sham and hypocrisy, and, bend myself to the work, well as I can, of destroying them; or, at least, of making them look mean and ridiculous. And, I fear, there is something of sham in those who are looking back in anger, encasing themselves within a bubble of dark hues, and calling it, or thinking it, the Universe. I prefer in imagination to lie in the bell of a cowslip, for it, at any rate springs from the earth, whence I came myself, and its top is beautiful.

By the way, you say you were depressed when you wrote your essay. It wouldnt appear to me that you had been in anything but a combative mood, which is a good mood, when it is sincere, and one is battling for an ideal. In future reflective thought and comments which I have in mind to write, I may touch on these things said by Wilson and Amis; but not just now, for I am too much occupied with many things.

I enclose the article which Nathan wrote about me[2]—I came across it when looking for notes I had jotted down—. This he used (or most of it) for the Preface to Five Famous Irish Plays.[3] Please return when you next write.

I hope you got your MS safely, and the letter I sent with it.

I think that is all.
With all good wishes,
Yours sincerely,
Sean O'Casey

[1] Kingsley Amis, "That Certain Revulsion," *Encore,* June–July 1957: "I am discouraged to think that among the most intelligent and progressive critics of any play I might write would be people who took their notions of the sublime from O'Casey." Colin Wilson, "In Touch With Reality," *Encore,* June–July 1957: "I have an intense dislike of Mr. O'Casey's work. When, years ago, the poet Maurice Willows pressed a copy of *The Plough and the Stars* on me, assuring me that it was far greater than *my* pet admiration, Granville Barker's *Secret Life,* I began to read it on the bus on the way home. I was so anxious to read this new 'great playwright.' Ten pages finished me. Shallow theatrics, sentimental Irishisms."

[2] See O'Casey's letter to Ayling, 23 September 1957, note 5.

[3] *Ibid.,* note 6.

To Dr. Frank Morrell

MS. MORRELL

30 SEPTEMBER 1957

My dear Frank,

So glad to hear from you that you are well and working—what more can a man want for the use of his talents? And on Labor Day, so tame here with us, so tame there with you: a few banners, a few bands, a few speeches, and all is over: neither dance nor song of the workers in either of them—yet; but both will come.

I am glad to hear, too, that you have added a lass to your life, without which a man's life, even with labor & health, is very incomplete. It is unimportant whether you contribute anything to my life or no; you contribute something to life around you; and that is the important thing; & terribly important thing too; whether we work within our orbit good or evil. I am, of course, very glad that what I said & what I wrote helped you towards commonsense & the tremendous responsibility of yourself: not of me, or of anyone else, but of you. Doesn't matter a damn how restless one may be, so long as it is not confusing or uncertain; but eager and assured, and, above all, sensible, so that it does not trouble the mind or weaken the body. Your research work seems, to me, to be your answer to God and man.

I am delighted to hear about Leonore, & hope you and she may have many many years of active & useful life together; even thro' an occasional "Montreal Autumn," which, sometime or another, in one way or another, comes to each of us. As we sang the song of life when the sun shone, so must we go on with the song as we walk thro' the falling leaves, passing the gaunt bare trees by; on even into the winter's harshness & venom-winds, looking toward another spring that comes to most, and never comes to the few, who, if they be brave, will sing on, strive on, and last out courage till their last day dawns & passes taking one here, another there, away along with itself; and the farewell to life is life itself, for life it is that gives the last long sigh of farewell to herself before the end comes.

So, even in the Autumn there is great beauty; even in the fall of her last leaf in its fluttering sigh, for it but lies in the earth that will give birth to the tender green thousands of them in the awakening Spring.

I do hope, my dear Frank, that Leonore & you may see us one day, even tho' I be much older now than when we met; but the song is still being sung.

My love to you both.

As ever,
Sean

To J. J. O'Leary

TS. O'LEARY

5 OCTOBER 1957

My dear J.J.,

Many thanks for your letter and for the remarks that enliven it about the beating of Father Ned's drums. Lord, J.J., I cant try to write it all over again. I havent the energy, nor the inclination. You see, I wrote almost all of it first in longhand, in pen and ink, going over what I had written, scratching a lot of it out, and putting other dialogue in; then I made a rough typescript of it, altering, amending, changing; then I did a third script—one I thought final, but after re-reading, I changed, took out, added in, till the script was alive with alterations. This I sent to a professional Typist, who did it well, but on the bill mentioned that it was "a much-corrected script" (quite too true), and so charged more. This script was sent to you, and you could see for yourself that even this had been emended in many places. Now, I get a suggestion that it should be altered near from beginning to end.[1] Oh, J.J., J.J., J.J.! You may well be right, of course, for a playwright isnt always a good judge of his own work, and not much of a one with the work of others either. But once a play is done, that is done as I did this one, a number of times with many alterations, it becomes almost impossible to make drastic changes, for the mood is gone, the whole continuing impulse disappated, and it must stand (bar maybe, a few minor changes in dialogue) for better or for worse; and even any minor changes can be made only during rehearsals when practical experience may show a speech too long or too vague, or in the wrong place, etc. Development of character is a big question. Development—if it comes at all—is very slow. It took millions and millions of years to give us the form and the mind we have, imperfect as both of them are in many ways; and how can one watch for development in two hours of transit on a stage? As for the P.P., I think I am right, for where is the liberal-minded P.P. to be found?[2] Father Ned represents the spirit of Dr. McDonald, Father Morgan Sheedy, Father O'Sullivan, and Father Flanagan; but where now is there one such as they were? My answer is Nowhere—in Ireland. They are still spouting out the messages of the Rerum Novarum, indeed, have colleges and schools teaching the laity; but read what Dr. McDonald said about the R.N. many years ago, seconded by Father Yorke, D.D. of

---

[1] In his 3rd October letter to O'Casey, O'Leary said the play was "excellent," but he offered some suggestions: "The second and third Acts do not come up to the extraordinary high level of the Prologue and first Act, but I would not cavil at them. You may before it goes into production find a way to make the final curtain more memorable and dramatic—and more box office."

[2] O'Leary had one objection, the satiric treatment of the P.P., Father Fillifogue: "The only character I do not like is the Parish Priest—your man belongs to the Ireland of the last century rather than to-day. You make him a lampoonish character. Could you not trim him a bit and bring him more up-to-date? More 'educated' and crafty and cagey."

San Francisco, when the two of them were having a chinwag in Maynooth. What happened to the worker-priests in France, or to the Dominican who got Matisse to decorate a church for him; a beautiful example, but followed by the Pope's denunciation for employing "atheists" to adorn a church—as if an Atheist couldnt honor God! No, J.J., I fear that the clerics are, on the whole, Protestant (especially Prods) as well as Catholics, are old-fashioned fogies, Fillifogies, and life—as Dr. McDonald warned many years ago—is passing them by. You know well as I do that if the Noras, the Michaels, McGuntys, Man of the Pike, Man of the Musket were to act as they do in the play, in any town in Ire. like Doonavale, there would be more than one explosion. Therefore the play is something of a dream-play.

I see they have appointed an Accountant, a Judge, and a Civil Servant to the Censorship Board, and what are these but nominees of the fathers Fillifogue? You mention that I should have made the good old Father (he isnt a bad fellow, and he is taken from one whom I knew intimately) more educated. The problem in Ireland is not to use the education you get, but to escape from it; and this applies now as it did then as far back as historical times! Wolfe Tone, for instance, Fintan Lalor, Parnell, Pearse, Larkin, Joyce, Shaw, F. O'Connor, Lady Gregory, J. Plunkett, they break away through new thought, or as thousands are now doing, by fleeing to another land.

Now Irish people are to be helped towards ed. by an Account. a Jud. and a C. Ser.! Oh, J.J., J.J.! As for a "memorable ending," that is easier said than done; but to strive for memorable ending would be bad drama, and I prefer, rather than kill meself striving, to give it a natural ending, but one of quiet, satirical, but significant fun—I hope.

I must be boring you stiff, so farewell to alarms.

It was indeed kind and patient of you to read the MS, and I am very grateful. It gives me a slant on the reaction of a generous and intelligent friend. By the way, I was afraid myself that the 1st act would be too long.

All good wishes to you and to Will [Barry Fitzgerald], if he be wandering through the Dublin streets, and to Miss Doyle.

Sean

To Robert Emmett Ginna

MS. GINNA

7 OCTOBER 1957

My dear Bob,

It was very pleasant to hear your voice coming over the waves; under them, rather, into my ear, bringing into the mind the days with Gjon

[Mili], & later on, the days with Bob G. and the men of the NBC.; when you and I walked the streets of Marychurch, under The Eye of the Kindly Camera. A most enjoyable experience withal its labor and its anxiety to persuade the Camera to do well.

Speaking to Eileen about you, she told me Gjon had tried several times to come to us; but that week I was prostrate with bad attacks of vomiting; & far from seeing Gjon, I was wondering if I was there myself. She had told me about Gjon, but I was in the condition of indifference to all things that week, & so, though I probably listened to her, I had no consciousness of hearing anything. So I done wrong in saying Gjon didn't think of us.

While you were speaking, I was trying to battle out of a whoreson cold; and it was fortunate my voice carried back under the waves to you.

Many thanks, Bob, for saying you would see Shivaun; but don't try to do too much for her. She is with a Community, and they might be, naturally, a little annoyed if she got too much attention. She will have to mingle with her fellows, who, Eileen tells me (I don't know them) are a very charming & interesting group. Today, we are in the midst of a thick Devon mist, as if all the dampest clouds had come down to envelop garden, tree, plant, and man; Can't distinguish the smoke from my pipe from the mist that absorbs it.

If you come thro' England, and have time to spare, come along to see the sights still lingering in the O'Casey household.

Love to all friends. Eileen sends hers to you, & so do I.

As ever,
Sean

In a Devon Mist

Love to all friends. Eileen sends hers to you, & so do I.

As ever,

Sean

In a Devon mist

To David Krause

MS. KRAUSE

7 OCTOBER 1957

My dear Dave,

Thanks for your kind letter. I am writing this bare reply under the dim banner of a heavy cold, with the good eye bunged half up with painful inflammation; otherwise all is well. Yes, indeed, "Juno" is to be sung not said sometime later on; but how it will go is a question. I know nothing about "musicals" so can't be either anxious or eager about the result—only curious. I hope "I Knock at the Door" went well, but haven't heard yet. Anyway, it couldn't be in better hands than those of Paul Shyre. I believe "Cockadoodle" will be a stiffer job for almost every character in it is important. Recently a young teacher from New York was here, gathering material for a Thesis which he said he hoped might become a book; and managed to collect material unremembered by me—a letter written by me to a Fergus O'Connor, a publisher of Christmas cards & ballad-sheets in Eccles St. (where Bloom lived) & a copy (rare) of "Songs of the Wren," written by me, and almost forgotten.[1] [Herbert] Coston is the lad's name, & Dave G[reene]. recommended him to me. He stayed about a week in Marychurch, for I became very ill for 2 days, & couldn't see anyone; could hardly see myself. He & his wife went off to Venice, & I haven't heard of, or from, them since.

I do hope you may get your grant giving you a year's freedom to do what you will. Teaching is a responsible task, and takes away almost all chance of thinking to look out of a new window. I spent years at it myself trying to teach Irish to souls who couldn't be bothered, for minds and hands were forcibly dedicated to the task of winning a sparse living from a grudging world of senseless competition. So, I hope fervently you get your holiday for a year and a day.

As for "The Plough," it was written by one who lived many years ago, the time he went to Coole and carved his initials on Lady Gregory's Copper Beech; entered by the gate, shown in inset,[2] and sat under the great catalpa tree spreading out over a pathway, shading her dignified frosty [brow] when the Connaught sun was hot. A tree she loved, & scorn darkened her face when anyone called the Catalpa a "weeping willow." The play "The Plough" began, as you know, in the midst of an uproar, and ended in a flame of fire; for this play was adoing when the Abbey Theater sought oblivion in a blaze. And the Theater has never come to life since:

[1] See O'Casey's letter to Fergus O'Connor, 13 February 1918, note 4, Vol. I.

[2] He had enclosed a line-drawing postcard, sent to him by his daughter Shivaun, of the copper beech Autograph Tree in Lady Gregory's garden at Coole Park, with an inset of the Coole Gates. This card apparently touched off the following memory of Lady Gregory.

dust to dust, ashes to ashes, and so the one who wrote it sees his shadow as he looks back, there under the Catalpa tree, with the old Lady sitting beside, watching the Connaught sun go down in a blaze of red, green, & gold, behind the Birnen Hills. One of my young friends, son of Barrows Dunham, a fine lad named Clarke, helped in the designing work of the Shakespearean series in Central Park; so O'Casey, was, in a way, near to it all. The play "The Night is Whispering" has changed its name to "The Drums of Father Ned." I've sent the Script to the Chairman of the Tostal (he asked for it), but I doubt they'll do it. The eyes gives out, so I close it & send a loving goodbye to you.

As ever,
Sean

To Coiril Ó Mathúna[1]

MS. Ó MATHÚNA

10 OCTOBER 1957

A chara,
    Buail ar aghaidh, ma's maith libhse cuig léirighthe P. On Demand; ach biodh fhios agaibh gur beag, suarach an drama é, is nach fiú é 'nochtadh os comhair aoinne.
    Fee dá sgilling is rael.

Mise
Sean O'Casey

[*Friend,*
    Go ahead and produce "Pound On Demand" if you want to; but understand that it is a miserable little play and not worthy of being exhibited before anyone.
    Fee two shillings and sixpence.

Yours]

[1] Coiril Ó Mathúna, director, Irish Theatre, Galway.

To Brendan Smith

TS. SMITH

11 OCTOBER 1957

Dear Mr. Brendan Smith,

Very well, I give my approval that THE DRUMS OF FATHER NED be given its World-premiere in the Gaiety Theater, Dublin, during the Tostal Festival, and may God be with the work.[1]

I am a bit uneasy still about the actors and the Director, but we shall have to leave this to God and to the best that all of us can do about it.

I am a bit troubled about the play being "a full-scale National Production." I dont want the play or the production to sound too big; so please try to modify this implication (Nat. Product.) as much as you reasonably can, so as to avoid any envy or sense of favor of choice by the other older or younger playwrights, who, indeed, may be working on a newer and a more original way.

One last thing is this proviso—the Agreement ends with the end of the run at the Gaiety Theater, unless additional arrangements be made by written consent of both parties to the understanding now agreed upon.

No more, now; I am struggling out of a heavy cold, influenza, lumbago, bad eye, and heaven knows what else or what others; and I'm busy starting on another possible book; so all I can add, have time to add is my best wishes to you and to all that you are doing.

By the way, our pal, J. J. [O'Leary] had some criticisms to make, and, if he hasnt mentioned them to you, you should ask him about them, and see what you think of what he thinks too.

All the best to J.J. and to you again.

Yours very sincerely,
Sean O'Casey.

[1] In his letter of 10th October, Smith stated that the Dublin Tostal Council and the Irish Tourist Board had accepted his recommendation of *The Drums of Father Ned* as "one of the main items for the 1958 Festival."

To Brendan Smith

TS. SMITH

[?] OCTOBER 1957

Dear Mr. Brendan Smith,

Some time ago, Eileen (Mrs O'Casey) read THE DRUMS OF FA-THER NED, and, talking about it a little, later on, said she didnt like the taking of the money episode between Skerighan and Bernadette. She thought that an Irish girl could be hardly so sophisticated (big word), so ready to seize a chance. Thinking over it, I think she is right. Irish girls (or Irishmen) arent clever at taking advantage of a condition of things which would mean money if they were a bit more brassy. They find it hard to make a bargain—bar at cattle fairs, where everyone is doing it. Alone, they are pretty hopeless; or dealing with one whom they know. They refuse what they are longing to take. Even the occasional lass on Leicester Sqr. isnt in it with her other-race competitors. We arent good for standing up for our right, unless they are political ones, and when dealing with these, too, we lose sense, and become frenzied.

So I send you herewith the amended part of the play, and shall be glad if you would give it to the Director chosen to set the play out on the stage.

With all good wishes,
Yours sincerely,
Sean O'Casey.

P.S. See additional changes in scene sheet. Some friends of mine discussing a Director have advised me to relinquish my Prejudice against Hilton Edwards; so, if you decide he might be best, go ahead.

Sean

THE DRUMS OF FATHER NED
Alterations made in Act II, pages 13 and 14.

Page 13, Act II, as follows—

> Bernadette (thoughtfully) If I only could keep quiet till I get some of th' terrible shock outa me system. (what follows to be cut.)

Page 14, Act II.

> Skerighan. I dinna mind ye warnin' me a wee kiss could send ye all agley, but gether your wuts taegither, an' it'll no be lang til ye're cantie again.

Then cut "Skerighan fussing a wallet from a breast pocket . . ." to "Go on, tak them, an' pop off to where you'll get a rest."

Bernadette (speech after Sker's "tll ye're cantie again.") Th' blessed ones
and th' sanctified ones will help me over this sore calamity. If anyone
questions, I'll just murmur it was a sudden spasm brought on be over-
doin' it for th' Tostal. I'll just have to sthrive all I can to piece some of
me scatthered parts together again. (she gives a long sad sigh) I must be
careful how I move. (she presses a hand to her heart) Now get over
from me far as you can for fear of another hot seizure takin' you when
I get up on me quiverin' feet.

(rest of her speech to be cut)

Page 15. Act II.
Change Sker's speech "confused about the news of Bernadette" . . .
to Sker (confused about the news of Bernadette galloping off) . . . add
at the end "She didna look fut fur a gallop."
Change Father F's following speech to

Father F. Oh, didnt she That's all you know. Sly little hussy scatterin' occasions of sin before her every time she meets a boy. (suspiciously)
What gab did she give to you, now?

The above eliminates the money scene, and still allows the play to flow on
without any break.
After

Skerighan (imploringly) Cant ye thry to pull yourself taeguther before
someone arrives tae mak a song about it?

add

(he puts some notes on the end of the table nearer to her) There's a few
wee pounds 'ull hulp ye tae come to your senses.

Before next speech by Bernadette put the following:

Bribin' me now maybe in me few last moments. Money didnt get me in
this state, an' money cant get me out of it. (as if to herself) Oh, wont
someone bring Mrs Binngton or Nora . . . etc.

On page 14

Bernadette . . . I forgive you th' dhreadful harrrm you have done to a
poor innocent counthry girl—

change following directions to

(She staggers to the table, picks up the money dreamily then moves to the
door, pressing her hand to her heart . . . etc.)

To Irish Times

15 OCTOBER 1957

IRISH FAMILIES[1]

Sir,—Kindly let my friend, Mr. E. Ó Mahony, know that Ó Casey was born Ó Casey, lives Ó Casey, and will die Ó Casey.

All good wishes to all the other Irish Families so finely set down and coloured in Mr. MacLysaght's lovely-looking book.—Yours, etc.,

Sean Ó Casey

St. Marychurch
Torquay, Devonshire
October 12th, 1957.

[1] Eoin O'Mahony, the well-known genealogist, in his review of Edward Mac-Lysaght's *Irish Families: Their Names, Arms and Origins* (1957), in the *Irish Times,* 10 October 1957, stated: "Sean O'Casey and Maureen O'Hara have no connection with families of these names, for they were born Cassidy and Fitzsimons." O'Casey had used the name Casside for his family in his autobiography, but he was born in Dublin as John Casey, son of Michael Casey, who came from the Limerick branch of the Casey clan.

To Miss Kay Carney[1]

TS. CARNEY

20 OCTOBER 1957

Dear Miss Kay,

My dear, England has had her turbulent periods as well (much more even) as Ireland—W. War, 1914 to 1918, and W. War II, 1939 to 1946, yet what have English dramatists made of it all—JOURNEY'S END! Looks like journey's end for English playwrights too. I have nothing to say about your "angry man outsider school." I dont know them, though I have heard them talking. I dont know what their ideas are "about the nature of man"; but hardly believe that the Descent of Man has arrived and ended at either [Colin] Wilson or [John] Osborne. They may be those, prophisied by T. S. Eliot, who will end the world with a whimper rather than with a bang. I dont know what they are looking back in anger at, and you havent told me. Are they looking back in anger at themselves? At things undone that should have been done; at things done that should not have been done—or what? Tell me, for devil a know I know. And

[1] Miss Kay Carney, 347 Bleecker Street, New York City 14.

I'm too busy to study to know why I dont know. These angry ones seem, to me, to be concerned, not with the bodies and souls of men, but with the buttons on their clothes.

By the way, I'm not reviewing or criticising what they have written or how they wrote it—that's another question. However we may disagree with a philosophy in book or play, the book or the play may, in itself, be a fine one. I am not a critic or a reviewer; I havent had the training, the experience, and I dont think I have got the gift to be either critic or reviewer.

Shaw was never an angry man, though he was at times a man who was angry—a big difference. He was angry only when anger ceased to be a deadly sin, and became a virtue—like Christ's anger against the Scribes and the Pharisees.

I dont know that any Irish authors emulate me; I certainly hope they dont. I never met Mr. B. Behan, and never had any contact with him. Bernard Shaw did not teach me to write or plot a play; I did a lot of work before I met him, and then knew only his JOHN BULL'S OTHER IRE-LAND, which taught me to look with open eyes all over Ireland. One thing he did: I always had courage—not spontaneous, it had to be created and developed, but my friendship for and with him strengthened the courage I already had. Now, Kay, I must end. I have answered hundreds of questions already—there are three letters like yours on the table; I am old, now, and easily tire. So fare thee well, allana, and God speed all you do to get your Master's Degree.

Yours very sincerely,
Sean O'Casey

Shaw sent me a grand letter about "The Silver Tassie,"[2] praising it highly, including the much disputed II Act; But the quotation you give, appeared in a letter from T. E. Lawrence of Arabia (Shaw's great friend) to Lady Nancy Astor.[3]

[2] See Bernard Shaw's letter to O'Casey, 19 June 1928, Vol. I.
[3] See T. E. Lawrence's letter to Lady Astor, 15 February 1934, Vol. I.

To Cyril Cusack

MS. Cusack

22 October 1957

My dear Cyril,

You are plunging into a big adventure, and your courage alone deserves success.

If wishing it on my part can give it you, it is yours. With all my heart, I send you my best wishes.

I have long thought, & sometimes said that Irish actors should practice in plays of Shakespeare and European playwrights so as to get a glimpse of, & feel a different current of action & thought within them from those they get in acting the usual way in the usual Irish plays—my own included.

So God be with you in the part of Hamlet.[1]

My love to pretty Maureen & to your children.

Sean

P.S. The change, too would tax the "Critics."

[1] Cusack's production of *Hamlet* opened in Dublin at the Gaiety Theatre on 28 October 1957, with Cusack in the title role and Micheál MacLiammoir as Claudius.

To Bjarni Benediktsson[1]

TC. O'CASEY

24 OCTOBER 1957

Dear Mr. Benediktsson,

Thanks for your kind letter. My answers to your questions must be brief—I get many of them; too many to be able to answer all.

1. I dont rightly know what you mean by "history." All my work deals with life as I lived it, and as, I believe, others around me lived it, too. Most of the characters described by me were, of course, known to me, but I have made them larger than life; and have added to their stature; though, had I been able to know each through and through, the characters might be smaller than life; for life—even the most insignificant, remember Darwin with the mullusks—is a big thing. Then, Life, Experience of life, love of life, a keen eye and a keen ear, with an imagination go to the making of my work.

2. Cant say which made the biggest impression: all did a lot to impress me. The flight of a gull, the presence of a linnet, a flower blooming, the Fall—all things impress me, for all are a part of life. This part of history or that doesnt mean a lot to me, for

[1] Bjarni Benediktsson, Langateigi 24, Reykjavik, Iceland. A journalist for a socialist newspaper, he saw a production of *Juno* in Iceland and sent O'Casey a questionnaire for an article.

all are part of a continuous flow, though to man some may stand out. Bunker Hill; French Revolution; and the Soviet Revolution giving us the Ten Days that Shook the World. But life began a long time ago; far, far beyond the year 1. A.D.; and we who live now are part of it all.

3. I dont try to teach anyone. I dont describe Man; I live and have my being with him, and I write about the experiences I go through as I live among the active world of man.

4. [Are there some main teachings in your plays] Not that I am aware of.

5. Morals are constantly changing, and no one can prevent this. As Shaw says, "Every man has a true morality, but everyman's true morality isnt the same." The Author should take his part in man's effort to make the world a more secure place in which to live. An author as well as being an A. is also a social being.

6. [How would you describe the kind of drama you have mostly written?] I havent an idea as to how to describe it.

8. Present state of the Theater in Ireland (and England) is in a very bad way. Economic conditions have deprived the commercial theaters of many who could afford to pay big prices, and so are declining—for which, God be thanked! A new theater more sensible, more democratic in price, and livelier, will, I think, ultimately take its place.

9. [Is the influence of literature on the wane today?] No; on the contrary, it is increasing. The great authors are coming closer to the people, in the schools among the young; in the libraries among the older.

10. [What is the most necessary quality for an author?] An irresistible desire to write.

11. No. I have never lost my faith in Man.

12. Facing what powers of destruction? Do you mean the power of nuclear energy? If you do, then this power can make life a much more extraordinary thing of light, joy, and security. The peoples of the world have declared for Peace so that this power may be used for the benefit of all. Who is to go against it? If anyone does, then, in my opinion, world revolution will sweep over us all, and those who cling to wealth and privileges will be swept away a little earlier than they would had they waited for the inevitable changes. Man is not prepared to destroy himself, and all, or almost all have spoken. Arent you going to join us, and mingle your voice with ours in the trumpet-call for Peace and friendship with the peoples of the world?

7. I dont know which is my best play; my favorite, personally, is COCKADOODLE DANDY. To find out its contents, I suggest that you should read it.

That's all, my Icelandic friend, that I have time or energy to set down; for age (I am just 78) now makes me tire rather quickly.

All good wishes to the People of ICELAND and to you.

Yours sincerely,
Sean O'Casey.

To Sean O'Rourke[1]

MS. O'ROURKE

24 OCTOBER 1957

My dear Sean,

Sad news. Another final break with the past; one more link gone. How vividly I remember all the days of long ago. I might as well be once more sauntering along Seville Place, with Frank Cahill beside me, deciding this or that about the Pipers, about Ireland, or, indeed, about the world. And now Frank rests quiet in St. Fintan's, Sutton. I've worked along there often; & up the Hill at St. Fintan's, near the Convent of Stella Maris. Well, at least, Frank did what he could for the old Parish of St. Lawrence O'Toole, & for Ireland; till the cross-grain came into so many souls following the stupid & calamitous Civil War over the Treaty. I read, somewhere, that Mick Colgan had gone, too; but it is good for you to have still the boul' Lar, Paddy & Johnny McD. [McDonald] & Fred Lynch (the drummer)—long life and good going to them all. I remember others, too—Matt Carroll, Mick Lawless, & Fay (a drummer, too)[2] whose first name I've forgotten; & Paddy Kinsella, the two Rooneys, cousins to Frank from Co. Meath, & the banner bearer, whose name I can't remember, who got married while I was with you all. How closely-knit the Parish was, & how I remember every stone in its streets, even the jumble of houses back of Mayor Street, where Jimmy Moore used to live with his mother, his father, Jack, an old docker, & his sister; the time Jimmy worked for Gleeson in O'Connell St., before he got a firm of his own, & made a mess of it; but pulled up, & lived happily with his wife & two? most charming children. And "the Cahills"—Mrs C., Mrs. Pollard, Martha, Mick, Tom, with his clarinet; Jack, Mollser, Kathleen, Josie, an' all. Most of them gone now. May God be good to them all, for they were kindly souls, good-natured, tolerant, and hard-working.

By the way, the St. L. O'Toole Pipers asked me some time ago to be a Vice President; but I pointed out that the name of a Communist as a

---

[1] Sean O'Rourke, 2 Seville Place, Dublin, one of O'Casey's old friends in the St. Laurence O'Toole Club.

[2] O'Casey drew a small sketch of a drummer here in the margin of the letter.

Vice President might do them no good. In memory of old & honored times, however, I'd like to send a token of good-will, & so I enclose a sub. of £ 3.3.0. to their funds, with all the good wishes in the world.

I often think of Kevin O'Loughlin & the loss he was to us the time he died in the full flush of his mental vigor.

Ah, well, we all have to go; but till we do, the old picturesque days in the Parish will linger in the minds of those who lived in them.

I hope you are keeping fit. My affectionate regards to you & all.

As ever,
Sean

24 October, 1957

Sean ó Rourke, Sct.
Flat 3, 40 Trumlands Road, St. Marychurch, Torquay, Devon.
2 Seville Place,
Dublin.
Tel. Torquay 87766.

My dear Sean,

Sad news. Another friend break with the past; one more link gone. How vividly I remember all the days of long ago. I might as well be once more saumtering along Seville Place, with Frank Cahill beside me, deciding, this or that about the Papers, about Ireland, or, indeed, about the world. And now Frank rests quiet in St. Fintan's, Sutton. I've worked along there often; & up the Hill at St. Fintan's, near the Convent of Stella Maris. Well, at least, Frank did what he could for the old Parish of St. Lawrence ó Toole, & for Ireland; till the cross-grain came into so many souls following the stupid & calamitous Civil War over the Treaty. I read, somewhere, that Mick Colgan had gone, too; but it is good for you to have still the loved Lar, Paddy & Johnny McG, & Fred Lynch (the drummer) — long life and good going to them all. I remember others, too — Matt Farrell, Mick Lawlers, & Fay (a drummer, too) whose first name I've forgotten; & Kneallen Paddy. The the two Rooneys, cousins to Frank from Co. Meath, & the banner bearer, who name I can't remember, who got married while I was with you all. How vividly I knit the Parish now, & how I remember every stone in its streets, even the jumble of houses back of Mayor street, where

To Coiril Ó Mathúna

MS. Ó Mathúna

26 D. Fomhair 1957

A chara,

Thaunig an Seic ar Punt a sgilling agus an ceann eile ar Deich sgilling is raol cugham go reidh slán; agus taim buidheach dhuit ar a son. Ach, tuige gur thugais an méid sin dhom, mar is cuimhin liom nar iarr mé acht cúig sgillinge mar ioch as an léirighthe?

Más rud e go bfuil an iomad airgead agaib, ta go maith; ach murra bhfuil, deanfaid, ar aon ocáid eile, cuig sgillinge mar iocach as aon leirighthe den dramín ud—"Punt ar uleamh."

Mo beannacht orraibh agus ar bhur n-obair.

Mise.
Sean Ó Casey

26 October 1957

Friend,

Your cheque for one pound one shilling and the other one for ten shillings and sixpence reached me safely; and I am thankful to you for them. But why did you send so much, because I remember I only asked for five shillings for a production?

If it happens that you have plenty of money, fair enough; but if not, five shillings will be sufficient for any future production of the play "Pound on Demand."

My blessing on you and on your work.

Yours.

To Jay Deiss

MS. DEISS

1 NOVEMBER 1957

Dear Jay Deiss,

I've read your book, "The Blue Chips";[1] read it slowly, but with un-fading interest. To read it at all is more than something, for nowadays, & for a long time past, I find it near impossible to read a novel. As a novel, I think it fine, and goes ahead like a burning building. In a lot of ways, it is a frightening book, and makes us, laymen, anxious about the way life-saving drugs can be controlled and exploited by profit-making Com-panies. The characters, I think, are well drawn, & the deterioration of the central character, fine fellow as he is, away from his scientific integrity is ruthless, but, as you do it, inevitable; and forms a sad and exciting requiem over a clever and a good man baring his soul for what will perish sooner than an autumn petal on a fading flower.

I wish I had the gift to comment in detail, but I have had neither the training nor experience of a reviewer. All I can say is that I read it, liked it, that I think it has conviction shown with power; and that it is worthy of the author of "A Washington Story."[2]

With my heart and mind, I wish "The Blue Chips" every success.

My warm regards to you & all.

Yours very sincerely,
Sean O'Casey

PS. You were a bit hard on "Daphne." She was a lovely lass, and that forgives a lot. S. O'C.

[1] Jay Deiss, *The Blue Chips* (London: Hamish Hamilton, 1957).
[2] Jay Deiss, *A Washington Story* (New York: Duel, Sloan and Pearce, 1950).

To Ronald Ayling

TS. AYLING

3 NOVEMBER 1957

Dear Ron,

Well, well! I've read with interest the extracts from the letters sent to you by St. John Ervine and Austin Clarke. Austin C. camouflages the events of 1926 very nicely; but hardly hides them all. "By collecting un-complimentary references"; and why not? They are often more interesting than the opposites; but, I fear, they went farther than being just "uncomplimentary." The "exploitation of the poorer class"[1] to me was a slander. I never said there was a "cabal" against me in Dublin. The outburst of opposition was probably spontaneous; but I did say in my biography that there was a cabal against Yeats. I know, because I was asked to join it. Whether Clarke had anything to do with it or not, I'm not sure. My own belief is that he hadn't, that he would be above it. [Liam] O'Flaherty[2] was the core of it, for he disliked Yeats for some reason. A.C. couldn't have read my biographical books when he ventures to say I never faced the fact that the biggest injury I suffered was the rejection of the S. Tassie. I think I faced the fact, faced Yeats, Lady Gregory, and L. Robinson pretty firmly; though it would have been better—materially—for me to have been humble, and keep my mouth shut. This is the first time I have heard that A.E. had "been running O'C as a sort of political propaganda for a long time." Isn't it obvious, too, that then, 1926, I should have been a damn bad propaganda weapon for A.E.—even were I willing to become one— seeing that then I was rather infamous than famous? As for "Nationalism," his [Austin Clarke's] anxiety to defend it amuses me. I was never aware that either he or F.R.H[iggins]. did much for it; I never heard of them in the Gaelic League, the Republican Movement, or saw them on a hurling field, the time I was half killing myself for them all—organising Camogie clubs, secretary of a hurling club, secretary of a Pipers Band, teaching Irish four nights a week, speaking on platforms, and doing a damn hard day's work before tackling any of them. Now, he comes along to hint or say that I was prejudicing the nationalism of the country. He isn't quite frank when he says that he never tried to assess the ultimate value of my plays. He has forgotten the long review he had in the Irish Times of Cocka-doodle Dandy,[3] the most peculiar and bitterest review I have ever received of that play. I quoted a poem of his in The Green Crow,[4] referring to him as being no mean poet and a man of no mean mind which he probably hasn't read. In Dublin, he mentioned this to my daughter, saying he heard I had said something kind about him in the book. But I don't want to think any harm of Austin. He has had a damned hard time of it, and doesn't make much from his work. I wrote to America about him, trying to get him some attention there, and wish I could help him more effectively. But he lacks the aggressive spirit, that of the fighter, so essential if one believes one has a mission, be it politics, poetry, painting, or playwrighting. I wish he were a bolder spirit; for he has been brave in clinging to his poetry against many odds, and he is a very good reviewer of other poets' work. Indeed, I have a cautious affection for Austin. A catholic in Ireland, if he has any thought, has a bad time of it. I think he is a proud fellow in his own way, and I admire him for that same.

1 See O'Casey's letter to David Krause, 5 January 1955, note 4.
2 *Ibid.*
3 *Ibid.*, note 1.
4 See "Foreword," *The Green Crow* (1956), p. xiii.

I wonder where St. John Ervine got his dogmatism? He is more dogmatic on everything under the sun than a newly-fledged Irish Bishop. I have no doubt that G.B.S. was a friend of his and of W[illiam]. Archer; but, I imagine, in a limited way. I imagine that it was St. J. who walked with Shaw rather than it was Shaw who walked with St. J. Mrs. St. J. was a friend of Mrs. Shaw rather than of G.B.S. I imagine that it was Mrs. St. J. who talked of God to Shaw rather than vice versa, possibly in an effort to win Shaw from his unbelief, as so many tried to do, the last, an Irish nurse when G.B.S. was in hospital with his broken thigh. I don't know what St. J. means by "You can do a man a kindness, and Shaw was incessant in kindness, without being his intimate." What is he hinting at here? If he means that I personally was beholden to Shaw, or that I received from him any of this incessant kindness, then, plainly speaking, St. John Ervine is a liar. As a matter of fact, St. J. wouldn't have understood, and can't now, the bond between me and G.B.S. Here are a few: He was a Dublinman, so was I; he was reared up a Protestant, so was I; he suffered the humiliation of living in the genteel poverty of the Irish lower middle-class, while I suffered the squalid, but more vigorous, poverty of the proletariat; Shaw was mainly a self-educated man, so was I; Shaw hated poverty in all its forms, so did I; Shaw fought against it most of his life, so did I and still do; Shaw thought Stalin a great man, so did I, and so do still; Shaw was passionately devoted to the USSR and all the USSR did and was doing, so was I; Shaw hated all British Imperialism, so did I; Shaw rejected the Christian beliefs, so did I; Shaw saw through the romantic idea of Irish Nationalism, so did I; Shaw was a fighter, and he knew I was one, too (I've never heard that he ever said in a letter to St. J. "Bravo, Titan!");[5] in almost his last words to Mrs. O'C he said, "It is for Sean now to carry on the fight";[6] Not St. J. but Sean; Shaw was a born Communist, so was I; Shaw called Jim Larkin "the greatest Irishman since Parnell," and Shaw knew how I had fought for the workers with Jim; Shaw was deeply interested in the Chinese Workers' and Peasants' Red Army and its long and terrible march from Kiangsi in the south to Shensi in the north, wondering if they could do it, and if they did, what effect it would have upon the whole of China, so was I, though I'm sure, St. J. never even heard of it till the Red Army eventually broke through in Manchuria, and, finally, won China for Communism; Shaw had a deep affection for Lady Gregory, so had I (I hope St. J. won't next say somewhere that I was never a friend of hers; but he'd hardly do that, for he disliked her, I imagine, or, certainly, she did him); his initials are carved on the great tree in Coole, so are mine, but I've never seen St. J's there; while St. J. mentions a number of American Drama Critics, I notice he never mentions Nathan, yet Nathan had a deep reverence for Shaw, and Shaw thought highly of him, and so did, do, I; although his name is [not]

[5] See Bernard Shaw's letter to O'Casey, 19 June 1928, Vol. I.
[6] See O'Casey's letter to George Jean Nathan, 3 November 1950, Vol. II.

mentioned either. Shaw was always delighted to see John Dulanty, the then High Commissioner for Ireland—it was he who brought the Roll of Dublin's Freeman to G.B.S.; Shaw loved his humour and his stories, and so did I; Shaw was always ready to talk about Ireland, and so was I.

Well, there are a few of the affinities that went to and fro between Shaw and me, cutting out, even, the tremendous interest we both took in the Theatre; affinities that could hardly have existed between St. J.E. and the Dublin sage. Again, if Mrs. St. J. was so dear to GBS, why didn't he ask to see her during his last days? He asked for Eileen, not once, but several times; and it was she who was with him just before he sank into his last long sleep. Why didn't he give his last message to St. J.? On the 22 Oct. a letter from a Dublin friend (now in a London job), Seumas Scully, 20 Mountview Road, Stroud Green, London N.4., says "Have been to Shaw's house, and saw your family photo there on the mantlepiece." How did that come there—will St. J. tell us? Perhaps he knows that O'Casey stole into the house on a dark night and placed it there. It is also odd that St. Jay never mentions—if I remember right—Shaw's friendship for Lady Gregory, though he was very fond of her. Why? Shaw's name is carved on the Coole tree, and I have a photograph of GBS sitting on the border of Coole Lake (sent to me by Shaw himself), with one of the Old Lady, and one of Yeats in his younger days (very handsome) standing before the background of Coole Park trees. Why wasn't she admitted to Shaw's friendship by St. Jay? I imagine because he disliked the Old Lady, and so shoved her out, as far as he could from Shaw's circle.

When I first came to London, I never sought out Shaw; it never entered my mind to do so; I never even thought of him much, never at all in the way of a visit, for [it never] dawned on me that he would be interested in any way with me or my work—very little at that time. I have never bothered to mingle with the famous; rather am I interested in the folk. When I was at Cambridge, I sought out, not the dons (though many of them have been great minds and great souls), but the students. I hadn't an idea even where Shaw lived, and I was very surprised to get an invitation to lunch, not to Whitehall Court, but to Adelphi Terrace. It may surprise St. Jay to hear that I went to Adelphi Terrace several times. Only once was Shaw and his wife invited by us, and by Eileen who thought we should ask them to us after so many visits to them. We couldn't afford lunches or dinners then, so we asked them to tea to Woronzow Road, where we lived. As GBS didn't drink tea, Mrs. Shaw came half an hour before the sage, and the two of them ate bread and salt in the O'Casey home. At all other times, the invitation came from Mrs. Shaw. I like the conceit of St. Jay when he says that if I had been asked to W. Court, he would have been asked too to provide the conversation! This shows some of the measure of the man. Without him, there would be silence. Well, at times, between Shaw and me no words were needed; we were one on most questions; I believe on all. But it is singular that I should be asserting to

St. Jay that I actually did visit Shaw. Even if St. J. wished to separate me from Shaw's friendship, he might at least have allowed me the privilege of knocking at his door. But I'd like to know what he meant in the implication of "Shaw's kindnesses," as applicable to me. Perhaps you might ask him.

I don't think Fox's book on Jim Larkin[7] worth a damn. I was asked to review it, but refused, because I dislike the man, and I might not have been fair to him. There's a young lad, an American, who is writing a Life of Larkin,[8] and I think this book will be a far, far finer one. He has secured all the official reports of Jim's trial in the USA, when Larkin defended himself, and he tells me they are amazing. To me, Fox hasn't the gift of writing; and, if he has, he hasn't got the guts to use the gift. St. Jay is, though not in the first class in fancy or imagination, I'm afraid, but forcible, though too dogmatic. His book on Shaw,[9] in my opinion, is a fine biography, and a great tribute to Shaw.

I can't give you George Jean Nathan's address for very good reasons. He is a very ill man, and has been so for a very long time, over two years. He came out of hospital just as I entered one, and, afterwards got a stroke that deprived him of the use of his right hand and weakened his left one, and he walks with difficulty. I can't have him worried. His references to me are scattered over his writings, mainly in his various articles. He saw but one of my later plays produced—Within the Gates. Though Purple Dust has been running in New York, and still is, he isn't able to go to see it, which is an annoyance to him, for this is one he likes well, and laboured for years, time and again, to get it produced there for me. His favourite is, I believe, the Cockadoodle Dandy, which he thinks to be a splendid play; and it is my favourite, too. I haven't heard his opinion of The Bishop's Bonfire, but he is sure to think the former a better play, which, indeed, it is. I usually send him the MS of any new play (a standing request from him), but I didn't send the B. Bonfire or The Drums of Father Ned, because I couldn't bother him in his illness. George is a very, very dear friend of mine, and his illness has been a great grief to me, and a great loss to the American Theatre.

I enclose an article showing that the attacking forces are still in the field.[10] What matter if they had in their saying a smut of honesty. I who had affection and reverence for Yeats and love for the Old Lady am accused of vilifying them. No hesitation at libel. Again "in those days he wasn't interested in tub-thumping for the Reds." Yet in 1925–26, I was corresponding with Raissa Lomonosa,[11] a member of the then struggling Soviet Embassy in London, and one of my reasons for deciding to come to

---

[7] R. M. Fox, *Jim Larkin: The Rise of the Underman* (1957).

[8] Emmet Larkin, *James Larkin: Irish Labour Leader, 1876–1947* (1965).

[9] St. John Ervine, *Bernard Shaw: His Life, Work and Friends* (1956).

[10] Ulick O'Connor, "An O'Casey Obsessed With His Critics," *The Standard*, 12 April 1957, a review of *The Green Crow*.

[11] See his 1925–1926 letters to Raisa Lomonosova, Appendix, Vol. IV.

London was to try to meet her. By then the Embassy had been pressured
out of the City, but a letter from her asked me to come and stay awhile in
the French Soviet Embassy; but I could get no letter through to her, and
soon, Paris pressured them out, too. It was almost impossible then to keep
in touch with the Soviets, but I still have photographs she sent me of the
first Diesel Locomotive arriving in the Soviet Union, and the crowds of
soldiers, men, women, and children gathered to see it—the acorn that produced the forest. I have still copies of *International Theater,* too, sent to
me from Moscow, arriving by a miracle, a good deal tattered; but alive.
Read that grand message of Ulick's "Artists don't need to think . . ."! I
return the photos. Design not quite right. I enclose sketch of my idea.

By the way, Nathan wrote a boisterous [review] of acclaim around
End of Beginning. He loved it. If I ever come across it, I'll send a copy.

Now, what about you? Your studies? Are you diffusing your energy
too much? Take it easier. So ends my article. I rejoice that you have swum
out of the 'flu, a pestilent thing. But go easy for awhile.

All good wishes.
Sean

To Lewis Funke[1]

TC. O'CASEY

6 NOVEMBER 1957

Dear Lewis,
Thanks for your letter and for the very kind thoughts wrapped up in
it. It is very good of you to ask me about my new play, and to tell you
something about it. I'm always put out a little when asked about my work,
not from any modesty, but because I find it hard to get my thoughts together to explain the shape it has taken and the things that it has tried to
say. In this respect, I am shyer even than Shaw—and he was shy enough—
and, also, I am far less competent in giving a synopsis of what I have tried
to do. Well, first, I have given the play another name. In the course of
writing it, it grew somewhat away from the original, and, in the making of
three drafts, many changes were made. The first title—THE NIGHT IS
WHISPERING—wasnt bold enough; it had within it a breath of melancholy which is absent (I think) from the play; and so I gave it the new
and bolder name of THE DRUMS OF FATHER NED. The play is about
Ireland, and hardly likely to have much interest for Americans. The back-

[1] Lewis Funke, Drama Editor, *New York Times.*

ground before which the figures go is what we call The Tostal, a yearly Festival in which Ireland, or a good part of her, goes gaily serious. There is heard again the old Irish Hurrah, a little less confident and resolute than the one which Thomas wrote about. For many years Ireland has been losing and surrendering her resolution and her courage. The land is now heavily sprinkled with the ideas of cynicism and derision; and we have lost faith in ourselves. Many public men and women have sadly lamented it, and most responsible members of the Press have, time and again, cried out against this spirit of apathy and indifference. Indeed, this spirit of indifference seems to be developing into positive hostility to Ireland and all her odd and cherished traditions. Only the other day, the head of the Roman Catholic Church in Ireland, the Cardinal-Archbishop of Armagh, said that "Young people were leaving Ireland as if she were a land of lepers." What a terrible saying! A true one, though; the young among us Irish have become a different kind of leppers: they are taking a lep over the Irish Sea to land in England, or a flying lep over the Atlantic Ocean to land in the United States, or further up in Canada—the leppers of Ireland!

Ireland's Tostal is an effort to activity and enthusiasm back to the people, activity in many things that alone make life a useful and enjoyable living. Houses are repainted, gardens tilled, special games are played, there are festivals of drama and music, and work is honored by an Industrial Procession. It is a spring bubbling out activities, and this bubbling may grow into a steady flow, watering the land and its people with new hope and new ideas.

The Tostal, then, is the background of the play, and the Spirit of Father Ned is the hero, symbolising (though he never appears) the desire to thrust out into new endeavor lurking in the hearts and minds of many of the younger clergy, not only in Ireland, but in all other lands where the Church is growing old and hesitant; where the old heads (some of them on young shoulders) look backward, and think it mortal sin, or, at least, dangerous, for the younger mind to look ahead and stretch a welcoming hand to new ideas in art, literature, architecture, music, politics, and peace. So the figures in the comedy move in and out among this background, prefaced by a "Prerumble" showing the Black and Tans in the main street of a burning town. There is a good deal of fun in it—at least, I hope it is fun, though the theme is the brave thrust forward of the new idea within the wider hope of resolution; hands and minds joined up with hearts and souls—the four good suits in the pack of life. In other words, if not the dream of a madman, the day-dream of desire in Ireland.

When it became known that I was working on a new play, the Chairman of the Festival wrote asking me to let him read it for possible production during the next Tostal Week. I was reluctant to do this, for I didnt wish to interfere with the chance a younger and newer playwright may have to get a play of his honored at the Festival. A friend of the Chairman's, who is also a friend of mine, appealed to me to send the play, and, finally, I sent the Script to what would be thought of it as a work for performance during the week of special Irish activities in art, drama, films, and music.

The Chairman read it, and wrote to say he "liked it immensely," and eagerly requested me to allow it to be set aside for production during the Festival, so, after some hesitation, I agreed that THE DRUMS OF FATHER NED should receive its "World Premiere" in Dublin next May, in the Gaiety Theater, Dublin. So there it is, and may the beat of the drums of Father Ned find a responsive echo in the hearts of many of my own people, the indomitable Irishry.

P.S. If this be printed,[2] I should, if possible, like it to be strictly copyright, for this reason: There was a great to-do before the actual production of my THE BISHOP'S BONFIRE, and I dont wish this to happen again, if it can be avoided. I want the play to be quietly done without any pre-fuss so that no bitter comments may be made of any "ballyhoo for O'Casey, and complaints of over-attention given to his work." I'd like the play to speak for itself as well as it can, and as well as I hope it may do.

S. O'C.

[2] A paraphrase of parts of the letter, including several quotations, appeared in Funke's regular column, "News and Gossip Gathered Along the Rialto," in the Sunday *New York Times,* 24 November 1957.

To Paul Shyre

TS. SHYRE

11 NOVEMBER 1957

Dear Paul:

Thanks for your letter. Of course, I'm glad that PURPLE DUST is hanging on, for the weekly dollars are very welcome; I was just worrying about the actors not getting all that they deserved to get from the hard work they put into the Play and the Reading. If they are contented to go on, then, as I said, the longer both last the better—for me.

I hope you may manage a tour, and that the Reading may go well wherever the artists may perform.

I had weeks ago given up the idea of a Film of the play, and had almost forgotten that anything had ever been said about it; but, if it goes through, it will be good news indeed, for both of us, and, I daresay for some of the actors who took part in the stage production.

It is fine that you have secured a home of your own, where you can walk about, and, maybe, look out of a window. Besides, it is always interesting—when one is young—to dress the home up, and show ones pictures on one's own wall. I hope you may be very happy there.

It is a pleasant thought that we have been able to help each other, and it was a good day for me when a lad named Paul Shyre came into my vision over the hills. I shall be glad if the Play reaches a year's run—a thing never dreamed of by me, or anything like it. Well, as Shaw so truly said YOU NEVER CAN TELL.

By the way, would you care to read the MS of THE DRUMS OF FATHER NED? If you would care to, I'll send it on; but I must hold to my agreement that the play shall have its world premiere in Dublin next May. However, I'd like to have your opinion as to whether it is possible that it might interest Americans. My personal opinion is that it wouldn't, but, again, I never can tell.

Shivaun is buzzing about all over the USA. She is very busy, working hard—I hope, not too hard, and can hardly find time to write to us; but Eileen, Breon, and the Dad, send her weekly letters. Eileen and Breon send their love to you, and so do I; and to all the Cast in the Play and in the Readings.

As ever,
Sean

By the way, Gordon Craig did get an honor.[1] I wrote the Prime Minister Harold Macmillan about it—a tempestuous letter; & he has replied that G.C. received the honor of "C.H." = Companion of Honor—whatever that may be, but I understand that it is considered—by the English People—as a high one. So there you are. Maybe G.C. forgot all about it; or, maybe, they never told him.

---

[1] See O'Casey's letter to Harold Macmillan, 11 September 1957.

To Michael Barry[1]

TC. O'CASEY

12 NOVEMBER 1957

Dear Mr. Barry,

Thank you for your letter of kind insistence.

Any letter of this kind could never be an intrusion, though your sincere arguments dont convince me. It is a long ideology as far as I'm concerned, beginning before Television came into existence. Thirty years ago, I

[1] Michael Barry, BBC Television Center, Wood Lane, London 12.

carried on a controversy with a Film Critic, Sydney Carroll,[2] who wrote, I think for THE OBSERVER; a long controversy in which I tried to point out that in Film Art (applying equally to Television) the actor was, not this one or that one, but the Camera. With all its devotion to words, both remain, to me, a visual art. But to me, it seems, those in control of both activities are concerned, not with art, but with popularity; not a bad thing in itself—for every artist likes to be popular; but to gain this great pleasure too much is sacrificed. I never wrote for Television—I wouldnt know how; but I have been in touch with the Theater since I was 11 or 12 years of age. Again, a lot of the Irish actors are pretty bad, and have a lot to learn; not only those in London, but the ones in Eirinn, and even in the Abbey Theater.

As for a visit to me, it "would serve no useful purpose"—how often have we heard that one! If in the coming summer—which may come with the help of God, and you happen to come to Torquay, and I be alive, then we might arrange a visit only as a visit of friend to friend, and not as an inquisitorial experiment. You are a persuasive man, but you could never assure me other than that the Television is one medium and the Theater quite another.

All good wishes,
Yours very sincerely,
Sean O'Casey.

[2] See O'Casey's letters to *Time and Tide,* "Stage and Screen," 17 February and 3 March 1934, Vol. I.

To Brooks Atkinson

TS. ATKINSON

24 NOVEMBER 1957

My very dear Brooks,
It is some time since I received your letter so it's about time I gave you word I got it with its enclosure—letter from Joseph Friedman, which I return, for you should keep some of these tributes to yourself which are so well deserved—and to tell you I'm still here, doing a little and thinking a lot.

A day or so ago, a letter from George Jean tells me he is slowly improving and mentions how you call to see him every week, an event which, from what he says, gives him great delight. I should have written sooner, but I get periodical bouts of inflammation in the corner of my good eye which has to be treated and, for a time, I have to be content to go slow. I sent your article to my Russian friend. He hasn't mentioned it, but I know he has read it, and that is what matters. As you say, all Art is religious, and is part of man's transfiguration; not religious in any dogmatic or institutional way; but art has its great canons and, as Shaw said, an apostolic succession going far and away beyond the church's consecrations. And what a glorious crowd of apostles, saints, prophets, and martyrs it has as witnesses! And Drama has her fair share of them, with apostolic critics interpreting them, lighting the lamps (as Nathan said) in the Temple of art so that all men may see to worship. A young lass, a teacher in a college in Saratoga Springs, has written asking me "what is religious drama," and I shall reply that all drama is religious.

Communists, dear Brooks, arent as difficult as many believe. Communism isn't just brought out to be exposed at some conference, the way the Blessed Sacrament is exposed for worship: the Roman Catholic churches; it is a force working everywhere towards the brotherhood of man, a force helped on by many who would be horrified at the very thought of Communism. It isn't always the center of gunpeal and slogan cry: there is the still, small voice as well as the earthquake and the great wind. Odd and wonderful influences in devious ways, some of them apparently forgotten, work towards a change in the thought of the mind, in the feeling of the human heart. In 1890 an English publisher issued THE WORKS OF EMERSON. I was then a garsoon of 10, going about Dublin with broken boots, patched trousers, and an empty belly. When I started to earn my eighteen shillings a week, or so, I scrooged from necessity an odd sixpense, saving them up till I had a shilling or two; then went on a hunt for second-hand books. The best books were on the cheaper shelves, none of them above a shilling. Strange, how the great minds offer themselves to the poor for next to nothing. One day, I went home with THE WORKS OF EMERSON under my protecting arm. What I read there helped to open my mind to Communism, though I was even then an ardent Labor man and staunch member of my Union; but Emerson put a new world before me. He may have been something of a mystic—whatever that may be—but what a wonderful lot of commonsense and wisdom is sown among his mysticism! I have that book I bought still, now over fifty years, lying handy on a shelf over the fireplace in my room; and he is more of today than many of the writers writing at present. A spiritual clock on the wall of Time, the pendulum still swinging widely, the hands pointing to wisdom and truth, the chimes still telling the hours of the day.

You write in the way of Brooks Atkinson—I would know the writing of Brooks Atkinson anywhere as I would know the writing of George Jean—but at times, I think I can get an echo of Emerson's style in yours; and, indeed, I shouldn't be surprised that there was in my Irish wildfire of words a faint echo of Emerson, too. As for Cocteau's "Art is a priesthood," isn't all life a priesthood, too, for bread that preserves all is blessed; there is the bread of physical life, and there is the bread of spiritual life; and both are holy. God Almighty, am I becoming a preacher, Brooks!

We all thank Oriana and you for your kindness to Shivaun. She seems to be absorbing the USA. Last we heard from her, she was in Chicago. Cargoes of picture-cards, programs, catalogs of museums, etc, are arriving from her—"to be kept safe till she comes back." Certainly she will have gotten a glimpse of your country anyway. PURPLE DUST will have soon reached its year's anniversary; a remarkable performance, thanks to Paul Shyre and his co-workers. It has given us all a lift.

I'm glad that George Jean seems to be allright financially. We had a good many years of that kind of worry, and we know well how wearing it can be; but the USA did a tremendous lot to give us our daily bread. I indeed agree with you about the Playhouse being unsuitable for the Readings. I told that to Paul, but he was more hopeful, and they seem to have gone fairly well; very well for me.

We all send our deep love to dear Oriana and to you.

As ever and a day.
Sean

Enclosure

To Miss Rosamond Jacob[1]

MS. JACOB

26 NOVEMBER 1957

Dear Miss Jacob,

If another World War falls on top of us, lady, take my word for it, Ireland won't escape—neutral or partial. Of course, I'm with you against foreign troops in Ireland, or foreign troops in any land; & I'm against native troops as well. We know enough now to know that we must learn to do without them. They're a damned expense & a damned nuisance wherever they may be. The day of the armed man should be over now. A gun is no longer as good as a guinness. In time of devastation, it's always the women who get the worst of it. They, at least, should say To hell with war; women'll have no more to do with it.

Yours very sincerely,
Sean O'Casey

---

[1] Miss Rosamond Jacob, an Irish woman in Dublin.

To Harry M. Ritchie[1]

TC. O'CASEY

[26 NOVEMBER 1957]

Questions   Questions   Questions

Well, my friend, my young friend Harry Ritchie, here are your questions and here are the answers as well as I can give them:

Where can you obtain copies of FROST IN THE FLOWER, THE HARVEST FESTIVAL, and THE CRIMSON IN THE TRI-COLOR? Answer: Nowhere, far as I know. Whether the manuscripts (written down in longhand) ever came back to me from the Abbey, I cant remember. The third play—C. IN THE TRI-COLOR—was kept by the Abbey for some years; it was lost for more than a year, then found again; and then put into typescript. I had an idea all along that some MS of the play— typescript or longhand, I dont know—was held by Mr. Lennox Robinson, for many years Manager and Director of the Abbey. He once wrote about some matter to me, and incidentally mentioned he had the MS of the play, and would send it on. I replied saying I'd be glad to have it back; but I heard no more about it. However, when Mrs. O'Casey went to Dublin to see the first production there of THE BISHOP'S BONFIRE in 1956 (I think), Mr. Robinson told her he had it, and that he would send it to me. Later on, in 1957, Trinity College, Dublin, held an Exhibition of Theater activities, and the Secretary asked me for the MS of one of my plays. I dont write plays straight out, and the first draft may be found here, there, everywhere in exercise books, note books, slips of paper, backs of letters received—on anything close at hand when a thought strikes me, or a gleam of dialogue flashes into me head. I wrote the Secretary to say that if he got the MS of C. in the T. from Mr. Robinson, he could exhibit it, provided that when the exhibition was over, he returned it to me. He said he'd be glad to do so; but wrote again saying that Mr. R. had lost the MS; that he had searched for it, but couldnt find it, and when he had, he would send it to O'Casey. I havent got it so far; and I dont think I ever shall.

Never had any personal contact with Toller, George Kaiser, Piscator, or any other plunger into Expressionism, German or otherwise. Dont know what it means; nor do I yet know what "Realism" is either. Heard the name of Piscator, but dont know what he does or did. Saw Toller's Masse-

---

[1] Harry M. Ritchie, graduate student at Yale School of Drama. In 1960 he earned a Doctor of Fine Arts degree from Yale and wrote his dissertation on "Form and Content in the Plays of Sean O'Casey."

Men done by the Dublin Drama League years ago (25 or so), read his HOOPLA, and saw his DRAW THE FIRES in London, long after W. THE GATES and SILVER TASSIE had been written. Dont think a lot of either. Toller was a poet, but seemed to me to pursue life in a dream; and was too sure that the right shape and only shape for the world was the shape that he formed in his own head. Read K's GAS and [Elmer Rice's] ADDING MACHINE, and liked both; but none of these dramatists influenced me in any way. Too much skeletonised; not enough of the plumpness of life, and little humor. The Elizabethans, on the other hand, were dizzy with life, prancing humor, and when the need is there, a sad journey through a via dolorosa. Gordon Craig would be more in my line than any you mention; and what about Dion Boucicault? Not that I'm trying to judge any theatrical ism; I simply dont understand them, and none has ever consciously moved me towards any hilarious acceptance. One of my favorite plays is Strindberg's DREAM PLAY. What form is it in? Divil a know I know. All I know, all I want to know is that it is a most moving, most beautiful play. As for S. and the Elizabethans, I was brought into their glorious company (and other great poets) by the stabs of circumstances. When I became inflamed with the lust of literature, I was damned poor, and so had little to spare for books after buying bread—you see, bread comes first, whatever the intellectuals may say. The great minds were readily present for those who wished to get to know them; second-hand copies were spread over the barrows, no book higher in price than a shilling ($0.20 to you). I bought all the WORKS OF SHAKESPEARE, plays, poems for One shilling, second-hand. The new book could be gotten from Macmillans for half a crown, a small fortune to me, so I waited till I could pounce on it on sale for a shilling. In the same way, I came on Shelley, Byron, Keats, Burns, Dickens, Thackeray, Milton, Whitman, and Emerson, and others; so you see how I came to be a friend of Shakespeare, and a pal of many other fine boys, and two girls—Jane Austen and Charlotte Bronte. But I dont try to imitate any of them; I sit down with them, talk to them, drink with them, have even whored with some of them, S, for instance; just for the holy and happy joy of it all. During that time, too, I bought literally hundreds of Dick's STANDARD PLAYS, mostly melodramas; but with a few fine ones—Goldsmith and Sheridan, Wycherly, Congreve—all for a Penny each (a cent to you). That was how, I daresay that my nature became infused with the Theater; naturally and unconsciously, but with great joy. Strindberg and Ibsen came later, for they werent to be gotten on the barrows, in Dublin, anyway; and then I had never heard of the EVERYMAN LIBRARY who printed these and the classics in new vols for a shilling.

These are the answers for you to make what you can of them.

S. O'Casey.

To Miss Joan McAlevey

MS. McALEVEY

28 NOVEMBER 1957

Dear Joan,

I am very glad that you have recovered from the Influenza, that is a plague in so many places. As for your longing to live in England, that may well be the depression the illness you had usually leaves behind it—a sense of being God-forsaken and man-forsaken too. So don't worry because you can't fly from where you are: it doesn't matter much where we may happen to be so long as we try to be true to ourselves: we are never far from all things that life brings; & they come just as surely in Saratoga Springs as they would in Oxford.

All Drama is religious; all Art is too: not only the plays that think they deal with special religious hope & beliefs; but the laughter of the clown as well as the prayer of the sorrowful or the saint. Falstaff is as religious a character as Hamlet, & more so than Wolsey. Religion is everywhere: Gothic Cathedral, Mahomedan Mosque, Savage's Totem Pole. All things on the stage giving thought, sorrow, pity, hope, sadness, & laughter are religious, and the Theater (as Shaw says) is a Temple, its priests having an Apostolic Succession far greater and stretching far further back than the oldest Christian Church. Yes, my latest play "The Drums of Father Ned" is to be given first performance next May during the Irish Tostal. It is a play of laughter, hope, & resolution for the future. It will, I hope, be published after production, and, Joan, don't be too afraid of a "gap" in your life—if one should come many of us have to bear these things. I have had many, and a bitter one not very long ago. So be brave, my lass. Your future is before you, but there may be difficulties to overcome. So overcome them, and all will be well. "Well, done, good & faithful servant"—At the moment, I'm writing down reflections on various things. Shivaun is roaming over the USA last time we heard, she was in Chicago. God be with her; and with you, my lass, too. As for the Sputniks—H. G. Wells said long ago that one day man would step from star to star, & we now step from stone to stone over a shallow river.

All affectionate wishes to you.

As ever.
Sean

To David Krause

MS. KRAUSE

1 DECEMBER 1957

My dear Dave,

It's some time since I wrote to you or you to me, and, while wondering how you are, I hope you are well and very busy with life in your flat and in the University. We go along doggedly, though changes have come as changes do, however we may try to keep things in a groove of complacency. Breon has a studio in Torquay, and spends a lot of his time there; Shivaun is rushing around the USA; the last time we heard, she was in Chicago facing the winds, and, during Christmas, she expects to be down south in Texas—think of that! Eileen does all the business end of our activities, and so I spend a lot of time on my own, still thinking out what life is, and delving into her complexities. So you see, the household has changed. This Christmas will be wholly different from all that have preceded it since Eileen and I began life together. We won't spend it here; we're going to pass the evening with two Jewish friends, Dubliners, who have settled in Torquay as doctors, and whom we know since we came to Marychurch. Odd, isn't it—two Gentiles spending Christmas with two Jews! They spent Christmas before last with us, so it is something of a quid pro quo. Eileen finds it impossible to be here during the festival because of Niall's death within the festival last year, and I am obliged to agree, though I shouldn't mind staying here on my own, and passing the day gaily on a couple of boiled eggs and a cup of tea, as I so often did in Dublin when on my own, regardless of all the gaiety and singing wailing out from the other rooms in the crowded tenement.

We are hoping that fewer cards will come this year to us—Eileen is, at any rate, and that the day will go by with the minimum of recognition; though it were really best to take things as they may happen to come, for life is safely oblivious to personal feelings, and is concerned only with the mass; as she has to be if the race is to go on living.

I think I told you that my last play—THE DRUMS OF FATHER NED is to be performed (first time) in the Gaiety Theater, Dublin, during the Irish Tostal. When they heard I was writing one, the Chairman wrote appealing for it, and I finally allowed it to go there. So, in spite of the odd boycott of the Abbey of later plays, O'Casey appears once again in the old town, and hangs his banner on the inner walls.

I am finding it harder to work these days with a corner of my one eye full of painful inflammation that harries me when I peer into anything. It comes periodically now, and is a nuisance, but one has to put up with it, and wait till it goes to hell, doing what one can while it stays.

I do hope you are enjoying yourself in the Flat, and that you get more chance of self-communion than you could get in the center of the Campus.

Some time ago, had an American [Herbert Coston] & his wife—friend of Dave [Greene's]—who are interested in me. He has poked about Dublin, & has even collected a letter written by me nearly 50 years ago. Had a letter from the Secretary of Assoc. for giving holidays to children in Irish-speaking districts. He tells me he is married to the daughter of a woman who, as a young lass, was taught Irish by me more than 50 years ago. How close we are to each other, often without knowing it.

My love to you Dave, me lad, & to all your students.

As ever,
Sean

To Mrs. Arthur W. Bromage[1]

MS. BROMAGE

3 DECEMBER 1957

This is O'Casey writing:

Dear Mrs. Bromage,

Lack of a photograph and inflammation in my good eye prevented me from writing sooner. I get all my pictures from Mr. [W.] Suschitsky—who was Camera Man the time N.B.C. took Television shots of me; and I now don't like anyone else to handle the Camera when I face it. My friend has been away since. He goes on long long trails, Malaya, Burma, Siam, & God knows where, with his Camera; & we are waiting for him to return to get some copies he took of me when he was here.

We have written to his London address several times, but he isn't yet anywhere near Greenwich Time; & so we wait on. When he comes back, I'll renew the stock, & shall be glad to send you one, if not for use now, then for some future time.

There was no timidity in writing to me, God knows. The one regret I have is that neither time nor condition of my eyes allow me to reply to as many letters from friends as I'd like to write.

Imagine now, you knowing about Dev. and writing his life.[2] With all their faults, his Party is the most Democratic we have & the one that may face the too-full power of the Church in Ireland.

My good wishes to your husband and to you; & success to your onerous & important vocation of Teaching.

Yours very sincerely,
Sean O'Casey

[1] Mrs. Arthur W. Bromage, 2300 Vinewood Boulevard, Ann Arbor, Michigan.
[2] Mary Bromage, *De Valera and the March of a Nation* (1956).

To Dr. R. F. Ewer[1]

TS. EWER[2]

5 DECEMBER 1957

Dear Mr. E,

Thank you for your very kind letter flinging me among the magnificoes; but I have decided not to stay there, but to come back to where common men congregate; and climb down from an apical point to a lower and a safer place.

By the way, I am very keen on listening over radio [to] all that's said about life before (and after) man came forth to have a look around. Two piers of stone flank the gateway to the house where we have our flat, and these piers are speckled with the fossils of primal worm and primal mollusk. Coming in or going out, I often have a look at the stony remains of what was life 60 million years ago or so. Life goes back a long way, and so does a fossil tooth; and a scientific imagination can form an amazing picture from a stony tooth. Now, it seems, there's life in matter, and we stand stunned by the energy of an exploding atom; fearful that some mad fool will use it one day so as to blast us into nothing; denying us even the scanty satisfaction of forming into the semi-immortality of the fossil.

Many thanks, again, for your very good words.

Yours very sincerely,
Sean O'Casey

[1] Dr. R. F. Ewer, Zoology Department, Rhodes University, Grahamstown, South Africa. Dr. (Mrs.) Ewer is a geologist, which explains the geological comments in the letter.
[2] From a copy made by Ronald Ayling.

To David H. Greene

TC. O'CASEY

6 DECEMBER 1957

My dear Dave,

I'm very glad to hear that you are getting on with the book on Synge; but I shouldnt go so far as 150,000 words, if you can help it, for I dont think his life was active enough to stand that length of reading, though, of course, this is but a queer guess, and the knowledge is with you. I gather that from what you say about your lunch with Mr. Budlong, that Macmillans are to publish it. Anyway, there seems to be a great demand these days for Biographies, which is all to the good. Shivaun has been in the USA now for ten weeks, visiting many places. Last we heard from her, she was in Chicago. I do hope she may be allright through the tour which is to last till next March. I've changed the name of my play to THE DRUMS OF FATHER NED—a change indeed. The Tostal Committee (at their repeated requests, I gave in to them) has taken it for a "world-premiere" Tostal Week, next May. I have stipulated that there is to be no beforehand ballyhoo and that it is to be taken to its performance in a quiet way, without much pre-blather; for I've no wish to evoke any envy among other playwrights because of any over-advertisement. I told the Committee first that I preferred some younger dramatist should get the honor of a Tostal production, and not an old campaigner like myself, but was assured that there was no play forthcoming from the younger fellows that would deserve such a showing. I cant understand why those who have their roots in Irish soil still cant write a play about Ireland suitable for a Tostal production. There is to be a dramatisation of "Ulysses"[1]—another exile, and one from Beckett[2]—a third exile, which makes it look like that the exiles are more fruitful than those who lag behind in their own townlands. I wonder what does V[ivian]. Mercier think of that? Cyril Cusack knew I was writing a play, but didnt ask anything about it, so I waited for a while, but when he kept silent, I decided he did not want to risk another venture with O'C. (I dont blame him, though, thank God, he made money out of it), and so allowed it to go to the T. Committee.

I'm sure that E[mmet]. L[arkin].'s book on Jim Larkin will be a fine one. [R. M.] Fox's book is a poor one—making Jim look like a lighted match instead of the flaming torch the man was. The other day, I wrote a long letter to an old warrior, Barney Conway, a loyal soldier of Jim's, with whom I went through all the turmoil of the 1913 Lock-Out, and the aftermath of the fight. A big fellow from the Dublin docks, six feet four and as broad in proportion, with a chest like an elephant's, a man of enormous strength in his young days. We two are about what is left of what Barney calls "the Old Guard." Fox didnt seem to bother about the mass of material that must be somewhere in Dublin Castle containing the account of the Inquiry into 1913, in which Tim Healy acted for the massed employers, and Jim defended himself and acted for the massed men, succeeding in covering himself with glory in his eloquent stand against all the limbs of the law. I cant remember if Fox even mentions it. I have one of the huge curved-shank pipes that Jim smoked holding a pound of tobacco.

I was sorry to read about the failure of Pat Kavanagh[3] to take ad-

[1] Alan McClelland's *Bloomsday,* a dramatization of Joyce's *Ulysses.*
[2] Two mime plays by Samuel Beckett.
[3] Patrick Kavanagh, the Irish poet.

vantage of getting a purse of American dollars, though maybe he despises them, though God knows why. I imagine his boobishness is an effort to conceal from himself (and others) that he isnt sure of himself; that he hasnt yet assimilated the good feeling and peace that flow from good manners. God knows, I can be violent myself, and fling thunderbolts, but only on matters of principle, trying my best to be what one should be when acting as guest or as host. I dont altogether accept what is said by so many, but when a man like Frank McManus confirms it, there can be no denying of it. Pat has lost a grand opportunity that shall never come again; and, worst of all, there was no earthly or heavenly reason for it. He doesnt seem to have done any work for a long time in the way of writing, bar his article in the I. TIMES, and a violent condemnatory letter about me in the same paper. However, I hear he has secured a job as Lecturer in University College, Dublin, and that should help him to find his feet, and soften his social outlook a lot. As usual, he who wrote to tell me this added "But how he got this job is another question." All envy and much gnashing of teeth in Ireland; and the young still flying out of the country, "as if," said Cardinal D'Alton, "it were a colony of lepers." A terrible saying, though I was denounced for saying a much milder thing in THE BISHOP'S BONFIRE. One unfortunate thing for P. Kav. is that he hasnt a job like some other Irish poets—one of them a District Justice [Donagh MacDonagh], another a Customs Officer [Padraic Fallon], another First Sec. to the Irish Embassy in London [Valentin Iremonger]. Now, if the Lectureship be any good, he may grow more mellow, mixing with the students and Professors of the College—I hope so.

I let Coston and his wife come here, though I was far from well. They stopped about three or four days, in one of which I couldnt see them, for I had a bad day of sickness, with bad vomiting. However, it passed off, and I gave them as much information as I could before they left for Vienna.

Glad you had such a long social vigil with Dave II [Krause]. I hope he isnt trying to do too much. I've just written a few lines to him. I am bothered at the moment with inflammation in my one good eye, which persists in spite of treatment, but I'm beginning to get used to it. We will be spending Xmas with friends this year. Eileen finds it too hard to stay here. I shouldnt mind, but she wont go unless I go too, so I have to agree, for I can understand the way she feels about the flat reminding her of the Xmas that brought the death of Niall upon us. Delighted that your dear family is keeping well. Give my love to Catherine.

[Sean]

To Peter Newmark

MS. NEWMARK

7 DECEMBER 1957

My dear Peter,

It was fine to hear from you and to hear that Monica & you and another (a babe) are going along well. I am fairly well, though I've gone through a hell of a lot during the past year and a half; and some of the trials have left me a little less buoyant; for at 78 one doesn't rise so quickly against a sea of troubles.

However, I've written another play—"The Drums of Father Ned"—which is to get its "World Premiere" during the Irish Tostal next May. I have heard Dublin is already becoming agitated about it. The Tostal Committee appealed to me to give it, and saying "I would ne'er consent, consented." I've read Worsley's exclamation, & those remarks that appeared in "Encore," but I am too occupied to bother my head about them. I have more thought for New York than for London. Readings from "K. at the Door" & "Pictures in the Hallway" got a fine show there, arranged by a clever young Jew, Paul Shyre, who has charge now of a lot of my work. I am putting down a few thoughts for a possible book of Comments on Theatre & Life in General, but, it is but a beginning & may never have an end.

Of course, Osborne is a far greater playwright than Rattigan, clever an' all as he is. His play "L. Back in Anger" has scored a hit on Broadway.[1] By the way, what do you think of Samuel Beckett? I can't think much of either Betti or Ionesco; but I love Giraudoux.

Well, Peter, a vic, with Monica's leave, I send a blessing to the bouncing toddler; & my love to Monica herself & to you.

As ever.
Sean

Eileen sends her love, too.

[1] John Osborne's *Look Back in Anger* opened in New York on 1 October 1957, and ran for 407 performances.

To Voja Čolanović[1]

TS. ČOLANOVIĆ

15 DECEMBER 1957

Dear Friend,

I enclose the best answers my poor mind can think of to the questions submitted to me. If they are not to your liking, just throw them out of the nearest window, or put them into the nearest fire.

Permit me to take this chance of sending my warm wishes for peace and prosperity to your People, to your Leader, to your Government, and to all they try to do together for the security and advancement of your Republic.

Yours very sincerely,
Sean O'Casey.

There Must be No More War[2]

Question 1[3]—Answer: As always, Art, Literature, and Science is against war; war of any kind that inflicts pain and horror upon the people of a nation, or the peoples of the world. At all times, the poets, the writers of literature, and, as far as I know, the Scientists, have had no love or veneration for war; the work they did and the work they do, has always, directly or indirectly, brought the peoples closer together within the space of friendship and the bond of peace—see Shakespeare's "Enter a father who has killed his son; enter a son who has killed his father"; and the talk between the common soldiers and the English King Henry the Fifth before the Battle of Agincourt. Now, of course, under the flaming threat of the nuclear weapon, there is but one way for all—the way of peace and the living together of all peoples in friendship and understanding; for if they dont, all shall sink together into the blasting arms of a flaming death. There should be more meetings of scientist, of writer, and of artist with their comrades of different nations to talk of ways that will bring our feet more surely into the way of peace.

Question 2[4]—Answer: In certain countries, persons born into privilege and wealth, are made into statesmen, and are often fools. These can hardly lis-

---

[1] Voja Čolanović, Cultural Editor, *Jugopress,* Belgrade, Yugoslavia, had asked O'Casey to answer three questions for a New Year Poll submitted to a number of distinguished artists and scientists.

[2] These answers appeared in *Jugopress Information Bulletin,* 7 January 1958.

[3] "At a time when the world is faced by the alternative of peaceful and creative cooperation of communities with different social systems, or a final nuclear catastrophe, what is the role art, literature and science can play in the rapprochement of peoples?"

[4] "Before deciding for given steps of far reaching significance the statesmen seldom lend an ear to the opinions of their humanistically inclined compatriots from the ranks of artists and scientists. What should be done with a view to rendering these consultations more effective, thus enabling them to exert a stronger influence on the course of international events?"

ten to any counsel other than their own. It would be waste of time for any artist to try to advise them. They are joined to the idols of their own conceits. In most wars, they expanded the means of making profits. That happy hope is gone now. Then they remained safe at home, while the many died for them. In any war of the future, the statesman will perish along with the common man; and they want to die in their beds. We should work to get the voices of scientist, artist, and writer, not to the statesmen, but to the people. Hitler would never have done as he did, could he have foreseen his own end. Any budding Hitler among the statesmen of the world knows now what his end will be, if he starts a nuclear war, and he will fight shy of beginning. The artists, writers, and scientists have spoken out in a multitude of places, and the peoples have heard them. I remember many years ago when twelve writers first made a call for peace; now these twelve have multiplied into six hundred writers signing their name to the people's call for peace. If statesmen haven't listened to poets and prophets, the people have; for often the still, small voice is heard rather than the earthquake or the big wind. Shelley and Blake in their day, Bernard Shaw in his, for instance, have had a wide influence on thought and action; and who can estimate the force given to the impulse for peace by Picasso's dove fluttering over the world. Because of writers, scientists, and artists, the shouts against the nuclear bomb have deepened into a great roar, and the statesmen have had to listen, for it has shaken them out of their complacency, and the banning of this horror is nearer than it was but a year ago.

Question 3[5]—Answer: When the world is free from the fear of mutual annihilation, science and art will not only offer, but will bring to the peoples of the world more abundant life in body, soul and spirit. Then shall we all know the fruits of peace, when all shall be working for the good of all. To quote Tennyson, the poet:

Oh, my comrades, oh, the workers, ever forging something new,
All that they have done but earnest of the things that they shall do.

Sean O'Casey

[5] "What could art and especially science in view of its latest epoch making discoveries offer to mankind finally freed from fear of mutual annihilation?"

To Brendan Smith

TS. SMITH

16 DECEMBER 1957

Dear Brendan Smith,
        Thanks for your letter of the 9th of this month.
        About Jim Fitzgerald: I'm neither convinced nor happy, for I know

nothing about the lad.[1] I'll have to wait to see how he does it. However, I have confidence in your judgement, for you have had a lot of varying experiences, and should know your left hand from your right by now. So, in that respect, I'm satisfied, with the proviso that I have permission to pray that Jim will do himself and the play proud.

About the choice of actors—all I know is that S. Kavanagh, C. Cusack, Eddie Byrne, and Maureen Cusack, are good. Maureen, for instance, I imagine, would make a good Bernadette; but Jim Fitzgerald already knows all this, and I leave it to him to make the best choice possible.

Regarding transfers to Liverpool, Belfast, and the London Court Theater: Take notice that in a previous letter, I laid it down that your licence for production of the play would end with the ending of the production in the Gaiety Theater, Dublin; so no transfer can be arranged without my written permission. I should like the play to be done in Belfast, of course. When Cyril wanted the Court Theater for the BISHOP'S BON-FIRE, he couldnt get it; and I'm in no way eager to let this play go there. I assume that Liverpool is the Theater under Sam Wanamaker—a very dear friend of mine—but I doubt that the play would suit Liverpool, and I dont want to hurt the great effort Sam is making there to bring the Drama to that part of England. (I assume that Jim F. has read the play, and that he is willing to take on the production. If he didnt like it, or is in any way reluctant, of course, I shouldnt like to press him into the work.)

Finally, regarding Advance Royalty: A sum of £20 to be paid as advance royalty; which isnt to be taken as any precedent. I am just willing to help the Tostal all I can; and wouldnt give the same terms to London or New York.

Now, to end the homily, all good wishes to all the work you are doing to try to jerk or coax Ireland out of her apathy, and produce more of the Smiles na gCopaleení.[2]

> *Go mbuanaidh Dia an Tostal.*[3]
> *Sean O'Casey*

---

[1] In a 9th December letter, Smith stated that "Jim Fitzgerald is the best man for the job . . . and he has done brilliant work here in recent years."

[2] A pun on Myles na gCopaleen (Brian O'Nolan-Flann O'Brien) who had frowned at the Abbey Theatre's revival of *The Silver Tassie* in 1951 and wrote a bitter attack against O'Casey. See O'Casey's letter to Brooks Atkinson, 25 October 1951, note 1, Vol. II.

[3] God Preserve the Tostal.

To George Jean Nathan

MS. CORNELL

17 DECEMBER 1957

My very dear George,

Perhaps, you were foolish to take on criticism in "Theatre Arts"; but, as you say, it is idle to try to keep still. And one has a gift, one has to keep going. It is a plague; but, on the whole, a pleasant plague.

Tom Curtiss spent a week-end with us recently, & we all had a most pleasant time with him. We are all very fond of Tom. He told us he was returning to New York to join in the celebration of your birthday. These birthdays! When one passes 50 they become a nuisance. If each year they knocked a year off, instead of adding a year on, how beautiful they would be; how beautiful!

I do hope you are keeping fairly fit. I, too, go up & go down; feel fine one week, feel anything but fine another. Still, I find the world good enough to linger long in.

I enclose a cutting telling of more prizes for poor drama. "None of the plays was particularly adventurous"! If they had been, they'd have frightened the life out of the Arts Council. John Gassner tells me the season has been a poor one. So here, too. Here, I fear, the Theatre is entirely in the hands of Cissies. Indeed, they seem to be prolific in all the arts here now. It is a pitiable state of affairs; but it cant last forever. Coward has a new play on[1]—one of the old old manner. Hobson heads his review with the announcement, "The Eternal Rebel"![2] A new honour for him. Take care of yourself.

As ever,
With love,
Sean

[1] Noel Coward's *Nude With Violin* opened in London on 7 November 1957.
[2] Harold Hobson, "The Eternal Rebel," *Sunday Times,* 11 November 1957.

To Vincent C. De Baun[1]

MS. DE BAUN

27 DECEMBER 1957

Dear friend,

No one can be, or should be, a stranger to another. We live in the same world, we feel as others feel, come into life the same way, and leave it, by different doors, maybe; but in the very same manner, & each, at his going, give the same last sigh of farewell. We are all seeking to understand more about life, feeling our way to a greater idea and manner of safe and busier living. You did well to gather as much life as you could into your arms, and I hope—you are very young still—you are still doing it. Even now, when I am within a few years of my 78th year, I feel life to have been too short, too hasty in its going by, and would, if I could, go back many years, or, if I could, add many years to those I have already lived—if it be that I remained alert in mind and mobile in my body. This present Century, maybe, isn't quite so crazy as we think. Many new minds have begun to take a part in the world's thinking; and more and more multitudes of people are calling for Peace; &, far as Peace is concerned, Vox Populi vox Dei, & the still small voice is becoming a roar for brotherhood.

My warm wishes to you.
Yours very sincerely,
Sean O'Casey

[1] Dr. Vincent C. De Baun, Wells College, Aurora, N.Y.

IV

THE ARCHBISHOP AND
DRAMA AND THE
HOLY GHOST

1958

IT is rather comic to think of a frightened Archbishop frightening the Tostal Council into closing the gate of Dublin on
Dubliners. Shut the gates! Quick; we have not a moment to
spare. The Archbishop doesn't know (or doesn't care) that a
work by Beckett, by Joyce, or even by O'Casey, performed in
Dublin, is of more importance to Dublin than it is to any of
those authors: that outside Dublin is a wide, wide world, and
that this wide place is Joyce's oyster, Beckett's oyster, and even
O'Casey's oyster; or that these voices, hushed in Dublin, will be
heard in many another place."

"What in the name o' God is 'religious' Drama? 'Samson Agonistes'? 'Murder in th' Cathedral'? Does it include 'Pagan Drama'
—the Greeks, for instance? Is Shakespeare, with his bawdiness

outside o' God's Portals? Or is it just solemn drama? Moses
on Mt. Sinai is drama, so is the terrible story of Tamor & Ammoses. Are these 'religious' Drama? My dear, to me all Drama
is Religious: it is the speaking of the Holy Ghost, & it isn't all
tears & all prayer."

Although O'Casey seemed to have a genius for controversy as well
as drama, much of his public fighting in this year was instigated by his
vindictive countrymen. Early in January, however, he had started one
argument in the *Irish Times* with a letter that chastised the Christians for
their virulent hatred of Communism; and it was evident that his ammuni-
tion came from his carefully kept record of attacks on Russia and Communism, as well as on himself, that appeared over the years in the Irish
newspapers. He obviously enjoyed this kind of verbal combat as he aimed
his ironic shafts at the unchristian Christians: "What, after 2,000 years of
Christianity, haven't you Christians learned to live in charity with your
neighbours? Is your house still in disorder? Do ye still fan the flames of
hatred?" As if to prove the validity of this accusation, within a week an
overt sign of hatred and disorder emerged when the supreme Christian in
Dublin, the Archbishop, started a new fire. He announced that he would
refuse to say the traditional Votive Mass for the opening of the Tostal
Festival if the names of O'Casey and Joyce were associated with the occasion.

Clerical pressure has always functioned as a form of unofficial censorship in theocratic Ireland, where there is no official censorship of the
theatre. Without having read *The Drums of Father Ned* or the dramatization of *Ulysses,* the Archbishop with his ecclesiastical ban had apparently
struck fear into the hearts of the people planning to produce these plays.
At the end of January the directors of the company appointed to produce
O'Casey's play fanned the flames by writing an arrogant and insulting letter—sent carelessly to the old Totnes address where he had not lived for
four years—telling O'Casey they were "not at all happy" with his play's
"structural state," and asking him to give their director "the necessary authority to make such alterations as he requires." Understandably, O'Casey
was not about to allow anyone in Dublin to rewrite his play; and the mystery of its so-called unsatisfactory "structural state" was never revealed to
him or anyone else. Confronted by such insolent and vague conditions, he
felt he had no choice but to withdraw his play. It is quite likely that the
mere presence of the names O'Casey and Joyce on the program appeared
as red flags of immorality to the Archbishop. It is also probable that the
frightened theatre people, except for Brendan Smith, the sympathetic Director of the Drama Festival, had their eyes on the Archbishop rather than

on the play. After O'Casey withdrew his play, the Joyce dramatization was dropped, and Samuel Beckett withdrew his mime plays in protest. Three internationally renowned Irish writers had been banished from Ireland. Small wonder, then, that three years later O'Casey wrote a satiric comedy on fear and censorship called *Behind the Green Curtains*.

Meanwhile he was busy defending himself and his play in letters to the Irish newspapers and to his friends. In February he told the drama editor of the *New York Times* precisely why he felt he had been treated unfairly: "I don't want people to like my style, or even to agree with it, if they cant do either; but when a play of mine is asked for, considered, and accepted, I take it for granted that the style and manner is accepted, if not liked, or even understood." He had also been treated unfairly for a year by the Irish Customs Office, which had without explanation prohibited the distribution and sale of his book of essays and stories, *The Green Crow*. In Ireland, it seemed, the O'Casey name on a play or book was sufficient cause for an unofficial religious or political ban. Mysteriously again, without any explanation, the prolonged ban on the book was lifted in March.

O'Casey therefore had good reason to protest once more, in a March letter to his Dublin Catholic friend, Frank MacManus, against the intolerant and uncharitable Irish Christians. They had distorted the spirit of Jesus and the meaning of the Incarnation, he wrote, by creating an unchristian climate of fear: "What angers me, Frank, is how so many seem to limit the scope of what they believe in—the Incarnation. They so often put Jesus behind barbed wire, telling Him you mustnt go there; you mustnt listen to that; you should turn your eyes away from this sight. As if He went about in constant fear of seeing us making fools of ourselves." Two weeks earlier MacManus had written to O'Casey to remind him of the time they first met in Dublin in 1935, when O'Casey had made his last visit to Ireland: "You had once said that if you could believe the bread and wine was Christ you'd go off your head with joy. It's the best sermon I ever had. You old pagan, I hope it's down in gold letters after your name." In 1963 both men were deeply moved when they were shown this comment. "Yes, in gold letters," MacManus said. "Red letters'll do me," O'Casey replied.

In a mid-March letter to a Russian woman who had asked for help with her book on the English Romantic poets, O'Casey uses something like red letters to give his version of a secular incarnation of the Romantic spirit. He begins by stressing the liberating "fire that blazes in Shelley, Keats, Byron, Whitman, Emerson, and even in Coleridge." In his typical eclectic way, however, he goes on to broaden the base of his vision and brings together some very unusual "Romantic" figures: "The inspiration doesn't only come from the poets, however, for many leaders have led us into the way of life—Lenin and Stalin, for instance, in your country, Kier Hardie here, Jim Larkin and Parnell in Ireland, and Eugene V. Debs and Bill Haywood in the U.S.A., not to mention Lincoln and Jefferson. But all these great souls were poets in their own way, in the way of vision." No doubt those people who are able to share some of this sweeping Romantic vision will find it impossible to accept Stalin as either a great soul or a poet.

George Jean Nathan died in April and undoubtedly O'Casey would have included his dear friend's name in the company of the great souls and poets. A month later he wrote to Richard Watts, Jr., to say he realized that the brilliant Nathan had also been a strange and aloof man: "One has to go warily with proud and arrogant souls. Yeats was another such man, too." O'Casey himself could be quite proud and arrogant at times, but with all his rough and bristling ways he could also be a man of lyrical warmth and humor, a loyal companion as well as a humble and insecure self-critic. In June he confesses to a young American teacher who admires his work: "Funny, praise invariably embarrasses me. I've no false modesty, & realise my value; but praise from others makes me shy: why, I don't know." Part of the answer must lie in the constant hardships he had to endure throughout his life, and the feeling of insecurity about his achievement as a dramatist, since so many of his controversial plays had fallen into the gray area of artistic merit shaken by financial failure.

O'Casey's artistic standards were never measured by notions of popular success, and he invariably defended writers who went against the grain of government or establishment approval, in Russia as well as in Ireland. When Boris Pasternak was awarded the Nobel Prize, O'Casey wrote to a Russian editor in November to say he suspected the "Prize was given for political reasons"; but he went on to protest that "it was a sad and pathetic mistake to expel the poet from the Soviet Writers Union. . . . Every artist is something of an anarchist, as Bernard Shaw tells us." In any conventional society, even in his idealized Russia, O'Casey himself would probably be considered something of an anarchic individualist, an artist who instinctively opposed all political and aesthetic orthodoxies.

After brooding about the humiliating treatment he had endured over the unofficial banning of *The Drums of Father Ned,* O'Casey decided in July to act against the political and theatrical orthodoxies in Ireland. He imposed his own official ban on professional performances of all his plays in Ireland, a prohibition that he stubbornly maintained for the next six years. He insisted in a September letter to an American friend that he was not only protesting for himself, but "for the great dead Joyce, and for the integrity and honesty of Samuel Beckett."

In the meantime, preparations were being made for the opening of two O'Casey plays in New York, *Cock-a-Doodle Dandy,* his favorite work, and *The Shadow of a Gunman,* both of which had to close after short runs at the end of the year. Somehow, he tried to believe, it was the productions, not the plays, which had failed. In a late December letter to Brooks Atkinson, he tried to ease his disappointment in the philosophical hope that the characters he created in his comedies would survive: "Somehow, some day, somewhere, the characters will leap & laugh a way into life. Meanwhile, they are safe in limbo."

The following day, after Atkinson's secretary had sent him the mixed reviews of the plays, O'Casey braced himself again for the ordeal of defeat. Still determined to survive, he replied with these brave and poignant comments: "Things haven't got on too well; but the Theater is just like life—one day up on a sunny hill, the next down in a dark, dark valley; & when we find ourselves in the valley, we must do our best to climb on to the sunny hill again. . . . So I'm hard at it climbing out of those dark valleys. Pray for me." The wounded old pagan was climbing and fighting back, but he felt the need of prayer.

To Irish Times

6 JANUARY 1958

CHRISTIANITY AND COMMUNISM

Sir,—Those who fear and hate Communism have, indeed, an odd way of blathering about it and about, and the very sight of a hammer and sickle makes them feel faint. The latest, Sir Cecil Stafford-King-Harman, says in a letter to you—"Partition and the Commonwealth," December 31st—that "the greatest problem with which we are faced to-day is the challenge which Communism has thrown out to Christianity," adding that "Communism is based on terrorism, hate and the substitution of the State for God. Christianity is founded on love, tolerance and freedom for the individual." Yet his own letter seems to show that the terrorism, the hate, the denial of freedom to the individual flourishes, not so much in the Communistic countries, but in the God-loved Christian lands, Ireland by no means lagging behind. He says: "If we are to give an effective answer to Communism, and live in charity with our neighbours—we must cease to fan the flames of hatred, we must begin by setting our own house in order."

What, after 2,000 years of Christianity, haven't you Christians yet learned to live in charity with your neighbours? Is your house still in disorder? Do ye still fan the flames of hatred? Indeed, it is in right disorder in many places, Cyprus, in Algiers, in Arkansas, in Uganda, with the reek of disease and poverty in every Christian country. Discrimination and oppression in the North by the Protestant, in the South by the Catholic. The beam in the Western eye—the beam, the beam! I suggest to Sir Cecil that he should read the little booklet of sermons written by Dr. [Donald O.] Soper, the Pastor of the West London Mission, which takes its title from the first line of a hymn written by W. Faber: "It is Hard to Work for God." Hard to work for God in a Christian country, when one would think it should be as easy as kiss a hand. . . . Let ye who hate Communism put your own house in order, sweeping out hate, intolerance, oppression, censorship, and an apathy in division that has the West unable to think of anything else, worship anything else, except the triad of rent, interest and profits.

Let us look at the other side of it. The Anglican Bishop of Chichester, speaking over television on New Year's Eve, said: "Communism, which we hate" (the Christian busy again with hate), "has a focus, an ideal that the West lacks." The Roman Catholic Bishop, the Most Rev. Vincent Sheen,[1] in an American broadcast, is reported as saying: "Christians have clung to the Cross and abandoned Christ; the Communists have clung to Christ and Abandoned the Cross." (By the way, there is a mural fresco in Dartmouth College, America, by the great Mexican mural painter, Orozco, showing Christ leaving His Cross as a protest against the use of it made by Christians for the exploitation of other men.) Here is an extract from a letter in the Catholic Universe, issue of December 27th, 1957, written by G. L. Canon Smith, The Presbytery, Hay Lane, London, N.W. 9: "Visitors who have returned from Russia describe with amazement the quiet decency they have observed there in the relations between the sexes. Russia denies God's existence, but observes His Commandments. The West ignores the existence of God and openly flouts His Commandments. Which is further from God?"

It is time we said farewell to this stupid hatred of Communism and Communists everywhere, and began to realise that this force is here to stay and to grow and conquer, unless Christianity can evolve a force grander and greater than this ideal, forged in historical realism, now moving the hearts, minds and bodies of so many millions of men and women in every land.

From what the Anglican Bishop of Chichester said, from what Bishop Sheen broadcast, from what Canon Smith's letter mentioned, and from what Dr. Walter McDonald, Professor of Theology in Maynooth College wrote so many years ago, God is on the side of Communism as well as Time.—Yours, etc.,

Sean O'Casey

Devon, January 1st, 1958

[1] He should have written the Most Rev. *Fulton J.* Sheen. See his letter to the Rev. Michael Sweetman, S.J., 8 January, note 2.

To Robert Emmett Ginna

TS. GINNA

6 JANUARY 1958

My dear Bob,

I greet you again with affection, and thank you for your kind letter, and for your generous attention to our Shivaun. She is speeding all over your Country, and paid a visit of two weeks to Mexico. I dont think she'll get much knowledge from the Company, that is, theatrically; but she is bound to benefit from the experience of travelling through the USA—the amazing majesty of its natural features, and the many-colored social life of your people, so different from that depicted on the Hollywood Films. She will meet the great American people as they are, their generous nature, their enthusiasms, their originality in their creations, music, architecture, dancing, and speech—a wonderful Race. She is sending home cargoes of postcards, catalogs, guide-books, art books, shirts for me, things for Eileen, things for Breon, and especially a brilliantly-crimson American worker's peaked cap for me; so I'm adding to my grand collection.

You will be a busy man, busier man, now than ever before, with the commitment of "words of the wise"[1] God help them and us! The idea of repeating the one you did of me is interesting—to me; but what about the American people? Do you think they'd stand (or sit) for a repeat performance? I doubt it very much.

The Irish remarks, well as I can remember, were *"Go Mbeannuigidh do Bhothar romhat—*Guh Mannee duh wohar routh—*May God bless your road before you; Tri Gartha ar gcnuic* Tree gorrha er knick—*Three shouts on a hill,* given at the end of a rally or of a meeting, equal to three cheers. Meetings to decide things in old days were often held on a hill or well-known eminence; and *Is leor do dhuine a dhichill-*Iss lore duh ginna a yeehill—*Enough for a man is his best:* good enough, for what can one do more than his best?

As for your attractive proposal to Televise "Shadow," with a subsequent production on the stage—oh boys! Oh, Bob! I havent a high regard for Televised plays on the whole, though I admit, some were done well on the screen. Mine is an old play, a bit tattered by now. I have refused the BBC permission to do THE PLOUGH in their "World Theater" series; I have refused it to GRANADA, Independent Television for North of England, and "The Shadow"; I have refused Radio Diffusion here, too. I enclose an extract from a letter received from Emmett Dalton Television asking for SHADOW. E. Dalton has been asking it for quite a time, and appealed to Eileen when she was in London. He offered £500; 1000,

---

[1] Ginna was working on the Wisdom Series of interviews with notable figures for NBC-TV, and he had already presented "A Conversation with Sean O'Casey and Robert Emmett Ginna" on 22 January 1956.

2000, and, now, as you see £3000; but I have written a letter of refusal. He also wanted THE PLOUGH for "spectacular" two or three performances in New York on Television, to be performed by the Abbey Co. on the Gaiety stage, televised there, and sent over the ocean My bonny is over the ocean. I have refused this, too. Emmett Dalton is a fine man, he is in partnership with an American Co.—dont know which; but in these things, one has to think of one's play.

By the way, all the above is between ourselves. I shouldnt like to let E.D. think I was telling on him. I'm not, just only letting you know that I have already given these refusals. However, any proposal from the USA is always attractive to me, for, in most cases, when they try to do anything for me, the effort is usually the best they can do; and that is a lot. So I suggest, you ask Miss [Jane] Rubin what she thinks of it. I have a good respect for her judgement regarding activities in America, and she has often given good advice; but dont say anything about E. Dalton's offer— that is confidential. The others arent, for comment appeared in the Press about my refusals to Granada and the BBC, and I was pestered over the phone; but refused all requests for an interview.

Think again, Bob, of this proposal of yours, and try to think against it. Remember, you have helluva lot to do, and shouldnt encumber yourself with other work and responsibility; even injuring your health, maybe, and I have too much affection for you to let you do this, if I can prevent it. So, unless you are sure you wont be doing too much, forget about it. But I am very grateful to you for your generous interest in my work—even in the old tattered Shadow—and thank you from my heart for it. If you still decide, then I shall think again of it, for I am, as I said, always attracted towards an American proposal, for the USA Lads have done a lot for me; and the lassies, too.

How is Kathy? Is she with NBC still? I owe her a letter, but I have had a lot of things to do; and, besides, for some time, I've been bothered with some whoreson inflammation in my one good eye, that prevents me from writing as constantly as I used to do. Eileen and Breon send their love to you. Remember me to t'other Bob, and his wife. I'll be dropping him a line soon to thank him and her for a kind Card. Busy on an article— a chapter for a possible new book in the years ahead, called IMMAN-UEL.[2] My love.

As ever thine,
Sean

[2] See *Under a Colored Cap* (1963), Ch. VII.

To Kay Carney

TS. Carney

7 January 1958

Dear Kay,

I think you are right, and I am on the same road of thought with you about our angry young man speaking out of an Osborne window to the world. I think you have made a very keen and intelligent analysis. No, I dont think Osborne has Original Sin in his mind, rather the fribbles and frabbles of life that can be so damned annoying, but do not measure into the importance that he seems to give them. There can never be pie in the sky, but there may be, and should be, some pie in every household. But I dont think Jimmy P.[1] was after pie above or pie below, but after getting his own desires, his own petty opinions honored by everyone else. He hasnt much wit, and his thought is not for others, but solely for himself. This is demonstrated by his disgusting treatment of the woman he lives with, the other woman, and even of his boy or man friend. He, to me, behaves like a snarling cur; and, if in any way thought of injustice to others, he would surely show it and fair play to those who were near to him, in place, if not in thought and affection. To me, there seems to be a great difference between the thought of your own personal young man and that of Osborne; one seems to be made of righteous indignation, the other merely of snarling futility. By the way, it isnt possible for all of us to reach the heights visioned by W. Stephens.[2] Many of us are limited in vision and in faculty, though I agree there is a height below which no one should go; but the highest are for the few; as it is said in the Bible, one star differeth from another in glory; we cannot all be stars of the first magnitude.

And there is really no intrinsic harm in a game of golf, or in any other game; it is good at times to enjoy ourselves, for there is joy, even now, in the world, and it is right we should take advantage of it; different joys at different times. I can no longer join in a game of hurling or handball, or dance—all of which I did vehemently when I was young; but I can enjoy the look of a sky, the beauty of the flowers and trees, the greatness of Mozart, of Shakespeare, and many others, and I am full of desire to take the chances of enjoyment when they come my way; for Grief will come, do what we may, and each of us will, one time or another, get his or her share of it.

[1] Jimmy Porter, the hero of John Osborne's *Look Back in Anger* (1956).
[2] Wallace Stevens. Miss Carney had quoted a stanza from Stevens' poem, "A Weak Mind in the Mountains," *Parts of a World* (1951):

> Yet there was a man within me
> Could have risen to the clouds
> Could have touched these winds
> Bent and broken them down
> Could have stood up sharply in the sky.

Neither your angry young man nor Stephens seems to be angry with Man; Jimmy is very angry with him, whereas he should be angry with himself. No sensible woman, not even a simple sane one, would stay more than a day with such a companion. You are right Kay: to change things we must do things, for no improvement can work its way out of wailing.

Thanks for your sympathy, dear lass. Our boy's swift death was a deep blow. He was a gallant lad, full of activity against the injustice we speak of; a fine athlete, an alert mind; a glorious sense of humor, promising to become a first-class biologist; yet he died at twenty-one under the glitter of a Christmas Tree.

The only tribute we can give to him now is to do what little we can to help those who are doing all they can to overcome the malady that killed him; and this little I and Eileen are doing, and will go on doing, in an effort to prevent the loss of other intelligent young lives so that they may live for full years, only going when their work is over, and tiredness of age makes them glad of a rest.

My love to your own young angry man and to you.

With warm wishes to you both.
Yours very sincerely,
Sean O'Casey.

To Rev. Michael Sweetman, S.J.[1]

TC. O'CASEY

8 JANUARY 1958

Dear Father Sweetman,

The Lord forgive me! He will, I'm sure, for the reversal was unintentional.[2]

I can, however, base my argument on Bishop Sheen's statement, for the principle is the same—the terrible lack of sincerity, the abandonment of practice, on the part of the Christians, which my first argument presented by what eminent Christians themselves said; they praise Me with their lips, but their hearts are far from Me; or, he that shutteth his bowels against the needs of his brother, how dwelleth the love of God in him? Turn the picture of Bishop Sheen's saying how you may, the contour and content show the same defects. Christians arent following Christ (*Geur-*

---

[1] Rev. Michael Sweetman, S.J., Rathfarnham Castle, Dublin.
[2] See the letter to the *Irish Times,* 6 January, note 1. Father Sweetman had replied to O'Casey's letter.

leanuinint Iosa),[3] but are dragging Him about and using His Majesty for their own materialistic purposes. Formal recognition is a poor way, a dangerous way for Christians, of following, for it isnt even the following afar off of Peter.

It was kind of you to send me the warning, and I thank you for doing so; though the argument is untouched.

Yours respectfully,
Sean O'Casey.

[3] *Geur-leanuint Iosa*, The Persecution of Jesus, including a pun on the name of one of the Irish versions of Thomas à Kempis's *The Imitation of Christ*.

To Tom Sutton[1]

TC. O'CASEY

10 JANUARY 1958

My dear Tom,

It was a surprise to get a letter from you that awakened many old memories of the lang syne. The days when we hurled together and danced together, and thought of no land but Ireland. Well, seas between us braid hae roared sin auld lang syne. I remember well a Ceilidh[2] in St. Margarets, held in the old church, no longer used because there was a new one. We went in Brakes, the old lumbering wagonettes out of which we had to get when the horse met a hill; the many dances I had and the hearty supper we all ate afterwards; and then the long walk home—for the wagonettes couldnt wait till two in the morning—a lovely experience, for it was summer, and we travelled on foot under a full moon, singing as we went the road. Days never to come again; but what harm, for we had them when they were there, used them to the full, so we should be satisfied.

Frank Kelly died about two years ago.[3] He had been ill in bed for a long time before. He wrote me several letters while he was ill, and an article which he asked me to look over, which I did for him. His wife wrote to tell me of his death; Go suaimhnigh sé i síochain.[4] I had a letter from S. Tallon, Secretary of Coisde na paisde,[5] who is married to a daughter of

[1] Tom Sutton, National Ploughing Association, Brougham, The Ward, Co. Dublin.
[2] A song and dance party.
[3] Francis J. Kelly died of TB on 27 January 1955, at the age of 66. See O'Casey's letter to his widow, Mrs. Elizabeth Kelly, 20 July 1955.
[4] May he rest in peace.
[5] The Children's Committee.

Maire Kavanagh; you may remember her. She and her sisters, Esther and Rosanna, lived in a little slum cottage on Drumcondra Road. Maire married Andy Hanratty who was an engine-driver on the old G[reat]. N[orthern]. Railway—many a time, going to a country job, I rode on the foot-plate with him. Joe Scully, a long, gangling, gay lad from Louth, was his fireman, and the three of us often had a merry chat as the train sped on its way, leaving me at Balbriggan, Gormanstown, Drogheda, or Dundalk. How times change! Now even the railway is going.

I am sorry to hear of the death of Frances Snowden, Paddy's wife— a gentle, charming woman. It was she who did the lovely banner for the O'Toole Pipers, the time I was secretary to the Band: crimson poplin with a white lion on either side done in silver thread. How well I remember the night of its unfurling in the C[hristian]. Brothers School, Seville Place. Dr. [Douglas] Hyde it was who broke the banner out to a burst of cheering. God be with those grand old times! May the fine woman rest in peace. If you ever see Paddy again, give him my love. Ask him if he remembers the night of decorating a float or lorry on the canal bank for the G[aelic]. League procession; when I slipped over a cord I didnt see—my sight wasnt of the best—and brought all down, so that we had to do everything again. By God, Paddy was in a temper! But he brought me home that evening, and forgave me over a fine cup of tea.

I remember Leo Rush and the girl he married—a Miss Walsh; Leo Keogh, a girl called McElroy, Cathal Lally, Sean Smith, Frank Hanratty, and Bennett who met with a bad accident climbing over the spiked rails of the Magazine Fort after a lost ball. I recollect others, but cant recall their names. You dont mention Paddy? Lawless and Maire? Lawless. Paddy that often played fiddle for us dancing in the slum-shanty in Seery's Lane. What a place! The dancing is done in very different places now. Well, it was all *we* could afford, and we certainly made the best of it. Sorry to hear of Tom Duke, but glad that Richard is still going. It wasnt either of these, was it, who went to the Agricultural College, Glasnevin, at that time? And Paddy Martin—the dark-eyed, shy lad from Donegal, who, too, worked, if I remember right, on the GNR. All this must be fifty years ago, or near it; and all you lads, like meself, must have the grey head now. You were a sturdy boy in those days.

Is my old friend, Paddy Callam as ardent a Gael as ever? So you are still farming. Devon is an English county which is mainly a farming one, mostly dairy-farming. Very fine cattle, butter, and milk. I know a number of farmers, and, I've often thought, had I a life to live over again, I'd be a farmer if the chance came my way. It's a hard task, a very anxious life, but it is near the earth, and, all in all, a healthy way of living; and there is much to be learned about all kinds of life in the fields and the meadows.

You mention that "I am doing well"; maybe so; I have what is called "a name," but a name is a thing I never cared much about. I have always realised, as I still do, that neither I nor anyone else knows very much; we have all a tremendous lot to learn.

My blessing on you, oul' son, and I embrace all the comrades of the long ago.

Yours very sincerely,
Sean O'Casey.

To George Jean Nathan

MS. CORNELL

11 JANUARY 1958

My very dear George,

Here we are within another year that I hope may bring better things to the both of us. I do hope you are stronger, & that you can get a little closer to things theatrical which miss you so much.

I am looking forward to the coming of the spring, the charming usherette who, I hope, will lead in a pleasant summer. Now, I don't cross any frontier away from a fire, for the days are cold and full of bitter winds; so I look for the days that will give the imprimatur allowing one to sit in the sun once more.

My last play, which is to be done during Tostal Weeks in Dublin, is causing a bit of bother. The Festival was always opened by the celebration of a Mass, but this year there's to be none, because (it is said) the Archbishop of Dublin disapproves of showing plays by Joyce & O'Casey.[1] However, the Chairman of the Tostal Council tells me they are going on with their arranged program; but I fear opposition will grow in the meantime, and there will be acrimony and division once again in Ireland. I hope not, but I'm fearful; for I'm tired now of all these many attacks on any play I venture to write.

The Gate Theater has re-opened, but with a debt on it of £13,000; which will be hard to come by. It isn't likely that Hilton Edwards & [Micheál] McLiammoir will ever again play there; they themselves have

---

[1] On 10 January 1958 the *Irish Times* reported: "For the past week, there has been some doubt whether these two plays [O'Casey's *The Drums of Father Ned,* and Alan McClelland's dramatization of Joyce's *Ulysses,* called *Bloomsday*] would be part of the festival programme. Last week the Council became aware that the Most Rev. Dr. McQuaid, Archbishop of Dublin, did not approve of their inclusion in the programme. As a result of their inclusion, this year's Tostal will not be marked by an official opening Mass."

divided, & both have gone away from Lord Longford who controls the Gate.

No need to ask if you are taking care of yourself, for Julie is there to see to that; but I hope the winter isn't proving too tedious to you—I know it is very tedious and trying to me.

I embrace Julie and you, my very dear George.

As ever,
Sean

To Mrs. John T. Cooper

MS. Cooper

12 January 1958

My dear Georgie,

It is lovely news you sent in your last letter—that of a baby coming to the Coopers; unto them a child is born. One more joy, one more anxiety in the world; one more voice to the voice of man. May the little one come into a deeper place than what we know—I think it will; and grow up to strength in a world of no war, and far less fear.

Take good care of yourself.

It was very kind of you to send the magazine showing Shivaun's picture.[1] She looks very well in it. I don't think you missed much in being unable to see the Co.'s "Arms & The Man." Between you, John, and me, the company is not a very good one; & I didn't wish Shivaun to join it; but she was eager to go, & I have (we rather, Eileen & I) never gotten between the wishes of our children, if it could possibly be avoided. Shivaun is seeing the American People as they are, and not as they are shown in so many Films; and that is, indeed, something to thank God for. She sends home piles of guidebooks, postcards, & other mementos, gathering them as she goes along; & will soon know more about the USA than many Americans themselves, greatly to her glory, and a little to their shame. You seem to be doing something about it now—"American Heritage" is one thing: I've been through it, & like it a lot. What a lovely Madonna & Child is the Mexican-Indian wood statue, done in New Mexico. I've just gotten the book "Life of A. Lincoln in Pictures"—two in fact: one from an NBC friend—he was with us in the making of a film; & the other from Shivaun herself. She is bent on telling us a lot about the Land in which she is a guest; & how vigorous and handsome a bird is the Bald-headed Eagle. Hav-

---

[1] O'Casey's 19-year-old daughter, Shivaun, was touring America as a member of Ronald Ibbs' Dublin Players.

ing looked at the pictures, I have begun to read "American Heritage"; tho' I do really know a good deal about you all. For instance, over my room mantel-shelf are two shelves of books, & one of them is a book of poems & articles I have often read, for the book has been with me now for 40 years—the "Work of Emerson."

Jan. 17: Had to stay my hand: the one chosen to direct my new play in Dublin has been down here discussing problems; the most prominent being that the Roman Catholic Archbishop of Dublin has declared the church will not offer a Votive Mass for the Tostal Festival if the O'Casey & Joyce plays are done. More trouble! He hasn't read the play, doesn't know anything about it; but I daresay, he's a bit angry because of the last one—"The Bishop's Bonfire"—the Committee say they will go on with the Productions; so we wait to see what may happen. It is all very tedious.

My love to John & to you. Mind yourself, Georgie, & my blessing on you & your hope.

As ever,
Sean

To David Krause

TS. KRAUSE

21 JANUARY 1958

My dear Dave,

Never fear about your article:[1] all of us have many a weary wait to get anything in a journal or on to a stage. The writer rarely has much of this world's wealth, but he must have a load of patience on his back, and carry it round wherever he goes unlike Christian's load (in Pilgrim's Progress), the writer can never dare to abandon it.

I am sure you enjoyed a fine time with your mother and father, and that they were delighted to see you, and have a hold on you for the holidays at least. When next you see them or next time you write to them, give them O'Casey's love. I daresay you'll be hard at it again now till Eastertide.

The Irish Tostal runs in May—12th to 26th. It comes, in my opinion, too early, for the weather is usually harsh and cold, bad for the out-door event. Dublin during Tostal holds the Drama Festival; and, already, clouds are gathering. You see the Council wanted to make the drama Festival as

[1] David Krause, "The Playwright's Not For Burning," *Virginia Quarterly Review,* Winter 1958.

attractive as possible, with as many new plays as they could get. They heard I was writing a new one, and appealed to me to let them read it. I held back, not wishing to put in on the younger dramatists, and said so to the Council's Chairman. He appealed again, saying the younger ones were doing nothing, or if they were, no play would come up to what the Festival wished to do. They read it, liked it "immensely," and asked me to let them make it one of the Tostal events. After holding back some time, I finally gave it to them. They are making a play out of Ulysses and S. Beckett is to give them one in Mime; and these three, they said, are to be the highlights of Dublin's Tostal Drama Festival. So far, so bad. At the beginning of the Tostal, the Tostal Flag is run up by the Lord Mayor in O'Connell St. and, at the same time, Dublin's Catholic Archbishop says a Votive Mass on behalf of the activities. So far, so good. A week or so ago, the Council were informed that if the O'Casey play and that of Ulysses weren't abandoned, the Archbishop would not celebrate the Votive Mass. So far, so bad again. At the moment, the Council has decided to go on with their Program, but heaven knows how it will all end. Since then, bar some resolutions passed by Committees of religious Societies and a few town councils, there is silence. No mention in the papers, which may be a good sign or a damned bad one. These attacks on O'Casey are getting to be tedious to the same O'Casey. Never have I had a play on that wasn't attacked, though I still write, well or badly, as the Spirit moves me. Irwin Ross should know that a writer hasn't always a good time, even when he's far, far away from the Iron Curtain. I have had the one-acter, BEDTIME STORY, refused twice, banned by Educational Committees in Kent and in Suffolk.

The pen must come to finish, for I give over typing at 11. oc. P.M., for fear of disturbing the people below. I amn't capable of surrendering the right to love all peoples, tho', naturally, I have a wide heart for Americans. I wish well to your article on Shaw and me. I'm afraid, Dave, Christians aren't interested in Christ; or, indeed, any remarkable soul that is brave enough to seek the Truth, whatever the facts may say. It is in no way astonishing if the Truth isn't quite what we imagined it should be. I know the "Catholic Worker," a brave little journal, though, to me, engaged in a fight too big for it to make a dent in the self-interest of Christians. I am glad your lads did so well with "The Plough";[2] & glad too, the audience responded to their work; for the acting of a full-length play is no damned joke. Give them all my thanks. I did intend to write suggesting they shouldn't bother about the accents; but finally decided to let them do it their own way, which is the only real way for all things.

We got the parcel you sent, Dave, & we enjoyed all that was within it; but it was extravagance, you know. In the Educational Journal, "Practical

[2] The Sock and Buskin Players of Brown University, Providence, R.I., performed The Plough and the Stars, 13–17 December 1957.

English," Shivaun tells an interviewer that while she packed here for the trip, "I sauntered in to give her fatherly advice," & gave her this warning, "Be careful of Americans: they are too generous. Io leor nod d'on Colach." A nod is enough to a learned man. In this, Dave, is a bit of fatherly advice for you: "Be generous; be not too generous."

Thank you, dear comrade, all the same for your kind & generous gift. My love to you & all the lads.

Eileen & Breon send their love.

Thank you for your gentle and dear reference to our beloved lost Niall. Eileen is, indeed, a brave lass.

As ever,
Sean

To Ronald Ayling

TS. AYLING

[22 JANUARY 1958][1]

Letter from Shaw to Lady Gregory. June, 1928.[2]

Why do you and W.B.Y. treat O'Casey as a baby? Starkie was right, you should have done the play anyhow. Sean is now hors concours. It is literally a hell of a play; but it will clearly force its way on to the stage and Yeats should have submitted to it as a calamity imposed on him by the act of God, if he could not welcome it as another Juno. Besides, he was most extraordinarily wrong about it on the facts. The first act is not a bit realistic; it is deliberately fantastic chanted poetry. This is intensified to a climax into the second act. Then comes a ruthless return for the last two acts to the fiercest ironic realism. But that is so like Yeats. Give him a job with which you feel sure he will play Bunthorne and he will astonish you with his unique cleverness and subtlety. Give him one that any second-rater could manage with credit and as likely as not he will make an appalling mess of it. He has certainly fallen in up to the neck over O'C.

I was looking up a date in *Story of the Abbey Theatre* by Peter Kavanagh, brother to Pat K., the poet. It was printed and published in the U.S.A., and never published here. I seem to remember your asking me

---

[1] Postmarked date.

[2] Originally published in *Lady Gregory's Journals, 1916–1930* (1947), edited by Lennox Robinson, pp. 110–111; reprinted in Peter Kavanagh's *The Story of the Abbey Theatre* (1950), p. 141. Following Kavanagh, O'Casey omitted the final two sentences, and for the whole letter, see Shaw to Lady Gregory, (?) June 1928, Vol. I.

about Shaw's letter to Lady Greg., and maybe, this is the one you were seeking.

S. O'C.

This letter itself should show to St. John E[rvine] some friendliness towards me.

To Miss Jane Rubin

TS. RUBIN

26 JANUARY 1958

Dear Jane,

I return the Gate Theater's Preface to Shaw's OVERRULED, and with it a few words which may do them as a preface to BEDTIME STORY.[1]

Shivaun has said nothing about bad business on the Tour, but she has written several times to say that acting and production are bad. She also told us that while they had three weeks holiday, and she with a few others were in Mexico, some others mishandled the bus they travel in so badly that it had to be repaired in a garage, the repairs costing upwards of a thousand dollars. This mishap, I think, is the reason for the delay in payment of royalties, for, I'm afraid, it will take some time to make up this net loss. That is my guess. As far as I am concerned, I wont worry, and, if you agree, I shouldnt like anything to be worrying Shivaun. All her letters deal mostly about America and America's People, which, to me, is the one and only benefit she'll get from the Tour; but it is a great benefit, and one she will remember with more than one thrill all her life long.

I hope PURPLE DUST had a good ending and a fine last night.[2] I'm sure the artists need, and are glad of, a rest.

I daresay you have heard that my latest play to be done by the Tostal Festival in Dublin during May, has fallen on a spot of bother. The Tostal is opened by a Votive Mass said by the Archbishop of Dublin. He has informed the Tostal Council that if the plays by Joyce and O'Casey are performed, no Mass will be said; so this has set all the religious com-

---

[1] This probably refers to the essay, "Badtime Story," *Blasts and Benedictions* (1967).

[2] *Purple Dust* had ended its run of just over a year in New York at the Cherry Lane Theatre on 5 January 1958. It opened on 27 December 1956. For details of the production, see O'Casey's letter to Paul Shyre, 28 December 1956.

munities talking. I dont know yet what will eventually happen, but the Council have declared they will go on with their Program.

The news that the NBC film of its interview with me has aroused mixed feelings. I fear the American People will be bored seeing me again, for I fear it is Bob [Ginna]'s affection for me that prompts him to put it out again, regardless of whether viewers will be interested or no; and that may do Bob harm, which would be far from agreeable to me. Dollars are, of course, always welcome, but not at somebody else's expense. That the idea of doing S. OF A GUNMAN will last till 1959 will give Bob a good chance of thinking it over. I hope, of course, that Paul will manage a Fall production of COCKA. DANDY; and that the singing Juno will be a success. All good wishes to you.

As ever,
Sean

To Godfrey Quigley and Norman Rodway[1]

TC. O'CASEY

29 JANUARY 1958

Gentlemen,

A letter signed by the above names, headed by the superscription of a Theater as named above also, has come to me, forwarded on from the town of Totnes; and, from what the letter says, I can but assume that you have made a mistake, confusing my name with someone else, for the whole tenor and expanse of the letter is inexplicable to me.

No play of mine has been submitted to your Theater for consideration, nor have I ever had any wish to do so; consequently, your comments

---

[1] Godfrey Quigley and Norman Rodway, directors, Globe Theatre Company, Ltd., playing at the Gate Theatre, Dublin. On 24 January 1958, Quigley and Rodway wrote a letter to O'Casey in which they stated they had not yet made a definite decision to produce *The Drums of Father Ned* at the Dublin Tostal for the following reasons: "Mr Brendan Smith is now pressing us for a definite decision and while we are most eager and proud to have the chance of producing this play, we are still not at all happy with its present structural state, which does not, in our opinion, make it produceable. Mr Elliman is also of the same opinion. Mr Fitzgerald says that while you are quite agreeable to changes being made 'on the floor,' you are chary of allowing any basic structural re-shaping in advance. We feel, on the other hand, that to attempt to re-shape the play at the last moment would be disastrous all round. Should an impasse be reached at that late stage it would leave things in a very difficult situation. It is for this reason that we are writing to ask you to give Jim Fitzgerald the necessary authority to make such alterations as he requires, before committing ourselves to any definite action with the Tostal authorities." (TS. O'Casey)

are ultra vires and altogether gratuitous, calling for no comments from me, that is, assuming the letter I received was really meant for me.

Yours sincerely,
Sean O'Casey.

P.S. It is evident that you must have an MS of my play. I must ask you to return this at once to Mr. Brendan Smith, Chairman of the Dublin Tostal Committee to whom I sent it. Thank you.

To Brendan Smith

TS. SMITH

29 JANUARY 1958

Dear Mr. Brendan Smith,

This morning I received a letter from *The Globe Theater* signed by Messrs Norman Rodway and Godfrey Quigley, which assumes that I have submitted my play to that Theater for consideration. You know that this isnt so. I wouldnt give a play of mine under any circumstances to them. I give you just one quotation—after a number of comments they make on the construction of the play, etc—Here it is:

"It is for this reason that we are writing to ask you to give Jim Fitzgerald the necessary authority to make such alterations as he requires, before committing ourselves to any definite action with the Tostal authorities." It is but necessary for me to say that it was I, and not Fitzgerald, who wrote the play; and it is I who shall stand or fall by the writing. The demand to sign over to Mr. Fitzgerald the right to make changes to Mr. Fitzgerald's "requirements" is, far as I know, an unprecedented one; and certainly one to which I would never agree—to Mr. Fitzgerald or anyone else.

It is plain to me now that there is no theater into which O'Casey can be allowed to fit, which is all OK by me; and that Mr. Fitzgerald doesnt understand what I am aiming at in the theater, and also, that the manner of my playmaking frightens him. Indeed, this demand left me with little to say: there is no answer to it, save silence.

I feared that Mr. F. would be timid about it from the talk I had with him; but tried to encourage him by pointing out that a play presenting no difficulty in production isnt much use to a living theater; but in my heart of hearts, I felt that this wasnt the man to make any attempt to do the play. Well, to end, I have come to the conclusion that there isnt a Director in Ireland today competent to do first-class drama, bar, probably, H[ilton]. Edwards. So I have fashioned the decision to withdraw the play from any production in the Republic of Ireland during the Tostal, or after the Tostal is done.

I shall be very much obliged, therefore, if you would return the Manuscripts to me—the copy I sent to you and the one given to Mr. Fitzgerald in the hope that a more familiar knowledge of it would prompt to a fuller courage in play production.

With all good wishes, and thanks for requesting the play in the first place.

Yours sincerely,
Sean O'Casey.

To Brendan Smith

TS. SMITH

5 FEBRUARY 1958

Dear Brendan Smith,

No, there is no change in my mind, nor will there be one. My letter to you concerning the one that came from the Globe Theatre Directors holds my refusal to permit the play to be done by the Tostal Committee; a decision I very much regret, but I am not prepared to have my play manhandled either by negotiations or without them. Your letter of the 4th but repeats the demands already made by the Globe Directors (why from them is a puzzle), but be it from these gentlemen or from the Members of the Dublin Tostal Committee, they cannot be accepted by me.

It is plain to me now that the Irish Producers, quite as strongly as the Critics, have neither sympathy nor understanding of my mode of playwrighting; that they have no desire to even tolerate experiment; that their blather about technique—which they do not understand—embraces, not technique as such, but embraces, with a view to destroy, the spirit and the structure of the play. If they are determined to defend that boxed-in mind, well and good; that is for them to do; it is a very safe attitude to take up; but it is not for me. Since that is so, another Producer (you mentioned [Tyrone] Guthrie) would have a bad time of it; and I am not willing that he should suffer for my sake. Besides, there's the Bishop's blast which Jim Fitzgerald seemed doubtful about: any outside Producer would have to contend with a lot, leaving aside the determination of the Council members and the G. Directors telling how the play should have been made. It is comic, all this demand for "requirements, arbitration, negotiations, technical discussions," making the acceptance of the play like a conference between international foreign ministers.

Jim Fitz. has an MS of the play, given to him (as I told you) when he was here, after telling me that you frequently borrowed the original script, and he badly needed one for himself so that he could study the play. He left one copy behind him in the hotel where he stayed, and Mrs O'C, searched for it in his bedroom but failed to find it. We looked through his bag again, but it wasnt there; then Mrs O'C. went back to the hotel, searched again, and found it beside the telephone. So both of the MS were given to him, the search and the finding of a lost copy fixing it all conclusively in our memory. It isnt just true to say he left it here. There isnt the shadow of a doubt that he had it safe when he left us, both copies in his bag. I shall be greatly obliged to you if you see that this copy is returned to me. I thought the giving of a second copy would help him, give him courage, and prompt him to throw himself into the play; but, alas, it would seem that he threw himself out of it!

By the way, neither I nor you were sent into the world to make producers. A gift from God cant be gotten from the hand of man; so neither you nor I is to blame.

By the way, again, the Globe's letter was sent to an address of Totnes, Devon, with name of neither street nor house; and only the kindness of Totnes P. Master brought it to me. I havent lived in Totnes for years. You knew my address, so did Fitz. It is known in Paris, Holland, all over the USA, in Warsaw, Buones Aires, India, Bulgaria, Moscow, Perm, Leningrad, Yugo-Slavia, Israel, Scandinavia, Berlin, etc; but evidently, still unknown in Dublin. Anyway, they didnt even pay me the courtesy of finding out my correct address before they sent the letter, which a phone call to you could have found for them. Yet they evidently think they can tell me how I am to make my plays. Surely, they should know by now that O'Casey, rightly or wrongly, is determined to remain himself.

I am deeply sorry that you have wasted so much time over the play, for you have enough to do; but, to make some amends, I have wasted a lot of time, too.

I most earnestly hope that all the other adventures you have in hands to do may be highly successful.

With all good wishes,
Yours very sincerely,
Sean O'Casey.

To Semerova Tatyana Fedorovna[1]

TC. O'CASEY

7 FEBRUARY 1958

Dear friend,

I cannot believe that my letter was so interesting as to be worth printing in your *Star*.[2] The exact year of my birth is 1880, and so, next March, I shall be 78 years old—alas! The confusion arose in this way: I never had any celebration for a birthday. We were too poor to bother, and so I never looked at a calendar. I had an idea that I had been born in the early eighties, but wasnt sure, and didnt care a lot when I had been born. It was good enough to be alive. I did not know the year till a few years ago. Then I had a play done in Paris. Before one can have a play done in France, the playwright must become a member of the French Society of Authors. This was no trouble to me, of course, so I immediately applied for membership. But one of the rules required every one who applied to furnish his Birth Certificate, and I had to set out to do this. I wrote to Dublin's Registrar, pointing out that I had been born somewhere between 1880 and 1888; but due to the circumstances of never having kept any birthday in mind, couldnt say which year recorded the event. After a big search, the Certificate was sent to me showing that the year was 1880, and so, from that day, O'Casey knew in which year he had been born. My latest play (I have written 15 other plays) is, I fear, not to be staged in Ireland, after all. Every year Ireland has a Festival called An Tostal; one of games, drama, music, opera, ballet, and literary competitions. It is opened by the hoisting of the Tostal Flag by Dublin's Lord Mayor, and a Votive Mass celebrated by the Roman Catholic Archbishop of Dublin. A few weeks ago, this Archbishop sent word to the Dublin Tostal Council that if any play by O'Casey was staged during the Festival, he would not allow the Votive Mass to be said. Then the man selected to produce the play demanded authority from me to change the play as he thought desirable, the Council supported him, and I have refused to allow them to make any change without my written permission; for I imagine they have been shaken by the cleric's outburst; and would try to mangle the play so that it would cease to have much resemblance to the one written by me. My first play written more than thirty years ago was first done in Dublin; but since then, I have met with a good deal of opposition,

---

[1] Miss Semerova Tatyana Fedorovna, 65 Kirov Street, Perm, USSR.

[2] When it was announced that a translation of *The Bishop's Bonfire* was to be published in *Zvedza* (The Star)—see O'Casey's letter to Brooks Atkinson, 11 September 1957, note 2—the editor asked him to write something about the play and its reception in Dublin. This piece, "K Chitatelyam 'Zvezydy': O Drame 'Koster Episkopa,'" appeared as an introduction to the play, *Koster Episkopa*, in *Zvedza*, January 1958. It was published in its original English version as "O'Casey's Drama-Bonfire," *Blasts and Benedictions* (1967).

mainly due to my political judgements. However, I am not worried in the least about the way they think of my judgements, for, since I believe them to be honest and true to me, they are not to be changed because some dislike them. I have asked two teachers if they would write to you, but both are not inclined to do this, not out of any dislike of your Country, but because they are too busy, and get very tired at the end of each day. They have very large classes to teach, and, at present, the whole system is in a hurried state of change. Previously, they have clung to an old-fashioned method of classicism, Latin, literature, and so on, setting science aside. Now they realise the importance of this subject in life and industry, but find it very hard to get suitable teachers, mainly because the Science teachers have been badly paid, and less thought of than those who teach Latin; a subject I have mocked in my books, for those who learn Latin, forget all about it when they leave school. If I meet with anyone who should be willing, I'll let you know. But I imagine, you would do better by good reading—say Shaw's Prefaces and Waldo Emerson's Essays (the great American writer and philosopher) in which are many beautifully-written essays on many subjects.

Yes, of course, you can be very busy and do many things, and have much enjoyment, even living so far away from Moscow. Indeed, every point, however far away it may be, is, in its own way, just as important as Moscow.

I enclose a photograph which I hope may get to you allright, and that you may like it.

Hearty congratulations upon the launching of the two Red Sputniks into the outer skies.

My good wishes to the Citizens of Perm, and my good wishes and warm regards to you, my dear.

Yours sincerely,
Sean O'Casey.

To Lewis Funke

TC. O'CASEY

12 FEBRUARY 1958

Dear Lewis,

I havent been able to devote a second to searching out an article that might or mightnt suit you, for two reasons—an ailing eye and the necessity to withdraw my play from the Tostal Council. I daresay, you have heard of the blast that came from the Palace of Dublin's R. Catholic Archbishop which thundered out that No Votive Mass would be said if any play by Joyce or O'Casey was performed during the Tostal Festival. Bang! Well, the Council decided to go on with the work (by, I have heard, a minority decision), and The Tostal Chairman chose a Director about whom I had some doubts. However, he came here to me, and we discussed things, but I saw that he was frightened of the play. He couldnt make himself comfortable with the blend of realism and fantasy, though there's less of it than in the BISHOP'S BONFIRE. I did all I could to instil courage into him, for I know that Ireland badly needs a good Director. He left, leaving me still doubtful, but hoping. Some time after, I got a letter from the Globe Theater (a little one showing plays in the Hall of the Gas Co.), signed by the two Directors. Now, I hadn't given the play to the Globe, but to the Tostal Council and they were to be responsible. The letter from the Globe told me that they considered the play "unproducable"; that they wouldnt commit themselves to a production till I signed an authorization Giving their Producer (Director) the power to change the play "according to his requirements." I answered this by a brief note, and wrote more fully to the Tostal Chairman withdrawing the play, for, under no circumstances, could I agree to such a proposal. I dont want people to like my style, or even to agree with it, if they cant do either; but when a play of mine is asked for, considered, and accepted, I take it for granted that the style and manner is accepted, if not liked, or even understood. Then came a letter from the Chairman saying "the Council were desirous of including your play in the Dublin Theater Festival, subject to the satisfactory outcome of negotiations on technical points already discussed (I have no knowledge of discussing any such thing). I am instructed to ask you too if you would change your attitude towards the question of negotiating such alterations." Negotiations! You'd think it was a summit meeting. So I have withdrawn the play. You may remember me saying in an earlier letter that I wanted to avoid the fuss and the ballyhoo that surrounded the production of the B's BONFIRE, and my hope that this one would go quietly. Quietness isnt for me, evidently. Now Ireland is bubbling over all this. What the inner motive of the Council may be, I know not; but I have a hunch that the Archbishop's blast shook them a little, and that they may have been eager to get away from the production in some way or another. Just as I received these letters from the Tostal Council, I got another from the English Publisher of THE GREEN CROW; copies of letters he had sent to the Irish Embassy and the Irish Revenue Commissioners. Here's what he says to the latter: "It is utterly monstrous that no decision should have been made although almost a year has passed. Mr. O'Casey is one of Ireland's great writers (Hurrah!), and is entitled to more courteous consideration. Why in any case it should be thought necessary to refer to the Censorship Board so obviously inoffensive a publication is beyond reasonable understanding.

On what prima facie grounds does a Customs Officer take it upon himself to decide that this book falls into a category warranting detention?

"Yours etc, Jeffrey Simmons."[1]

There you are, Lewis—Tostal Council, Globe Directors, Censorship Board, Archbishop, and Customs Officer, not counting Legion of Mary, C.Y.M.S. [Catholic Young Men's Society] Monsignors, and Canons, all in battle array against a bird, sniping at the Green Crow as he flies past, or perches for a minute on an Irish tree.

I am just letting you know the news; not in any spirit of complaining, for I am used to it all by now; and it doesnt take a feather outa me.

I hope you and Brooks are well.

All good and warm wishes to him and to you.

Yours very sincerely,
Sean O'Casey.

[1] See O'Casey's letter to Jeffrey Simmons, 14 March 1958.

To Paul Shyre

MS. SHYRE

14 FEBRUARY 1958

Dear Paul,

Enclosed is script of play. I think, I shall go back to its first name— "The Night is Whispering"; or would it be better to keep to the later name, since all the present Ree Raa (confused noise-Irish) is around "The Drums of Father Ned"?

The Tostal Council has issued a long statement saying O'Casey refused to agree "to structural changes to make the play suitable for the Dublin public,"[1] a most curious statement, indeed, since they add that there is no moral objection to the play. I haven't the slightest definite knowledge of what the structural changes they wanted to make, for they give no hint of them; but from what the prospective Director of the play said to me when he was here, I gathered they wanted to cut out the fantasy incident; & leave only the realistic ones; but even this was inconclusive, for you can't get these people to talk frankly, & tell you what they're thinking

[1] From a report in the *Irish Times*, 12 February 1958: "A spokesman for the Council said yesterday–'The Dublin Tostal Council, through its festival director (Mr. Brendan Smith), rejected this play because it was not allowed to make structural alterations to make it suitable for the Dublin public.'" See also O'Casey's letter to Brooks Atkinson, 25 May 1957, note 3.

about. I told the newspaper men who rang me up about the "Withdrawal," that if the Tostal Council would publish the letters they sent to me, & the replies I sent to them, the facts would be plain, & the readers could judge for themselves. I've been taught one thing—bar Hilton Edwards, there isn't a Director in Ireland fit to direct any play, worthwhile production, that is new, & which has never been done before. They direct plays that have been done by others already, & so have grounds to go on. It was pitiful to watch the laddo who was here trembling before the difficulties in the "Drums," but, of course, fearful of saying he was afraid; & not knowing really what he was afraid of. It is odd they couldn't see how full the play is of Ireland as she is. The structure is even aimed at showing the confusion current in the present efforts to keep Ireland alive; to "bring her out of an almost deathlike coma," as a writer in today's *Irish Times* says—after the Tostal Council had decided to give up the O'Casey play; & an article (leading) in the *Irish Press* yesterday dealt with an appeal to "tidy & brighten up Irish Towns," one of the lively items in the play; yet the play has been refused. Again, the two Parties, hating each other, yet as like as tweedledee & tweedledum; & so on, almost ad infinitum.

Regarding proposed production in Boston, do what you think best; but don't let it put you to too much waste of energy. You have a lot of other things to do. In a prologue-verse, that might be spoken before the play begins, I have called it "an idle, laughing play";[2] & this is what I hope it to be.

Eileen & Breon send their warm regards & affectionate greetings, and so do I, a mhic o.

As ever,
Sean

---

[2] This "prologue-verse" appears in the published edition of the play, 1960, p.x:

> This comedy's but an idle, laughing play
> About the things encumbering Ireland's way;
> A flag shoved from a window, and a cry
> To wake up drowsy girl and drowsier boy,
> To snatch from Erin's back the sable shawl,
> And clothe her as she was before her fall;
> In cloak of green as bright as spring's young call;
> Beside her Tara's harp from off a time-stain'd wall,
> To play new dandy airs; holding high the poet's hazel rod,
> String tied to tip, hook-holding a crimson berry,
> With myrtle and with laurel wove, deep-dipp'd in wine,
> Champagne or sherry;
> That mobled minds may all new courage grow,
> And miser'd hearts be merry.

To Kay Carney

TC. O'CASEY

15 FEBRUARY 1958

Dear Saint of Bleecker Street,[1]

The quotation at the start of the B.'s Bonfire is taken from a well-known Gaelic song—The Keen of Kilcash,[2] a lament for the death of a Kilcash chieftain. It means, What shall we henceforth do without timber—the last of the forest trees is down. It has a haunting air, and is rather lovely in spirit and cadence. Now, my dear, you know.

It is very appropriate at the moment, for I daresay youve read what has happened to my play that was to receive its world premier in Dublin during the Tostal Festival. The Tostal Council quailed before the thunderbolt of the Archbishop; deliberately made impossible conditions, demanding the authority to alter it as they thought fit to "make it suitable for the Dublin public." There was nothing unsuitable in it; it was an excuse to get out of it, and so that event is over, after wasting a deal of time that at my age, I can ill spare. Tonight, I have gotten news that the proposed play made from Ulysses has gone west, too: the Council have decided to abandon it; so the Archbishop has had his way.[3]

K. Listens In, as far as I know, exists no longer.[4] The original MS probably burned up during the Abbey Theater fire. The other—Nannie's Night Out doesnt either. There may be some of the MS buried under my papers, but I doubt it, for I never had any intention of publishing either.

I do hope you may get a job. It is a sad state that man or woman should find it hard to find work. Many a year I passed myself within the same danger. But one shouldnt lose courage, for when courage is gone, all goes with it.

I have had many bitter times, and, recently, was called upon to withstand the bitterest sorrow my life has yet experienced; but we must go on with life while life lasts, and never, never cease to fight the good fight till we finish the course.

---

[1] Miss Carney lived on Bleecker Street, New York City, and Gian-Carlo Menotti wrote a musical drama called *The Saint of Bleecker Street* (1954).

[2] See O'Casey's letter to Cyril Cusack, 19 February 1955, note 4.

[3] The decision to drop Alan McClelland's dramatization of *Ulysses* was reported in the *Irish Times,* 15 February 1958: "It was learned that the decision to drop the play had come from Bord Failte [the Tourist Board] which subsidises the Festival. The board, it is understood, felt that recent 'adverse publicity' which had followed the expression of the Most Rev. Dr. McQuaid, Archbishop of Dublin, made the production of *Bloomsday* inadvisable." Several days later Samuel Beckett announced in Paris that he was withdrawing his two mime plays from the Festival as a protest against the Council's decision to drop O'Casey and Joyce from the programme.

[4] *Kathleen Listens In* and *Nannie's Night Out* are printed in *Feathers From the Green Crow* (1962).

So, be brave, my friend, and just fight on, being as prudent as you can.
With all good wishes,
Yours sincerely,
Sean O

To Irish Times

17 FEBRUARY 1958

DRUMS OF FATHER NED

Sir,—I should like to say a few words about the Dublin rejection of the above-named play, in fairness to myself.

I did not ask the Tostal to take an interest in the play, much more to do it. While writing it, and when it had been finished, I had no thought of the Tostal Council wanting to get the play for production in Dublin. The Council, through their hard-working Chairman, asked, not once, but several times to see and read the typescript. I was very reluctant to comply, instancing my desire that the opportunity of publicity the Tostal gave should be used for the benefit of some younger or newer playwright; but was met with the reply that none of the younger playwrights had come forward with anything suitable, and, now, that the Tostal Drama Festival has been postponed (which is an elegant word for abandonment), it would seem that this opinion was the right one. The Script was sent to Dublin at the beginning of September, 1957, so that those concerned had plenty of time to consider the play, yet it was only after the Archbishop had issued his fiat that the discovery of structural changes was made. Further, it was pointed out in the letter saying the Script had been sent, in reply to suggestions of possible producers of the play, that "(my) play has something in it besides its 'realism,' and it is this odd breeze within a wind that worries me in direction." I was afraid that the selected producer might not be capable of embracing my intentions. However, no complaint came over the months, and I settled down to other work. It wasn't till 24/1/58, that I received a letter signed by the Directors of a Theater to whom I had not given the play demanding that I should give the producer "the necessary authority to make such alterations as he requires"; and that "its structural state made the play unproduceable, Mr. Elliman agreeing with that opinion."[1] This was followed by a letter from the Tostal Council saying the

[1] See O'Casey's letter to Godfrey Quigley and Norman Rodway, 29 January 1958, note 1.

same thing within a few different words. I at once surmised that this was not an attempt to improve O'Casey (in my opinion, none of those who objected were at all competent to do it), but an untidy way of getting rid of him, for, undoubtedly, the outcry from Drumcondra[2] was dinging their ears. When news came of the dropping of the Joycean play, this surmise became a certainty. As I had no desire to battle a group into keeping a play they wished to get rid of, I withdrew it.

When the script returned, I found—though it was quite obvious that it had been read by far more than one person—there wasn't a single mark on it (other than alterations I had already made myself) to indicate any tentative idea of questionable construction. To this day, I haven't the slightest notion of what part of the play, in their opinion, needed an alteration. It is rather comic to think of a frightened Archbishop frightening the Tostal Council into closing the gate of Dublin on Dubliners. Shut the gates! Quick; we have not a moment to spare. The Archbishop doesn't know (or doesn't care) that a work by Beckett, by Joyce, or even by O'Casey, performed in Dublin, is of more importance to Dublin than it is to any of those authors: that outside Dublin is a wide, wide world, and that this wide place is Joyce's oyster, Beckett's oyster, and even O'Casey's oyster; or that these voices, hushed in Dublin, will be heard in many another place.

Regarding Quid Nunc's remark that I withdrew the play because of a demand for "tightening it up,"[3] let me say that this is a far call from "structural alterations." Tightening up is often done after production, it may mean only a change of tempo; and what is called "formlessness" may be a form in itself, as for instance in J. Bull's Other Island, Chekhov's plays, and Shaw's HEARTBREAK HOUSE. Life is like that at times. Few places can be so formless as Ireland's at the present time. It is like a kaleidoscope, but giving—as kaleidoscopes do—not settled or discernible pattern, however one may twist it slow or with speed. This the play tried to show, with the confusion animated by the activity of the Tostal in which there was hope and resolution (If the last issue of INNIU is read some of this confusion and uncertainty can be felt). An ironical item in INNIU, within the article by Beann Mhadagain,[4] which says that if we let the Language die, or leave it weak as it is today, "níorbh fhéidir dúinn a chur abhaile choiche ar Phrotastúnaigh an Tuaiscirt nach rud lom-Chai-

---

[2] The Archbishop's Palace is in Drumcondra.

[3] Quidnunc, "An Irishman's Diary: 'The Blinds is Down,'" Irish Times, 15 February 1958: "The play was not regarded technically as up to the high standards expected from the Grand Old Man of the Irish Theatre, I understand, but the G.O.M. himself thought it quite good enough and refused to tighten it up; hence the present impasse."

[4] Beann Mhadagain, "An Bord Failte agus an Fheile Dramaiochta" (The Tourist Board and the Drama Festival), Inniu, 28 February 1958. O'Casey must have received an advance copy of this article by Beann Mhadagain (Cave Hill, near Belfast, where Wolfe Tone founded the United Irishmen), the pseudonym of Ernest Blythe, managing director of the Abbey Theatre.

tiliceach 1 an Náisiúntachas Éireannach."[5] They might listen, even partly believe, if a Gaelic Nation went back to Colimbkille, Aidan, and Bridhid, but that is hardly likely; and now they have the experience of an audience waiting for certain plays to appear, when a few quiet words from an Archbishop are heard, and the whole Tostal Drama Festival dissolves away from the Irish stage.

Co-incidental with the quiet voice from the Palace of Drumcondra, I received from the publisher of the *Green Crow* copies of two letters, one to the Counsellor, Irish Embassy, the other to the Revenue Commissioners of Dublin Castle (ominous name, ominous place), which says, "It is monstrous that no decision should have been made although almost a year has passed. Mr. O'Casey is entitled to more courteous consideration (aha!). Why in any case it should even be thought necessary to refer to the Censorship Board so obviously inoffensive a publication is almost beyond reasonable understanding. On what prima facie grounds does a Customs Officer take upon himself to decide that this book falls into a category warranting detention? 7 Feb. 1958. Jeffrey Simmons."[6]

With an Archbishop in his palace, fortified by the rights of the church and a Customs Officer on the Quay vive at the docks, Dublin is kept safe for freedom of thought, and the Drums of Father Ned have been silenced—for a time. My sympathy is with the courteous and good-natured Brendan Smith who has had a rotten time of it, as Mr. Hilton Edwards knows better than I do.[7] In all this banishment of Irish effort, where are the indomitable Irish about whom the poet sang? Gone to cover? Looks like there isnt an arm or a leg of them left. They have left for other lands to get outside of the ecclesiastical iron curtain; a cause of emigration that is never mentioned. It may be just as well that Ireland's population is getting less and less, for it will leave plenty of room for the elect people of God, the faithful few, with all the rascals gone; those that stay safe from any touch of pitch that might defile them; for at present, reading the Lenten Pastorals, it would seem that the Irish people are becoming a nation of delinquents. All the same, citizens of the Republic bad or good, have a claim on the State. His Grace, the Archbishop, in a democratic State is no more than a citizen of the Republic, even though such a claim comes from an accident of birth; well, so am I a citizen of the Republic, not only by accident of birth, but also by definite intent.

So, by demand of Dublin's Catholic Archbishop, this citizen, with a

[5] "we would never be able to convince the Northern Protestants that Irish Nationalism is not a baldly Catholic thing."

[6] Jeffrey Simmons of W. H. Allen, London, publisher of *The Green Crow* (1957). See O'Casey's letter to Simmons, 14 March 1958.

[7] An allusion to a comment by Hilton Edwards, who was to have directed *Bloomsday* at the Dublin Gate Theatre, reported in the *Irish Times,* 15 February 1958: "What this really means is that there is, as there always has been, a rigid censorship of plays and everything else. It is working in different ways, and putting pressure on things."

tear in his eye, a pain in his heart (While the other Archbishop doesnt
say a word), has to say a second time—Inisfallen Fare Thee Well.—Yours,
etc.

Sean O'Casey

DEVON.

To Francis MacManus[1]

TS. MACMANUS

22 FEBRUARY 1958

My dear Frank,

Could you thank on my behalf the kind soul that thought of putting
on JUNO over Radio Eireann on the 11th May next? I imagine that this
was meant as a gesture of friendliness, and it struck a chord in my pagan
soul that was very pleasant. It was a kind gesture, and I appreciate it
very much, although I had to refuse it; but not the shake of the hand that
I imagine, went with it. I have passed through many bitter times, but I
amnt yet hardened enough yet not to welcome a kind thought.

Now, greetings to you and to yours. You, too, have had your share
of sorrow, and, to that extent, a very deep one, really, we are akin.[2]

You are aware of what has happened, all a pity to me, for the play
was one of hope and courage embedded in the Tostal activities. On the
wall of my room a Tostal Poster hangs, and, even now, I've no intention
of removing it. One ironic thing in this matter of banishment is that the
play was first thought of through the life and work of Canon Hayes,[3] who
died too soon, and a remembrance of the thoughts of Father Sheedy[4]
with whom I came in contact when I was in New York many years ago;
he was a life-long friend of Dr. McDonald's,[5] and the old priest gave me
his blessing, which, believe it or no, I still remember and still value. Indeed, I had intended to dedicate the book of the play to those two fine

[1] Francis MacManus (1909–65), schoolteacher, writer, Director of Talks and
Features, Radio Eireann, 1947–65. See many letters to him in Vol. II.
[2] MacManus's young son died of a heart disease.
[3] Canon John M. Hayes (1877–1957), founder of *Muintir na Tire* (People of
the Land), a society to help and preserve rural communities in Ireland.
[4] Dr. Morgan Sheedy (1853–1939), Rector, Cathedral of the Blessed Sacrament, Altoona, Pennsylvania.
[5] Dr. Walter McDonald (1854–1920), Professor of Theology, Maynooth College.

priests; but, now, I fear such a dedication would be reckoned an insult to their memories.[6]

With warm regards and all good wishes.

Eadrainn féin, a chroidhe, an litir seo.[7]

Sean

[6] Nevertheless, in honor of five courageous priests, he changed his mind and wrote the following dedication for *The Drums of Father Ned* (1960): "*The Memory be Green*, Of Dr. Walter McDonald, courageous theologian in Maynooth College for forty years; of Dr. Morgan Sheedy, his lifelong friend, banished for venturing to defend a Parish Priest against a Bishop, and who sent me 'an old priest's blessing' from Pennsylvania to New York in 1934; of Father Yorke of San Francisco, who warned Irish Ireland of fond delusions many years ago, and who told Dr. McDonald, his friend, that in the *Rerum Novarum* the Church was offering the workers no more than a string of platitudes; of Canon Hayes, Founder of Muintir na Tire, bringing a sense of community life and co-operation to rural Ireland, and brightness with them; and of Father O'Flanagan who, when his poor flock were shivering through a black winter, bade them go to a private-owned bog, and take from it all the turf they needed, led them there to do it, and was, consequently, banished from his Parish and from County Sligo by his Bishop. Each in his time was a Drummer for Father Ned, and the echoes of their drumming sound in Ireland still." (Father Michael Flanagan [1876–1942] was the Republican priest who, due to his radical views and actions, often clashed with religious and secular authorities. Father Yorke appears in Dr. McDonald's *Reminiscences of a Maynooth Professor* [1925], pp. 215–17.)

[7] This letter is between ourselves, dear friend.

To Jane Rubin

MS. RUBIN

22 FEBRUARY 1958

Dear Jane,

Thanks for check and for Contracts, which I am returning, signed and witnessed as directed, under another cover, by ordinary mail—not by air mail. You should get them safely.

By the way, Jane, I've been thinking that it might be tactful to wait till this year had gone—100th Anniversary of Bernadette—before putting on "Cockadoodle Dandy." Then the storm of emotionalism will have subsided; the participants tired, as always afterwards, be it pietistic or jingo demonstrations; & many will be ready for a break, seeing disease cant be banished by miracles at Lourdes; but only by the discoveries of Science as to what diseases are, & how they can be conquered. I'd like you to consider this; tho' maybe a cry against the play would do no harm. Eileen is writing a note to Paul touching the same thought.

Don't worry about our Film failure—these things are common occur-

rences. I myself had little hope—a hunch of some kind—that it would come
to a successful conclusion.

The Tostal Drama Festival has been abandoned because no suitable
plays could be gotten to replace those banished.

So there Dublin goes again. At Paul's request, I have sent the Script
of "Drums of Father Ned" to him.

I do hope the snow is all gone from New York. We here had a bad
fortnight of it all Devon roads blocked with drifts.

All good wishes
As ever,
Sean

To Eric Gorman

TS. GORMAN

27 FEBRUARY 1958

Dear Mr. Gorman,
In case that you [the Abbey Theatre] should be thinking of putting
any play of mine (JUNO, I think, was done last time) during the weeks
of the Tostal this year, or within the octave before or after them, this is
a formal note to say I cannot permit it; and, I'm sure, you'll understand
the reason why.

It isnt likely that you are thinking of it, but I wish to make sure. Indeed, if at any future time you should think of putting on a play of mine,
I shall be grateful if you told me beforehand.

With all good personal wishes,
Yours sincerely,
Sean O'Casey.

To Ronald Ayling

MS. AYLING

28 FEBRUARY 1958

Dear Ron,
A short note to you. You may quote whatever you like about what
I've written. I care not for Ulick [O'Connor]'s opinions; but am always

ready to allow quotation from anything written that has my name appended at the end: that is, if I know I wrote it.

Yes, I'd like to have a preliminary try-out of my last play before sending it to publishers. There is a chance now: a Massachusetts College is interested, and a Script has gone to Paul Shyre, who was responsible for the Biograph. Readings and Purple Dust, which came off last month, after more than a year's run. I send you a letter (which I want back) about what happened to The D. of Father Ned, which I intended to send to the Irish Times, but held back, just to leave them wondering. Even this doesn't contain all the details of how they begged for the play. The only play left to them now is one by Denis Johnston sent to the Abbey Theatre, to be done Tostal Week, but Johnston will probably withdraw it too.[1]

By the way, you say nothing about yourself. How do you live? Are you teacher or student? I do hope that asthma doesn't bother you, and that you will shake it off completely: you are young enough to do this: you should be in the air as much as you possibly can; and eat moderately but effectively.

> *Very busy.*
> *All good wishes*
> *as ever*
> *Sean*

Enclosure. There may be a word or two left out, or a misspelling; but you'll be able to read it.

---

[1] Denis Johnston's *The Scythe and the Sunset* opened at the Abbey Theatre on 9 May 1958. O'Casey later felt that Johnston had acted as a scab by refusing to withdraw his play from the Tostal, in the same spirit of sympathetic protest for O'Casey and Joyce that led Samuel Beckett to withdraw his mime plays. See O'Casey's letters to Ayling, 20 January 1960, note 4; and to Peter J. Ryan, *Theatre Arts,* February 1960, note 3, Vol. IV.

To May Keating

MS. KEATING

28 FEBRUARY 1958

Dear May,

A letter even, not to mention an article, would do the *Plough*[1] more harm than good. You have seen what a word from an Archbishop can do to those who lead the Irish at home; &, at times, too, the Irish abroad.

---

[1] *The Plough,* a Socialist newspaper in Dublin.

Not a word from any politician, a writer—bar [Padraic] Colum—haven't let a murmur out of them. The Protestants go about their business, & live as if they heard nothing, saw nothing, knew nothing. The liberal-minded Catholics see-saw with this opinion contraventing that one, each from the one mouth, colliding like timid atoms, & dissolving in vapor. And I'm told, I'm out of touch with present-day Ireland. She is as she was before, only worse. It began in the older days of the Gaelic League—the case of the Rory O'Moore Branch & the Gaelic League Quoir; all dictation from the clerics taken sheepishly; a slinking away and a silence. The Republic, in spite of its pre-natal valor, its hope, its terrible beauty, was still-born in the end: it was snapped up by the prelates. Well, they are having it their own way, but they are paying heavily for it. The Bishopric of Ross is gone—there is no longer a Diocese. Hundreds of Parishes are perishing for want of parishioners. Take what you want, says God; take what you want, and pay for it.

Well, May, I'm busy, and no longer have the energy I once had: I grow old, & can't sing so constantly now. I can't write articles as I am asked for them. I've just refused to do two, though each would have gotten me £25. And I have many, many letters to write.

I enclose a subscription, the only help I can usefully give.

> *All good wishes*
> *Yours very sincerely*
> *Sean O'Casey*

To Mrs. John T. Cooper

MS. CSU FULLERTON LIB

[?] MARCH 1958

My dear Georgie,

You Americans are dangerous people—You run wild in your generosity. You don't wait even to think that it is more blessed to give than to receive; you give because it seems to be part of your nature. It is a beautiful quality, but, often, it seems to me, it is unfair to yourselves. You are not a wealthy lady nor is John a wealthy gentleman; both of you have a long time in front of you, and responsibilities will increase as a few years pass; & so, dear ones, be careful: if you give with one hand, don't give with two. Americans seem to look upon what they have, not as easy come, easy go; but it comes hard, let it go easy. All the same, & in spite of your wild generosity, I was greatly touched by your gift, and by the thought that you remembered me; so, dear ones, I accept your kind gift as a sign of affectionate regard for me by John & you, an affection very dear to me.

I hope you are taking care of yourself, & that you are weathering the cold of Iowa. Here, in England, we have had a big share of it, with traffic on many roads impossible, villages cut off, and snow above and below. As I write, snow is falling heavily a few miles away, coming nearer & nearer; & soon it will be falling outside of the O'Casey windows. The daffodils brave it all well enough, even tho' they cannot close their golden bells to keep the cold winds out; but the white, orange, and purple crocuses force their petals to cling close, shutting up their inner beauty from the bite of the winds and the icy touch of the falling snow; and I never stray far from a fire.

Don't worry yourself about Father McLoey. Some of what he thinks of me has a grain of truth in it, but, by and large, he knows me not. It is evident he has never read the book written by Dr. Walter McDonald, who was Professor of Theology in Maynooth (he has probably heard of Maynooth, anyway), for 40 years.[1] The things said, & written down, by Dr. McDonald would make him cry out with anger and anguish. He shouldn't worry about me "leaving the Church," for 50,000 leave the Catholic Church, in England alone, yearly. 50,000!, and they can't do anything about it. I know a Professor of Notre Dame University, Dr. O'Brien, who raised an outcry in Ireland when he edited a book called "The Vanishing Irish"; even quoting me in it.[2] I wonder did Father McL. read that one?

As for the Archbishop banning any O'Casey play, or the play made from Joyce's "Ulysses"; his ban caused a panic in the Tostal Council; they banned Joyce & me; then S. Beckett, in protest, withdrew his two mime plays, and the whole Drama Festival fell down like Dagon's image.

The whole affair has given me some annoyance, and wasted a lot of time I can ill spare. They could find no plays of Irish origin good enough for a Festival; & so the whole scheme lies scattered in the dust and ashes of fear that clutter every effort Ireland tries to make for a more liberal outlook.

Thanks, dear, for the clipping telling of Cavanaugh's cry for Catholic intellectuals more fitted to stand today in the urging, surging world of thought and endeavor. One like me can hardly sympathize, for one of their own braver Scholars, Dr. McDonald, warned that this was bound to happen; warned them more than forty years ago; but they refused to listen, & used any means they could think of to force him to shut his mouth; and even today, never venture to murmur his name.

[1] See many references to Dr. Walter McDonald in Vols. I and II. See also the chapter devoted to Dr. McDonald, "Silence," in *Inishfallen, Fare Thee Well* (1949).
[2] *The Vanishing Irish: The Enigma of the Modern World* (1953), edited by Dr. John A. O'Brien, Research Professor of Theology, University of Notre Dame. See O'Casey's letter to him, 8 March 1954, Vol. II.

But what you have to do now, lass, is not to bother about these things; but only about the life to come.

If there be a God, may he bless and keep you, now, when the Babe comes, & forever after.

My love to John and you.
As ever,
Sean

To Irish Press

1 MARCH 1958

O'CASEY MAKES A CHALLENGE

Sir—Your predumbinent "drama critic" in Monday's issue (February 24) of your valuable Journal, in the course of other remarks, says "I think it is fair enough to record the statements (record the statements—what pompous phrases!) of responsible people who have read the O'Casey manuscript. . . . Well, I regret to say (he regrets to say!) that competent theatre personages (personages!) who have read the script carefully (carefully!) have made no secret of their disappointment (disappointment!). In brief, and without mincing words, they have informed me (not told him: informed him) that it is 'very mediocre stuff.' "[1]

Whispered it to him, eh? I have to remind this critic of yours, the important personages, and the competent theatre people, that the first three "great plays," that this critic again hails, were declared too, in their time to be "very mediocre stuff," by equally important people and competent theatre personages, with this big difference, namely, that they had the decency to say so publicly, and add their names to what they wrote.

So I challenge this critic of yours to publish the names of these important people and competent theatre personages in the columns of THE IRISH PRESS. They need have no fear that His Grace will mind their poor opinion of O'Casey's work, nor will O'Casey molest them in thought or word or deed. If they refuse to permit their names to be known, then they must indeed be a cowardly bunch, or, on the other hand, Carroll has invented the information for his own satisfaction. This is a statement that is unfair to an author, to say the least of it, a statement by unknown persons who may not have even read the play, a statement, for all we know, may have been made by the reporter himself. It is easy for him to settle this by telling us who these important people and competent

[1] Niall Carroll, "That O'Casey Play," *Irish Press,* 24 February 1958.

theatre personages are. If he wont, then we must be content to know our own know.

Carroll disputes his ignorance of drama by emphasising the merit of the "great trilogy of his (O'Casey's) realistic writings." In an effort to teach him a tettle about drama, I quote from an article by a "competent theatre personage," and an important one of the people," in "The Virginia Quarterly Review" (if Carroll is interested—or anyone else, the article can be found in the Magazine mentioned, Vol. 34, Number 1: Winter 1958): "Unlike O'Neill and Strindberg, O'Casey used non-realistic and realistic material in the same play—an approach, incidentally, which has been subsequently employed by many modern dramatists, for example, Giraudoux and Anouilh, Denis Johnston and Thornton Wilder, Tennessee Williams and Arthur Miller."[2] In the same issue of your Journal, a speaker is reported as saying "In the elements of culture, including drama, we (Irish Writers) seemed not only satisfied with mediocrity but made it our ideal."[3] It would be useful, maybe, if Carroll began to think of his own deep depth in it.

Sean O'Casey

Devon, Feb. 26, 1958

[2] David Krause, "The Playwright's Not For Burning," *Virginia Quarterly Review,* Winter 1958.

[3] Sean Og Ó Tuama, vice-principal of Capel Street Technical School, in a lecture on "Irish Culture" at the Dublin Institute of Catholic Sociology, *Irish Press,* 24 February 1958. He also stated: "From Irish writers of international fame—Shaw, O'Casey, Joyce, Yeats—he got the idea that Ireland was a breeding ground of drunkards and amoralists."

To David Krause

TS. KRAUSE

1 MARCH 1958

My dear Dave,

Thanks a lot for the copy of THE VIRGINIA QUARTERLY, the whole of which I am reading with great interest. I liked your article (naturally) very much, for it has placed one more weapon in the hand fighting the Irish "writers," actors, and all the ree raa yelping at O'Casey's heels. I have already quoted it against a "drama critic" of THE IRISH PRESS, a lad who has been born without, or has deprived himself of, the power to think out, not only a review, but even a sentence. He has gone on to the old road of the first "three great plays," and the assertion that the rest is a mass of mediocrity. I have reminded his readers that the first "three great plays" were also deemed to be a mass of mediocrity, but these writers deliberately and with malice aforethought, restrain this information from those who read them. Now they are busy circulating the news that the *D. of Father Ned* was abandoned because it was a bad play, mediocre stuff. He tells us of "important personages and important and competent people of the theater" who "had read the script" as "informing him" that the play was about as bad as it could be, admitting that he hasn't read it himself. I have challenged to let us know the names of these important personages, and I have asked how important they are, and why do they go about whispering without having the courage to tell the world who they are. But I imagine I am but wasting my time. They carefully steer clear of mentioning the Archbishop's declaration against the production of an O'Casey play during the Tostal. He hasn't read the play either, but I'm sure he read THE BISHOP'S BONFIRE, and that it was this play that soured his archiepiscopal soul.

I enclose some of the clippings that may give you a bird's eye view of what happened, but the Tostal Council have ignored my suggestion that all letters between them and me should be printed, if they wish to give those interested a clearer view of what happened. The Green Crow's view has yet to come, but I'm taking my time so as to let the Irish "writers" tease their minds over the whole question; for a more cowardly lot of leaders of opinion I verily believe lives in no other land outside Ireland.

The Director sent down here to me (the man for your play, said the Council chairman) was a lad who wasn't thirty years of age, and I expected to welcome the courage and enthusiasm of youth. God, he was terrified at the realism and the fantasy in the same play, and kept muttering that he thought it wouldn't do; but I labored at trying to put spunk into him, and he went away, I thought, convinced that it would be a feather in his cap to do the play. They had had the play for months, and I had concluded it had been studied and sorted out in at least a tentative way; but when I got the scripts back, there wasn't a single mark positive or negative on either of them. Then a week after he had gone, I got a letter from the Globe Theater (to whom I hadn't given the play), signed by two Directors (actors) saying they considered the play unproducable, and they wouldn't commit themselves to doing it till I sent them the written authority giving power to the Director full permission to alter it according to his requirements. Some time, I'll type out the short letter I sent them in reply.

Oddly enough, the priestly spirit of the play, (Father Ned who never appears) is built from the thoughts of an old priest who was exiled to Altoona, Penn., and Canon Hayes, who labored to make rural Ireland brighter, and full of self-reliance in creating a new and active life, with hand, mind, and imagination. This clashed with business, parochialism, and out-dated clericalism (a humorous figure and kindly withal), all against the background of the work for the Tostal. This microcosm is meant (successfully or not, I don't know) to portray the whole condition of Ireland as she is;[1] for today, in confusion of politics, art, literature, and sex, Ireland is a colorless kaleidoscope, a kaleidoscope, twist it how you may, never shows a settled or colorful pattern; that is the technique which no one seemingly could accept; though I am convinced they wanted to rid themselves of the play when the Abishop spoke; and after events proved it. Now, they are trying to fix the fact of a mediocre play, as the reason, dumb about the Abishop's camoflaged curse on O'Casey. And all are concerned only about O'Casey's "prestige"! So for the second day, I have had to say Inishfallen, Fare Thee Well.

My hope, dear lad, that you are well, not too tired, and content in your flat.

My love as ever, and Eileen's too. Breon is now away, living on his own in Torquay in a self-contained room, and painting away fiercely.

As ever again,
Sean

[1] The published text of the play bears the subtitle: "A Mickrocosm of Ireland."

To Robert Hogan

MS. HOGAN

3 MARCH 1958

Dear Bob Hogan,
Here's a script of the play for you to have a look at it. It's a bit rugged, for I do a number of drafts, rereadings, changing as I read or not as I think the need may arise. This is the Script I sent to the Tostal Council last Sept. 1957. They had a long time to look it over; they, thro' their chairman, "liked it immensely"; and it wasn't till the archbishop spoke that comments began to fall on it. Now, it is only concerned with the "mediocrity" of the play, but most who say so haven't read it. The Archbishop's ban is very calmly camouflaged by this curious criticism.

Yes, you may quote anything that has my name written at the end as a warrant of authenticity. I have been made to say a few things I never said; & so I allow only quotations bearing my name as a pennon.

I enclose some clippings to give you an idea of what happened; also a letter I put together for the *Irish Times* but which I didn't send; deciding not to satisfy enemy curiosity, but abide my time for speaking out;

inclined to wait and see if many, or any, protests be made. So far, only a few timid ones, flooded over by many hurrahing his Grace, the A.Bishop. (I'd be glad for the return of this letter.)

I send, also, a letter (copy) to a friend of mine giving an idea of what I aimed at in the play; & the form was an effort to do something like what R. Strauss did in his music to Don Chichote, picture following picture in sounds of lovely music. The play tries to show some dramatic pictures of present-day Ireland, of course, the dram. form in no way comparable to Strauss's lovely creation; tho' when I was writing it, I didn't think of Strauss, hadn't even heard it; but some time ago, I listened to Strauss, & said to myself—"That's something like what I aimed at doing in *The Drums of F. Ned.*"

I read your article in Dub. Mag. & thank you for it.[1] It has had repercussions as you can see by reading the clipping called "Irishman's Diary."[2] Please return "Letter to Irish Times" & my copy of letter to friend when you are done with them; &, of course, Script of play. I don't need the Press clippings.

"Green Crow" is still banned in Eire. Held up a Year now by the Customs, & the harassed Publisher can't get a word out of them about what they intend to do: ban or release it.

With all good wishes,
Sean O'Casey

I return the check you so kindly sent to me.

[1] Robert Hogan, "The Experiments of Sean O'Casey," *Dublin Magazine,* January–March 1958; see also "Riches Scorned," *TLS,* 31 January 1958, a leading article inspired by Hogan's article.
[2] Quidnunc (Seamus Kelly), "An Irishman's Diary," *Irish Times,* 15 February 1958.

To Francis MacManus

TS. MacManus

7 March 1958

My dear Frank,

Thanks a lot for your kind letter. I'm afraid the good idea of small theaters is a bad one. The actors couldnt live on the wages given, the playwrights on their royalties. A theater of this kind isnt possible without Socialism. Even the Abbey has fallen from a very high place, helped by a Government subsidy; and actors and playwrights are afraid to write anything they think might offend the Church, the religious societies, and THE STANDARD. As for the Poster—it hangs on the wall because it is intrinsically charming: Eire holding a harp, with her gown showing in outline her activities, sport, music; but no book. It is odd that your description of what is going on is precisely what the play tries to show—the formless confusion of Ireland today, stemming from the B[lack]. and Tan period; the echo of business is business, gain alone uniting the members of both parties, with the young mind, the newer mind, revolting, and trying to get things done, led by the spirit of Father Ned. It was a shabby ending, for I didnt intend that the Tostal should have it, or any Irish theater; but was persuaded to give it as an eminently suitable drama-offering for the Festival by members of the Council themselves. They had it for months, and not till the ABishop spoke was there a word about alterations, or the demand that I should give written authority to the Producer to "alter the play according to his requirements." Well, I'll just read again what Dr. McDonald says about the Episcopacy in general, opinions that got him into a fine row; but then, he was seldom out of one. It is hard, as you say, to measure with comfort or any tittle of satisfaction the sorrow that struck you and me. However we may differ, at least we are brothers in this sad trouble.[1] I dont remember what you say I said to you, but coming from you, I must have said it.[2] On reflection, I cant see why I should be ashamed of it, though many things I have done and said since, all foolish, have rubbed away any gold that happened to be on the words. All I can do now is to try to realise the responsibilities that a belief puts upon every believer in the recognition that I am one with all men. What angers me, Frank, is how so many seem to limit the scope of what they believe in— the Incarnation. They so often put Jesus behind barbed wire, telling Him you mustnt go there; you mustnt listen to that; you should turn your eyes away from this sight. As if He went about in constant fear of seeing us making fools of ourselves; or as if He were afraid of seeing a bad line in a lovely picture, of hearing a false note in a burst of music; as if He didnt see, hear, know all things (if what they believe in be true), and was afraid of nothing; making Him into a timid member of the Y.M.'s Catholic Asso-

---

[1] Both men lost young sons.

[2] In reply to O'Casey's letter of 22 February 1958, in which he told MacManus about the blessing he had received in New York in 1934 from the "banished" old priest, Dr. Morgan Sheedy, MacManus replied to O'Casey on 24 February 1958. In this letter MacManus recalled that when O'Casey paid his last visit to Ireland in September 1935, the two men met in Dublin, and MacManus remembered what O'Casey had said to him: "You tell me you still remember and value the blessing of the old priest you met in New York many years ago. Well, I'm going to give you a jolt by telling you about something you said many years ago to me. It came back to me the other morning in the church here at the Consecration. You said once that if you could believe the bread and wine was Christ you'd go off your head with joy. It's the best sermon I ever had. You old pagan, I hope it's down in gold letters after your name." (MS. O'Casey) In the summer of 1963, in Dublin and in Devon, I read these remarks to both men, and they urged me to put it in the record—MacManus: "Yes, in gold letters"; O'Casey: "Red letters'll do for me."

ciation. I hope these sayings dont hurt you, for I wouldnt offend you for the world. I have a deep respect for you and a deeper affection.

Dave G[reene]. has been busy for a long time at The Life of Synge. It is a long and a hard job, and I do pray that it may be a fine success for the book's sake, and for Dave's too. We here, or rather Eileen, managed to put him in touch with Peggy O'Neill, Maire's daughter, whom she met in London, and Dave got valuable information from her which helped him. I shouldn't try to write the life of anyone else.

I pray a blessing on your gallant son, so bright and humorous in his affliction, and another on your wife, your family, and on you, a mhic mo chroide.

As ever,
Sean

To George Jean Nathan

MS. CORNELL

7 MARCH 1958

My most dear George,

Though not hearing from you for some time, our friend Tom C[urtiss]. rang me from Paris, telling me you had a troublesome time recently, but had now recovered. I've been told he is in New York now, and visits you each day: that is an interesting comfort; and I hope Tom will be near you for some time, for he is a dear lad. Here, things go quietly. The crocuses are showing purple and orange caps, but I've enjoyed them but once, for the weather has been bad, and I'm no longer able to face, even grimly, either an East wind or a wind from the North: red one from the east and black one from the north. I don't go for much of a walk now, even under the sun, for too many memories collide in my mind; & I prefer to stay put, writing letters, doing a little work, and listening to music—now a great calmer of sad thought.

I daresay, you have heard most about Dublin's Drama Festival, & how it tottered and tumbled when Dublin's Roman Catholic Archbishop banned O'Casey & Joyce from the Irish Tostal; & Sam Beckett withdrew his two mime plays as a protest; so now there is to be no Drama Festival for there seemed to be nothing else to put in their places. So we in Ireland go from worse to worser. No prominent man or woman has uttered a word of protest, bar a mild minor leading article in the Irish Times. However, I won't bother you more with our scant regard for courage, letting Ireland be a country of barking dogs.

I do hope you are getting back a little strength, & that the Summer may do something to revive both of us.

Breon now lives on his own, & with Shivaun in your country, the flat is quiet, & full of echoes. However, in a few weeks, we expect her back again, with many tales of all she saw, & of all whom she met, in your great Land.

Eileen sends her love to Julie & to you; & so do I, dear comrade of the Theatre; the Theater that misses you so much, & so longs to have you back again.

> *My love again, dear lad.*
> *As ever,*
> *Sean*

To Tyrone Guthrie

TS. GUTHRIE

9 MARCH 1958

Dear Tyrone,

No, I'm not prepared to give Radio Eireann the right to do the Readings. I have had enough of Ireland for a few days to come. Hilton Edwards wanted this Reading for the Gaiety more than a year ago, but neither I nor Paul Shyre (who has the License for the work) liked the idea, and so we refused. It was a good production in New York, of which I know something, for I have the Tape Recording of it, and have listened to it several times.

There is another thing, however, in which I take more interest, that I'd like to mention to you. A week or so ago Lewis-Crosby, Secretary to the Arts Council of N.I., wrote to me asking to be let read the script of DRUMS OF F. NED for possible production in Edinburgh for the Festival there, by the Group Theatre. I sent him the script and am waiting for a reply. It may well be that he (or the Group) may think the play too good or too bad for them to do; but the thought crossed my mind that you might be interested in the possible event; or, if they didnt like the play sent, I thought that, maybe, they might prefer the BISHOP'S BONFIRE, and that you might be interested in its production, seeing that you are out of a job; though this would mean entering the hurly burly again. However, if you needed a little money, it might be worth while considering.

I sympathise with you in the difficulty of keeping a home going, for I have had years of difficulty myself, and I'm by no means certain that the struggle is ended; for in the Theatre, if one tries to do one's best, the reward isnt always a golden one.

The address of L-Crosby is—in case you might like to write to him—
    The Secretary,
    Council for Encouragement of Music and the Arts,
    Tyrone House,
    Ormeau Avenue, Belfast, Northern Ireland.
All good wishes to Mrs. Guthrie and to you.

Yours very sincerely,
Sean

To Irish Times

11 MARCH 1958

THE THEATRE FESTIVAL[1]

Sir,—Permit me to say a few words about my preview and past-view of what has happened to the hustling out of Dublin of O'Casey by a Voice from the Silence.

When I wrote the play, I didn't for a moment think of Tostal or Tostal Council for the play's production. The fact of a "new play" was announced in the press, and I received a letter in July (I think) asking me to let the Council read the script. I didn't bother to reply to this request till I received a second one asking for a reply to the first letter. I then told the Council that the play was in a script form, but pointed out that I was hesitant about giving it to be read, preferring that the Tostal should be kept for the work of younger or newer Irish playwrights, but was met with the reply that no younger or newer playwright had come forward with anything suitable for the Festival. After further hesitation, I sent the script to the Council, and nothing said afterwards (except that the play was "liked immensely") came my way to warn me.

This was in early September, so that all concerned had plenty of time to mark, learn, and inwardly digest it; but no objection came till the Face appeared at the window and the Voice spoke from the air. Then fright paraded Dublin. The Bord Failte, apparently, got a fit and, running over to the Drama Festival Council, infected the members with the same fright; and the question became one of how to get rid of O'Casey, all the

---

[1] A modified version of this letter appeared as "Sean O'Casey and His Critics," *Enquiry,* June 1958, University of Nottingham. See O'Casey's letters to Ronald Ayling, 15 March 1958, note 4; and 1 August 1958, note 2.

time pretending not to see the Face at the window, or hear the Voice in the air. These infected actors, writers, columnists, and various members of the people from Dublin on to Galway; all of them running breathlessly round in widening circles to get as far away as possible from the sound of the Voice in the air and the glance from the Face at the window.

All this can be understood from your correspondence columns, in which most of the letters closed their eyes from the Face in the window, and covered their ears from the Voice in the air. The latest I have read is a long article, titled *An Bord Failte agus an Fheile Drumaiochta* (Athar Ned), by Maisie Bean Mhadagain.[2] She tells us that the Tostal Council did well to get away from the Drama Festival, for, in three or four ways, it would have done harm.

First, she says the Council will have to do deep thinking about the next Drama Festival, so that proper aims and ideals may come from what is done; that there was nothing in the whole prime-plan that wasn't clumsy and of little sense; that it was *amaideach* [foolish] to connect Tostal with the Festival, and to say that the Tostal had failed, and that the interest of the people had died down; that it was foolish to hold the Festival in May when interest in the theatre is declining, for then the people will be seeking the sunny airs of the evenings—forgetting that May has an Arctic air, and often has had one, as Goldsmith well knew when he wrote, "And departing Winter chills the lap of May."

Maisie complains that an O'Casey play was accepted without first finding out if it was worthy, and that it would be pleasant to all who came to see it (Oh, God; oh, Montreal!) They just wanted the O'Casey name, she says, and ditto with that of Joyce. Well, a good choice, and all might have been well, but for the Face at the window and the Voice in the air. She recommends that a permanent committee should be formed by the Ministry of Arts, away from An Bord Failte—a committee that would be one of sound knowledge and a true national feeling in them. This committee would have to think a long time, and wade through much troublesome work before they could hit on, or beat out, a plan that would be of the best for a Drama Festival in Dublin. She tells us it might take a year, two, three, or more to do it. It might be for years and it might be for never.

So, she goes on, her article more *amaidaighe* [foolish] than anything, or everything, the poor Festival Council has done. They can coin a committee, but where are the dramatists? Where are the plays? The drums of Father Ned would beat in vain. Nowhere does Maisie mention the be-all and end-all of the offending—that Face at the window, and that Voice in the air. O'Casey ordered out of his city, and Joyce along with

---

[2] See O'Casey's letter to the *Irish Times,* 17 February 1958, note 3. He makes a pun on Ernest Blythe's pseudonym, Beann Mhadagain, by alluding to Mrs. Maisie Madigan, a character in *Juno and the Paycock.*

him. When O'Casey goes, the Festival totters; when Joyce and Beckett follow it tumbles down.

There are other watchers guarding Ireland against enemies coming through the rye. The English publisher of "The Green Crow" sends me copies of letters he sent to the Counsellor of the Irish Embassy, London, and another to the Revenue Commissioners at Dublin Castle (ominous place, ominous name). Here is the latter letter: "It is monstrous that no decision should have been given, although almost a year has passed. Mr. O'Casey is one of Ireland's great writers (God forgive the man!) and is entitled to more courteous consideration. Why in any case it should even be thought necessary to refer to the Censorship Board so obviously inoffensive a book is almost—almost? Nay, it is—beyond reasonable understanding. On what *prima facie* grounds does a Customs officer take it upon himself to decide that this book falls into a category warranting detention? Yours, etc., Jeffrey Simmons. January 27, 1958."[3] I wonder if the poor publisher has even got a reply, even an acknowledgment, to his letters?

There we go: the streets of Dublin echo with the drum-beats of footsteps running away. The Archbishop in his Palace and the Customs Officer on the quay viva watch out to guard virtue and Eire; the other Archbishop draws the curtains and sits close to his study fire, saying nothing; and so the Hidden Ireland becomes the Bidden Ireland, and all is swell.—Yours, etc.,

Sean O'Casey

Devon, March 5th 1958

[3] See O'Casey's letter to Jeffrey Simmons, 14 March 1958, note 1.

To Irish Press

12 MARCH 1958

O'CASEY PLAY

Sir,—Permit me a few last words about—not to—Niall Carroll.

He has become very excited indeed; so much so that it cascades into an apocalyptic vision—very frightening: "When the fires of world argument are out there will be found among the residual ashes a few hard stony facts, so hot that even Mr. O'Casey will not dare to look at, never mind handle them."[1] Dear me, what a fate! By the way, aren't ashes residual in themselves?

[1] Niall Carroll, "Reply to O'Casey," *Irish Press,* 3 March 1958.

Well, he hasn't told us the names of his gossips, as I was sure he wouldn't; perhaps he couldn't.[2]

So I leave him alone with his prodigious mind and his Nameless Nobodies, sitting among his residual ashes.

Sean O'Casey

Devon. March 5, 1958

[2] Ibid., "Well, isn't this man of the theatre, who has some claims to be classed as one of the world's greatest figures, displaying a rather naive attitude in asking a man of the newspapers to break the first law of his trade, namely, that he does not disclose the source of his information." This was Carroll's explanation of why he could not reveal the names of the "competent theatre personages" who had called *The Drums of Father Ned* "very mediocre stuff"—see O'Casey's letter, "O'Casey Makes a Challenge," *Irish Press,* 1 March 1958, note 1.

To Mrs. Hugh Doran

MS. DORAN

14 MARCH 1958

Dear Mary,

You'll have to forgive me for not going to your Birthday on Saturday. I have been working a lot, & still have innumerable letters to answer, as well as to give opinion on British Romantic poets for a Moscow friend who is writing a critical work about their Poetry—though, God help me, I know little about what to say. I've enjoyed their work, & that is really all I know.

Please accept my warm wishes for many more birthdays to you, and a happy time during the hours of the coming one. Could you give enclosed stamps to Hugh. I am tired, and expect to be prostrate after saying what I can say about the Poets.

Affectionate regards,
Sean

To Jeffrey Simmons[1]

MS. SIMMONS

14 MARCH 1958

Dear Mr. Simmons,

Congratulations, though I'm afraid the Irish Sales won't make either of us rich.

I sent copies of your letters to Ireland early on, and in one commentary on the banning of the O'Casey play from the Irish Tostal Festival, gave your letter to the Irish Revenue Commissioners in full. This was published in the *Irish Times* of March 11th.[2]

It is fine that the "Green Crow" will be allowed to perch on an Irish roof or two without being stoned.

All good wishes,
Yours sincerely,
Sean O'Casey

[1] Jeffrey Simmons, W. H. Allen Company, London, publisher of *The Green Crow* in 1957; published in New York by George Braziller in 1956. The W. H. Allen edition was seized by Irish Customs Officers when the book was released in February 1957, and this unofficial ban was maintained until March 1958, when, without any explanation, it was released for sale in Ireland. See O'Casey's letter to Mrs. John T. Cooper, 23 April 1957, note 1. The book was probably seized because it contained the short story, "I Wanna Woman," which had led to the official banning of *Windfalls* in 1934, a prohibition that the Irish Censorship of Publications Board never revoked.

[2] See O'Casey's letters to Lewis Funke, 12 February 1958, note 1, and to the *Irish Times*, 17 February, note 5, and 11 March 1958, note 3, where he quotes from Simmons's letter to the Irish Embassy and the Irish Revenue Commissioners.

To Ronald Ayling

TS. AYLING

15 MARCH 1958

Dear Ron,

Got your letter. Glad to hear that you have a job, for I was afraid that you were just a poor student, finding it hard to keep things going; but now my mind is easy about sending you letters that would be wasting you away from your studies before you were earning a living.

I am afraid you and I are wasting our time, but, at any rate, you have something to fall back on in the way of wage, though I suggest that you should give more time to that M.A., than you do to my affairs. I sent another letter to the Irish Times, and attach here the appearance of it in that paper. I thought the first one clumsily written in one or two ways, and sent out another, the one I now send to you. I shall need it back again. So far, one reference has been made to it—which I enclose, which declares it inaccurate and unfair, and rebukes me indirectly for bringing the matter to the front again: they all want to bury it in silence. That was one reason why I waited till all had sunk to sleep before rousing them with an unexpected shout—a bit sardonic, but it's something they deserve. I also enclose a cutting of a criticism by the IRISH PRESS critic alleging that competent drama personages had informed him that the D. OF F. NED was "a mediocre affair"; and my reply to his comment. I am getting a bit tired of it all, for it really doesn't matter what they think or what they say.

Thanks for the quotation from Manchester G[uardian]. I may write a short note to the paper. Now about Lady G. and WBY, and their help to make me a dramatist. To save time and get away from weariness, I might say that they, helped by Mr. Robinson, wrote the plays from beginning to the end; looked over my shoulder as I wrote the TASSIE, and the other "later" plays, saying dtch dtch dtch, he's going from bad to worse; and that they edited, improved, advised, and corrected the proofs of all the biographical volumes; and that I only, with a desperate effort, signed my name to the work they did. That would be very pleasant for the Irish criters, Irish writers, and the D. Greenes;[1] but it isn't so. The one help they gave me (Lady G. and WBY) was to create the Abbey Theater for me (and others and themselves—a tremendous work) and to put my plays on when they came. That was their help, and it was good and great help, and I am grateful to them for it. I'm not sure what Lady G. refers to in her Journal. It may be that when *The Plough* had been accepted, Yeats sent me a wish to pay a visit to him—described in one of my books. He didn't like the short Love scene in the First Act—I think it's the first—between Nora and Jack; Couldn't I make it less sentimental? I didn't agree with him, and the scene remains as it was first written. This was the meeting that gave me a first shock about WBY's bona fides (he had his weaknesses). The moment I entered, he exclaimed "O'Casey, you are the Irish Doistievesky"! Now, I had just returned from a visit to L.G. in Coole Park, and there she had told me that she had been astonished WB. had never read this Author; and that she had given him THE BROTHERS KARAMAZOV to read. He didn't know that I knew he had just gotten up from reading one book by this author, and his impulsive assumption staggered me, and made me cautious of everything he said. Or, again, it may be that before this play was written, I had sent in two one-acters— KATHLEEN LISTENS IN and THE COOING OF DOVES. The first, a squib, was taken: the other returned without thanks, though it was by far the

---

[1] Professor David Greene of Trinity College, Dublin, not to be confused with Professor David H. Greene of New York University.

better of the two. I liked this one-acter a lot, and again I felt cautious
about the Abbey Directors knowing all they claimed to know about drama;
so from this rejected one-acter grew the PLOUGH AND THE STARS,
the rejected play forming the second act of the work. So, in a way, the
rejection helped me to a bigger work, but the help was never intended, and
I doubt they ever noticed its inclusion, for as far as I can remember, they
never mentioned it. I think I remember Mr. Robinson writing after *The
Gunman* had been sent in (I believe it was the Gunman) saying that it was
a pity I didn't come to him beforehand, and then we could have worked
out a Scenario together! Well, I never write a scenario. The play grows
out of an idea or from one or a group of people. Bernard Shaw, when I
mentioned this incident to him once, gave a laugh and said he didn't write
scenarios either; and that a play grew, and if it didn't it never came alive;
I agreed heartily with him.

Of course, I remained a friend of Lady Gregory's (rather she remained a friend of mine), and we wrote a good many letters to each
other; but since I lived in England, we didn't see each other afterwards.
She wished to see me shortly after the row over The Silver Tassie, but I
was too indignant to risk a meeting, for fear I might hurt her by anything
I might say: this, however, was a mistake, as I see things now. Mrs. O'C
appealed to me to see the old lady, but I just couldn't quell my indignation. I have still a bunch of her letters, but her handwriting was so terrible
that now I find it impossible to make them out; I could, if I tried hard
enough, but haven't the time. I made one into typescript, but gave it up
then.

What are "independent critics"? Every critic must be independent; if
he isn't, he just isn't one. One isn't without revenge, however. It is amusing
to read how these critics squirm into trying to let down the new play
Roger Casement[2] with fair words. I send one from the Irish Press, done
by a clever writer, Benedict Kiely[3]—evidently, they thought he'd be more
subtle than [Niall] Carroll; and another, more explicit, from the TIMES,
but with no name attached—a citizen of the hidden Ireland; afraid to give
his name to honesty. There is a Leader in yesterday's Irish Times commenting on the tweedledee and tweedledum nature of both Irish pol.
parties which in its comments shows forth the identical implication por-
trayed by two characters in The D. of F. Ned, written more than a year
ago. Still they say O'C. doesn't know a thing about Ire now!

I got Enquiry, and am writing to Mr. Gibbon to thank him for sending me a copy. I like it well, for itself, and for the reason that I have long
been wishing and telling my wish to the world, that there are more Universities in England than Ox and Cam; and that it is near time for these
to speak out about the life England lives and the life she shall live in the

[2] Roger McHugh's and Alfred Noyes's *Roger Casement* opened in Dublin at the
Gaiety Theatre on 10 March 1958, with Cyril Cusack in the title role.
[3] Benedict Kiely, "Casement Play a Simple Lesson," *Irish Press*, 11 March 1958.

future—first, of course, doing away with the threat of War on the earth, on sea, under it, or in the sky above.

You can, if you wish, publish the letter appearing in The Irish Times,[4] or make use of the one held back, or mingle bits together from both—just as you wish; but, for God's sake, don't waste too much of your time; and don't tire yourself while the asthma is bothering you. By the way, a friend of mine, another David Greene, Profess. in New York University (I knew him when he was a Harvard student, and when he was a lieutenant in the USA Navy in the last war), has written a Life of Synge. He is just getting into shape for publication, and has found it a damnably difficult job.

All the best,
Sean

Try to let me have clippings back—when you've finished with them.

[4] See O'Casey's letter, "The Theatre Festival," *Irish Times,* 11 March 1958, note 1.

To Robert Hogan

MS. HOGAN

[18 MARCH 1958][1]

Dear Bob,

Enclosed is a letter I sent to the *I. Times,* which may interest you.

An Irish critic has said, in *The Manchester Guardian,* that "the Tostal Drama Council made a mistake in arranging a play for production before its completion"; and that the "judicious help from Lady Gregory really made the early plays of O'Casey."

I have written a short reply saying that whosoever said either or both of these things are liars.

Before, he had referred to the play & "poor stuff" from what he (or she) heard.

All good wishes.

Sean

[1] Postmark. Letter is undated.

To Anne Elistratova[1]

TC. O'CASEY

19 MARCH 1958

Dear Anne,

Your letter is no nuisance, but a most interesting one, though it presents, in one or two ways, a difficulty in answering.

First, let me say that I have been plunged into the midst of a row, a dispute about an event that happened in Dublin, my native city, recently: Ireland for some time has been holding a yearly Festival of drama, music, opera, sport, games, and ballet, which is called the Tóstal. The Drama Council hearing that I had written a new play, asked, appealed for the favor of giving it a world premiere in Dublin during the Tóstal. After hesitating for some time, I sent it to them; they "liked it immensely," and everything went on well till the Catholic Archbishop of Dublin declared against any play by Joyce or O'Casey appearing during the Festival. The Council got frightened; the Irish Tourist Board, who were helping the event with a money guarantee, refused or revoked their guarantee; the two plays were dropped, and Samuel Beckett who had sent in three Mime plays, withdrew them in protest; and the whole Drama Festival had to be abandoned. I have been answering many enquiries from England and the USA, and so hadnt time to reply to yours sooner. I enclose some press-cuttings which may explain the row in more detail.

You ask me if I think the fire that inspired the best work of the romantic poets of the last century be still glowing and its pulse beating still. Here in England and in Ireland, I should say it doesnt glow; but there is still a red center—what we in Ireland call "the seed of the fire"; and I believe that this fire will blaze again; not, perhaps, in the same way, for the flames may have different colors. Science and a new conception of psychology have made us more aware of the strange forms of living activity, and, of course, we respond to the new discoveries of man and his nature; but these in themselves have a romanticism all their own. We know more now about the flower, its form and its biological activity, but its color, its shape, its perfume is as beautiful and as enjoyable as ever. Most of our English reviewers are soaked in an impression of Freudian conceptions, coming from their own minds rather than from Freud's, for they are versed in the study of this new and still misunderstood psychical science; but they carry on a never-ending chant which is a perpetual sneer, and cynically declare that man's nature can never change; and that his unconscious mind is conceived by the lower passions of the animal—as if any passion in any animal could be low! They pull up a rose-bush and

---

[1] Miss Anne Elistratova, Union of Soviet Writers, Moscow; author of "Sean O'Casey," *Soviet literature,* No. II, Moscow, 1952; work in progress, a book on the Romantic Poets.

point out the roots, saying, Look there; look at its crookedness, and the mud clinging to it; but seem to be blind to the scarlet, the white, or the yellow petals, so bright, so lovely, surrounding the one that holds it with its delightful scent. These reviewers, and, indeed, the novelists, are obsessed with the idea of "original" sin, seeming to accept as eternal truth the Psalmist's biblical slogan, "I was born in iniquity, and in sin hath my mother conceived me." They go about as if no bird sang on a tree, no song is ever sung, no flower blooms in either wood or wayside; and all is darkness. Well, in spite of this "original sin," the birds do chant on the trees, many lads and lasses sing their songs, and the flowers bloom in the wood and the wayside.

Well, here is where they go out, and I come in. I am sure as I can be that there is a swing against this stupid idea that all is woe; and that many are turning away from this crowd of cowled miseries. Just recently, a writer in THE TIMES LITERARY SUPPLEMENT, influenced by an article in THE DUBLIN MAGAZINE, written by an American teacher in Ohio University, wrote that it was time to give O'Casey a new evaluation;[2] that he was the one dramatist who faced life with hope; and that though in his plays the dirge was heard, the dance of life was always there, too; and I got this information from a young teacher in a Secondary High School in Nottingham, England. The young are beginning to sing, to laugh, and to demand a fuller life. The upsurge for life and peace, against all war, shown among the workers, the women, mothers, wives, sisters, and sweethearts, the graduates and under-graduates, in the Universities, is one great fact that will bring about a condition of life which will banish the wails of those who can see no hope or loveliness in life; and these new conditions of sensible life will bring into existence such a change that will do away with many of the reasons for selfishness, fear for ourselves, and restore the fire of romance into an amazing flame again. As long as men have their senses, they'll have something of romance within them. Long as there's sunrise, sunset, the ebb and flow of tides, the birds sing, and the flowers bloom; long as the mountains stand; long as a lad desires a girl and a girl desires the desire of man, there will be romance of life, like Keats in his poem, when he is sad—

> life is but a day;
> A fragile dew-drop on its perilous way
> From a tree's summit;

changes to

> Why so sad a moan?
> Life is the rose's hope while yet unborn;
> the reading of an ever-changing tale.[3]

---

[2] "Riches Scorned," *TLS,* 31 January 1958, a leading article inspired by Robert Hogan's "The Experiments of Sean O'Casey," *Dublin Magazine,* January-March 1958.

[3] Keats's "Sleep and Poetry" (1816), ll. 85–91.

It is but a day, a dewdrop on its way down a stem; but it is a lovely day and a sparkling dewdrop; and when we learn to live sensibly, it will be a longer day, and a less fragile drop of dew. So I believe that the people everywhere, even here, will realise this, and go their way towards achieving it. The inspiration doesnt only come from the poets, however, for many leaders have led us into the way of life—Lenin and Stalin, for instance, in your country, Kier Hardie here, Jim Larkin and Parnell in Ireland, and Eugene V. Debs and Bill Haywood in the U.S.A., not to mention Lincoln and Jefferson. But all these great souls were poets in their own way, in the way of vision.

To let you know the "significance of the Romantic poets of the last century for our times in general, and for yourself, personally, in particular" is more than I am able to do. I never had time to take thought to study these poets, but had time only to enjoy them. You see, when I had passed my fourteenth year, I was still damnably ignorant, and through a poor and painful time, I had to learn grammar, spelling, geography, the elements of arithmetic, and these had to be mastered before I could even venture to think of reading the simplest of literature. When I had done something for myself in the way of education, I set about developing the little knowledge I had, and began to buy books.

(I broke off writing to you here to go watch Television to see your Ukrainian State Cossack Company doing their wild and their graceful dances—the Battle, the Weaving of a Carpet, the Flirtation—very beautiful and ROMANTIC, and the famous Gopak. I had already seen your Red Army Assemble. My wife and children saw them in London; but I am too old now to go places, and have to be content to see them on Television— through a glass, darkly.)

When I began with books, I had to limit myself to the Classics (very, very fortunately, though I didnt know this then). These books could be picked up second-hand—books discarded by others, and sold cheaply. One could get any of them for anything no more than a shilling; mostly for sixpence or so, though, often, it was a hard job to spare even a sixpence. These books were Shakespeare, Byron, Keats, Shelley, Whitman, Emerson, Browning, Goldsmith, Coleridge—Blake came to me much later. So you see how the romantic poets came to influence my first impressions of English Literature. To describe minutely, to delve deep into how they influenced me, is more than I am able to do, for the prime reason, I think, that I am not a Critic. The Critic must have a gift for his or her Art, for Criticism is an Art like any of the others. As Bernard Shaw says somewhere— when someone asked him about honesty in a critic—There is no such thing as an "honest" critic: one is a Critic or one isnt; and I believe what Shaw said. A Critic is one who cant help criticising, and honesty doesnt enter into the art: he or she has just to set down the opinions the gift gives; a very important and very precious gift, which must, of course, be developed (like other gifts) by study, thought, and experience. I have had no experience, never gave a lot of thought to it, practised only by setting down a few random opinions, as in THE GREEN CROW, and so cant help you much in any analysis of the works of the romantic poets. One thing I am sure of—Wordsworth never influenced me; I never liked his work a lot. To me, he lacked fire; the fire that blazed in Shelley, Keats, Byron, Whitman, Emerson, and even in Coleridge. I imagine Keats to be a finer poet than Shelley; more graceful in his choice of words, and lovelier in his images, though lacking the thrust and the fiery enthusiasm of Shelley. All the same, Keats could be forthright in a declaration as when he says in twelve or thirteen lines[4] what—as Shaw said—is the essence of all that Marx and Lenin said and set down in writing.

Touching the Drama, I was influenced by none of these, for none of them was anything of a dramatist. Here Shakespeare comes first, though in my young days, before I met any of these poets, I knew a lot about melodrama; saw many of these kind of plays; and later, when a brother of mine was a carpenter in the Theater Royal (afterwards burned down), I saw at matinees, my brother getting me a grand seat for nothing, a lot of the plays by Shakespeare, then done by Frank Benson and his company; and saw Henry Irving too, a great event in my life. When I became secretary of a little National Drama Group, I began work on a play of my own, and all that I had seen and heard in the way of drama, bad and good, flooded back into my mind; so I became immersed in the dramatic mood which has remained with me, more or less, ever since.

To my mind, the present-day poets lack fire, and mutter rather than speak out, so that few can recognise what they say; though they be true poets—Eliot for instance, whose theological philosophy has no echo in either my mind or my heart.

By the way, you dont mention him who is said to have been the last of the romantic poets—W. B. Yeats; nor do you mention Olive Goldsmith, a gentle, and, to me, delightful writer. I enclose a review of a new life of him recently published which may interest you.[5] The paragraph you give from THE NEW YORK TIMES came from a personal letter I sent to Brooks himself. You may, of course, quote it as often as you wish. I was amazed at Communists here so often declaring with apparent delight their ignorance of the great works of past generations. I had a group of local Communists taking tea with me once in Totnes, and was indignant to discover that not only were they ignorant of Dickens, but despised him as what they called a Bourgeois; one of them declaring that he had never read a line of Dickens, and never would; and that they had expelled a member who had tried to vindicate his love for that great writer. I'm afraid, I gave my comrades a shock, pointing out that the ignorance of, and contempt for, great works of a past time was no mark of Marxism; but

[4] Two stanzas in Keats's "Isabella: or The Pot of Basil"; see O'Casey's letter to David Krause, 12 April 1955, note 2.

[5] Ralph Martin Wardle, *Oliver Goldsmith* (1957).

that this Deposit of Art to the glory of man was to be honored and pre-
served, not only for ourselves, but for the generations to come. Well,
there's an end, my dear Anne, to this letter. I'm afraid it wont be a damned
bit of use to you, but a waste of your time reading it. I wish you every success in the great work before you, thanking God I havent to do it; but I'd
say you were a natural Critic, and what is feasible, though hard, to you,
would be utterly impossible to me. My warm regards.

Sean

To J.E.C. Lewis-Crosby[1]

TC. O'CASEY

20 MARCH 1958

Dear Mr. Lewis-Crosby,
     I am sorry that I have decided to keep THE DRUMS OF FATHER
NED away from your Ulster Group.
     The other day, in THE IRISH PRESS, an account of a Drama Festi-
val in Meath gave us the written picture of a Very Rev. J. Holloway,
deputising for The Most Rev. Dr. Kyne, Bishop of Meath, (Revs. Revs.
everywhere) gesturing out of him as he said "The Church would condemn
in no uncertain fashion anything that would lower or destroy man's moral
life. Dramatic art must not be divorced from religion," and a helluva lot
more. That didnt matter a damn; but this Rev. was followed by a James
Boyce of the Ulster Group, the Adjudicator for the Drama Festival of
An Uaimh,[2] who said "He was in whole-hearted sympathy with Rev. Holloway," and a lot more. You can read it yourself in THE IRISH PRESS,
issue of 17 March, 1958. These canting fools!
     I want no more bother with these fellows, and so must ask you to
return Script of the play to me. I've been pestered with inquiries about
what happened at the Tostal Drama Festival. Last night THE NEW
YORK TIMES was on the phone asking further questions about what is
happening now. Ireland is being made to look a sorry sight over the whole
world. Two days ago, a young Belgian writer has been asked to write about
it all in the Belgian papers; and it has gone forth as far as Moscow. Well,
I want no repetition. Boyce can keep his whole-heartedness safe as far as
I am concerned.

[1] J.E.C. Lewis-Crosby, Secretary, Council for Encouragement of Music and of
Art, Belfast.
[2] Navan, Co. Meath.

Let Ireland say Not this Man, Joyce, but Boyce! Oh, Joyce, oh Boyce, oh boys oh boys!

The Script of the play is now in New York and I prefer it to be there than that it should be among the spitters of the Irish Republic or of Northern Ireland.

With respect to you in a very difficult job, I remain, Yours sincerely,

Sean O'Casey.

To Ronald Ayling

TS. AYLING

21 MARCH 1958

Dear Ron,

Where shall I begin, and how shall I end is becoming a problem with me. I've just sent off a long, long letter to a Moscow friend. She is writing a critical book on the romantic poets (English—Shell; Byron, Keats, Wordsw), and has asked me a lot of questions about their work, their views, and if there is any room for them in present-day life.

Well, so much for Anne [Elistratova]; now for Ron. The question of the way Lady G. made the "first great plays": This curious belief always puzzled me, and now it puzzles me as much as ever; but I was about to write to you an addendum about it which, I believe solves the whole question. The "early plays" referred to, and the changes made in them by suggestions (by Yeats or Lady G) meant, without much doubt, the *earliest* plays: looks like I'm going to have early plays, earlier plays, and earliest plays—like the Gov, the other gov. the otherest gov. in OUR MUTUAL FRIEND. These earliest plays were those which were never accepted; and these were the ones that were altered by suggestion to my terrible cost in time and effort. It was all a history of frustration that only a gaum [fool] (or a titan) like myself could have withstood. The first play was THE FROST IN THE FLOWER.[1] This came back with a review saying that the central character was too dominant, and reduced the stature of the other characters too great a degree; that if he was modified, they would consider it favorably. Well, I took their advice, and sent it in again. They returned it to me saying I had modified it too much, and that the first draft was on the whole better than the second. I flung the play aside. Then I sent in THE HARVEST FESTIVAL.[2] This got an answer saying it was

[1] See the Abbey Theatre's "Reader's Opinion," 26 January 1920, Vol. I.
[2] *Ibid.* The MS. was eventually found and published, *The Harvest Festival* (1979).

well, or splendidly conceived (I forget which), but badly executed. I hadnt the slightest idea of what "executed" meant; and, even now, I've but a hazy idea of its meaning. I flung that one aside, too, and began another— THE CRIMSON IN THE TRICOLOR—all these plays were written out in pen and ink, and no copy kept, though, of course, I had had the first two scripts returned to me. Now came a long drawn-out waiting. After I dont know how long, a letter came from Lady G. saying that she had read it through one night in bed—if I remember right—adding that she loved three of the characters in it; but that they would have to get it typed, for no one could profitably read such writing.[3] So I waited. Then came a letter from Lady G. saying that they might produce it. Then a letter came from Mr. Robinson asking for a copy of the play, for, in moving to Foxrock, he had lost [the] original script. I had no copy, couldnt rewrite it, and so had to bear it, sit down, and begin another—THE S. OF A GUNMAN. A year later, R. found the play; it was typed, and a letter from R. quoted a criticism (from WBY),[4] to which I sent a hot reply;[5] adding that I was in the middle of a new play, and so wasnt a lot concerned. (Then it was, I think, that Mr. R said it was a pity I hadnt talked it over with him, so that we could make out a scenario together!). Anyway, the play was never accepted finally, and I asked for the MS to be returned. The play was lost again. Since then, R. declared he had recovered it, and would send it back. I wrote again, but he couldnt find it. Then while Eileen was at THE BISHOP'S BONFIRE [Dublin, 1955], he mentioned he had it, but would send it on later. It never came. Then Trinity College held a book exhib showing MSS as well, and the Librarian asked me for an MS.[6] I thought this a good chance to get the long-lost MS back, so wrote Librarian telling him of it, and if he got it from Mr. Robinson, he could show it, and welcome, and then could return it to me when the Exhib. closed. He wrote R. who told him that the MS couldnt be found: that an American had searched through his papers, but couldnt discover it. So there it lies still, wherever it may be; and it will never come back. A long history for a play. Now, I've no doubt that the play wasnt too good; but I'm convinced that HARVEST FESTI-VAL and FROST IN THE FLOWER were a damn sight better than many done before and since by the Abbey. So after *The Gunman* had been written, I had decided that the advice of these counsellors was rather to be avoided than to be taken; and so separated myself from them forever. I dont understand why it was said about the love scene in P. and the S. that I was writing about something I had read in books. What books? I had read then only the classics, for they were the only books that could be picked up second-hand for sixpence or so. From what I discovered later

3 See Lady Gregory's Critique of *The Crimson in the Tri-Colour*, ? October 1921, Vol. I.

4 See W. B. Yeats's Critique of *The Crimson in the Tri-Colour*, 19 June 1922, Vol. I.

5 See O'Casey's letter to Lennox Robinson, 9 October 1922, Vol. I.

6 See O'Casey's letters to R. D. Dougan, 16 April and 11 May 1957.

on, I'm sure it was Yeats and Lady G. who read "the books." By the way, when the Abbey returned from Paris, and did their production of *The Plough,* G. Fallon gave a bitter suggestion (nearer a demand) to the Abbey that the phrase "my little red-lipp'd Nora" should be cut out of the play as silly and sentimental. If I remember right, one of Brahms' songs has in it a similar line. Anyhow, I've said the same thing myself to more than one girl in my time. The fact is, I believe, that Yeats for one reason or another, wanted to be my boss; to dictate to me the way I should go, but I wasnt having [any] of that now; for I had learned that none of them could teach me anything in the way of drama.

Since writing the last letter sent to you, I remembered that there was one change made in the **P. AND THE S.**; but not suggested by Y. or Lady Gregory. It was the song in the pub scene, the bawdy one. Lady G. had read the script but hadnt mentioned it. After the play had been accepted, before Yeats asked me to visit him, I spent a week or more in Coole Park—when she told me of Yeats's ignorance of Doistievsky [sic]; I guessed in some way, she had missed out the song, or didnt get its bawdy meaning; and I was very fond of her, and didnt wish to hurt her in any way. So I casually mentioned the bawdy song in the 2nd act. My! how she fluttered. Well, I hushed her by telling her that I had no objection to its removal—simply for her sake. Years after, when I read about the Abbey, I learned that Mick Dolan was in a terrible way about it, and wrote letters to her, quotations from which (where I learned about it) were in, I think, Peter Kavanaugh's book on the Abbey published in America; or was it in her own Journals?[7] What strikes me as odd is that so many of the Irish dramatists (there are hundreds, for in the last competition for plays organised by the Abbey Thea., over two hundred were sent in, all so bad, they said, that no prize was given), buried all their lives up to the neck in their own green sod, dont seem to be able to write a play, in Eng. or Gaelic, worth a damn. The oul' sod doesnt give them a second's inspiration.

What was in my mind in 1929 is hard to say: I was writing to Lady G. off and on just because I knew she liked to hear from me, having, for some reason or another, a "gradh" [love] for me. I was then in a bad way financially, and wrote without (to her) thinking very much about what I was saying, for the affair of *The Tassie* lingered on in my mind, and home problems were uncertain and trying—we then had the big lad to think of, and all the outlay that meant an anxious time (years in fact) for Eileen and me; so I cant remember very much about what I thought then when I wrote the letter mentioned to her. However, one thing is certain: England had

[7] *Lady Gregory's Journals, 1916–1930* (1947), edited by Lennox Robinson. See the entry for 2 September 1925, p. 87: "[Michael] Dolan writes objecting to *The Plough and the Stars.* 'At any time I would think twice before having anything to do with it. The language is—to use an Abbey phrase—"beyond the beyonds." The song at the end of the second act, sung by the "girl-of-the-street," is impossible.' "

given me a new conception of things, not only in Drama, but in other arts as well. We went to picture galleries and revelled in all we saw, and started collecting, when we could, prints of the Impressionists, Post-Impressionists, and these, as well as exhibits of living artists, had a big influence on Eileen and on me. I learned a helluva lot from England, and, inevitably, my thoughts changed on many things, drama included. I began to know a little about music by listening to it, and reading Ernest Newman's articles. All this widened my conception of life, and, indeed, the Abbey Theater gradually began to shrink in my mind, and I saw how meagre and mean were the plays that the Abbey did, so I wandered into a wider field of drama; reading Strindberg, talking to Shaw, with Charlotte listening, at times, disapprovingly murmuring an objection to something I said; and also, I began (had begun) to write to G. J. Nathan, to read his books, and to send (at his request) articles for his new venture *The American Spectator*. The chapter, "A Protestant Kid Looks At the Reformation,"[8] first appeared in this brave and witty monthly. So you see, all these things were flowing through my mind, and I began to feel that the drama needed a new conception, a fresher life, such as were appearing in Music and painting. Joyce, too, was speaking to me now, my Dublin brother, and I loved his voice. There was no question of abandoning the "O'Casey idiom," for that would mean the abandonment of life; but I judged dimly and vaguely then that music and painting should appear in any future play I tried to write. This I have since aimed at, how successfully or unsuccessfully, I dont know. There is a quote in a clipping of a reply I sent to an article by the critic of *The Irish Press*, taken from the *Virginia Quarterly*,[9] which seems to show that this element of fantasy has been adopted by other dramatists. Brooks Atkinson in an article, said that he "noticed a change in the form of drama since the writing of *The Silver Tassie*," instancing the DEATH OF A SALESMAN, by A. Miller as an example. Whether he be right, or the author of the article in the V. Quarterly, I dont know. I think your assumption is right—that I had no "radical" intention of altering my plays, for that would mean altering myself; but just meant that the present-day drama (1929) wasnt what I conceived the drama should be. There is, though, a distinct difference between the first three plays and the *Tassie*, and, I think, in all that follow.

The version the Sister gave to L.G. of my experience in hospital is incorrect, told, I imagine, as it appears intentionally.[10] This letter is long

[8] Sean O'Casey, "A Protestant Kid Thinks of the Reformation," *American Spectator*, July 1934; reprinted in *I Knock at the Door* (1939).

[9] David Krause, "The Playwright's Not For Burning," *Virginia Quarterly Review*, Winter 1958.

[10] *Lady Gregory's Journals, 1916–1930, op. cit.*, p. 320: "*1929 (Dublin, in hospital)*. On Sunday Sister Baptist had come and sat beside my bed. She asked a great deal about Sean O'Casey. He had come to their dispensary just about the time his first play was being rehearsed, *Shadow of a Gunman*, for some remedy for his eyes. He had brought a bottle for it. And he was vexed when some poor woman came for some stuff she wanted, and the Sister said No, she had not brought a bottle, she had

enough already without recounting it here. In a subsequent one, if you are still interested, I'll retell it.

About A. Clarke: Somewhere the clipping lies, but I havent the energy to search for it. I sent it when it appeared, to G. J. Nathan, and he replied to say he couldnt understand it, that it was due to envy, and not to waste time thinking of it. I dont [want] to hurt Austin Clarke, for he has had a tough time of it financially. He cant sell many of his books, and how he lives has often been a wonder to me. He is timid by nature; a poet undoubtedly, but lacking fire and thrust. I believe he is bound to be a little envious of those who do better than he does, and this is natural; but he has integrity, and that is hard to keep in a country like Ireland. I really have a respect for him, and wish he was more courageous because I think he'd do better if he were. Recently, I read in *Irish Writing* a chapter of autobiography, and it seemed to me to be the best thing he had done, promising well for the whole book, which, I understand, he is working at.[11] I do hope it may be a fine success. Let us forget about the article on *Cockadoodle Dandy*.[12]

I wasnt very interested in the Hawthornden prize.[13] While in Dublin, John Good, then sub-editor of *The Irish Times,* meeting me in the Abbey Foyer, told me I had won it, but that I should have to go to London to get it. I'm afraid I told him rather rudely that they could keep their prize. One rule was that a book or a play had to be sent in for judgement (in a competitive way) before the prize could be formally awarded. I refused to do this. I have never sent anything of mine to anyone without first receiving a request to do so. For instance, G. J. Nathan wrote asking me for an article for his AMERICAN SPECTATOR, and any article of mine appearing anywhere was first asked for; for I'm a proud fella, though, in my mind's center, I realise how foolish all this is. I dont like publicity. I refused to go on Television (MONITOR) to talk of drama with Tyrone Guthrie; I refused an appeal by my English publisher to do a television interview with Attenborough to talk about THE GREEN CROW. I dont think it was any sense of fear that kept me back, for I did a more than half an hour interview and actions—walking through the Marychurch streets, walking in the garden, etc, chatting away, for the National Broadcasting Co. of America, and got a universal acclaim as "a born actor." I just dont like exhibiting myself. When I came to London, Lady G. was there, and it was she

---

been told before that they give the medicine free but they don't supply bottles. Sean was vexed, and then he and the Sister went to the store where empty bottles are kept and they found one for her. . . ."

[11] Austin Clarke, "Capel Street, A Chapter of Autobiography," *Irish Writing No. 37,* Autumn 1957. The first volume of Clarke's autobiography was later published as *Twice Around the Black Church* (1960).

[12] Austin Clarke, "Cock-a-Doodle Dandy," *Irish Times,* 6 November 1954, an unfavorable review of *Sunset and Evening Star* (1954).

[13] See "London Honours Mr. O'Casey," *Irish Times,* 24 March 1926, an account of the awarding of the Hawthornden Prize to O'Casey; reprinted in Vol. I.

who persuaded me to go to Aeolian Hall to take the prize publicly. I didnt like the experience.

Lastly, and by the way: HALL OF HEALING wasnt furnished from experiences in St. Vincent's Hospital, but from a Poor Law Dispensary in North William Street, N.Strand, Dublin. The old cod was just as I drew him; so was the doctor, so are the patients. The episode of the three bottles actually occurred. I mentioned this Dispensary in one of my books; but fearing a libel action, I gave the name of the good doctor to the bad one. Afterwards, I got a letter from the doctor's daughter saying how she rejoiced that her father wasnt what people thought him to be; that she herself, even thought him to be the reverse of what I said he was! I didnt try to deliver the poor girl from her illusion. Well, a long letter; longer to me, for I am tired of all these unhappy, far-off things, and battle long ago.

I hope you are feeling better. Weather very tiring here; haven't ventured out for weeks; bitter winds, snow showers, and slashing sleet.

All good wishes. Are you wasting your time with these things?

As ever,
Sean.

To Paul Shyre

TS. SHYRE

25 MARCH 1958

Dear Paul:

Glad to get your letter. Shivaun landed this morning at Southampton, and Eileen was there to meet her. I wasn't feeling fit enough to go with her, for all, and more, of the pains of old age prick and pinch me, so that I feel black and blue like poor Caliban after Prospero's sprites have gotten to work on him. We expect Shivaun and Eileen home in a few hours time, and I shall be very glad to see her again; indeed, I will. I understand she brings back a cargo from your USA. Well, it was a grand experience, and I'm delighted that her first wide one brought her into such close communion with your country. The thanks of my heart to you and Kathy for your kindness to her.

It will be fine if you can get the [Theatre] De Lys, and that the COCK will give its first American crow. About [Tyrone] Guthrie coming over to do—Direct—DANDY, I don't know; but here's an opinion or two: It would mean an added expense, fares, etc; I fear, he doesn't care for the play. When Eileen was in Dublin during production of THE B'S BONFIRE, she had a number of chats with him about me, and she was surprised, to learn that he didn't like that particular play; why neither she nor I know. However, if you did decide to ask him, and he consented, he would be too much of an artist not to do his best with it; but, personally, I'd prefer one who liked the play. To take over the Irish Drama Festival and do what they rejected, would be fine, but why in the SUMMER? I'd rather, looking at it selfishly, hope for a longer run for my own play; but the idea is a very attractive one, indeed.

Now, a question for you to answer: The head of Northern Ireland's Council for Encouragement of Music and Art (an Arts Council) asked me to let him read Script of D. of F. NED, for THE ULSTER GROUP THEATER, so that they might do it at the coming Edinburgh Festival. I sent the Script to him to read, not committing myself in any way. Since then, I've read of an Adjudicator of plays, judging a drama festival in Co. Meath, whereat the Right Rev. someone declared the Church would speak with no uncertain voice about any play that was dangerous to decency, faith, or morals, and the Adjudicator agreed "wholeheartedly" with the R.Rev. even, that when such a play was in rehearsal, actors should walk out of it, and "prevent it from taking the air," and this Judge was one of this Group Theater. So I am hesitating about giving it to them. It might be a good thing, maybe, to put on THE D. OF F. NED while the ban was in the minds of all, even before the DANDY. What do you think? It would take some doing, but no more than, I think, P. DUST. But, I daresay you are damned busy, and I shouldn't be bothering you. No use, Paul, of worrying about the Film—any how, we didn't lose what we never had. I never thought much about it, for I've been so often left wanting, that I never now long for anything till it's on the table before me, and my hand holds it tight.

If things allow, I, we, shall be delighted to see you again. I understand that someone—was it [Robert] Briscoe or [James] Carroll, the former, lord mayor of Dub. last year, the latter of this—said had he had anything to do with the Tostal, he would have banned the plays, too.

Let me know quick as you can what you think of the idea of doing "Drums" in Edinburgh.

As ever, with love to Kathy,
Sean

To Brooks Atkinson

TS. ATKINSON

31 MARCH 1958

My dear Brooks,

Thank you for your letter. I hope you passed your slight vacation quietly, not even reading the NYT[imes], for you needed a rest. Shivaun is home with us again, and brought with her a cargo of souvenirs from almost all places in the USA; very charming a lot of them, too; with a host of Tourist booklets, and quite tidy-sized vols. describing the various States, which I am reading myself, learning more and more about your heroes and historic places. She is still delighted with all she saw and met on her travels. By the way, I hope Oriana took a few days off from her never-ending vitality. She should take an odd spell away from work, too. We all need a rest. Even the heart that can never safely stop rests between the beats.

I am as happy as you are that my name appears on the Silver Tray: an engraven thought of respect and affection.

The Tostal affair was a miserable business. Ironical, too, for the play was one full of hope and endeavor animated by the spirit of a young priest who, though he doesn't appear, is the soul of the young in their Tostal activities. It was built on, and conceived by, the work of a Canon Hayes leader of Muintir na Tire—People of the land, and a contact I had with another priest when I was in N. York in 1934, Father Sheedy, a life-long friend of Dr. McDonald's. I daresay the ArchB. was mad and had it in for me over the B's Bonfire. These men are a dreadful pull-back to the younger clergy.

I enclose a letter appearing in the *Irish Times,* which, I think, helps me to explain what happened. It was wholly unexpected by me. I had given the play with great hesitation, wishing that a younger fellow would have the chance, and reduce envy. They had the play for months, liked it immensely, and had begun to discuss Director and Cast with me. Then came the fiat from the AB, not against the play specifically, but against O'Casey. Since then, not a single writer of any kind has said a word against the fiat, only the *Irish Times.* The universities remain silent, so do the politicians, so does the Irish Academy of Letters, so do the leaders of the Protestant churches—the whole land has been enveloped in a web of silence. The remarks made, mostly by those who haven't read it, are telling the people that the play was "sorry mediocre stuff indeed." Now, a lot of the major clerics are exclaiming that if any plays appear that they think bad, the "Church will speak with no uncertain voice." It isn't that there aren't many (there are a lot) of the intelligentsia who abominate the fiat, but they are afraid to say a word. It is ironical that I place the play in the town of Doonavale which means "Shut his mouth"! Paul Shyre has the play now, and thinks it a fine one. He is thinking it might be a good thing to do the whole Irish Tostal Drama Festival in New York—my play, BLOOMS-DAY, and some Mime plays by S. Beckett.

However, these things are what I most wanted to tell you. A young literary critic, Anne Elistratova, of The Union of Soviet Writers of Moscow, has written to me. She has written a History of English Literature, and now is preparing a criticism of the works of the Eng. Romantic Poets—Shelley, Byron, Keats, Blake, Coleridge, Wordsworth, and I have also suggested Goldsmith. She was asking me to give her a few opinions, seeing that I, too, seemed to be romantic in a lot of my work; and asking if I thought the influence of these poets had ceased to have any influence. Now comes the more interesting question: "There is also one more question which I feel tempted to ask you. In a review of your "Green Crow," by Brooks Atkinson /NYT18.III.1956/ you are quoted as saying 'I am a Shelleyan Communist, a Dickensian one, a Miltonic one, a Byronic one, and a Whitmanian one, like all those who thought big and beautifully and who cared for others, as I am a Marxian one, too.' Could you tell me whence are these words taken? I wish very much to be able to quote them in my turn." I have written her telling her that the quote comes from a personal letter written to you, and (assuming that you wouldn't object) I gave her ready permission to quote them. Of course, if you object, I shall write to her withdrawing my permission; but I'm sure you won't mind. Odd how a letter goes; to you, into the NYT. into Moscow, read by A.E., and probably now, into other magazines in Russia. She has already written a review of the G. Crow in the Russian Magazine, "Literary Questions."

Well, dear Brooks, that's all for the present, except to send my love, and our love, to Oriana and to you. I'm afraid that poor George [Jean Nathan] will have to put up with many limitations now. We all have to when the time comes. I don't like to write to him too often for fear of bothering him. I too have had to realise that what was common to me a few years ago, has gone forever from me now; but we must just make the best of what is left. Again, my love, and our love to you both.

As ever,
Sean

To David Krause

TS. KRAUSE

31 MARCH 1958

My dear Dave,

Many thanks to you for your kind cable-greeting on my birthday, when I reached my 78th year of blossom and battle. You have heard, I daresay, of the scuttling of the Tostal drama by the Archbishop of Dublin, who declared he would say no prayer while O'Casey was in Dublin; O'Casey and Joyce, the two Dubliners. It looks like the most cowardly and meanest things that has happened in Ireland so far, and that's saying a lot. I enclose some clippings which will give you a synopsis of what happened. Don't spend much time over them, for the incident is of little importance to any other than the Irish, and to those only who are in Ireland. A bit of news: Last quarter an article on my later plays appeared in THE DUBLIN MAGAZINE. I get this, and read it. It was written by a Bob Hogan. Later, there appeared in the TIMES LITERARY SUPPLEMENT a Leader called "Riches Scorned," built on this article, and I wondered who Bob Hogan might be.[1] I have never met nor seen him. Then came a letter from him, and I discovered he was an American, attached to the Staff of Ohio State University. He requested very earnestly for a look at THE D. OF F. NED. I sent it to him, and he liked it very much, saying it "was one of my best plays." He has sent a letter to the T. Lit. Supplement saying this, and, he tells me, an article to COMMONWEAL. However, the real news is that he read your article in the VIRGINIA QUARTERLY,[2] and has told me he's writing to you.

I sent a script, too, to Paul Shyre, and he tells me that he loved it, and that it is a grand play. I fear, though, that these two—the one I don't know and the one I do—have a slant towards my work; and whether their verdict on the latest play be right or mistaken, I don't know. Of course, I hope they are right.

Give my loving thanks to your 155 Students who sent me the cable-greeting of affection of my birthday. May they all be right good Americans, and take a fearless part to make their Country greater in all the busy stir of industry and all the arts of peace. I have just sent an article in honor of May Day for the May-day number of NEW TIMES, called "The Day the Worker Blows a Bugle,"[3] all workers, students as well as the teacher. I ended it with "On this first day of May, in the city squares, under the birch tree or the oak; under the cedar of Lebanon or the palm; in the sandy places and the cold snows; or where the rich grapes grow, the worker blows a bugle: a moment for a dance and a song; a kiss from a girl, and a merry meal for all of us who are "too busy with the crowded hour to fear to live or fear to die." So may it be through life with all my comrade-students, and with you, my dear friend, Dave.

The mistakes in this letter are due to a violent influenza cold that has me only half aware that I am here; but I'm fighting it with care. Shivaun is home again, and has brought a cargo of brochures, pamphlets, and tourist

---

[1] See O'Casey's letter to Robert Hogan, 3 March 1958, note 1.
[2] See O'Casey's letter to David Krause, 21 January 1958, note 1.
[3] Sean O'Casey, "The Day the Worker Blows a Bugle," *New Times,* May 1958, Moscow; reprinted in *Blasts and Benedictions* (1967).

slips home with her—the History of the USA; and very interesting a lot of them are. I learn more and more about your Country.

My love,
As ever,
Sean

To Joan Littlewood[1]

TC. O'CASEY

31 MARCH 1958

Dear Miss Littlewood,

Here's a coil! Before I got your letter, I had sent a subscription to the Defence Fund (as mentioned in THE STATESMAN AND NATION), and I can see no chance of doing anything else for you.[2]

An Irishman isnt a suitable one to interfere in England's internal affairs, theater or state; and this long-pressing question of the Lord C. must be solved by the English themselves. If you have ignored the law before, why not ignore it now? You'll not win in any court of law over the L.C. You will have to fight on your own home ground: refuse to pay any fine, and resist any attempt to close your theater; as the Irish used to do when the landlords sent police and soldiers to evict them from their farms. England is cluttered with these pest-pets of a long-dead past—mayoral robes, maces, swords, horse guards blue and red, knights and barons, this order and that one, searching the vaults of parliament for gunpowder, while hydrogen bombs hover overhead; court wigs and gowns, lord's day observance society, tall hats at garden parties, eton suits and harrow hats, and in the midst of them all, this old stuttering carcase of an effigy of a lord chamberlain getting in the way of the drama-artist, supported by the alberys, the littlers, and the tennants,[3] who believe in a way they dont be-

---

[1] Miss Joan Littlewood, Theatre Royal, Stratford, London, E. 15.

[2] Miss Littlewood's Theatre Workshop production of Henry Chapman's *You Won't Always Be On Top,* which had opened on 12 October 1957 at the Theatre Royal, Stratford, London, had been prohibited by the Lord Chamberlain because the actors were adding improvisations not in the script originally submitted to the Lord Chamberlain's office. A report of the Lord Chamberlain's action appeared in the *New Statesman and Nation,* 29 March 1958, in a letter setting up the Theatre Workshop Defence Fund, signed by Kenneth Tynan, George Devine, Peter Hall, Wolf Mankowitz, and Richard Findlater. Miss Littlewood wanted O'Casey to give her a statement of protest that her solicitor might use for her case.

[3] Bronson Albery, theatre director; Prince Littler and H. M. Tennant, theatre managers.

lieve the gospel, that drama has everything to do with making money; with the phila or the BBC symphony orchestra playing at the proms, amid great cheering, Elgar's land of hope and glory.

It is many years now since I had anything to do with the English Theater, and I'm in no way eager to have anything to do with it now. It might be better if the young people who are fit and old enough to fight and die for their queen and country (doing a grand job—as the bemedalled bastards of generals say standing over their heap of dead) had a vote so that England might be cleaned up, and all these effigies thrown into the ashcans.

All good wishes to you.
Yours sincerely,
Sean O'Casey.

To J.E.C. Lewis-Crosby

TC. O'CASEY

1 APRIL 1958

Dear Mr. Lewis-Crosby,

I regret that I must ask you to send back the script of THE DRUMS OF FATHER NED. I have now arranged for the first production of the play to be given in New York.

It is all very well to say that Mr. [James] Boyce has not, and had not, any connection with the Ulster Group Theater (Mr. [Harold] Goldblatt in a letter to me, says so, too; but admits that Mr. Boyce did act "semi-professionally" for his Theatre; so it is quite possible that other members of the Group may have similar opinions as expressed by Mr. Boyce; unfelt at the moment, but ready to arise if an occasion occurred such as arose in Dublin when the R.C. Archbishop issued his fiat against O'Casey; so I can never be sure).[1] On a number of occasions, both in THE IRISH PRESS and THE IRISH TIMES, Mr. Boyce has been set forth as belonging to the Ulster Group Theater, and no contradiction of this claim has been made by you or by Mr. Goldblatt, or any other member of the Group.

As the Script was sent to you, and not to Mr. Goldblatt, for whom I have great respect, I am asking you for its return.

I have received such bitter and persistent opposition in Ireland, that

[1] See O'Casey's letter to Lewis-Crosby, 20 March 1958.

it is much easier for me to shake her dust from my feet, and go where they know how to respect an honest and an open mind.

With all good wishes to yourself,
Yours sincerely,
Sean O'Casey

To Paul Shyre

TS. SHYRE

4 APRIL 1958

Dear Paul,

Thanks for your letter. Shivaun is settling down, but she was very tired, for the Tour was a rushabout one, and took a lot out of her. However, she saw much of your Country, and loved it a lot, which was the main thing of the tour, for if it had been to any other country, I'd have done my best to persuade her against going. She returned with a cargo of goods, and I have now a whole colony of fine shirts of American shape and texture; with your fine Russian cap to shelter my aged head from the sea winds that sweep over us and into the house during the winter and spring. Weather here still bitterly cold, with sharp frosts at night, and snow falling a few miles away. Thanks a lot for the cap.

I agree with you about the Group Theater, and have written a refusal and have asked for the Script back. A previous letter (written before I wrote to you did the same thing, but they have replied appealing to me to reconsider my decision, so I've sent the 2nd letter confirming my refusal). They have had the play for three weeks, but in two letters asking me to alter my decision, they never said a damned word as to what they thought of the play! I haven't the faintest idea whether they like it or no; whether they consider it good or bad. It is quite likely that they are influenced by the opinions of the Dublin lads who never read it, and would play it in such a way as to make it appear to bear out the opinions of those who have already declared it to be the worst ever written by O'C. I had an experience in the first time of the PLOUGH when Eileen Crowe doing Jenny Gogan got frightened, saw her priest, who advised against her playing it, and she refused to do the part in the middle of rehearsals, a week before the play was due for performance.[1] Fortunately I got an actress who was,

[1] Eileen Crowe objected to many of Mrs. Gogan's speeches and, after consulting her priest, refused to say the line, "Ne'er a one o' Jinnie Gogan's kids was born outside of th' bordhers of the Ten Commandments." She was replaced by May Craig. See O'Casey's letter to Lennox Robinson, 10 January 1926, note 1, Vol. I.

not only as good, but a damned sight better, to do it; but the fact remains that I can no longer trust an Irish player, living and working in Ireland, to act in any play of mine other than the first three. So I have decided to refuse the chance to the Ulster Group, and await the return of the script. I, of course, prefer that THE DRUMS should get its first performance in the USA if at all possible, and welcome your idea of trying to get it on. I'm afraid I can't advise you about a Director for the COCK. What about him [Stuart Vaughn] who directed the Readings? Or P[hilip]. Burton? But this is a decision you'll have to make yourself; even do it yourself, if you feel fervently enough about doing it, and have full confidence in yourself to do it.

By the way, were the Readings ever published?[2] I have a vague idea that booklets came to me of the printed version, but I was ill then, and can't remember clearly. Perhaps, I'm confusing them with the booklets of PURPLE DUST that did come, or am I?

I have just come out of a bout of Influenza, and still feel a little unaware of the world and of myself, but am nearly allright again.

I am looking forward to the summer, as is everyone here, but wondering has it gone astray on the way home.

By the way, if you decide anything definite about the DRUMS, I have a few little phrases—two—to add, and a few to take out, with a word change in a few places, about six or seven trivial changes in all; and these I'll send on when you are in need of them. I think I sent the music for the airs in the play; but if I haven't, let me know, and I'll let you have them when you want them.

Today, I restarted the peeling of potatoes.

This morning, I got a letter from the Chancellor of Kansas University telling me that the O'Casey "WISDOM" film was shown again by NBC. I hope to God the poor American people won't get fed up looking at the old Irish gob pottering around his estate in the village of St. Marychurch.

By the way again, a Robert Hogan who is on the staff of Ohio University, Athens, has written to the London TIMES LITERARY SUPPLEMENT praising THE D. OF F. NED. He had an article on my later plays in the DUBLIN MAGAZINE praising them, and this was the subject of a Leader in the TLS. recently. Now he has written, he tells me, an article on THE DRUMS OF FATHER NED for COMMONWEAL, the American Liberal Weekly. I daresay they may publish it. It probably goes for the Tostal Drama Council (as he did in his letter to the TLS), and the Irish writers who declared against the play. You might be interested in the article, specially as you think of doing it.

Shivaun wants to know if you have any knowledge of Ray V. Johnson & Charles R. Wood, James's Theater Building, as play producers. A

---

[2] Shyre's three adaptations were published: *I Knock at the Door* (New York: Dramatists Play Service, 1958); *Pictures in the Hallway* (New York: Samuel French, 1957); *Drums Under the Windows* (New York: Dramatists Play Service, 1962).

friend of one of the touring Co. has written a play, and this company wants to get it; but playw. is hesitating because he never heard of them. He should, of course, have sent his play to an Agent, and have let them deal with it. If you have to make inquiries, don't bother—you've enough to do with Shyre & O'Casey already.

Eileen, Breon, send their love; Shivaun sends her thanks and love; and I send you all the bessins I can think of. Amen.

Thine,
Sean

To Robert Emmett Ginna

TS. GINNA

5 APRIL 1958

My dear Bob,
Greetings to you! It's some time since I wrote to you, but I was busy with my last play, and then busier with the miserable happening that fell out over its Dublin production when his lordship, the Dublin Catholic Archbishop spoke out against an O'Casey play being done during the Tostal Festival. The Tostal Drama Council sagged at the knees immediately they heard the VOICE. Well, it's over now, and Paul [Shyre] has the play, and is to try to get it done in the late spring if he can get a suitable theater. At the moment, I've just recovered from a sharp attack of influenza, which let me in a condition fit only to throw stones at anyone who came in my way.

I have to thank you for the fine book about Abe Lincoln you sent to us, with its host of pictures, which I am now beginning to read and enjoy; for, before, I was busy, and a bad spell with my one good eye kept me from reading as much as I wanted to. So now, I am walking along with Lincoln, talking with him, and generally, and in particular ways, thoroughly enjoying his gallant company. Thank you so much for sending such a fine and intensely interesting book to the O'Casey home.

I daresay, you are busier than I am, getting material for future programs in the WISDOM series. It must be a hard job finding a suitable figure, and harder, when youve found one, to get him into shape for the televising; for we who are so bloody wise tremble before the THING that shoots out into the watching and the listening world.

Breon is painting away, and seems to have suddenly jumped into a helluva good improvement with his work, and is painting now with a confidence and surety that he didnt seem to have before; and he is satisfied himself that he is suddenly doing work much, much better than any he did previously. At the moment, he is organising an exhibition of a group of younger painters here in Torquay and district to be held in Torquay in less than a fortnight's time—seven or eight artists and about fifty pictures. I hope it may be a success, anyway it is a fine experience for him. He has enlisted Shivaun in the work of designing the programs, posters, etc, and both of them are very busy. I have just passed by my 78th birthday. 78 of Yeats's "great black oxen" have passed over me, and, if I'm not broken yet by their passing feet, be God, I have a few deep bruises; but still one of "the indomitable Irishry."[1]

I have to thank you and Kathy for your great kindnesses to Shivaun while she was under the New York sky.

The weather here is just indescribable. The winds are black and bitter, snow falls on Dartmoor and in Cornwall, and bus loads of holiday makers have had to be ploughed out of the snow-drifts. Our daffodils, that stood up to and faced the winds of march with beauty, are bet, and sink level to the chilly clay, lost and bewildered. Ice gathers round you if you venture to look out of a window, and all Marychurch is in the deep freeze. Looks like it'll be a long time before the summer is acumen in. The Hebrides are now the one warm place in England, and if I had the way, it would be Over the sea to Skye with me.

Here I am blethering away, and not asking a question about yourself. Well, Bob, agradh, how are you, and how do you stand? How is the work going, and what are your plans for the future? If the summer ever shows her nose here, maybe we might have the pleasure of seeing you, and of having a long chat with you as in the days of lang sin.

Give my love to Kathy, to Bob G. if you see him (I shall write to him one of these days), and take a good share of the love for yoursel'.

As ever,
Sean

[1] A double allusion, one to Yeats's play, *The Countess Cathleen* (1892):
> The years like great black oxen tread the world,
> And God the herdsman goads them on behind,
> And I am broken by their passing feet.

and another to his poem, "Under Ben Bulben" (1938):
> Cast your mind on other days
> That we in coming days may be
> Still the indomitable Irishry.

To Franklin D. Murphy

MS. MURPHY

5 APRIL 1958

Dear Mr. Murphy,

Thank you for your letter telling me of the Television show. I hope the NBC won't wear out the patience of the viewers—they must be a little tired of watching the old face smile, and tired of hearing the patter of the foolish old Irishman.

I have a collection of "Beanies" now—not precious like your books: a fez from Egypt; a gay, sparkling cap from India, a false fur one from Russia; a skull-cap from Switzerland; a big-peaked crimson cap from USA, one worn by those on the land; maybe the farmers of Kansas State.

It will be fine when the sun shines hard. I've just been reading about your University, and a great University it is, a glory of the sunflower State.

Thanks, too, for the story of the long, long trail after books for the Library—many of them never heard of by me; and all giving out the perfume of an older & more leisurely age.

Why don't you wear a "beanie" if you feel like it, or if it makes you feel a little less uncomfortable when the air blows bitter on the head? As for me, I never cared what people thought of what I did, or what I wore, so long as what I wore was decent, & what I did could not possibly do harm to my neighbour. God can have no objection to an elder head wearing a "beanie"; & this opinion counts more than man's.

I am learning a lot more about your great Country from my daughter, Shivaun, who has just returned from travelling through the U.S.A. from one end to the other; & she is a living chorus of chanting praise.

All good wishes to you.
Yours very sincerely,
Sean

To Zöe and Jessica Wanamaker[1]

MS. WANAMAKER

[5 APRIL 1958]

My dear Zöe and Jessica,

My love to you both & my thanks for the wonderful Fudge and the Wonderful Turkish Delight. I have been ill, and I have had to swallow

---

[1] Zöe and Jessica Wanamaker, the young children of Sam Wanamaker.

medicines—oh, I didn't like them; no, I didnt! They left a horrid taste in my mouth, so I had to leave your wonderful sweets aside for awhile; but I kept them safe, you bet, though, of course, I'm sharing them now with Eileen and Shivaun—one at a time for each of them, and two at a time for myself, you understand. Oh, yes; the sweets are too lovely to be too generous sharing them out.

And I loved, dear Zöe, the grand pictures you painted on the box of Fudge. I love Fudge and I love Turkish Delight, and, now, that I'm better, and free from medicines, I can sit down and eat them, keeping them from disappearing as long as I can; which is a hard thing to do. I remember you, Zöe, well, & all the lovely things you showed me when I was sleeping in Abby's room. I haven't seen Jessica yet, but I hope to when the summer begins to come again.

Thanks again, my dear Zöe and Jessica, for your very kind thought of me an my Birthday.

The God of Jacob, Isaac, and Abraham, bless you both, and Abby, and Mama and Daddy as well.

Your old friend
Sean

To Rose Russell[1]

TS. RUSSELL

9 APRIL 1958

My dear Rose,

Thank you for the clippings. I've read quite a bit about these young people who have found a harmony in life—I read "The Guardian,"[2] a brave and very sensible Journal. The boy you mention is, of course, a physical misfit. We are near helpless before these diseased elements of life: all we can do is to fight for a Social life that can no longer create these piteous types. Don't brood over individual cases where thought is futile. You see, dear, in any case, the mind was allright; in fact, even then, vivid, and so the love of Mrs. Casside was vital and of a sure substance of encouragement & help.

I imagine the NBC did make a mistake of some kind. Anyway, I

---

[1] Rose Russell (1900–1965), union leader, for twenty years Legislative Representative of the Teachers Union of New York.

[2] *The Guardian*, the Progressive news-weekly, formerly *The National Guardian*, founded in New York in 1948 by Cedric Belfrage, James Aronson, and John T. McManus.

know the organisers of this program, & they are grand lads, and great friends of the O'Caseys.

I enclose a few words to Dr. Pauling. I have been fighting this fight now for years. I was thinking as I typed it of the words—said in all the churches just before Easter: Consummatus est, falling from the lips of Jesus on the cross. What an irony it would be now, if the same words flashed from the lips of humanity falling asunder in the ball of flame from the H. Bomb—"It is finished!" Humanity, lovely life becoming a hideous and a terrible vapor.

Personally, I never believed it would. I never felt anxiety about the world use of it. I felt in my inner soul that Life would not suffer it to happen, though I fought with all who were fighting against it from the beginning. Indeed, I began it before the Bomb came into existence, as shown in "The Silver Tassie" where in one scene, the Stretcher-Bearers chant a verse, replied to by the maimed men on the stretchers chanting.

> Carry on, carry on to the place of pain,
> Where the surgeon spreads his aid, aid, aid;
> And we show man's wonderful work, well done,
> To the image God hath made, made, made."

Done some few years ago in Vienna & Berlin, it was banned and denounced as a play written as propaganda for the World Peace Council— "a gang of Communists"; though the play was written more than 30 years ago. It all seemed futile, but thoughts never fail to fall on some ear somewhere; and today there is a world conscience for peace and commonsense man has never known before. Hurrah!

I'm just getting myself out of a sharp experience of an influenza cold, so this writing may seem a bit shaky; but the heart of it is sound and vibrant. Hurrah again!

My love to you & all your Comrades.

As ever,
Sean

I have just lost a very, very dear friend in George J. Nathan[3]

[3] George Jean Nathan died on 8 April 1958, at the age of 76. See O'Casey's letter to Brooks Atkinson, 16 April 1958, note 1.

To Dr. Linus Pauling[1]

TS. RUSSELL

9 APRIL 1958

My dear Dr. Pauling:

I give you an Irish handclasp enclosing a prayer for us and a song for you as a tribute to what you are—a Leader of those determined to deliver the peoples from a prison of anxiety, fear, and death. It has been a long struggle, and there is still some way to go, to the strife's center, till the military-minded politician and the gaudy-coated general are shattered into silence by the shout of the people for peace.

I have known three young people in our little village of St. Mary-church who have died of Leucaemia—the son, the only child, of a widow working-woman, the son of a local Anglican Rector, and a son of my own; die of the disease that the effect of atomic radiation eagerly seeks to plant deep into the vital forces of the human body. Doctors dread its entry into their hospitals, for they know that they are helpless to interfere with it: those who carry it within them are bound to die. It is the greatest curse that God or nature has inflicted upon the stupidity of man. This glorious and terrifying power that Science has delivered into the hand of man brings him disease, darkness and death, or it brings him light, health, and a surer life; and it is for man to choose which it is going to be.

You, Dr. Pauling, have chosen the better three, and we, too, make the same choice, and I fervently believe that the peoples of the world are hurrying to make the same choice, too.

I have taken an interest in the atom since Rutherford rent it asunder. I have been an Associate Member of the British Atomic Scientists' Association for many years, and have read all their monthly bulletins; I read the English NEW SCIENTIST and your own THE SCIENTIFIC AMER-ICAN, so I know a little about the possibility of thermo-nuclear power to blast us all or to bless us all, and so, for me, it is a happy and most worthy thing to be allowed to go with you in your fight to abolish the very conception from the mind of man of this power's use for the destruction of human life, or any other life, anywhere upon this beautiful earth of ours.

My deep regards to you, Dr. Pauling, and my blessing upon the great work you have done and are doing for all our sakes.

Sean O'Casey

[1] Dr. Linus Pauling (1901–   ), American scientist and fighter for peace; awarded the Nobel Prize for Chemistry in 1954; devoted much of his energy after World War II to the struggle to abolish nuclear weapons and war.

To S. E. Capper[1]

TC. O'CASEY

10 APRIL 1958

Dear Mr. Capper,

Thank you for your kind letter. I have had one from Mr. [Harold] Goldblatt saying practically the same thing about our friend Mr. [James] Boyce. Thanks, too, for the return of Script of the play—DRUMS OF FATHER NED.

I'm afraid I shall never cross that particular Border over which there are so many damned disputes. Another Border is looming in front of me now, which must be crossed, willy nilly, one day or another. I should hope indeed that the reaction of Belfast to my play (had it been produced) would have been far different from that of Dublin, for Belfast's sake, not for mine; for it would be of deep indifference to me whatever the reaction might have been; as I am indifferent to Dublin's as concerning myself. Not boasting this, merely a fact. The play's in N. York now, where they think something of it. My heart's a crowd of wishes, and one of the biggest is that Belfast, Dublin, or Cork (Galway's outa the question till Time or God bears Bishop Browne off) might lead, not only Ireland, but Europe in some art, Lit. Mus. Paint. Sculpt. or even Jazz; but there's no sign of it yet. I dont agree that the Newspapers always win; it depends on many things that I havent time to go into. It wasnt the newspapers said that about Boyce; it was some local reporter, and he must have gotten the tale from Boyce himself. I couldnt go to Belfast to talk; I talk now only through my books and my plays.

By the way, I was wondering what you, Mr. Lewis-Crosby, or Mr. Goldblatt might think of the play; but you three wise men answered not a word. Well, silence is golden now all over Ireland: the less said the sooner mended. Sweet is the mouth that keeps closed (a Gaelic proverb). Ireland has learned them all. Dublin is braver: those who hadnt even read the play said the most about it. However, the event may make a fine chapter for a new book—The Silencing of the Drums. I dont remember your father, though I remember "the Ivy Church."[2]

All good wishes to you and the Council.

Yours sincerely,
Sean O'Casey.

p.s. I hope I got your name right.

[1] S. E. Capper, Council for Encouragement of Music and the Arts, Belfast, Northern Ireland.
[2] The Ivy Church, North Strand, Drumcondra, Church of Ireland.

To Robert Hogan

MS. HOGAN

11 APRIL 1958

Dear Bob,

I hope Commonweal will publish your article, and, if they do, I shall be most interested in reading it. Your letter to TLS was a fine one, from my point of view, and I thank you for taking the trouble to write it.

I've just had a bout of Influenza, & am engaged in fighting a way back to feeling normal; otherwise I'm busiest in trying to select from piles of letters those I must answer; and, in between, trying to put down a few reflections in words for a possible book in the far, far future. One article—rough draft of thoughts—is called "Immanuel,"[1] so you can see I need your prayers. I have a number of notes, serious, quizzical, & satirical, for other articles; but God knows when I'll get a chance to coax them to grow into a fuller plant. I don't know what happened to MS of first plays—the ones previous to "Gunman," except one MS. of "The Crimson in the Tricolor." L. Robinson has it, and I can't get it from him. When I sent it in first—all written in longhand—he lost it for a year; found it, it was read; L.G. liked it; they got it typed, & thought of doing it; but finally rejected it. Then L.R. lost it again when changing to another address, & wrote to me saying he'd send it on. He didn't. When Mrs. O'C. was in Dublin for the "B.'s Bonfire," he told her he had it, & must send it on; I wrote to him, and got word he'd lost it again. Trinity College had a Book Exhib. & asked me for an MS.[2] I suggested they should get the MS. L.R. had. They wrote to him, & were told he couldn't find it: so there it is. It's of no value, except the value of having a MS written by me so many years ago. I can't recollect very much about it.

Paul Shyre has the Script of "F.Ned," & hopes to do it in N. York one day. He thinks like you about it; &, naturally, I hope he's right. It was a great pity about the Tostal Drama Festival going west. I wish I hadn't sent them the play; but they begged me for it, & I thought it might help (God forgive me!) on a sturdier spirit in a land soaking itself in despair and cynicism. Ironically, it was born out of the efforts of Canon Hayes, of Muintir na Tire (lost now by recent death;[3] and a big loss, too), & words written to me by an old priest-friend, Dr. McDonald, when I was in N.Y. in 1934.[4]

Do look after your young ones; these colds & coughs are sometimes dangerous. I hope they are better now. Warm regards to them, Mrs. Hogan, and to you.

[1] Sean O'Casey, "Immanuel," *Under a Colored Cap* (1963).
[2] See O'Casey's letters to R. D. Dougan, 6 April and 11 May 1957.
[3] See O'Casey's letter to Francis MacManus, 22 February 1958, notes 3 and 6.
[4] *Ibid.,* notes 4 and 6.

I feel pretty sad over George J. Nathan's death. George Jean was a very dear friend of mine: I loved him very deeply; & I believe he was very fond of me. He is a great loss to the American Theater, and to the Irish Theater, too.

My daughter Shivaun has just told me she was in Athens during the tour of Dublin Players—a pretty poor Group.

We have a son 26 & Shivaun 17 now: we had another son once.

Again, I hope your young ones are allright now.

Sean.

To Miss Marguerite Buller

MS. BULLER

14 APRIL 1958

Dear Marguerite,

Thanks for your kind letter. We are all well—now. Mrs. O'C. had a bout of Influenza, and I, eventually, imitated her; but both of us are alive again. I have, too, been busy answering many inquiries about the Tostal Drama affair. It was, of course, the Archbishop's ban on any play by O'Casey during the Tostal that frightened the Council in demanding power to change the play. They knew I'd refuse, and so tried to get out of it gracefully. They had the play for months, liked it "immensely"; it was "eminently suitable" for the Tostal, &, in fact, they were quite excited about it, till the Archbishop spoke. The failure to hold out, from my viewpoint, is of very little importance; it is Ireland I grieve about. There they are (some of them, young lads with no deep thought) carrying on a senseless, destructive fight against Ulster, killing their own kin; while the rest of them cower down before a finger shaken at them by a Roman Catholic cleric.

I'm not competent to give any expert opinion on what is called "Modern Art," even "Modern Drama." All I have to offer is my personal feeling towards a lot of it. There's no doubt about such men as Matisse— whom I love—Picasso, & Braque; but quite a lot of the more recent artists give me no enjoyment: tho' I think "Genesis" a tremendous work. It isnt a portrait of a woman; but a Symbol of the Genesis of all life; and the sum of life itself, & all that life has done, calls for a tremendous figure. Whether Epstein has succeeded or no, I can't tell. I haven't the glorified opinion of Osborne that all others have; but beware! This is one playwright commenting on another. I can't understand any woman putting up for an hour with J. Porter;[1] and, I think, he, and the rest, lacks a sense of humour. Ionesco I just can't stick. Beckett is very clever, very sincere, & compassionate; but again, I can't believe that life is lived in a never-ending tenebre despair.

I have had a hard life, many trials, many sorrows, but my eyes insist on seeing the lilac bloom, the laburnum's golden glory, my sense inhales the hawthorn's fragrance, & my ears will go on listening to the song of the birds, the laughter of children, and my mind frequents the active thoughts of life.

I hope your sister may be with you again, and that you may renew the joy of her companionship.

My love to you.
As ever,
Sean.

[1] Jimmy Porter, the hero of John Osborne's *Look Back in Anger* (1956).

To Brooks Atkinson

TS. ATKINSON

16 APRIL 1958

My dear Brooks,
Thanks for your letter and the clipping giving a picture of the solemn and sad yew and cypress trees. It is a big loss in many more ways than one, but not a too mournful one. George had a full life, made the most of it, and gave a lot of himself to the world of the Theater; and so we can lay him to rest with resignation; and then turn to go on with life.

Eileen and I sent a cable of sympathetic grief to Julie, but I haven't written to her, having nothing to say. I, too, hesitate to say anything just now, considering the conversion as a disturbance of spirit, and shouldn't like to say anything, however unintentional, that would hurt her in such an emotional time.

Two surprises came to me from the accounts of George's last days— this odd and almost inexplicable conversion to the R.C. Faith,[1] and the

[1] The secret of George Jean Nathan's conversion to Roman Catholicism a year before he died was disclosed the day after his death, in the *New York Times,* 9 April 1958: "A solemn requiem mass will be offered for George Jean Nathan, drama critic, author and former magazine editor, who died early yesterday morning. . . . Mr. Nathan, sharp-tongued iconoclast who prided himself on being a hedonist most of his life, was baptized a Roman Catholic on October 9, 1957, it was announced yesterday. The 76-year-old dean of Broadway critics died in his apartment in the Royalton

fact that he was so well-off. It is a comfortable thought that Julie will have no cause for financial worry (if as you say, she minds her step), and that she will be free to live safely without any necessity to take a lot of thought. Odd, too, that George didn't leave anything to the Church. However, he made a wise division of all he had, and the award should be very interesting, though I haven't a lot of faith in awards.[2] The big loss is that of the Theater, but he leaves a grand lad behind him to carry on the great work.

As for entry into an Order, Brooks, they'll take her, I imagine, readily enough, if she brings in a good dowry to them.[3] I think I remember George telling me once that Father McGinley (now Monsignor) was a law-relative—brother to George's sister-in-law, or something of that kind. He sent me his Breviary from Philadelphia when I was in New York—why I don't know. It all seems strange to me; but then there are a damn lot of things in this world that are strange to me; and one must take them as they come and as they go.

I agree with you that Julie must experience some sense of relief now that the unequal struggle is over, and that George is at rest after a strenuous and well-filled life.

I have seen death so often and in so many shapes—in hospitals, on the streets, at home, at work on railway buildings, in quarry, that it has no surprise for me now. I've reached the age myself—going on 79—that leaves me for the remaining time in a waiting wayside station for him to come.

In the meantime, we must go on in life, and you must not be too mournful, me lad.

I'm glad you liked the letter in the I. TIMES. Lord Longford, of the Gate Theater, has refused to let A VIEW FROM THE BRIDGE to be done "in his premises." A new play has had to take the name of God out of it, and a crozier has had to be changed to a crutch. Ireland is now entangled by clerical laocoon serpents; they are spiralled round everything done, everything said; but a new monthly—THE PLOUGH—liberal paper is busy making a brave fight for a little freedom. I do all I can to

---

Hotel, 44 West Forty-Fourth Street, at 12:15 o'clock yesterday morning. He had been ill for two years. Mr. Nathan had received the last rites of the church last Friday from the Rev. Charles McManus of St. Patrick's Cathedral, the priest who had given him instructions and baptized him in his apartment last October. The Rev. Timothy Flynn of the Chancery office said yesterday that Mr. Nathan had been a weekly communicant since his conversion and had spent much time developing arguments for 'doubters.' Miss Haydon was also received into the Catholic Church, a month following her husband's conversion. His parents, the former Ella Nirdlinger of Fort Wayne, Ind., and Charles Naret Nathan, a Parisian lawyer, were both partly Jewish, but his mother was a practicing Catholic, a close associate said yesterday."

[2] In his will he had set up a fund for the award of an annual George Jean Nathan Prize for the best drama criticism in America.

[3] His widow, Miss Julie Haydon, announced that she planned to enter a Convent. She later changed her mind.

help it; and the Protestants have gotten out a new monthly, too—FOCUS—which may help Ireland to be a little more liberal in thought and idea.

Meantime, I go on adding to my colored caps. I have now a fez from Persia, a gay sparkling one from India, a brilliant crimson cap with a big peak worn by the American lorry-driver, a Russian one of false fur, and, as I write this, I'm wearing a blue-black cap, red button on top, red peak, and a big Red K to its front; worn by the students on Kansas University Campus, sent to me by the Chancellor. So you see, Brooks, I'm adding to my riches.

There is a trenchant article about the Tostal Drama Festival Council in the last number of the English magazine, PLAYS AND PLAYERS by an Irish drama critic[4] that couldn't appear in any Irish journal—a pity, but it is good to see it even in England.

You must be damn tired of this letter; so I send my love to Oriana and to you.

As ever,
Sean

[4] John Keyes Byrne, "Playwright Under Pressure," *Plays and Players,* March 1958. Byrne is the Irish playwright who writes under the pseudonym of Hugh Leonard.

To Paul Shyre

TS. SHYRE

21 APRIL 1958

Dear Paul,
Many thanks for your letter. Peter Ustinoff may be a good choice. He is certainly a man of the theater, a fine sense of humor, very clever, and unafraid of a little fantasy; but I can't advise you definitely, though I imagine you might make a worse selection, always provided that Peter likes the play.

I agree with you that the theater vacant willing to take D. of F. NED was altogether too small; and I agree with Jane [Rubin] that it is a bad time to put a play on when the weather is beginning to let the people think of the open air; it would be hard for a play to "catch on." I'm in no hurry about it, for, if it be any good, it won't waste waiting. I could get it published, but want to wait, if possible, till production so as to be sure of its final form. It is always a nuisance to find that the published form of a play needs a change here and there, discovered in rehearsals. My first 3 plays were done first, and so needed no change, so too was

THE B'S BONFIRE, and it needed none; but RED ROSES, PURPLE DUST, SILVER TASSIE, and W. THE GATES did. Few changes needed, except in the case of the last play; but I don't like to find that even a change of one word can't be inserted into an already published form. So, I shall wait till I see if we can do the play before I send MS to a publisher.

After writing to you, I saw Breon reading a paper-covered booklet, looked at it, and found it was PICTURES IN THE HALLWAY, published by French. So I must have these booklets hidden away somewhere safely. I have the scripts of PURPLE DUST. I'll have a look for those of **P.** in the Hallway: they must be somewhere. I hope you may manage a tour of the play so as to have a few dollars falling into both our pockets; but don't kill yourself trying to forge out one—COCKADOODLE is more important.

Don't bother any more about those two producers that Shivaun asked about. You have too damn much to do already. I've told her to tell those interested that they should get an Agent, and not expect persons 3000 miles away to advise them.

Thanks for the photos. They were fine, and I shall keep those showing my name displayed from a Theater in New York City.

I've read about the reception of the Russian Assemble by New York in the English papers—Irish ones haven't mentioned it. The Tostal Affair is in the news again; they have now "Abandoned the scheme for a Drama Festival in September, which they had hoped to arrange, and don't know whether there will be any Drama Festival next year or no." Irish Actors Equity are in an uproar about it, and are holding a general meeting on the 27th to deal with it, and the loss of employment it means. They are to "discuss the situation. Correspondence between the Union and the Board will be read, and there will be a full discussion of the events which led up to the original postponement of the Festival on February the 19th."

So it hasn't died down, because the Actors don't get too much work to do, and many are idle, and all were looking forward to a full time during Tostal Week. Maybe, the Archbishop's victory won't be such a hilarious one as some think it was. I hope so. Equity asked me, or extended a warm invitation to me to come to their Garden Party held during the T. Week; but I told them at my age the only G. Party I could think about was one in the G. of Eden.

Well, so much for the news here. Breon has organised a Torquay Group into showing a number of pictures in the Municipal hall at Torre Abbey, and it has turned out to be a fine success, and has aroused an interest never shown so far in the exhibition of pictures. He is, naturally, very pleased about it, and so are we all. Seven or eight young lads and lasses showed six or five pictures each, and a number of students here had a little room of their own. Breon and Shivaun worked like trojans making curtains, dyeing hessian for the walls, and painting posters, and they made a very colorful and attractive display. I went myself, and I was well pleased with it all.

Had a visit from a young English lad [Ronald Ayling] (23) a teacher in Nottingham and student in N. University, who is keenly interested in my work. He lost mother and father by a bomb when he was nine, and a sister who was six—a terrible experience. Oh, war, war!

Give my love to Jane and Kathy.
All the best, with love, to you,
from Eileen and me.
As ever,
Sean

To Mrs. John T. Cooper

MS. CSU FULLERTON LIB

22 APRIL 1958

My dear Georgie,

I have to make this a short one—have been ordered (advised) to read little, write less. A painful corner of my one good eye stays a fortnight or more, goes for a week, and returns so I find it easier then to sit with eyes closed; but, damn it, I can't keep them closed forever.

Thanks, dear, for the Magazine, and it was very interesting reading, tho' I couldn't get over it all. Curious that a relative of Ibsen should find a home in Iowa; but a helluva lot have found homes in all the States. The Rev. Mr. Pike is going to have a hard time if he persists in being as brave and broadminded as Jesus. Odd how so many try so hard to fence in God; and they call us, Communists, atheists! The Tostal affair gave me some trouble—letter-writing—but no anxiety. I am personally indifferent; but Ireland is harmed. The Actors (Irish) Equity is in an uproar: they expected a hectic period of work during the Tostal weeks, but now many of them will be idle; there is to be no drama festival in Sept. (they thought they could get substitute plays by then, but couldn't) and they say there will probably be no drama festival next year either.

Well, Georgie, May is coming close to us now. I hope you are minding yourself, and not doing too much gardening. Stooping may be bad; walking is the best exercise for you.

You will soon have a lot more to do, &, probably, Mrs. Taylor may be a help (it is wonderful the way mothers talk together. I have listened to them scores of times, when I was a boy; when I lived in the slums; and when I became a father of children meself), for experience with children brings much wisdom, if we be fit to receive it.

I need hardly say, Georgie, how I hope you will have an easy time, & that your little one may be a good comrade for your friend's ruddy-headed son.

My blessings on you, & my love to John, & to you.

As ever,
Sean

To Seumas Scully

MS. SCULLY

24 APRIL 1958

Dear Seumas,

Thanks for your letter and for the clippings. Someone poured a shower of the new "Catholic" paper, "Hibernia" over my head the other day—why, I don't know. Wasn't the "Standard" sufficient? This must be but a note—my good eye is troublesome, & it is too painful to use it for long.

I haven't been in Belfast, &, I fear, shall not be able to go there anytime.

I am very glad you have found a new job, which, as things go, seems to be a fair one. I take it you've given up the idea of carving feet.

I don't think we're going to get many remarkable plays from Ireland. Johnston's "Scythe and Sunset"[1] should be something worth seeing. The Tostal Drama is off for Sept., & they say it isn't likely there'll be any next year either. The new Deers' Cry is echoing still.

All good wishes
Sean

[1] Denis Johnston's *The Scythe and the Sunset* opened at the Abbey Theatre on 9 May 1958. In his Introduction to the published edition of the play, "Up the Rebels," *Collected Plays* (1960), Vol. I, Johnston says that this play about the 1916 Easter Rising is linked only by its ironic title to O'Casey's *The Plough and the Stars,* "the play of which the title of mine is an obvious parody." See also O'Casey's letter to Ronald Ayling, 28 February 1958, note 1.

To Robert Hogan

TS. HOGAN

25 APRIL 1958

Dear Bob,

I have had to read your article slow.[1] I have developed some whore-son infliction in the corner of my good eye, and it handicaps continued reading because of its nagging pain. It is lasting, coming for a fortnight or so, then hiding itself for a week or, maybe, more, then coming again. One just has to put up with it, for I've been advised to stand it rather than risk a permanent removal.

Perhaps it is just as well to have to read slow instead of skimming over a page like the flight of an indifferent Ariel. Anyway, I read your article with great interest and unexpected amazement. I have seen myself in a strange glass—one more mirror in my house. You are certainly a Critic. Of course, you are right about the early verses (and about some of the later ones, too), but I am not ashamed of them, for I have a vital (and maybe everlasting) defence to make for them: If there be a God, and I was brought before Him by some aesthetic apostle to answer for them, I should say: Lord, they were the best I could do at the time; they were an effort towards the development of the talent which Thou Thyself hadst given me.

One remark only of yours I am inclined to protest—the white laughter of children and the red joy of grave youth goin' gay.[2] I can't see much wrong in this: there's My luv is like a red, red rose; the red badge of courage, the red rose of youth; the red wind from the east, the white wind from the south; and the red and grey spirits of Middleton and Macbeth. I was more than surprised to see myself anyway near Swift, for I have read little of him. I still love Shelley, but Keats I love more; and Milton, Byron, and most of the romantic poets. I have never consciously studied any poetical law or rule; I don't know one of them; and I have often declared that I am no poet. Any rhythm or any melody in what I have written is made by the ear: I seem to hear, though I don't even murmur a word, the sentences as they are written at first go, or at a second look, or again when the ear listens for a third time.

Yet mistakes come and mistakes go, but full satisfaction at what has been written never eases the heart.

Now for the amazement: It was caused by the inclusion in your

[1] Hogan had sent O'Casey the MS. of an article, which later appeared as "The State O' Chassis: A Study in Style," in his *The Experiments of Sean O'Casey* (1960).
[2] In his article Hogan had objected to the language in one of the songs in Act III of *Red Roses For Me:*

Fair city, I tell thee that children's white laughter,
An' all th' red joy of grave youth goin' gay,
Shall make of thy streets a wild harp ever sounding
Touch'd by th' swift fingers of young ones at play!

article of the fable of the spun-glass houses.[3] No one else ever mentioned it. It was written first for TIME AND TIDE, whose editors didn't like it; didn't like anything I wrote about the theater. The Editors, Lady Rhondda and Miss Phoebe Gay[4] (I hope I have the name right) begged me to become the drama-critic of their paper. I refused, saying I was not a critic. They insisted, coming to my play in London several times to persuade me. At last I consented to try for awhile. I wasn't the sort of critic they wanted. They thought I'd hop off to the West End to see every tom and dick who put a play on the stage; but I was interested in the Theatre, not the W. End. It wasn't long till I saw that I was no longer needed, and the one dignified thing to do was to let TIME AND TIDE, with its two editors, go to hell.

So as no one mentioned the fable, as no one seemed to think of anything of it, I thought, too, that it was no more than a quip. Then it suddenly comes again before me as something worth including in THE GREEN CROW, though I hadn't even thought of adding it to the nest of articles there. Well, well. Still, it is gratifying to realise that the little effort was worth a kindly nod from a very intelligent and critical mind.

I think your chapter to be a well-reasoned and clever review, and I wouldn't venture to dispute anything you say in it; though I do hope that I am really half as good as you make me out to be.

The Tostal affair is still busy with itself. The Irish Actors Equity is in an uproar over it. They have sent delegates to the Drama Council, to Bord Failte, and got cold comfort. The attempted substitute drama festival in Sept. has been abandoned, and it seems that it is very unlikely that any drama festival will be held even next year. Many idle actors expected a hectic time of employment during Tostal time; but, now, they realise that in the theater things will be more idle than ever. They are holding a big general meeting on the 27th to argue out the whole question. I can't see that they can do anything, for they can't say anything critical of the Archbishop's ban. Here, in England, the Bishop (Anglican) of Coventry arranged to hold a great Art and Music Festival in the ruins of C. Cathedral, but the Protestant Lord's Day Observance Society pointed out this was illegal, and the Bishop had to abandon it. The Bishop said he believed this Art Festival would be pleasing to God, but Protestants think it would hurt God's feelings if it were held on a Sunday; and, besides, more important than God's feelings, it would be illegal. What a lot the poor artist has to put up with! By the way, I think I remember you asking me to return your MS in a previous letter. Did you? If so, let me know, and I'll return it immediately; but I'd like to keep it.

All good wishes, with the hope that your children have gotten over their colds.

Sean

---

[3] Sean O'Casey, "Sainte-Beuve, Patron of Poor Playwriters, Pray For Us!" *The Flying Wasp* (1937).
[4] See his letters to Lady Rhondda and Phoebe Fenwick Gaye in Vol. I.

You may well be right about last act of "D. F. Ned." I'll look at it again, tho' I fear nothing can be done now.

To Joseph Stein[1]

MS. STEIN

28 APRIL 1958

Dear Joe,

Eileen has sent some old pictures of the first production of "Juno." They aren't much good, but they are all we have. I don't think we ever had photos of this play. But why go with these old far-off methods? Why not try newer shapes & signs? Since it is to be a musical, so somewhat gayer in another form, why not go in for dress a little more fanciful: & maybe, more colorful? A brass button or two on Boyle's coat, bell-bottomed moleskin trousers, a ship as a badge on his peaked cap, etc; Joxer having on his dress some of the signs of a clown; Mary flippantly dressed; Mrs. Boyle as the only sensible one, neat & soberly dressed: Johnny's face pale, lined & haggard, with haunting lines on it. Maisie Madigan a cascade of Jewels—big beads of many colors. Bentham gaudyily-dressed, & so on.

And, by the way, having heard you are thinking of Tony Richardson as Director, why not Bobby Lewis, the Director of "Brigadoon"? I think, too, Jacky McGowran would be better as Joxer (if you can get him) than Cusack.

Excuse this hasty note. Haven't been too well; but, of course, am eager the show should be a success. If these remarks don't interest you, don't let them bother you. Just forget them all.

All good wishes to your wife, your children, & to you.

As ever,
Sean

---

[1] Joseph Stein (1912–   ), playwright and librettist of musical comedy.

To Joseph Stein

MS. STEIN

10 MAY 1958

Dear Joe,

I strained a heart-muscle recently, somehow, & had to cover my head away from the world for a week or so, but I'm allright now. Thanks for your letter. I am an old friend of Melv. Douglas (he directed "Within the Gates" for me years ago), & we got on fine. I'm sure he would be good; but tell him not to bother too much with the "Irish" accents—there's a score of different accents in Ireland. I imagine Eileen Herlie would make a fine "Juno."

For "Joxer," I prefer Jackie McGowran to C. Cusack; but C. is certainly a fine actor.

Records haven't come yet; but it takes a long time for anything to come over the sea from America now; ships seem to go at the pace of a row-boat—over the sea to Skye manner.

Regarding shape of arrangement, as I said, I've no experience of "Musicals"—I wish I had, for playwrights should be well up in all forms done in the Theater; but circumstances forced me to begin late, and I had no time, no time, no time.

One thing only: I think the musical should be brighter in spirit & look than the play, for it is in another form, &, actually, a different work.

That is why I made the suggestions sent in my last letter to you.

My love to Sadie & to you, with a blessing on your young ones. Amen.

As ever
Sean

To Richard Watts, Jr.[1]

MS. WATTS, JR.

10 MAY 1958

Dear Dick,

Thanks for the clipping of your Article about George.[2] It was, I think, a very fine tribute to a comrade-critic; and, in my opinion, an accurate es-

[1] Richard Watts, Jr. (1898–1981), drama critic of the *New York Herald Tribune*, 1936–1942; drama critic of the *New York Post*, 1946–74. Retired in 1974. See O'Casey's first letter to him in Vol. II.

[2] Richard Watts, Jr., "Two on the Aisle," *New York Post*, 17 April 1958. He devoted part of this column to a consideration of the important influence of the drama criticism of the late George Jean Nathan.

timate of that strange man, strange in the hour of death as he was throughout his hours of life. I knew him by his reviews, & by intimate association
with him during my few months stay in your Country; and we got on very
well together. He had all the charm and kindness you praise, not only to
me, but to others which both of us met from time to time where I was in
New York; but, as you say he could be very cold and unkind when a
darker spirit possessed him; and I've seen him be even cruel, according to
my way of looking at things, with some who, as far as I could see, did not
deserve it. But George's nature couldn't bear irritation, &, I think he was
cruel merely to protect himself from any inrush on him of irritation by any
chance meeting, or by any attempt of one to associate himself in company
and conversation with George, which many seemed eager to do. One has
to go warily with proud and arrogant souls. Yeats was another such man,
too. But, all in all, George had a deep and abiding love for the Theater, &
labored hard to preserve the Theater's dignity, humor, grace, and pathos.

Shivaun had a passionately fine time in the USA, and came home
laden with reminders. She didn't care for the touring Co., (all Irish), but
loved the American scene, and led me through many a place up north,
down south, & in the middle states; giving me a life (or some of it) of
General S[tonewall]. Jackson (one of my early heroes, fifty years ago,
after reading his life). Washington, and Lincoln, & Jefferson, too. She is
half-American now; so am I and so's Eileen. After having had a touch of
Influenza, somehow, I strained a heart-muscle; & had a timid week of it;
but am all right again by all appearances.

It was fine to hear from you, & realize you hadn't forgotten an old
warrior in the battle of life & battle of the Theater.

> *My love to you, a mhic o.*
> *As ever,*
> *Sean*

To Elizabeth Coxhead[1]

MS. COXHEAD

14 MAY 1958

Dear Miss Coxhead,

I knew Mr. [Lennox] Robinson had planned to write a Life of Lady
Gregory, but did not know that the family would not allow it. I, too, think
Lady G. is under-estimated as a Writer; but the old Lady was, I fear, too

---

[1] Elizabeth Coxhead (1901–   ), The Red House, St. Mary's Way, Gerrards
Cross, Bucks, British writer; author of *Lady Gregory: A Literary Portrait* (1961);
Daughters of Erin (1965), Five Women of the Irish Renaissance; editor of Lady
Gregory's *Selected Plays* (1962), with a Foreword by Sean O'Casey.

frank for Ireland, & for some of those with whom she worked. Far as I am concerned, you may quote as you wish from the Coole Chapters in "Inishfallen, Fare Thee Well"; but you must also get permission from the Publishers, Macmillan & Co. St. Martin's Street, London, W.C.2. By the way, you might mention I have already agreed.

My first visit to Lady G. in Dublin was to the Russell Hotel, corner of Stephen's Green and Harcourt St.; afterwards to the Standard Hotel, Harcourt St., a few steps from Stephen's Green. I visited her once when she stayed in a house in Adelaide Road. I never knew of her staying anywhere in Nassau St. She was photographed with me several times; once with Sally Allgood, I between the two of them, outside, I think, of the Fortune Theater, Covent Garden; again when I got the Haw haw thornden Prize[2] (God forgive me), as she sat on the platform. She was staying then in Sloane Sqr with her daughter-in-law. I called for her there, & she escorted me down to the Aeolian Hall; and I escorted her back to her daughter-in-law's flat. I have no copies of these pictures—I never bothered to gather photos of persons or plays. The Abbey Theatre may have a picture of her. There is a good one in an Anniversary programme. You might find something with the photo theater & paper agencies round the year of 1926, when the ones I mention must have been taken.

I'm afraid that's all I can do for you.

All good wishes for the Novel & the Life.

Yours sincerely
Sean O'Casey

[2] See "London Honours Mr. O'Casey, Award of Hawthornden Prize," *Irish Times,* 24 March 1926, Vol. I.

To Miss Joan McAlevey

MS. McAlevey

20 MAY 1958

Dear Joan,

I am glad to hear that you are well and full of the hope of life. It will be a big change when you no longer are yourself, but one in another, & the other one in you; a very important partnership. I have been married now for thirty-two years; we have had many troubles and one very bitter sorrow; but Eileen [and I] are as close to each other today as we were in the earlier time of over thirty years ago: closer in fact. May it be so with all young people deciding to make a home and live a new life together.

I have been ill—with a touch of Influenza, &, afterwards strained a heart-muscle, & had to hide my face from the world for awhile. Allright

604 THE LETTERS OF SEAN O'CASEY

now; but my old eyes get tired quick, and I've been advised to read little & write less; so I've cut down my letter writing—had to; it is a nuisance, can't be helped.

Weather here very bad still: cold, bitter winds & much rain. Well, it was often so, for Goldsmith tells us it was so in his day "When parting Winter chills the lap of May."

My love & best wishes to you

As ever
Sean

~~Joseph Stein, Esq~~ *to shoots a little!* 21 May. 1958
Flat 3, 40 Trumlands Road, St. Marychurch, Torquay, Devon.
Tel. Torquay 87766.

Joseph Stein, Esq.   *Mc Dauran*

Dear Joe,
        Glad to get your letter and glad to hear you have cap-
tured Miss Shirley Booth; also that you may get Jackie Magauran. I
dont like recommending anyone for such a big task, but believe to
that Jackie will be good. However, my opinion goes for little
if the Director thought differently. It is fine to hear that he
too thinks Jackie the better man for the work, for it is he, ~~fixs~~
first of all, who must be satisfied with his team.
        Glad, too, that you didnt take much not-
ice of the costumes shown by the old old photos. What I said
regarding fancy dress was but a throw-in opinion. The work, in
my opinion, will be virtually a new play; its spirit more lively,
as you say, and, I think, everything around it should be livelier
too; but mind you dont go too far, and make it to gaudy. If I
had a theater myself, plus enough money to make things safe, as
well as a team sure of constant work - a State independent
theater, I'd sail ahead with experiment in color, dialogue, acting, and costume; but things arent that way, and we have to remember others are concerned, and that the team will have to put
a damned lot of work into the venture; so it is necessary that
we should do all we can to reward all with a satisfactory run.
        I have never had a chance of having my
own way, and so have no experience; and in these things, one k
must have that, coming into efficiency through a morass of mistakes; but this is what a commercial theater cant permit.
        Well, Joe, I have read the script
and I have listened to the music, and find it hard to comment.
I find it hard to get my ear to adapt itself to the newer rhythms.
I used to wonder at our boy, Niall, changing the tempo of old
airs I knew ell into a kind of jazz time on i his trombone, and
jotting it down for use in the band to which he belonged. So the
fact is I cant give a safe or a convinced opinion about the music.
However, Eileen, Breon, and Shivaun have declared they like the
music and songs well, with the one exception of Eileen thinking
that the song sung by old women could be better - I believe she
has written to say so. Another thing: I listened in the other
night to the BBC Third Programm giving Poulenc's "Chansons Francaises", and when they ended, I ejaculated "Well, the music of
JUNO is as good as that," Eileen, who was listening too, adding
"Better; a lot better." So there I'll leave it. Poulenc is a
present-day composer, and did the opera "The Carmelites" recently.

To Joseph Stein

TS. STEIN

21 MAY 1958

Dear Joe,

Glad to get your letter and glad to hear you have captured Miss Shirley Booth; also that you may get Jackie McGowran. I don't like recommending anyone for such a big task, but believe that Jackie will be good. However, my opinion goes for little if the Director thought differently. It is fine to hear that he too thinks Jackie the better man for the work, for it is he, first of all, who must be satisfied with his team.

Glad, too, that you didn't take much notice of the costumes shown by the old old photos. What I said regarding fancy dress was but a throw-in opinion. The work, in my opinion, will be virtually a new play; its spirit more lively, as you say, and, I think, everything around it should be livelier too; but mind you dont go too far, and make it too gaudy. If I had a theater myself, plus enough money to make things safe, as well as a team sure of constant work—a State independent theater, I'd sail ahead with experiment in color, dialogue, acting, and costume; but things aren't that way, and we have to remember others are concerned, and that the team will have to put a damned lot of work into the venture; so it is necessary what we should do all we can to reward all with a satisfactory run.

I have never had a chance of having my own way, and so have no experience; and in these things, one must have that, coming into efficiency through a morass of mistakes; but this is what a commercial theater can't permit.

Well, Joe, I have read the script and I have listened to the music, and find it hard to comment. I find it hard to get my ear to adapt itself to the newer rhythms. I used to wonder at our boy, Niall, changing the tempo of old airs I knew well into a kind of jazz time on his trombone, and jotting it down for use in the band to which he belonged. So the fact is I cant give a safe or a convinced opinion about the music. However, Eileen, Breon, and Shivaun have declared they like the music and songs well, with the one exception of Eileen thinking that the song sung by old women could be better—I believe she has written to say so. Another thing: I listened the other night to the BBC Third Programme giving Poulenc's "Chansons Francaises," and when they ended, I ejaculated "Well, the music of JUNO is as good as that." Eileen, who was listening too, adding "Better; a lot better." So there I'll leave it. Poulenc is a present-day composer, and did the opera "The Carmelites" recently.

Yes, me lad, I'm better, and out walking again; walking the ways of Marychurch & the ways of the world.

My love to Sadie, to the children, & to you.

Yours very sincerely,
Sean

To Abigail Wanamaker[1]

MS. WANAMAKER

22 MAY 1958

Miss Abigail Wanamaker.

Flat 3, 40 Trumlands Road, St. Marychurch, Torquay, Devon.

Tel. Torquay 87766.

22. May. 1958:

My dear Abby,
Thanks a lot for your
kind letter. I haven't been too well, an' d
feel very tired — as you can see by the
sketch below. No sun has come to us here
to give a chance to us to revive; but I'm
sure it will come one day. Then when I feel
better, I may make an effort to go to
London, & so see you all again. Hurrah!

But I am sorry to hear that Jessie isn't
well. Tell her she should try to keep quiet — as
she can for a week or so, till she is really,
really well again. I saw all ⚹ the delightful
pictures of Dad, Mam, Zoe, Jessica, & You
in the 'Woman's Journal: all looking lovely
and bright. My love to your Mother,
to Dad, Zoe, Jessie, & yourself—
As ever,
Sean

11

---

[1] Abigail Wanamaker, daughter of Sam Wanamaker, the American actor, director, producer, who directed *Purple Dust* in 1953. For details of the production, see O'Casey's letter to him, 28 April 1953, Vol. II.

To David Krause

TS. KRAUSE

28 MAY 1958

My dear Dave,

Thanks for your kind letter. I am glad to hear the good news (good news! how is it good news?) about the Fellowship, giving you a year's holiday in the shape, apparently, of a year's hard work. Life does strange things. Dont let the damned work on the book be a burden to you, if you can avoid it. At times I worry that you may be wasting your time over me. I do hope not. About where you should pitch your tent is a question. I think, at any rate, that you should see more of Ireland than only Dublin and Wicklow. I imagine you should see something of the West; Clare-Galway, Sligo—the one Lady G's counties, the other, the county of Yeats. Croagh Peatrick and the Twelve Pins, and the Burren mountains. I have a friend in Tralee—I hope he is a friend still. He keeps a general store there; a lad—he was such fifty golden years ago, and his name is O'Connor. A few years ago, he wrote me a friendly letter, remembering old times when he was a student with his brother Vincent in Dublin; and many's the time he and I played hurley together, and when the play was over, sang National ballads on our way home. I remember one particularly—Up with the Green flag, down with the red rag; but mon uar! [alas!] the words have faded from my memory. I think his first name was Donal. Maybe, he is gone the way of all flesh now. I do hope not. There's another who wrote to me, Mr. Glazier, a Stationer and Printer of the same town, who must have been one of the descendants of Cromwell's soldiers, but national and a catholic now. I had another friend in Dublin, a Tom Glazier, an Orangeman, who remained an old Ironside to the last. He used to send me a christmas card every year till the end, though in the old days I stood for all ideas opposite to his; yet we remained good friends, for both were sincere, and each knew that of the other. Tom came from Tipperary. But Tralee is too far, away in C. Kerry.

We shall be glad to see you again, Dave; and though August is the hub of the season, we'll ferret out some near by place for you. I have just had a letter from Dave [Greene], and will reply when I get a second. You are a full-blown Professor now; and Dave is proud of his Student, as he may well be. I hope you will have a pleasant time with the drama, though it's a pity the University is not away in the country, a place so full of sweet airs and sweet noises. The Tostal is now ended, but there are still arguments in the papers about Joyce's indecency and his blasphemy, too. I have had to stay quiet for awhile with a strained heart-muscle, but am allright once more. Paul Shyre tells me he is working on the "Cock" for a

spell on the stage this Fall, and he also has ideas about D. of Father Ned.,
for the Fall, too.

As ever,
Sean

To Mrs. John T. Cooper

MS. COOPER

16 JUNE 1958

My dear Georgie,

How are things with you? Receipt of clipping would point to your being allright. I dearly hope you are.

Very busy, myself with visitors to England wanting to come down,
but I haven't now the energy to see so many. Tom Curtiss—Paris Drama
Critic of Her-Tribune, and Dick Watts, of the New York Even. Post,
coming here in a few days, & a young New York lass who is with our
Shivaun in London, coming on Wednesday; then a young English teacher,
23, who, when he was nine & his sister six, lost father, mother, & home in
a bomb explosion during the war; most intelligent, with a great knowledge
& love of books & drama; and a Photographer begging a visit to put me in
a book he's composing of pictures of famous persons; but I have refused.
This appeal, not in any way desirous of appearing among the famous.

I enclose clipping of R. Tattoo Case, ended now.[1] It puts the Archbishop in a comic dilemma, for the law allows it, &, following the decision
on "Cat on a Hot Tin Roof," too! This after banning me from any Production in the Diocese of Dublin; though the "Drums of F. Ned" is a little innocent lamb compared with these two wolfish dramas. What will he say
now, & what will he do?

My love to you & all & John.

As ever,
Sean

---

[1] It was reported in the *Irish Times,* 10 June 1958, that Alan Simpson of the
Dublin Pike Theatre was finally acquitted of the charge of "producing for gain an indecent and profane performance" of *The Rose Tattoo.* The case had been in the
courts for 13 months, and Justice Cathal O'Flynn, ruling in favor of Simpson, stated:
"I can only infer that, by arresting the accused, the object would be achieved of closing down the play. But surely if that was the object nothing could be more devastating than through restraint of production before even a hearing is held. It smacks to
me of the frontier principle, 'Shoot first and talk after.'" Nevertheless, Simpson's
legal victory rang hollow in reality, for there was no award of costs and he was faced
with legal debts of £2,600, and irreparable damage to the reputation of the Pike
Theatre, whose membership had fallen from 2,000 to 300. See O'Casey's letter to
Brooks Atkinson, 25 May 1957, note 3.

To Robert Hogan

MS. HOGAN

20 JUNE 1958

Dear Bob,

Many thanks for your article in "New Republic";[1] the one, I assume, you sent to "Commonweal." Very odd, they didn't take it: eventually got cold head, I think. Keep cool; don't risk putting out any pennant for O'Casey.

Your article embarrassed me, not because of the criticism of the last act, but because of the volleys of praise. Funny, praise invariably embarrasses me. I've no false modesty, & realise my value; but praise from others makes me shy: why, I don't know. Thank you very much for sending it to me.

The case against "Rose Tattoo," after going from District Court to Court Supreme, has been dismissed; & literary people are jubilant. Now Dublin is threatened with a Revival, and also with "Cat on a Hot Tin Roof"! Don't know what Archbishop will say or do, if this happens. Having banished O'Casey with "Drums of Father Ned" under his arm, he'll feel funny if he has to allow "C. on a H.T. Roof."

I hope your little ones are safe out of the measles, a trying disease, & not a little dangerous; so I hope your & your wife's share of our future life is safe again.

My warm regards to Mrs. Hogan & to you.

Yours very sincerely,
Sean

[1] Robert Hogan, "O'Casey and the Archbishop," *New Republic,* 19 May, 1958.

To Rev. Michael E. Gallagher, S.J.[1]

MS. GALLAGHER

27 JUNE 1958

Dear Mr. Gallagher,

Thank you as acht mo chroidhe[2] for your very kind letter—a little embarrassing in its unstinted praise; for praise frightens me a little, tho' blame very often acts as a stimulant: as Blake says somewhere (Marriage of Heaven & Hell, I think) "Damn braces; bless relaxes." Very wise man. Regarding "The Bishop's Bonfire," of course, you have no Bishops to bother you. The old priest who gave me his blessing was Father Sheedy, a life-long friend of Dr. W. Macdonald, Professor of Theology in Maynooth for 40 years.[3] Father Sheedy was banished for daring to give evidence for a Parish Priest who had been brought before his Bishop; & he had little regard for the mitred ones, I imagine.

The new play you mention has now a little history attached to it; it was to receive its world premiere in Dublin during the Tostal (The Tostal had appealed to me to give it to them for their Drama Festival); but suddenly Dublin's Archbishop declared against the production of any play by O'Casey or by James Joyce; so the Drama Festival had to be abandoned. The play is named "The Drums of Father Ned." It is the most innocent of my plays, played actually against the background of Tostal activities, the spirit moving the young people into hope, color, and action, is that of "Father Ned," who never appears, but who is the soul of the play. It was an effort of mine to combat the spirit of despair & cynicism now smothering Ireland. It is a great pity it to have been banished. G[raham]. Greene is, of course, a powerful writer; but I don't think he understands Catholicity: he revels in the sorrowful mysteries, but completely forgets the Joyful ones, & Those that give out beams of glory. So does Mauriac, a greater writer even than Greene, in my opinion. I should have written to thank you sooner; but I get periodic attacks of eye-trouble, so that I have to rest them, reading little and writing less.

Your youthful blessing is very acceptable—I need all I can get; and I am grateful to you for it. I daren't return a Communist blessing; but, believe me, I wish you a good, useful, and active life, so as to earn a "well-done" at its end.

Yours very sincerely,
Sean O'Casey

[1] Rev. Michael E. Gallagher, S.J., St. Mary's College, 1–710 Kamishakujii Nerima-ku, Tokyo, Japan.
[2] from the bottom of my heart.
[3] See O'Casey's letter to Francis MacManus, 23 February 1958.

To Merrill Pollack[1]

TC. O'CASEY

27 JUNE 1958

Dear Mr. Pollack,

I am very glad that you and your wife have had such a successful holiday.

As for the article, I have decided not to go any further with the idea. I have given it, from time to time, some thought, discovering at the end of the meditation that such an article is not for me to do. The fee offered was a very tempting one, and reading over what I had written, I found that in trying to arrange its form so that it might be suitable for THE S. EVENING POST, I should be doing it, not because I wished so to do, but because of the lure of $1500 (if I remember the amount right). To do this would mean for me afflicting myself with the feeling of having changed or arranged something for a reward; a thing which would be, to me again, a sin against the Holy Ghost, in whom I dont believe.

I know this is a damned foolish attitude of mind, but it is my foolish way, and I beg you to excuse me.

My good wishes to Mrs. Pollack and to you.

> *Yours very sincerely,*
> *Sean O'Casey.*

I didna remember the count right—it was $2500.

[1] Merrill Pollack, of the *Saturday Evening Post*, Philadelphia, Pa., had asked O'Casey to write an article for his magazine's "Adventures of the Mind" series.

To Paul Shyre

TS. SHYRE

9 JULY 1958

Dear Paul,

As you are aware, I daresay, I have given Cheryl Crawford the go ahead with SHADOW OF A GUNMAN. I don't think it can hurt any production of COCKADOODLE, and Jane [Rubin] thinks as I do, too.

But that isn't what I wish to write about. Yesterday, George Devine of the Court Theatre, London, again appealed to me to let him do COCKADOODLE in that theater. He has been asking me time and again for the play (and Eileen too). I am not eager to give it to him, and had an argument with Breon about it, who thinks I should. Now he (George) has suggested that he should write to you, and has asked me if you agree to allow a London performance, will I give my consent too? Very embarrassing. However, I said I myself would write to you to learn what you think about it. My first feeling is that the English Theater doesn't care a damn about my work, and the English who go to the theater even less, and the indifference they have for me is fully reciprocated; the second is that I imagine that G. Devine doesn't really care about my work either. During our talk (over the phone), to escape from the Cockadoodle, I suggested THE B.'S BONFIRE, and to my surprise got the answer that he had never read it; that he did not know that it had been published, and I had to tell him the name of the publisher—that after the hullabaloo the play caused when it had appeared in Dublin, and though the London critics had attended the show, and had written about the play and the commotion; and, also, in spite of the fact that it was this play that had prompted Dublin's Catholic Archbishop to ban O'Casey and DRUMS OF FATHER NED from Dublin during Tostal Week. So you can understand why I haven't a lot of enthusiasm for his proposal to do the Cock, or any other play of mine. Anyway, I told him I had promised you the first world production, adding that in any case, you would want to do the N. York production first of any others. I am all for this too; so I suggest you write to me saying something like this, and that you are against any production that would precede the New York one. This will save Eileen and me from future requests—at any rate, till the New York production has flowered into a fact.

Pity you couldn't get the Bijou, but it can't be helped. However, I shouldn't take any theater you don't think suitable; better to wait till one can be found.

Enclose a few stamps may be useful. All the best.

As ever,

Had promised Gunman before getting your letter. You never said anything about a film idea before. Anyhow, Paul, agradh, there's plenty of other plays would make good ones.

Sean

I've taken out a few words from last part of "Dr. Father Ned." I want part of Chopin's Funeral March to be heard faintly as the Deputy-Mayor, Mayor, & Parish Priest sink into a semi-coma broken by Haydn's Trumpet Call & the roll of Drums in the "Military" Symphony preceded by a playing of his mazurka-like march in the same work, & ending, too, with this music. The music occurs nicely at the extreme end of the 2nd movement.

S. O'C

To Eric Gorman

TS. GORMAN

11 JULY 1958

Dear Mr. Gorman,

Thank you for your inquiry about SHADOW OF A GUNMAN for Horse Show Week.

I do not wish my play to be done during this event. I suggest that you give the entire week to the play by the young dramatist.

After what happened during Tostal Week, or rather before it came, I have no eagerness to appear in Dublin, or make any manifestation, any epiphanical appearance calculated to frighten his grace of Drumcondra.[1] So I cannot give permission for performance of the play.

For a change, it is to be done in November in New York.

With all good wishes to you personally.

Yours sincerely,
Sean O'Casey.

[1] The Most Rev. John Charles McQuaid, Archbishop of Dublin, whose palace is in Drumcondra, Dublin.

To Robert Hogan

TS. HOGAN

12 JULY—THE TWALTH—1958

Dear Bob,

I didn't think your article[1] too fulsome at all; all I meant to say was that praise always makes me feel shy. I thought it well reasoned, and I hope all the fine things you said about my work were right—quite a natural desire on my part.

I am sorry your MS wasn't taken by the Rutgers Press; but it is always damned hard to get a work accepted. It is always strange what readers see in the things one tries to do, due, no doubt to the inadequacy of words to explain one's thoughts. Words on the whole are very feeble symbols for thought; but we must put up with them. One can see how Manley-Hopkins strove to make his thoughts go by jostling words together, and Joyce using them as a kind of catalyst to give a variety of meanings to the one word written.

[1] See O'Casey's letter to Hogan, 20 June 1958, note 1.

I think Beckett a very clever writer, a very sad one, but intensely sincere. He may be coming down here to see me with a friend this coming week. Shivaun (our daughter knows him, and says he is a very charming man, shy, but very very attractive). The human mind is a very vague mystery; sending, often, sweet and bitter thoughts out in the one stream. Ionesco isn't in the same street with B. I have no concept of respect or admiration for him. I hope you may be happy in your new post. Glad the children are again like wild Indians, as they should be while youth lasts.

I enclose an unexpected letter I got from a young Jesuit: a copy of the original.

I imagine myself (as a vague explanation) that there are many young priests who are in silent revolt against things as they are in the Church; against old-fashioned ideas, even theological ones. Dr. McDonald bitterly complained against the stagnation in matters of theology, saying that Theology like all things, must go ahead, and must base its promises on the newer physics. That was why he wrote his banned thesis on MOTION.[2] What would he think now with the atom blazing, were he alive!

All good wishes to Betty, the children and to you.

And success to you in the State
where the Zinnias grow.
Sean

[2] Walter McDonald's *Motion: Its Origin and Conservation* (1898) was condemned by the S. Congregation of the Index in Rome in 1898. See McDonald's "My Book of Motion" and "The Sequel to the Condemnation," *Reminiscences of a Maynooth Professor* (1925).

To Merrill Pollack

TC. O'CASEY

21 JULY 1958

Dear Mr. Pollack,

Thank you for your very kind letter. You argue very well, and almost persuade me to become a contributor to the series of articles appearing in your WEEKLY.[1]

You tell me that the fee is $2500—not $1500, as I thought at first. But this is worse and worse, since your correction has made your offer more tempting than ever.

Woe is me that I cannot decide to agree to do what you ask. I shall

[1] *Saturday Evening Post.*

certainly consider what you so kindly say; but what you ask would introduce an element of haste into what I try to write, and this would, unfortunately, provoke a pricking of conscience, or, as Joyce says, "agon-bite of inwit," making me feel uncomfortable, a feeling which I dont like.

Believe me, I like dollars as well as any American can; so I shall think over what your letter says, and, if the article I am trying to write (I have begun it all over again) should feel suitable, I shall let you know.

With all good wishes to your wife and to yourself.

Yours very sincerely,
Sean O'Casey.

To Hume Cronyn and Jessica Tandy[1]

MS. CRONYN

25 JULY 1958

Dear Hume Cronyn and Jessica,

Many thanks for your very kind letter. I fear, though, you clothe me in a garment of so many bright colors that I'm dazzled, and a little frightened. If I'm quarter of what you think, I'll have a chance of heaven. When I look back on life, what I have done gives me no pride; but all I have left undone makes me ashamed of myself. An Irish proverb says "If a man's sins were written on his forehead, he would pull his cap well over his eyes." He would that; and, be god, so should I!

Thanks, a lot, too, for the fine Brochure of so many things done by you and Jessica. England was very backward in not holding on to the handsome, graceful Jessica of yours. The few things I saw her do here, showed me at once that here was a lass who was bound to be a great Tribune of the Drama. The Brochure is a wonderful window looking into what you have both done. You certainly have been dazzling yourselves with fine achievements. I like the phrase "The Cronyns refuse to make solemnity a qualifying condition either of beauty or the total effect of FACE TO FACE." By God, I do! It's harder to be comic than tragic; Comedy is the most difficult Muse to serve, & her face & figure are just as beautiful as any of the other Eight. This phrase has given me a thought to add to what I am presently trying to write.

I do hope your Tour will be a very successful one.

---

[1] Hume Cronyn and Jessica Tandy, actor-producers, planned a tour of the summer theatres with a program of one-act plays, including O'Casey's *A Pound on Demand* and *Bedtime Story*. See O'Casey's letter to Cronyn, 15 December 1958, note 1.

My warm Regards to you Both. Go n-eirigheach an uile go geal le na Cronyns.

"May all things rise brightly with the Cronyns"—Gaelic.

Yours very sincerely
Sean O'Casey

Thanks for the clipping holding the blessing of Dick Watts.

To Paul Shyre

MS. SHYRE

29 JULY 1958

Dear Paul,

Thanks, Paul, for your letter of the 14 July. I'm sorry about the Bijou Theater. As a matter of fact, I confused theaters: I thought it was the De Lys Theater you were after, & took no notice of the Bijou name. It can't be helped now. However, if you can't get a theater you think suitable then, lad, why not put it off till you can? However, I leave this entirely to your judgement.

George Devine was convinced by the quotations taken from your letter, & has abandoned his appeals for "Cockadoodle." He has asked me to let him do "Plough & the Stars" instead, and I have given him permission. I indeed appreciate your warning about persons wanting to do my plays now; but this matter is in the careful & wise hands of Jane [Rubin]. I got a letter from an old friend, Barrows Dunham, who tells me his son, Clarke, wants to start an "off Broadway" theater in Philadelphia, & wishes to open with "Cockadoodle," presumably with the N.Y. Company. He also wants to call the theater, "The Sean O'Casey" Theater! This is very embarrassing, & I could never allow a theater to be called after me—while I'm alive, anyway. I've sent this letter to Jane, &, when, you see her, she can show it to you. I've written B.D. to say any scheme of this kind must be dealt with in New York and not in Marychurch; & that I can't give my name for such a purpose of naming a Theatre.

Sol Jacobson, his wife, & his daughters, July & Barbara, were here with me a week ago. He took two pictures of me wearing the Brittany Beret—the one you sent me.

All good wishes for your health & happiness.

Yours as ever,
Sean

To Franklin D. Murphy

MS. MURPHY

31 JULY 1958

Dear Mr. Murphy,

I have gotten the lovely Tashkent Cap, and am delighted with it. Thank you so much.

Here was I thinking you wouldn't be able to bear (to hear) the name of the USSR; and now finding that you have travelled near from one end to t'other of the land! I'm glad you liked your trip so much. I have been a friend of the USSR since 1923, years before I left Dublin; & have many friends there. At the moment, I'm sending a John Gassner vol—"The Theater in Our Times"—to a young Leningrad girl who is writing about the English-speaking Drama, & a book on the Romantic Poets to a young woman of Moscow who is writing about these poets, & to whose many questions I have sent opinion-answers as to my belief that they are far from dead.

Since we are friends, I say we should drop the "Misters"—there's no such word in Gaelic—& so, I begin now: Dear Franklin, I'm sending by ordinary registered mail a few sheets that may be interesting: on one, the reverse sides contain other examples (economy!), & a few interesting letters; the 2nd is the first rough draft of "Bishop's Bonfire"— you will see how it grew into a different work; even the name I thought of using "McGilligan's Daughter" changed to "B.'s Bonfire," a booklet in German for "Shadow of a Gunman" has a reproduced sketch of me I did when I was very ill— like a bearded pard.

My warm regards,
Sean

To Ronald Ayling

MS. AYLING

1 AUGUST 1958

My dear Ron,

I'm sending this to Brighton by the sea, where I assume (and hope) you are having a fill-up of sea-air and sun. I haven't yet come to a time in ease or eye-goodness to begin your letter of questions again, and to try to answer some of them. I think I shall have to wait till you are by my side to answer them viva voce; for it is really a painful task now to write more than necessity demands. Time has gone away with a good many visitors from the U.S.A., and more are signalling their designs and intentions to invade St. Marychurch and pour through our open gateway. Domini dirige nos.[1] By the way, "Quid Nunc" of the Irish Times has given a column replying to your comments on O'Casey in Enquiry[2]—a vigorous little magazine, by the way. Soon as I get to know where you are fixed, I'll send the clipping—if you'd like to read it. The controversy is on again as enclosed clipping will show; but most of them fight shy of any mention of the A. Bishop's ban. However, I have had a few letters of approval and support—one from a District Justice in the South of Ireland—of all people! I have just refused an invitation from Hugh Wheldon to take a place in a Television Programme of "Monitor."

I hope, my dear lad, you are taking a good rest immersed in good air, and letting your young mind quietly stroll away from serious questioning of the ways of the world.

Yours very affectionately,
Sean

[1] Lord guide us.
[2] Quidnunc (Seamus Kelly), "An Irishman's Diary," *Irish Times*, 12 July 1958, writes a reply to Ayling's "Rowdelum Randy: Sean O'Casey and His Critics," *Enquiry*, June 1958, University of Nottingham, and to O'Casey's letter in the same issue, a modified version of the letter which appeared in the *Irish Times*, 11 March 1958.

To Irish Times

7 AUGUST 1958

O'CASEY RECORDS

Sir,—Under the heading of "Crux Over O'Casey Recordings" (July 30th), you report that some body calling itself Connoisseur Records has made recordings of my works for distribution in the U.S.A. and in Ireland.[1]

This firm, body, or shop has no authority from me for any recordings of my work whatsoever now, and will receive none in the future. Some

[1] Connoisseur Records, Ltd., Fownes Street, Dublin, announced that it had suspended distribution of a recording called "Sean O'Casey's Pictures in the Hallway," a stage adaptation of O'Casey's autobiography, which it had made without his permission.

time ago, this body—or another—wanted to do recordings held by Radio Eireann, and permission was refused, a letter from R.E. (after a protest from me) telling me that no record held by them would be given to anyone without my written permission. A day or so ago, a press agency rang me up to tell me that recordings had been made. I wrote at once to R.E. and am waiting for a reply. This firm or body which made recordings without my permission will be called upon, not only to suspend distribution in Ireland, but also in the U.S.A., unless an agreement has been come to between the responsible persons in the U.S.A. who are in charge of my work there.

Under no circumstances will I be willing to allow the recordings held by R.E. to be recorded by anyone anywhere, and R.E. would oblige me very much by destroying them.

O'Casey is easily found; both the Abbey Theatre and R.E. know where I live, and Connoisseur and Records could have discovered the place readily by asking either. Some time ago, I refused an American request to use these broadcasts, and I don't intend to change my mind about them.— Yours etc.,

Sean O'Casey.

AUGUST 1ST, 1958.

To Ronald Ayling

MS. AYLING

11 AUGUST 1958

Oh, my dear Ron,

What are you doing to yourself? What possessed you to fling yourself into such a job! For heaven's sake, clear out of it, fast as you can: your mind is far too sensitive to be harried by the company of the mentally sick; sensitive minds are not common, and what we have of them are the most precious things within England's heritage of time. I should have written this at once were it not that I have been, and still am, in bed with a bad bronchial attack that made a nasty entrance into one lung: much better now.

Don't worry about your visit. It's just possible, I won't be able to see you; but I'd love to see you, and unless I'm very ill, I'll certainly look forward to it. Now, we can get you settled in a comfortable worker's home a few minutes walk from our place.

Got what the doctor calls a "kick-back" with temperature up again, and forced back to a quiet life in bed.

You'll distress me if you worry about coming down—put it out of your mind till the time comes, and then, we'll see.

I'm venturing to send you a little loan that can be paid back later or when you are flush. Please, Ron, do just take it, and say nothing about it to anyone else, or mention it to me. You will please me well by doing this for me; and, please do it.

I enclose Quid Nunc's article.[1] I kept it back so's you couldn't reply to him, just read—take no notice. And one—which I want back—by G.F.[2] who has falsified every incident—story later on.

Love,
Sean.

[1] See O'Casey's letter to Ayling, 1 August 1958, note 2.

[2] Gabriel Fallon, "He's Wrong-shipped This Time!" *Dublin Evening Press,* 2 August 1958, an article on O'Casey's decision to ban all professional performances of his plays in Ireland, as a result of the controversy over *The Drums of Father Ned.* Late in July O'Casey had announced his ban: "If Dublin isn't allowed to see my new play, I am withdrawing my old plays as well." (Dublin *Sunday Press,* 27 July 1958.)

To Philip Burton[1]

MS. BURTON

19 AUGUST 1958

Dear Philip,

I was very glad to hear (Paul told me) that you had taken charge of Cockadoodle Dandy,[2] leading him on at last where he should ha' been long ago; better late than too late. I'm sure you'll give the bird a chance to give a lusty crow, & I hope it may be a long one too.

I have been in bed some weeks with Bronchitis which "infiltrated" into a lung—"unprovoked aggression," & I was laid low; still am, but much better. This is why this is but a note to acknowledge your letter. Eileen & I think your idea for the opening to be a fine one; most appropriate, & more important, very poetical: a grand beginning.

The song you mention is a well-known one; or used to be. I remember these lines only now—

[1] Burton had directed the highly successful New York premiere of *Purple Dust,* which ran for just over a year at the Cherry Lane Theatre. For production details see O'Casey's letter to Paul Shyre, 28 December 1956, note 1.

[2] Burton directed the New York premiere of *Cock,* which opened at the Carnegie Hall Playhouse on 12 November 1958. For production details see O'Casey's letter to Clara Rotter, 18 November 1958, note 1.

> Only to see her face again,
> Only to hear her speak:
> One little wish is all I ask—
> Only to hear her speak!

Shivaun may be here next week, & she might be able to jot down the air. I see your point about Sheanaar, but though deadly serious, he's a comic character, & "a dangerous old cod," symbolising, too, all the silly & vulgar superstitions of the Irish. Long ago, some of them had poetry in them (the pagan ones) but the Christian ones have nothing but a grovelling stupidity in them. I should think Paul would do well. One-eyed Larry is, I imagine, the younger progeny of Sheanaar. Paul didn't mention he was to do the part.

Glad, too, you have gotten Lester Polakov to design. You could go farther & fare far worse. I'm sure he'll "be a credit to you."

You have certainly made a fine start.

Writing even this much has tired me. Several visitors are due end of week—one from Toronto, so I must rest all I can.

Good fortune go with all you do.

All the best to you from Shivaun, Breon, Eileen & me.

As ever
Sean

"What didja say, mr. o Casey?"

To Mrs. John T. Cooper

MS. COOPER

26 AUGUST 1958

My dear Georgie,

A lovely little babe, my dear; a lovely new life in the world; or, as we Irish say, a lovely child, God bless it.

A charming picture of the grandmother; & of Dad and his daughter.

Odd, how naturally the mother crooks the arm; the lass with no experience instantly gives the right bend; while the Dad's is clumsier—a little more of a grip. I often & often noticed this charming instinct in the young mother.

Of course, the little one thinks of naught but sleep & food; but, just as important, terribly important, is the warmth of the mother's love; the feeling the growing life has of protection & care.

My blessing on Sarah.

This must be but a note of welcome to the little one.

I have been chained to the bed for a fortnight (still am) with bronchitis that "infiltrated" into a lung; but am getting better; but not energetic enough to think or write much; but I had to cry out "hail" to the little newcomer.

My blessing on her, on you, on the Dad, & the Grandmother.

"Unto us a child is born"—a chant that never fails to bring a new message to life.

As ever,
Sean

To B. Leontyev[1]

TC. O'CASEY

[2 SEPT. 1958]

O'Casey Sends a Rose to Tashkent

I send a rose of greeting, a full-blown blossom to all Comrade Asian and African Writers gathered in Tashkent to talk together about what they

[1] B. Leontyev, International Editor, *Literaturnaya Gazeta,* Moscow. O'Casey's message appeared in the magazine on 4 October 1958.

have to do as writers in the service of man; to break forever the bitter hold of Colonialism everywhere, forcing peoples back from a full development; to banish the governors and the masters, till all races are equal and all men are comrades.

The poet, Shelley, had a high opinion of the power in the art of writing, and so had [Arthur] O'Shaughnessy [in his "Ode"] when he said,

> One man with a dream, at pleasure,
> Shall go forth and conquer a crown;
> And three with a new song's measure
> Can trample a kingdom down.

Man has gone a good way forward; in the West through the march of the Soviet peoples; in the East through the march of the Chinese People; and Africa is waking up, and her Peoples are beginning to set forth on a great march forward, too; and we, writers, must be there in the march—in the van, in the center, and bringing up the rear.

I send an Irish blessing on all that the Tashkent gathering may say or do, and my cordial wishes to all Asian and African comrade-writers gathered together in a meeting that is bound to be historic, and to give encouragement and inspiration to all of us who are in the fight for peace, for racial equality among men, and for the full and free development of the differing, but beautiful cultures of all peoples.

With my love,
Sean O'Casey.

To David Krause

TS. KRAUSE

14 SEPTEMBER 1958

My dear Dave,

Well, thank God, agradh, that I hadnt to lead over a rescue party to search for you, and to pull you out (God helping us) of the lost regions of Glenmalure. You are safer and warmer where you are.[1]

I have managed to shake off the touch on the lung, coaxed away the bronchitis, am skirling round Marychurch, and once more beating the drums of a literary offensive.

I enclose the copy of DRUMS OF FATHER NED. Dont let anyone

[1] I was in Ireland for the year, June 1958 to September 1959, on a Howard Fellowship, finishing my book on O'Casey. I had thought of living in the Wicklow mountains, but finally settled in Dublin.

bar yourself read it, for there are many who are anxious to do so, and pose as knowing all about O'Casey. I havent been quite satisfied with the ending of the last act, and—as you will see—have introduced an excerpt from a Haydn Symphony that, I believe, will give the play a much more dignified end. You are certainly having a busy time—though, I fear, far from a wonderful one. Dont take my part too vehemently, for, I think, you may hear more, if you speak less on my behalf. The only thing that worries me is that you may be wasting your talents on doing this work. That wouldnt please me a bit.

I sure would have wished to hear you talking over the Irish world through Radio Eireann. Frank McManus is a fine lad. I have a deep respect for him; kindly, broad-minded, and very clever; and a fine critic as well as a fine writer. I wish he was one of Dublin's drama critics. I am glad you met Jim Plunkett. He wrote a radio drama about Jim Larkin[2] and sent me the book of what he had written. I thought it good, and recommended him to lengthen it, and make it fit on to the stage. I'm glad he did this, and I wish the work every possible success.[3] He is as you say an Honest writer, and brave, too; he has written some first-class short stories,[4] and has a fine literary talent. But he too must walk warily.

A word about the Ban:[5] I am not standing up, or protesting, for myself alone; I am standing up for the great dead Joyce, and for the integrity and honesty of Samuel Beckett, who withdrew his Mime Plays as a protest against the clerical ban on Joyce and me: we form, incidently, a three-leaved Dublin Shamrock.

Give my warm regards—should you see them again—to F. McManus and to Jim Plunkett.

Eileen and Breon send their love to you, and so do I.

As ever,
Sean

[2] James Plunkett, *Big Jim* (1955), a play for radio.

[3] The radio play was revised and expanded to a full-length drama, *The Risen People*, which opened at the Abbey Theatre on 23 September 1958.

[4] His short stories, originally published in *The Bell* and *Irish Writing*, appeared in two collections, *The Eagles and the Trumpets* (1954); *The Trusting and the Maimed* (1959).

[5] As a result of the unofficial "banning" of *The Drums of Father Ned*, O'Casey had banned all professional productions of his plays in Ireland.

To Brooks Atkinson

TS. ATKINSON

15 SEPTEMBER 1958

My dear Brooks,

It was indeed a fine thing to get your kind letter today, and to hear you are in the Fray fought by the regiment of reasonable men and women for a kinder and more sensible way of living with all the world. I fervently believe that we shall win, but it is a hard fight, and may be a long one. I'm too old to carry a banner now, but I still hold a pennon in the right hand.

I didn't write to you simply because I wanted you to rest quietly in the country, and decided to wait till you had gotten back to the ree raa of work. From what you say, it looks like Oriana was more sensible than you, may heaven bless her.

One thing is certain, and the rest is lies, Brooks, I'm not going to visit America. I wish to God I could, but the gods forbid. The old body is too outworn to make the journey. To make matters worse, I've just had five weeks of bronchitis that crept down into a lung—unprovoked aggression. It has left me limping a little more through the remainder of life. However, I'm again skirling round Marychurch; but I couldnt venture across the salt say, or sail to your land under the skies. Yesterday, the doctor warned me wisely against attempting any such thing; so I have had to reconcile myself to journeys through the locality; and I had a fight to get back into the state of being able to even do this. I don't think Shivaun will go with Eileen, for Eileen insists that someone should be here to "take care of me." I don't need anyone, but it is hard to convince Eileen. Eileen would like to see all the productions,[1] but longs especially to see COCKADOODLE; so if this comes first, she will, if all be well, go over (if we can afford it), and if the musical comes later—in January or so—she could pop over again having seen that I am still there in Devon. Talk of being swamped there— I'm swamped here, too, with letters, theses, poems, plays, questions of all kinds, till me poor head whirls. I've just had to hide from the most of them. I've refused a Canadian television interview; one for a BBC program called "Monitor," and an interview for an Ontario Newspaper—I haven't really got the head or heart to do these; for let God so speed me as I speak the truth, I hate talking about myself, and am far and away more interested in others. I have just written a short thing for Mr. [Arthur]

---

[1] Three productions of O'Casey's plays were scheduled to open in New York in the months ahead: the first New York performance of *Cock-a-doodle Dandy* on 12 November 1958 at the Off-Broadway Carnegie Hall Playhouse; the Actors' Studio production of *The Shadow of a Gunman* on 20 November 1958; and *Juno,* a musical by Joseph Stein and Marc Blitzstein, based on *Juno and the Paycock,* on 9 March 1959.

Gelb, and I hope all who read it (if it be published)[2] will realise that all I say are opinions, and not the words of God. At present I am setting down some thoughts on things mysterious; the chapter I am working at, off and on, is called IMMANUEL,[3] and tells what O'Casey ventures to let into his mind about religion, death, fair play, and commonsense; also I'm setting down some thoughts on the recent hunt from Dublin of the O'Casey-Joyce plays by the Catholic Archbishop of Dublin; the muteness of the Protestants—the other day, THE IRSH TIMES referred to the Protestants who were on the Censorship Board as spineless—who keep their mouths closed fast against the utterance of any controversial matter. So I keep myself going.

By the way, the Cronyns—Jessica Tandy and Hume Cronyn—are doing a successful round of some Summer Theaters with BEDTIME STORY, POUND ON DEMAND, and a play by Ben Levy. We have here now a great number of new young dramatists, and hope is high. I send under another cover a copy of ENCORE which deals mostly with these "new commencers," and which you may be interested to read. In the heel of the hunt, I find I've been talking a helluva lot about myself; but you have been a dear friend for a long time, and I find it simple to take you into my confidence.

Sept. 16. Left writing to soak myself in the sun shining down on our tiny garden. We had a wretched summer, so I rush out whenever the sun shines.

As you say, things are restless in the Far East. It is a pity that the U.S.A. is wasting so much of her wealth, and so her energy; and, as Ruskin said, "the waste of energy is the greatest waste of all." I heard a Senator over the BBC the other night talking in defence of the Dulles policy, saying that the USA had poured billions of dollars into the defence of Formosa and Quemoy, and we couldn't afford to back down now. A terrible waste of energy to keep Chiang on his unsteady feet. The sooner the USA learns that She has a responsibility far and away above Formosa and Quemoy, the better it will be for all of us. In this matter of Quemoy, it seems to be that She is like Emerson's Mountain trying to crack a nut. She has her own big problems to face, too; but even facing these, if She were but a little wiser in Her political foreign ways, what a gigantic friend She could be to all the world. But I have no doubt that the American People will solve all these things in their own way and in their own time.

If you could mention in some way or another through the Drama Department, that I can't possibly come to the USA, I shall be grateful. It will save me from a crowd of letters.

[2] Sean O'Casey, "O'Casey's Credo," *New York Times,* 9 November 1958. In this article, which he had titled "Cockadoodle Doo?" O'Casey gives his views on life, drama, and "my favorite play," *Cock-a-doodle Dandy.*
[3] This chapter appeared in *Under a Colored Cap* (1963).

And now, sad and all as I am that I won't see New York again (1 guessed I never should when I gazed at the receding skyline from the liner away aback in the years), I hope to see Oriana and you some time in the future, to embrace two dear friends once more.

My deep love to Oriana and to you.

As ever,

Sean

PS. I'm sending this to your office *The New York Times,* for fear you wouldn't yet be fixed at home in 120. R.D.

To Harold Goldblatt[1]

TC. O'CASEY

29 SEPTEMBER 1958

Dear Mr. Goldblatt,

I enclose a copy of DRUMS OF FATHER NED for you to read; just, at the moment, for you to READ. I shall have to consider your request further. In the meantime, let me know what you think of the play, and what you think of your Group's ability to play it (assuming, of course, that you like the work, and wish to do it). Then I can decide whether to give it or no.

I can hardly trust Ireland now, my friend, after all that has happened. The Abbey ignoring everything written by me since 1926; the clerical opposition to all I try to do; and worse still, the malicious opposition of the critics and writers, not one of whom ventured a word of protest against the recent ban on Joyce-O'Casey during the Tostal week.

So, I cant let the play go to Dublin. I have banned production of my plays in Ireland in protest, and I must stand by the memory of Joyce and by Samuel Beckett who very manfully withdrew his plays as a protest. I cant allow my play to be done there in S. Ireland, till these other plays find a footing there too. In all honesty to my brother writers, Joyce and Beckett, I cant do anything else.

I have no such objection to Ulster, and am prepared to consider a performance in Belfast, provided you like the play, and feel your Group can manage it; but I must think over this a little longer. In the meantime, read the play, and tell me what you think when that is done. For the life of me, I cant help wondering why you dont prefer to do the other play— THE BISHOP'S BONFIRE; and I cant help a suspicion that you want

---

[1] Harold Goldblatt, Ulster Group Theatre, Belfast.

to do D. of FATHER NED because of the Archipiscopal ban. A bad reason, you know, for wanting a play.

With all good wishes,
Sean O'Casey.

To David Krause

TS. KRAUSE

3 OCTOBER 1958

My dear Dave,

The play-scripts came back safely.[1]

Try not to get yourself entangled into this curious controversy about me and my work, remembering that you have a life of your own to live. These controversies can be very alluring, but they are usually futile as you can see in Ireland, which has become a land of a host of disputes, wasting energy, unsettling hope, and smothering life itself. So dont be too eager to defend one who is out of favor. Remember in Lear the Fool presenting his cockscomb to one who is out of favor?

By the way, I remember you mentioning in a letter you were trying to sort out dates of what happens in the Tostal affair. I've just looked up the letter I got from Godfrey Quigley and Norman Rodway (signed by them) demanding me to "give Jim Fitzgerald the necessary authority to make such alterations as he requires."[2] The date of this letter is 24/1/58, a long time after the Abishop's fiery fiat.

I'm glad you still like F. Ned. I dont consciously try to teach anyone in talk or in play: I am a kind of a searcher, and things said in a play or chat are just opinions deeply felt, which may be right or may be wrong. I ask no one to take them to his or her bosom, but I'll fight against any try to smother them in raging aversion or in the method of a mute silence. Regarding Joyce's "rabblement," Dave, there are two families of this genus: the roaring crowd is one, the silent or malicious intellectuals another; and of the two, the second is the more dangerous. It is this second family that still hates Joyce—see Frank O'Connor's review of P. Colum's book—"My friend, James Joyce."[3] This review appeared in the N.Y.

---

[1] *The Drums of Father Ned* and *Kathleen Listens In,* which O'Casey gave me to read when I visited him in July 1958, on my way to Ireland.

[2] See O'Casey's letter to Godfrey Quigley and Norman Rodway, 29 January 1958, note 1.

[3] Frank O'Connor, "Shadows on the Artist's Portrait," *New York Times Book Review,* 24 August 1958, a review of Mary and Padraic Colum's *Our Friend James Joyce* (1958), in which O'Connor denigrates Joyce.

Times. I have been something of a prophet, and so have no honor in Ireland; but let me make it clear that I am and have always been on the side of the Gaelic Language as the right one for Ireland. I simply knew that the methods used would fail, as they have failed, and pointed this out more than 30 years ago in the then Irish weekly, THE IRISH STATES-MAN:[4] and years before that in W. P. O'Ryan's paper, THE IRISH PEASANT AND NATION.[5] I am very glad that J.P. did so well;[6] but he will never sweep away the rubbish flooding the stage of the Blithe Theater;[7] but it is a stand, and that is to the good. I hope his play may have a good run. I'd have sent a telegram of good wishes, but have to be careful against doing harm rather than good. Ireland is the one place that I dont ever put my name on an envelope for fear of drawing attention to the fact that the addressee is in contact with the "notorious" O'C. Free-dom-loving Nation! Think well before going to the debate on my work.[8] All the best to a vic no croidhe [friend of my heart], as ever, with love,

Sean

P.S. As you suggested, I've put in an Echo ending first & Second Acts; and have kept Murray back to the end.[9] Roughly done, but will look again when I've time.

S.O'C

[4] See O'Casey's letters to the *Irish Statesman:* "The Gaelicisation of Irish Edu-cation," 5 July 1924; "The Innocents at Home," 10 January 1925; "Barr Buadh and Piccolo," 7 February 1925; Vol. I.

[5] "Sound the Loud Trumpet," *The Peasant and Irish Ireland,* 25 May 1907, by "An Gall Fada" (The Tall Foreigner or Protestant), O'Casey's first pseudonym and first published article; reprinted in *Feathers From the Green Crow* (1962).

[6] James Plunkett's *The Risen People* opened at the Abbey Theatre on 23 Sep-tember 1958, and had a successful five-week run.

[7] A reference to Ernest Blythe, Managing Director of the Abbey Theatre.

[8] The Technical Student's Debating Society debated the motion, "That Sean O'Casey is no longer a fair playwright," on 18 October 1958 in Dublin. Gabriel Fallon was the guest chairman, and I spoke against the motion after the debate.

[9] Changes made in *The Drums of Father Ned.*

To Joseph Stein

MS. STEIN

5 OCTOBER 1958

Dear Joe,

Thanks for letter. I've been down with bronchitis, & so sought sleep. However, I'm awake again. I understand—to some extent—the complicated co-operation necessary in a Musical; I, as I have said, have had no experience with this kinda art, & so I have said little about it, leaving it to you & your colleagues to do your best—which I know you'll do for all our sakes. The one comment I have to make—we played the music, etc. over to Jackie McGowran, who is here with us now—& I think you have too many "daarlin' mans" in it; it seems to be overdone; & the dialogue between the women (chorus) in pub. It's bad. I think Eileen wrote about this to you. The Irish used to hard drinking (women or men) don't vomit mornings; they'd like to, but can't. I knew them well, & I never heard the word "vomit" used; "spew," yes; but the fact is after a night of it, they feel rotten, but don't vomit, unless there's something else wrong; & I never heard women asking for "a pint." They act more "genteely," & say they'll have "glass of plain" or "small tumbler o'stout." Though they lower as much in the end as if they had asked for & gotten "pints."

These, of course, are trivial faults, but I thought I'd mention them so as to shift a mistake by a correction.

I agree that "Juno" isn't a good title. I suggest simply as a reverse way of using "Juno" to call it "The Paycock," or, maybe, "The Daarlin' Paycock"; but I prefer the first & simpler title.

Well, God speed all you are doing.

Love to Mrs. Stein & to you.

As ever,
Sean

To Paul Shyre

TS. SHYRE

6 OCTOBER 1958

Dear Paul,

Got your letter and enclosed clipping. Glad you think the play went well, and hope it may go better and better.[1] Thank the Company, Director, and Designer for me.

As for Father Sheridan's remarks—while they express his mind on the matter of the play, they express nothing. One of the Staff of a Canadian paper rang me up, told me a few sentences, and I said a few words. I wish I had gotten the clipping beforehand. I also have written a short article

---

[1] *Cock-a-Doodle Dandy*, produced by Lucille Lortel, Paul Shyre, and Howard Gottfried, opened at the Playhouse Theatre in Toronto, Canada, on 2 October 1958, for a brief run prior to its opening in New York on 12 November 1958. For details on the New York opening, see O'Casey's letter to Clara Rotter, 18 November 1958, note 1.

for the *New York Times,* at the request of Mr. [Arthur] Gelb, called COCKADOODLE DOO?[2] which is to appear a week before the opening date in New York.

As for Father Sheridan's criticism, I find it impossible to say much. What answer can there be to the statement that the play "is absolute and complete rubbish"? His English style! If it is absolute rubbish, why the need for "complete"? How is it rubbish, why is it rubbish, where is it rubbish? What reason, or reasons has he for making this assertion? He gives ne'er a one. There is, therefore, nothing to answer. He says the play "lacks realism." By God, what hurts them is that, in the midst of the fantasy, there's too much realism! The striking of the man, because he refused to drive a woman was living with him away was actual—a fact; and the blow killed him. So is the part where the employer refused to sack a splendid workman, and, in his rage, the priest struck. Very little was made of the case. So also, the scene of Loreleen and the "rough fellows" actual; and the words used by Father Domineer were almost identical with those in the play. It is a FACT that an engaged couple were fined for Kissing each other in the street; there was not even a hint (it was acknowledged in court) of indecency—just kissing; yet they were fined forty shillings each or a month in jail. Today the papers are carrying on a criticism about a case in Kilalloe, where some evangelists attempted to preach in the street near a church.[3] A violent little crowd gathered, and the police advised the evangelists to go. They obeyed at once, but on the way to their car, the crowd attacked, and one of the evangelists had his teeth knocked in and a skelp on the head with a stout stick left him senseless for half an hour. Charged in court, the District Justice attacked the evangelists, suggested they got what was coming to them, and declared in open court that "religion was above the law." Not the evangelists' religion, of course, but the religion of the assailants; in spite of the fact that the Irish Constitution guarantees freedom of religious propaganda to all, which of course the catholics do everywhere—for instance in Hyde Park without interference. The tale of the possessed girl and the advice that she should be sent to America formed a Gaelic story in THE IRISH PRESS. A possessed girl, having an evil spirit in her, picked up in England (like a virus!) which a priest exorcised, killing himself in the process, appeared in a play per-

[2] The title was changed to "O'Casey's Credo," *New York Times,* 9 November 1958.

[3] The Killaloe Case, which O'Casey goes on to describe, had begun on 26 June 1958 in Killaloe, Co. Clare, when three Protestant street preachers were assaulted outside a Catholic church. The case was dismissed in court on 15 September 1958 when District Justice Gordon Hurley, in releasing the three Catholic farmers accused of the assault, stated that the Protestant evangelists had deserved their beating, that "religion is above the courts" (*Irish Times,* 16 September 1958), meaning in this instance only the Catholic religion. This immediately provoked a controversy over constitutional freedom for religious minorities in Ireland that continued for many months, particularly in the editorial and letters columns of the *Irish Times,* to which O'Casey refers.

formed in the Abbey Theater, running for weeks; and was done in Liverpool, the then Archbishop giving special permission to all priests in his Archdiocese to attend and see and be (I suppose) exalted by the drama. The play is called THE RIGHTEOUS ARE BOLD,[4] and, if Father Sheridan wants to learn what "absolute rubbish" is, he couldn't do better than to read this play.

A few weeks ago, the Forestry Commission of Ireland carrying out work in the West, had to set up fences to their plantations. The western laborers found that part of the fencing cut through a "fairy rath." They refused to do it. The Forestry C. then sought out the oldest men there to do it, convinced that they, being so close to death anyway through age, and the good money they'd get, would do it. They refused as vehemently as the young ones, and the F. Commiss. had to make a big detour. No bishop or priest ventured to tell the workers that this objection of theirs was superstitious and all balls—maybe, if they had been asked, they, too would have run away from the job. How long, oh, Lord, how long! The Father calls the play "fantastic." Well, it is a fantasy, and so MUST have fantastic elements within it (as well as heart-tearing realism). Well, so is MIDSUMMER'S NIGHT'S DREAM, so is THE TEMPEST, so is PEER GYNT, so is THE DREAM PLAY, so is THE ENCHANTED, so is the SHADOWY WATERS, so is EMPEROR JONES. As for CURES, the cures for diseases at present mysterious, are alone buried in the mind of some eager scientific researcher, and nowhere else—certainly not in Lourdes. All diseases, diphtheria, cholera, smallpox, were conquered, not in Lourdes, but in the MIND OF MAN. I've never yet heard of any prelate or cardinal going to Lourdes for a cure, they run to the doctors like sensible souls. One last question: Leucaemia is incurable; doctors dread a case coming to them, for they are helpless. Here's a chance for Lourdes! Why not send the afflicted there? My word is that man alone must discover the cause and find out the cure: there is no other way. God has given man a mind, and this mind alone must solve man's problems. Let the faithful pray by all means, for it gives them consolation, and so no one would despise it; but it is only through the mind of searching man that disease will be defeated over the whole world of men. So much for Father Sheridan's charge of a play of absolute rubbish.

Your remark about the play seems to show it didn't get an enthusiastic reception; but there is still New York, a mhic. All the best, Paul, and a good run to us all.

As ever,
Sean

---

[4] See O'Casey's letter to Anthony Harvey, 14 December 1955, note 2.

New York Times

7 OCTOBER 1958

SHOUTERS AT PLAY CHIDED BY O'CASEY
Dramatist Scores Manners of Couples
Who Interrupted His Drama in Toronto

TORONTO, Oct. 6 (Canadian Press)—Sean O'Casey said yesterday the two couples who caused a commotion at a performance here of his play, "Cock-a-Doodle Dandy," had bad manners. The playwright added:

"The couples had a right to oppose my views; they had a right to express themselves, but not to interrupt the players."

Mr. O'Casey was interviewed by telephone by The Telegram here at his home in Torquay, England.

Two men leaped to their feet in the third act of the performance here Saturday night and cried "you're a liar," when a dying girl returns from the shrine of Lourdes, France, without being cured and rejects the belief in miracle healing.

They had urged the audience to leave at the second intermission. The men continued their shouts until escorted out.

Mr. O'Casey said yesterday "the play is based on fact." He said commotion at his plays is not new to him. He said he wrote the play to amuse people and was not trying to put across any message.

"Its only message is what the public wants to find in it. I don't believe in messages. I think it's one of my best plays," he added.

Mr. O'Casey's play has a modern Irish setting. It is a fanciful comedy attacking superstition and fear. It is to go to New York next month.

The first objections came from the couples when a priest knocks down and accidentally kills a man who has been living with a common-law wife.

An understudy in the play, Elsa Dawson, said the couples complained during the intermission at the front of the theatre and said the play should be banned.

"Does the church know about it?" they asked.

A spokesman for The Playhouse, where the play had its professional world premiere last week, said the men apparently considered the play anti-Roman Catholic. A few members of the audience had walked out at every performance, he said.

One of the actors, Dennis Drew, said four youths asked him as he was leaving, "Are you with the O'Casey show?"

Assuming they were fans, he said "yes," and one of them grabbed him. He slipped from them and ran back into the theatre.

To Franklin D. Murphy

MS. MURPHY

8 OCTOBER 1958

Dear Franklin,

I had written for you on a photo (taken a week ago), when your letter and your own picture came. Thank you very much. It is a fine one, and I am very glad to have it. You look handsome & very young, in spite of the furrowed brow and the looking-out eyes of a Searcher.

State of health and age—I'm but a few months from 79—keep me from going to the USA, much as I'd love to do; but Mrs. O'Casey (Eileen) is going in my place, and will be, I'm certain, a very worthy Deputy.

With the photo, I enclose the original "Notice to Quit" handed to me in 1921—the scene is shown in "The Shadow of a Gunman." I thought it might be an interesting item to go with your collection. I came across it when looking for a song (which I didn't find) written a good while ago, & which I wished to include in an article. You'll notice my name is given the English form, & not that which I used, & had used for many years— Sean ó Cathasaigh—, this is because the Irish form would not be recognised in the English Courts, & so it would make the notice to quit null and void. Many a one, in those days, was fined or imprisoned for having his name in Irish on his cart or over his shop. I myself got into trouble over giving my name in Irish to the Police—a comic interlude in one's life.

I wish I could have gone over the sea to you; but time and my doctor have said no; & "we must be satisfied."

All good wishes and cordial regards to you, my friend.

As ever,
Sean

To William Patterson

TC. O'CASEY

12 OCTOBER 1958

Dear Mr. Patterson,

I'm afraid I cannot be of much use to you. I do not know anything about Mr. North[1] (other than what your letter says), and so I cannot

---

[1] Joseph North, an editor of the *Daily Worker,* New York, founder-editor of the *Sunday Worker* and *New Masses.*

honestly do what you ask. Elizabeth Flynn I know of well, and of Howard Lawson, too, and give them a blessing of an Atheist—if they be willing to take it. Mike Gold I know of, too, but my knowledge of him is mainly of a lot of nonsense he has written from time to time—including a fierce aspersion upon me in 1934, the time of WITHIN THE GATES appearing in New York, and an equally foolish paean of praise in the NATIONAL GUARDIAN some little time ago.[2] Blows will always be levelled at Communism till Communism is in force everywhere; but the worst blows hitting Communism are given (have been given rather) by Communists themselves. They have been too rigid, understanding only the letter of Marxism, knowing nothing, seemingly, about its spirit. Their heads have been packed with theory, but they have never been able to apply them to the world of life as it is (not all, of course, for if that were so, we should indeed be in a bad way), but many; sincere, honest, but ignorant of the needs of life, and unaware of its infinite variety. They have been (and many of them are so still) strangers to many men; and so many of them, when a crucial time came (or what they thought to be a crucial time), they fell asunder. [J. B.] Priestley went all over the USSR, was feted, came back, wrote many articles in Lord Beaverbrook's EXPRESS (and got a good reward) when the going was good, and all favored the USSR; but came a time when an article of his appeared in COLLIERS—which you may have read. Many years ago, a few writers put their names to a letter calling for abolition of the atom bomb, but P's name wasnt there, nor Bertrand Russell's either. Now, of course, it is a good and safe thing to do. You there took the tyke [Louis] Budenz to your bosom; here they took the other tyke, [Douglas] Hyde to their bosom, making him sub-editor of the WORKER, without, seemingly, able to see that such a spirit could never be a Communist; knowing as much about Communism as he knows now about Catholicism; but the latter knowledge doesnt matter—as long as he stupidly opposes Communism— which he knows nothing of—he is on the road to heaven. Then there was the ultra-realist, the rigid Howard Fast, whose book on Socialist realism I have read, and couldnt then understand what S. realism was or was not— a dull writer; not to be compared with Jack Lindsay of whom very little is heard. So Howard Fast, the rigid socialist realist, when realism faced him, ran away, and hid himself in the cave of his conscience. There was a flight here, too, when it was discovered, or mentioned by Khrushchev, that Stalin had made mistakes (though ne'er a soul here or there yet knows what K. exactly did say). They forgot the many times Stalin made no mistake; and they have but to look at the USSR to see the amazing achievements of the Man. A Communist must have as well as being of human flesh subsisting, the iron of Communism in his nature; not to strike at people, but to stand firm in every crisis, in bad times as well as good times. You saw how many couldnt see the realism in the Hungarian crisis; how, though of

[2] See O'Casey's letter to Ken Coates, 17 July 1955, notes 3 and 4.

course the workers in the revolution were genuine, the leaders were not, and out only to restore again the old times; not only this, but to create a state by the side of the USSR that would aim always at destroying Socialism there, which, the USSR dare not permit, and was powerful enough to stop; with the pudden-headed and cowardly [Cardinal] Mintzentzy, eager to be the Prince-Primate of Hungary again, with all its power and wealth, taking care to stay on the doorstep of the American Embassy so that when the end of his dream came, he could bolt into safety, leaving the workers to their fate.

A Communist should be all things to all men (read DISTANT POINT,[3] and remember the character of the Communist general); a farmer to the farmer, a scientist to the scientist, a poet to the poet, a worker to the worker, even a christian to the christian, still with the iron of Communism firm within him, if he is ever to have any impression of the people with you there and the people with us here.

At beginning, I forgot to say I know Paul Robeson, whose lovely voice has so often enchanted me, and who should not tax that precious voice too much by public speaking. It is a rare gift, and the use of it enriches all who hear it; that is his true Communism. So all great men and women who excel at their work or art—they are Communists in spirit if not in name; they enrich humanity, which is what Communism is aiming at the world over. Remember what Picasso's Dove did for the creation of a longing for Peace everywhere. I havent yet read Mr. North's book[4] (I shall), for physiological reasons; I have but one eye, and that not too good, and always painful, so I must read slow; and I am not permitted to read half as much as I'd like; but it cant be helped. Please take my best wishes to you all, and I hope brother North's book will be a great success.

Yours for peace and brotherhood the world over.

[Sean O'Casey]

[3] Alexander Afinogenov, *Distant Point* (1934), first performed in London in 1937.
[4] Joseph North, *No Men Are Strangers* (1958), an autobiography. Patterson had asked O'Casey to comment favorably on North and his book.

To Walter Starkie[1]

MS. STARKIE

14 OCTOBER 1958

Dear Professor Starkie,

Thank you for your letter. Chancellor Murphy[2] and I are old friends now. I have sent him some MS, but I destroyed a lot of the earlier pieces. I've just sent him the original Notice to Quit delivered to me by the landlord of 35 M'joy Sqr, when I digged in the little Return Room there, the incident & room depicted in *Shadow of a Gunman*—quite a relic that I came across when looking for the MS of a song for a chapter of what I'm trying to write now—& couldn't find it; so had to re-write from memory of the lost one. I hope you may have a very successful tour. Lecturing isn't an easy job. I gave a "lecture" in Harvard & one in Philadelphia; but never again. I did well, but it was a damnable strain. Yes, I have many friends in the USA, in many other Countries, including China & USSR; but damn a one in Ireland. I'm afraid, I don't take much interest in the affair of Killaloe;[3] quarrels of this kind seem to be inevitable among good Christians. It's their way of loving one another; an odd way, but apparently effective. The fights take place even with educated & cultured men. We had (during the war) two USA Naval lieutenants, who fiercely contested each other's beliefs, one Catholic, the other Protestant; & the poor Atheist had to make peace by explaining what Protestant & Catholic had really to believe. It's a waste of time—even for fiery Evangelists, to bring their brand of Protestantism to Kilalloe—unless they preach it in Irish which no one would understand, more shame for them. I personally ignore the dogma (they give solace to millions), but hate the vulgarities ribboned on to them. The Prot. are as superstitious with "The Book" as Catho. are with miraculous medals.—Tho' the Foundress wasn't afraid to mix among the Communists. I don't believe the legends of the Bible, but I love their beauty. If a religion hasn't truth (and what is truth?), then it should have beauty. The Preaching of the Evang. & the sticks of those holding the "true faith" were equally vulgar and dangerous.

> *All good wishes to you.*
> *Cordial regards.*
> *Sean O'Casey*

[1] Walter Starkie (1894–1976), Irish author; a Director of the Abbey Theatre, 1927–1942.
[2] Dr. Franklin D. Murphy, who had left Kansas University to become Chancellor of the University of California at Los Angeles, where Dr. Starkie was teaching.
[3] See O'Casey's letter to Paul Shyre, 6 October 1958, note 3.

To Paul Shyre

MS. SHYRE

22 OCTOBER 1958

Dear Paul,

Hope all things went well, go well with you, company, & play. Enclosed is a clipping telling of a younger Lorna & Loreleen in Gorey, Wexford. God knows how many of these things happen & remain hidden. This episode would never have been shown had the parents of the girls not finally—after long hesitation—decided to take law action. Frightened for a long time, someone must have persuaded them into a public protest. The final result was: Teacher forced to apologise; girls allowed back to school; payment of £50—I think that was the amount—compensation. The case shown in play of Loreleen happened a few years ago, fresh when the play was written. Then there was a case of a young girl working as a maid in a bachelor-farmer's home. She had the consent of her parents, but the priest demurred—& you can guess what that meant. Anyway, a Postman on a frosty morning found the maid in her nightdress chained to a telegraph-post; nearly dead; & the bachelor-farmer was found unconscious & bloody from a stick-beating he got from some pious protestors; stretched out on the floor of his farmhouse kitchen. This happened in Sligo—Yeats's County—; it never appeared in the Press; there were no arrests: all was silence. I shouldn't have known had not a young Sligo man sent me a full account in a confidential letter.

These are the things that happen often. Today there's a furore over two Protestant Evangelists beaten—one knocked unconscious for half a hour from a skelp of a shilhlagh in Killaloe, Clare. In Court—the Police arrested assailant this time—the District Justice rebuked the Evangelist for provocation; declaring that "religion was above the law"—presumably the religion of the attackers; & the police will be more careful in future. So you see Cockadoodle's Dance is no illusion. And still the pilgrims go to Lourdes, & still they come back as they were before they listed.

A new Runway at Shannon Airport had to be diverted around a Hill said to be inhabited by the shidhe—the fairies. They're moving carefully now around the Hill so as not to disturb the good little people. Oh, Jasus!

All the best,
As ever,
Sean

To Brooks Atkinson

MS. ATKINSON

23 OCTOBER 1958

My dear Brooks,

Your letter came carrying your mild rebuke. I am really not fit to go anywhere far now: my chest is always a trouble, & my one good eye constantly painful. I genuinely wish to God I could once again wander the streets of New York; and more wonder at its Buildings, & view the new gigantic nest of the United Nations. However, I'm sure Eileen will be a good ambassador for the O'Casey Clan.

Brendan Behan of "The Quare Fella" has had another play—THE HOSTAGE[1]—performed, & has got wonderful notices & reviews from the London Critics. I hope it may be a great success; & that B.B. will settle down sensibly now to future work; for he is badly needed to quicken the pulse of the younger Irish playwrights: & widen their frightened minds, too.

A Northern Irish Director & Manager wants me to let him do: "Drums of Father Ned"—the play Dublin's Archbishop banished—& suggests he'd ask Tyrone Guthrie to do it. This is tempting; but I'm afraid it would be unfair to Guthrie, for he wouldn't get much out of it for a N. Ireland Production. The N. Irish manager of the "Group Theatre"—clever Jew—has read it, and likes it a lot (as he says anyhow), & is eager to do it, with help from a grant that might be given by the N. Ireland Arts Council.

I am trying to write a few reflections on things real and things abstract: on religion & politics, in an odd O'Casey-Emerson way. May God strengthen the effort!

I have refused an Irish offer to film "Shadow of a Gunman." They have a huge film set of Studios now in Co. Wicklow, & are turning out Abbey plays as films by steam-power. Julie Harris was in one of them. I enclose a picture of the proposed new Abbey Theater. The building looks fine; but a new Directorate is sorely needed.

My love to Oriana & to you.
As ever,
Sean

---

[1] Brendan Behan's *The Hostage* opened in London at the Theatre Royal, Stratford East, on 14 October 1958, directed by Joan Littlewood.

To Edward B. Connolly[1]

MS. CONNOLLY

23 OCTOBER 1958

Dear Mr. Connolly,

Your letter which was mislaid, has just come in front of me; so I send a belated reply. Maybe just as well, for I'm a poor hand at making comments on any kind of literature—novel, poem, or drama; and I have forgotten the mood of "Juno"; gone far away from it, so that, to me, it is no longer "an O'Casey play." Still, I am connected with you all by the title of "Cap and Bells." I am a Jester who walks in a garden, once a noisy and tumultuous one; now quieter, and growing still as the years pass. I just try to set down an odd song in the form of a play; include an odd tap dance to the bells a jingle, censure what is said with many a laugh, and, at times, silence the bells with a deep sigh. There, then, you have me.

I hope you had a successful production. If you hadn't, never mind— it was an effort, & from effort comes experience, from experience knowledge, &, at times, truth. By the way, the lowering of a curtain, denoting passing of time, does not destroy a mood. In "Juno," it is in the scene that follows, the laugh of censure, following the deep sigh. One more thing: never bother about "brogue" or accent; there is a different accent for every Irish County, & there are 32 of these. Speak your own American accent, for none other can come natural. As you with ours so we with yours—we could never speak as Americans speak. We should be fools to try: fools without any jingle of bells.

My warm regards and good wishes to all your members, and to you.

Yours very sincerely,
Sean O'Casey

[1] Edward B. Connolly, Cap and Bells Club, St. Joseph's College, Philadelphia, Pa.

To Miss Agnes Agatha Robinson

MS. ROBINSON

23 OCTOBER 1958

Dear Miss Robinson,

Thank you for your kind letter. I am well used to attacks on my plays by now. Each of them has suffered one or more, in one place or another, from Houston, Texas to Toronto in Ottawa. I take it all with life.

I know a good deal about Lourdes. It is possible that one afflicted with a nervous disorder, causing apparent paralysis, can be cured by an emotional shock. One is splendidly described by Zola in his "Lourdes." Hundreds went to this place while I was living in Dublin; year by year, they went, & always came back the way they went. Efforts are being made to make a local place, Knock, a miracle worker; the same kind of vision; seen by children—always by children, in Knock, in Lourdes, in Fatima.

You do well to hold on to your job. Writing of any kind is the most precarious living of all. I shouldn't advise even an enemy to take it up. All good wishes.

Yours sincerely,
Sean O'Casey

To Herbert Coston[1]

TC. O'CASEY

30 OCTOBER 1958

Dear Herb Coston,
Glad you both got home safely, and that Eva recovered from the cold she had when she came here. As for an understanding of the plays—different minds understand them in different ways, and, in one way or another, all of them, I suppose are right; but it isnt possible for me to give a detailed plan of conception or of execution of any one of them: they simply grew. I dont make a scenario, and so there is nothing like a frame-work similar to a skeleton of a steel-framed building. I dont think any method was "logically required by my material." It could have been done as well, maybe, in a different way. There is I daresay a logic in growth (in plants for instance, but it is determined by hereditary qualities and environment), and so there is in a play in somewhat the same way; but no dramatist of any standing can ever tell how his play will eventually form itself into a whole. I didnt use the TASSIE method just because that method was demanded by the scope of the idea. I happened to be interested in Plainchant (I am still), and I used what was humming in my mind for part of the presentation of the play; it had nothing to do with Expressionism, a method I still dont understand, and have never given it any attention. I hadnt read Strindberg before I wrote the PLOUGH, nor Toller; not

[1] Herbert Coston, Hunter College, New York. He wrote a doctoral dissertation at Columbia University in 1960, "The Idea of Courage in the Works of Sean O'Casey." See his article, "Sean O'Casey: Prelude to Playwriting," *Tulane Drama Review,* September 1960.

even before I had written the TASSIE. I have been always fond of fantasy. I wrote a play ROISIN'S ROBE (Roisin—a name for Ireland: Little Dark Rose) long before I thought of writing for the Abbey. It was published in a weekly called THE PLAIN PEOPLE. I didnt know this till many years after (I hadnt then even the penny to buy the paper each week); till a Priest, Father Behan from Killorglan, Kerry, who had read it in that paper told me. Then, before I had written PLOUGH before JUNO, I had written KATHLEEN LISTENS IN, a Phantasy in One Act, before I had even heard of "Expressionism"; but this was "E," but O'Casey's way. My real ambition is to wed all the arts to Drama. In COCKADOODLE for instance, we have dancing, pictures, for some of the scenes form paintings in the grouping, music, though it be only voice song and an accordion, and architecture in the formation of the whole play; and this has nothing to do with the official idea of "E," far as I guess. Again, to bring comedy and pathos together, arm in arm, as they so often are in life. The "realism" blathered about isnt real life at all; if it is anything. Walk any where, any day, keep your ears and eyes open, and you'll see fantasy everywhere you go. This is all I've time for. Henceforth, I'll answer questions no more. I've answered them hundreds of times, and must give up, for the sake of my eyes and the work I still hope to do. Of course, Dave [Greene] can do it; and, by all accounts, has done it damn well. May God speed him! All good wishes to Eva and you.

Yours very sincerely,
[Sean O'Casey]

To Gerard Fay[1]

TC. O'CASEY

3 NOVEMBER 1958

Dear Gerard Fay,

In your interesting book THE ABBEY THEATER,[2] mentioning me, you say that I "was a Trades Union leader" or Official. I was never a Trades Union Official in Dublin or out of it. I was a Communist (and am), a part of revolutionary Labor, a comrade of Jim Larkin from 1910 till the great man's death. I was never an official, paid or unpaid, but a constant worker, speaker, and Secretary of the Citizen Army. "Trade Union Organiser" is the term you use, I think, but that isnt correct as

---

[1] Gerard Fay, London Editor of the *Manchester Guardian;* son of the Abbey Theatre actor Frank Fay.

[2] Gerard Fay, *The Abbey Theatre, Cradle of Genius* (1958).

implying that I was a paid worker for Labor—no shame attached to being so, of course; but the fact is I wasnt one. The one financial relationship I had with any Movement to which I belong was that of paying my dues— to the Irish Transport and General Workers Union (Larkin's, not Bill O'Brien's); The Gaelic League; and the I.Republican Brotherhood. I am still a Republican, a Communist, and, in a way, a member of the Gaelic League, for I read INNIU, FEASTA, subscribe to an t-Oireachtas,[3] and am a member of CLUB LEABHAR.[4]

Have you me? as Polonius asked Reyaldo.

I shall be glad, should another issue of your book be printed, if you would correct the statement which appears in the first one; an event which I hope may happen to you.

With all good and sincere wishes to you.

> *Yours very sincerely,*
> *Sean O'Casey.*

[3] The annual Arts Festival organized by the Gaelic League.
[4] The Book Club run by *Inniu.*

To Paul Shyre

MS. SHYRE

5 NOVEMBER 1958

Dear Paul,

Your letter came this morning. Eileen has written giving details of her departure and arrival—you should have it by now.

Glad things go well. Hope for a good run. Pasternak isn't the only one who has had to give up glittering rewards.[1] I myself was offered from $150,000.00 to $200,000.00 to write a Film Scenario for "Look Homeward Angel," & refused.[2] The other day, I refused £700 for Film rights of "Shadow of a Gunman," & a month ago, refused to write an article of 2000 words of "Saturday Post" for a fee of $2500.00;[3] so you see, with a little more sense, I could be richer than I am. But then, had I taken the Film job of "Homeward Angel," maybe, I'd have never written "Cockadoodle

[1] Boris Pasternak was awarded the Nobel Prize for literature for his novel *Doctor Zhivago* on 23 October 1958; he was denounced by the Russian press on 25 October, and expelled from the Writers' Union on 29 October; he declined the prize on 30 October. See also O'Casey's letters, "Pasternak and Joyce," *Irish Times,* 19 and 26 July 1960, Vol. IV.
[2] See O'Casey's letter to William Herndon, 17 January 1945, Vol. II.
[3] See O'Casey's letters to Merrill Pollack, 11 June and 21 July 1958.

Dandy," & I prefer to have written the play than the scenario, tho' I won't get any Nobel Prize for it.

You didn't say much about experience in Canada. Bad houses? Well, never mind. New York has a better heart and head for Drama than Toronto.

It was a pathetic mistake to expel Pasternak from the Writers' Union. I'm writing a few words about this to my friend, the Editor of Moscow's "Literary Gazette."

Give my warm regards & good wishes to the Caste, to Philip, & to Mr. Polakov.

> *All the best to you.*
> *As ever,*
> *Sean*

P.S. Eileen leaves on 10 November at 7. o.c. evening, and arrives New York at 6.30 on 11th. Flight no. P.A.A. 101.

> *S. O'C.*

To Mrs. Helen Kiok

MS. Kiok[1]

6 November 1958

Dear Helen,

Thank you for your kind letter. It was good of you to think of how we felt after the swift going of our beloved boy. It is a deep ache still, and always will be, in both our hearts and minds; but it also links us closer to the many who have suffered the same sorrow.

I agree with you about the sad and unpleasant treatment of the poet, Pasternak. West and East are at his heels, for the West's concern is not about the poet, but an effort to make the most of something by which to humiliate the Soviet Union; & I believe, myself, the Nobel Prize was given so as to try to sharpen & intensify what has happened. There was no outcry when Joyce was banned everywhere, bar France; & it took years before he was allowed to put his nose into the USA & England; & he is still rigidly kept far out from holy Ireland. He never got the Nobel Prize; nor did any University ever give him even a whisper of honorable mention.

I do hope you may thoroughly enjoy "S. of a Gunman" and "Cocka-doodle Dandy."

I have been ordered to write less, & to rest my eyes as often as I can;

---

[1] This letter was printed in the *Sean O'Casey Review*, Fall 1976.

so I have had to cut away at the desire to reply to many letters that come to me. It is a nuisance, but one that must be borne.

All warm regards and good wishes to you.

As ever,
Sean

To O. Prudkov[1]

TC. O'CASEY

7 NOVEMBER 1958

Dear friend,

Thank you for your very kind letter, and for sending me the copy of the Gazette holding my message to our Asian and African brother-writers.[2] I have heard from a friend, who was in Tashkent that the Congress was a fine success. It may interest you to hear that I am wearing a Tashkent skull-cap, black and silver-embroidered, which I got as a present from a Vice-Chancellor of an American University. The embroidery is very lovely, and I am very proud of it.

I was very sorry, and not a little distressed, to read about the commotion caused by Boris Pasternak's book. I havent the slightest doubt that the Nobel Prize was given for political reasons, and a great furore has broken out in the West about the quarrel; but I believe it was a sad and a pathetic mistake to expel the poet from the Soviet Writers Union. I am convinced that the poet loves his people and his country, and even that the book was written with the best intentions, for we often criticise sharply what we love deeply. As a friend of your magnificent Land since 1917, I would plead for the withdrawal of this expulsion order. I do not know B. Pasternak; he has never written to me or I to him; but I have good friends in the Union of Soviet Writers, and it is to these I beg to send my plea.

The West comes out in defence of authors very vehemently when it serves their political purpose, but when it doesnt they usually keep their mouths shut; for instance, when James Joyce was banned in England and the USA for years, we heard damned few voices raised on his behalf—he is still banned in Ireland, his own country. A play of his, along with one of mine, was banned from Dublin by the Roman Catholic Archbishop of Dublin, during Tostal Week, and few indeed were the voices either in Ireland or England that raised any protest about the banning. Every artist is

---

[1] O. Prudkov, Deputy Foreign Editor, *Literary Gazette,* Moscow.
[2] See O'Casey's message to B. Leontyev, 2 September 1958.

something of an anarchist, as Bernard Shaw tells us in one of his prefaces, and the artist should be forgiven many things. Pasternak is, I think, without a doubt, a Poet, and there is ample room for him in the world of so many activities in your wide and great Country. I venture to say all this as a friend for many, many years, and I hope I myself may be forgiven for saying them.

With cordial regards and good wishes to the USSR, to her people, to your Gazette, and to you personally—

[*Sean O'Casey*]

To Dr. and Mrs. Hugh Doran

MS. DORAN

18 NOVEMBER 1958

My dear Hugh and Mary,

Don't be angry with me for asking you to forgive me not going to your home in Southover. I hate going out o' nights. I'm completely blind in the dark, and have to be guided hither & thither, into a car & out of it, etc. I hate and loathe this, always anxious to be able to do all for myself; to walk free everywhere I go. That's why I dread illness; & when I'm down this way, why even then I do all I can for myself without help from others.

So I love my own habitat where I can go quickly from one place to another, free and independent. Besides, I'm in the middle of a chapter-fantasy called "Figuro in the Night," & want to give all the time I can to it, for a "Fantasy" is a slow & thoughtful thing to try to write.

Why not come here instead some night? Then you won't have to lug me back, & so save a journey.

I can give Mary & you a wee drop o' whiskey, a glass o' sherry, or a cup o' tay; and what could be better, answer me that!

I enclose a few stamps, & with them my love to you both.

As ever,
Sean

To Clara Rotter

MS. ROTTER

18 NOVEMBER 1958

Dear Clara,

My thanks—all heart and hands can hold—to you for sending me the pages from *The New York Times*.[1]

Mr. Atkinson is terribly right about my wanton belief that comedy can be played as it has been, & will be again, please God, as Joyce's Citizen says. It has long been a weary woe in my heart that Fitzgeralds and Sinclairs are so scarce among the artists of the stage;[2] a woe made known by the knowledge that I'm able to play them myself at home, & could do it on the stage, had I not within me the fear that paralyses me at any attempt at a Public showing. There are those who could do comedy parts well, but they aren't to be had—lost in the waste of the film erred & the deserts of Television. I'm so glad Paul Shyre was so good; but playing Comedy will always, in my opinion, be harder than playing Tragedy. It is fine, too, that so many of the artists are so good, & that so much of the play shines so well. I am very proud of the Gold, Frankincense, & Myrrh of the lovely Review Mr. Atkinson gives of the play.

Thanks, again, dear friend.

My love,
Sean

[1] Miss Rotter, Brooks Atkinson's secretary, had sent him Atkinson's review of *Cock-a-Doodle Dandy*, "O'Casey's Defense of Joy," *New York Times*, 13 November 1958. The play opened on 12 November at the Carnegie Hall Playhouse, an Off-Broadway theatre, directed by Philip Burton, scenery and lighting by Lester Polakov, costumes by Don Jensen, produced by Lucille Lortel, Paul Shyre, and Howard Gottfried. Leading members of the cast were: Carlo Mazzone as The Cock, Will Geer as Michael Marthraun, Ian Martin as Sailor Mahan, Paul Shyre as Shanaar, Gaby Rodgers as Loreleen, Rae Allen as Lorna, Anne Meara as Marion, Jack Betts as The Messenger, George Ebeling as Father Domineer.

[2] Atkinson had commented: "Since it was written on the amiable assumption that all actors are as pungent as Barry Fitzgerald and F. J. McCormick, it also sets the theatre serious problems . . . The Celtic tone is uneven throughout the cast. Probably there is nothing that Philip Burton, the director, can do about that. And some of his actors are first-rate, Irish or not: Paul Shyre as an addle-headed soothsayer and moralist; George Ebeling as a harsh, bellowing priest; Anne Meara as a giggling, high-spirited servant; Rae Allen as a fiery-eyed young wife to an old codger; Gaby Rodgers as a shameless hussy; Jack Betts as a mysterious messenger, who is not intimidated by superstition or authority."

To Paul Shyre

MS. SHYRE

25 NOVEMBER 1958

My dear Paul,

First congratulations on the fine way you filled the part of the Old Cod, Sheanaar; one of the hardest parts in the play to do. Quite obvious, the comic characters can be done well; but there's a big element of chance in selecting who's to do them. I know many Irishmen, actors, who would ruin the parts if anyone gave them leave to do them; tho' there are a few who could probably do them well. Well, you done well. Me soul man, Paul!

It is a sad thing the play hadn't the same gusty reception given to "Purple Dust"; but I guessed something was wrong in Toronto. However, I was near certain it would go hilariously in New York. But these disappointments are part of the Theater; one never can tell what may happen.

Perhaps, you may be able to pull part of a season out of the Production. I hope so for all our sakes. The play has great competition now what with "Shadow,"[1] "Playboy"[2] & "Quare Fella,"[3] which, I hope, for Behan's sake, maybe a success. He has a lot of wit & courage, & deserves one.

Never mind, too much, Paul, a mhic. You have done your best, & hope is still with us. Anyway, you have come well out of it from the acting point.

I was dubious about your doing it, for it is a curious character; but you evidently fleshed out the part fine. My thanks.

And thanks to the Company who worked so hard. May they all get a run long enough to get something for their efforts.

My love to all & to you.
As ever,
Sean

[1] *The Shadow of a Gunman* opened in New York at the Bijou Theatre on 20 November 1958, directed by Jack Garfein, sets by Peter Larkin, costumes by Ruth Morley, presented as an Actors' Studio production by Cheryl Crawford and Joel Schenker, with the following cast: William Smithers as Davoren, Gerald O'Loughlin as Shields, Stefan Gierasch as Tommy Owens, George Mathews as Mr. Grigson, Katherine Squire as Mrs. Grigson, Susan Strasberg as Minnie Powell, Daniel Reed as Mr. Mulligan, Bruce Dern as Maguire, Zamah Cunningham as Mrs. Henderson, Arthur Malet as Mr. Gallogher, James Greene as An Auxiliary.

[2] The Irish Player's production of Synge's *Playboy of the Western World,* which had opened off-Broadway at the Tara Theatre on 8 May 1958, with Dermot McNamara as Christy Mahon and Helena Carroll as Pegeen Mike, was still running.

[3] Brendan Behan's *The Quare Fellow* opened off-Broadway at the Circle-in-the-Square Theatre on 28 November 1958.

To Mrs. R. S. Beattie[1]

MS. BEATTIE

27 NOVEMBER 1958

My dear Joan,

So the great change has come on you. May you manage it well and face it bravely; for married life brings burdens & new responsibility. Things can never be the same again, & we must learn to tune ourselves to the new rhythm, so that we may live in harmony with ourselves, & so living, live in harmony with others, too. I don't wish you happiness, for happiness has various shapes, good & bad; but I wish you an active and useful life which is the Spring of any happiness due to us.

You have been places! Up on the high mountains, down in the deep valleys: just like life as most of us experience it one day or another; & now, you are snug at home, walking the plain road of routine life, which is never plain, &, if we think of it, is never routine either.

I am fairly well, though my eyes get tired quicker, and I amn't able to write so often or so long; I have to take more time over it. Still, I've no reason to complain, for they—the eyes—have given me long and good service.

Eileen has been over in New York since the 11th, & she is expected back on the 19th, just, maybe, as you get this note. I shall be glad, for I miss her very much.

By the way, Joan, I don't think there's such a thing as "religious" Drama. What in the name o' God is "religious" Drama? "Samson Agonistes"? "Murder in th' Cathedral"? Does it include "Pagan Drama"—the Greeks, for instance? Is Shakespeare, with his bawdiness outside o' God's Portals? Or is it just solemn drama? Moses on Mt. Sinai is drama, so is the terrible story of Tamor & Ammoses. Are these "religious" Drama? My dear, to me all Drama is Religious: it is the speaking of the Holy Ghost, & it isn't all tears & all prayer. My love to your Mother, Father & Brother; to Sherman, and to you.

As ever,
Sean

[1] Mrs. R. S. Beattie was the former Miss Joan McAlevey, one of O'Casey's regular correspondents.

To Hume Cronyn

TS. CRONYN

15 DECEMBER 1958

Dear Hume,

Hold your horses—I didnt mean you to take my lament so seriously; I spoke (or wrote) more in sorrow than in anger.

You may well have mentioned the "cut" in one of your letters to me.[1] My eyes arent too good, and I get periodic bouts of pain in them so that it is painful to read, and a bit difficult too (Eileen reads a lot of letters for me, but she isnt always here to do it); so I sometimes miss a line in a letter, and usually have to read it again to get it right. So I may well have missed that line or two in which you mentioned the "cutting." It isnt necessary to look over them again to find out. I quite understand (too well) the condition of things in the Theater that necessitates an economy that should not be necessary, if we were civilised enough to realise that the Theater was a common part of our culture; and that its full activity everywhere should be but a matter of course in our life of leisure after the day's work. Neither I nor you nor Jessica [Tandy] nor Jane [Rubin] is to blame: we are all within the grip of economic circumstances as they now are, and must try to make the best of them. There are many ways of making art difficult, even of quietly suppressing it in countries other than that one where Pasternak lives. I have myself experienced it many times, and, probably will again; but we must go on working—fighting too—for better conditions when those concerned with production and acting will not have to worry in any way about costs or capital.

So go ahead, if you should decide to risk a one-act show in New York. I know that you and Jessica will do your best with the plays, and that your best will be damned good.

I knew "Mossy" and have a lingering affection for the old lady, so I hope that some better time to come you and Jessica will be able to include her in some performance, and bring the old figure back to life again.

All good and affectionate regards to Jessica and to you.

Sean O'Casey.

[1] Cronyn decided to eliminate four characters from O'Casey's *Bedtime Story*, which was part of *Triple Play*, a program of short plays he produced and acted in with Jessica Tandy in New York on 15 April 1959. The characters eliminated were Miss Mossie, the Policeman, the Doctor, and the Nurse. This reduced the cast from seven to three. For details of the production see O'Casey's letter to Jane Rubin, 19 April 1959, note 1.

To Joseph Stein

MS. STEIN

22 DECEMBER 1958

Dear Joe,

I understand you've been riddling brains for a TITLE, & have chosen "Juno,"—not a good one: too like the play, & leaving out mention of Paycock. Eileen & I have chanted titles, & I think the under-mentioned better than either "Daarlin' Man" or "Juno." It is

"*JUNO AND JACK*"

It is short, crisp, & musical. It is alliterative, & suggests a connection with the Nursery song "Jack & Jill," (as "My Fair Lady" does with another); Jack falling, & Juno tumbling after him, as happens in the play. It also gives a fair showing to the 2 chief characters. "Juno" calls Boyle "Jack" in the play, & so this title is eminently suitable. "Juno" coming first allows a soft falling cadence on the name of "Jack." "Juno and Jack."

This title pre-eminently fits & suits the Musical. "Juno" is too terse; "Daarlin' Man" too exclusively attached to Boyle. The Title, too, suggests the gayer aspect of the Musical as compared with the play.

I've sent a cable to you giving this title to give you time to think of it before this letter comes your way. I am, of course, as eager as you are for a success.

Eileen sends her love to Sadie & to you; & so do I, & the children, too, of course.

Adieu for the moment
Sean

To Jessica Wanamaker

MS. WANAMAKER

22 DECEMBER 1958

Flat 3, 40 Trumlands Road, St. Marychurch, Torquay, Devon.
Tel. : Torquay 87766.

22 December.
1958

Miss Jessica Wanamaker.

My dear Jessica,

A HAPPY CHRISTMAS

TO YOU. from

EILEEN'S SEAN.

SHIVAUN'S DADDY.

---

[1] Jessica and Zöe, the young daughters of Sam Wanamaker. See the letter to Abigail Wanamaker, 22 May 1958.

To Zöe Wanamaker

MS. WANAMAKER

22 DECEMBER 1958

December. 22. 1958

Flat 3, 40 Trumlands Road, St. Marychurch, Torquay, Devon.
Tel.: Torquay 87766.

Miss Zöe Wanamaker.

My dear Zoe,

A HAPPY CHRISTMAS
TO YOU.
Your old friend.
SEAN.

To Brooks Atkinson

MS. ATKINSON

29 DECEMBER 1958

My dear Brooks,

Thank you so much for your kind notices;[1] & for all you did to coax the Cock to keep crowing; but, from all I have heard from letters & reviews, there wasn't any vitality in the Production. The Cock crowed allright; but the others; or, most of the others, refused to wake & greet the glowing morn. It was a great disappointment to me, for, right or wrong, I like this play the best of all. Fact is, Brooks, comedy artists are hidden away like needles in haystacks: they are very scarce; for comedy is far harder to do than serious work. It is a gift born in one; & when such a one as Barry [Fitzgerald] leaves stage for film, the Theater totters. Jack McGowran (who is to play in the musical [*"Juno"*]) is a born comedian, I think; but he's damned hard to get now, too. I was born under a curse, Brooks: I love to hear people laughing, and I love to laugh myself. Consequence is, I see the comic side of things, and can't keep them secret. In my last play, "The Drums of Father Ned" lies the same problem: comicality. Dave Krause, of Brown University, ardent lover of the Theater, says it's "next to the 'Cock'," & that the character, "Mr. Murray is one of the finest yet done by me." I don't think he's right. I knew "Mr. Murray"— that *was* his name—well; & loved him a lot. But who can play him? Others, like Mr. Murray, strut thro' the play; so what am I to do? Somehow, some day, somewhere, the characters will leap & laugh a way into life. Meanwhile, they are safe in limbo.

I've had a sharp touch of bronchitis again, & it has left me a whoresome hoarseness I can't shake off. Ordered today not to talk, not to smoke for some days, till, if the hoarseness isn't gone, a minute examination may be made. Mister, will you laugh; mister will you talk; no, Ma'am: I will neither smoke nor talk till a bright day comes. Day before the order came, Dave Krause came here—he is in Dublin now—, and I talked and I talked till Dave had to go. Now, the door is closed & the window barred.

Thanks again, Brooks, for your great kindness. Please give my love to Oriana.

Yours very sincerely,
As ever, my dear Brooks,
Sean

[1] Besides his reviews of *Cock-a-Doodle Dandy* and *The Shadow of a Gunman* in the daily *New York Times,* 13 November and 21 November 1958, Atkinson wrote about both plays in his regular Sunday column, "Two By O'Casey," *New York Times,* 23 November 1958. *Cock-a-Doodle Dandy* closed on 7 December, after 31 performances. *The Shadow of a Gunman* closed on 3 January 1959, after 52 performances.

To Miss Clara Rotter

MS. ROTTER

30 DECEMBER 1958

Dear Clara,

Just a note to give thanks to you for sending me the Press-cuttings reviewing the plays. Things haven't got on too well; but the Theater is just like life—one day up on a sunny hill, the next down in a dark, dark valley; & when we find ourselves in the valley, we must do our best to climb on to the sunny hill again.

From a bout of bronchitis—another dark valley!—I've lost my voice. And have been set in a cage, & given in charge to Mater Silenti: I have been ordered to keep my mouth shut. Easy enough when there's no one knocking about with whom to talk; but that is seldom; & I've been told to lay off smoking, which is worse than all.

So I'm hard at it climbing up out
of those dark valleys. Pray for me.
All warm regards.
Yours as ever,
Sean

Every evening when there are
two knocking about it's when
to bed; but that is seldom; & I've
been told to lay up smoking,
which is worse than all.

So he's hard at
it climbing up
out of these dark
valleys. Pray for
me.

All warm regards

Yours as ever.

Sean

INDEX OF LETTERS
BY O'CASEY

INDEX OF
LETTERS TO AND
NEWS REPORTS ABOUT
O'CASEY

GENERAL INDEX

Note: Footnote page entries in bold-
face indicate references with bio-
graphical or background information.